MORE Windows® 98 Secrets®

MORE Windows® 98 Secrets®

Brian Livingston and Davis Straub

IDG Books Worldwide, Inc.
An International Data Group Company

Foster City, CA ◆ Chicago, IL ◆ Indianapolis, IN ◆ New York, NY

MORE Windows® 98 Secrets®

Published by
IDG Books Worldwide, Inc.
An International Data Group Company
919 E. Hillsdale Blvd., Suite 400
Foster City, CA 94404
www.idgbooks.com (IDG Books Worldwide Web site)

ISBN: 0-7645-3360-6

Printed in the United States of America

10 9 8 7 6 5 4 3 2 1

1O/RS/QX/ZZ/FC

Distributed in the United States by
IDG Books Worldwide, Inc.

Distributed by CDG Books Canada Inc. for Canada; by Transworld Publishers Limited in the United Kingdom; by IDG Norge Books for Norway; by IDG Sweden Books for Sweden; by IDG Books Australia Publishing Corporation Pty. Ltd. for Australia and New Zealand; by TransQuest Publishers Pte Ltd. for Singapore, Malaysia, Thailand, Indonesia, and Hong Kong; by Gotop Information Inc. for Taiwan; by ICG Muse, Inc. for Japan; by Norma Comunicaciones S.A. for Colombia; by Intersoft for South Africa; by Eyrolles for France; by International Thomson Publishing for Germany, Austria and Switzerland; by Distribuidora Cuspide for Argentina; by Livraria Cultura for Brazil; by Ediciones ZETA S.C.R. Ltda. for Peru; by WS Computer Publishing Corporation, Inc., for the Philippines; by Contemporanea de Ediciones for Venezuela; by Express Computer Distributors for the Caribbean and West Indies; by Micronesia Media Distributor, Inc. for Micronesia; by Grupo Editorial Norma S.A. for Guatemala; by Chips Computadoras S.A. de C.V. for Mexico; by Editorial Norma de Panama S.A. for Panama; by American Bookshops for Finland. Authorized Sales Agent: Anthony Rudkin Associates for the Middle East and North Africa.

For general information on IDG Books Worldwide's books in the U.S., please call our Consumer Customer Service department at 800-762-2974. For reseller information, including discounts and premium sales, please call our Reseller Customer Service department at 800-434-3422.

For information on where to purchase IDG Books Worldwide's books outside the U.S., please contact our International Sales department at 317-596-5530 or fax 317-596-5692.

For consumer information on foreign language translations, please contact our Customer Service department at 800-434-3422, fax 317-596-5692, or e-mail rights@idgbooks.com.

For information on licensing foreign or domestic rights, please phone +1-650-655-3109.

For sales inquiries and special prices for bulk quantities, please contact our Sales department at 650-655-3200 or write to the address above.

For information on using IDG Books Worldwide's books in the classroom or for ordering examination copies, please contact our Educational Sales department at 800-434-2086 or fax 317-596-5499.

For press review copies, author interviews, or other publicity information, please contact our Public Relations department at 650-655-3000 or fax 650-655-3299.

For authorization to photocopy items for corporate, personal, or educational use, please contact Copyright Clearance Center, 222 Rosewood Drive, Danvers, MA 01923, or fax 978-750-4470.

Library of Congress Cataloging-in-Publication Data

Livingston, Brian.
    More Windows 98 secrets / Brian Livingston and Davis Straub.
        p. cm.
    Includes index.
    ISBN 0-7645-3360-6 (alk. paper)
    1. Microsoft Windows (Computer file). 2. Operating systems (Computers) I. Straub, Davis, [DATE] II. Title.
    QA76.76.063L586 1999
    005.4'469–dc21   99-28102
                                                                    CIP

ABOUT IDG BOOKS WORLDWIDE

Welcome to the world of IDG Books Worldwide.

IDG Books Worldwide, Inc., is a subsidiary of International Data Group, the world's largest publisher of computer-related information and the leading global provider of information services on information technology. IDG was founded more than 30 years ago by Patrick J. McGovern and now employs more than 9,000 people worldwide. IDG publishes more than 290 computer publications in over 75 countries. More than 90 million people read one or more IDG publications each month.

Launched in 1990, IDG Books Worldwide is today the #1 publisher of best-selling computer books in the United States. We are proud to have received eight awards from the Computer Press Association in recognition of editorial excellence and three from Computer Currents' First Annual Readers' Choice Awards. Our best-selling ...For Dummies® series has more than 50 million copies in print with translations in 31 languages. IDG Books Worldwide, through a joint venture with IDG's Hi-Tech Beijing, became the first U.S. publisher to publish a computer book in the People's Republic of China. In record time, IDG Books Worldwide has become the first choice for millions of readers around the world who want to learn how to better manage their businesses.

Our mission is simple: Every one of our books is designed to bring extra value and skill-building instructions to the reader. Our books are written by experts who understand and care about our readers. The knowledge base of our editorial staff comes from years of experience in publishing, education, and journalism — experience we use to produce books to carry us into the new millennium. In short, we care about books, so we attract the best people. We devote special attention to details such as audience, interior design, use of icons, and illustrations. And because we use an efficient process of authoring, editing, and desktop publishing our books electronically, we can spend more time ensuring superior content and less time on the technicalities of making books.

You can count on our commitment to deliver high-quality books at competitive prices on topics you want to read about. At IDG Books Worldwide, we continue in the IDG tradition of delivering quality for more than 30 years. You'll find no better book on a subject than one from IDG Books Worldwide.

 John Kilcullen
Chairman and CEO
IDG Books Worldwide, Inc.

 Steven Berkowitz
President and Publisher
IDG Books Worldwide, Inc.

IDG is the world's leading IT media, research and exposition company. Founded in 1964, IDG had 1997 revenues of $2.05 billion and has more than 9,000 employees worldwide. IDG offers the widest range of media options that reach IT buyers in 75 countries representing 95% of worldwide IT spending. IDG's diverse product and services portfolio spans six key areas including print publishing, online publishing, expositions and conferences, market research, education and training, and global marketing services. More than 90 million people read one or more of IDG's 290 magazines and newspapers, including IDG's leading global brands — Computerworld, PC World, Network World, Macworld and the Channel World family of publications. IDG Books Worldwide is one of the fastest-growing computer book publishers in the world, with more than 700 titles in 36 languages. The "...For Dummies®" series alone has more than 50 million copies in print. IDG offers online users the largest network of technology-specific Web sites around the world through IDG.net (http://www.idg.net), which comprises more than 225 targeted Web sites in 55 countries worldwide. International Data Corporation (IDC) is the world's largest provider of information technology data, analysis and consulting, with research centers in over 41 countries and more than 400 research analysts worldwide. IDG World Expo is a leading producer of more than 168 globally branded conferences and expositions in 35 countries including E3 (Electronic Entertainment Expo), Macworld Expo, ComNet, Windows World Expo, ICE (Internet Commerce Expo), Agenda, DEMO, and Spotlight. IDG's training subsidiary, ExecuTrain, is the world's largest computer training company, with more than 230 locations worldwide and 785 training courses. IDG Marketing Services helps industry-leading IT companies build international brand recognition by developing global integrated marketing programs via IDG's print, online and exposition products worldwide. Further information about the company can be found at www.idg.com. 1/24/99

Credits

Acquisitions Editor
Andy Cummings

Development Editors
Heidi Steele
Katharine Dvorak

Technical Editor
Heidi Steele

Copy Editors
Heidi Steele
Zoe Brymer
Marti Paul

Production
IDG Books Worldwide Production

Cover Image
©TSM/Lester Lefkowitz, 1999

Proofreading and Indexing
York Production Services

About the Authors

Brian Livingston is the author of IDG Books Worldwide's best-selling *Windows 3 Secrets*; *Windows 3.1 Secrets*, 2nd Edition; *More Windows 3.1 Secrets*; and coauthor of *Windows Gizmos*, a collection of shareware and freeware tools and games, *Windows 95 Secrets*, and *Windows 98 Secrets*. His books are printed in more than 30 languages. In addition to writing books, Mr. Livingston is a contributing editor of *InfoWorld* magazine, and has been a contributing editor of *PC/Computing*, *PC World*, *Windows Sources*, and other magazines. He was a recipient of the 1991 Award for Technical Excellence from the National Microcomputer Managers Association.

Davis Straub is the coauthor of *Windows 95 Secrets*, *Windows 98 Secrets*, and technical editor for *Windows Gizmos*. He previously worked as a Windows multimedia software developer. He is the former president of Generic Software (a successful CAD software company) and Personal Workstations, Inc. (a successful CAD VAR). When not furiously digging for Windows secrets, he spends his time hang gliding.

To those people who have helped their fellow Windows 98 users by answering their questions on the Windows 98 support newsgroups. We list a number of the most generous of these good-hearted individuals in our Acknowledgments, and mention others throughout the book.

Acknowledgments

This book is not the sole work of its authors. While we focused our efforts on writing and researching this work, many others provided the help we needed to complete it. Belinda Boulter researched and wrote the Outlook Express chapters, and edited all the other chapters. Without her efforts, this book would have been too difficult to write.

We would have been lost and our readers wouldn't have had a readable book if it weren't for our development editor and technical editor, Heidi Steele. An accomplished author in her own right, Heidi checked everything we wrote and made us rewrite until it was understandable. We can't thank her enough.

We spent a considerable amount of time on the Microsoft Windows 98 newsgroups, including the Microsoft private beta newsgroups. Our fellow Windows 98 and Internet Explorer beta testers and newsgroup participants provided us with crucial assistance and guidance. We especially thank those individuals who have provided ongoing and consistent support to their fellow Windows users on the Microsoft support newsgroups. They include: Tom Porterfield, Jeff Richards, Attila Szabo – MrScary, Tom Koch, Eric D. Miller, Don Lebow–don lebow, Mark Stapleton – Sporkman, John Hildrum, Lee Chapelle, Bill Drake, Tom Pfeiffer, Sky King, Michael Santovec, Steve Howland, Robert Moir, Rick Halle, Robert Scoble, Brian Sullivan, Brett I. Holcomb, Bill Sanderson, Sean Chappell, Matt Adres, Danny Falknov, and Juan Flowers at Microsoft.

Wherever we have included a tip or secret from someone on a newsgroup, we have included a thank you to that individual in the book. We hope that we haven't missed anyone. We also thank Chris Pirillo, whose Lockergnome e-zine (http://www.lockergnome.com) was a constant source of inspiration and clues.

Contents at a Glance

Contents

Chapter 1

Read This First

In This Chapter

▶ Why a book like *MORE Windows 98 Secrets* is needed.

▶ How to find answers to your questions.

▶ How to correctly type Windows 98 commands as used in this book.

▶ Where to get the best technical support.

Why More Windows 98 Secrets

We couldn't fit all the cool secrets into the 1,200 pages of *Windows 98 Secrets*. We've found a lot more secrets since Windows 98 was first released. We wanted to produce a book that was a good companion to *Windows 98 Secrets*. We wanted to write a book that just stuck to the cool secrets and didn't provide a more comprehensive guide to Windows 98.

We've found a great number of new and interesting secrets as well as Windows 98 system-oriented shareware and freeware. We provide step-by-step instructions on implementing these secrets and using the software to enhance Windows 98.

It's hard to overestimate the depth and complexity of Windows 98. There is almost always a way around a problem, or a different switch setting that you can use to change the way Windows operates. Our job is to give you the secrets that transform (as much as possible) Windows 98 from Bill Gates' operating system into your operating system. Of course, we are using Bill Gates in a mythological sense here.

How to use this book

We hope that you use this book in conjunction with your computer. Open it up and crease the binding so that it stays open to your page. We don't expect you to read this thing like a novel. This is a reference work, so you should hunt and peck around looking for things of interest.

We've included an electronic version of the book on the enclosed CD-ROM. The e-version is in the form of a help file. We provide it in a new format that includes contents, index, and search capabilities in the left pane of the help window. We have found this format to be quite convenient. If you install the help file on your computer, you will be able to search on any word in the book to find information about a particular topic. To get the most out of your searches, we suggest making a full text index. The first time you use the help file, just click the Search tab and mark the Maximum Search Capabilities option button in the Find Setup Wizard that appears.

If you install the help file, you'll also be able to click the various web addresses as you read along to travel to the sites referenced in the text. There are plenty of surprises that show up when you click a URL. We've tied the text in the book to what you'll see, often without revealing everything. The feel of the book comes through when you follow along with us and see what's live up on the web. This book includes hundreds of URLs.

Of course, some of our URLs are going to be dead. The web changes and we can't keep up with it, especially in a book. If you hit a dead URL, try to back out a ways in the Address field. Delete everything past the last slash and then click the Go button or press Enter.

We've given you plenty of freeware and shareware download sites to visit. We hope that you have a chance to download some of the packages that we recommend. They make an incredible difference in how Windows 98 operates as an operating system.

We decided not to put the shareware on the CD-ROM because we assume that it will be past its freshness date by the time that you get this book. With the proliferation of shareware web sites, it's now easy and cheap to download the software, at least here in the United States, and we hope it will be cheaper for the rest of the world soon.

Secret

We've used the Secret icon to indicate secrets that we thought were especially cool or hard to figure out on your own.

Tip

The Tip icon calls attention to intriguing bits of information or clever solutions to the problem at hand.

STEPS

We often give you step-by-step instructions on how to carry out a specific task. One of our goals in creating these steps is to make sure that nobody gets lost. So even if you're unfamiliar with the theory, we include enough details in the steps for you to complete specific tasks. You can breeze through some of the steps as you learn more about Windows 98.

Getting commands right the first time

You'll be able to use the secrets in this book faster if you know exactly how to type the many Windows commands shown in the text.

Throughout this book, we've indicated many commands like this:

```
WORDPAD {/p} filename
```

or

```
Wordpad {/p} filename
```

In this command, *filename* is shown in *italics* to indicate that you should change *filename* to the actual name of the file you want to open in the WordPad text editor. The command /p is shown in curly braces {like this} to indicate that this command line parameter is optional. You should *not* type the curly braces if you decide to add /p to this command. Because Windows often uses square brackets [like this] to indicate the beginning of sections in initialization *(ini)* files and in the text version of the Registry, we do not use square brackets to indicate optional parameters. If you see a line that contains square brackets, you must type the square brackets along with the rest of the line.

If you want to print the Readme.txt file using WordPad, for example, you could click the Start button, click Run, type this line, and then press Enter:

```
Wordpad /p Readme.txt
```

When a command that you should type appears within a paragraph, it is shown in **boldface**. Often, you can enter commands in any combination of upper- and lowercase — all lowercase, ALL UPPERCASE, or a mixture of both. However, some command line parameters, such as /p, are case sensitive. When something you need to type is case sensitive, we let you know.

Whenever you see the term *filename* in italics, you can change it to any form of a valid filename that DOS or Windows will recognize, including drive letters and directory names. For example, if C:\Windows\Command is your current folder, any of the following names for the Readme.txt file are valid in this WordPad command:

```
WORDPAD README.TXT
Wordpad Readme.txt
WORDPAD C:\WINDOWS\COMMAND\README.TXT
WORDPAD \WINDOWS\COMMAND\README.TXT
```

We denote special keys on your keyboard with an initial capital letter, like this: Enter, Tab, Backspace, Shift, Alt (Alternate), Ctrl (Control), and Esc (Escape). If one of the shift keys (Shift, Alt, or Ctrl) should be *held down* at the same time that you also press another key, the two keys are written with a plus sign between them. For example, *press Ctrl+A* means *hold down the Ctrl key, then press the A key, then release both keys.* If you are supposed to *let up* on a key *before* pressing another one, those keys are separated by commas. If we say *press Alt, F, O,* this means *press and release Alt, then F, then O.* This sequence activates the menu bar of a Windows application, then pulls down the File menu, then executes the Open command. This is the same as saying *click File, Open*.

Getting technical support for Windows 98

All Windows programs (and books about Windows programs) have bugs. Every program, no matter how simple, has some unexpected behavior. This is the nature of software, and existing bugs are usually fixed and new ones introduced with the release of a newer version.

It is not possible for the co-authors or IDG Books to provide technical support for Windows 98 or for the many applications that may cause conflicts in your system. For technical support on the CD-ROM, see the section "Technical support for the CD-ROM" later in this chapter.

For technical support for Windows 98, you will be better off contacting Microsoft directly — or using electronic support (which we describe in a moment).

Microsoft provides telephone technical support for its DOS and Windows products through these numbers:

Type of Support	Number to Call at Microsoft
Microsoft Windows 98 Support 90 days of free support starting with your first phone call	425-635-7222 905-568-4494 (Canada)
Microsoft Pay-Per-Call Support ($35/incident)	800-936-5700 (U.S.) 800-668-7975 (Canada)
Microsoft International Support (for referral to a non-U.S. office)	425-882-8080 or 888-877-9095
Microsoft Fast Tips — automated touch tone	800-936-4200 (U.S.)

If you're really desperate, have read *Windows 98 Secrets* and this book, reviewed the newsgroups, and checked out the Microsoft Knowledge Base, and still need help, I'm always available at www.davisstraub.com/secrets. I've answered every e-mail message I've ever received from a reader, and from many non-readers. Of course, if it gets out of hand, I'll go back to the Australian Outback and cut the phone lines.

Online news about Windows 98

Here are some good places to seek technical support and read the latest news about Windows 98:

Where to Get Help	How to Get There
Microsoft general support	www.microsoft.com/support
Microsoft Knowledge Base	support.microsoft.com/support/search/c.asp
CompuServe	Type GO WINNEWS
AOL	Go to the keyword Winnews
Prodigy	Type Jump Winnews
FTP	ftp:/ /ftp.microsoft.com/Softlib

Accessing Microsoft support newsgroups

The best place to get Microsoft support is from the Microsoft support newsgroups. These newsgroups combine peer support (for the most part), support from Microsoft volunteers (MVPs, ClubWin, and ClubIE members), and every now and then (depending on the newsgroup), actual support engineers from Microsoft.

Microsoft hosts the newsgroups on its news server, msnews.microsoft.com. While some Internet service providers carry the newsgroups, they aren't generally available to other news servers at Internet service providers. To access the newsgroups, choose msnews.microsoft.com as your news server (or as one of a number of news servers) in your newsgroup reader. Outlook Express, the mail and news reader that comes with Windows 98, allows you to subscribe to multiple news servers.

Log on to the Microsoft news server after logging on to your Internet service provider. Choose from the long list of product and interest area-specific newsgroups hosted by Microsoft and be prepared for a lot of reading. You can start here: support.microsoft.com/support/news.

If you want actual one-on-one contact with Microsoft support engineers, you are pretty much going to have to pay for it on a per-contact or contract basis. You get support for the first ninety days, but after that, it's pay as you go.

Accessing technical support on CompuServe

The CompuServe Information Service (CIS) is a worldwide computer service (one of many). Many vendors of Windows products maintain forums on CompuServe. A *forum* is a message area that technical support people may monitor, answering questions and comments left by users of each vendor's products.

To get electronic technical support from Wugnet on CompuServe, for example, you call a CompuServe local number with your modem, and then type **GO MICROSOFT** at any CompuServe prompt to get to the Microsoft

Connection. You will see a list of services, including several Microsoft Connection forums. You can also go to the Microsoft Knowledge Base from this area.

You can type **GO WINNEWS** to go to the WinNews forum and get the latest information about Windows 98. The Microsoft Knowledge Base is available at **GO MSKB**. For Windows 98 shareware, type **GO WINSHARE** or **GO WUGNET**. To get to the Windows 98 help switchboard, type **GO WIN98**.

If you need support from someone other than Wugnet, type **GO SOFTWARE** or **GO HARDWARE**. You will see a listing of scores of companies, each with its own forum or forums filled with technical messages posted by company technicians and users.

Once you're in the forum for your particular vendor, choose the menu option Announcements from Sysop. This displays a listing of system operators (sysops), along with the latest news about the forum, such as new program enhancement files you can copy (download) to your computer, for example. Write down the name and CompuServe number that corresponds to the sysop in your particular area of interest. Then switch to the Messages section of the forum, compose a detailed message about your problem, and address it to the number of the sysop you wrote down.

When you *post* a message in this way, it is seen not only by the sysop you addressed it to, but also by anyone else who reads the messages for that forum. Check the Messages section 24 to 48 hours later, and you'll probably find several responses. Some of them will likely be from people who are not employees of the vendor but are more expert users of the company's products than many employees!

To gain access to CompuServe, call the Customer Service Dept. at 800-848-8990. Customer service is available 8 a.m. to 1 a.m., Eastern Time, Monday through Friday, and 10 a.m. to 10 p.m. Saturday, Sunday, and holidays. CIS will send you a packet of information on how to find the closest local number in your area and how to use the service.

Technical support for the CD-ROM

If the CD-ROM that comes with this book is damaged, you should of course contact IDG Books Worldwide (www.idgbooks.com), which is committed to providing you with a CD-ROM in perfect condition.

If there are any updates to *MORE Windows 98 Secrets*, you'll find them at the IDG Books Worldwide web site at www.idgbooks.com or at www.davisstraub.com/secrets.

What are secrets?

Where do secrets come from? And what makes something a secret?

In about the order that we used them, secrets come from knowledgeable users, from our own tests and experience, and from the Microsoft Knowledge Base. We got some clues from the *Windows 98 Resource Kit*, but if it was adequately explained there, we showed you how to find it on your Windows 98 CD-ROM. If it didn't cover a secret well, we wrote it up.

We had plenty of help from the many participants on the Microsoft support newsgroups. By far most of what is written in these newsgroups is not of any use to anyone, but every once in a while a real nugget of clear thinking arrives. One of our filtering strategies was to clue in on the consistently brilliant participants. After reading a few thousand messages, you can figure out who they are.

We thank those newsgroup participants who made an effort to help their fellow man at no evident reward to themselves (see the Acknowledgments). Wherever we use one of their generously and freely provided secrets, we give them their much due credit.

Web sites devoted to Windows 95 and Windows 98 have proliferated. Several of them are quite good, although most only provide beginner level tips. Whenever we've found a secret at such a web site, we've given the site credit, as well as tested and rewritten the secret into a series of easy steps.

Microsoft has significantly expanded access to its Knowledge Base through its web site. There are plenty of substantial Windows 98-related Knowledge Base articles that were well worth the effort we expended in finding them, and we provide their URLs throughout the book. We suggest that you keep up with the latest articles published in the Knowledge Base by going to the KB site often and asking it to display the latest articles.

Microsoft provides the *Windows 98 Resource Kit* on the Windows 98 CD-ROM. This is their real documentation for Windows 98, and we suggest that you install it on your hard disk or at least access it from the Windows 98 CD-ROM. It is an invaluable and comprehensive resource, and it comes at no additional cost.

The "secrets" in *MORE Windows 98 Secrets* were there, waiting for us to find and document. Something is a "secret" if it is useful and isn't found in the standard Windows 98 documentation (either in the "manual" or in the online help) that you get when you purchase Windows. We didn't repeat what was available in the *Resource Kit*.

Of course, as soon as a secret becomes well known, it isn't a secret anymore. The problem with writing a book about secrets is that it is a pretty good way to make some people (who now have learned the secrets) feel that your book isn't about secrets at all. How ironic.

This book is a collection of secrets and tips that we feel will be immediately useful to you. We suggest that you find the secrets in your area of interest and implement them right away, as you're reading the steps in the book.

We feel that if you find just one really clever trick that helps you use Windows 98, then your purchase of this book will be worth it. Perhaps that is a bit self-serving, but at least we are sincere. We have striven to provide you many more than one really neat insight into how to effectively master this operating system.

We hope you enjoy this book.

Summary

We've found a lot more secrets since Windows 98 was first released, and we've written this book to share them with you. This chapter describes how to use this book and where to go for more information.

▶ If you have a question about Windows 98, load the e-version of this book onto your computer and search the text.

▶ We tell you how to recognize commands that you need to type from your keyboard.

▶ We tell you how to get the best technical support for Windows 98 — by phone from Microsoft and electronically through the Microsoft support newsgroups.

Part I

Internet Secrets

Chapter 2

Internet Explorer

In This Chapter

The Internet Explorer chapter is right up here at the beginning of this book just to emphasize its importance and introduce some key changes. For example, the offline web pages feature works in version 5 of Internet Explorer (unlike in version 4.01), and you can save complete web pages. In addition, we'll show you how to customize Internet Explorer for your individual uses.

▶ Take twelve steps to configure offline web pages to work for you.

▶ Save complete web pages with the graphics included.

▶ Add power to AutoComplete with a shareware package.

▶ Instead of copying and pasting a shortcut to a URL, copy and paste the actual URL.

▶ Rename the Internet Explorer.

Favorites and offline web pages

Unlike version 4.0 of Internet Explorer, version 5 actually allows you to successfully download Internet HTML documents and return later to view them offline. This can turn the World Wide Wait into the World Wide Web on your local hard disk.

You can also make your Favorites even handier by providing access to them where you find it most convenient.

Favorites off the Start menu

The Windows 98 Start menu includes the Favorites folder. When you click Favorites on the Start menu, you'll notice that the URL shortcuts to your favorite web sites are displayed in a menu fashion (as opposed to folder window fashion).

You can also get to your favorites by clicking the Favorites button on the Internet Explorer toolbar, or the Favorites menu item in your Explorer or Internet Explorer. If you don't use the Favorites Start menu item very frequently and would like to remove it from your Start menu, you can do so with TweakUI. (In TweakUI, click the IE tab, clear Show Favorites on Start Menu, and click OK.)

If you've removed the Favorites item from your Start menu, you can create an alternate method of getting to your Favorites folder by right-dragging the folder \Windows\Favorites to your Desktop and choosing Create Shortcut(s) Here. You can also create a Favorites toolbar by following these steps:

STEPS:

Creating a Favorites Toolbar

Step 1.   Right-click your Taskbar, click Toolbars, New Toolbar, browse to \Windows\Favorites in the New Toolbar dialog box, and click OK.

Step 2.   Drag the sizing bar at the left edge of the Favorites toolbar over to the right until only the word *Favorites* is still visible.

Step 3.   Click the arrow next to the word *Favorites* to display a vertical menu of Favorites, as shown in Figure 2-1. Click a menu item to open a folder window of Favorites.

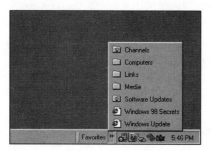

Figure 2-1: The Favorites menu, as displayed on a Favorites toolbar.

Easy access to your Offline Web Pages folder

Speaking of favorites, it can be a bit difficult to get to your Offline Web Pages folder if you've removed the Favorites item from your Start menu. You can get easy access to this folder in a couple of ways.

One option is to right-drag the \Windows\Offline Web Pages folder to your Desktop and create a shortcut to it there. You can also right-drag the folder and drop it on your Start button. (In this case, you can also left-drag to create the shortcut, but this is not standard behavior when you left drag a folder.)

Secret

If you use the Offline Pages resource identifier when dragging the Offline Web Pages folder to the Start menu, you can create a cascading menu instead of opening a folder window, as described in these steps:

STEPS:

Easing Access to Your Offline Web Pages

Step 1. Right-click the Start button and click Open. If you want the Offline Web Pages item to appear on the main Start menu, stop here. Otherwise, continue to open up windows of menu items until you open the menu folder that you want to contain it.

Step 2. Right-click an open area of the window and choose New, Folder.

Step 3. The temporary name New Folder is highlighted so that you can type over it with a new name. Type the following text exactly as we have printed it here:

Offline Web Pages.{F5175861-2688-11d0-9C5E-00AA00A45957}

Step 4. Press Enter, and the New Folder icon is replaced with the Offline Web Pages icon.

Step 5. Click the Start button. The Offline Web Pages icon appears as a menu item, and all of the offline web sites are listed in a cascading menu attached to it (see Figure 2-2).

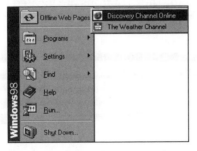

Figure 2-2: The offline pages are now available on the main Start menu.

You might find two settings related to this in TweakUI that don't work. In the Desktop tab, you can ignore Subscription Folder and Shell Favorite Folder.

Download web sites for later perusal

Assuming that you've created a shortcut to your \Windows\Offline Web Pages folder on your Desktop, click it to display your offline web pages, as shown in Figure 2-3.

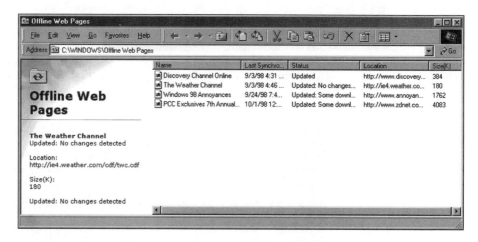

Figure 2-3: The web pages you download for offline viewing are displayed in the Offline Web Pages folder.

The toolbar at the top of the Offline Web Pages folder contains two new buttons, Sync and Sync All. These buttons are located just to the left of the Cut (scissors) button. You can use them to download a web page or site immediately.

Clicking the Sync or Sync All button will by default download only one page of a web site, unless the web site publisher has specified other pages. If you want to go deeper, you can let Internet Explorer download a pretty complete set of HTML documents from a web site — up to three links deep starting from any web page that you choose. To do so, take these steps:

STEPS:

Downloading a Web Site

Step 1. Connect to the Internet, and use your Internet Explorer to navigate to a web page on a web site that you want to view offline. If you have already added this page to your Favorites, you don't need to go online — right-click it in the Favorites, click Make Available Offline, and go to step 4.

Step 2.   Navigate to a central page of the web site that provides links throughout the site to information that you are interested in.

Step 3.   Click Favorites, Add to Favorites. In the Add Favorite dialog box that appears, mark the Make Available Offline check box, and select a Favorites folder for saving the shortcut. Than click the Customize button.

Step 4.   This brings up the Offline Favorite Wizard shown in Figure 2-4. (If you haven't run the wizard before, you will see an introductory screen that tells you about the wizard. You can choose not to show this again.) Click the Yes option button, choose how deep to delve into the web site by selecting 1, 2 or 3, and then click Next.

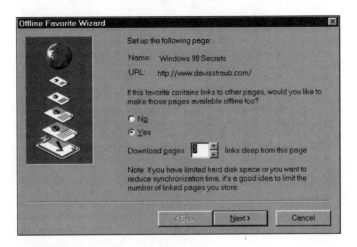

Figure 2-4: The Offline Favorite Wizard.

Step 5.   The wizard now asks how often you want to update (synchronize) the web page/site. Unless you already have a schedule set up, click Only When I Choose Synchronize from the Tools Menu, as shown in Figure 2-5. Click Next.

Continued

STEPS

Downloading a Web Site *(continued)*

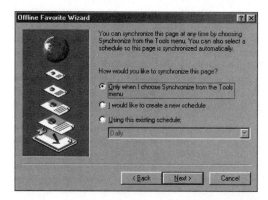

Figure 2-5: Mark the first option button in this Offline Favorite Wizard dialog box unless you have established a schedule for downloading.

Step 6. If the site doesn't require a password, click the Finish button. Otherwise enter your user name and password (twice), click Finish, and then click OK to close the Add Favorite dialog box.

Step 7. Internet Explorer will attempt to download (synchronize) the site right now. You can do this now, or wait until after you've refined your synchronization schedule using the remaining steps. To wait until later, click the Stop button shown in Figure 2-6.

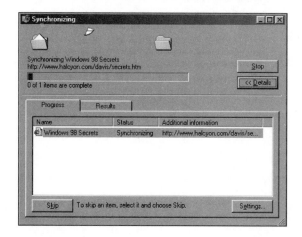

Figure 2-6: Click the Stop button if you want to refine your schedule before synchronizing.

Step 8.   Click your Offline Web Pages shortcut on your Desktop or in your Start menu, or navigate to \Windows\Offline Web Pages. Right-click the shortcut to the offline web page that you just created, and click Properties. Click the Download tab in the Properties dialog box, as shown in Figure 2-7.

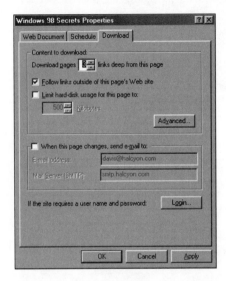

Figure 2-7: The Download tab of the Properties dialog box for the Windows 98 Secrets offline web page.

Step 9.   Adjust any of the parameters in the Download tab. If you want to exclude graphics files, sound, video, ActiveX controls, or Java applets, click the Advanced button.

Step 10.   To set up a regular schedule to update your downloaded web site/page at a time while you're asleep or away from your computer, click the Schedule tab, shown in Figure 2-8. You can select a daily, weekly or monthly schedule, or create a custom schedule. Highlight the schedule you want, and then click the Edit button.

Continued

STEPS

Downloading a Web Site *(continued)*

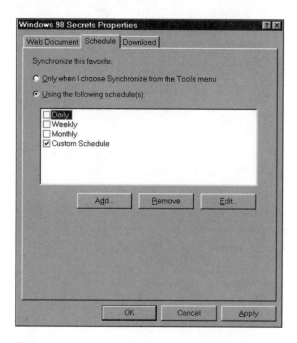

Figure 2-8: Select one of the preset schedules, or set up a custom schedule.

Step 11. Click the Schedule tab in the dialog box for your schedule, display the Schedule Task list, and choose a frequency for synchronizing the web site, as shown in Figure 2-9. Depending on what you have selected, you may also need to choose a time or specify other information.

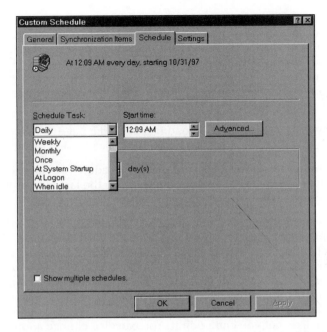

Figure 2-9: Select a frequency for synchronizing from the Schedule Task drop-down list.

Step 12. If you chose Weekly or Monthly in step 11, click the Advanced button. In the Advanced Schedule Options dialog box, choose a start date for your schedule, as shown in Figure 2-10. and then click OK twice.

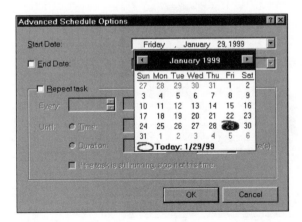

Figure 2-10: You can set your weekly or monthly schedule to start today.

Your web page/site will now be downloaded at the date and time that you've chosen, as long as you have your computer on at that time. During synchronization, the icon for the Synchronization Manager will appear in your system tray. Later, you can click your Offline Web Pages shortcut on your Desktop or in your Start menu, and click the new web page to view it. If your computer tries to go online, click File, Work Offline in the Internet Explorer window.

If you find that the download has missed a page or two (hey, it's a jungle out there on the web), just go online and click the links that seem to be missing.

Internet Explorer will go out on the schedule you have set up, and will check whether a page has been changed since the last synchronization. It won't download the page to your offline web page store again if it hasn't changed.

If your web page is a channel, the Offline Favorite Wizard won't give you the option of choosing how many pages deep to download. The channel operator is limiting access to the site. The Download tab of the Properties dialog box for a channel gives you two options: download the content specified by the channel operator, or just download the home page and a table of contents. Channel operators have recommended schedules, which show up in the Schedule tab of the Properties dialog box. You can choose their schedule if you like, but you can't edit it. You can also choose another schedule.

Windows 98 tracks the offline web pages separately from the temporary Internet files. You can manage them with the Disk Cleanup applet (Start, Programs, Accessories, System Tools, Disk Cleanup), as shown in Figure 2-11. Notice that this applet can distinguish between the two types of files.

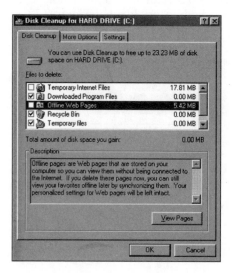

Figure 2-11: The Disk Cleanup dialog box. You can delete the temporary Internet files while leaving the offline web pages intact.

Deeper offline viewing

The Internet Explorer offline viewer limits your web page gathering to three levels starting from any given page. If you want to go a little deeper and have a bit more control and flexibility, check out SiteSnagger, a freeware package from Steven Sipe via PC Magazine. SiteSnagger lets you follow the links up to 20 jumps away from the original page. You can set the maximum number of web pages, whether or not you'll download GIFs, JPEGs, and other multimedia or non-HTML files, and whether to follow the links to another server.

SiteSnagger stores all the pages and multimedia files associated with the site in a separate subfolder for each site (or user-defined project), as shown in Figure 2-12. You can have SiteSnagger create an HTML table of contents that just lists the names of the web pages, but it's not really as useful as the pages and their own links.

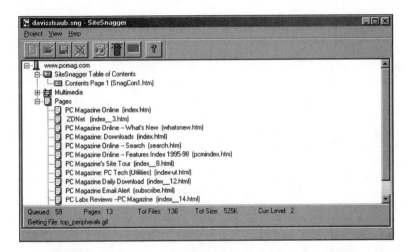

Figure 2-12: SiteSnagger makes it easy to navigate among the pages you've downloaded from a web

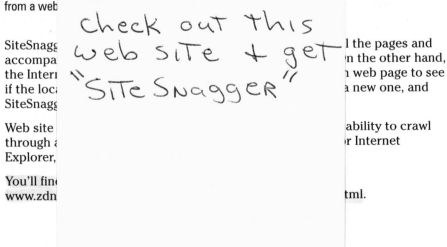

SiteSnagg [...] l the pages and accompa [...] n the other hand, the Inter [...] a web page to see if the loc [...] a new one, and SiteSnagg [...]

Web site [...] ability to crawl through a [...] r Internet Explorer, [...]

You'll fin [...]
www.zdn [...] tml.

Save complete web pages

Internet Explorer 5 has added the ability to save a web page as a single document. The Microsoft HTML format (*mht*) incorporates the graphics and the HTML text into one text file. The graphics are encoded using MIME (and Uuencoding) so everything is stored as text characters, but Internet Explorer can decode the file on the fly and display the graphics.

This feature greatly expands the power of the Internet. If a document is displayed as one web page, you can download it and all of its associated graphic files, and save everything in one very convenient document. If you do this, you don't have to save the document as an offline page to keep it readily available.

All you do to save a web page in this format is click File, Save As, and choose Web Archive for Email in the Save As Type field. This secret isn't hidden, but it sure is powerful. Turns the web into something that you can actually use as a publishing arena.

Tip

You can see the entire underlying text file if you open a file with an *mht* extension in WordPad. If you click View, Source in the Internet Explorer when viewing an *mht* file, you'll only see the HTML code, and not the encoded graphics that are in fact there in the file.

Internet Explorer also lets you save a document as a "complete" web page (click File, Save As, and choose Web Page, Complete in the Save As Type field). In this case, the graphic files are not included in the HTML source text. Instead, Internet Explorer creates a subfolder in which it saves the downloaded graphics files. It rewrites the saved web page to reference the graphics files in this subfolder, and enters the web page's URL as a comment at the top of the page. We wish Save As, Web Archive for Email saved the web page's URL as a comment.

Turn your favorites into a web page

The Favorites menu and submenus are fine for starters, but sometimes it is a bit of a drag to search repeatedly through all these menus. How about creating a single web page of all your favorites? Or separate web pages for different subsets of favorites?

Internet Explorer 5 includes the Import/Export Wizard, which can export your favorites or cookies. It writes them in a format that Netscape can read. You can also use the wizard to import cookies and favorites from Netscape. The wizard writes out your favorites as an HTML file. This makes it easy to look through your favorites and edit them if you like.

Choose File, Import and Export to run the wizard.

Move Favorites to Links

We're not big fans of the Favorites Explorer bar on the left side of the Internet Explorer window. Maybe if we had 21-inch monitors, it would be a different story. This gets even worse if you remove Favorites from your Start menu. You might like to have a way to get to your Favorites other than the Internet Explorer menu itself.

One way out of this dilemma is to move your Favorites subfolder into the Links subfolder. Before you do this, you might create an additional subfolder for all of your existing links, and store the subfolder under the Links folder. Now you'll have a Links toolbar that contains menu items for your favorites as well as your links. This process is detailed in these steps:

STEPS:

Moving Your Favorites to Your Links

Step 1. Open your Explorer and navigate to \Windows\Favorites\Links.

Step 2. Right-click your right pane, click New, Folder, and rename the new folder **Links**.

Step 3. Drag all of the shortcuts in your \Windows\Favorites\Links folder to your \Windows\Favorites\Links\Links folder.

Step 4. Drag the rest of your Favorites shortcuts and subfolders into your \Windows\Favorites\Links folder.

Step 5. Position your Links toolbar in your Internet Explorer window so that you can see all of your favorites on the toolbar, as shown in Figure 2-13.

Continued

Moving Your Favorites to Your Links *(continued)*

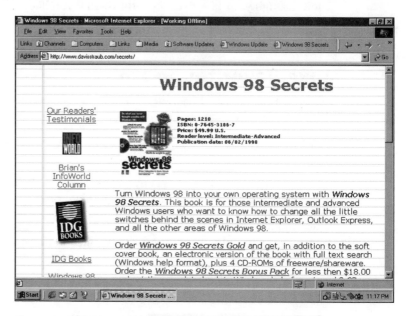

Figure 2-13: The new Links toolbar appears at the top of the window, just above the Address bar.

Now you can use the Links toolbar to get to your favorites.

Thanks to Jim Schott for this tip.

Navigating with the Internet Explorer

Internet Explorer gives you many tools for navigating and searching on the Internet. In this section, we show you some new tools and some new ways to use the old ones.

The complete AutoComplete

Internet Explorer has a feature called AutoComplete that helps you complete your entry in the Address bar as soon as you type in the first few letters. For example, type www.davis, pause for a few seconds, and you'll get a drop-down list of sites you have previously visited that start with www.davis,

Check out This web Page

in … re is a long list of URLs th … ou can easily use your m … itry in the list, and then p…

If … s bar is active, Internet E… resses you've recently ty… ist than the AutoComplete d… you click the down arrow a…

T… Internet Options, click the C… the AutoComplete S… AutoComplete for web a… ds (see Figure 2-14). (We c… section.)

Figure 2-14: You can control the AutoComplete settings.

Tip

If you want Internet Explorer to preface your entry with www. and end it with the suffix .com, just type the domain name in the Address bar and then press Ctrl+Enter. For example, type **davisstraub**, press Ctril+Enter, and you get www.davisstraub.com. This is different from actually searching on the Internet for the address; see "Autosearch for a web address" later in this chapter for more on that.

Fill in forms by clicking a button or two

According to a Microsoft Intelliform developer document, when you submit a form on a web page, Internet Explorer encrypts and saves on your computer the name of each text field with the value you have entered in that field. The next time you visit a web page and begin typing in a text field of the same name, AutoComplete will prompt you with a list of previously used data.

So, if the name of the field on a web page form is Address, the next time you run into a web page form with a field named Address, your previous input value will be displayed in a drop-down list. You can then choose to enter it or not.

While it's really great that Microsoft built in the AutoComplete capability, it is also nice to enter text by clicking a single button. The great thing is that you can do either or both.

TypeItIn is a simple — and simple-minded — utility that puts a toolbar on your Desktop (see Figure 2-15). You can define and name up to 50 buttons. Click a button, and the associated text is squirted into the active window at the current location of the insertion point.

Figure 2-15: The TypeItIn toolbar inserts the associated text when you click one of its buttons.

You can add, edit, rearrange, and delete buttons. A right-click lets you undo an erroneous entry. You can also use TypeItIn to insert the current date and time, or use it as a Start menu to start programs. Keep it always on top or not. TypeItIn stays in the system tray so you can call it up at any time. It's very fast, and it handles special characters.

In addition to the freeware version, you can get a professional version that lets you group your buttons — by application, for example. You'll find TypeItIn at www.wavget.com/typeitin.html. Nothing fancy, but very functional.

Autosearch for a web address

Internet Explorer 5 will automatically search on the Internet for a web address if you ask it to. Type a fragment of an address in the Address bar, press Enter, and Internet Explorer will treat the fragment as a search term. After a minute or two, you will see a list of URLs containing the text you typed, and Internet Explorer will navigate to the site that is the most likely match according to its criteria, as shown in Figure 2-16.

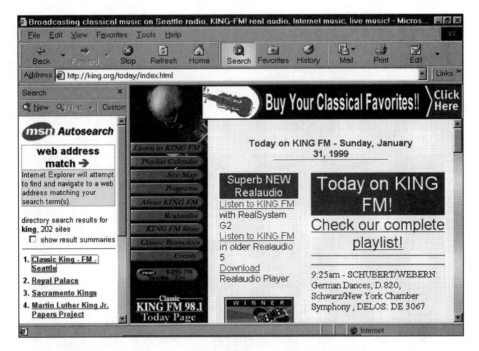

Figure 2-16: The results of an autosearch for a web address containing the word *king*.

You can choose to turn this feature off or change how it functions by taking these steps:

STEPS:

Changing Your Autosearch Settings

Step 1. Click Tools, Internet Options in your Internet Explorer.

Step 2. Click the Advanced tab and scroll down to Search from the Address Bar.

Step 3. Mark the option button that you prefer, and click OK (see Figure 2-17).

Continued

STEPS

Changing Your Autosearch Settings *(continued)*

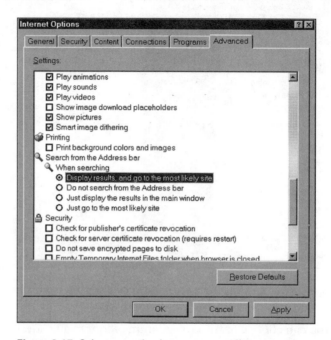

Figure 2-17: Select an option button to turn off Autosearch or to change the way it behaves.

The Search pane

Click the Search toolbar button, and the Search pane opens on the left side of the Internet Explorer window.

Microsoft has provided a Windows Search Assistant Workshop web site that includes a set of specifications and design criteria that developers can use to make their sites more Search-pane friendly. For example, search engine developers must display their output in a manner that fits within a 200-pixel wide window (the width of the Search pane). Microsoft also asks that ads be placed at the bottom of the Search pane. The payback for the developers is that they get to be on the list of sites that comes up in the Customize Search Settings window. (You display this window by clicking the Search toolbar button and then clicking the Customize button at the top of the Search pane.) You'll find the Windows Search Assistant Workshop at microsoft.com/ workshop/browser/configuration/searchbarguide/searchbar_reqs.asp.

Microsoft's search feature doesn't search with all the web search engines, just the first one on the list you create in the Customize Search Settings window. Mark the search engines that you want to have available in the Search pane, and then use up and down arrows to change the order of the engines in the list. This will be the order they are used for searching.

Because Customize Search Settings doesn't provide any information about the individual search engines, it may be hard for you to choose which one to use. You may need to run a sample search or two, starting with the default search web site. Once you have tried a search with it, you can use the Next button at the top of the Search pane to try each search engine in the order listed and see how it handles your queries. There are many more search engines than the ones shown in the Customize Search Settings window.

You can still search the old fashioned way, by typing the web address of a search engine in your Address bar. Or, you can use a search engine front end that searches multiple search engine sites for you. We discuss Copernic and Express, which do just that, in the next section.

Search multiple search engines at once

It may seem a bit redundant to search the search engines, but there are some advantages that aren't clear at first. First, local agent software on your computer can manage searches more effectively than the front ends of the search engines. For example, you can more easily save the results of previous searches so that you can go back later and review them. You can organize and group the search results into categories that you find helpful.

Also, a package such as Copernic, shown in Figure 2-18, can keep track of up to 130 search engines, which would be a bit of a pain for you and me. You can organize the results by rating, date found, address, and so on. You can browse the results and create a web page from them. Send the web page of results to a friend.

You'll find Copernic at www.copernic.com. The freeware version is somewhat limited in the number of search engines it will search; the professional version will search through 130 of them.

Express is another freeware tool that performs searches using multiple search engines at once, then retrieves only those web pages you say are the most relevant. It retrieves data from up to seven search engines you specify and combines the ratings from all these engines into a single ranked list.

Express is a free download from Infoseek, itself a major search engine. To its credit, Infoseek doesn't seem to get any preference in the ranking of the listings, although Express doesn't let you control this yourself. Express is free, but it does present a lot of advertising, including ads from the other sites its listings come from (this is apparently intended to give something back in exchange for the use of those databases). Express also manages to place itself in every conceivable menu, toolbar, and nook and cranny of your Windows user interface to a level that we found annoying.

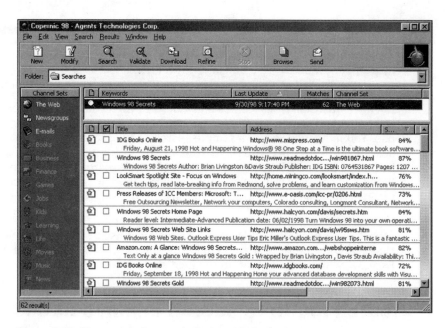

Figure 2-18: The results of a search displayed in Copernic.

The professional version of Copernic offers far more in the sheer number of search engines it can manage, and much better flexibility in saving, managing and using past searches. However, we found Express' tab-based user interface makes it especially quick and easy to select and view the most relevant results. If relevance and convenient viewing are your emphasis, you might prefer Express.

Set up a search on Express' Search tab and let it run. You then see a listing of results from your search on the Results List tab. Express includes check boxes to the left of the listings, as shown in Figure 2-19, that let you quickly mark the web pages you actually want to see.

When you mark a check box to select a listing, Express begins to download that page in the background. After you've marked a few pages, click Express' View Results tab to display the first downloaded page. Clicking the Next button on the View Results tab takes you to the next page, and so on. The pages come up quickly, and there is no need to repeatedly click your Back button to jump between your search results and the actual web pages.

Express is available for download at express.infoseek.com. It requires 10MB of disk space, an 800 x 600 display, and Microsoft Internet Explorer 3.0 or higher or Netscape Navigator 3.0 or higher.

If you prefer your search listings without advertising, you need to buy a different software package that eschews ads. Danny Sullivan's Search Engine Watch contains a page that briefly reviews such products as BullsEye, Copernic, Mata Hari, and WebFerretPro. See searchenginewatch.com/sereport/9809-utilities.html. A good comparative review of five commercial search utilities (plus the free Express utility) is available at Chris Sherman's Mining Co., websearch.miningco.com/library/weekly/aa100998.htm.

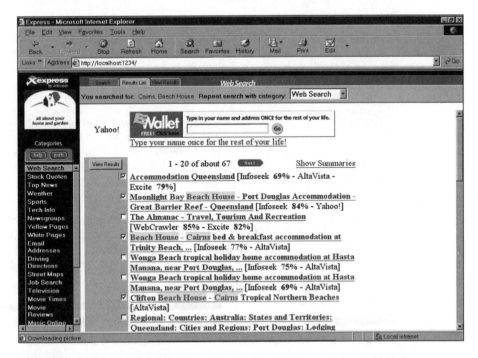

Figure 2-19: The Results List tab shows the results of an Express search. Mark the pages that you want to view.

Standardizing search engines

Search engines often return far too many results to find the one item you want, and different search engines refine their searches in completely different ways. Now someone is doing more than just complaining about this. Danny Sullivan, the editor of Search Engine Watch, an Internet analysis service, has a goal to bring together major search engine executives so users need learn only one set of search techniques that will work across all engines. For details, see searchenginewatch.com/standards.

By "major" search engines, Sullivan means AltaVista, AOL NetFind, Excite, HotBot, InfoSeek/Go, Google, GoTo, LookSmart, Lycos, MSN Search, Netscape Search, Northern Light, Snap, WebCrawler, and Yahoo. All of these engines exist because no single engine can fill all users' needs.

Choosing which engine to use for a particular task is daunting even for experienced data miners, much less occasional users. Sullivan's project to standardize search procedures may help users who must jump from engine to engine to find the information they need.

Most queries return thousands of hits, and narrowing your search becomes a painful but essential step. Fortunately, there are many little-known ways to make fine tuning easy. And this is exactly where Sullivan's standards project may be able to help.

One fast way to narrow your focus is to search only the titles of web sites. This eliminates many sites that have mere passing references to your subject. AltaVista, HotBot, InfoSeek, GoTo, MSN, Snap, and Northern Light allow you to do this with the prefix title: (as in title: windows bugs). But Yahoo uses the prefix t: and Lycos makes you go to an "advanced search" page.

If you are still getting too many hits, you can narrow your search to a single web site that has many relevant pages. The syntax for this type of search is even less standardized, however. AltaVista uses the prefix *host:* (as in *host:infoworld.com windows bugs*). InfoSeek uses *site:*. HotBot, GoTo, MSN, and Snap use *domain:*. And other engines don't yet support this useful refinement (though some do on "advanced search" pages).

Even the most basic searches, such as *windows bugs*, aren't foolproof. Most engines treat this entry as *windows OR bugs*, but HotBot, Lycos, MSA, and Northern Light treat such entries as though you typed *windows AND bugs*. AltaVista and Google default to *"windows bugs"* (they treat it as a phrase).

A complete description of all these rules can be found at searchenginewatch. com/facts/powersearch.html. A handy chart summarizing the rules is available at www.davisstraub.com/secrets/searchenginerules.htm.

The site www.searchengines.net/ makes it easy to quickly review different search engines. If you have a web site and want to place a link on one of your web pages to a search engine, this site makes that easy. Many search engines provide small forms that you can incorporate into your site, thus allowing your visitors to do a quick, perhaps specialized, search of the net from your site. You'll find all the forms here.

Jump to a site without searching

If you had a database that associated a company name with its web site address, it would be a bit easier to find the company's web site (assuming you knew the company's name). 1jump is an Internet Explorer add-on that comes with just such a database.

1jump is another example of the continuous growth in web services. Take an address format that only technicians could love, and put a user-friendly front end on top of it. Type the name of the company, its stock symbol, or a brand, and click the Jump button to open up its web site (see Figure 2-20).

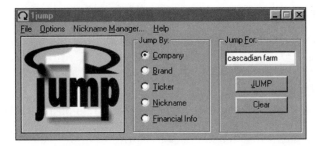

Figure 2-20: Use 1jump to jump to a company's web site even if you don't know its address.

You can download 1jump from www.1jump.com.

Placeholder for images on web pages

Tip

It isn't the default, so you might miss it. Internet Explorer will not put in place-holder borders for images yet to be downloaded. If you want this feature turned on so that the text can wrap around the images as yet unseen, you can turn it on in your Internet Options dialog box. Choose Tools, Internet Options, click the Advanced tab, and scroll down to Multimedia. Mark the Show Image Download Placeholders check box. Click OK.

Clear the frames

Sometimes you just want to get rid of the menu frame on the left side of a web page. One of those times is when you click a link to another web site and the frame from the old one remains in the browser window.

A quick way to get rid of the frame is to drag the link of the page you're viewing to the Address bar and drop it there. This sends you to the URL associated with the link, whether it is to another site or just to another web page at the same site. In either case, the menu frame goes away.

Thanks to Chris Pirillo at www.lockergnome.com/ for this tip.

png graphics

Internet Explorer can display the *png* graphics format. You probably haven't seen any graphics files using this format, but perhaps you will in the future. Check out www.w3.org/Graphics/PNG/Inline-img.html for an example.

The PNG format is described by the World Wide Web Consortium (W3C) as: "an extensible file format for the lossless, portable, well-compressed storage of raster images. PNG provides a patent-free replacement for GIF and can also replace many common uses of TIFF."

Copy and paste links

Wherever there's a hot link, there's a way to cut and paste it. If you receive an e-mail message in Outlook Express that contains a link, you can of course, just click it to invoke an Internet Explorer window (if it's a link to a web site or an FTP address).

You can right-click a link and click Copy Shortcut. Then paste this URL into the Address bar, into a text file, onto the Desktop, whatever you like. You can also click Add to Favorites instead of Copy Shortcut.

Right-click a web page name in your History Explorer bar, and you can click Copy or Add to Favorites. You can do the same with a web page name in search results displayed in the Search Explorer bar.

Copy and paste URLs

Internet Explorer saves web pages as URL shortcuts. You'll find lots of them in your \Windows\Favorites folder. You can easily copy and paste these shortcuts into e-mail messages, other folders, to and from your Desktop, and so on.

Sometimes you don't want to copy the shortcut, you just want to copy the URL embedded in the shortcut. CopyURL, a freeware applet, makes this easy. It adds three items to the context menus associated with URL shortcuts. Right-click a URL shortcut, perhaps on your Favorites menu, and you will see the three additional options, as shown in Figure 2-21.

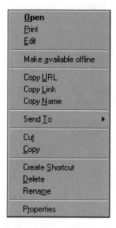

Figure 2-21: This context menu has been modified using CopyURL. The three new commands are in the third section of the menu.

The Copy URL command lets you copy just the URL — for example, www.davisstraub.com/secrets.

The Copy Link command lets you copy the URL as a link—for example, <A HREF="http://www.davisstraub/secrets">Windows 98 Secrets</A>. This text with HTML tags is ready to be inserted in an HTML document.

Finally, the Copy Name command lets you copy the URL along with the title of its web page—for example, Windows 98 Secrets: http://www.davisstraub/ secrets. This gives you a handy way to create a list of names and URLs if you highlight and copy a whole bunch of shortcuts at once (the other two commands also work with multiple selected shortcuts).

Extract the CopyURL.zip file to a temporary folder. Right-click CopyURL.inf and click Install. You can then delete the files in the temporary folder.

You'll find this little hummer at www.moonsoftware.com/.

Stay online

Does your Internet service provider (including AOL and Prodigy) kick you offline after a period of inactivity? Would you like to have an applet that simulates user input and keeps your connection open even when you are away from the computer?

StayOn Pro will randomly ping URLs on its list to simulate user input over a PPP connection to an Internet service provider. If you are on AOL, it will let you stay online by helping you identify the dialog box that AOL sends out requesting that you respond.

StayOn Pro isn't pretty, and it doesn't do much, but if you need what it does, it does it.

You'll find this applet at rclabs.simplenet.com.

Protect your e-mail address

One thing we don't like is people sending us commercial e-mail when we haven't requested it. The Internet's popular SendMail program has recently been revised to give Internet service providers more tools to stop spam, such as refusing to deliver messages that have bogus return addresses. And vigilant ISPs continue to find new defenses against the tide of junk e-mail from lists we can't seem to get removed from.

Still, there are ways that web sites can capture your e-mail address without your knowledge. Some web sites can make your browser silently download a tiny file using FTP. To start the FTP download, your browser sends your e-mail address.

Glenn Fleishman has created a small demonstration at his own web site of how this trick works. Visit www.glenns.org/cgi-bin/nph-ftpgrab to see what information your browser gives out. The script takes several seconds to work—click Refresh if you don't see any results on the first try.

The scam doesn't work with recent versions of Internet Explorer, which send web sites a generic e-mail address such as ieuser40@ (the @ fools the web site script). You can increase Internet Explorer's resistance to other similar tricks, however. To do so, choose Tools, Internet Options, click the Security tab, click the Custom Level button, scroll down to Logon under User Authentication, and mark either Anonymous Logon or Automatic Logon Only in Intranet Zone.

In our opinion, it's unethical for commercial entities to collect personal information from you or about your computer without your consent. Closing this loophole won't stop all spam. But it's one step toward more privacy on the web.

Toggle Internet Explorer between full-screen mode and restore

Open up Internet Explorer and press the F11 key. If you weren't before, you are now in full-screen mode. If you were maximized before, hitting F11 again will get you back there.

Did we say Internet Explorer? Because Windows 98 integrates Internet Explorer and Explorer, you can use the F11 toggle switch to "blow up" your Explorer, My Computer, Control Panel, or any folder window.

Thanks to Dave Adams and Jason Nadal for these tips.

Internet Explorer shortcut keys

This is where Microsoft help actually does a good job. While we've pointed out a few keys that are of special interest, and you can look in Internet Explorer help for more.

One that we thought was pretty cool was Ctrl+F5. This forces Internet Explorer to download and refresh the page even if it thinks it has the latest version in the cache.

Tom Pipinich at Microsoft pointed this out to us.

We provide you with a table of Internet Explorer keyboard shortcuts in Chapter 9 of *Windows 98 Secrets*. Table 2-1 lists a few more:

Table 2-1   Keyboard Shortcuts for Internet Explorer

Key or Combination	Effect
Alt+D	Jumps to the Address bar
Ctrl+F	Brings up the Find dialog box
Ctrl+P	Brings up the Print dialog box
Ctrl+Shift+Tab	Moves backward among frames
Ctrl+Tab	Moves forward among frames
F4 (or Alt+down arrow)	Displays the Address bar history
F6	Jumps to the Address bar
F11	Toggles full-screen mode
Page Down	Scrolls down, one screen at a time
Page Up	Scrolls up, one screen at a time
Spacebar	Scrolls down, one screen at a time

A key resource for keystrokes

Michael Maardt, a Danish writer/publisher, decided to publish English versions of his best selling booklets (in Scandinavia) to get them out to more users and build interest in his efforts among a wider audience. The books are free in the PDF format. To view the files, you need to download the free Acrobat reader from Adobe Systems at www.adobe.com/supportservice/custsupport/LIBRARY/acrwin.htm.

We found his Escape from the Mousetrap booklet to be quite well done and useful. It was written for Windows 95, so it doesn't have all the latest Internet Explorer 5 and Windows 98 keystrokes, but it does have the ones that Windows 95 and 98 share in common.

He has a few other booklets online that you can download for friends who are just beginning to use Windows 98. Michael encourages users to ignore their mouse and use their keyboards to accomplish all their Windows task.

You'll find his booklets at www.knowware.dk/eng/windows.htm. Alan Eldredge told Chris Pirillo at www.lockergnome.com about this site, and that's how we found out about it.

Customizing Internet Explorer

Internet Explorer 5 gives you more ways than ever to customize the user interface. Here are some secrets for making it look and act the way you want it to.

Microsoft's tweaks to Internet Explorer

Microsoft has released its own add-ons and tools that help you change and use Internet Explorer. You can zoom in and out on images, customize your searches, open a frame in a new window, paste URLs, and more.

All of these tools are available from the "Web Accessories" page on the Microsoft web site at http://www.microsoft.com/windows/ie/webaccess/default.asp.

Do away with the Go button

Microsoft added the Go button to the Internet Explorer because the whuffos who they brought in from the real world would sit back after they typed a URL in the Address field and wait for the web page to display. It sometimes took quite a while for people to figure out that they had to press Enter to "go" to the site — hence, the Go button.

If you've been trained to press Enter to execute a command, you'll find the Go button a bit much. To banish the offending helper for dummies, in Internet Explorer, choose Tools, Internet Options, click the Advanced tab, and clear the Show Go Button in the Address Bar check box. Notice how high up this item is in the list of check boxes in the Advanced dialog box — makes it real easy to get rid of.

Your own "addresses" in the Address bar

Microsoft makes available at no cost an Internet Explorer Administration Kit that allows you to easily change the Internet Explorer to be more the way you want it to be.

A system administrator using this kit can create a list of friendly names that correspond to the unfriendly URLs where useful information is stored, on an Intranet or otherwise. For example, users could type *401K* in the Address bar to reach a document that had a URL of http://benefits/employee/401K.

You can find the Internet Explorer Administration Kit at ieak.microsoft.com/.

Thanks to Ray Sun at Microsoft for pointing this out to us.

Rename Internet Explorer

Secret

You can use the Internet Explorer Administration Kit described in the previous section to rename the Internet Explorer window. But if you'd rather not use this kit, you can manually rename Internet Explorer with a little Registry editing. Here's how:

STEPS:

Changing Microsoft Internet Explorer to a New Name

Step 1. Open your Registry editor and navigate to HKEY_LOCAL_MACHINE\ SOFTWARE\ Microsoft\ Internet Explorer\ Main.

Step 2. If the value Window Title doesn't exist in the right pane, right-click the right pane, and click New, String Value.

Step 3. Give the string value variable the name **Window Title**. Press Enter.

Step 4. Double-click Window Title. In the Edit String dialog box, type the name you'd like to see instead of Microsoft Internet Explorer (see Figure 2-22). Press Enter. Exit the Registry editor.

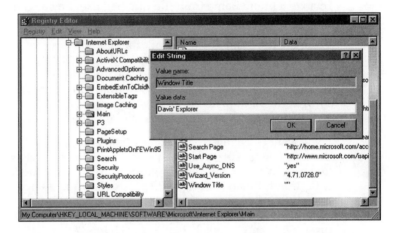

Figure 2-22: In this example, Internet Explorer will now be called *Davis' Explorer*.

The next time you open Internet Explorer, it will use your new title in the title bar.

Thanks to Peter Lara and many others for this tip.

You can also use the little freeware program IE Tweakin' Tool to accomplish this task and a few others. You'll find it at www.digitalspider.co.uk/tweak/.

Clear out the Internet Explorer brands

Some computer suppliers and Internet service providers put their own brand logos in the copies of Internet Explorer that they provide. They may substitute their own logo for the animated Internet Explorer logo in the upper-right corner of the window, or even add an additional logo pane in the Internet Explorer window. If you prefer to do without the third party branding, you can clear out these brands and put in your own.

Tip

The easiest way to do this is to use WinBoost, discussed in "Tweaking the Windows 98 Desktop" in Chapter 13. Click WinBoost's Internet toolbar button, and then mark Changing IE and OE Logo Animation and Putting Text in Internet Explorer Title Bar. You can decide whether to change the values or get rid of existing values to go back to the Internet Explorer defaults.

Instead of using WinBoost, you can edit your Registry directly. If you want to remove a brand name from the title bar, use the steps in the previous section and delete the Window Title entry.

To delete the animated icons of other companies that may run in your Internet Explorer window, use the Registry editor to navigate to HKEY_ CURRENT_USER\ Software\ Microsoft\ Internet Explorer\ Toolbar. You can delete the string values labeled BrandBitmap and SmBrandBitmap if you see them in the right pane of the Registry editor. (You won't see them if you don't have a third party branded version of Internet Explorer.)

Secret

If you want to change these values (and add them to this key), you can also do that. Just be sure to specify the value of a correctly sized graphics file. To fit correctly in the Internet Explorer window pane, the file that is associated with BrandBitmap should be 30 pixels wide and 38 pixels high for each image. A file that is 38 x 722 x 256 (colors) allows for 19 frames in an animation sequence. The graphics file associated with SmBrandBitmap should be 22 pixels wide and 22 pixels high for each image.

If you have a branded Internet Explorer, you can find the existing graphics files by looking in the Registry at the branch given above, and then edit the files with MS Paint, if you like.

Ask to open media files

Secret

Normally, Internet Explorer automatically opens and plays media files when it downloads them from the Internet. These files include sound files in the *wav* format and video clips in *avi*, *mov*, and *qt* formats. You can force Internet Explorer to ask whether you want to open or save the files, instead of just playing them. This gives you the option of saving media files under recognizable filenames in your designated locations.

STEPS:

Confirming Open After Download

Step 1.   In your Explorer window, choose View, Folder Options, and click the File Types tab.

Step 2.   Scroll down the Registered File Types list to the media type that you want to change — Wave Sound, for example.

Step 3.   Highlight the media type, and click the Edit button to display the Edit File Type dialog box.

Step 4.   Mark the Confirm Open After Download check box, as shown in Figure 2-23.

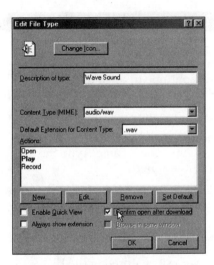

Figure 2-23: The Confirm Open After Download check box is in the lower-right corner of the Edit File Type dialog box.

Step 5.   Click OK.

Step 6.   Repeat this process for other media file types, and then click OK to close the Folder Options dialog box.

Add History to your Start menu

Secret

Accessing your history menus through the History button on the Internet Explorer toolbar is a bit of a pain. You can access them as a toolbar off your Taskbar (create a toolbar for the \Windows\History\History folder), but that requires that you hold down the Ctrl key when you click the button for any given week to get a menu of the previously visited sites (otherwise, clicking the button opens a folder window).

It is possible to put the History folder directly on the Start menu and access all the sites easily as menu items. Follow these steps to do this:

STEPS:
Getting Quickly to your Internet Explorer History

Step 1.   Right-click the Start button, and click Open. If you want to have the History menu item on the main Start menu, stop here. Otherwise, continue to open up windows of menu items until you open the menu folder where you want it stored.

Step 2.   Right-click an open area of the window. Choose New, Folder.

Step 3.   The temporary name New Folder is highlighted so that you can type over it with a new name. Type the following text exactly as we have printed it here:

History.{FF393560-C2A7-11CF-BFF4-444553540000}

Step 4.   Press Enter, and the New Folder icon is replaced with the History icon.

Step 5.   Click the Start button. The History icon appears as a menu item, and all the web sites stored in the History folder are listed in a cascading menu attached to it.

We feel that this is an absolutely necessary change to be able to run history effectively. The history function is much improved with Internet Explorer 5, and it is well worth your effort to be able to get to it easily and often.

Tip

We also suggest that you greatly expand the range of your history file, far beyond the 20 days that are standard. Choose Tools, Internet Options. In the General tab of the Internet Options dialog box, increase the number of days to keep pages in the History folder.

Edit the Links toolbar

You can rearrange and edit the items in the Links toolbar just as you can in any other Windows 98 Desktop toolbar or menu. Just because it sits in your Internet Explorer window doesn't mean that you can't treat it like you do the other Desktop toolbars.

To move an item in the Links toolbar, drag and drop it to another location on the toolbar. Drag and drop to add an item, too. Right-click any item on the Links toolbar to bring up its context menu. Click Delete to get rid of that item.

Remember, you'll find the items in the Links toolbar in the \Windows\Favorites\Links folder.

Restore Open in New Window

Secret

Internet Explorer lets you open a new Internet Explorer window by right-clicking a link in a web page and clicking Open in New Window. It is possible to lose this capability.

You can restore your ability to open new windows from links by taking these steps:

STEPS:

Restoring Open in New Window

Step 1.   Click Start, Run.

Step 2.   Type **regsvr32 shdocvw.dll** and press Enter.

Step 3.   Click Start, Shut Down, Restart, and click OK.

Thanks to Adam Vujic for this secret.

Set Work Offline before you open Internet Explorer

Secret

By changing your Registry settings, you can make a pair of shortcuts that let you switch between online and offline mode before you open Internet Explorer. This is useful if you have marked Always Dial My Default Connection in the Connections tab of the Internet Options dialog box. If you have done this and you use a home page that is not stored in your Temporary Internet Files folder, Internet Explorer will try to dial a connection as soon as you open it, and you'll have to cancel the dialing. It's much easier if you can set your system to offline mode before this happens.

These steps walk you through the creation of two files, Online.reg and Offline.reg. You'll find these files on the CD-ROM that accompanies this book. If you like, you can just copy them onto your hard disk and skip to step 3.

STEPS:
Setting Online/Offline Status

Step 1: In Notepad, start a new text file and type the following:

REGEDIT4

[HKEY_USERS\.Default\ Software\ Microsoft\ Windows\ CurrentVersion\ Internet Settings]

"GlobalUserOffline"=dword:00000000

Save your file as Online.reg (if you have created a My System folder as we suggest in *Windows 98 Secrets*, that's a good place for it), and then close it.

Step 2: Start another text file and type the following:

REGEDIT4

[HKEY_USERS\ .Default\ Software\ Microsoft\ Windows\ CurrentVersion\ Internet Settings]

"GlobalUserOffline"=dword:00000001

Save this file as Offline.reg in the same folder you used for the file in step 1, and close it.

Step 3: You can make shortcuts to your two new files on your Desktop. Better yet, put the shortcuts on a toolbar so they'll always be handy. See "New folders for new toolbars" in Chapter 12 to learn how to make a new toolbar for shortcuts like these. Drag the toolbar's sizing bar to the right until only the toolbar's name is visible, and click the arrow to display your shortcuts, as shown in Figure 2-24.

Figure 2-24: You can put your Online and Offline shortcuts on their own toolbar. We put the toolbar just to the left of the Quick Launch toolbar.

Step 4:   Click the Offline.reg shortcut. You will be asked if you want to add the information in Offline.reg your Registry. Click Yes. When you see a confirmation that the Registry has changed, click OK again. Now open Internet Explorer, and notice that it will not try to make a connection. When you click File, you should see a check mark next to Work Offline. Click File, Work Offline to remove the check mark and switch to online mode.

If Internet Explorer is closed and you want to switch to online mode, click the Online.reg shortcut, click Yes and then OK, and reopen Internet Explorer.

To eliminate the warning and confirmation in step 4, right-click the icon for each shortcut (in the Explorer, not on the toolbar) and select Properties. At the beginning of the Target field, type **regedit /s** followed by a space in front of the path to the target, and then click OK. You'll find more on this in "Autoinserting into your Registry at startup" in Chapter 15 of *Windows 98 Secrets*.

Thanks to Tom Koch for this secret!

You might find it easiest to download InkSwitch, a small Windows 95, 98, and NT program available from Inkland. InkSwitch indicates whether you are working online or offline, and lets you change the status by clicking its icon. You can put it in your system tray, and set Windows 98 to always start in offline or online mode. You can even define hot keys for it. InkSwitch is freeware, and it's available at www.inkland.demon.co.uk.

Replace the Internet Explorer shell

You can think of the Internet Explorer as just a user interface to built-in Windows 98 capabilities. Microsoft certainly has made the case that the Windows 98 operating system and the Internet Explorer browser are "integrated." This means that they consist of dynamic link library files that can be called by any other program.

Neoplanet is an Internet browser front end that takes advantage of the Internet services provided by Windows 98, as illustrated in Figure 2-25. It uses the online service SNAP as its organizer and portal, although you can change that if you like.

Figure 2-25: The Neoplanet user interface.

We like Neoplanet's look and feel, especially the buttons. You can run it at the same time that you run Internet Explorer. It comes with its own integrated e-mail, and you can import your Outlook or Outlook Express settings to it automatically. It uses your existing Favorites folder.

Is it competing or cooperating with Microsoft? Yes.

You'll find it at www.neoplanet.com.

Get stronger encryption

You may find that your online banking connection is complaining about the lack of security and refusing to download data. This is a sign that your browser isn't supporting 128-bit encryption.

Neither Netscape nor Internet Explorer support strong encryption right out of the box. To upgrade Internet Explorer, you'll need to download the 128-bit encryption patch from Microsoft. It is only available to U.S. and Canadian citizens who are connected to Internet service providers in the U.S. or Canada.

You'll find the 128-bit patch at www.microsoft.com/ie/download/128bit.htm.

Get rid of Compaq programs that interfere with Windows Internet access

Compaq adds to its computers a set of programs that come between you and the programs that Microsoft includes with Windows 98 and Internet Explorer. If you like these programs, fine — if not, you can uninstall them, or at least stop them from running every time you start up your Presario computer.

Secret

To get rid of the Compaq Encompass browser, Compaq Internet Access Wizard, and/or Compaq Watchdog, click Start, Settings, Control Panel, Add/Remove Programs, and scroll down to Easy Internet Access (or Internet Access on older Presarios). Highlight this entry and click the Add/Remove button.

To simply disable these programs, click Start, Programs, Accessories, System Tools, System Information. Choose Tools, System Configuration Utility, click the Startup tab, and clear the check marks next to monitor.exe and watchdog.exe.

Thanks to Kelly at the Compaq Presario Users Group at www.tiac.net/users/alext6rh for this secret.

Internet Explorer opens partially off screen

Secret

If you open an Internet Explorer window only to find that most of it is off your Desktop, it may be because you have bad values stored under window placement in your Registry. It's best just to delete the relevant keys and then let them get rebuilt.

STEPS:

Clearing Your Window Placement Keys

Step 1. Use your Registry editor to navigate to the following key:

HKEY_CURRENT_USER\ Software\ Microsoft\ Internet Explorer\ Main

Step 2. Right-click Window_Placement in the right pane, and then click Delete.

Step 3. Navigate to the following key:

HKEY_CURRENT_USER\ Software\ Microsoft\ Internet_Explorer\ Desktop\ Old WorkAreas

Step 4. If you see OldWorkAreaRects in the right pane, right-click it and then click Delete.

Step 5. Exit your Registry editor and restart Windows.

What's missing from Internet Explorer

As our expectations continually rise, there will always be something that we just have to have. Give us six months and suddenly what was pretty darn cool is as lame as it gets.

Here are a few of our wishes for Internet Explorer:

■ Add a real print preview feature. This is a bit ironic because Microsoft pioneered this feature as a standard part of the operating system. Any application could use print preview by referencing the function in a dynamic link library. Internet Explorer just doesn't show you what the printed HTML pages will actually look like.

■ Add a graphical progress bar to show the percentage of a file that has been downloaded. Sometimes we get the percentage value and sometimes we get the amount downloaded. It isn't clear why one or the other appears.

■ Add to the print feature to allow table backgrounds to be printed independently of the page backgrounds. Web page designers usually add page backgrounds to enhance the user's enjoyment of the page displayed onscreen. Page backgrounds usually don't do well when printed. Table backgrounds, on the other hand, often enhance printed information. There should be separate toggles for each type of background in Internet Explorer's Print dialog box.

There is one way around this problem, but it requires the cooperation of the web master. Web masters can use Cascading Style Sheets to define backgrounds that are only displayed on your monitor. The trick is to set the media attribute for the style used by the background image to Media Display.

Keep the browser window behind the current window

Wouldn't it be great if when you clicked a link, the browser window didn't pop up over what you are currently doing? We realize that this wouldn't be a good thing for new users because they would wonder what happened to the web site that they just tried to invoke, but it sure would be good for the rest of us.

We would hope for a check box under Tools, Internet Options, Advanced that allowed us to keep the browser window in the background filling in from our little wire going to our Internet service provider. After a decent interval, we could click the browser window and see what's up. Meanwhile, we could continue reading the material in the current window.

Ok, here's a solution that, while not perfect, works well enough. TopIt! allows you to designate windows that stay on top. If you want your Outlook Express window to stay on top when you click a link to a web site in your e-mail, just make sure that your Outlook Express window is set to stay on top.

The problem is that if you have set the Outlook Express window to stay on top, you can't click a window underneath it and have that window go to the top. You have to minimize Outlook Express. Outlook Express will now stay on top of any other window, unless the other window is also marked to stay on top.

You can download this $5 program from CyberTech at members.tripod.com/cybertech_software/.

Summary

Use our fixes and shareware packages to tune up your Internet Explorer.

▶ Search the search engines with third party add-ons.

▶ Do away with the Go button.

▶ Restore your Internet Explorer to the default version by getting rid of your third party brands.

▶ Replace the Internet Explorer shell, but not the underlying functionality.

▶ Make sure that your Internet Explorer window stays in the background when you click a link in your e-mail.

Chapter 3

Outlook Express

In This Chapter

Outlook Express 5 uses a new data structure and offers lots of new features. We show you some of the most important changes and how to really take advantage of them.

▶ Move all your mail and news documents to one place where they're easy to back up.

▶ Use multiple identities to handle several users on one computer.

▶ Schedule sending and receiving mail.

▶ Access your HotMail account with Outlook Express.

▶ Put a shortcut to a New Message window on your Desktop.

Working with Outlook Express data files

Outlook Express 5 has a whole new data structure that works differently from earlier versions. It helps to know about the files that Outlook Express creates — what they are, where they are stored, and how to make them easier to back up.

The new Outlook Express data structure

The Outlook Express message folders and their contents are referred to collectively as the *message store*. Earlier versions of Outlook Express used separate file formats for the mail (*mbx* and *idx*) and news (*nch*) portions of the message store, and stored them in separate folders. These have been replaced in Outlook Express 5 by a new *dbx* file type for both news and e-mail messages. The new structure is designed to be faster and to eliminate what Microsoft felt were design limitations of the old one.

The *dbx* files for both mail and news are now all stored together — the default location is \Windows\Application Data\Identities\{*your identity number*}\ Microsoft\Outlook Express. Your identity number will be a long hexadecimal string, something like {6DAF96CE-A1A7-11D2-87AD-0040055B596B}. If there are multiple Outlook Express identities set up on your computer, you will see a different Outlook Express message store for each one. See "Using identities" later in this chapter for more on what identities are and how to use them. See "Save all your documents," also in this chapter, to learn how to tell which identity belongs to you.

In your message store folder, you'll see a separate file for each message folder and newsgroup, identified by its familiar name. So, for example, the file containing your Inbox data is called Inbox.dbx. This makes it easy to selectively back up message files.

Mark Lium, Outlook Express Beta Support Engineer at Microsoft, described the key files in this folder:

- **Pop3FolderName.dbx:** Contains the index and the messages contained in the POP3 folder.

- **newsgroupname.dbx:** Contains the index, headers, and messages contained in the indicated newsgroup.

- **ImapServerName-FolderName.dbx:** Contains the index, headers, and messages contained in the indicated folder on the indicated IMAP4 server.

- **Offline.dbx:** Contains all of the IMAP4 actions you carry out while offline. Upon reconnecting to the IMAP4 server, these actions are carried out on the server.

- **Folders.dbx:** Contains the list of all newsgroups and IMAP4 folders available, the newsgroups and IMAP4 folders you're subscribed to, and the folder hierarchy of your store. You can actually rename or delete this file while troubleshooting and it will rebuild itself based on the files in the store. If you do this, your newsgroup list will need to be re-downloaded and your folders will all be placed on the top level of the hierarchy.

- **Pop3uidl.dbx:** Contains the list of POP3 messages you've already downloaded. It is used primarily if you choose to leave a copy of messages on the server so that Outlook Express doesn't download the messages more than once.

- **Cleanup.log:** Contains a log of compaction activity.

To find out the name and location of a particular item such as your Inbox, right-click its icon in the Folders pane, the Folders list, or the Outlook bar, and select Properties. The Properties dialog box for that item will show you the filename and its path (see Figure 3-1). The path will most likely be too long to fit in the dialog box. Click the path and use your right arrow key or End key to scroll the rest of the path into view.

If you delete a message folder in Outlook Express, you will still see its *dbx* file in your Explorer as long as it is in the Deleted Items folder. Once you permanently delete the message folder, its *dbx* file will disappear from the Explorer.

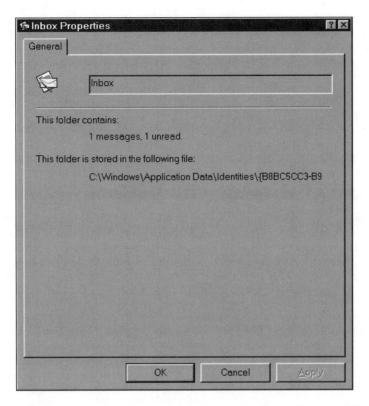

Figure 3-1: The Properties dialog box shows the path and filename of the Inbox.

Upgrading to Outlook Express 5

When you upgrade from version 4 to version 5, Outlook Express looks for your old *mbx*, *idx* and *nch* files and makes new *dbx* files from them. This happens automatically the first time you open Outlook Express 5.

Your old files remain in their old Mail and News folders, but their contents have been duplicated in your new message store. They are there in case you need to go back to using Outlook Express 4. According to Mark Lium at Microsoft, during the Outlook Express 5 installation process an importer for *dbx* files is placed on your system, and it stays there even if you uninstall version 5 and go back to using version 4. To convert and import your Outlook Express 5 message store into Outlook Express 4, click File, Import, Messages, select Outlook Express 5, and then choose to import your old message store. Be sure to indicate that you want only Outlook Express 5 messages — this will help you avoid downloading duplicates.

We did not test this process ourselves. However, using Microsoft's tools in Outlook Express, we have successfully translated among various e-mail formats during the beta test process, and have no reason to be concerned about this working correctly.

Your old message store may be quite large, and it's no longer needed. After you're convinced the conversion to Outlook Express 5 is successful and you won't be going back to version 4, it's fine to go ahead and delete the old Mail and News folders and their contents.

Tip

Because of the new data structure, you cannot run two different versions of Outlook Express on your computer. If you are dual-booting two different operating systems (Windows 98 and Windows NT, for example), they must both be running Outlook Express 5 if you want your messages and newsgroups to be available in both operating systems.

Beware of sharing with Outlook

Outlook is a Microsoft personal information management product that is completely different from Outlook Express, though it bears a similar name. These two products have a history of causing problems for each other. Although by the time you read this the problems may have all been fixed, one in particular has been so widespread that we thought it worth mentioning.

Secret

When you install Outlook, it will offer to import your messages and address book from Outlook Express, as shown in Figure 3-2. If you do this, your messages and address book will no longer be available to Outlook Express (even if you uninstall Outlook). At the very least, you'll have to reimport them into Outlook Express, and some people have had to reinstall Outlook Express to get it to work again. We recommend waiting until you are certain that you want to migrate to Outlook before you do any sharing.

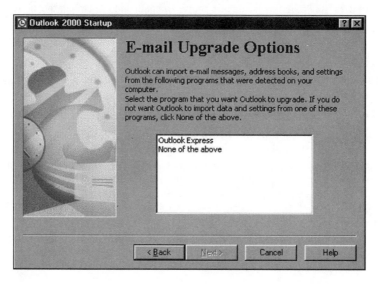

Figure 3-2: Outlook will offer to import your Outlook Express messages and address book.

Save all your documents

One of the convenient features of the My Documents folder is that it organizes all your documents into one place for easier backup. Unfortunately, Windows 98 places all e-mail and news messages and your address book — very important documents indeed — someplace else.

On the other hand, it is now much easier to move your messages to subfolders under your My Documents folder, as described in these steps:

STEPS:

Moving Your Outlook Express E-mail

Step 1.   Using your Explorer, navigate to My Documents. Right-click the right-pane of your Explorer, and choose New, Folder. Name the new folder **Outlook Express**.

Step 2.   In the Outlook Express window, choose Tools, Options, click the Maintenance tab, and click the Store Folder button. The current location of your message store appears in the Store Location dialog box, as shown in Figure 3-3. If you can't see the whole path, click inside the path field and press your End key to scroll to the end.

Figure 3-3: The Store Location dialog box shows where your messages are stored.

Step 3.   Click the Change button to display the Browse for Folder dialog box (see Figure 3-4). Navigate to the folder you created in step 1, highlight it, click OK three times, and then restart Outlook Express.

Continue

STEPS

Moving Your Outlook Express E-mail *(continued)*

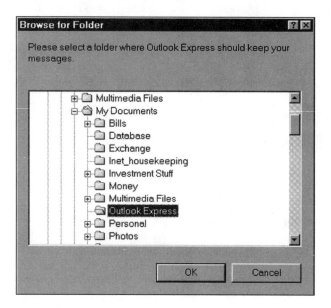

Figure 3-4: Navigate to your new folder.

Step 4.   When you restart Outlook Express, you will see a message stating that your message store is being moved. Use your Explorer to verify that your messages have moved to their new location.

If you have trouble with these steps for any reason (or just like the challenge of doing it the hard way), you can move your message folders by making a couple of changes in the Registry to show Outlook Express where everything is stored. This is also still the only method for moving your Windows address book.

STEPS:

Editing the Registry to Move Your Outlook Express E-mail

Step 1.   Exit Outlook Express.

Step 2. Start your Registry editor, navigate to HKEY_CURRENT_USER\ Identities\ {*your identity number*}\ Software\ Microsoft\ Outlook Express\ 5.0, and locate Store Root in the right pane. (See Figure 3-5.)

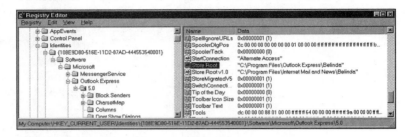

Figure 3-5: The Registry location of Store Root.

As you can see from Figure 3-5, identities are listed in the Registry by their hexadecimal numbers (see "Using identities" later in this chapter for more on what identities are). If you have more than one identity set up on your computer, you can easily tell which one is which. Select an identity in the left pane of the Registry editor, and you'll see Username in the right pane, listing the user name associated with the identity, as shown in Figure 3-6:

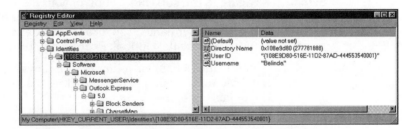

Figure 3-6: Select an identity to see the associated user name.

Step 3. Double-click Store Root in the right pane of your Registry editor. In the Edit String dialog box, change the folder where the message folders are stored to C:\My Documents\Outlook Express, as shown in Figure 3-7. If you have multiple profiles set up on this computer, the path should instead be **C:\Windows\Profiles\ *Username*\My Documents**. (See "User profiles and My Documents" in Chapter 12 for more on this.) If your My Documents folder is on some other drive, or if you've changed its name, use those values instead.

Continued

STEPS

Editing the Registry to Move Your Outlook Express E-mail *(continued)*

Figure 3-7: Type a new location for your message store.

Step 4. Click OK, and close the Registry editor.

Step 5. Using the Explorer, navigate to My Documents. Right-click the right pane of your Explorer, and choose New, Folder. Name the new folder **Outlook Express**.

Step 6. Navigate to the current location of your Outlook Express message store. It may be in your \Program Files\Outlook Express folder, under your user name. If so, drag the folder with your user name to \My Documents\Outlook Express and drop it there.

If your Outlook Express folder is \Windows\Application Data\Microsoft\Outlook Express, drag that folder to \My Documents and drop it there.

Secret

Now that you've moved your message folders, you need to move your address book.

STEPS:

Moving Your Windows Address Book

Step 1. Exit Outlook Express.

Step 2. Start your Registry editor, and navigate to HKEY_CURRENT_ USER\Software\ Microsoft\ WAB\WAB4\ Wab File Name.

Step 3. Double-click Default in the right pane of the Registry editor, and type the new location and address book filename in the Edit String dialog box — for example, **C:\My Documents\Outlook Express\ Belinda.wab** (see Figure 3-8).

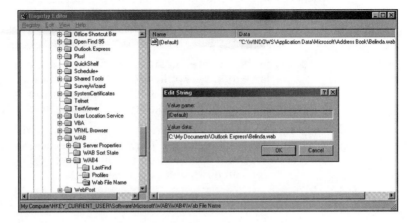

Figure 3-8: Type a new location for your address book.

Step 4. Click OK and close the Registry editor.

Step 5. Using the Explorer, navigate to the current Windows address book location at \Windows\Application Data\Microsoft\Address Book.

Step 6. Drag the address book (*wab*) file from this location to \My Documents\Outlook Express.

Recover from corrupted messages

If you're having trouble opening your Inbox or reading its contents, it's possible that you have downloaded a corrupted message, or a message with an attachment that's so big it's causing problems. You can recover from these situations by having Outlook Express rebuild your Inbox.

STEPS:

Recovering from Corrupted Messages in Your Inbox

Step 1. In the Outlook Express Folders pane or Folders list, right-click Local Folders and select New Folder. Name the new folder something like **Temp**. If you have any messages in your Inbox that you want to save, drag and drop them into your new Temp folder.

Step 2. In the Explorer, navigate to the message store (the default location is \Windows\Application Data\Identities\{*your identity number*}\Microsoft\Outlook Express). Rename Inbox.dbx to Inbox.old. When you see the warning, click OK.

Step 3. Now when you open Outlook Express, it will automatically create a new Inbox folder. You can drag the messages you saved in step 1 back into your Inbox if you like. If everything is working properly, you can now delete the Inbox.old file.

Background compaction

Although you can still compact individual newsgroups, Outlook Express now automatically compacts your entire message store in the background. Normally you should not even notice that this is happening.

According to Mark Lium, Outlook Express Beta Support Engineer at Microsoft, compaction begins thirty seconds after you open Outlook Express, and by default reoccurs every thirty minutes while Outlook Express stays open. Background compaction is not applied to a folder where there is activity such as downloading, copying or deleting.

To enable or disable background compaction, choose Tools, Options, and click the Maintenance tab (see Figure 3-9). Mark or clear the Compact Messages in the Background check box.

You can change the frequency with which background compaction occurs by changing the number in the Compact Messages When There Is [   ] Percent Wasted Space. A smaller number in this box (5 for example, as shown in Figure 3-9) will cause compaction to occur more frequently.

To see a record of compaction activity, close Outlook Express and use Notepad to open the Cleanup.log file in your message store folder (the default is \Windows\Application Data\Identities\{*your identity number*}\ Microsoft\Outlook Express). This file is emptied when it reaches 64K and then starts over, so as to take up a minimum of space on your hard disk.

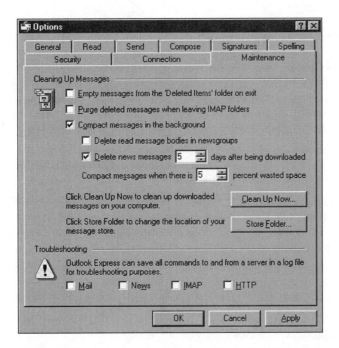

Figure 3-9: Mark the Compact Messages in the Background check box to enable background compaction.

Tip

When Outlook Express compacts your messages, it creates temporary files with the *dbt* extension. These should automatically disappear when the compaction process is complete. If there is a problem, however, they may not be deleted, and they may be quite large. If you notice that your hard disk is suddenly full, check for any *dbt* files in your message store folder, and delete them.

When Outlook Express won't open

If something in your message store becomes corrupted, you may not be able to open Outlook Express at all. You may see an error message such as:

```
Outlook Express could not be started. The application was unable to
open the Outlook Express Message Store. Your computer may be out of
memory or its disk is full. (0x800C0069, 8).
```

Secret

This error message means that Outlook Express could not start because the Msoe.dll file could not be loaded into memory (probably because it could not be found). Despite the message's wording, lack of memory or a full disk are not probable causes of this problem. A more likely cause is that Outlook Express is not installed correctly. This is a side effect of having everything in one big message store. Still, it's possible to recover.

STEPS:

Recovering When Outlook Express Won't Open

Step 1.   In the Explorer, create a new temporary folder. Then navigate to the folder that contains your Outlook Express message store. The default location is \Windows\Application Data\Identities\{*your identity number*}\Microsoft\Outlook Express.

Step 2.   Move the contents of the message store folder (*dbx* files) to the temporary folder you created in step 1. If you have a *wab* file in this folder, leave that where it is.

Step 3.   Now open Outlook Express. When it doesn't find your message store files, it will rebuild your Inbox and other system folders. Your mail accounts, news accounts, and other settings should be intact.

Step 4.   Choose File, Import, Messages to launch the Outlook Express Import Wizard. Choose Microsoft Outlook Express 5 in the first wizard dialog box, and click Next.

Step 5.   The Import From OE5 Wizard appears. Click Import Mail from an OE Store Directory, and click OK.

Step 6.   In the Location of Messages dialog box, click the Browse button and navigate to the temporary folder where you moved your *dbx* files. Mark All Folders, and Click Next. After your message store is reimported into Outlook Express, click Finish.

You may lose the hierarchical structure of your message folders during this process. You will certainly lose all your newsgroup subscriptions and their contents. But at least you will be back in business.

Recover deleted message folders

In earlier versions of Outlook Express, if you deleted a message folder by accident, there was no way to recover it or its contents. But in Outlook Express 5, when you delete a message folder it is moved into your Deleted Items folder, as shown in Figure 3-10. It won't be permanently deleted unless you delete it from the Deleted Items folder or empty the Deleted Items folder.

To recover a deleted folder and its contents, use the Folders pane to drag it from the Deleted Items folder to another place under Local Folders.

Figure 3-10: You can now recover a deleted message folder and its contents.

Get those dialog boxes back

Lots of Outlook Express dialog boxes include a check box that says Don't Ask Me This Again. It's possible that you might mark one of these check boxes, and later wish that it *would* ask you again. Luckily, the Registry settings for these dialog boxes are all neatly stored in one place. Open the Registry Editor and navigate to HKEY_CURRENT_USER\ Identities\ {*your identity number*}\ Software\ Microsoft\ Outlook \ 5.0\ Don't Show Dialogs. You'll see a list of the warning dialog boxes in the right pane, as shown in Figure 3-11. A value of 0 means the box is turned off; double-click the one you want and set its value to 1 to reactivate it.

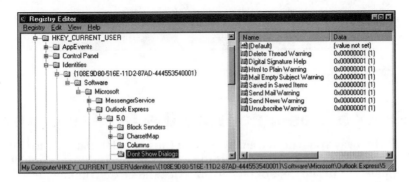

Figure 3-11: The Registry location of the Don't Show Dialogs key.

Panes in the window

The Outlook Express window is divided into a number of different panes. Some are more useful than others.

Start in your Inbox

The Welcome screen in Outlook Express 5 has been redesigned, as shown in Figure 3-12, and it actually gives you access to some additional features, such as Find a Message and Identities. But probably the most important feature in this screen is the little check box at the bottom of the window labeled When Outlook Express Starts, Go Directly To My Inbox. Mark it now, and you'll never need to see the Welcome screen again.

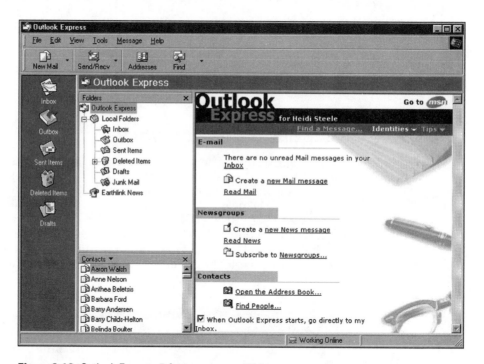

Figure 3-12: Outlook Express 5 features a new Welcome screen.

Start a message from the Contacts pane

Right away you'll notice a new pane in the lower-left part of the Outlook Express 5 window that displays the entries in your address book. If you prefer not to see the Contacts pane, click the Close Window button in the upper-right corner of the pane. To get it back, choose View, Layout, and mark the Contacts check box.

To send a message to someone in your address book, simply double-click the name or group and a New Message window will open. This works even while you are using the newsreader, and without making you lose your place—answering a long-time request from Outlook Express newsgroup members.

The Contacts pane is not the address book

Although the Contacts pane in the Outlook Express window is handy for quickly picking a name out of your address book, it does not have all the address book features. For example, you do not have the ability to sort other than by first name.

The Outlook Express 5 address book lets you organize your contacts in folders and share them with other identities (see "Folders and groups and sharing an address book" in Chapter 8). But in the Contacts pane, you cannot add a new group or address book folder, add a contact to any folder other than the main Contacts folder, or even see your other folders for that matter. In the Contacts pane, the contents of all folders, including your Shared Contacts folder, are shown in one alphabetical list, with addresses and phone numbers not visible.

You can access the full address book properties for a contact by right-clicking it in the Contacts pane and choosing Properties. You can add a new contact by right-clicking any contact in the Contacts pane and choosing New Contact. And to open the real address book from the Contacts pane, right-click any name and choose Address Book.

Rename Outlook Express

Secret

Some newer versions of Outlook Express include the words *provided by Microsoft* in the title bar at the top of the window. If you'd rather have your window without the additional advertising—or if you'd like it to say something more personally meaningful, you can change it. Here's how:

STEPS:
Changing the Outlook Express Title Bar

Step 1. Open your Registry editor and navigate to HKEY_CURRENT_USER\ Identities\{*your identity number*}\Software\Microsoft\ Outlook Express\5.0. If you aren't sure which identity number is the right one, click a number and you'll see the associated user name in the right pane. If you only have one identity set up in Outlook Express, you'll only see one number.

Continued

STEPS

Changing the Outlook Express Title Bar *(continued)*

Step 2.   If the value WindowTitle doesn't exist in the right pane, right-click the right pane, click New, and choose String Value.

Step 3.   Give the string value variable the name **WindowTitle**, and press Enter.

Step 4.   Double-click WindowTitle. In the Edit String dialog box, type the name you'd like to see in the title bar, as shown in Figure 3-13. Press Enter, and close the Registry editor.

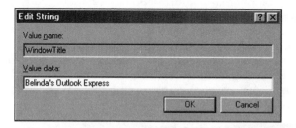

Figure 3-13: In this example, Outlook Express will now be called *Belinda's Outlook Express*.

The next time you open Outlook Express, it will use your new title in the title bar.

Thanks to Marc Butenko and many others for this tip.

Disable the Info pane

If you have a "branded" version of Outlook Express — that is, one that carries the logo of a third party such as a computer vendor — you will see an additional pane in the Outlook Express window when you first open it. This is called the Info pane. In fact, even if you have uninstalled the branded version, the old Info pane may still be displayed when you open Outlook Express. You may feel you have a better use for that real estate.

Secret

To temporarily disable the Info pane, open Outlook Express, choose View, Layout, and clear the Info Pane check box. To permanently disable the Info pane, you must edit the Registry, as described in these steps:

STEPS:

Permanently Disabling the Outlook Express Info Pane

Step 1.   Start with Outlook Express closed.

Step 2.   Open the Registry editor and navigate to HKEY_CURRENT_USER\ Identities\ {*your identity number*}\ Software\Microsoft\ Outlook Express \ 5.0.

Step 3.   Find the string called BodyBarPath and delete it. Press F5 to refresh your Registry, and close the Registry editor.

Step 4.   Open Outlook Express, and choose View, Layout. You will no longer see the Info Pane check box.

Secret

You can create your own Info pane if you like.

STEPS:

Creating Your Own Info Pane

Step 1.   Create artwork using MS Paint or another pixel-painting application. A good dimension is 720 pixels wide by 72 pixels high. Save your image as a *bmp* file.

Step 2.   Close Outlook Express.

Step 3.   Open the Registry editor and navigate to HKEY_CURRENT_USER\ Identities\ {*your identity number*}\ Software\Microsoft\ Outlook Express \ 5.0.

Step 4.   If you already have a string called BodyBarPath (because you have a branded version of Outlook Express), double-click it. In the Value Data field, enter the path and filename of the *bmp* file you created in step 1 and click OK.

   If you don't have BodyBarPath, right-click the right pane of the Registry editor, and click New, String Value. Rename the value to **BodyBarPath**. Then double-click it and, in the Value Data field, enter the path and filename of the *bmp* file you created in step 1. Click OK.

Step 5.   Find the DWORD called ShowBodyBar and look at its value. If the last digit is set to 0, double-click ShowBodyBar, type **1** in the Value Data Field, and click OK. Close the Registry editor.

Continued

Creating Your Own Info Pane *(continued)*

Step 6.   Now open Outlook Express. You should see your new image in the Info pane at the bottom of the window, as shown in Figure 3-14.

Figure 3-14: You can put your own artwork in the Outlook Express Info pane.

You can change your artwork as often as you like without editing the Registry. Just save it with the same name and path you entered in step 4. You must close Outlook Express and reopen it to see the change.

Toolbars

There are lots of ways to combine and customize Outlook Express toolbars. It pays to experiment to find out which combination matches the way you work.

Customize your toolbar

One feature that has disappeared with Outlook Express 5 is the ability to put your toolbar any place you want — at the top, side, or bottom of the window. According to Microsoft developers, putting the toolbar on the side made the drop-down menus work incorrectly and caused other problems, so they eliminated this ability. Many users are grieving its loss.

On the plus side, Outlook Express now has the same drag and drop toolbar capability found in Internet Explorer and Windows 98 itself. You can gain some room by moving the toolbar next to the menu bar. Point to the sizing bar at the far left edge of the toolbar. When you see the resize arrow, drag the toolbar to the right or left of the menu bar, as shown in Figure 3-15. You can adjust the relative width of the menu bar and the toolbar by dragging the toolbar's sizing bar.

Figure 3-15: Drag the sizing bar at the left end of the toolbar to move it up next to the menu bar.

Putting the toolbar next to the menu bar works best if you turn off the text labels for the toolbar buttons. To do this, right-click the toolbar and choose Customize. In the Customize Toolbar dialog box, display the Text Options drop-down list and choose No Text Labels. While you're in this dialog box, you might want to add a few buttons to your toolbar. Two good ones to add are Preview, which toggles the Preview pane on and off, and Save As, which works from the Message pane so you don't have to open a message in order to save it. If you don't use the Outlook bar or the Folders pane, it's also handy to put an Inbox icon on your news toolbar. (If you want to customize the news toolbar, highlight a news server or newsgroup before displaying the Customize Toolbar dialog box.) When you're done customizing, click Close.

The Views bar

Right-click your toolbar and you'll see a new menu item — Views Bar. Click it to display a handy drop-down list of views, as shown in Figure 3-16. Now you can easily see whether you've chosen Show All Messages, Hide Read or Ignored Messages, or perhaps a custom viewing filter. You can drag the Views bar up to the same row as the menu bar and toolbar. If there's not enough room to display the down arrow to the right of the Views list, you can click the currently selected view to display the list instead.

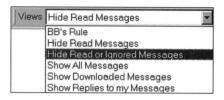

Figure 3-16: The Views bar makes it easier to see and select your view.

The Folders list

The Folder bar is a thick gray stripe under the toolbar that lists your current message folder and identity. When the Folders pane is not displayed, you can use the Folder bar to verify which folder you're in and navigate to another. Click the name of the current folder in the Folder bar to display a drop-down Folders list, as shown in Figure 3-17. The Folders list works similarly to the Folders pane, in that you can right-click folders in it, and use it to drag and drop.

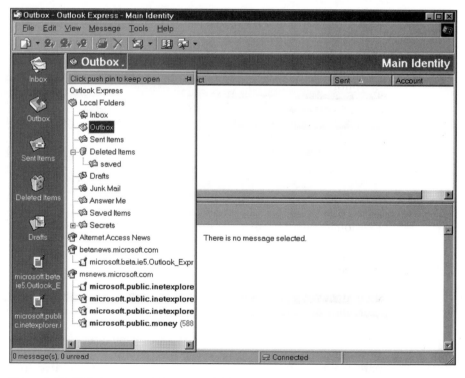

Figure 3-17: Click the name of the current folder in the Folder bar to see a drop-down list of message folders.

You may decide not to display the Folders pane, and to use the Folders list instead. This gives you a wider Preview pane and makes it easier to read messages without opening them. To turn off the Folders pane, click the Close Window button in the upper-right corner of the pane — or choose View, Layout, clear Folder List, and then click OK.

If you prefer to display the Folders pane, you might find that the Folder bar takes up too much real estate in your Outlook Express window. To turn the Folder bar off, choose View, Layout, and clear the Folder Bar check box. If you do this, you may want to put the Folder List button on your toolbar so you can toggle the Folder List pane on and off without using the Folder bar.

The Outlook bar

The Outlook bar, a popular feature of Outlook 98, is new to Outlook Express. It contains shortcuts to message folders. The Outlook bar appears on the left side of the Outlook Express window, where many of us used to keep our toolbars.

You might prefer to use the Outlook bar for navigation instead of the Folders pane, especially if space is at a premium. Right-clicking a blank area of the Outlook bar displays a context menu for controlling the Outlook bar's appearance. To switch from large icons to small ones (or vice versa), choose Large Icons or Small Icons. To hide the Outlook bar, choose Hide Outlook Bar. If you want to add a new shortcut to the Outlook bar, choose New Outlook Bar Shortcut and select the desired folder in the New Shortcut dialog box (see Figure 3-18). Another simpler way to add a shortcut is to drag and drop the icon for the desired folder from the Folders pane or the Folders list onto the Outlook bar (or right-click the icon and click Add to Outlook Bar). To rearrange the order of the shortcut icons, just drag and drop them to suit yourself. To remove a shortcut icon from the Outlook bar, right-click it and choose Remove from Outlook Bar.

If you don't have an icon for a folder in your Outlook bar, and you don't have your Folders pane open, you won't be able to tell if you have unread mail in that folder. For example, you might have something new in your Junk Mail folder that's not really junk (this happens all too frequently). You can always see which folders have unread mail in the Folders list, but you have to remember to display the list to look there.

If you right-click a shortcut on the Outlook bar and choose Find Message, the Find Message dialog box opens, allowing you to search for and open a message from any folder without opening the folder itself. So, for example, if you're reading a large newsgroup, you can search for and read a message in your Sent Items folder without losing your place in the newsgroup. You can also empty the Deleted Items folder by right-clicking its icon in the Outlook bar and choosing Empty Deleted Items Folder. Right-click and select Properties to see the properties of the folder itself (not the shortcut), with a quick summary of the number of files in that folder, the number unread, and the location where the folder is stored.

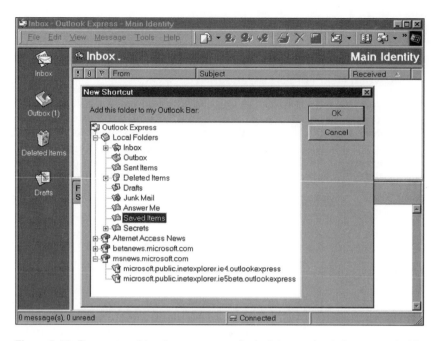

Figure 3-18: Browse to add a shortcut to your Outlook bar — the dark gray vertical bar on the left.

Who am I?

You can have multiple personalities on the Internet: employee, family member, and hobbyist, to name the most prosaic. Outlook Express lets you use multiple automatic signatures to reflect your various personae. And for a real split personality (or two people sharing the same computer) you can take advantage of the identities feature that is new with version 5.

Signatures

Signatures are now in the Signatures tab of the Tools, Options dialog box (see Figure 3-19). Instead of only allowing one signature each for mail and news, Outlook Express 5 lets you create several signatures for different uses. You can create signatures for specific accounts, and set up a separate set of signatures for each identity.

Figure 3-19: The new Signatures tab lets you create and manage multiple signatures.

STEPS:

Creating a New Signature

Step 1. Choose Tools, Options, and click the Signatures tab.

Step 2. In the Signatures area, click the New button. The words *Signature #1* appear in the Signatures list, and your insertion point jumps to the Edit Signature box. You can type the text for your signature in the box, or click the File option button and type or browse to a file that contains your signature. Your signature can be a text file, an HTML file, or an animated *gif* file. However, there is a 4K size limit on signature files, so it's best to keep your ego in check.

Step 3. To give your signature a short name so that you'll remember which one it is, click it in the Signatures list. Now click the Rename button, type the new name, and press Enter.

Step 4. To set a signature as your default, select it in the Signatures list and then click the Set As Default button next to the Edit Signature box.

Continued

STEPS

Creating a New Signature *(continued)*

Step 5.   If you want to associate your signature with an Outlook Express account, select it and click the Advanced button. In the Advanced Signature Settings dialog box, select the account(s) and click OK. You can only associate one signature with a particular account.

Step 6.   To automatically insert your signature in all messages, mark the Add Signatures to All Outgoing Messages check box at the top of the Signatures tab. If you prefer to insert your signature at the time you compose a message, clear this check box. Click OK to close the Options dialog box.

To insert a signature in a message as you're composing it, make sure your insertion point is in the text area of the message (not the header), choose Insert, Signature, and click the one you want. To replace a signature, highlight it before inserting the new one.

If you marked Add Signatures to All Outgoing Messages in step 6, and if you have multiple mail accounts going into the same Inbox, the signature for your default mail account will be the default. The exception is that if you reply to a message sent to a non-default account, the signature inserted will be the one for that account. If you have not associated a signature with your default mail account, the default signature will be inserted. If you are sending a message from a news or IMAP folder, the signature associated with that account will be inserted, or the default signature will be used if none is associated with that account.

You can add a Signature button to the toolbar of your New Message window (but not to the main Outlook Express toolbar). To do this, start a new message, right-click an empty spot on the toolbar, and choose Customize. In the Customize Toolbar dialog box, double-click the Insert Signature toolbar button, and then click Close. You'll need to do this separately for mail and news. After you've added this button to your toolbar, you can click it to insert the default signature (as described in the previous paragraph). If you have created more than one signature, you can select the signature you want from a drop-down list attached to the button.

Tip   If you don't have any signatures defined, you may find that extra blank lines are being added in your messages where the signature would otherwise be. To fix this, choose Tools, Options, click the Signatures tab, and make sure that Add Signatures to All Outgoing Messages is cleared.

If you have set up Outlook Express to insert a signature automatically, it will do this for all messages and all accounts, both mail and news. What if you only want to sign newsgroup postings, not mail messages? You can't set up an empty signature and assign it to an account. But you can set up a signature that consists of nothing but one space. This will add a blank line to your message, so it's not the ideal solution, but you might be able to live with it.

In keeping with a generally accepted standard on many newsgroups, Outlook Express precedes signatures in newsgroup messages with two hyphens on a line above, with an empty line above that. You don't need to add the hyphens or the line; Outlook Express inserts them automatically. So, for example, a signature for a news account might look like this:

```
--
Belinda
```

This is not the case with signatures in mail messages, however. No hyphens, no extra line. If you want them, you'll have to create a different signature for use in mail messages and put them into that signature yourself.

Using identities

Identities make it a lot easier for several people to use the same computer to get their mail and read their favorite newsgroups. Unlike profiles, which affect all of your Windows 98 settings and must be set up before you install Outlook Express, *identities* affect only Outlook Express and you can easily manage them at any time. Each identity has its own accounts, newsgroup subscriptions and maintenance, signatures, and Options settings. You have to set up all of these items separately for each identity. When you first install Outlook Express, you have only one identity, called Main Identity, and it is set as the default.

Because it's easy to switch among different identities, you may find it convenient to use multiple identities for yourself. For example, you might use your laptop on a local area network at the office, and then take it home to follow your favorite hobby newsgroups on a dial-up account. Or you might have one identity with a password and one without. Maintaining a different identity for each situation makes it easy to globally switch all of the settings that change with each environment.

STEPS:

Adding a New Identity

Step 1. In the Outlook Express window, choose File, Identities, Add New Identity.

Step 2. In the Type Your Name field of the New Identity dialog box, type a name for your identity (different from all other identity names). Click OK, and click Yes in the Identity Added dialog box to switch to your new identity. Outlook Express will close, and after a few seconds it will reopen along with the Internet Connection Wizard.

Step 3. If you have already set up an Internet mail account in Microsoft Exchange, Windows Messaging, or Outlook (not Outlook Express, however), you can import it into this identity by marking Use an Existing Internet Mail Account and clicking Next. The wizard will step you through to confirm the settings.

To set up a new mail account for this identity, mark Create a New Internet Mail Account and click Next. The wizard will step you through the settings for a new account.

If you want, you can click Cancel to exit the wizard. Your identity will have a name, but will have no accounts or other settings. You can then import an account that you have first exported from another Outlook Express identity by following the steps in the next section.

Step 4. If you have a message store from Microsoft Exchange, Windows Messaging, or Outlook, the Outlook Express Import Wizard now prompts you to import the messages and/or address book from that application. You can choose Cancel here and do it later if you like by choosing File, Import in the Outlook Express window for this identity.

Step 5. After you have finished or canceled the wizards, Outlook Express closes and reopens at the Welcome screen, with the name of your new identity displayed at the right end of the Folder bar. Choose File, Identities, Manage Identities to display the Manage Identities dialog box, as shown in Figure 3-20. If you want to make your new identity the default, highlight it in the Identities Names list and click the Make Default button.

Step 6. To always start Outlook Express in your new identity (regardless of whether it is the default), select it in the Start Up Using list. If you want to be prompted for an identity when you open Outlook Express, choose Ask Me.

Step 7. To add password protection for this identity, click the Properties button, and mark the Ask Me for a Password When I Start check box in the Properties dialog box. Type your password (twice) in the Enter Password dialog box, click OK twice, and then click Close in the Manage Identities dialog box.

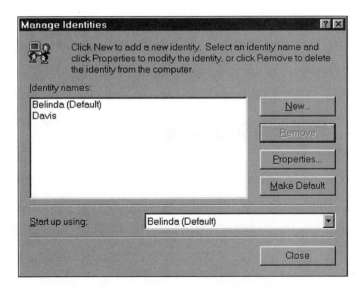

Figure 3-20: The Manage Identities dialog box.

Adding password protection to your identity is a simple way to protect your e-mail messages and newsgroups from the prying eyes of your co-workers or family members. It does not protect anything on your system outside of Outlook Express, and it offers only a basic level of security — a truly malicious, computer-savvy person could most likely get around it. For more robust security, you'll need a more "corporate" program such as Outlook 98.

You will only be prompted for your password when you switch identities, or if you log off your current identity before closing Outlook Express. To do log off your identity, choose File, Identities, Logoff *YourIdentityName*. The next time you open Outlook Express, you will have to enter your password to use this identity.

As you go about your business under this new identity, you will quickly notice that all settings are set to the default, *not* to what you had for your original identity. For example, you'll need to create new signatures for your new identity, you'll need to set up the toolbars and panes the way you like them, and you'll need to set up all new newsgroup accounts. In essence, it's as though you had just installed a new copy of Outlook Express.

Import an account for your new identity

When you first create an identity, the Internet Connection Wizard opens to help you set up a new Internet mail account. Although the wizard can import an account from a Microsoft Exchange client such as Outlook, it cannot import an account directly from another Outlook Express identity. But it's very likely that you will want to do just that. Luckily, you can export an account from the first identity as an *iaf* file. Then you can import it into your new identity.

STEPS:

Exporting and Importing a Mail Account

Step 1.   In the old identity, choose Tools, Accounts, and click the Mail tab.

Step 2.   Highlight the account that you want to use in the other identity, and click the Export button (see Figure 3-21).

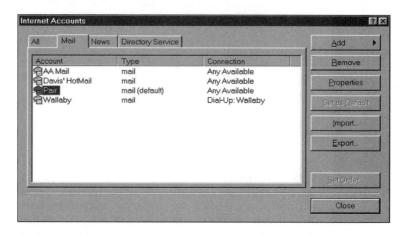

Figure 3-21: Click the Export button to export your mail account.

In the Export Internet Account dialog box that appears, navigate to the place where you want to save this *iaf* file — your default Outlook Express folder is a good choice — and click Save. Then click Close in the Internet Accounts dialog box.

Step 3.   Choose File, Switch Identity. Select your new identity in the Switch Identities dialog box, and click OK. Outlook Express closes and reopens in your new identity.

Step 4.   Choose Tools, Accounts, click the Mail tab, and click the Import button. The Import Internet Account dialog box opens to the default Outlook Express folder. Select the *iaf* file you saved in step 2, and click Open. This account now appears in the Internet Accounts dialog box. Click Properties if you need to change the e-mail address or other information, and then click Close.

These steps describe exporting and importing a mail account, but the process is the same for news accounts. If you import a news account, it will not have any subscriptions; it will just contain the server information.

Import messages from another identity

It may seem odd to import messages from one identity to another, because one of the reasons to use identities is to keep one set of messages separate from another. But maybe you've just set up a new identity, and previously your messages were all mixed up with someone else's in the same Inbox. You can move your messages to a different mail folder, and then import only that folder from the other identity.

To import messages from another identity, choose File, Import, Messages, select Microsoft Outlook Express 5 in the Select Program list, and click Next. Mark the Import Mail from an OE5 Identity option, select the identity from which you want to import messages (*not* your current identity), and click OK. You will see the message store location for the identity you have chosen; click Next if it is correct. In the Select Folders dialog box shown in Figure 3-22, mark the Selected Folders option button and highlight the folder(s) that contain the messages you want to import. Click Next, and then click Finish. Your imported folders should now appear in the Folders pane. These folders and messages have not been moved from the other identity, only copied.

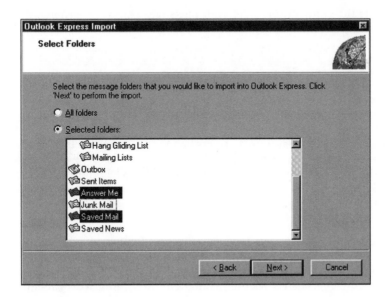

Figure 3-22: Use your Shift and/or Ctrl keys to select multiple folders to import.

Sheddding old identities

To remove an identity, you must first switch to a different identity — click File, Switch Identity and select an identity other than the one to be removed. Now click File, Identities, Manage Identities. Highlight the identity to be removed and click the Remove button, click Delete, and then click Close. Although that identity will no longer appear in the Manage Identities dialog box, its folder and data still appear in your Explorer. You'll need to delete this folder manually.

Identities are stored at \Windows\Application Data\Identities. The folders have hexadecimal numbers for names. This makes it very hard to tell in the Explorer which identity is which, so you'll have a hard time figuring out which folder you can safely delete.

Secret

To sort this out, start the Registry editor and navigate to HKEY_USERS\ .Default\Identities. Click the folder for an identity in the left pane, and you'll see a Username string in the right pane. The value of this string is the name of your identity. Only current identities appear in the Registry. Make a note of the number, and now go back to the Explorer and delete the folders for the identities that no longer appear in the Registry.

Connecting with Outlook Express

Making the connection to get your messages can be less than automatic. Here is some help for making it as painless as possible.

Working online or offline

Unlike earlier versions of Outlook Express that used a separate (and sometimes competing) dialer to make dial-up connections, Outlook Express 5 now shares the Internet Explorer dialer. This eliminates lots of previous problems, such as Outlook Express hanging up a connection that was initiated by another application. It also makes for a more consistent user interface. In fact, you can now access the Internet Explorer connection properties from Outlook Express. To do this, choose Tools, Options, click the Connection tab, and click the Change button. The changes you make here also affect Internet Explorer.

Because Outlook Express now uses Internet Explorer's connection management system, the concept of working online or working offline has become considerably more significant. If you have a constant Internet connection, you can work online all the time without worrying about it. But if you dial up to connect to the Internet, you sometimes need a way to use communications applications such as Outlook Express and Internet Explorer without trying to communicate with the server.

For example, when you move from your Inbox to a news folder, Outlook Express attempts to connect to that news server if you are working online. This might also happen when you highlight the header of an e-mail message that links to a web site. If you just want to look at the messages without connecting, first switch to working offline. This setting is global for all of your applications that use it, so if you are offline in Internet Explorer, you are also offline in Outlook Express.

If you have chosen Never Dial a Connection in the Connections tab of the Internet Properties dialog box (click Tools, Options, click the Connection tab, and click the Change button), you might think that this would keep Outlook Express from trying to make a connection. But choosing that setting only makes Outlook Express assume that you have already established a connection (perhaps over a network). If you are set to work online and you go to a news folder, Outlook Express will still attempt to connect to that news server, but will fail to find the server because there is no Internet connection. You should choose an Internet Properties setting that is appropriate for the way you connect to that mail or news account in general, and use the work online/work offline settings to tell Windows 98 how you want to work at the moment.

The standard way to change your work online/work offline setting is by choosing File, Work Offline in either Outlook Express or Internet Explorer. But Outlook Express offers two other ways to both see and change your current state. One is an Offline button that you can add to your mail and/or news toolbar, shown in Figure 3-23. When you are working offline, it appears to be depressed. The button's icon and text change to show you what will happen if you click it, *not* your current state. Some of us find this confusing.

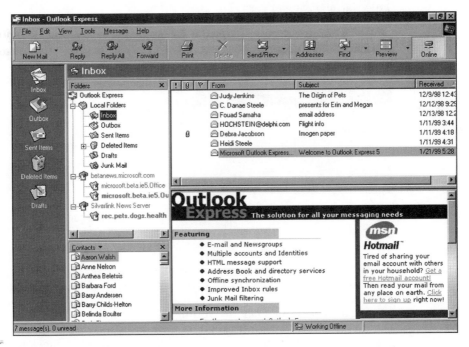

Figure 3-23: The Offline toolbar button is depressed when you are working offline. The text and icon indicate the state you would switch to if you clicked it, *not* your current state.

More convenient than the toolbar button is the status bar at the bottom of your Outlook Express window, shown in Figure 3-24. Not only does the status bar clearly indicate your current online/offline state, but in Outlook Express it toggles on and off with a simple double-click. If you don't see a status bar in Outlook Express, choose View, Layout and mark the Status Bar check box. (The Internet Explorer status bar only shows you an icon if you are working offline; it looks slightly different and is only a status indicator, not a toggle button.)

Figure 3-24: The status bar clearly indicates that we are offline at the moment.

You can also make a pair of shortcuts that let you set your Registry directly to work in online or offline mode. See "Set Work Offline before you open Internet Explorer" in Chapter 2 for the steps.

Disable the disconnect message

Normally, when you close an Internet application and there are no others running, you will be prompted to disconnect from your dial-up account. This is a useful reminder if you are paying by the minute for access. However, if you switch applications often and like to leave your connection open, this little warning can get very old.

The easiest way to disable this message is to mark the Don't Use Auto Disconnect check box in the Auto Disconnect message box itself, shown in Figure 3-25.

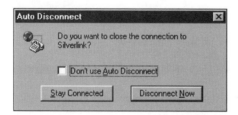

Figure 3-25: When the Auto Disconnect message appears, you can disable it by marking the check box.

There is another, longer way to do this that doesn't require you to go online. Choose Tools, Options, click the Connection tab, and click the Change button. In the Connections tab of the Internet Properties dialog box, highlight your dial-up account, click the Settings button, and then click the Advanced button under Dial Up Settings. In the Advanced Dial-Up dialog box, clear the Disconnect When Connection May No Longer Be Needed check box, as shown in Figure 3-26. Click OK four times to close all the dialog boxes.

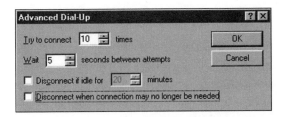

Figure 3-26: Clear the Disconnect When Connection May No Longer Be Needed check box to disable the disconnect warning.

Using a non-default mail or news account

If you have set up more than one mail account, when you start a new mail message you will see a From field at the top of the New Message window displaying your default mail account. If you reply to a mail message, the From field in your reply will display the account to which the original message was sent. News messages include a News Server field in the message header. This field displays the news server for the newsgroup that you are currently reading.

It's now really easy to choose a different mail account or news server for your message. Click the down arrow to the right of the From (or News Server) field in the message header and select from the list of active accounts. Once a message is in your Outbox, you can look in the Account column to see which account it will use. (If you don't see that column, right-click a column header, click Columns, mark the Account check box in the Columns list, and then click OK.)

Set the connection for an account

If you need to always use a specific connection for a particular mail or news server, you can set that up. For example, many Internet service providers refuse access to their news servers if you dial in from another service, so you need to associate that news account with the correct dial-up connection. If you need to always use a local area network to access a certain server, you also need to be able to specify that. Designating a specific connection in this way overrides the default connection.

To associate a connection with a mail or news account, choose Tools, Accounts, highlight the account in question, click the Properties button, and click the Connection tab. Mark the Always Connect to This Account Using check box (see Figure 3-27), and then select the dial-up connection in the drop-down list.

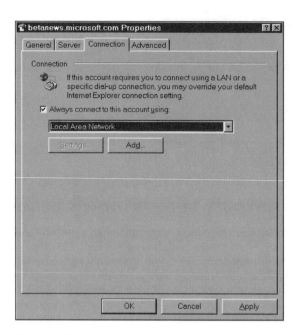

Figure 3-27: If you need to use a specific connection with a mail or news account, specify the connection in the Connection tab of the Properties dialog box for the account.

Your Outbox can contain messages associated with several different mail and news accounts, each associated with a different connection. When you click the Send and Receive button, Outlook Express uses the default dial-up connection to connect with the Internet. When it comes to a message in the Outbox that is set to use a different connection, Outlook Express will either hang up and dial the other connection or it will prompt you with the message shown in Figure 3-28. You control this by marking or clearing the Ask Before Switching Dial-Up Connections check box in the Connection tab of the Options dialog box.

Usually it works just fine to use the current connection to look for the other server. In fact if you travel, this is a good way to access your mail server back home while using a dial-up connection that's a local call from the place you're visiting.

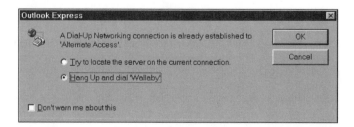

Figure 3-28: You'll see this warning if you try to use a different dial-up connection.

Tip

In the lower-left corner of this dialog box, you can mark the Don't Warn Me About This box to avoid getting this warning in the future. But beware: If you mark this box, in the future Outlook Express will automatically choose the second option, always disconnecting and establishing a new (possibly long distance?) dial-up connection. To restore the original setting, choose Tools, Options in the Outlook Express window, click the Connection tab, and mark the Ask Before Switching Dial-Up Connections check box.

Scheduling the mail

Secret

You can use the Task Scheduler that comes with Windows 98 to automatically open Outlook Express and retrieve your mail at a set time every day, as long as your computer is running.

STEPS:

Scheduling Send and Receive

Step 1. In Outlook Express, choose Tools, Options.

Step 2. In the General tab, mark Send and Receive Messages at Startup.

Step 3. On the Connection tab, make sure that Hang Up After Sending and Receiving is marked. Click OK and close Outlook Express.

Step 4. Click Start, Programs, System Tools, Scheduled Tasks. In the Scheduled Tasks folder window, click Add Scheduled Task. In the Scheduled Task Wizard that appears, click Next and be patient while the Task Scheduler examines all the applications on your computer. When the wizard presents you with a list of programs, Highlight Outlook Express and click Next. (If for some reason you don't see Outlook Express, click the Browse button and navigate to \Program Files\Outlook Express. Click msimn.exe and click Open.)

Step 5. Type **Outlook Express** at the top of the next dialog box if it's not already there. Mark the Daily option button, and click Next. Set the start time and start date. Then indicate whether you want to do this every day, just weekdays, or at a particular interval of days, and click Next. (If you want to test your task now, enter a time in the next couple of minutes — it's easy to change later.) Mark Open Advanced Properties for This Task When I Click Finish, and click Finish.

Continued

Scheduling Send and Receive *(continued)*

Step 6. The Properties dialog box for your task opens. On the Settings tab, mark the check box next to Stop the Scheduled Task If It Runs for [   ] hour(s) [   ] Minutes(s), and set the length of time to something like 5 or 10 minutes — long enough to make a connection and do a Send/Receive. Click OK, and minimize the Scheduled Tasks folder window.

Step 7. Once you are satisfied that your scheduled task works, restore the Scheduled Tasks folder window and click the Outlook Express task to open its Properties. Go to the Schedule tab and enter the correct time when you want Outlook Express to open (for example, midnight, or 7 AM). Click OK, and close Scheduled Tasks.

Remember to leave your computer turned on with Outlook Express *closed* in order for this to work!

What's that pushpin for?

You may have noticed a pushpin icon in the lower-right corner of Outlook Express' Send and Receive dialog box (shown in Figure 3-29). Or you may never have noticed it. The purpose of the pushpin is to tell you how the dialog box will behave. Normally, the "point" of the pushpin points to the left. This indicates that the dialog box will close automatically after your e-mail messages are downloaded. But if you click the pushpin, it will appear as though it's sticking into the screen, indicating that now the dialog box will stay visible after the download is complete. That can be useful if you want to review the tasks Outlook Express went through in sending and receiving messages. If Outlook Express encounters any errors, the dialog box stays visible with the Errors tab in front, even if the pushpin is "out." In either case, you can just click the Hide button to send the dialog box away.

Previewing your mail

If you want to be able to look over your message headers and choose which messages to download, you might want to try something like Magic Mail Monitor. This small, fast, freeware program sits in your system tray, checks for incoming mail, and lets you view message headers and even delete messages without downloading their bodies. This is great if you occasionally receive files with large attachments that take too long to download or cause your dial-up connection to time out. Check out the Magic web site for more details and to download the software: www.geocities.com/SiliconValley/Vista/2576/magic.html.

A similar (though much larger) freeware product is POP3 Scan Mailbox, available at www.netcomuk.co.uk/~kempston/smb/.

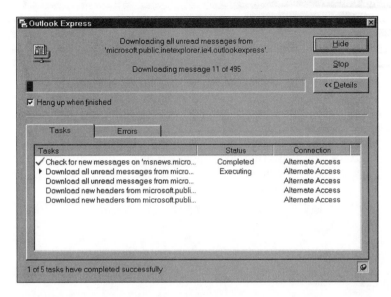

Figure 3-29: This pushpin appears to be "pushed in." The dialog box will continue to be displayed after the download is complete.

Monitor web-based e-mail

If you are using Juno, Yahoo, or some other web-based e-mail system, you have to remember to check if you have new mail. If you have multiple accounts, this can be a bit much. One solution is to use a program that checks all your accounts for you.

Ristra Mail Monitor may be just the ticket for you. It will check your web-based e-mail account at a pre-set interval or on demand, and let you know if you have new mail. You'll find it at ristra.hypermart.net/.

Access your HotMail with Outlook Express

Many people would like to be able to access their web-based e-mail accounts using Outlook Express. It's nice to be able to read your mail offline and to save it on your computer. Outlook Express now has the built-in ability to do this for users of HotMail, a service of Microsoft's MSN online service.

To set up a new HotMail account from within Outlook Express, choose Tools, New Account Signup, HotMail. The Setup HotMail Account Wizard launches, initiates a dial-up connection, and walks you through the account setup sequence online. It also creates a new mail account on your computer for HotMail and a new HotMail folder in your Folders list.

If you already have a HotMail account, don't use the New Account Signup command. Instead, click Tools, Accounts, Add, Mail. After entering your name, click Next. In the next wizard dialog box, mark I Already Have an E-mail Address That I'd Like to Use, enter your HotMail address, and then click Next. Outlook Express recognizes that you have entered a HotMail account and sets the defaults accordingly. Continue through the wizard to enter your password, click Finish, and click Yes to download your HotMail folder.

Your new HotMail folder contains its own Inbox and Sent Items folders, separate from the main Outlook Express Inbox and Sent Items folders. These will only be created when they have contents. The HotMail folder actually behaves more like a newsgroup server than like e-mail, as you can see in Figure 3-30. The synchronization settings work the way they do in a newsgroup. Messages that you download reside on your hard disk, while those you don't download remain on the HotMail server.

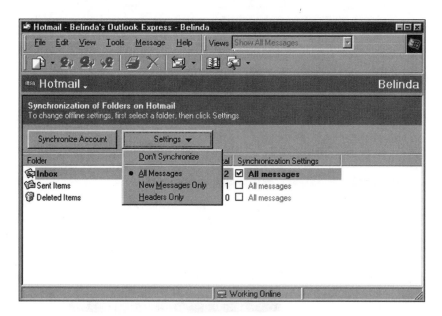

Figure 3-30: The HotMail folder lets you choose synchronization settings as you would for a newsgroup.

Instead of choosing the synchronization setting All Messages, you might prefer to use Headers Only (select the HotMail folder in the Folders pane, click the Settings button in the right pane, and choose Headers Only). Then you retrieve only the messages you want by right-clicking their headers and selecting Download Message Later. In fact, you may find this method of mail management to be a reason for using HotMail instead of standard e-mail.

If you prefer to have your HotMail messages go into your regular Inbox and be managed in the same way as your other e-mail, you might want to try a shareware package called HotMail Express from C-WebMail. HotMail Express gives you POP3 access to your HotMail account, letting you download messages using any POP3 e-mail software. It even gets rid of the advertising messages. And you can still get your mail by logging onto the web when you are using a different computer.

In early 1999, the C-WebMail web site said the company planned support for other web-mail accounts in the near future, so users of other web-based mail services might want to investigate. Find out more and download the software at www.cwebmail.com.

Mail management for small businesses

The great thing about the Internet is that your company can look bigger than it really is. For example, a shareware product called The Tiger lets you run e-mail conferences and mailing lists, and set up forwarding and sophisticated automatic e-mail replies, without having to have your own mail server. You use it with your regular e-mail software over a standard dial-up connection. Developed by the English web consulting firm Clevett Vella, a fully functioning copy of The Tiger can be downloaded free from www.betterwebdesign.com/free_software.htm. The registered version includes a manual and costs $39.

Shortcuts in Outlook Express

Sometimes you only want to use part of Outlook Express, and you want to get to it fast. Here are a number of ways to do that. We also point out some useful keyboard shortcuts.

Shortcut to the New Message window

If you want to be able to write e-mail messages quickly, you can create a shortcut to the Outlook Express New Message window. Place the shortcut on your Desktop or drag it to a toolbar.

STEPS:

Creating a Shortcut to the New Message Window

Step 1. Right-click an empty part of your Desktop and click New, Shortcut.

Step 2. Insert the following text into the Command Line field of the Create Shortcut dialog box, as shown in Figure 3-31:

"C:\Program Files\Outlook Express\Msimn.Exe" /mailurl:%1

Continued

STEPS

Creating a Shortcut to the New Message Window *(continued)*

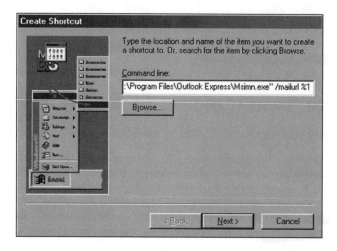

Figure 3-31: Insert the command to open the Outlook Express New Message window in the Command Line field.

Step 3. Click the Next button, rename the shortcut **New Message**, and click the Finish button.

Step 4. You can now drag the shortcut to a toolbar and drop it there. After dropping it on a toolbar, right-click the shortcut on the Desktop and click delete to get rid of it from the Desktop.

Thanks to Ryan Coe for this tip.

When you click your shortcut icon, a New Message window opens without opening Outlook Express. After you've composed your message, when you click the Send button, the message will be put in your Outbox unless you have marked Send Messages Immediately in Tools, Options, Send. In that case, you will still need to open Outlook Express and do a Send and Receive in order to send the message.

Copy a shortcut from a message

Right-click an e-mail address or URL in a message and click Copy Shortcut. The message needn't be open; you can do it from the Preview pane. Now you can paste this shortcut into the To field of an outgoing message, paste it as a live link in a message body or an HTML document, or paste it into your Address bar and press Enter to open a New Message window or a web site. If you paste it onto your Desktop (right-click your Desktop and click Paste Shortcut) you will create a URL shortcut, which you can use over and over, as described in the next section.

Creating a command line shortcut

A URL shortcut is like a shortcut to a web page, but instead of starting with http: to indicate a web address, it starts with the Internet mailto: command. With a URL shortcut, you can pre-specify the contents of all the header lines, and even the message body. This is useful if you frequently send mail messages to the same person or group of people, or if you frequently send the same short message to various people. You must have Outlook Express set up as the default MAPI client for this method to work.

If you have received the address in an Outlook Express message, you can skip the Creating a Mailto Shortcut steps below. Just right-click the link, click Copy Shortcut, and then right-click your Desktop and click Paste Shortcut. If you want to add some command line parameters, as discussed later in this section, right-click the shortcut on your Desktop, click Properties, add the parameters to the end of the Command Line field, and click OK.

Another way to make this type of shortcut is to type your mailto: command in the Address bar (in the Internet Explorer or on your Desktop). Click the Go button, close the New Message window that opens, and then drag the icon from the Address bar onto your Desktop (see Figure 3-32).

Figure 3-32: Drag the icon for your mailto: command onto the Desktop to create a shortcut.

Here's how to create a mailto shortcut from scratch:

STEPS:

Creating a Mailto Shortcut

Step 1. Right-click an empty part of your Desktop and click New, Shortcut.

Step 2. In the Command Line field of the Create Shortcut dialog box, type **mailto:**. You can add an e-mail address (for example, **mailto:davis@halcyon.com**) or one or more other fields using the syntax described in a moment. Click Next.

Step 3. Type a name for your shortcut and click Finish.

Secret

If you want more of the message to be filled in automatically than just the To field, you can add more parameters to the command line for your shortcut. To do so, right-click the shortcut and click Properties. In the Web Document tab of the Properties dialog box for the shortcut, you'll see the URL field containing your mailto: command line. Make your edits here, using these guidelines:

- Precede the first parameter with a question mark (?).

- Separate fields with an ampersand (&).

- Separate addresses within fields with a semicolon (;).

- Separate the name of the field from its contents with an equal sign (=).

- If a field contains only one address, you can type a name as it is displayed in your address book — if there are two people in that field, you must type their actual addresses.

- The fields that can have parameters are: subject, CC, BCC, and body.

- The total number of characters in your command line must be less than 457 characters; otherwise you'll get an error message and your shortcut won't work. Keep this in mind if you are planning to include body text or a whole lot of addresses; it's best to keep it short.

Here's an example of a command line using lots of parameters; the results are shown in Figure 3-33.

```
mailto:davis@halcyon.com?subject=Hi
There&CC=mom@ix.netcom.com;joe@eskimo.com&BCC=
belindab@aa.net&body=Hello everyone!
```

Figure 3-33: You can use parameters to fill in more of the message if you like.

The next time you click the shortcut, the changes you made to the command line will be reflected in the message. The New Message window opens without opening Outlook Express. After you've composed your message, when you click the Send button, the message will be put in your Outbox unless you have marked Send Messages Immediately in Tools, Options, Send. In that case, you will still need to open Outlook Express and do a Send and Receive to send the message.

Drag and drop to an Outlook Express message

If you want to send a new message containing some text from another message or document, all you have to do is drag and drop. Outlook Express must be open for this to work, but it can be minimized.

STEPS:
Dragging Text to a New Message

Step 1. Highlight the text that you want to send. If the text is in an Outlook Express message, you can highlight it in either the message window or the Preview pane. If it's in another document, such as a text file or a Microsoft Word document, highlight it there.

Step 2. Drag and drop the highlighted text onto any message folder except the Outbox. If Outlook Express is minimized, hover over its Taskbar button until it opens. If the Folders pane is not displayed, hover over the folder name on the Folder bar until the Folders list appears. Drop onto a mail folder for mail, or onto a news folder for news.

Step 3. A New Message window appears containing only the text you highlighted. No header information appears in the new message, and no quote characters are included.

Shortcut to the Windows address book

You can also create a shortcut to the Windows address book. Keep it on your Desktop, or drag it into your Quick Launch toolbar. The shortcut makes it easy to add or update contacts without waiting for Outlook Express to open. You can compose a new message directly from the address book by right-clicking a contact and choosing Action, Send Mail. With the address book's new telephone dialing capabilities (see "The address book does more than e-mail" in Chapter 8), it makes even more sense to keep your address book as handy as possible.

STEPS:
Creating a Shortcut to Your Address Book

Step 1.   Right-click your Desktop and click New, Shortcut.

Step 2.   Click the Browse button. In the Browse dialog box, choose All Files in the Files of Type field.

Step 3.   Navigate to \Windows\Application Data\Microsoft\Address Book to find your address book, unless you've moved it to your My Documents folder, or you have multiple user profiles. In this latter case, you can find your address book by using the Find command (Start, Find, Files or Folders) to search for *.wab.

Step 4.   Click your Windows address book name, click Open, and then click Next.

Step 5.   Rename the shortcut **Windows Address Book** and click the Finish button.

Because the *wab* file contains the address books for all the identities set up in Outlook Express on your computer, when you open the *wab* file from outside of Outlook Express, the focus is on the Shared Contacts folder. Unless you have shared some contacts, it will appear empty. To make your own contacts appear, mark View, Folders and Groups in the Address Book window. In the left pane that appears, highlight the folder for your identity's contacts (or Main Identity's Contacts if you haven't set others up). You should now see the contents of your address book. While your shortcut will now always open with the Folders and Groups pane open, it will unfortunately still open with the focus on Shared Contacts.

Keyboard shortcuts in Outlook Express

In addition to the standard Windows 98 keyboard shortcuts, there are a number of shortcuts more or less unique to Outlook Express. Most are listed in Table 3-1:

Table 3-1   Keyboard Shortcuts in Outlook Express

Action	*Key*
Go to Inbox	Ctrl+I
Go to the Newsgroup Subscriptions dialog box	Ctrl+W
Send and Receive	Ctrl+M
Download all (news)	Ctrl+Shift+M
Open a New Message window	Ctrl+N
Forward a message	Ctrl+F
Reply to author	Ctrl+R
Insert signature	Ctrl+Shift+S
Send	Ctrl+Enter or Alt+S
Next message	Ctrl+Shift+>
Previous message	Ctrl+Shift+<
Next unread message	Ctrl+U
Next unread news thread	Ctrl+Shift+U
Next unread newsgroup	Ctrl+J
Mark as read	Ctrl+Enter or Ctrl+Q
Mark all news messages as read	Ctrl+Shift+A
View full header and body	Ctrl+F3
Edit HTML source	Ctrl+F2

Summary

Outlook Express 5 is even more configurable than previous versions. You can set it up to look and act the way that works best for you.

▶ You can make your mail and news files much easier to back up by moving them to My Documents.

▶ The Contacts pane and the additional toolbars make navigation more flexible. We recommend changing things around to gain as much message-reading space as possible.

▶ Identities are an important new tool that let multiple users share a computer for e-mail.

▶ It can be helpful to work offline to minimize unwanted dialing. We show you how to toggle back and forth between online and offline mode more easily.

▶ You can make a Desktop shortcut that lets you start composing a new message without opening Outlook Express.

Chapter 4

Outlook Express — Mail and News Messages

In This Chapter

Reading, composing, and saving mail and news messages is the heart of Outlook Express. We show you how to make your everyday communication look the way you want it to.

▶ Send a message as a web page.

▶ Change the default font for your stationery.

▶ Publish an Outlook Express e-zine.

▶ Save animated *gif* graphic files from the messages you receive.

Reading and managing messages

If you get a lot of e-mail, you know that managing all those messages can become a significant effort. Outlook Express 5 has lots of new bells and whistles to make it easier to read and keep track of the messages you receive.

Make messages and threads easier to find

You can now flag mail and news messages that are important or that you want to find easily later. You can flag a message in two ways: either highlight the message header in the Message pane and click Message, Flag Message, or simply click next to the message header in the Flag column, as shown in Figure 4-1. A little flag icon appears next to the header of a flagged message, and when you open the message you'll see flag icon and the note "This message is Flagged" in the header.

The Flag column is turned on by default in mail message folders, but in news folders it is turned off. To see the Flag column when you are reading news, right-click a column header button at the top of a column and select Columns. In the Columns dialog box, mark the Flag check box and click OK. The Columns setting can be different for each message folder.

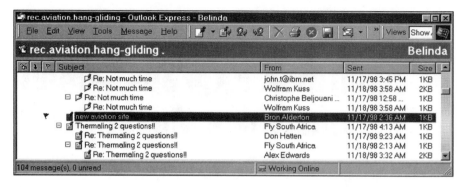

Figure 4-1: It's easy to flag messages for later reference.

You can also flag a message header that appears in the Find Message dialog box (Edit, Find, Message), so that you'll be able to locate it later in the Message pane. Just click in the Flag column as you would in the Message pane.

A similar tool for tracking conversations in a newsgroup is the Watch/Ignore icon (a pair of glasses or a red X), which you can use to mark threads that you want to watch or ignore (see Figure 4-2). To mark or unmark a thread, choose Message, Watch Conversation or Message, Ignore Conversation — or simply click next to a message in the Watch/Ignore column. Your first click marks the thread to be watched, your second click marks it to be ignored, and your third click unmarks it. You only have to select and mark one message to mark the entire thread. As you download headers for new messages in a thread, they will also be marked. When you open a watched or ignored message, you see the glasses or X icon and a note saying either "This message is being Watched" or "This message is being Ignored."

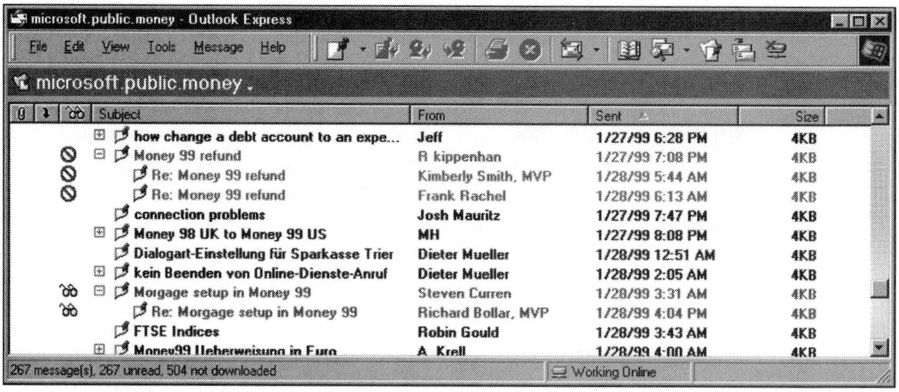

Figure 4-2: It is easier to keep track of what's going on in a large newsgroup if you mark conversations that you want to watch or ignore.

Threads now function in mail as well as in news, but the Watch/Ignore column is not turned on by default for message folders. You might want to use this if you save messages in a message folder over a period of time, or if you have a very high volume of messages. To turn on the Watch/Ignore column, right-click a column header button at the top of a column and select Columns. In the Columns dialog box, mark the Watch/Ignore check box and click OK.

To make watched threads even easier to see, they are by default highlighted with red, as shown in Figure 4-2. To select a different color, choose Tools, Options, click the Read tab, and select the color you want from the Highlight Watched Messages with the Color drop-down list. (To turn off color highlighting, select Default from the drop-down list.) Not only will watched threads will be highlighted in color, but folders containing unread watched messages will be highlighted in the Folders pane (see Figure 4-3).

Figure 4-3: The red folder contains watched messages.

A big advantage of flags and watch/ignore icons is that you can sort by them. Just click the column header button (the flag or glasses icon) at the top of the column to bring the flagged or watched messages to the top of the list. While the author sets the priority of a message, the reader gets to flag it or mark it to be watched.

If you have chosen Hide Read Messages in the Views bar (or View, Current View, Hide Read Messages), you won't be able to see a message you have read even though you have flagged it or marked it to be watched. But if you have collapsed a thread you're watching so that you only see the first message, that message will appear to be unread as long as there is at least one unread message in the thread.

Depending on your settings, Outlook Express may still download headers for ignored threads, but you can choose not to view them by choosing Hide Read Or Ignored Messages in the Views bar. Outlook Express will only download the body of an ignored message if you select the message header while online. If you clean up your newsgroups, as we describe in "News maintenance" in Chapter 5, Outlook Express may delete flagged or watched messages. For messages you really want to keep, it's still best to create a local folder and drag those messages into it.

What are those little arrows?

The icons for messages in the Message pane now change to indicate if a mail or news message has been forwarded or replied to. The open envelope icon next to a message you've read shows a little red arrow pointing to the left if you've also sent a reply, and a blue arrow pointing to the right if you've forwarded it (see Figure 4-4). No more trying to remember whether you've responded, or hunting through your Sent Items folder!

From △	Subject	Received	▽
Bill Greening	Thanks	9/3/98 2:25 PM	
Jeff Winchell	Full Moon Poker Club Meeting ...	9/4/98 1:05 AM	

Figure 4-4: The first message has been replied to. The second message has been forwarded.

Choose your columns

You can choose which columns to display in the Message pane. To do this, right-click any column header button and click Columns (or choose View, Columns). In the Columns dialog box, mark the columns you want to see and clear those you don't. Use the Move Up button and the Move Down button to set the order in which columns will appear (or you can drag the column header buttons to position them). Each message folder can have different column settings.

For example, if you find the Flag and Watch/Ignore columns aren't useful and are just taking up space, you can turn them off. While you will still be able to flag a message or mark a thread to watch or ignore, you won't see the icons in the Message pane and will be unable to sort by flag or by thread state.

Tip

If you have more than one incoming mail account, you might want to view the Account column. That way, you can easily see where a message came from without bothering with message rules. The Account column can also be very helpful in your Outbox.

Finding

Outlook Express' find utility has been improved quite a bit with version 5.

You can now use two different search approaches. To scan through the current folder for messages that contain a certain piece of text, choose Edit, Find, Message in This Folder. Type your text in the Look For field (see Figure 4-5), and click Find Next. The header of the first message that contains your text appears highlighted with gray in the Message pane. To see the next message, press F3 — in this way you can quickly scan through a folder to find the message you want, viewing the contents in the Preview pane.

Figure 4-5: Mark Search All the Text in Downloaded Messages if you want to search the message body as well as its header.

The other approach gives you much more flexibility in designing your search, and it displays the results differently. You can initiate this type of search in a number of ways: Click the Advanced Search button in the Find dialog box shown in Figure 4-5; choose Edit, Find, Message; or right-click a folder in the Folders list, the Folders pane or the Outlook bar, and click Find. You can also go to the Outlook Express Welcome screen (click Outlook Express at the top of the Folders pane) and click the Find A Message button. Any of these actions will bring up the Find Message dialog box, shown in Figure 4-6.

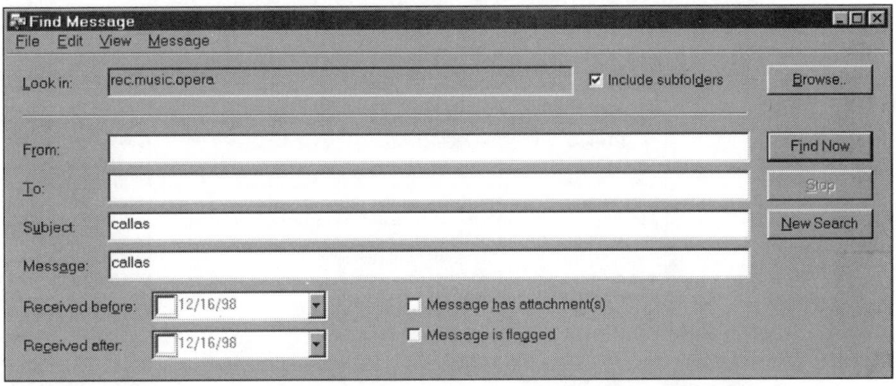

Figure 4-6: The Find Message dialog box offers more flexibility in searching.

You can search for a text string in the bodies of messages, as well as in their headers. You don't need to type the complete name or subject, just a partial name or a keyword. For example, if you type msn.com in the From field, you'll retrieve all the messages from everyone who sent e-mail using MSN.

By default, the search starts from the current folder or the folder you have right-clicked. If you start from the Welcome screen, the search by default includes all of your mail and newsgroup folders. To change the folder or folders that will be searched, click the Browse button in the Find Message dialog box.

Secret

The search results appear at the bottom of the Find Message dialog box, as shown in Figure 4-7. You can open the messages in the results by double-clicking their headers in the list. To sort them, click the column header buttons. You can add a flag to a message by clicking next to it in the Flag column. The flag will also appear next to the message in the Message pane of the Outlook Express window, allowing you to easily locate the message later without doing another search. Right-click the message header to access the same context menu you see in the Message pane. You can save a copy of a message to an Explorer folder without opening it — just drag it directly into the Explorer.

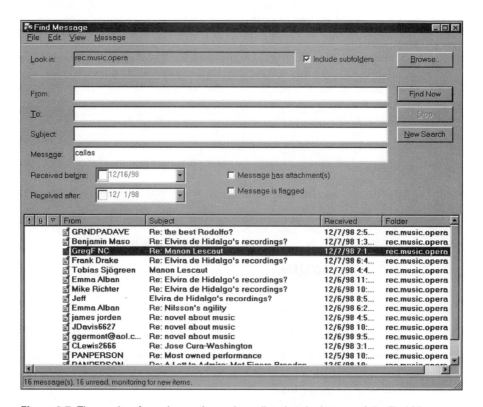

Figure 4-7: The results of an advanced search are listed at the bottom of the Find Message dialog box.

Install on Demand

With previous versions of Outlook Express, if someone sent you a message using a character set that you had not installed — Hebrew, for example — you would see what appeared to be gibberish, with no easy way to find out how to fix it. Now, if you open a message that uses a language or other component you don't have, the Internet Explorer Install on Demand dialog box appears and offers to download the components you need, as shown in Figure 4-8.

Figure 4-8: In the example shown here, a language pack is required to read the message. Install on Demand offers to download and install it.

To download and install the necessary component, click the Download button. Outlook Express initiates a dial-up connection if necessary, downloads the component from Microsoft, and installs it for you. If you don't want to download the component, just click Cancel.

Install on Demand applies not only to languages, but to other components that you might need to see animation or hear sounds. You no longer need to worry about whether to install everything in advance, because you'll be able to get what you need easily whenever you need it.

Install on Demand should be enabled by default. If it is not, choose Tools, Options, click the Connection tab, and click the Change button. In the Internet Properties dialog box, click the Advanced tab, and mark Enable Install On Demand.

Time stamps on e-mail

Occasionally, you may find that the time and date shown in the header of a mail or news message is different (earlier or later) than what you expect. The header might even indicate that the message was sent at a time later than when you received it. While the time stamp isn't actually controlled by Outlook Express, it's interesting to understand.

If you highlight a message header in the Message pane and press Ctrl+F3, the complete header information for that message appears in a separate Message Source window, as shown in Figure 4-9.

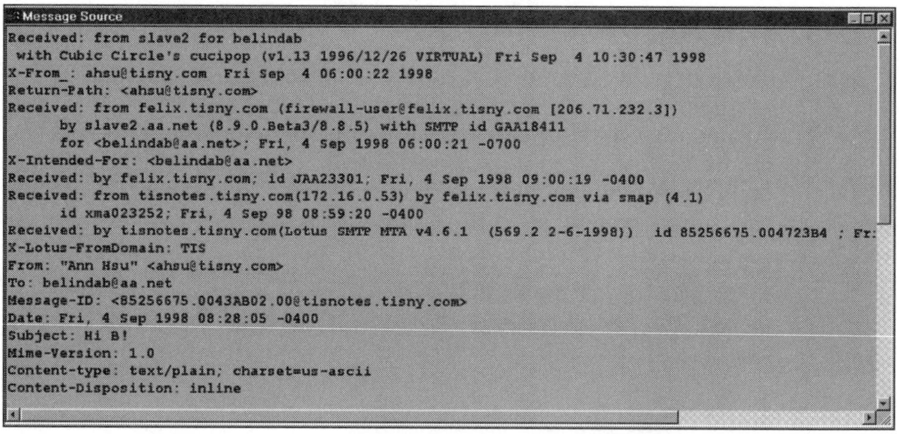

```
Message Source                                                                    _ □ ×
Received: from slave2 for belindab
 with Cubic Circle's cucipop (v1.13 1996/12/26 VIRTUAL) Fri Sep  4 10:30:47 1998
X-From_: ahsu@tisny.com  Fri Sep  4 06:00:22 1998
Return-Path: <ahsu@tisny.com>
Received: from felix.tisny.com (firewall-user@felix.tisny.com [206.71.232.3])
       by slave2.aa.net (8.9.0.Beta3/8.8.5) with SMTP id GAA18411
       for <belindab@aa.net>; Fri, 4 Sep 1998 06:00:21 -0700
X-Intended-For: <belindab@aa.net>
Received: by felix.tisny.com; id JAA23301; Fri, 4 Sep 1998 09:00:19 -0400
Received: from tisnotes.tisny.com(172.16.0.53) by felix.tisny.com via smap (4.1)
       id xma023252; Fri, 4 Sep 98 08:59:20 -0400
Received: by tisnotes.tisny.com(Lotus SMTP MTA v4.6.1  (569.2 2-6-1998))  id 85256675.004723B4 ; Fr:
X-Lotus-FromDomain: TIS
From: "Ann Hsu" <ahsu@tisny.com>
To: belindab@aa.net
Message-ID: <85256675.0043AB02.00@tisnotes.tisny.com>
Date: Fri, 4 Sep 1998 08:28:05 -0400
Subject: Hi B!
Mime-Version: 1.0
Content-type: text/plain; charset=us-ascii
Content-Disposition: inline
```

Figure 4-9: Display the complete message header to see all of its time/date stamps.

Notice that there are a number of time stamps in the header shown in Figure 4-9. The time on the second line (Fri Sep 4 10:30:47 1998) is the time that Belinda's computer retrieved this message from her Internet service provider's POP3 mail server. You have to go down to line seven to see when the message was received by her service provider's SMTP mail server (Fri, 4 Sep 1998 06:00:21 –0700). This is the time displayed in the Received column in the Outlook Express Message pane. Both of these time/date stamps were put there by the Internet service provider's servers — if the clock in one of the servers was wrong, the time shown will be incorrect. The very last time/date stamp (Fri, 4 Sep 1998 08:28:05 –0400) was put there by the author's computer when she clicked her Send button. This time is displayed on the Date line in the message header when the recipient opens the message. In between are stamps from all the servers that this message passed through on its way.

At first, it looks as though this message was sent three hours before it was received. The author was in the U.S. Eastern time zone and the recipient was in the U.S. Pacific time zone, and the times are local for each computer. You can see time zone codes in two of the time stamps above: -0700 indicates that the recipient's server was seven hours earlier than Greenwich Mean Time (GMT), and –0400 indicates that the sender's server was only four hours earlier than GMT. (GMT doesn't recognize Daylight Savings Time.)

While some messages may show a time zone code (for example, PDT for Pacific Daylight Time), the international standard is GMT. If Outlook Express comes across a time zone code that it doesn't recognize (most non-U.S. codes are in this category), it will treat it as GMT. In addition, if the time stamp doesn't contain the expected number of characters and spaces, Outlook Express may not recognize it, and will treat the stamp as 00:00:00 GMT. In either of these cases, the times displayed by Outlook Express could be several hours off. If the time doesn't look right, check the original message header by pressing Ctrl+F3 to see what might be going on.

Thanks to Eric Miller for his insight into these issues.

The character issue

In Outlook Express 4, a non-Western character set changed the fonts in succeeding messages. In Outlook Express 5, this problem has been fixed. It's also much easier to get to the character encoding settings — click View, Encoding, and select the character set to use for the message you are viewing (see Figure 4-10).

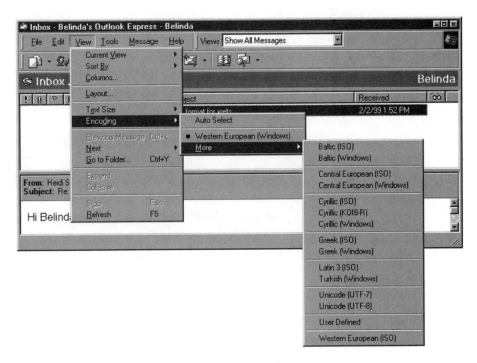

Figure 4-10: The Encoding menu lists all the available character sets on this system.

Secret

If you leave Auto Select marked, as it is in Figure 4-10, Outlook Express uses the message's header information to apply what seems to be the most appropriate character set. But you might come across some messages that contain odd characters or symbols. If you click View, Encoding, you may discover that the new Western European (Windows) character set is marked. Try selecting Western European (ISO) instead — it should clear up the problem. Of course, this assumes that the message was written using a Western alphabet — you might need to apply non-Western encoding instead.

Composing and sending messages

Outlook Express 5 offers more flexibility in how you compose and send your messages. Some features are more intuitive than others — here are some suggestions for getting the mail out.

Associating a message with an account

You can associate a new mail message with a specific account at the time that the message is composed. This is especially helpful if you have multiple users with different accounts on the same computer.

STEPS:
Associating a Message with an Account

Step 1: Open a New Message window by clicking Message, New Message.

Step 2: Click the down arrow at the right end of the From field to display a list of your accounts (see Figure 4-11).

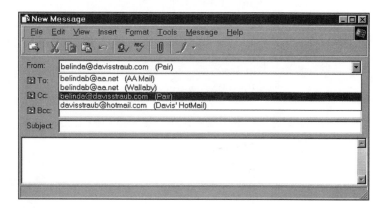

Figure 4-11: Select your account in the From drop-down list.

Step 3: Select the mail account you want to use when sending the message.

What's the Drafts folder for?

The Drafts folder is a place to keep messages that you're not yet ready to send. When you are composing a message and you choose File, Save, your unfinished message is automatically stored in the Drafts folder. If you close a New Message window without sending the message and click Yes when asked if you want to save it, the message will be stored in Drafts. To finish editing a message in stored in the Drafts folder, double-click the message to open it. When you click the Send button, Outlook Express moves it from the Drafts folder to the Outbox.

If you save a plain text message in the Drafts folder and then close it, when you reopen the message and add text you will find that the line endings behave differently. Instead of rewrapping to accommodate your new text, the lines now have "hard" line breaks (called *carriage returns*, a legacy of the prehistoric days when we used typewriters with moveable carriages), which were inserted at the default line endings when you saved the message. These are not the places where the lines appeared to break while you were composing in the New Message window. Rather, the lines break where necessary to fit your message to a width of 76 characters, or whatever you have set as the default under Tools, Options, Send, Plain Text Settings.

These carriage returns are necessary in a plain text message that's ready to be sent (in the Outbox), because otherwise your recipient would see one long line of text instead of a paragraph. On the other hand, they're annoying in a message that you haven't finished composing. When you insert text in the middle of a paragraph, the existing text to the right of the insertion point wraps to the next line, pushing the line breaks to the wrong place. And every time you save and close the file this effect is compounded.

One way around this behavior is to compose messages in HTML format (Format, Rich Text (HTML)) and convert them to plain text if necessary (Format, Plain Text) just before you click the Send button. HTML-formatted messages don't have a fixed line length, but retain the ability to wrap text "on the fly."

Quoting in replies and forwards

When you reply to an e-mail message, it's helpful if you can distinguish the text you write from the message text you are replying to. In plain text messages, the standard is to place a > symbol in front of each quoted line of text. To make this happen automatically, follow these steps:

STEPS:

Automatic Quoting in Plain Text Replies

Step 1.   Choose Tools, Options in the Outlook Express window, and click the Send tab.

Step 2.   Make sure that the Include Message in Reply check box is marked. (This is the default.)

Step 3.   On this same tab, click the Plain Text Settings button under Mail Sending Format. Make sure Indent the Original Text with [   ] When Replying Or Forwarding is marked (see Figure 4-12). If you like, you can use the drop-down list to choose : or | as your quote character instead of >.

Continued

STEPS

Automatic Quoting in Plain Text Replies *(continued)*

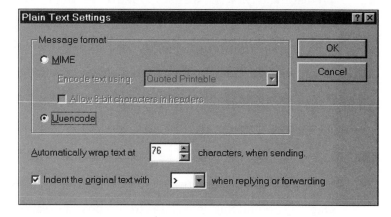

Figure 4-12: Use the Plain Text Settings dialog box to automatically insert a reply character in plain text messages.

Step 4.   Click OK.

So far so good. But this kind of quoting only works as long as you are replying to a message sent using plain text. Messages sent using MIME/Quoted Printable (such as HTML-formatted messages) don't insert line endings, so there are no line beginnings for Outlook Express to mark with >. Instead, the text is formatted in paragraphs. Even if you tell Outlook Express to reply in plain text, it will still not place a > at the beginning of quoted lines if they weren't originally composed in plain text. See "UUENCODE or MIME" in Chapter 19 of *Windows 98 Secrets* for a fuller discussion of message encoding formats.

If you reply in HTML format, you can use the BLOCKQUOTE paragraph tag to mark paragraphs. However, this is not one of the paragraph styles available via the Paragraph Style toolbar button in the New Message window. To be able to use it without editing the HTML source, you must choose Tools, Options, and click the Send tab. Click the HTML Settings button under Mail Sending Format, and mark Indent Messages on Reply in the HTML Settings dialog box. Now your quoted HTML text will be indented with a vertical bar along its left side, as shown in Figure 4-13.

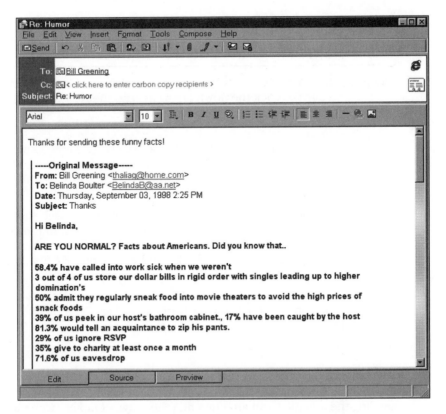

Figure 4-13: In this reply to an HTML-formatted message, the quoted text is indented with a vertical bar.

Secret

There is a downside to marking Indent Messages on Reply, however, if you like to intersperse replies with quoted text to simulate a conversation. If you insert your reply after a section of quoted text, you'll find the new text is also indented with the vertical bar. To get rid of the indent and the bar, first place your insertion point in the quoted text where you want to insert your reply text and press Enter — this inserts a line break. Then with your insertion point in the new paragraph, click the Paragraph Style toolbar button and click Normal. Even though the drop-down list shows that the current paragraph is already Normal, this will work. Your new text will be flush left and will not have a vertical bar.

Send a message as a web page

You can use Outlook Express to e-mail a web page from the Internet without having to open your browser.

Mailing a Web Page from Outlook Express

Step 1. In Outlook Express, choose Message, New Message Using, Web Page (or click the down arrow next to the New Message toolbar button and choose Web Page).

Step 2. In the Send Web Page dialog box, type the Internet address of a web page and click OK. Outlook Express will initiate a dial-up connection if necessary. The address must start with http. Even if the web page is available offline, you can't send it without actually going to it on the Internet.

Step 3. A New Message window opens, displaying the web page you have indicated. You can click in the page and insert additional text if you like. You can also do more extensive HTML editing by choosing View, Source Edit and then clicking the Source tab at the bottom of the page.

Step 4. Address your message, add a subject, and click the Send toolbar button to send it to your Outbox.

You can send an HTML file that resides on your hard disk by opening it in Internet Explorer, saving it in Web Archive for E-Mail (*mht*) format, and then sending the *mht* file as an attachment. (See "Save complete web pages" in Chapter 2 for more on the *mht* file format.) However, if you use this method the web page will not appear in the body of your message.

Remove hyperlinks from HTML text

While composing a message, if you type a sequence of characters that looks something like an e-mail address or a URL, Outlook Express automatically makes it into a clickable hyperlink. Sometimes, however, what you've typed might not be a real link, or there may be some other reason why you'd rather not have a link associated with that particular text.

To remove a link from an HTML message, click anywhere in the link, and then choose Edit, Remove Hyperlink. The text remains in your message, but it is no longer highlighted and will not produce a clickable link when the message is sent. The Remove Hyperlink command only works with HTML-formatted messages; it's dim for plain text messages, even though these messages can still contain links.

Break up large messages

You can tell Outlook Express to automatically break apart messages larger than a certain size. This is a courtesy to your recipient, and may be necessary depending on your ISP. When Outlook Express receives mail files that have been broken apart, it will combine and decode them automatically. For newsgroup files you must do this by choosing Message, Combine and Decode, as described in "Multi-part files" in Chapter 19 of *Windows 98 Secrets*.

STEPS:

Breaking Up Large Messages

Step 1: In Outlook Express, choose Tools, Accounts. Highlight the name of the account you will use to send large files, and click the Properties button. In the Properties dialog box for that account, click the Advanced tab.

Step 2: Under Sending, mark the Break Apart Messages Larger Than [ ] KB box, as shown in Figure 4-14. Enter a file size, or keep the default of 60K, and click OK. Then click Close.

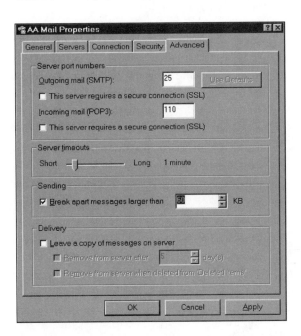

Figure 4-14: Outlook Express will automatically break apart files that are larger than the size you enter in the Advanced tab.

Step 3: Send the large file using the usual method. It will look normal in your Outbox. But when you do a Send and Receive, you will see that the message is being broken into two or more messages.

Outlook Express often has difficulty combining HTML files, so it's best to send files with big attachments as plain text in MIME/Quoted Printable in case they have to be broken up.

Stationery

More and more people are using stationery to make their messages more personal and colorful. Stationery works much better in Outlook Express 5 — here are some tips for getting started using stationery.

Use the wizard to design new stationery

A stationery style is more than just the background you see in a message. It also defines the font, font color, sounds, and images that make up the total "look and feel" of your message (everything but the content, that is). All of these parameters are defined in an HTML document that you can store and apply to HTML messages.

Although you can use the stationery samples that come with Outlook Express, you don't need to be an HTML programmer to define a new stationery style. To do so, choose Tools, Options, click the Compose tab, and click the Create New button. In the Stationery Setup Wizard that opens, click the Next button to move to the dialog box shown in Figure 4-15.

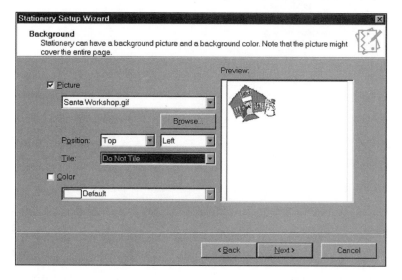

Figure 4-15: The Stationery Setup Wizard walks you through the design of a new stationery style.

The wizard contains a drop-down list of *gif* files you can use in your background, or you can use the Browse button to point to a different one — the Preview area lets you see what you'll be getting. After you have set the information about background graphics for your stationery, click Next to display a dialog box for selecting the font that will be part of this stationery. The information you set here only applies to this stationery. When you're done, click Next. The next dialog box lets you set margins (in pixels). Use the Preview area to see how the text and graphic will work together. Click Next when you've defined the margins. Now give your stationery a name, and click Finish. Outlook Express saves your stationery with the other stationery; the default location is \Program Files\Common Files\Microsoft Shared\Stationery.

To make your new stationery the default for mail or news messages, mark the Mail or News check box under Stationery on the Compose tab of the Tools, Option dialog box, and click the Select button to select your stationery. If you mark the Mail or News check box, your default format will be HTML, regardless of what you have marked on the Send tab — see "Get back to plain text" later in this chapter.

If you only use stationery occasionally, you can apply it to an individual message by choosing Format, Apply Stationery in the New Message window (this command is only active when Format, Rich Text (HTML) is marked), or by clicking the down arrow next to the New Message toolbar button and selecting the stationery from the drop-down list, as shown in Figure 4-16. The stationery you used most recently appears at the top of the list.

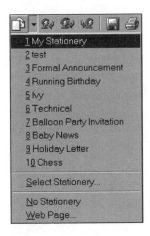

Figure 4-16: Select stationery from the New Message drop-down list for occasional use.

Change the default font for your stationery

In earlier versions of Outlook Express, the default Compose Font settings shown in Figure 4-17 (Tools, Options, Compose) affected your message regardless of whether you applied stationery, as long as the stationery did not contain font information. That is no longer true; these settings now only apply to HTML messages in which you have not applied stationery. You may find that your old stationery now uses Times Roman instead of the font you used to use.

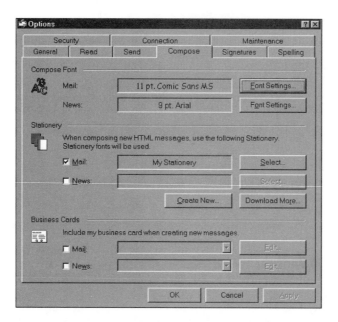

Figure 4-17: The Compose Font settings no longer affect messages that use stationery.

You can edit an individual HTML message in the New Message window by clicking View, Source Edit, and using the Source tab. But of course you don't want to do that every time. You can also (theoretically, at least) access an application that will let you edit stationery from within Outlook Express. (To do this, choose Tools, Options, and click the Compose tab. In the Stationery area, mark the Mail or News check box, and click the associated Select button. In the Select Stationery dialog box, select your stationery and click the Edit button.) However, doing this may not work for you.

Secret

Unless you have set things up otherwise, the default application associated with editing HTML files (including stationery) is most likely Front Page Express. Unfortunately, the header information placed in a file by Front Page Express when you save it will make that file unusable as stationery. You must use a plain text editor such as Notepad for editing stationery instead. While it's possible to change the file association so that the Edit button in the Select Stationery dialog box opens Notepad (see "Creating and Editing File Types and Actions" in Chapter 13 of *Windows 98 Secrets*), it's probably easier just to open Notepad and edit the HTML file for your stationery from there.

If you are planning to change the default font color, you will need to know the HTML hexadecimal code for the color. If you have Paint Shop Pro 5, it's easy to find this information. Open Paint Shop Pro 5, click the color that you want to use in the Color Palette, and then click the foreground color box at the bottom of the Color Palette. The Color dialog box appears with the hexadecimal code for the color listed at the bottom of the dialog box. If you don't have Paint Shop Pro 5, you'll find an HTML color chart at desktoppublishing.com/

color-codes.html, www.btinternet.com/~paulr/color/ msie4/index.htm, home.earthlink.net/~jjtompkins/Color.html, and numerous other places.

If you are unfamiliar with editing HTML code, you may want to save a backup copy of your stationery file before you edit it. Open Notepad, choose File, Open, and browse to the stationery file that you want to edit (the default location is \Program Files\Common Files\Microsoft Shared\Stationery). Figure 4-18 shows part of the HTML code for one of the stationery samples that come with Outlook Express. Notice that within the <STYLE> tag, the font attributes for various paragraph styles are listed. You can edit the font family and other characteristics for each paragraph style, and then save your stationery file when you're done. Now test your stationery in Outlook Express by opening a New Message window using the stationery you edited. Use the Paragraph Style toolbar button to change your current style if necessary.

```
Baby News.htm - Notepad
File  Edit  Search  Help
<html>
<head>
<title></title>
<style>
<!--
body {
margin-top: 120;
}
UL, OL, DIR, MENU, DIV, DT, DD, ADDRESS, BLOCKQUOTE, PRE, BR, P, LI
{
color: 006699;
font-size: 14pt;
font-weight: bold;
font-family: "Arial Narrow""Comic Sans MS", "Arial";
}
h1
{
color: FF0000;
font-size: 36pt;
font-weight: regular;
font-family: "Script MT Bold", "Comic Sans MS", "Arial";
}
h2
{
color: 006699;
font-size: 60pt;
font-weight: regular;
font-family: "Script MT Bold", "Comic Sans MS", "Arial";
}
-->
</style>
</head>
```

Figure 4-18: In this stationery sample we have changed the color of the H1 paragraph style from blue to red.

We find it much easier to just start over fresh using the New Stationery Wizard.

Get back to plain text

If you mark the Mail or News check box under Stationery in the Compose tab of the Tools, Options dialog box (see Figure 4-19) and select a stationery to use for your mail/news messages, your new messages will always start in HTML. This happens even if you have marked Plain Text under Mail Sending Format or News Sending Format on the Send tab (see Figure 4-20). In other words, if you have set a default stationery style, it will be your default for *all* messages. If you prefer to use plain text as your default, clear the Mail or News check box. Then when you want to use stationery, choose Format, Apply Stationery in the New Message window, or choose the stationery from the drop-down list attached to the New Message toolbar button in the Outlook Express window.

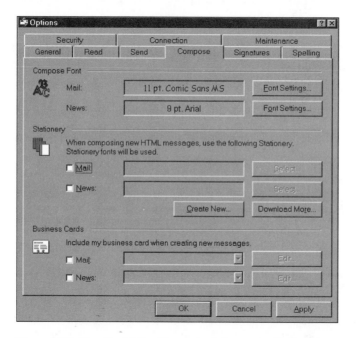

Figure 4-19: Clear the Mail or News check box under Stationery to get your plain text default back.

Move your stationery folder

Secret

If you've spent a lot of time developing stationery files, you might want to put them some place that's easier to back up — under My Documents, for instance. To do this, you need to edit the Registry. If for some reason you find you have two Stationery folders, you can use steps 1 and 2 below to determine which is the default. Then move into the default folder anything from the other one that you want to save, and delete the non-default folder.

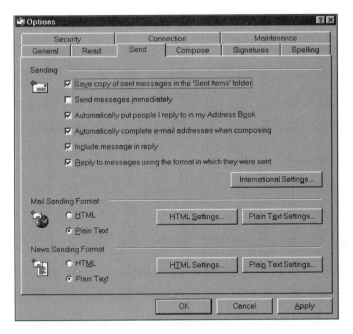

Figure 4-20: Even if you set plain text as the default in the Send tab, your setting will be overridden if you have marked the Mail or News check box under Stationery in the Compose tab.

STEPS:

Moving Your Stationery Folder

Step 1. Open the Registry editor.

Step 2. Navigate to HKEY_LOCAL_MACHINE\SOFTWARE\Microsoft\ Shared Tools\Stationery. Highlight Stationery in the left pane. In the right pane, you'll see Backgrounds Folder and Stationery Folder, with the current default location for each. The default is for backgrounds and stationery to be stored in the same folder, so they most likely have the same string value in the Registry (you can change this if you like).

Step 3. Double-click Stationery Folder. In the Value Data field, change the location for your Stationery folder, and then click OK. Do the same for Backgrounds Folder. Close the Registry editor.

Step 4. In the Explorer, navigate to the Stationery folder (in its old location) and drag it to the location you gave it in step 3. If you have set a different location for the Backgrounds folder, you'll need to create the new folder and drag the background files into it.

No default stationery for replies

Even if you have set Outlook Express to always send in HTML and to always use stationery, you will find that you cannot use your default stationery automatically in a reply.

Of course, if the original message contains stationery, you can use that in your reply. If you have set HTML as your default for sending mail, or if you have marked Reply to Messages in the Format in Which They Were Sent on the Send tab of the Options dialog box, the stationery of the original message will be the default for your reply.

If you want to use your default stationery in a reply, click Format, Apply Stationery and select it from the submenu that appears.

More stationery

If you're sick of stationery that looks like notebook paper, try Kenja's Stationery at www.kenja.com/stationery/. Kenja has created quite a variety of colorful stationery that you can download as a zip file for personal use.

David Guess of Bowling Green, Kentucky, has created a web site in which he reveals ways to insert scrolling messages, sounds, and marquee backgrounds into Outlook Express messages. His "Majik's Stationery Help Page," www.mindspring.com/~majik/docs.htm, is packed with tricks to make your e-mail distinctive.

To find a host of other sites with stationery files and how-to information, take a tour of the OE Stationery Web Ring at www.webring.org/cgi-bin/webring? ring=oestationery;list.

And for lots of ideas and help in designing your own stationery, don't forget the Outlook Express stationery newsgroup at msnews.microsoft.com\ microsoft.public.inetexplorer.ie4.outlookexpress.stationery. This is a very active group with lots of large files, so don't try downloading the whole thing at once!

Publish an Outlook Express e-zine

Because Outlook Express can produce and read HTML-coded text, you can use it to produce an HTML-formatted newsletter or e-zine that contains all of the formatting possible with HTML. If your readers have HTML-based e-mail clients, they'll be able to read the formatted version of your newsletter or e-zine.

Originally, HTML was used to format decent looking web pages. Early on, Outlook Express incorporated an HTML display engine to display HTML-formatted text in e-mail. Once HTML-compatible e-mail clients became widespread, it became practical to publish e-mail delivered e-zines using HTML-formatting.

You can use Outlook Express as a low-end HTML editor. It's easy to design stationery that includes a background and font information specifically for your newsletter. If you combine Outlook Express with FrontPage Express (which also comes with Windows 98), you can post the newsletter on your web site after you've sent out copies by e-mail.

There are plenty of HTML-formatted newsletters already available for you to sample. For example, you can subscribe to Jesse Berst's Email Alert, a daily fix of computer news, at www.zdnet.com/anchordesk/, or Chris Pirillo's Lockergnome, a daily Windows shareware review (see Figure 4-21), at www.lockergnome.com.

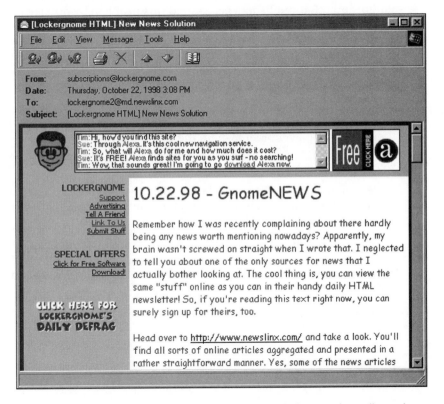

Figure 4-21: Lockergnome is a good example of an HTML-formatted e-mail newsletter.

Unfortunately, incompatibilities continue to exist among various implementations and definitions of the advanced features of HTML. It is precisely these advanced features that you will want to use to make your e-zine as attractive as possible. One way of dealing with these incompatibilities is to use the agreed upon HTML standards in tricky ways to make your text look good.

A good example of an advanced feature is in-line graphics — pictures inserted directly into the body of your e-mail messages. This is a great option that really adds to the power of your e-zine. (To keep your e-zine small, be sure to send out only *gif, jpg,* or similarly compact graphics files.)

Standard HTML doesn't support the inclusion of a graphics file in the same file as the HTML text. This is exactly what you want to do though — send the pictures and the text as one file. Fortunately, Outlook Express lets you do this. It places a pointer and a resource ID at the inserted location of the graphic and adds the graphic, encoded in text, at the end of the message file.

However, not all e-mail clients can read in-line graphics. Jesse Berst, Chris Pirillo, and other publishers get around this problem by not inserting graphics files, and instead inserting links to graphics files located on the publishers' web servers. When you receive and display one of these newsletters, the graphics are updated from files on the author's web site and stored in your Temporary Internet Files folder. This technique also gives the authors the opportunity to place continuously updating banner ads in their newsletters.

If you go offline before you display one of these newsletters, you'll find that there are only placeholders where the graphics would normally be displayed. Because you went offline before you displayed the newsletter, no commands were sent to the web server to download the graphics files.

Once you have viewed the newsletter online — and thereby downloaded the graphics files — the files will be in your Temporary Internet Files folder so that Outlook Express can find them after you go offline.

You can see the difference between these two methods of handling graphics files by looking at the underlying HTML source text. To display the HTML source of an e-mail message, double-click it in Outlook Express and press Ctrl+F2.

For example, here is a portion of Jesse Berst's newsletter:

```
<CENTER><A href="http://ads.zdnet.com/cgi-
bin/accipiter/aamr.exe/RGROUP=r128"><IMG
src="http://ads.zdnet.com/cgi-bin/accipiter/aami.exe/RGROUP=r128"></A>
```

You can see that the reference to a graphics file is a reference to the Ziff Davis web server.

Here is a pointer to a graphic that is contained within the Outlook Express e-mail message:

```
<P><IMG align=baseline
src="cid:011b01bdeb2e$8ddf8160$aa058d0a@fujitsu"></P>
```

Notice the resource ID — the string of letters, numbers, and punctuation that identifies the graphic. This graphic is stored at the end of the e-mail message that contains it.

If you include in-line graphics and the recipients of your e-zine use Outlook Express or a compatible e-mail client, they'll be able to view your e-zine with the graphics files located where you inserted them when you composed the message. If the recipients use e-mail clients that don't support in-line graphics, the pictures will either not show up at all or will be displayed as file attachments. These readers will have to click the attachments to display them.

If you want a separate web page that displays the contents of your e-zine, you can copy the contents of your e-zine into a blank FrontPage Express file. FrontPage Express doesn't know what to do with the pointer to the enclosed graphics files and will display broken references to them. You will have to copy the graphics files into the folder where you store your local copy of the new web page, and edit the web page to refer to the external graphics files. Just right-click each broken graphics symbol in FrontPage Express, select Image Properties, and use the Browse button to enter the filename and path for each image.

If you used stationery when creating your e-zine, you'll need to copy the stationery graphic over to the new folder that contains the web page. You'll most likely find the stationery in \Program Files\Common Files\Microsoft Shared\Stationery.

We often find when we have copied text from Outlook Express into a new blank FrontPage Express file that the text styles are forgotten. Hopefully Microsoft will fix this. You'll have to select all the text in FrontPage Express, click Format, Font, and choose the font again. Similarly, the background color may be altered; to fix this, choose Format, Background, and change the background color.

You can create a template file that you can then reuse to create new issues of your e-zine. It should include any background or stationery, and any repeated text. This could be nothing more than the last issue of your e-zine, saved in an Outlook Express Local Folder. To use it as a template, you simply delete the existing content and add the new content.

You might want to include a comment in the HTML source that warns people if their e-mail client is unable to display HTML. Here is an example of the kind of comment that you can add:

```
<META HTTP-EQUIV="Content-Type" CONTENT="text/html;charset=Windows-
1252">
<!- ***
This is Lockergnome's Daily HTML Newsletter, not the Text Weekly one.
If you can see this paragraph, then you are not using an HTML
compliant e-mail client. Don't worry, you may remove yourself from the
Daily (and still retain the Classic Text Weekly Lockergnome) at:
www.lockergnome.com/options.html or e-mail removehtml@lockergnome.com
- Sorry for any inconvenience this may have caused you.
*** ->
```

Attachments and multimedia

These days, messages come with all kinds of things attached, including sound and animation. Luckily there are some helpful ways to read, manage, and save these attachments.

Read attachments without opening the message

Sometimes a message is nothing but attachments. For example, some mailing list digests arrive as an empty message with a bunch of text files attached. The easy way to deal with attachments is to use the big paper clip icon that appears at the right end of the preview pane header of the message. If this header isn't visible, click View, Layout, and mark Show Preview Pane Header. (You must of course also have Show Preview Pane marked.) Click the paper clip to display a list of all the attachments, as shown in Figure 4-22.

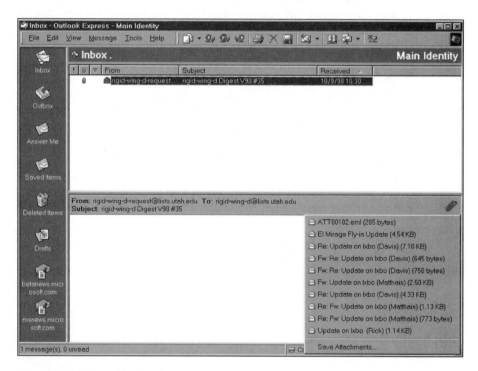

Figure 4-22: This mailing list digest contains a series of attached messages.

Click an attachment in the list to open it. Alternatively, you can choose Save Attachments at the bottom of the list (or choose File, Save Attachments) to display the Save Attachments dialog box, and then save any or all of the attachments to disk.

Unfortunately, you can no longer save an attachment by dragging its little paper clip icon out of the Message pane. Now if you do that, you'll save a copy of the whole message.

Strange attachments

Occasionally you may receive attachments that you can't seem to view or open. They may have a *dat* or *doc* extension. Usually these are files that were saved in Rich Text Format (RTF) — it's likely they were sent by someone using Windows Messaging or Outlook 9*x*. RTF is not an Internet standard and cannot be decoded using Outlook Express. Your only option is to ask your correspondent to re-send the attachment as a plain text file.

On the other hand, Outlook Express can now read many attachments encoded using Binhex, a popular Macintosh format. This decoding is transparent; you shouldn't have to do anything special to read these files. If you do receive one that doesn't open, you can decode it using Wincode, available as shareware on the Internet from www.jumbo.com, www.hotfiles.com, and many other shareware sites (be sure to get version 2.7.3 or later).

For an interesting, fairly technical discussion of encoding and decoding, see Michael Santovec's article, "Decoding Internet Attachments - A Tutorial" at pages.prodigy.net/michael_santovec/decode.htm.

Why all those little envelopes?

Maybe you've had the experience of opening a mail message to find no text, but only an attachment that looks like a little envelope in the message's Attach field. When you open the attachment, you discover that it contains nothing but another attachment, and maybe even the next one is the same. Finally you open an attachment containing the actual message. This is a common experience with humor that gets passed on from person to person. This is not a behavior of Outlook Express at all; instead, each reader has chosen to forward the message as an attachment (this is called *redirecting* in some mail applications). Many users of other mail software such as Netscape don't even realize they are doing this.

Tip

In fact, there may be times when you do want to redirect, or forward a message as an attachment. For example, you might want to do it if you are forwarding a message to a mailing list, troubleshooting a problem message, or complaining to an ISP about junk mail. To forward a message as an attachment, highlight the message header in the Outlook Express window, and choose Message, Forward As Attachment. You will see the message's icon in the Attach field of the New Message window that appears.

Save messages without attachments

Some people keep copies of all the messages they send for their records. But attachments can take up a lot of hard disk space, especially since you have probably already saved the file somewhere else.

After sending a message, open it from your Sent Items folder, and then use File, Save As to save it as a *txt* file. The attachment will be stripped out in the process. You can then delete the message from your Sent Items folder.

Put sound in your messages

HTML-formatted messages can include sound as well as graphics. To add a *wav* file to a new HTML message, click Format, Background, Sound to open the Background Sound dialog box shown in Figure 4-23. Use the Browse button to select a file, and then click Open. You can choose whether to play the sound only once or continuously (hope it's something very pleasant if you choose the latter). After you click OK, you'll get a preview of the sound, continuous or not depending on what you have chosen, in the New Message window.

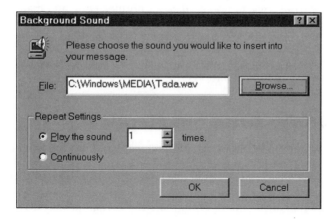

Figure 4-23: The Background Sound dialog box lets you select a sound to include in your message.

Add URLs to your favorites without going online

If someone e-mails you a link to a URL, you don't need to connect to the Internet to add the site to your Favorites. This works for any URL that functions as a hyperlink in Outlook Express. Just right-click the link and choose Add to Favorites.

Unfortunately, at the time we tested this it wasn't working quite right. You could choose Add to Favorites, but you weren't prompted to add it to a

Favorites subfolder or to give it a name. After saving the shortcut you had to go to the \Windows\Favorites folder in the Explorer to name it something other than "Favorites from Outlook Express" and to move it to a subfolder. We hope that by the time you try it things have improved.

Saving GIFs

Secret

It's fun to collect the animated *gifs* you see in newsgroup postings or messages from your friends. But if you try to save a file by right-clicking and choosing Save Picture As, your only choice is to save it as a *bmp* file, thus losing the animation. Here's a way to save a *gif* as a *gif*:

STEPS:

Saving Animated GIF Files

Step 1: In Outlook Express, choose Tools, Options, click the Send tab, and under Mail Sending Format, mark Plain Text. Clear Reply to Messages Using the Format in Which They Were Sent. Click OK.

Step 2: Highlight the header of the news message containing the *gif* file you want to save, and click the Forward button. The message should come up in plain text format, with the original *htm* file and any included *gif* files shown as attachments in the Attach field (as shown in Figure 4-24).

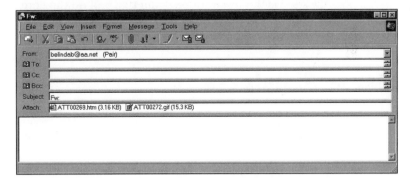

Figure 4-24: The *gif* file is shown as an attachment when you forward a message in plain text format.

Step 3: Right-drag the icon for the *gif* file you want to save directly into your Explorer and choose Copy Here.

ASCII Art

If you read your e-mail with a fixed space font, you get to see the ASCII art signatures. While HTML e-mail provides much more artistic power than that available to plain text messages, ASCII art is a fun way to turn dots, dashes, letters, and punctuation marks into art. Give an artist a limit and it's still art.

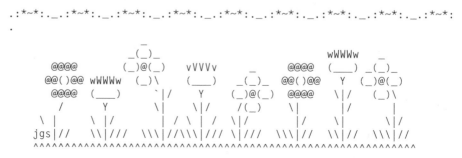

This example came from Joan Stark's ASCII art gallery at www.geocities.com/SoHo/7373/.

There is an easy way to convert existing graphics files (in *bmp* format) to ASCII art. You'll want to use an appropriate graphics file that translates well. Also, if you are going to use the ASCII graphic as a signature, you'll want to resize the graphics file so that after it is translated it is small enough to look good in an e-mail message. Each pixel in the graphics file is translated to a character, so a 600 x 480 graphics file is going to look really big. You might try 15 x 15 pixels.

ASCII Pic is the freeware program that will do the conversion, and you'll find it at members.xoom.com/5679soft/asciipic.zip. Thanks to Chris Pirillo at www.lockergnome.com.

Message helpers

There are lots of tools available online to help you get your message across. Here are a few we've tried.

Spell check help

Outlook Express uses the Microsoft Office spell checker. But what if you don't use Microsoft Office? Speller for Microsoft Internet Products is shareware produced by CompuBridge. They also make spell checkers for Microsoft Office and WordPad, and they make AutoSpell for other e-mail products such as Netscape and Pegasus. A main benefit of Speller is spell checking in multiple languages, such as Danish, Dutch, French, German, Italian and Spanish, as well as a couple flavors of English. CompuBridge is promising to support spell checking of the Subject line in Outlook Express messages — a helpful touch.

You can download free evaluation copies of Speller for Microsoft Internet Products from www.spellchecker.com. Registration (gets rid of the nag screen) is $14.95.

Reformatting and cleaning up your e-mail

When we looked at the interface for this utility we weren't greatly impressed, but when we read what it did and then watched it do it, Wow! OK, it doesn't seem like much, but it has always been a pain to get rid of "greater than" symbols, and especially to get rid of the incorrectly placed line ends in e-mail messages.

Tip

We found the easy way to use the Cleaner was to cut and paste the contents of a given e-mail message into the Cleaner. If you do it this way, you don't have to create a new file. You can then paste the cleaned up text back over the "unclean" text in your Outlook Express message.

You'll find the Cleaner at ftp://mirrors.aol.com/pub/simtelnet/win95/email/clean102.zip. Chris Pirillo at www.lockergnome.com told us about it.

Talking E-mail

Now you can have a pleasant voice announce the arrival of your e-mail and read your messages to you (up to 30 lines each). Choose a friendly animated cartoon character to do the talking (see the example shown in Figure 4-25). The registered version gives you a choice of characters and voices.

Developed by 4Developers, Talking E-mail is shareware that uses Microsoft's advanced text-to-speech technology. It works with your standard mail account, and leaves messages on your mail server so you can download them later with Outlook Express. No special hardware other than a sound card is required. You can download Talking E-mail from Shareware.com at www.shareware.com/DD/sw/0%2C156%2C1112-1-005%2C00.html

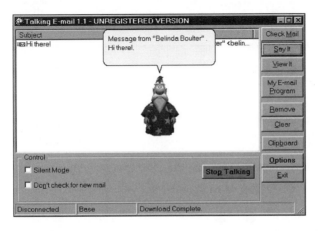

Figure 4-25: The cartoon character reads your e-mail to you while you do something else.

Jazz up your mail announcement

If you're looking for something a bit more entertaining to announce the arrival of mail, check out this page on the Eudora FAQ site: wso.williams.edu/~eudora/eudora-alert-sounds.html. They also have *wav* files for announcing the arrival of spam (including the entire Monty Python Spam Song) — it might as well be good for something, after all.

Outlook Express can use any *wav* file to announce mail, so even though this site is geared toward users of Eudora the files will work fine. Right-click the link to the file you want and choose Save Target As, and then save the file in your \Windows\Media folder or some other place where you keep sound files. Click the Sounds icon in your Control Panel to associate this file with the New Mail Notification action. For specifics on using *wav* files to announce mail, see "Waving When the Mail Arrives" in Chapter 19 and "Applying Sounds to Application Events" in Chapter 16 of *Windows 98 Secrets*.

Another good source of sounds is G-Man, gman.simplenet.com/email.

Summary

Outlook Express gives you a lot of tools for composing and managing mail and news messages.

▶ You can use Flag, Watch, and Ignore to make it easier to see the messages you really want. Use them with Find so you only have to find them once.

▶ Quoting in HTML files works better than before, or you can send plain text with customized quote characters.

▶ The Stationery Setup Wizard will help you design your own stationery. You can use the stationery to publish an illustrated e-zine.

▶ The preview pane header lets you open an attachment without opening the message.

▶ You can save an animated *gif* graphic from a message by forwarding it to yourself.

Chapter 5

Outlook Express – Keeping Up with the News

In This Chapter

The Outlook Express news reader is your link to the thousands of Usenet newsgroups on the Internet. We show you how to sort through the clutter and make newsgroups work for you.

▶ Set the synchronization to download the messages or headers you want.

▶ Design a custom newsgroup view to sort your messages.

▶ Put a shortcut to your favorite newsgroup on your Desktop or toolbar.

▶ Save a whole thread at once and preserve its order.

▶ Add a custom header to your news messages that can help protect your privacy.

▶ Forward a mail message to a newsgroup.

▶ Keep old news from filling up your hard disk.

Synchronizing and subscribing

How do you get started participating in newsgroups? How do you keep up to date with the discussion? The first step is to subscribe, and then to synchronize your computer with the news server.

Sync one newsgroup or the whole shebang

Outlook Express uses the term *synchronize* to refer to downloading a newsgroup. It's true, you are synchronizing the header list on your computer to the one on the newsgroup server. But all those folks who have wasted time looking for the "download" command are wondering if the change was really necessary. To avoid confusion, though, we'll stick with Microsoft's terminology.

You determine what synchronization entails for each newsgroup in the Synchronization pane for the newsgroup's news server (see Figure 5-1). Highlight the server in the Folders pane or the Folders list to display its Synchronization pane. In the Synchronization pane, highlight a newsgroup or use the Ctrl and Shift keys to highlight several at once, and then click the Settings button and select the desired option from the menu that appears. You can change the synchronization settings for a single newsgroup by right-clicking it in the Folders pane or the Folders list and choosing Synchronization Settings. This brings up the same menu as the one that's displayed when you click the Settings button in the Synchronization pane (see Figure 5-2).

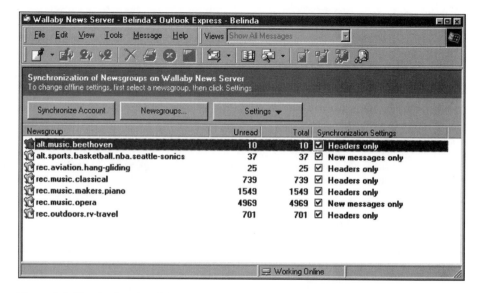

Figure 5-1: Use the Synchronization pane to control the synchronization of all the newsgroups on a news server.

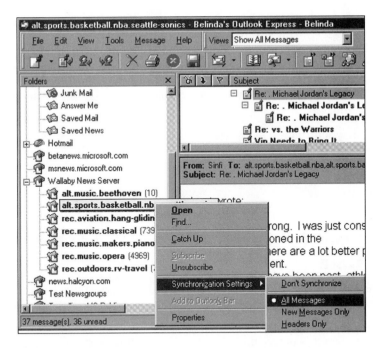

Figure 5-2: The menu for changing your synchronization settings.

Here is a description of the commands in the Settings menu:

- **All Messages:** Outlook Express first downloads all of the headers for this newsgroup that aren't already downloaded, and then downloads all of those messages. This can take quite a while if there are thousands of messages (often the case).

- **New Messages Only:** Outlook Express retrieves the headers and messages for a predetermined number of the newest messages (see the next section for how to set this number).

- **Headers Only:** Outlook Express downloads only the headers. You can then mark the headers that look interesting (right-click the message header and choose either Download Message Later or Download Conversation Later — or click in the Mark for Offline column if you have it displayed) and download only those messages the next time you synchronize (this will automatically be added to the tasks that will be carried out during a Send and Receive). A blue arrow appears next to the message in the Mark for Offline column if you have this column displayed.

- **Don't Synchronize:** Outlook Express skips this newsgroup when it synchronizes the others. (You can also clear the newsgroup's check box in the Synchronization pane.)

To synchronize all of your newsgroups on all news servers, choose Tools, Synchronize All. This action performs a Send and Receive for your e-mail at the same time. You'll see all of the tasks listed in the Outlook Express dialog box. While you can stop the whole process by clicking the Stop button, there's no way to skip a task and continue with the others once the process begins. Put a Synchronize All button on your news toolbar if you use this command a lot.

You can synchronize a single newsgroup or a single news server (which could include numerous newsgroups). To do this, highlight the newsgroup or account in the Folders pane and then choose Tools, Synchronize Newsgroup if you've highlighted a newsgroup, or Tools, Synchronize Account if you've highlighted a server.

Get more (or fewer) than 300 headers at a time

By default, Outlook Express downloads 300 headers at one time, starting with the most recent ones. To get the previous 300, choose Tools, Get Next 300 Headers.

You may feel this is too many headers to digest at once, or it may not be enough to suit you. To change the number of headers that Outlook Express downloads, choose Tools, Options, and click the Read tab. Under News, either clear the Get [ ] Headers at a Time check box, or set the number higher, as shown in Figure 5-3. The highest number you can enter is 1000. If you clear the check box, you'll get all of the headers.

If you prefer to download headers in small batches, you'll probably want to take advantage of the Headers button on your toolbar. This button is the equivalent of the Tools, Get Next *X* Headers command.

Secret

If you have Outlook Express set to download a set number of headers at a time, you may occasionally find that when you go to a newsgroup it downloads another, previous group of headers — without prompting. To stop this behavior, use the Catch Up command, described in "Catch up" later in this chapter.

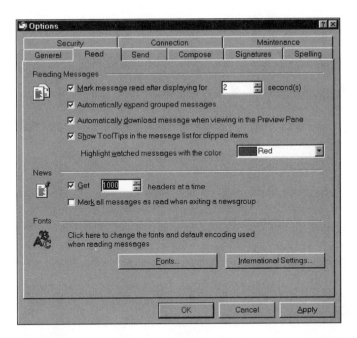

Figure 5-3: Clear the Get [   ] Headers at a Time check box, or increase the number of headers.

Read messages without sync-ing

When you switch from mail to news or switch to a newsgroup on a different news server, and you are working in online mode, Outlook Express will begin downloading message headers. This happens regardless of what your synchronization settings are. In fact, you never really need to synchronize at all if you have a continuous Internet connection or don't mind staying connected while you read the news. Each message will be downloaded individually when you highlight its header.

Secret

If you read newsgroups this way and have the Preview pane displayed, you will notice that it can take a moment for a message to download. It's easy to select a header by mistake, when you really didn't want to read that message. If you like, you can tell Outlook Express to download a message only when you tell it to.

To do this, choose Tools, Options, click the Read tab, and clear the check box labeled Download Message When Viewing in the Preview Pane. Now when you highlight a header, you'll see the message shown in Figure 5-4 in the Preview pane.

Figure 5-4: You'll see this message in the Preview pane if the message has not been automatically downloaded. Press the Spacebar to download the message.

Keep the downloads coming

If you frequently use Synchronize All to download lots of big newsgroups, you know how frustrating it can be to get disconnected in mid-download when you were away from your computer. (For that matter, it's a pain if you often receive very large e-mail attachments.) If this is a frequent problem, you might want to try InLook 1.03 for Outlook Express 4 and 5.

During synchronization, InLook checks every minute for the Reestablish Connection dialog box. If it's there (meaning you've been disconnected), InLook reconnects for you and starts another Synchronize All. This lets you go off and have lunch or go to bed instead of babysitting your computer.

InLook only works over a dial-up connection. You must have already made the connection and have your Inbox open for InLook to work (so you can't use it with the Task Scheduler to schedule a synchronization, for example).

InLook is freeware, available from Edgemeal Software at www.ameritech.net/users/edgemeal/home.html.

Add a news account to Send and Receive

You can have Outlook Express check your news server as part of the standard Send and Receive operation or an automatic poll (Tools, Options, General, Check for New Messages Every [   ] Minutes). To do this, choose Tools, Accounts, click the News tab, highlight the account you want to add, and click the Properties button. In the Properties dialog box for this account, mark Include This Account When Checking for New Messages, as illustrated in Figure 5-5.

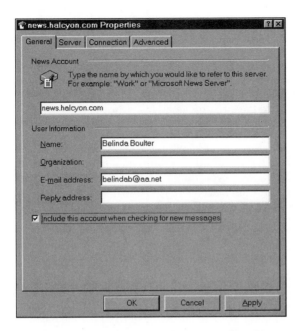

Figure 5-5: Mark the Include This Account When Checking for New Messages check box to include this news server in a standard Send and Receive operation.

You might think that this means Outlook Express will synchronize the newsgroups on this server when you perform a Send and Receive. So, for example, you might expect to see new headers or new messages after the process is complete. However, all that actually changes is the message count. In other words, when you go to a newsgroup on this server, you'll be able to see if there are unread messages, and how many there are. At this time there is still no way to automatically download unread headers or messages.

In fact, at the time this book was written, this check box wasn't working at all. It may be gone by the time you read this, or it may be working again. Try it out and see.

The message count seems to be inaccurate

When you are downloading a newsgroup, the status bar lists the number of messages on the server, the number that have been downloaded, and how many of those you have read. But sometimes the numbers seem to be inaccurate. Steve Serdy, a Microsoft Outlook Express Developer, wrote about this:

> Most, if not all, newsreaders suffer from problems like this. The problem stems from the fact that the message count information we can get quickly from the news server are all *estimates*. Based on that, OE comes up with the estimated number of messages we're going to

download so that we can show some approximate progress. Depending on the sparseness of the data in the newsgroup, this number can be fairly accurate or not even close.

I've spent an enormous amount of time over the last few years trying to come up with some better algorithm to make this number more accurate, but I haven't been able to without significantly increasing the amount of data we'd have to download from the server. Obviously increasing the download time is not acceptable.

Despite what Steve says, we believe we have seen some improvement in this area. If you are having a consistent problem, make sure you have set the view filter to Show All Messages — you may have hidden some. And remember that if you have chosen Edit, Catch Up, there will be messages on the server that you can't download because they have been marked as read. See "Catch up" later in this chapter for more about this.

Secret

If you have a newsgroup with wildly inaccurate message counts, try resetting it. To do this, right-click the newsgroup in the Folders pane or the Folders list, click Properties, click the Local File tab, and click the Reset button. If that doesn't help, unsubscribe from that newsgroup and then subscribe again. Of course, the work you put into downloading and sorting messages you've already read may make the cure worse than the disease.

You don't need to subscribe to read

If you're just curious about a newsgroup, you don't need to subscribe to it. Right-click the newsgroup's server in the Folders pane or Folders list, and choose Newsgroups. In the Newsgroup Subscriptions dialog box, highlight the newsgroup in the list, and click the Go To button. If you like, you can browse through the messages one-by-one online. If you'd rather work offline, you can still right-click headers of interest and choose Download Message Later or Download Conversation Later. Then later click Tools, Synchronize Newsgroup to download the message bodies. You cannot set synchronization settings for a non-subscribed newsgroup, and the newsgroup will not appear in the Synchronization pane for the server to which it belongs. If you choose Synchronize All, this newsgroup will not appear in the list of Send and Receive tasks (although individual messages you've marked to download will).

When you leave the newsgroup, you will be asked if you want to subscribe. If you click No, the newsgroup will still appear in your Folders pane, and the messages and headers will still be available, but only until you close Outlook Express. If you mark the Don't Ask Me This Again check box, the button that you click (Yes or No) will govern future behavior for this situation. To get the warning box back, see "Get those dialog boxes back" in Chapter 3.

Earlier problems with removing unsubscribed newsgroups in Outlook Express have been resolved. So if you think you'll want to go back to a newsgroup, there's no harm in subscribing to it — you can easily unsubscribe whenever you like.

Force plain text for an account

Secret

Even if your default message format is HTML, you can force Outlook Express to send messages for a particular news account using plain text. To do this, choose Tools, Accounts, double-click an account, and go to the Advanced tab. Mark the Ignore News Sending Format and Post Using check box, and then mark the Plain Text option button, as shown in Figure 5-6. This overrides whatever option you have chosen under News Sending Format in the Send tab of the Tools, Options dialog box.

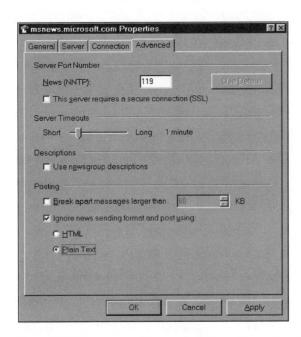

Figure 5-6: You can override your default sending options for a news account and send plain text messages.

Reading the news

Reading a newsgroup sounds like a pretty simple thing to do. But if you don't have all day to wade through the messages on some of the more popular groups, you might want to take advantage of some techniques to make it a little less cumbersome.

Moving around in a newsgroup

When you go to a newsgroup and you're in online mode, Outlook Express automatically tries to download headers. If you don't have a connection, you will be prompted to connect. Select a header, and the message will be downloaded. If you like, you can read the whole newsgroup this way without ever synchronizing.

When you click a newsgroup in the Folders pane or the Outlook bar, Outlook Express takes you to the first unread message. To see the next unread message, conversation, or folder, choose View, Next, and select from the menu shown in Figure 5-7. Because this is a bit cumbersome to do constantly, you may want to add a button to your news toolbar for one or all of these commands. Or just use the keyboard shortcuts shown in the menu: Ctrl+U for the next unread message, Ctrl+Shift+U for the next unread conversation, and Ctrl+J for the next unread folder.

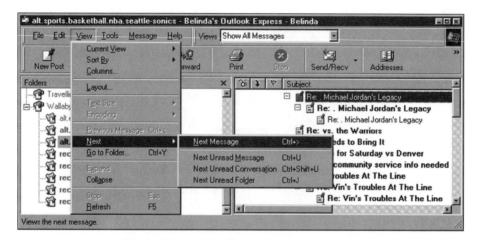

Figure 5-7: Choose Next Unread Message, Conversation, or Folder in the View, Next menu.

When you reach the bottom of the Message pane, the Next Unread command cycles the focus back to the top if there are still unread messages in this newsgroup. If you have read all of the messages and click the Next Unread Message button, you will be prompted to go to the next news folder with unread messages (see Figure 5-8).

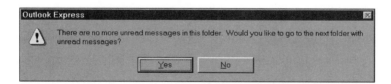

Figure 5-8: Click Yes to go to the next news folder with unread messages.

You may have unread messages in a thread where the first message has been read. If you have not marked Automatically Expand Grouped Messages on the Read tab of the Options dialog box, these will be hidden. In this situation, the top message will be shown in bold type as if it were unread. When you press Ctrl+U, the thread will automatically expand, and the unread message will be selected.

Next Unread Conversation (Ctrl+Shift+U) takes you to the first message in a conversation containing an unread message, regardless of whether the first message is read. Use Next Unread Message to expand the thread if necessary and go to the unread message.

Setting the view

It's a good thing we have the new Views bar, because the current view is now set individually for each newsgroup and mail folder. You can set the view to View All Messages in a smaller newsgroup, but Hide Read or Ignored Messages in a group with lots of flame wars. When you move to a newsgroup, the view setting changes to what it was when you were there last. You'll soon develop the habit of glancing at the Views bar to check the current view.

Secret

If your Views bar isn't showing, right-click the Outlook Express toolbar and click Views Bar. You can drag the Views bar up next to the menu bar to get it out of the way. Now you have a handy drop-down list of all the View settings, including the custom views you design yourself (see Figure 5-9).

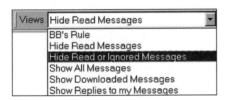

Figure 5-9: The Views bar is a boon to newsgroup addicts.

Design a custom view

You can design a custom view and save it to use whenever you read newsgroups. For example, sometimes you might want to see just the news messages from particular people (the ones whose comments you find most helpful, maybe, or the ones with the best gossip). Or you might set up a different view for each of several subject keywords, so you can read the messages for each subject as a group. Because it's easy to switch views, you can get to just the part of the newsgroup you're interested in at the moment without having to wade through the rest.

The easiest way to create a custom view is to modify the one you're currently using. Select the view that most closely matches the one you want, and then choose View, Current View, Customize Current View. (You will still be able to change any part of the view definition, so the view you start with is not critical, but it can be helpful.) The Customize Current View dialog box appears (see Figure 5-10), showing the definition of the current view.

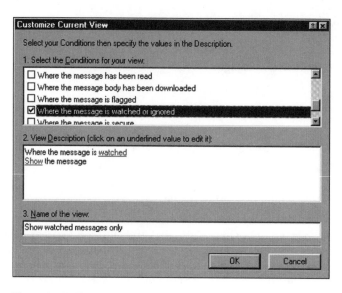

Figure 5-10: The current view in this example is Show Watched Messages Only.

The Conditions area lets you change or add conditions to describe the messages that you want to show or hide. You do this by marking or unmarking the check box for that condition. When this dialog box first appears, the conditions for your current view will be marked, but you can clear them if you want. These conditions are very general. For example, you can specify that the From line must contain people. Later you get more specific about which people. You can mark more than one condition, and later specify whether the messages must match all of the conditions or any of them.

As you select conditions, you will see a summary of all your choices in the View Description area. This is where you make each of your conditions specific. Click each blue underlined word or phrase in the Description area to display a dialog box that lets you define it or change the definition. The dialog boxes vary depending on what you are selecting, be it people, subject words, or something else. For example, the Select People dialog box, shown in Figure 5-11, lets you use the Address Book button to browse for people you want to select, or type their addresses and click the Add button — you can add as many people as you like. Other dialog boxes may contain only a drop-down list or option buttons.

Secret

You can further refine your selection by clicking the Options button available in some of the dialog boxes that appear when you click a blue underlined word or phrase in the Description area. The Rule Condition Options dialog box, shown in Figure 5-12, lets you change your condition in either of two important ways. The first pair of option buttons lets you select by *exclusion* rather than by *inclusion* — in other words, you can set the condition to view all messages that do *not* contain the keywords or addresses you have indicated. The second pair of option buttons lets you change the OR operator to AND — so that a message must contain *all* of the keywords or addresses you have indicated in order for the condition to be met.

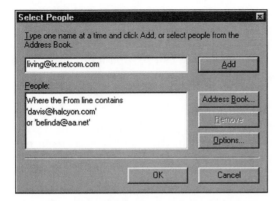

Figure 5-11: The Select People dialog box lets you select one or more people whose messages you will choose to show or hide.

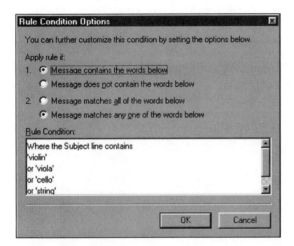

Figure 5-12: You can use the Rule Condition Options dialog box to change the way your condition will work.

Any changes you make in the Rule Condition Options dialog box affect only that one condition. If you have set multiple conditions by marking more than one check box in the Conditions area, the blue underlined word *And* appears between each condition listed in the Description area. This means the messages must match all of the conditions you have set. To change the And to Or, click the *And*. In the And/Or dialog box that appears, mark the Messages Match Any One of the Criteria option button, and click OK.

When you have finished editing all of the values in the View Description area, type a name for your view in the Name of the View field, click OK, and your view will be added to the Views bar and to the Current View menu.

Secret

While a custom view may seem similar to a news message rule, there are some significant differences. Message rules offer more possible actions than simply showing or hiding. And views do not affect what is downloaded, only what you can see at the moment. You can set up lot of views and quickly switch from view to view as you read, while message rules are designed to operate all or most of the time. For more on message rules, see "Setting up message rules" in Chapter 6.

If none of the existing views is similar to what you want, or if you're planning to set up several views at once, you might prefer to start from scratch instead of basing your custom view on the current one. That way you don't have to clear all of the existing conditions before marking the ones you want. This method also lets you edit a view without actually having it current. Click View, Current View, Define Views. You will see a list of all the views, along with their descriptions. You can add a new view definition or modify an existing one in the same way we have just described.

After you've defined a new view, you must still apply it to a message folder, normally by selecting it from the Views bar. To apply your new view to your current folder (or globally to all your Outlook Express folders) while your view is still highlighted in the Define Views dialog box, click the Apply View button (and if you want, mark the All of My Folders option button, as shown in Figure 5-13). You might also find this a convenient way to reset all of your folders to Show All Messages.

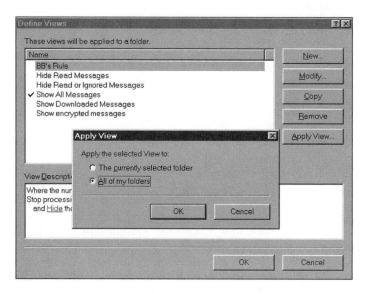

Figure 5-13: You can apply a view to all of your folders.

A shortcut to a newsgroup

Secret

You can't set Outlook Express to open anywhere except the Inbox — but you can create a shortcut on your Desktop to a favorite newsgroup.

STEPS:
Creating a Newsgroup Shortcut

Step 1. On an empty part of your Desktop, click New, Shortcut.

Step 2. In the Command Line field of the Create Shortcut dialog box, type **news://** followed by the exact name of your news server, a forward slash, and the name of the newsgroup. For example, your command might look something like this:

```
news://msnews.microsoft.com/microsoft.public.win98.internet
```

Use the full server and newsgroup names listed in the Synchronization pane for that news server. Click Next.

Step 3. The Select a Title for the Program dialog box appears. Type a name for your shortcut and click Finish.

Step 4. Click your new shortcut to go directly to your newsgroup.

Secret

If you have a bunch of newsgroups, you could make a newsgroup toolbar. Make a shortcut to each newsgroup, and then create a new folder called Newsgroups (perhaps under your \My System folder) and move all of the shortcuts from the Desktop to the folder. Now right-click the Taskbar, click Toolbars, New Toolbar, navigate to your Newsgroups folder in the New Toolbar dialog box, and click OK. Drag the sizing bar at the left end of the new toolbar to the right, so you only see the name of the toolbar. Then click the toolbar name to display a menu of your newsgroup shortcuts, and click the one that you want to open.

Threads

You can sort both mail and news messages by subject. These subjects are called *conversations* in Outlook Express, but they're known as *threads* in the wider Internet community. To see your messages in threaded order, choose View, Current View, Group Messages by Conversation. Unlike the current view, this setting applies to either all your news folders or all your mail folders, depending on whether you are in a news or mail folder when you choose it. Grouping messages in this way helps to make sense of the responses and counter-responses as a newsgroup discussion develops. An example of a long thread is shown in Figure 5-14.

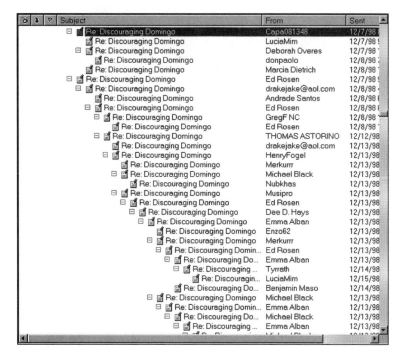

Figure 5-14: An example of a thread (conversation) taken from the rec.music.opera newsgroup.

According to Steve Serdy, a Microsoft Outlook Express Developer, Outlook Express uses the References line in a message's header (placed there automatically by the sender's news software) to decide whether it belongs in a thread. But because many news clients don't use this header, Outlook Express then does a secondary sort by subject. Although this means that some messages will be added to threads where they don't belong, at least all of the messages that do belong will usually be grouped together.

If you're contributing to an ongoing discussion, it's helpful to preserve the threading so that your message doesn't end up a disconnected orphan. To do this, highlight the message to which you're replying and click the Reply to Group button (*not* the New Post button or the Reply to Sender button). This will add the appropriate References line to your message's header, with a pointer to the message that you're replying to. You can see this line once your message is in your Outbox by highlighting the message and pressing Ctrl-F3.

If you have quoting enabled (Tools, Options, Send, Include Message in Reply), you will also see a reference to the original message at the beginning of the quoted portion of the body of your message, for example:

```
Somebody <somebody@isp> wrote in message
news:#waO#RgK#GA.193@uppssnewspub04.moswest.msn.Net...
```

You can set whole threads to be watched or ignored. For more about this, see "Make messages and threads easier to find" in Chapter 4.

Save a thread

You can save a whole conversation (or any group of messages) together in an Outlook Express folder. Highlight the messages and click Edit, Copy to Folder — or right-click and click Copy to Folder in the context menu. In the Copy dialog box, select or create a folder for saving the messages, and click OK. The threading information in the message headers will be preserved in the new folder.

Secret

If you save the messages to an Explorer folder, the threading information will not be preserved. Not only that, but because the default filename is the subject, if all the messages in the group have the same subject (the usual case) you'll have to save each message individually and rename each one. A much easier way to save a thread, and a way that preserves the order of the messages, is to save them in one file. Here's how:

STEPS:

Saving a Group of Messages As One File

Step 1.   In the Message pane, highlight the headers of plain text messages you want to save by using Shift+click (for consecutive messages) or Ctrl+click (for non-consecutive messages).

Step 2.   Click Message, Combine and Decode.

Step 3.   The Order for Decoding dialog box, shown in Figure 5-15, appears. Use the Move Up and Move Down buttons to select the order of the messages, or just drag the messages up and down the list with your mouse (a little black arrow appears on the left to indicate where the message will be dropped). When you're finished, click OK.

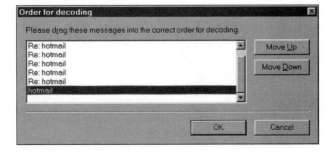

Figure 5-15: The Order for Decoding dialog box.

Continued

Saving a Group of Messages As One File *(continued)*

Step 4. The text of all of the messages appears in one message window. Now click File, Save As to save your file to a folder outside of Outlook Express. You can choose to save it in either mail *(eml)* or text *(txt)* format.

Combine and Decode now works on mail as well as news. It works best if the messages are in plain text format, because otherwise you see all of the HTML code along with the message. We have heard that using Combine and Decode with an HTML message can cause Outlook Express to crash, but we have not experienced it. The only other drawback with this method is that header information is only preserved for the first file.

Secret

Saving a batch of messages to a *txt* file is a good way to print a batch of messages at once. In fact, with the new message store structure, it's now the only way.

Posting to newsgroups

Spend any amount of time on a newsgroup, and pretty soon you'll want to participate. The collective expertise of a newsgroup can be a valuable resource for learning about that newsgroup's subject. While posting a message to a newsgroup is as simple as sending a regular e-mail message, there are some things to be aware of.

Track replies to your postings

It can be hard to find your own posts among the hundreds of messages on a newsgroup. To see only your messages and the replies to them, choose View, Current View, Show Replies to My Messages. But you can also set up a message rule to watch threads containing your messages. This way, they'll be highlighted regardless of the current view. For a more detailed discussion of message rules, see "Setting up message rules" and the other topics in Chapter 6.

Watching Your Own Posts

Step 1. Click Tools, Message Rules, News. In the Message Rules dialog box that opens, click the New button.

Step 2. In the New News Rule dialog box, set up the rule following the example in Figure 5-16. Use your own address in the Rule Description field. (Mark the two check boxes in the Conditions and Actions fields. You will see a *contains people* link in the Rule Description field. Click this link, type your address in the Select People dialog box, click the Add button, and click OK. Then click the *watched or ignored* link, mark Watch Message in the Watch or Ignore dialog box, and click OK.) Make sure to name the rule at the bottom of the New News Rule dialog box. When you're finished, click OK.

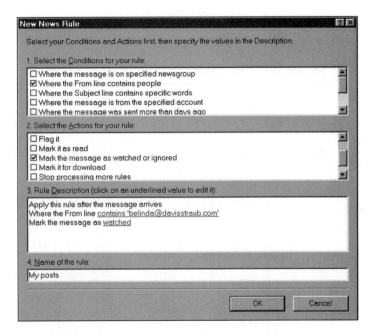

Figure 5-16: Follow this example for setting up the message rule, using your own address.

Step 3. Move this rule to the top of the list in the Message Rules dialog box, and click OK.

Now your messages and the threads they appear in will be marked as watched. The headers will appear marked with glasses and highlighted with red. If you prefer to mark only your own posts, you can set up the Action field in the rule to flag your messages instead of watching their threads. A big advantage of using the thread state (watch or ignore) or the flag is that you can easily reverse them. If you instead choose the Highlight It with Color action in the rule definition, it can be a chore to change the colors of all those headers when you decide that lime green is hard to read.

Handling cross-posted messages independently

Secret

Outlook Express has the normally very useful feature of automatically marking cross-posted messages (messages sent to more than one newsgroup) as read. That way, if someone has posted the same message to every newsgroup on your server, you only have to read his or her spam once. Still, some people find that a message they overlooked in one newsgroup is more useful in the context of another. If this applies to you, you can disable this feature with a simple Registry change.

STEPS:
Handling Cross-Posted Messages Independently

Step 1.   Open your Registry editor and navigate to HKEY_CURRENT_ USER\Identities\ {*your identity number*}\ Software\ Microsoft\ Outlook Express\ 5.0\ News.

Step 2.   In the right pane, locate MarkXPostsRead, as shown in Figure 5-17, and double-click it.

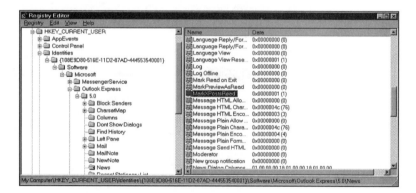

Figure 5-17: Double-click the MarkXPostsRead dword.

Step 3.   In the Edit DWORD Value dialog box that appears, change the Value Data field from 1 to 0. Click OK and close the Registry editor.

Thanks to Eric Miller for this tip.

Which group to reply to?

Cross-posting is generally frowned upon because it is so abused. Nobody wants to read messages that have no relevance to the newsgroup they are reading, and that have been sent to a hundred other off-topic groups as well. But occasionally you may feel that your message is of genuine interest to more than one newsgroup, so you choose to send it to two or three.

If you do this, you'll want to indicate in the message header a newsgroup where people should send their replies, as described in the steps below. This helps to keep conversations from spreading all over by putting all the replies in one place, so there's less duplication and it's easier for you to keep track of replies. Even if someone reads your message in a different newsgroup, the reply will automatically go to the one you indicate.

STEPS:

Setting the Followup Newsgroup

Step 1.   From one of the newsgroups to which you want to post a message, open a New Message window by clicking the New Message toolbar button or by choosing Message, New Message.

Step 2.   In the New Message window, click View, All Headers. Your message header changes to include additional lines, including a Followup-To line, as shown in Figure 5-18.

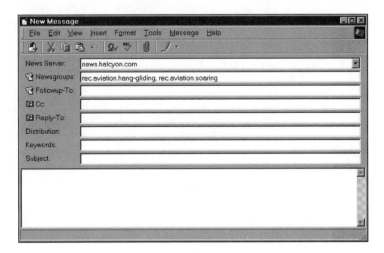

Figure 5-18: Choose View, All Headers to display additional header lines in your New Message window.

Continued

STEPS

Setting the Followup Newsgroup *(continued)*

Step 3.   Click the *Followup-To* label at the beginning of that line to open a list of the newsgroups you have subscribed to on this server (see Figure 5-19). To see all of the newsgroups available on this server, click the Show Only Subscribed Newsgroups button to disable it. Double-click the newsgroup where you want to have replies sent, and click OK. Although you can select multiple newsgroups in this dialog box, doing so pretty much defeats our purpose in this case.

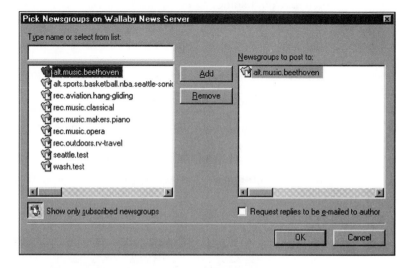

Figure 5-19: Select from the list of newsgroups in the left column to designate where followup messages should be posted.

If you also want to have replies sent to you as e-mail, mark Request Replies to Be E-Mailed to Author. This places the word *poster* in the Followup-To line. (You could also just type this word in that field instead of designating a newsgroup.) When someone replies to your message, you will automatically be sent a copy. This doesn't prevent the person from also replying to the group; it's more an indication of your preference.

Just as Outlook Express will only let you cross-post to newsgroups on the same server, it only lets you designate a followup newsgroup on the same server as the one to which you are posting.

Reply To

Another line that appears when you click View, All Headers (see step 2 in the previous section) is the Reply To field. Ordinarily, if someone replies directly to you instead of to the newsgroup, his or her message goes to your default e-mail address. But you can use the Reply To header line to direct replies to a different address if you like.

Many people use this as a way to keep their addresses from being "harvested" by companies that sell address lists to spammers. It isn't a wholly successful way to keep spammers from getting your address, though, because your regular mail address still appears in the From field in the message header. But it can be very useful if you send a message from work (or from someone else's computer) but want replies to come to your home address.

The Reply To line in a news message header is controlled by the properties for the news server associated with that newsgroup. To see this, choose Tools, Accounts, click the News tab, and double-click the name of your news server. The contents of the Reply Address field, shown in Figure 5-20, control the Reply To line for messages you compose for this server. If the field is empty, or if it is the same as your default e-mail address, the Reply To line will be empty in messages that you compose. But if you put something different here, that address will be used in your message header.

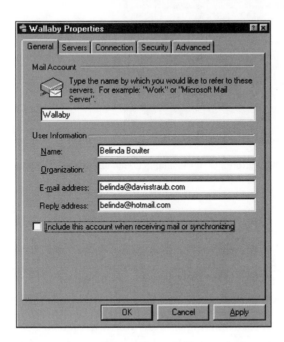

Figure 5-20: The Reply Address field controls the content of the Reply To line in message headers.

Thanks to Sky King for help with this topic.

Replying politely

Some newsgroups include a lot of pictures and sound. For example, microsoft.public.inetexplorer.ie4.outlookexpress.stationery on the msnews.microsoft.com news server is specially designated as a place for people to share their multimedia stationery. Many of these files are quite large. On the other hand, in most newsgroups, it's the information that people want, and they don't appreciate having to download a big file for only a few lines of text. Newsgroups are international, and in many places people have to pay by the minute for Internet access. Newsgroup participants who are in this situation appreciate receiving smaller messages.

It's possible to set Outlook Express so that if you are replying to a message that uses stationery, your reply will use the same stationery. In fact, this is the default setting for HTML mail messages. It's a very good idea *not* to use this setting for news, however, because a whole thread of messages using the same stationery can get big fast. If you find that your replies to newsgroup postings include the original stationery, choose Tools, Options, and click the Send tab. Click the HTML Settings button under News Sending Format, and then clear the Send Pictures with Messages check box, as shown in Figure 5-21.

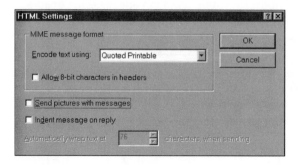

Figure 5-21: Clear the Send Pictures with Messages check box to avoid sending stationery with your news reply.

Custom headers in news messages

Click View, All Headers in a New Message window, and you'll see some additional header lines appear. But there are some header lines used in Internet newsgroups that are not normally available in Outlook Express. One of these keeps your message from being archived indefinitely on Usenet archiving servers such as DejaNews. Once a message has expired from the news server you sent it to, archiving servers are supposed to delete it if the header contains the line X-No-Archive: Yes. This helps protect your privacy somewhat by keeping someone from seeing every message you have ever posted to any newsgroup.

Secret

Although it's not particularly easy, you can insert X-No-Archive: Yes in your news message headers.

STEPS:

Adding X-No-Archive: Yes to Your News Headers

Step 1.   While in a news folder, open a New Message window. Click View, All Headers if you haven't already done so.

Step 2.   In the Keywords field, type **World** and press Enter. On the new line, type **X-No-Archive: Yes** (see Figure 5-22).

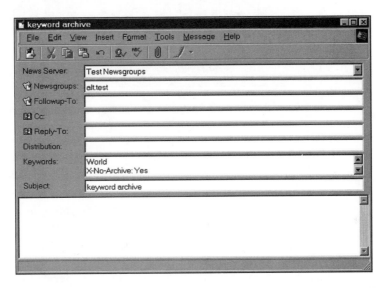

Figure 5-22: The Keywords line in your message header should look like this example.

Step 3.   Finish composing your message and post it without opening it in the Outbox. You might want to post the message on a test newsgroup before you send it to your regular group.

Step 4.   When you see your message in the newsgroup, press Ctrl+F3 to view the full header. You should see the text you added in the header, as shown in Figure 5-23.

Continued

STEPS

Adding X-No-Archive: Yes to Your News Headers *(continued)*

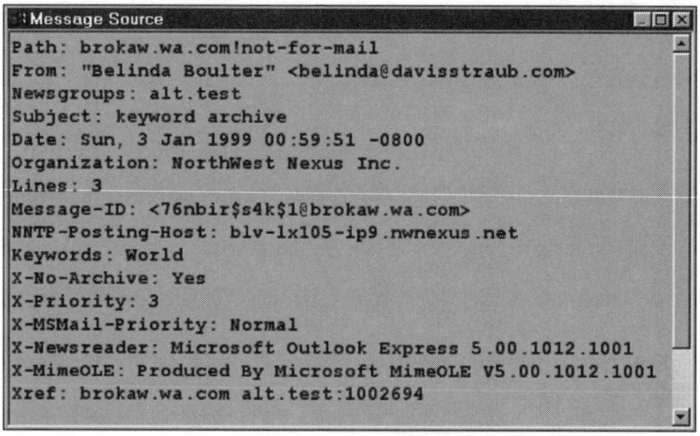

```
Message Source                                                    [_][□][X]
Path: brokaw.wa.com!not-for-mail
From: "Belinda Boulter" <belinda@davisstraub.com>
Newsgroups: alt.test
Subject: keyword archive
Date: Sun, 3 Jan 1999 00:59:51 -0800
Organization: NorthWest Nexus Inc.
Lines: 3
Message-ID: <76nbir$s4k$1@brokaw.wa.com>
NNTP-Posting-Host: blv-lx105-ip9.nwnexus.net
Keywords: World
X-No-Archive: Yes
X-Priority: 3
X-MSMail-Priority: Normal
X-Newsreader: Microsoft Outlook Express 5.00.1012.1001
X-MimeOLE: Produced By Microsoft MimeOLE V5.00.1012.1001
Xref: brokaw.wa.com alt.test:1002694
```

Figure 5-23: The full header of the message shown in Figure 5-22 after posting it to a test newsgroup.

Thanks to Eric Miller at www.okinfoweb.com/moe for pointing us in the right direction.

You might like to know about another custom header line that's used mostly by newsgroup moderators. (See "Start your own newsgroup" at the end of this chapter for resources on becoming a moderator.) This line adds a stamp of approval to your message header, indicating that as the moderator you have approved it for posting.

STEPS:

Adding an Approved Line to Your News Headers

Step 1. While in a news folder, open a New Message window. Choose View, All Headers if you haven't already done so.

Step 2. In the Keywords line, type **World** and press Enter. On the new line, type **Approved:** *username@yourisp.com*, using your own e-mail address.

Step 3. Finish composing your message and post it without opening it in the Outbox. You might want to post the message on a test newsgroup before you send it to your regular group.

Step 4. When you see your message in the newsgroup, press Ctrl+F3 to view the full header. You should see the text you added in the header.

Thanks to the pseudonymous mcwebber for this variation.

Secret

To automatically add the Approved line to the headers of all your newsgroup postings, you can make a simple change to the Registry. Open the Registry editor and navigate to HKEY_CURRENT_USER\Identities\{*your identity number*}\Software\Microsoft\Outlook Express\5.0\News. In the right pane, scroll down to the Moderator dword, double-click it, and change the Value Data field to 1.

Now when you open a New Message window from a mail folder, the message header will include the line Approved: *username@yourisp.com*. The only drawback to doing this is that it adds this line to *all* of your news posts, regardless of newsgroup or server, and it cannot be edited from the New Message window. To make use of this feature, you'll probably need to set up a separate identity for your moderator persona (see "Using identities" in Chapter 3).

Forwarding a mail message to a newsgroup

You might receive a private e-mail message that you'd like to forward to a newsgroup. (Of course, courtesy dictates that you would first get permission from the author.) Although there's no obvious way to forward a mail message to a newsgroup, it's actually very simple. Just drag the message from the Message pane and drop it onto the name of the newsgroup in the Folders pane or the Folders list. A New Message window opens, addressed to that newsgroup and with the body of the mail message in the body of the new message (no quote marks). You can add a subject, plus comments to indicate the original author before clicking Send.

Can't get news through the firewall

If Outlook Express can't access newsgroups on your local area network, the problem could be that your firewall uses the SOCKS proxy, which is not supported by Outlook Express. Luckily, you can use SocksCap to get around it. SocksCap is freeware that intercepts the networking calls from WinSock applications such as Outlook Express, and redirects them through your SOCKS server. You can download SocksCap from www.socks.nec.com/sockscap.html

Thanks to Mike Santovec for this tip.

Use test groups for testing

Sometimes you need to post a message to a newsgroup to test something about the way your news reader is set up. But newsgroup members can become quite irate about test files cluttering up the group—and who can blame them? That's why most news servers carry test newsgroups.

To find a test newsgroup, go to the Synchronization pane for your news server and click the Newsgroups button. In the Display Newsgroups Which Contain field at the top of the Newsgroup Subscriptions dialog box, type **test** to search for newsgroups with the word *test* in their names. You should see a list such as the one in Figure 5-24. Subscribe to one of these and post to your heart's content—nobody reads anything but their own posts on these newsgroups.

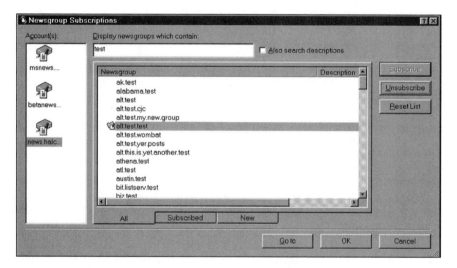

Figure 5-24: Search for a newsgroup with *test* in the name.

News maintenance

Ideally, you would the useful news messages you have downloaded to be available whenever you want them, while the non-useful messages cease to take up space on your hard disk. Although Outlook Express 5 makes it much easier to maintain your newsgroup messages than previous versions did, you still need to occasionally give some attention to housekeeping.

Catch up

If you have just subscribed to a very active newsgroup or if you've just come back from vacation, it can be quite overwhelming to deal with downloading thousands of messages. The same is true if you need to reset a newsgroup when you have already read all the messages. The Catch Up command lets you start fresh by marking everything on the news server as "read," including the messages you haven't yet downloaded.

To catch up on a newsgroup, right-click it in the Folders pane or the Folders list, and select Catch Up — or click Edit, Catch Up while the newsgroup is selected. Now if you synchronize this newsgroup, you'll see something like "0 message(s), 0 unread, 1607 not downloaded" in the status bar. The messages on the server are not downloaded because Outlook Express believes they are already read.

Secret

You might wonder about the difference between Catch Up and Mark All Read. The latter command only affects messages you've already downloaded, not those still waiting on the server.

No need to keep messages forever

After you have been reading a newsgroup for a while, its folder can get pretty big. Because no hard disk is infinitely large, and most messages have only ephemeral value at best, you'll want to limit their stay on your system. To do so, choose Tools, Options and click the Maintenance tab (see Figure 5-25).

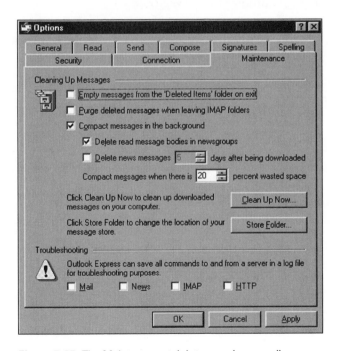

Figure 5-25: The Maintenance tab lets you clean up all your newsgroups.

If you work with very large newsgroups and are especially concerned about disk space, you might want to set Delete News Messages [ ] Days After Being Downloaded to three days or less instead of the default five days. Remember that this only deletes the message bodies from your computer — message headers are removed as part of the synchronization process, when those messages are no longer available on the newsgroup server (the length of time varies with the newsgroup). To get rid of old messages even faster, you can mark Delete Read Message Bodies in Newsgroups. If you do this, be sure to save messages you might want to see again in a separate folder.

In addition, you can reduce the setting for Compact Messages When There Is [ ] Percent Wasted Space from the default 20 percent to 10 percent. Compaction occurs automatically in the background unless you clear the Compact Messages in the Background check box. See "Background compaction" in Chapter 3 for more on how this works.

For more newsgroup maintenance options, click Clean Up Now. This takes you to the Local File Clean Up dialog box discussed in the next section.

If you haven't been on a newsgroup for a while, you may see lines through many of your headers (see Figure 5-26). These messages have been removed from the newsgroup server, but their headers are still on your computer. These headers will be removed from your computer automatically the next time you open or synchronize the newsgroup.

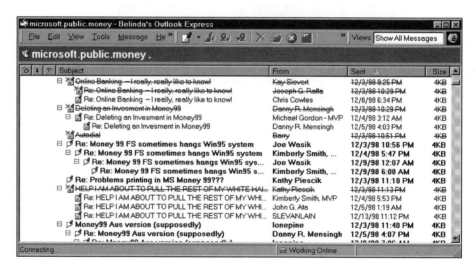

Figure 5-26: If a header has a red X and a line through it, its message is no longer on the newsgroup server.

Tidying up

Right-click a newsgroup in the Folders pane or the Folders list, click Properties, and then click the Local File tab, shown in Figure 5-27. This is the place for tidying up that particular newsgroup folder. (You can reach a similar dialog box by choosing Tools, Options, clicking the Maintenance tab, and clicking Clean Up Now. In the Local File Clean Up dialog box, you can select individual newsgroups or an entire news server for cleanup.)

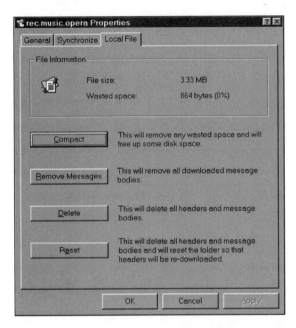

Figure 5-27: The Local File tab is part of the properties of a specific newsgroup.

If you have plenty of room on your hard disk, you may never need to use the Compact button. Outlook Express now performs compaction in the background while you are reading your mail or doing other things, so you really don't need to manually compact your newsgroups at regular intervals. See "Background compaction" in Chapter 3 for more about this.

If you find that you're short on disk space, one way to regain it is to use the Remove Messages button. Outlook Express keeps the message headers, but deletes all the message bodies you have downloaded for that newsgroup. Keep in mind that most news servers delete messages after a certain amount of time, so you may not be able to re-download the message bodies later if you decide you need them after all. For messages you really want to save, it's best to save them in a separate folder.

The Delete button removes not only the message bodies, but their headers as well. However, the index for this newsgroup will still remember what has been downloaded and what hasn't, so you will not be able to retrieve deleted messages later, even though they might still be on the newsgroup server.

Once you've removed or deleted the messages, you won't see a change in the file size until you click the Compact button. It's no longer necessary to compact everything after unsubscribing from a newsgroup — the disk space will be reclaimed immediately after you unsubscribe.

If you want to both delete the messages *and* reset the index (or to just reset the index after you've deleted messages), click the Reset button. You would most likely want to use this if you had a corrupted file that prevented you from opening this newsgroup. Reset starts everything fresh, as though you had never downloaded any messages from the newsgroup. Of course, it will also remove any record of what you have read, so when you go back to this newsgroup, you will end up downloading lots of messages that you have already seen. You can use Catch Up after resetting to mark all the messages on the server as read and keep them from being downloaded, or you can download the headers and sort through them manually.

You can't remove or delete individual messages from your newsgroup folder. If you don't want to see them, mark them as read or ignored, and set the view filter to Hide Read or Ignored Messages.

Start your own newsgroup

Mike Santovec pointed out four resources that can help you start a new newsgroup or just answer your questions about how they work:

- "So You Want to Create an Alt Newsgroup" at www.cis.ohio-state.edu/~barr/alt-creation-guide.html
- "All About Newsgroups" at www.learnthenet.com/english/html/26nwsgrp.htm
- Deja News at www.dejanews.com
- Usenet Info Center at sunsite.unc.edu/usenet-i

Summary

Newsgroups can be overwhelming, but if you manage them well, you can find the truly useful information.

- The synchronization settings can help you control the flow of messages that you download.
- You can create custom views to look at only some of your messages at one time.
- You can use a rule or a view to keep track of replies to your posts.
- Threads let you follow a newsgroup conversation over time. You can save a whole thread together to preserve its order.
- You can use a line in your message headers to specify the reply path, and add a custom line requesting that your message not be archived.
- The Maintenance tab of the Options dialog box and the Local File tab of the Properties dialog box for a newsgroup contain important features for controlling the size of your newsgroup folders.

Chapter 6

Outlook Express – Rules for Mail and News

In This Chapter

Outlook Express lets you set up rules for both incoming mail and newsgroup messages. We show you how to make them work to your advantage.

▶ Get your rules in the right order so they'll work properly.

▶ Cut down on unwanted mail messages.

▶ Set up automatic e-mail replies.

▶ Sort your Sent Items folder.

▶ Back up your rules.

Make up your own rules

The message rules feature was called Inbox Assistant prior to Internet Explorer 5. Many people also refer to rules as *filters*. They are used for sorting (or blocking, or forwarding) incoming mail based on criteria that you define. Message rules are applied automatically every time you have incoming mail, unless you disable them.

Setting up message rules

The user interface for editing mail message rules is now simpler and more explicit, and you now have a similar dialog box for creating news message rules. If you have set up Inbox Assistant rules in an earlier version of Outlook Express, they will be preserved as mail rules and displayed in the Mail Rules tab of the Message Rules dialog box (Tools, Message Rules, Mail), as shown in Figure 6-1.

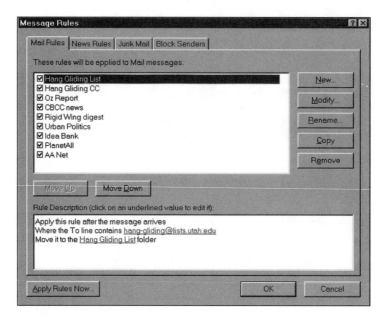

Figure 6-1: The Mail Rules tab of the Message Rules dialog box.

To define a new rule that applies to incoming mail messages, use these steps:

STEPS:

Designing a New Mail Rule

Step 1.   In Outlook Express, choose Tools, Message Rules, Mail. The Mail Rules tab of the Message Rules dialog box appears. Click the New button to open the New Mail Rule dialog box, shown in Figure 6-2.

Step 2.   In the Conditions area, select one or more conditions that will cause this rule to be applied to a message. For example, mark Where the To Line Contains People if this rule is based on the contents of the To line. Don't worry yet about what the actual content will be (you'll specify it in step 4). As you select conditions, they will appear in the Rule Description area.

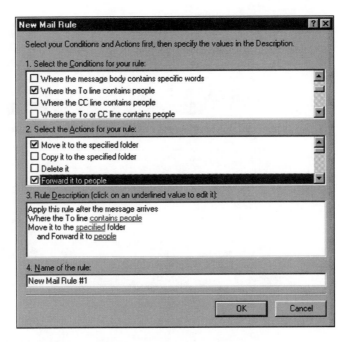

Figure 6-2: The New Mail Rule dialog box gives you a step-by-step approach to setting up or changing message rules.

Step 3. In the Actions area, mark one or more actions that will be applied to messages that meet the conditions of this rule. For example, you might want the message moved to a specific Outlook Express folder, or forwarded to a different address. You can mark more than one action here — both Move It to the Specified Folder and Forward it to People, for example.

Step 4. In the Rule Description area, you define the specifics. Click each piece of highlighted text to define what it will mean. For example, click the word *people* to enter one or more e-mail addresses in the Select People dialog box, as shown in Figure 6-3. For a folder, click the word *specified* and you'll see a Move dialog box with a folder tree. Click the phrase *contains specific words* to list one or more keywords in the Type Specific Words dialog box.

Continued

STEPS

Designing a New Mail Rule *(continued)*

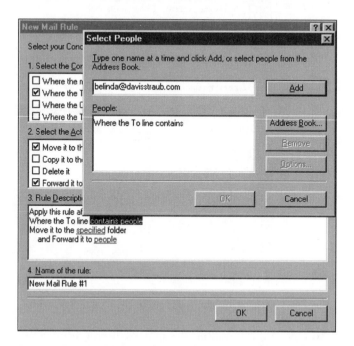

Figure 6-3: Type an address in the Select People dialog box, then click Add. Or use the Address Book button to copy names or a group from the address book.

Step 5.   The Select People dialog box and the Type Specific Words dialog box contain an Options button. Clicking this button displays the Rule Condition Options dialog box, in which you can further refine your selection (see Figure 6-4). You can change your condition in two important ways. The first pair of option buttons lets you select by *exclusion* rather than by *inclusion* — in other words, you can set the rule to act on all messages that do *not* contain the keywords or addresses you have indicated. (The default is inclusion.)

The second pair of option buttons (active if you have entered more than one address or keyword) lets you change the OR operator to AND — so that a message must contain all of the keywords or addresses you have indicated in order for the condition to be met. (The default is OR.)

Any changes you make in the Rule Condition Options dialog box will affect only that one condition. You don't need to bother with the Options button if you want to use the default settings.

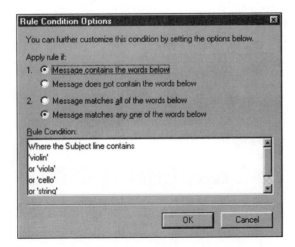

Figure 6-4: You can use the Rule Condition Options dialog box to change the way your condition will work.

Step 6.   If you selected more than one condition in step 2, a highlighted *and* will connect each condition in the Rule Description area. Click it, and the And/Or dialog box appears, giving you a choice between having messages match *all* of the criteria (AND) or *any* of the criteria (OR).

  If you don't set up a definition for each highlighted word in the Rule Description area, you will see a warning and the undefined phrases will be highlighted in red.

Step 7.   Enter a descriptive name for your rule in the Name field at the bottom of the New Mail Rule dialog box. When you are done defining your rule, click OK. Your new rule appears in the Mail Rules tab. Highlight it and use the Move Up and Move Down buttons to put it in the correct spot. (The reasons why rule order matters are explained immediately after these steps and later in this chapter.)

Step 8.   If you have messages in your Inbox and you want to apply your new rule to them, click the Apply Now button to open the Apply Mail Rules Now dialog box (see Figure 6-5). Select your new rule and click the Apply Now button, wait for the filter to work, and then click Close. Click OK.

  You can also use the Apply Mail Rules Now dialog box to apply a rule to a folder other than the Inbox. (In fact, this is the only way you can apply a rule to a folder other than the Inbox.) The settings you apply here are used on a one-time only basis, and do not become part of the rule definition. See "Sorting your sent messages" later in this chapter for another way to use this feature.

Continued

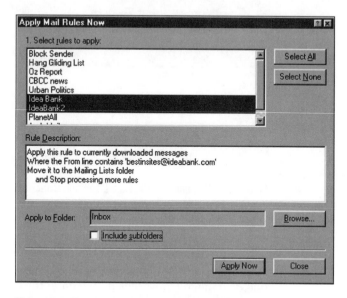

Figure 6-5: The Apply Mail Rules Now dialog box.

Outlook Express carries out message rules in the sequence they are listed in the Message Rules dialog box. Give each of your rules a meaningful name helps you keep them in the correct order. See "It's all in the order" later in this chapter for more on why this is important.

Secret

You can temporarily disable a rule without deleting it by clearing it in the Message Rules dialog box. Then mark it when you want to enable it again. This can be especially helpful in troubleshooting, when you think one rule might be affecting the rules below it. And it's essential for some rules — for example, the ones we discuss in "Sorting your sent messages" later in this chapter.

To set up rules that apply to newsgroups, click Tools, Message Rules, News. The news rules work in the same way as the mail rules, but you choose from a slightly different set of conditions and actions. You might want to set up a news rule to flag messages from a certain newsgroup member, as shown in Figure 6-6.

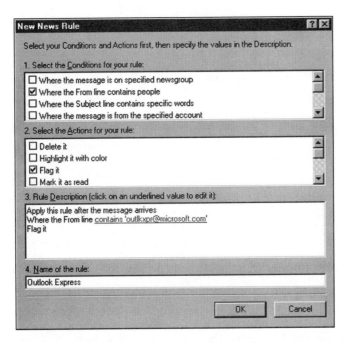

Figure 6-6: A sample news rule that will flag newsgroup messages from a specific address.

Play by the rules

If you highlight a rule in the Mail Rules (or News Rules) tab of the Message Rules dialog box, you'll see its description in the Rule Description area. To change one of the values specified in the rule, click the value in this area and change it in the dialog box that appears. To change a condition or action for a rule, double-click the rule to open the Edit Mail Rule (or Edit News Rule) dialog box.

Read through the list in the Conditions area to make sure you select the most accurate one for your rule. For example, to capture messages where an address is contained in *either* the To line *or* the CC line (a common occurrence), mark Where the To Or CC Line Contains People. That way, you don't have to make one rule for the To line and another rule for the CC line.

Notice also that you can select Where the Message Body Contains Specific Words. This could be much more powerful than depending on messages to have particular keywords in their subject lines. On the other hand, you will be more likely to catch unrelated messages.

Secret

You can enter an address book group when setting the values for a rule involving people. Click the highlighted phrase *contains people* to bring up the Select People dialog box, click the Address Book button, double-click your group name, and then click OK. The members of your group will appear in the People list — you don't have to type their addresses individually. You might use this in setting up a rule where the action is to forward certain messages to a number of people at once.

Rule values are not case sensitive. So if you set up a rule that looks for *Birds* in the subject line or the message body, it will also apply to messages where the subject contains *birds*.

Only the basic ASCII character set will work in defining values. ASCII Extended characters — such as accented letters, graphics characters, and special symbols — cause Outlook Express to skip that rule and go on to the next. (This could have dire consequences if the next rule involves deleting messages.)

Wild card characters are not allowed either, but you don't really need to use them. If you type the word or characters you want to select for, any string containing those characters will meet the conditions. So if you have several e-mail addresses, each containing the string *yourname*, just use *yourname* as the value in the rule description and the rule will apply to messages containing any of your addresses.

If you move a folder that is used by a rule, Outlook Express adjusts the rule so that your messages will still be sent to that folder. This will happen even if you move the folder to the Deleted Items folder. If you permanently delete the folder, the rule will be disabled and marked with a big red X in the Message Rules dialog box.

It's all in the order

Outlook Express carries out rules in the order in which they are displayed in the Message Rules dialog box. Changing the order can often affect the results, so plan carefully and test before you set up a rule that deletes messages you haven't seen.

Once a message has been acted upon by a rule, other rules further down the list can still apply to it. For example, one rule might move a message to a folder based on the person who sent it, while a later rule changes its color (or even deletes it) based on a keyword in the message's subject line. If you want to prevent this, select the Stop Processing More Rules action as an additional action in the last rule that you want to apply.

Actions within a rule are carried out in the order listed in the Actions area, and you can't change their order. For example, if you mark both Move It to the Specified Folder and Copy It to the Specified Folder, the message will be moved out of your Inbox before it can be copied. This makes it difficult to use message rules to distribute messages to more than one user – see "Multiple users for one account" later in this chapter for more on this.

If you define a rule that creates an "endless loop," it will be skipped. For example, if you wanted to forward a file to yourself as a test, that would create an endless loop of forwarding the file again and again every time you receive it. In that case, Outlook Express ignores your rule (and your test appears to fail). If you find your rules aren't working as you expected, this could be a cause.

When you are defining rules, it may be helpful to set up only one or two at a time. This makes it easier to detect problems with individual rules, or with their order, as your mail comes in. Don't set up an action such as Delete It or Delete It from Server until you are sure everything is working properly. Instead, have those items moved to a different subfolder so that you can see what you will be deleting, until you're sure it's really all junk.

Secret

If you are having trouble understanding why a certain rule fails or behaves differently than expected, try setting up a rule just above it with the condition For All Messages, and the action Move It to a Specified Folder (a folder you create). You may find that the real trouble is a rule further upstream. For example, you may have set up an action to copy messages when you should have moved them, with the unintended consequence that they are still there for the next rule to act on.

Create a rule from a message

The easy way to create a new rule with a condition based on the From line is by using a message as an example. This works with both mail and news messages. Simply select the message header and choose Message, Create Rule from Message. The New Mail Rule (or New News Rule) dialog box appears with the Where the From Line Contains condition set to the address of the person who sent the message. Although you may have different criteria in mind, more often than not this will at least give you a helpful head start. Then follow steps 2 through 8 in the "Setting up message rules" section earlier in this chapter to finish your rule.

Unwanted mail

Everybody gets it. Nobody wants it. Here are a few things you can do about it.

The Junk detector

The Junk Mail Detector was part of Outlook Express 5, but was removed before release because of an injunction brought against Microsoft by Blue Mountain Arts. While it is not part of the official release, we hope to see it back soon — and it may be back by the time you read this. With that hope, we've included some information about using it.

Even without the detector, Outlook Express still gives you a Junk Mail folder as one of its built-in system folders. You can use this with rules you create, as described in the next section. If you right-click this folder, you'll see the additional command Empty Junk Mail Folder in the context menu. This command will permanently delete the messages instead of sending them to the Deleted Items folder.

The purpose of the Junk Mail Detector is to keep unsolicited mail messages (spam) from getting mixed in with the messages you want to see. If this feature is available in your version of Outlook Express, you can adjust how it works by clicking Tools, Message Rules, Junk Mail to display the Junk Mail tab of the Message Rules dialog box, as shown in Figure 6-7. (If you don't have a Junk Mail tab, you don't have the Junk Mail Detector.)

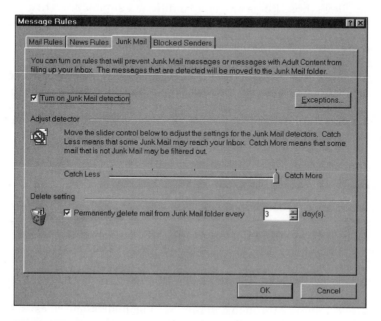

Figure 6-7: Mark the Turn on Junk Mail Detection check box on the Junk Mail tab to turn on the Junk Mail Detector.

The rules used by the Junk Mail Detector are secret, so spammers can't figure out how to get around them. You can turn the detector on and off, and set it for different filtering strengths, although there's no way to know what these settings really mean. When the Junk Mail Detector is turned on, messages that meet Outlook Express' criteria for spam are sent to your Junk Mail folder, one of the Outlook Express system folders.

Used alone, the Junk Mail Detector often sends "good" messages — e-mail newsletters, for example, or automatic responses from web sites — to the Junk Mail folder, where they could languish for days and even be deleted before you see them. But you can set exceptions to keep this from happening. Click the Exceptions button on the Junk Mail tab to open the Exceptions List dialog box, shown in Figure 6-8. At a minimum, you'll want to mark Always Treat People in My Address Book as Exceptions.

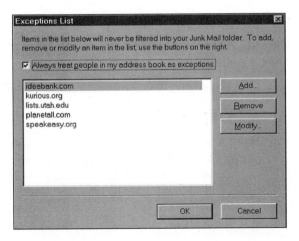

Figure 6-8: Domains and addresses you add to the exceptions list will not be treated as sources of junk mail.

The exceptions list contains domains and addresses that you do not want to have treated as the sources of junk. If you subscribe to an Internet mailing list, the messages are all forwarded from one domain even though they may come from a large number of different addresses. You can add that domain to your exceptions list to keep all those messages out of your Junk Mail folder — to see what the domain is, open a message from the mailing list and press Ctrl+F3 to display the full message header. Click the Add button, and type the domain address in the Exception field of the Add Exception dialog box.

Secret

We have found that setting the detector is an iterative process. Start with your slider bar adjusted to Catch More, and check your Junk Mail folder regularly to see what ends up there. When you find a "good" message in the Junk Mail folder, use it to make an addition to your exceptions list. If you're still getting too many "good" messages, you can turn down your slider bar. Over time, detection should get more accurate. If and when you feel confident that you're catching only junk in the Junk Mail folder, you can mark Permanently Delete Mail from Junk Mail Folder Every [　] Day(s).

You can use the Junk Mail Detector with your other mail rules. The junk mail detection occurs after all of your other rules have been carried out.

A do-it-yourself spam filter

The strategy behind the Junk Mail Detector described in the previous section is to compare incoming mail against a set of rules that describe probable spam; this includes a list of suspect domains that are often the source of spam. But even without the Junk Mail Detector, many people have a certain amount of success setting up their own rule, based on the principle that most of the unsolicited e-mail you receive has something other than your own address in the To or CC line.

Secret

To the delight of many users, the regular message rules now allow for exclusionary searching, which lets you leave the "good" mail in your Inbox where it belongs. You can set the action to send the unwanted mail to the Junk Mail folder, where it's easy to delete permanently.

To define this additional rule, choose Tools, Message Rules, and click New. In the Conditions area of the New Mail Rule dialog box, mark Where the To or CC Line Contains People. In the Actions area, mark Move it to the Specified Folder. In the Description area, click the highlighted phrase *contains people*. In the Select People dialog box, enter your own address (or addresses if you have more than one) and click Add, and then click the Options button. In the Rule Condition Options dialog box, mark the Message Does Not Contain the People Below option button, and then click OK to return to the Select people dialog box (see Figure 6-9). Click OK. Also in the Description area, click the highlighted word *specified*. In the Move dialog box, highlight the Junk Mail folder, and click OK. Give your new rule a name, and click OK.

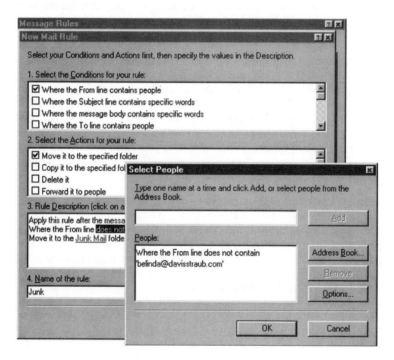

Figure 6-9: A sample rule to separate mail addressed to you from that which is not.

This rule should go below any other rules you may have set up. If you subscribe to a mailing list or newsletter that does not place your address in the To or CC field (most do not), you'll need to add a rule above this rule that specifically addresses those messages — otherwise they'll be treated as junk.

Anti-spam software

A rule such as the one described in the previous section can be a helpful step in the battle against unwanted e-mail. Still, if you get a lot of the stuff, you may want to take a more active approach to the problem.

Spam Exterminator (SpamEx), from Unisyn, not only lets you keep spam out of your mailbox, it automatically sends messages of protest to the postmaster at the spammer's domain. This can sometimes get a spammer kicked off a server.

SpamEx lets you view your message headers on the server before downloading, and it filters messages against a list of over 17,500 known spammers. You can set up your own additional rules similar to those in Outlook Express. In addition to reporting abuse to the source domain, SpamEx also automatically reports junk mailers to Unisyn for addition to their master list. SpamEx supports multiple mail accounts, and it is downloadable in a free trial version from Unisyn at www.unisyn.com/spamex/SpamEx.htm. The registered version costs $27.95.

SpamEater (Standard and Pro versions), from High Mountain Software, checks your e-mail on your POP3 server and determines if it is coming from a known spammer. You can have it just check for spam or check and eat the spam, as shown in Figure 6-10. You can also create a list of acceptable e-mail addresses. Only messages addressed to these addresses will be allowed through. SpamEater's database of 5,000 known spammers is upgradeable from the program's menu bar.

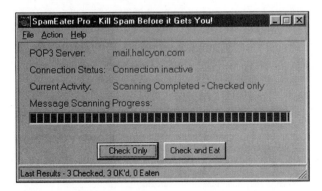

Figure 6-10: SpamEater Pro's status bar tells you how many messages it's scanned and eaten.

Because it can take a while to scan your e-mail headers on the server, you may want to have SpamEater run in the background and then call Outlook Express to get the uneaten mail. Unfortunately, SpamEater doesn't call your DUN and dial in to your Internet service provider.

This is a thoroughly professional package. The Standard version is freeware and is only missing a few of the nicer features of the Pro version. We are quite impressed with the shareware/freeware products by High Mountain Software. We also discuss their iSpeed software in "Test your download rate" in Chapter 17. You can find more details about SpamEater and download it at www.hms.com/spameater.htm.

Your Internet service provider may have installed filters that do essentially what SpamEater Pro does. Northwest Nexus here in Seattle has installed anti-spam filters, and we rarely receive any. If your service provider isn't providing this service, perhaps they should.

Blocking senders

You don't have to set up a rule just to avoid mail from a specific address. Instead, you can use the Blocked Senders tab of the Message Rules dialog box, shown in Figure 6-11. Blocked Senders works on both mail and news, so if someone from a newsgroup starts sending you abusive personal mail, you can more or less avoid seeing any of it.

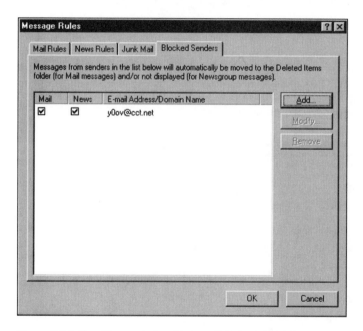

Figure 6-11: To add a sender's address, click the Add button. At least one of the check boxes must be marked for an address to remain on the list.

You still can't avoid downloading mail messages or news headers from these addresses. But the mail messages will be moved automatically to your Deleted Items folder, and news messages will be marked as read. To completely avoid seeing blocked mail messages, you should mark Empty Messages from the 'Deleted Items' Folder on Exit in the Maintenance tab of the Tools, Options dialog box. To avoid seeing headers for blocked news messages, set your current view to Hide Read Or Ignored Messages. If you're having a real problem with mail, you might prefer to use a mail rule with the action Delete It from Server to delete messages from that address. You can't delete a message from a news server, however — you can only tell Outlook Express to ignore it.

Mail filtering strategies

Once you get started setting up rules, you may start wondering about some strategies for making them work for you. Here are some to get you going.

Big messages

In addition to filtering messages based on their To, From, or Subject lines, you can also restrict them by size. That way you won't get stuck spending fifteen minutes downloading some misguided person's 750K JPEG file — just mark the condition Where the Message Size Is More Than Size and the action Do Not Download It from the Server. Of course, you might miss some cute pictures of your sister's new baby that way — and there's no way in Outlook Express to download just the message headers so you can see who sent the messages.

If you frequently receive large files and really want to know what they are before downloading them, you might want to try something like Magic Mail Monitor. This small, fast freeware program sits in your system tray, checks for incoming mail, and lets you view message headers and even delete messages without downloading their bodies. It has lots of other convenient features too. Check out the Magic web site for more details and to download the software: www.geocities.com/SiliconValley/Vista/2576/magic.html. A similar (though much larger) freeware product is POP3 Scan Mailbox, available from www.netcomuk.co.uk/ ~kempston/smb.

Mailing lists

Secret

Subscribing to a mailing list can be a great way to keep up with the news on a particular topic. But popular mailing lists can generate dozens of messages a day (or more!), making it hard to find the more urgent messages in your Inbox. You can't always tell from the message header that a message is from a mailing list. While some lists are available in digest format, this isn't true for all — and digests can be hard to browse. As an alternative, you can easily set up a message rule using Message, Create Rule from Message that will put messages from the mailing list's server into a separate Outlook Express folder. Make sure that you set your criteria to use the line where the server's address appears – it may be the To line, as shown in Figure 6-12, but this is not always the case.

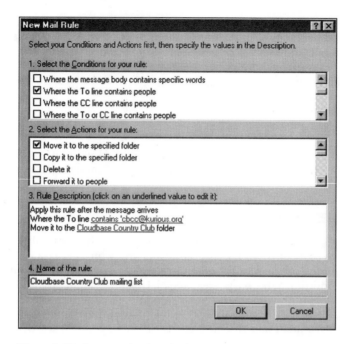

Figure 6-12: An example of a rule that sends messages from a mailing list to their own folder.

Setting up automatic reply rules

You can set up a rule to automatically reply to messages that meet certain criteria. For example, if people send you messages with a certain subject or send messages to a certain address, you can send them an automatic pre-written message or file in response. This is a great way to distribute a Frequently Asked Questions document, a current price list, or your résumé.

STEPS:

Setting Up an Automatic Reply Rule

Step 1. In Outlook Express, choose Tools, Message Rules, Mail. The Mail Rules tab of the Message Rules dialog box appears. Click the New button to open the New Mail Rule dialog box.

Step 2. In the Conditions area, mark Where the Subject Line Contains Specific Words.

Step 3. In the Actions area, mark both Reply with Message, and Move It to the Specified Folder (or mark Delete It if you don't want to keep the incoming messages).

Step 4. In the Rule Description area, click the underlined text *contains specific words*. In the Type Specific Words dialog box that appears, type the text that people should put in the subject line of their messages in order to receive your reply, as shown in Figure 6-13. It doesn't matter if you use capital letters or not. Click Add, and then click OK.

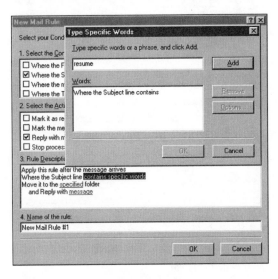

Figure 6-13: In the Rule Description area of the New Mail Rule dialog box, click the underlined words to define them.

Step 5. In the same area, click the underlined word *specified*. (If you did not mark the action Move It to the Specified Folder in step 3, this text won't appear. Go on to step 6). In the Move dialog box that appears, select the mail folder that will be the parent of your new folder, and click New Folder. In the New Folder dialog box, type a name for the mail folder — for example, Resume Requests. Click OK, and then click OK again to close the Move dialog box.

Step 6. Also in the Rule Description area, click the underlined word *message*. The Open dialog box appears to let you browse to the file that you want people to receive as your reply. Double-click to select the file you want to use, as shown in Figure 6-14. You can send news (*nws*), mail (*eml*), HTML (*htm*), or ASCII text (*txt*) files. If you want the file to appear in the body of the reply, choose *txt* or *htm*. If you want it to appear as an attachment, choose *nws* or *eml*. Select your file, and click Open.

Continued

STEPS

Setting Up an Automatic Reply Rule *(continued)*

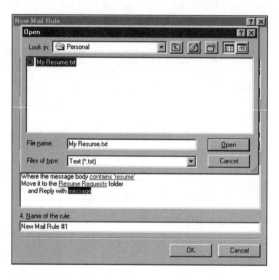

Figure 6-14: You can browse to select the file you want to use as your automatic response.

Step 7. Type a name for your rule in the Name field. When you are finished defining your rule, click OK.

If you have forgotten to define any values in steps 4, 5, and 6, the New Mail Rule dialog box stays open and Outlook Express displays a message box telling you that some information is missing or incorrect and asking you to correct the highlighted items. Click OK. A similar message appears at the top of the Rule Description area, and the problem is highlighted in red. When you've entered the information, click OK again, and you'll be back at the Message Rules dialog box.

Step 8. Your new rule appears in the Mail Rules tab. Highlight it and use the Move Up and Move Down buttons to put it in the correct spot in the list. You will probably want to put your auto-reply rules at or near the top of the list, where the other rules can't affect them.

Step 9. If you have messages in your Inbox and you want to apply your new rule to them, click the Apply Now button. In the Apply Mail Rules Now dialog box, select your new rule and click the Apply Now button, and then click Close. Click OK.

Now when a message comes in with the word you have specified in its Subject line, a reply message will be created automatically and sent to your Outbox, where it will wait for the Send and Receive command to be issued.

If you have set Outlook Express to save copies of your sent messages, your automatic replies will also be saved. There is no automatic way to filter *outgoing* mail, so your auto-replies will be mixed in with your other replies in the Sent Items folder (see the next section for a non-automatic solution). If you don't want to save *any* replies, automatic or otherwise, choose Tools, Options, click the Send tab, and clear Save Copy of Sent Messages in the 'Sent Items' Folder. Any other options you have set in the Send tab, such as the mail sending format or including the original message with a reply, will also apply to your automatic responses.

You may find that after people receive your automatic response, they reply to it without changing the subject line in their message. For example, you might get messages with the subject Re: Resume from people who received your resume. You don't want these messages (job offers?) to get caught by your auto reply rule, because the senders already received your resume once. But Outlook Express doesn't offer an obvious way to limit a condition to an exact match. You must set up a separate rule that goes before your auto reply rule to move these replies to a different folder. You might try setting the condition with a colon before the phrase (for example, : Resume) because replies in any language will use a colon. Thanks to Tom Koch for pointing out this solution.

Secret

Another way to use the automatic reply is to send a kind of "receipt" to people who send you mail. Outlook Express doesn't have the capability to request confirmation that a message has been received — and such a confirmation wouldn't really guarantee that anyone had read it, only downloaded it. However, if you correspond with someone who needs to know you've received a message, even though you're too busy to answer at the moment, you can use the automatic reply to send that person — or everyone — a notice that you've downloaded their messages. If you're one of those people who must cope with hundreds of incoming messages each day, this gives you a way to respond politely and still get your regular work done.

Secret

You might also think of using an automatic reply to let people know when you're on vacation. Remember, though, that you must be able to download your e-mail for this to work. This requires that you leave your computer running, and that you set up a schedule for automatically sending and receiving mail. If your circumstances allow this, it might be worth a try. See "Scheduling the mail" in Chapter 3 for details on the scheduling aspect. And remember to disable this rule by clearing it in the Message Rules dialog box when you get back.

Sorting your sent messages

Secret

Outlook Express' message rules feature is designed to only apply to incoming messages, not the ones you send. It would be nice, though, to be able to sort certain messages from your Sent Items folder into their own separate folder, so you could easily see everything you've sent on a particular subject or to a particular person. While you can't do this automatically, you can use message rules to sort messages in your Sent Items folder after the fact. Tom Koch showed us how.

STEPS:

Sorting Your Sent Items

Step 1: Choose Tools, Message Rules, Mail. Click the New button to display the New Mail Rule dialog box.

Step 2: In the Conditions area, set the condition for the messages you want to sort into their own folder. For example, this might be Where the To Line Contains People. In addition, be sure to set the condition Where the From Line Contains People.

Step 3: In the Actions area, set the action Move It to the Specified Folder.

Step 4: In the Rule Description area, enter your own address for the From line and one or more addresses for the To line. Click the highlighted *and*, mark Messages Match All of the Criteria in the And/Or dialog box, and click OK. Click the highlighted word *specified* to define a folder where these messages will be sent (you can create a new folder if you like), and click OK. Name your rule, and click OK. Set up additional rules that will apply to other folders, if you like.

Step 5: In the Mail Rules tab, click the Apply Now button. In the Apply Mail Rules Now dialog box, click the Select None button, and then select only your new rules (Shift-click to select sequential rules, Ctrl-click to select non-sequential ones). Click the Browse button next to the Apply to Folder field and select your Sent Items folder. Click OK. Now click the Apply Now button, wait while your messages are sorted, and then click Close.

Step 6: Clear the check box for this rule in the Mail Rules tab, and click OK to close the Message Rules dialog box.

Secret

You can only target a folder other than your Inbox if you use Apply Now, so be sure to leave your rule cleared during normal use. Then when you want to sort your Sent Items, open the Mail Rules tab of the Message Rules dialog box, mark your sorting rule, and repeat steps 5 and 6.

Multiple users for one account

Another way you can use the mail rules is to separate messages for two different users of one e-mail account – a husband and wife, for example. You do this by setting up two mail accounts in Outlook Express, with the same server settings, account name, and password, but with different "friendly" names. Then you can set the rules to look for messages that contain the "friendly" names in the To line, and send them to different local folders. Of course, this only works if your correspondents use the Reply button, or if you have alerted them to put the same friendly names you use in their address books.

The new identities feature is designed to address multiple users, and is a cleaner solution overall. Still, if you'd rather try this technique, Eric Miller describes the steps in detail in his article "Multiple Users of the Same Email Addresses" at www.okinfoweb.com/moe/mail/mail_036.htm.

Using news rules

Newsgroup rules are helpful for gleaning the messages you find relevant from the large mass of messages contained in a large newsgroup. These rules are different from the news viewing filters that we discuss in "Setting the view" in Chapter 5, though they work in similar ways and overlap somewhat in functionality. Here are some examples of ways you might use news rules.

You can define a rule so that messages on a specified newsgroup and posted more than a certain number of days ago are marked as read. Then you can set that newsgroup's synchronization to download All Messages and still only get the newest ones. This could be a very good alternative to getting a batch of 50 or 100 at a time. Instead, you get all of the messages that are one or two days old, and only those messages.

You subscribe to rec.music.opera and are primarily interested in baroque opera. You can set up conditions with keywords in the subject line for your favorite composers, performers, or names of operas (one rule for each). Set the action to highlight these messages with a different color for each composer.

You have posted a question on microsoft.public.money, and you don't want to miss any of the responses. Set a condition with specific words in the subject line (the subject line of your message), and set the action to move all those messages (the thread on your subject) to a separate folder for saving.

There are one or two regular contributors to your favorite newsgroup whose postings you especially enjoy. Set up a rule for each one, to flag his or her postings. Then after you download, you can sort the view by flag to read their postings first.

Secret

If your favorite newsgroup occasionally contains messages on a subject that you never want to see, you can mark messages with that word in the subject line as read. In this way, you avoid downloading the message headers as well as the bodies.

Backing up your rules

Secret

To back up the rules you have created, open the Registry editor and navigate to HKEY_CURRENT_USER\ Identities\ {*your identity number*}\ Software\ Microsoft\ Outlook Express\ 5.0\ Rules\. This branch contains sub-branches for Mail, News, and Junk Mail, so you can select the Rules branch itself to export them all or select only one of these folders. Now click Registry, Export Registry File, navigate to where you would like to save your backup, give it a name (the extension should be *reg*), and click Save. (You can see the name associated with an identity in the Registry by highlighting the number in the left pane and looking under Username in the right pane.)

You can move the *reg* file to a diskette or another computer if you like. If you should need to restore your rules, close Outlook Express, and then double-click the registry backup file. Now start Outlook Express again; your rules should be restored.

If you use this process to move rules to a different computer that already has rules set up, the two sets of rules will be merged. After you merge two sets of rules, you'll need to adjust the rule order to make sure they still work.

Summary

The Outlook Express rules act as filters to control what you see and download to your computer from your mail and news servers, and what happens to those messages.

- ▶ It's easy to set up one or more rules using the Message Rules dialog box, or to create a rule from a mail or news message.
- ▶ You can develop a rule or take advantage of shareware to help minimize unwanted mail messages.
- ▶ You can set up a rule to send an automatic mail reply to messages that request it.
- ▶ You can use a rule to sort the contents of your Sent Items folder, but it's not automatic.
- ▶ News rules operate similarly to mail rules and can be helpful for wading through large newsgroups.
- ▶ You can back up your rules by exporting a branch from your Registry.

Chapter 7

Outlook Express — Secure E-mail

In This Chapter

Outlook Express supports certificates and encryption, important tools that can help assure privacy in e-mail. We show you how to send and receive digitally signed and encrypted messages.

▶ Tell Outlook Express to automatically verify that a digital signature is still valid.

▶ Set the level of trust for a certificate or for the organization that issued it.

▶ Archive your certificate or move it to a new computer.

▶ Enable Outlook Express to read the encrypted messages you send.

Using digital certificates

It's almost a cliché that "on the Internet no one knows you're a dog." The truth is, sometimes we need to prove we are who we say we are — and that's where digital certificates come in.

Certificates — what's the point?

Certificates, also called *digital IDs* and *digital signatures*, serve two different but related functions in Outlook Express. First, a certificate gives your correspondents some level of assurance that a message you send is actually from you. Second — and much more importantly — a certificate contains the information required for sending and receiving encrypted messages. This information includes a *public key*, a *private key*, and a *digital signature*. (Public and private keys are discussed further in "Public key encryption" later in this chapter.)

You can always receive messages that are digitally signed. But you can't receive encrypted messages from someone unless that person has a copy of your certificate. Likewise, in order to send an encrypted message, you must first have a copy of your correspondent's certificate.

Certificates are issued by third party certification authorities such as VeriSign or BelSign, and are also sometimes issued by individuals or companies for internal use. Each certificate is associated with a specific e-mail address. Outlook Express lets you look at the certificate's source information, so you can decide how trustworthy you think it is.

Receiving digitally signed mail

A digitally signed message is indicated by a red ribbon icon in the Message pane. Highlight the message header and you will see a button with the red ribbon icon in its preview pane header, as shown in Figure 7-1. And after you have opened the message, a red ribbon appears on the message header. Encrypted messages also show a padlock icon in these locations.

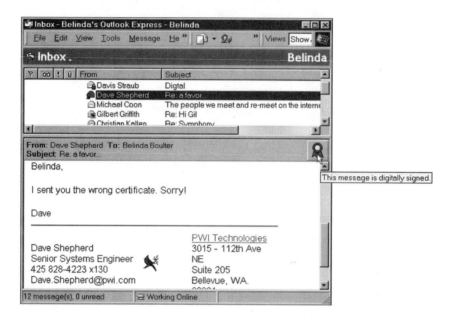

Figure 7-1: The red ribbon icon indicates that this message has been digitally signed.

The first time you receive a message with a digital signature, you will see a special help screen in the Preview pane. If VeriSign or another organization recognized by Microsoft issued the sender's certificate, the screen will simply indicate that the message was digitally signed, as shown in Figure 7-2. If you like, Mark Don't Show Me This Help Screen Again before clicking Continue. As soon as you click Continue, the message itself appears in the Preview pane.

If the issuer was a source unknown to Microsoft, or if the certificate has expired or has another problem, you will see a help screen such as the one shown in Figure 7-3. You can still open and read the message by clicking the Open Message button in the help screen. And you can still reply to it once it is open. But you should not reply with sensitive or confidential information until you have resolved the security issues. If you try to send an encrypted reply, you will see an error message such as the one shown in Figure 7-4.

Figure 7-2: This screen indicates the message has been digitally signed with a certificate you haven't seen before.

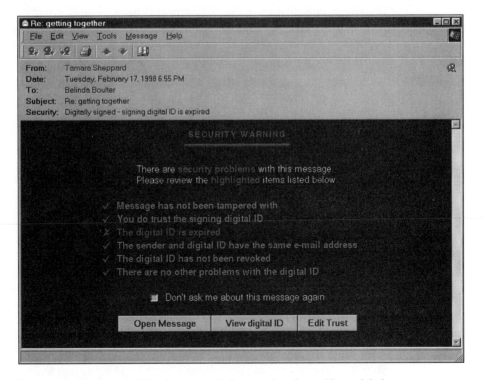

Figure 7-3: The Security Warning screen indicates what the problem might be.

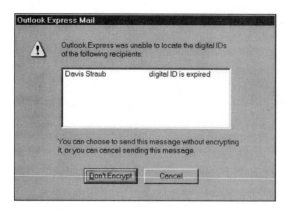

Figure 7-4: If you try to send an encrypted reply to an expired certificate, you'll see this warning.

Setting the level of trust

One reason you might see the Security Warning screen is if you haven't set the level of trust. You can tell Outlook Express how much trust you have in a particular certificate. Ordinarily, though, it makes more sense to set the level of trust for the agency or company that issued the certificate, and apply that to the individual certificate.

STEPS:

Setting the Level of Trust for a Digital Certificate

Step 1.   If you are looking at a Security Warning screen, click the Edit Trust button in that screen. Otherwise, highlight a message signed with this certificate in your Outlook Express Inbox. In the message's preview pane header, click red ribbon icon and choose Edit Trust. This opens the Trust tab of the Signing Digital ID Properties dialog box, shown in Figure 7-5.

You can also edit a certificate's trust level by editing the properties of its owner in your address book. Right-click the sender's name, select Properties in the context menu, click the Digital IDs tab, highlight an ID and click the Properties button, and then click the Trust tab in the Certificate dialog box. This Trust tab functions the same as the one in the Signing Digital ID Properties dialog box.

Step 2.   In most cases you will base your trust for the individual certificate on the organization that issued it (if you don't want to do this, skip to step 5). For example, looking at Figure 7-5, if I believe that a certificate issued by PWI Certificate Authority is valid, then anyone who sends me one of their certificates should be trusted to be who they say they are. To see where the certificate came from, go to the Certification Path tab, shown in Figure 7-6.

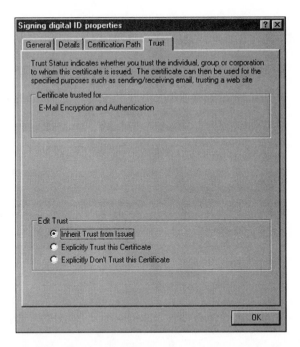

Figure 7-5: The Trust tab of the properties for a sample certificate.

Figure 7-6: The Certification Path tab shows the hierarchy of trust for a specific certificate.

Continued

STEPS

Setting the Level of Trust for a Digital Certificate *(continued)*

Step 3.   If the issuer of the certificate was not VeriSign or another group automatically trusted by Microsoft, you may need to set a level of trust for the issuer before you can pass that trust along to the individual certificate. To do this, highlight the issuer's name in the Certification Path tab and click View Certificate. A new Certificate dialog box opens for the issuing authority. Check the General and Details tabs for information about the issuer, and then click the Trust tab. Highlight the issuer's name in the hierarchical list, either mark Explicitly Trust This Certificate or Explicitly Don't Trust This Certificate (see Figure 7-7), and click OK.

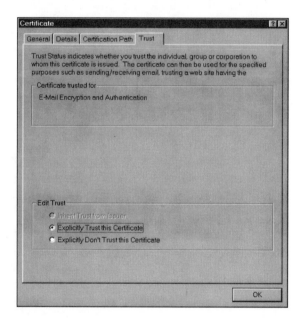

Figure 7-7: The Trust tab for the issuing authority is similar to the one for a certificate, only the first option button is dimmed. (If the issuer is automatically trusted by Microsoft, all of the buttons will be dimmed.)

Step 4.   Now go back to the Trust tab for the individual certificate, mark the Inherit Trust from Issuer option button, and click OK twice.

Step 5.   If this certificate has no issuer to inherit from, or if for some reason you want to treat this certificate differently from others issued by that organization, you can set its level of trust individually. In that case, skip steps 2 through 4 and mark either Explicitly Trust this

Certificate or Explicitly Don't Trust this Certificate on the Trust tab. Your choice will depend on what you know about the certificate and its source — you can use the information on the certificate's General and Details tabs to help decide. After you've marked the Trust tab, click OK, and then click OK again and close the address book if you opened it.

If you mark Explicitly Don't Trust this Certificate, you will not be able to send encrypted e-mail to the certificate's owner, or to the owners of any certificates whose trust is inherited from this one.

Secret

To see and edit a list of issuers that are trusted by default, choose Tools, Options, and click the Security tab. Click the Digital IDs button to launch the Certificate Manager, and click the Trusted Root Certification Authorities tab (see Figure 7-8). Highlight an authority and click the View button see information about its certificate. You can remove an authority from this list by highlighting it and clicking Remove (but if you do this, certificates issued by this body will not be trusted).

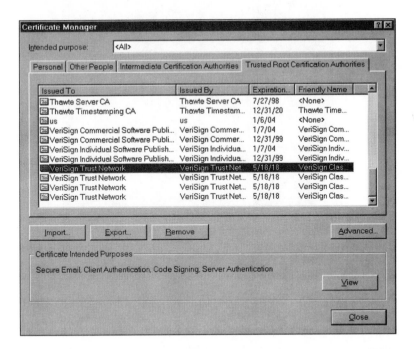

Figure 7-8: The Trusted Root Certification Authorities tab shows the certification authorities that are automatically trusted by Outlook Express.

Saving a certificate

Outlook Express lets you save a digital ID in your address book along with its owner's address. This is necessary if you want to send encrypted e-mail to the certificate's owner.

STEPS:

Saving a Digital ID in Your Address Book

Step 1. Highlight the digitally signed message in your Inbox. In the message's preview pane header, click the red ribbon icon and choose View Security Properties. Or highlight the message, choose File, Properties, and click the Security tab (see Figure 7-9). This tab shows you the security status of this specific message — you will only see it if the message is digitally signed.

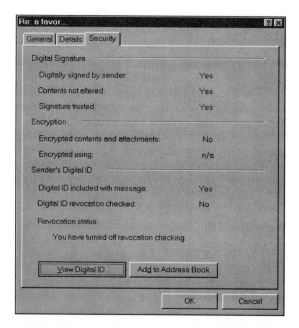

Figure 7-9: The Security tab is part of a digitally signed message's properties dialog box.

Step 2. If you want more detailed information about this certificate, click the View Digital ID button to open the Signing Digital ID Properties dialog box, and click the Details tab (see Figure 7-10). Here you can see what organization issued the certificate, along with the certificate's serial number, expiration date, and public key. Click OK when you're finished viewing the information.

Figure 7-10: The Details tab of the Signing Digital ID Properties dialog box.

Step 3. In the Security tab of the Properties dialog box for the message (refer back to Figure 7-9), click the Add to Address Book button, and then click OK twice.

The next time you receive a message with this person's certificate attached, Outlook Express will recognize it as valid. In addition, you have stored the digital signature and public key you need to send an encrypted message to the certificate's owner.

Address book entries for people with certificates appear with a red ribbon icon in the address book and in the Contacts pane. You can view and edit the digital ID for anyone in your address book by right-clicking his or her name in the Address Book window or your Contacts pane, choosing Properties, and going to the Digital IDs tab (see Figure 7-11). Select the ID and click the Properties button to open the Certificate dialog box.

Secret

To see and manage a list of all the digital IDs stored in your address book, open the Certificate Manager by clicking Tools, Options, clicking the Security tab, and clicking the Digital IDs button. Click the Other People tab to see a list of certificates such as the one in Figure 7-12. As you can see, this is a handy place to import, export, and remove certificates (see "Exporting and importing certificates" later in this chapter for more on what this means). Use the View button to check the certification path and details for a digital ID.

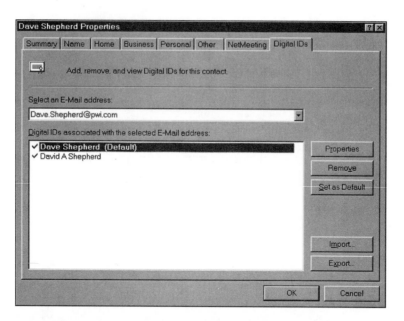

Figure 7-11: To view or edit information about a certificate, select it and click the Properties button. The person in this example has certificates from two different issuers.

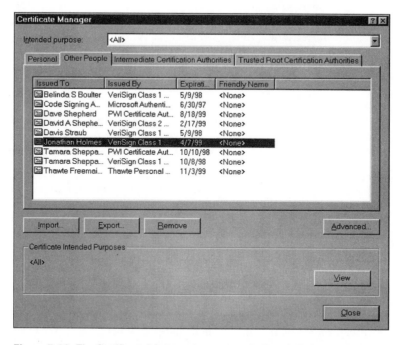

Figure 7-12: The Certificate Manager lets you see a list of all the certificates you have stored, including their expiration dates.

It's possible that someone might send you e-mail without digitally signing it, but with a certificate sent as an attached file. The certificate looks like an ordinary file with the extension *p7c* or *cer*. To verify the trust level and add the certificate to your Windows address book, click the file attachment to open it, and then follow the Saving a Digital ID in Your Address Book steps earlier in this section.

Revocation checking

Certificates contain an expiration date, so Outlook Express knows when a certificate has expired. Still, a person's certificate may be revoked before the expiration date if he or she switches jobs or changes e-mail addresses. How can you verify that a certificate is still good before you send that person a sensitive or encrypted message? Outlook Express can do this for you if you tell it to.

To enable revocation checking, choose Tools, Options, click the Security tab, and click Advanced. In the Advanced Security Settings dialog box, mark the Only When Online option button (see Figure 7-13), and then click OK twice.

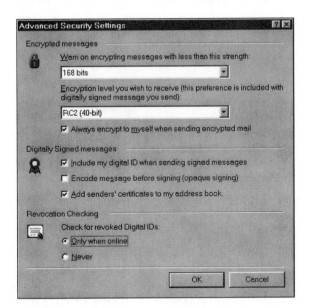

Figure 7-13: Mark the Only When Online option button to enable revocation checking.

Now if you open a digitally signed message while you are online, Outlook Express will automatically send a message to the issuer of the certificate to verify that the certificate is still valid. If you are not online, you can read the message, but its certificate will not be verified.

Getting your certificate

To send messages with your own digital signature, you must first register with a certification authority and receive a certificate from them. (The certification authority will most likely charge a fee for this service.) Your digital signature lets other people send encrypted messages to you by sharing your public key—it does not contain any sensitive or private information about you, so you can feel fine about sharing it.

The easiest way to find a certification authority is to choose Tools, Options in the Outlook Express window, click the Security tab, and click the Get Digital ID button. (You can also get to this button by clicking Tools, Accounts, highlighting a specific account, clicking the Properties button, and clicking the Security tab.) The Get Digital ID button launches Internet Explorer and takes you to a Microsoft web site with links to the web sites of some certification authorities. There you will find detailed information on security levels, pricing, and steps for buying and downloading your certificate. You may also find useful technical information about data encryption and Internet security. Some additional certifying authorities include:

Belsign	www.belsign.be	(based in Belgium)
Compusource	www.compusource.co.za/id	(based in South Africa)
UniCert	www.baltimore.ie/cert	(based in Ireland)
BT Trustwise	www.trustwise.com	(based in Great Britain)

Because the process of registering your certificate will vary with the certification authority, we can only provide general information here. At a minimum, you will be asked for your name and e-mail address. These will be permanently associated with this certificate, so make sure they are correct. You will only be able to use this certificate with this e-mail address; if you get a new address or change your name, you will probably have to apply for a new certificate. Depending on the level of security you require for your certificate, you will be asked for more information about yourself, and you may even need to submit to a credit check.

When you are asked to select a cryptography provider, be sure to choose the MS Base Cryptographic Provider v1.0—otherwise, Outlook Express won't be able to find your private key.

After you register, the certification authority will send you e-mail (confirming that the address you gave is correct) with directions for completing the certificate download. During this process a private key, which is required for you to be able to read the encrypted messages you receive, will be generated on your computer.

Your private key will be stored in the Registry in encrypted form. Windows 98 sets a default security level for access to your private key, as shown in Figure 7-14. To change the security level, click the Set Security Level button, mark the High, Medium, or Low option button (see Figure 7-15), and click Next to continue through the wizard. These security levels have nothing to do with the level of encryption; they are for controlling access to your digital certificate in case someone else might use your computer. If you choose High, you will have to enter a password in order to encrypt a message.

Figure 7-14: To choose a security level other than the default indicated, click the Set Security Level button.

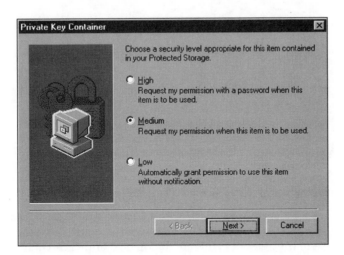

Figure 7-15: Select a level of security for use of your digital ID.

Using your certificate

Secret

Once you have registered and installed your digital ID, if you have more than one e-mail account set up in Outlook Express you must associate your certificate with the appropriate account, as described in these steps. (If you have only one account, there's no need to do this.)

STEPS:

Associating Your Digital Certificate with Your E-mail Account

Step 1: In the Outlook Express window, click Tools, Accounts. Highlight the account that you want to associate with this certificate (the one for the address you gave to the certification authority), and click the Properties button.

Step 2: Click the Security tab, and mark the Use a Digital ID When Sending Secure Messages From check box, as shown in Figure 7-16.

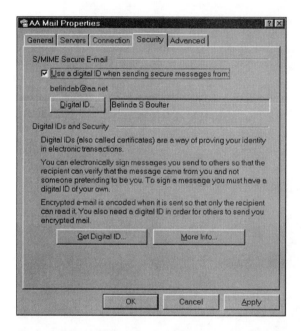

Figure 7-16: Mark the Use a Digital ID When Sending Secure Messages From check box to associate your certificate with a mail account.

Step 3: Click the Digital ID button, highlight the certificate you want to use in the Select Certificate dialog box, and click OK.

Step 4: Now click the General tab and remove any entries in the Reply Address field (this field must be blank for encryption to work). Click OK, and then click Close.

Secret

It's a good idea to add your certificate to your own address book. You can do this by sending yourself digitally signed e-mail, and then following the Saving a Digital ID in Your Address Book steps in the "Saving a certificate" section earlier in this chapter. Now when you send an encrypted message to someone else, you will be able to read your copy of it.

To attach your digital ID to an outgoing e-mail message, follow these steps:

STEPS:

Sending a Digitally Signed Message

Step 1. In Outlook Express, click Tools, Options, click the Security tab, and then click the Advanced button.

Step 2. In the Advanced Security Settings dialog box, mark Include My Digital ID When Sending Signed Messages. This will include the public key portion of your digital ID with your digital signature, so that others can reply with encrypted mail if they wish. See "Sending and receiving encrypted mail" later in this chapter for more on keys and encryption.

Step 3. Open a New Message window and choose Tools, Digitally Sign (or click the Digitally Sign Message toolbar button). Compose and send your message as usual.

If you want to attach your digital ID to *all* of your outgoing messages, choose Tools, Options, click the Security tab, mark the Digitally Sign All Outgoing Messages check box, and then click OK.

It's possible to send your certificate as a file attachment, without using it to sign the message. To do this, you would export your certificate without including your personal key (see "Exporting and importing certificates" later in this chapter for more on exporting). The certificate is saved as a *p7c* or *cer* file, depending on the format you choose during export. However, this method seems like a lot of trouble, with no real advantage over simply digitally signing a message.

Get rid of old certificates

Prior to Windows 98, Outlook Express did not give you a way to remove old certificates from your system without editing your Registry. Now it's easy, as described in these steps:

STEPS:

Removing a Digital Certificate from Your Address Book

Step 1. Open your Address Book window and right-click the name of the owner of the certificate that you want to delete. Click Properties, and go to the Digital IDs tab.

Step 2. Click the Remove button, and click OK.

Step 3. Notice that the address book listing no longer has the red ribbon icon associated with it. Close the Address Book window.

Exporting and importing certificates

Until recently, a certificate could only be used on one specific computer. Although Outlook Express now makes it easy to export your certificate to another computer — the one you use at work, for example — when you download your certificate, you should use the computer that you want to primarily associate with it. Because the whole point of using a certificate is to verify your identity for security purposes, and because it contains your private key for reading encrypted messages, you should be cautious about putting your certificate on other computers.

It is a good idea to keep a backup copy of your digital ID in case you ever have to reinstall Windows or Outlook Express, or in case your hard disk becomes damaged. It will save you the trouble and expense of re-applying for a new ID. For security reasons, your digital ID is not accessible as a file, or directly through your Registry, so you must export it in order to back it up. While you might have occasion to export other people's certificates — to pass one along to a friend, for example — it's not necessary to back them up because they are stored as part of your address book. (See "Save all your files" in Chapter 3 for how to make your address book easier to back up.)

If you change your e-mail software after you have installed a certificate, you must either get a new ID or export it from the old application and import it into the new one. For example, if you originally installed your ID using Netscape, you must export the ID from Netscape and import it into Outlook Express in order to use it there. (If you simply upgrade Outlook Express, your certificate is automatically preserved.) This ability to import and export is a relatively recent feature of both Netscape and Outlook Express, so you may need to download and install the most current version of Netscape before you can export the ID. Other e-mail applications may not give you the ability to export; in that case you must apply for a new certificate.

STEPS:

Exporting a Copy of Your Digital ID to a Floppy Disk

Step 1. In Outlook Express, choose Tools, Options, and click the Security tab. Click the Digital IDs button to launch the Certificate Manager, shown in Figure 7-17.

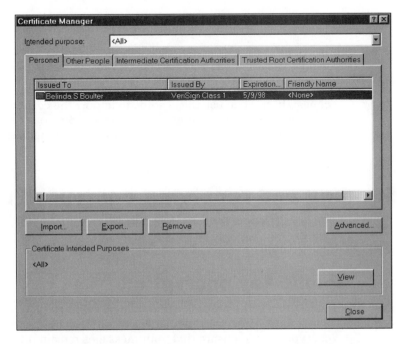

Figure 7-17: The Certificate Manager allows you to manage certificates belonging to you and others.

Step 2. Insert a disk into your floppy disk drive. Then highlight the certificate that you want to export, and click the Export button. Your own certificates are listed on the Personal tab, while other people's certificates are on the Other People tab.

Step 3. The Certificate Manager Export Wizard opens to walk you through the export process. Be sure to mark the Yes, Export the Private Key option when you are asked, unless you are exporting this certificate to send to someone else. This will include assigning a password that you use only for importing and exporting this certificate. The wizard will export your certificate with the *pfx* extension to your floppy disk (or to another location of your choosing). After you have completed the wizard, click Finish to save your new *pfx* file.

Continued

Step 4.   Click OK to confirm the security level, and then click OK again to acknowledge that the export process is complete. Close the Certificate Manager dialog box.

To import a *pfx* certificate, click it in the Explorer. The Certificate Manager Import Wizard opens and guides you through the import process.

For directions on exporting from Netscape, see digitalid.verisign.com/chngsw.htm. Then use these steps to import the certificate into OE. You can learn more about exporting and importing from your certification authority. For example, VeriSign has helpful information at digitalid.verisign.com/info_ctr.htm.

Sending and receiving encrypted mail

Once you have someone's digital ID, it's easy to send encrypted messages to this person that only he or she can read.

Public key encryption

Encryption is the process of encoding a message (and any attachments) so that it must be decoded with a *key* before it can be read. The purpose of encryption is to ensure that your messages remain private; this can be extremely important if you are exchanging sensitive personal or financial information. Outlook Express has some encryption capabilities built in, and if you live in the United States, more capabilities are available in the form of upgrades and plug-ins.

These days, the most commonly used encryption scheme is *public key encryption*. This involves two keys, a *private key* that you use for reading encrypted messages sent to you, and a *public key* that lets other people encrypt messages for you to read. Anyone can obtain your public key, either when you send him or her a digitally signed message or a message with your certificate attached, or by downloading it from your certification authority. But only you have access to your private key.

Encryption protocols

Until recently, the strongest encryption legally available in the United States was 40-bit encryption, a relatively weak level of encryption. (The more bits, the harder the code is to crack). Outlook Express automatically supports the RC2 (40-bit) encryption protocol. Residents of the United States and Canada can now download and install a 128-bit upgrade for Internet Explorer (available from www.microsoft.com/ie/download/). The upgrade allows you to send and receive the DES, RC2 (128-bit), and 3DES encryption protocols in addition to RC2 (40-bit). All of these protocols use the S/MIME algorithm created by RSA Data Security and licensed to Microsoft and many others. Both the sender and the recipient must have installed the 128-bit upgrade to use this higher level of encryption. Otherwise, the message will be sent in the RC2 protocol (but Outlook Express will still be able to encrypt it).

Outlook Express can tell from the certificate what protocol to use when sending encrypted e-mail. If you want to see what protocol was used to encrypt a message in your Inbox, Outbox, or Sent Messages folder, highlight the message in the Message pane, click the encryption (padlock) icon in the preview pane header, and choose View Security Properties. You will see the protocol shown under Encrypted Using (see Figure 7-18).

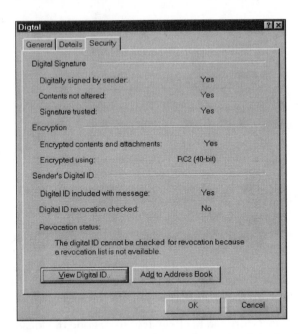

Figure 7-18: The Security tab of the Properties dialog box for this message shows that it was encrypted using the RC2 (40-bit) protocol.

Secret

To see the protocol preference associated with a certificate in your address book, open your Address Book window, right-click the name of the certificate's owner, click Properties, click the Digital IDs tab, and click the Properties button. In the Certificate dialog box, look on the Details tab for the Signature Algorithm. You will see the associated preference in the Value column, as illustrated in Figure 7-19.

Figure 7-19: The Details tab for this digital ID shows that it is set to use md2RSA encryption.

Sending an encrypted message

Say for example that you want to send an encrypted message to your friend Joe. To do this, you must first have a copy of Joe's digital certificate, which contains Joe's public key, stored in your address book. Joe's certificate also contains information about the encryption protocol that he prefers to receive. Outlook Express will automatically encrypt your message to Joe using the preferences contained in his certificate (*not* the preferences you set up for your own certificate). When Joe receives your message, his e-mail software will use his private key (stored in his Registry) to decode the message.

Because you don't have Joe's private key, you won't automatically be able to read (decrypt) the message you sent to Joe, even though you wrote it. When you send an encrypted message to Joe, you will see the error message shown in Figure 7-20. You will still be able to send the message, but you won't be able to read it in your Sent Items folder. To be able to read the encrypted messages you send, follow these steps:

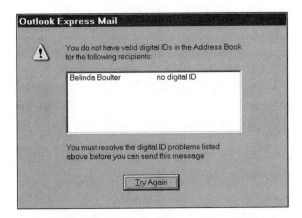

Figure 7-20: This message appears if you haven't added your own public key to encrypted messages you've sent.

STEPS:

Reading Encrypted Messages You Send to Others

Step 1.   Register for your own digital ID with a certification authority, and add your certificate to your own address book. (See "Using your certificate" earlier in this chapter for more about this.)

Step 2.   In Outlook Express, choose Tools, Options, click the Security tab, and then click the Advanced button.

Step 3.   Under Encrypted Messages, mark Always Encrypt to Myself When Sending Encrypted Mail, as shown in Figure 7-21. Click OK twice to close the dialog boxes.

Continued

STEPS

Reading Encrypted Messages You Send to Others *(continued)*

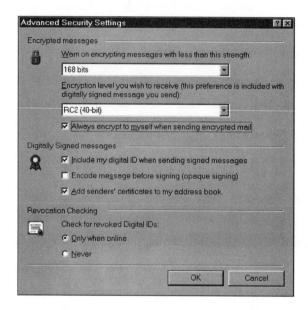

Figure 7-21: Be sure to mark Always Encrypt to Myself When Sending Encrypted Mail if you want to be able to read the encrypted messages you send.

Now when you send an encrypted message to Joe, Outlook Express will make a second encrypted message using your public key and put it in your Sent Items folder, where you will be able to read it with your private key.

When you receive an encrypted message for which you already have the public key, Outlook Express will display a dialog box asking if you want it to automatically decrypt the message. You don't have to do anything else to read it, just click OK.

If you want all of your messages to be either digitally signed or encrypted (or both), click Tools, Options in the Outlook Express window, and click the Security tab. Under Secure Mail, mark Digitally Sign All Outgoing Messages and/or Encrypt Contents and Attachments for All Outgoing Messages. If you have 128-bit encryption, click Advanced, and select the algorithm you prefer in the Preferred Encryption Algorithm drop-down list. Click OK, and then click OK again to close the Options dialog box.

Tip If you save an encrypted or digitally signed message in your Drafts folder without sending it, the security settings will be lost. In Outlook Express 4 there was no warning — version 5 at least gives you a warning when you save the message. Be sure to re-add the encryption and/or the digital signature before sending the message. Thanks to Eric Miller for pointing this out.

Learn more about encryption

You can learn a lot about cryptography at RSA's web site, www.rsa.com/rsalabs/newfaq. For more on S/MIME and how it works, see "S/MIME Capabilities" and "Troubleshooting Enhanced Encryption" on Eric Miller's web site, www.okinfoweb.com/moe/smime/encrypt/index.htm.

Another popular encryption protocol is Pretty Good Privacy (PGP), originally written by Philip Zimmermann and available in both commercial and freeware versions. PGP and S/MIME are not compatible; a message encoded using S/MIME cannot be decoded using PGP, and vice versa. You and your correspondent need to agree in advance on a protocol before you can exchange encrypted messages.

PGP Inc. is now part of Network Associates, at www.nai.com/default_pgp.asp. They offer a plug-in for Outlook Express that's designed to make OpenPGP somewhat integrated with your regular e-mail. The plug-in and PGP freeware are available from the Network Associates site; the freeware is also available from the MIT PGP distribution web site, web.mit.edu/network/pgp.html. Some excellent articles about OpenPGP are located at www.cnet.com/Content/Features/Howto/Encryption.

If you have trouble using PGP with Outlook Express, check www.geocities.com/~tombeck/privacy/trouble.html for troubleshooting tips and workarounds.

If you are having trouble sending encrypted messages to someone who is not S/MIME enabled, take a look at Eric Miller's article "Sending DIDs to Non-S/MIME Readers" at www.okinfoweb.com/moe/smime/DIDs/did_011.htm.

Patch Outlook Express

Older versions of Outlook Express may be vulnerable to a much-publicized virus that can affect Windows e-mail programs. An e-mail message with an attachment that has a very long filename (more than 256 characters) can crash Microsoft Outlook 98, Outlook Express 4.0, and Netscape Communicator 4.*x*. Once this occurs, the malicious e-mail can run a hidden "Trojan Horse" program. A similar problem that involves Java applets and scripts has also been reported with Qualcomm's Eudora.

No e-mail virus that actually exploits these security holes has been reported as of this writing. But that doesn't mean you shouldn't correct these flaws now, before you wish you had.

Fixes for Outlook and Outlook Express are available from Microsoft at www.microsoft.com/security/bulletins/ms98-008.asp. This bulletin is part of the Microsoft Security Advisor web site; while you're there, you may want to check out the current security bulletins as well. The virus problem does not affect Outlook 97, Outlook Express prior to or after 4.0, or Outlook Express on Windows 3.*x*.

Netscape posts its security announcements and fixes at www.netscape.com/products/security/. Qualcomm has fixes for Eudora available at eudora.qualcomm.com/security.html.

Summary

A certificate contains information you need to send encrypted messages to its owner, and it assures you that its ownership is valid.

▶ You can set the level of trust for an individual certificate or for the organization that issued it.

▶ Revocation checking tells Outlook Express to automatically verify on the Internet at the time of receipt that a certificate is still valid.

▶ If you obtain your own certificate, you can receive encrypted messages from people you send it to.

▶ You can export and import certificates for backup purposes.

▶ If you send an encrypted message, you won't necessarily be able to read it. You can read the encrypted messages you send if you have your own certificate.

Chapter 8

The Windows Address Book

In This Chapter

The Windows address book is coming closer to being a truly useful contacts manager. We show you how to take advantage of some little-used or new features.

▶ Use address book folders to organize your contacts and share them with other identities.

▶ Use multiple address books on one computer.

▶ Dial your phone from your address book

Add new entries to your address book

It's now easier than ever to add addresses to your Windows address book from messages you've received. Just right-click a message in the Message pane and choose Add Sender to Address Book. You can also right-click an address in the body of a message (or in the Preview pane), or in the header of an open message window, and choose Add to Address Book.

Secret

In the toolbar of an open mail or news message, click Tools, Add to Address Book. In the submenu that appears, choose Sender, or Everyone on To List, or select individual addressees. The Everyone on To List option is an easy way to capture a whole group of addresses at once. For example, if you get a message that's been circulated to everyone working on a certain project, you can add them all with one command. Unfortunately you can't specify a folder or a group, so if you want to keep the addresses together, you'll have to go into the address book, hunt each address down individually, and drag it into a group or folder.

If you get mail from someone new, you can automatically add him or her to your address book when you send a reply. In Outlook Express, choose Tools, Options, click the Send tab, and mark Automatically Put People I Reply to in My Address Book. If you don't reply to a message, the new address will not be added unless you specifically add it.

The only drawback to using this option is that if you have already entered this person with a slightly different name (Bob instead of Robert, for example), Outlook Express will create a second entry for the new name. If your correspondent has not bothered to enter a "friendly name" in his or her account setup, you will see an e-mail address instead of a name in your address book. You are pretty much forced to live with the name the way your correspondent has it set up, or else have a lot of duplicates in your address book.

We thought that using the Nickname field would get around this, and it almost does. The Nickname field is illustrated in Figure 8-1. If you give someone a nickname for which the first few letters are unique in your address book, you can type those letters in the To field and Outlook Express will enter the e-mail address. But if another entry starts with those letters, you can type the whole nickname and it will still not insert the person's address. So for example, in our address book the nickname Goofy works fine as an alias for a contact whose first name is Robert, but Bobby does not work because we already have a couple of other names starting with Bob. You may want to test this out for yourself, because it may work better in future versions.

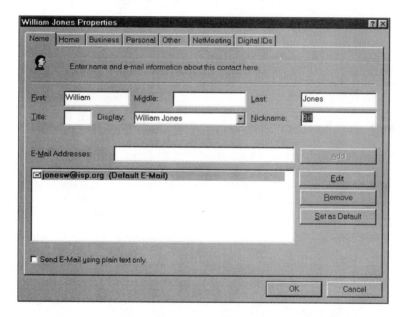

Figure 8-1: You can add a nickname that's different from a contact's name.

Folders and groups

A *group* is a set of pointers to address book entries, not the entries themselves. If you regularly e-mail information to the same people (people in your department at work, distant family members, or fellow hobbyists, for example), you can put all of their addresses into a group. If you do this, you can avoid having to enter each contact individually in the To line every time you send a message to these people. A contact can belong to multiple groups.

A *folder*, on the other hand, is a way of subdividing actual address book entries to make them easier to find and manage. A contact can belong to only one folder. All folders must be part of either the Shared Contacts folder or your identity's main Contacts folder. (These two permanent folders are explained further in the next section.)

Secret

If you open your address book and don't see any entries, it's most likely because the focus is on the Shared Contacts folder instead of your main Contacts folder. To see your Contacts folder, along with subfolders and groups you have created in the address book, click View, Folders and Groups. A left pane opens in the Address Book window, as shown in Figure 8-2.

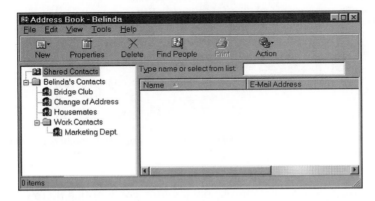

Figure 8-2: The hierarchy of folders and groups is visible in the left pane. Because the focus is on the Shared Contacts folder, and because we haven't shared any contacts, the right pane is empty.

You can't copy contacts, groups, and folders between folders — only move them. You can move a group to another folder without affecting the folder locations of the contacts in the group. You cannot move or copy a folder from one computer to another; if you need this kind of portability, you'll need to create a separate address book (see "Multiple address books" later in this chapter).

Secret

To make a contact appear in more than one folder, create a new group, add the contact, and then drag and drop the group into the other folder(s). Now if you open the group you can see that contact.

If you double-click a group to view its Properties dialog box and click Select Members, you will see a list of all the contacts in the main Contacts folder, as shown in Figure 8-3. Add any of these contacts to the group by highlighting them and clicking Select, and then click OK. To add contacts from another folder to this group you must drag and drop them. (The contacts will be copied, not moved.) To remove a contact, highlight the name in the right pane and press your Delete key (the contact will only be removed from the group, not from your address book).

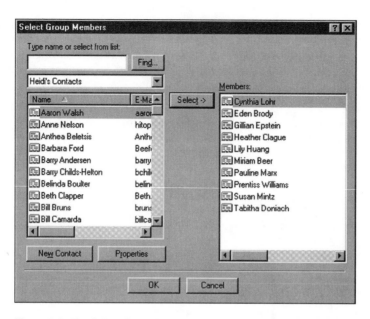

Figure 8-3: The Select Group Members dialog box lets you add members to a group, or remove them.

When you right-click an address book folder, you'll notice there's no Rename menu option. Instead, to rename a folder select Properties. The folder name is the only value in the Properties dialog box. You can't change the name of your main Contacts folder (or remove it, for that matter). We can only surmise that this is to prevent two identities from accidentally giving their main folders the same name.

You can type a contact directly into a group or a folder. Simply select the group or folder before clicking New, New Contact. This is different from the behavior of the Contacts pane, where you can only add contacts to your identity's main Contacts folder. You cannot import contacts from another address book directly into a folder or group, you must first import them into your identity's main Contacts folder (File, Import, Address Book (WAB)), and then move them to a folder or add them to a group individually.

Sharing an address book

Every address book contains at least two permanent folders — one for each identity, and one called Shared Contacts. No matter how many identities there are for a particular user profile, there is only one default address book (*wab*) file, named for the current user. (Remember that profiles are different from identities in that they govern your entire system, not just Outlook Express.) Ordinarily you can only see the entries for your identity's main Contacts folder, plus the Shared Contacts folder.

When you add a contact to your address book—for example, by right-clicking an address and choosing Add to Address Book—that information is stored in the Contacts folder for the current identity. To share a contact or group with other identities, drag the icon for that item into the Shared Contacts folder in the left pane, as shown in Figure 8-4. That contact or group will now appear in the Shared Contacts folder (and thus the Contacts pane) of every identity on this computer, instead of in your main Contacts folder. If you use a lot of shared contacts, it's probably desirable either to keep the Contacts pane open in Outlook Express (View, Layout, Contacts) or to add the Contacts icon to your Outlook Express toolbar.

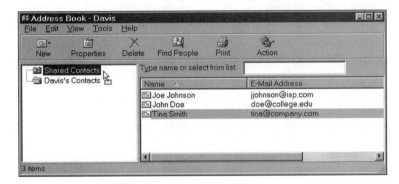

Figure 8-4: Drag the contact into the Shared Contacts folder to share it with other identities.

Multiple address books

Now that the Windows address book can contain multiple folders, the need for multiple address book files is significantly decreased. Address book folders are certainly easier to set up and use. But you can still have multiple address books if you choose, and this may be the best option if you need to move a subset of your address book between computers.

You can have as many *wab* files (address books) as you want, but only one default *wab* file. The default *wab* is the one you see in the Contacts pane, and the one used when you click To in the header of a New Message window. The path to the default *wab* is stored in your Registry (see "Save all your documents" in Chapter 3 for instructions on moving your default address book).

Secret

To create a new address book, click Start, Run, type **WAB /New**, and press Enter. Browse to the place where you want to keep your new address book (probably the same folder where you keep your other one). Then type a name for your new address book and click Open (see Figure 8-5). A new, empty address book appears.

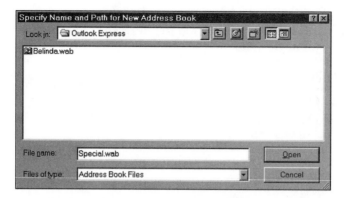

Figure 8-5: In this example, the new address book will be called Special and will be stored in the same folder as Belinda's default address book.

You can open the non-default *wab* files by clicking them in the Explorer. You can easily make shortcuts to them on your Desktop, on a toolbar, or in the Start menu. Or you can make shortcuts to Registry files that will automatically change the default *wab*. To see how this is done, take a look at "Using Multiple WABs" on Eric Miller's User Tips web site, www.okinfoweb.com/moe/wab/wab_015.htm.

Tip

It's easy to copy address book entries from one *wab* file to another. Just open both address books side-by-side, select one or more contacts to be copied (you can use the Shift and Ctrl keys to select the ones you want), and drag them into the other address book. This makes it quick to add multiple contacts from your address book at the office to the one on your computer at home, for example.

The address book does more than e-mail

You don't have to open Outlook Express to send mail to someone in your address book. From the address book, highlight the person's name, click the Action toolbar button, and click Send Mail. A New Message window opens with that person in the To line.

You can also use your address book to dial the telephone or initiate a NetMeeting conference. You must first have entered the information to do this, of course. To dial the telephone, highlight a contact for whom you have entered a phone number, click the Action toolbar button, and click Dial. This launches the Windows Phone Dialer applet (discussed in "Phone Dialer" in Chapter 32 of *Windows 98 Secrets*). A New Call dialog box opens, as shown in Figure 8-6. Click Call to dial the phone, pick up your receiver, and then click the Talk button in the Call Status dialog box before you start to talk. The Phone Dialer remains open but minimized after you end the call and click the Hang Up button.

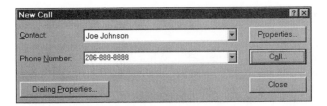

Figure 8-6: Click the Call button to dial the number you have selected.

To start a NetMeeting conference, double-click a contact to open its Properties dialog box, and then click the NetMeeting tab to enter Internet conferencing information for a contact. (This tab will be called Conferencing if you have not installed NetMeeting.) Enter the server and address information in the appropriate fields (see Figure 8-7), and then click Add. To initiate a conference, click Call Now.

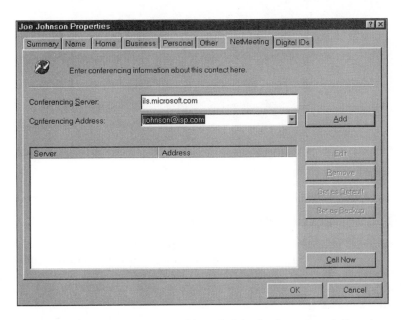

Figure 8-7: The NetMeeting tab will be called the Conferencing tab if you have not installed NetMeeting.

See "Connecting to other NetMeeting users" in Chapter 9 for more on how to use NetMeeting.

Print a phone list

If you click the Print button in the Address Book toolbar, you'll see a dialog box such as the one shown in Figure 8-8. What makes it different from a normal print dialog box is the choice of print styles. The Memo option prints all of the contact information for your contacts, Business Card prints the information on the Business tab, and Phone List produces a nice alphabetized phone list that you can carry with you. With all three print styles, you can print the information for all of the contacts in your address book or only for the selected ones. On the downside, you don't have much control over the layout, and you're stuck with printing on 8 1/2 by 11 paper.

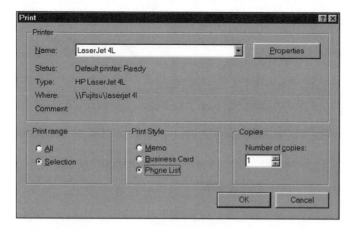

Figure 8-8: The address book's Print dialog box lets you select a print style.

Copy a contact into Word

Although you can't do anything as sophisticated as mail merging with your address book, you can at least get contact information into a Microsoft Word document pretty easily. Just drag and drop one or more contacts from your address book into a Word document, or right-click to copy and paste in the normal way.

If you do this, you'll find that all the non-empty fields for the contacts are pasted into your document — you'll need to delete the extraneous stuff if all you want is the mailing address. Still, it's better than typing.

If you have a lot of names and you want to do a full-scale mail merge, you'll need to export your address book to a comma-separated value (*csv*) text file.

You have to open this file in Microsoft Excel and save it in Microsoft Excel Workbook (*xls*) format before Word can use it as a mail merge source. Kind of a project, but again, better than typing.

To create the *csv* file, choose File, Export, Other Address Book, select Text File (Comma Separated Values) in the Address Book Export Tool dialog box, and then click Export. The CSV Export Wizard opens. Browse to a location for saving, enter a name for your file, click Save, and then click Next. You can select the fields to export by marking their check boxes, as shown in Figure 8-9. When you're done, click Finish, and then click OK when the export is complete.

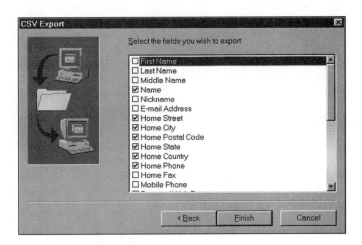

Figure 8-9: Mark the check boxes for the fields that you want to export.

Converting between address book formats

Outlook Express lets you import address book files from Eudora, Netscape, and several other formats (click File, Import, Other Address Book). But if you have some format that Outlook Express doesn't handle, or if you want to convert from Outlook Express to another format, you may find the InterGuru's E-Mail Address Book Conversions web site helpful. The conversion page is shown in Figure 8-10. This is a shareware service that performs the conversion for you online, and also offers links to some other helpful sites. Please note that we have not tested this conversion service. You'll find it at www.interguru.com/mailconv.htm.

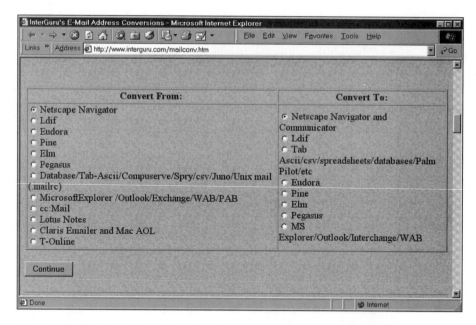

Figure 8-10: The conversion table at InterGuru's web site lists the possible conversion combinations.

Summary

The Windows address book has added some tools for managing your contacts. While the method leaves a lot to be desired, you can export contact listings into Microsoft Word.

▶ You can easily share address book contacts among identities if you put them in the Shared Contacts folder.

▶ You can use the address book to initiate a telephone call or an Internet conference.

Chapter 9

NetMeeting

In This Chapter

Microsoft will not leave an Internet stone unturned. To keep the Internet from becoming the operating system, they need to turn the operating system into the ultimate Internet client. NetMeeting lets you use the Internet as a video phone line, a chat room, a whiteboard, and a place to share applications.

▶ NetMeeting is an Internet phone, but you've got to make sure your audio doesn't echo.

▶ The capabilities of your sound card and driver determine whether NetMeeting acts like a phone or a two-way radio.

▶ Fix your microphone and sound card so that NetMeeting can detect them.

▶ How to contact the other guy.

▶ Use NetMeeting as an answering machine?

▶ Explore NetMeeting-related web sites.

Audio and video issues

You can not send audio and video information between NetMeeting users unless they are connected via a TCP/IP network. The Internet is such a network, as are properly configured local area networks, as well as Direct Cable Connection. NetMeeting will work over IPX and NetBEUI networking protocols, but it will lack the audio and video features.

In addition to the help provided in this chapter, you can find assistance on audio problems at the Microsoft Knowledge Base. Check out these articles:

■ "NM: Participants Cannot Hear During Audio NetMeeting Conference" at support.microsoft.com/support/kb/articles/q174/6/11.asp

■ "NM: Audio: Poor Quality, Distortion, Echoing, No Sound" at support.microsoft.com/support/kb/articles/q165/6/22.asp

■ "NM: Audio May Echo with Microsoft NetMeeting" at support.microsoft.com/support/kb/articles/q166/0/38.asp

■ "NM: Must Take Turns Speaking in NetMeeting" at support.microsoft.com/support/kb/articles/q155/0/24.asp

Feedback and echo

It is possible to test NetMeeting using two computers connected to each other through a null modem cable or over a TCP/IP network. If these computers are close to each other and if both sound cards are operating in full duplex mode, you'll find that the audio output from one computer can register as the input to the other, creating unpleasant feedback.

In addition to feedback, you may find that both microphones pick up what one person is saying. This produces an echo because both computers' speakers broadcast what is being said, with a slight delay. To reduce echo, you can reduce the volume on the speakers in NetMeeting, or use an anti-echo or noise-canceling microphone. You'll find them at www.andreaelectronics.com.

Tip

Some computers also produce feedback on their own when output from their speakers is picked up by their own microphones. To avoid both forms of feedback, turn down the volume on the speakers or the level on the microphone, so that the microphone does not pick up output from the speakers. The best option is to plug headphones into your sound card to cut the feedback loop.

Why do I have to stop talking before my friend can talk?

NetMeeting uses your sound card to both send out your voice when you speak and to play the voice of the person with whom you are speaking. In some cases, your sound card may only be able to support half duplex — that is, only one speaker at a time.

Half duplex is like two-way radio communication. First one person transmits, then the other. Unlike radio, NetMeeting doesn't require that you push the push-to-talk button. NetMeeting automatically senses your voice when you speak and also senses when the other person isn't speaking. This automatic sensing capability can be a source of problems (see the next section).

Sound cards with full duplex capability allow you to speak and listen in the same manner that your phone allows. These sound cards can transmit your voice at the same time as they play the voice of the person to whom you are speaking.

If either you or your friend's sound card does not have full duplex capabilities, you'll each have to wait for the other to quit speaking before you commence to speak. For a full duplex conversation to occur using NetMeeting, both parties must have full duplex sound cards and drivers. You may both have to upgrade if this is not the case and you want this capability.

You can determine whether your sound card has full duplex capabilities by starting NetMeeting and taking these steps:

STEPS:

Checking for a Full-Duplex Sound Card

Step 1. Click the Start button, Programs, NetMeeting. (If you've never run NetMeeting before, you will see the NetMeeting Wizard and then the Audio Tuning Wizard. Follow both wizards to set basic options, and then continue with these steps.)

Step 2. In NetMeeting, choose Tools, Options, and click the Audio tab.

Step 3. If either your sound card or your sound card driver doesn't support full duplex audio, the first check box will be dim, as shown in Figure 9-1. If this is the case, you will not be able to use full duplex audio.

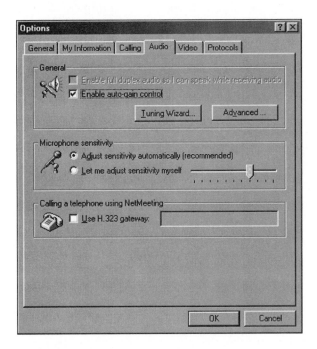

Figure 9-1: The Audio tab of the Options dialog box. The first check box is dim if your sound card or its driver doesn't have full duplex capability.

Tip You may be able to get an updated driver for your sound card that provides full duplex operation. Click Start, Settings, Windows Update to connect to the Microsoft Windows Update site through the Internet. It will download and install a new sound card driver if one is available.

To turn on full duplex capabilities for Sound Blaster drivers (the industry standard), take these steps:

STEPS:

Turning on Full Duplex

Step 1.   Click the Start button, Settings, Control Panel, System, and Device Manager.

Step 2.   Click the plus sign next to Sound, Video and Game Controllers. Highlight Creative Sound Blaster Plug and Play.

Step 3.   Click the Properties button. Then click the Settings tab, and mark the Allow Full-Duplex Operation check box, as shown in Figure 9-2. Click OK. Click OK.

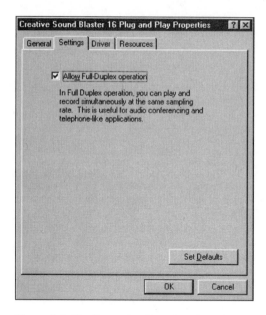

Figure 9-2: The Properties dialog box for a Sound Blaster driver.

Step 4.   Restart your computer and NetMeeting to allow these changes to take effect.

Why can't I hear the person I'm talking to?

If you are running NetMeeting with a half duplex sound card and/or driver, you may have difficulty receiving audio from the people with whom you are connected. This may be because your microphone is picking up sounds in addition to your voice, and blocking the incoming audio.

To correct this problem, turn down your microphone level in the NetMeeting window. This prevents NetMeeting from switching to the mode it uses to send audio from your computer (Transmit Audio mode). You can also get a directional or anti-echo microphone. You'll find them at www.andreaelectronics.com.

NetMeeting also can have trouble with DirectSound (Microsoft's sound drivers). You can turn off DirectSound using NetMeeting Super Enhancer. See where to get it in "How can I log on to a new NetMeeting directory server?" later in this chapter

Have the person you are trying to hear check to see that his or her microphone is working by clicking Start, Programs, Accessories, Entertainment, Sound Recorder. Your friend should be able to click the Record button (the red dot), and record and then play back his or her voice. If your friend can't record and hear the playback, check out the suggestions in the next section.

The Audio Tuning Wizard doesn't find my microphone

The first time you start NetMeeting, the Audio Tuning Wizard runs automatically. You can also run it after you start NetMeeting (click Tools, Audio Tuning Wizard).

If you run the Audio Tuning Wizard, you'll get to the dialog box that tests your microphone, shown in Figure 9-3. If nothing shows up on the decibel meter (the horizontal green line just above the volume slider that moves to the right as you speak louder), it may be because your microphone is muted.

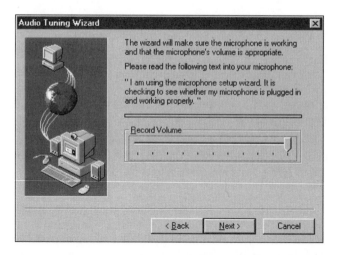

Figure 9-3: The Audio Tuning Wizard. This dialog box displays your microphone volume as you speak into your microphone. If you don't see a green line, NetMeeting isn't receiving any input from your mike.

To check out your mike, take these steps:

STEPS:

Checking Your Microphone

Step 1. Right-click the Volume icon in your system tray and click Adjust Audio Properties. Or, click Start, Settings, Control Panel, Multimedia, Audio.

Both of these methods display the Audio control panel (see Figure 9-4).

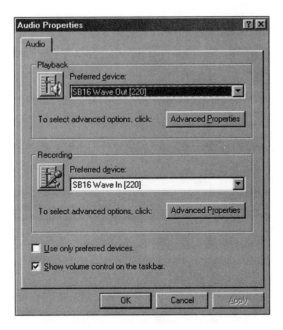

Figure 9-4: The Audio control panel. Both the Volume and Recording control panels are accessible from here.

Step 2. Click the icon directly under Recording to display the Recording control panel (see Figure 9-5).

Step 3. If the Select check box in the microphone control is not marked, the Audio Tuning Wizard won't find your mike. Be sure to mark this check box, and click OK.

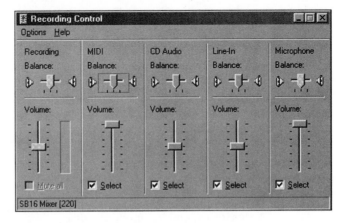

Figure 9-5: The Recording control panel.

Step 4. If you don't find the Microphone column on your Recording control panel, you can add it by choosing Options, Properties to display the Properties dialog box shown in Figure 9-6.

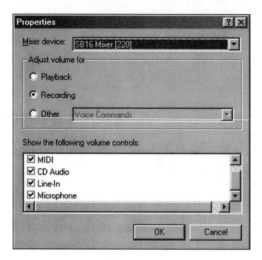

Figure 9-6: The Properties dialog box for the Recording control panel.

Step 5. Scroll down the volume control list and mark Microphone. Click OK.

As soon as you mark the Select check box for the microphone in the Recording control panel, the microphone will be available to the Audio Tuning Wizard. You can take these steps while you are running the wizard.

While you're adjusting your mike, you should also check out its volume setting in the Volume control panel. To do so, take these steps:

STEPS:

Adjusting Microphone Volume

Step 1. Right-click the Volume icon in the system tray and click Open Volume Controls. Or, click Start, Settings, Control Panel, Multimedia, Audio, and then click the icon below Playback. (A third option is to click Start, Programs, Entertainment, Accessories, and Volume Control.)

Step 2. The Volume control panel, shown in Figure 9-7, doesn't have the microphone volume control by default. To display it, click Options, Properties. Scroll down to the Microphone check box, mark it, and click OK.

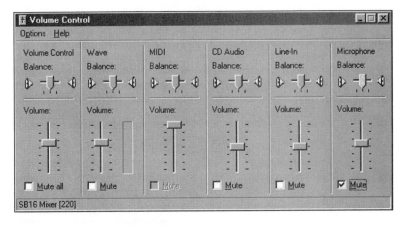

Figure 9-7: The Volume control panel.

Step 3. You can mark the microphone's Mute check box in the Volume control panel without affecting NetMeeting. If Mute is marked, your voice will not be played out of your speakers when you speak into your mike.

If the Mute check box is cleared, you'll hear yourself speak through your computer's speakers as you communicate using NetMeeting.

You may find that your computer's speakers put out a fair bit of electronic noise if the microphone volume isn't muted. We found that marking the Mute check box provides the most pleasant experience with NetMeeting.

Secret

You can have the Volume control panel, the Recording control panel, and the Audio Tuning Wizard all visible and running at the same time, if you have enough real estate on your monitor. You'll notice that as you adjust the microphone volume control in any one of these panels, the volume slider in the other panels is also adjusted. This lets you know that all of these controls are working together.

Different sound cards and drivers have different capabilities. Some sound cards don't support microphone volume control, so the microphone volume control in the Recording control panel doesn't do anything.

The Audio Tuning Wizard has trouble with my sound card

If you run the Audio Tuning Wizard and you get the error message "Microsoft NetMeeting may not be able to use audio correctly," this could be due to an outdated audio driver. You can run the Windows Update Wizard (Start, Settings, Windows Update), or you can check at the sound card manufacturer's web site to find the latest driver updates.

For example, for the latest Sound Blaster16 drivers, go to www.creaf.com/wwwnew/tech/ftp/ftp-sb16awe.html.

NetMeeting may have trouble with your DirectSound drivers. You can turn off DirectSound using NetMeeting Super Enhancer. See where to get it in "How can I log on to a new NetMeeting directory server?" later in this chapter.

In NetMeeting Super Enhancer, click File, Disable DirectSound. You can store NetMeeting Super Enhancer in the \Program Files\NetMeeting folder. Place a shortcut to it on your Desktop or in the Start, Programs, Internet Explorer menu (the \Windows\Start Menu\Programs\Internet Explorer folder). In fact, if your NetMeeting shortcut is in your Programs menu, you may consider moving it to the Internet Explorer menu as well, so that you keep all of your Internet Explorer related applications in one place.

Can a group of NetMeeting users share audio together?

You can address your audio to more than one listener if you log onto a NetMeeting server that provides these capabilities. Use your web browser to check out conference.databeam.com/net120, www.labtam.com.au, or www.wpine.com. The first and last sites provide a publicly available server.

You can also download server software for Windows NT from the first two sites. This software allows you to configure your own NetMeeting server with these enhanced capabilities. Thanks to Jeffery Durham, Robert Scoble, and Roger Tragin for pointing out these sites.

You should also check out www.databeam.com/meetingtools/ for additional add-on tools that enhance NetMeeting functionality. Microsoft incorporates DataBeam technology in NetMeeting.

There are other software packages that do multi-party video and audio. You can find them at www.ivisit.com and www.wpine.com. Thanks to Robert Scoble at www.vbits98.com for reminding us about these other sites.

Neither audio nor video works

If you can't get an audio and video connection, click Tools, Switch Audio and Video, and select your correspondent. NetMeeting has a bit of a problem if either you or your friend is using an Internet service provider that doesn't support header compression, and one of you has enabled it. You'll need to right-click your DUN connectoid, click Properties, Server Types, TCP/IP Settings, and clear Use IP Header Compression.

You can find additional help on video problems at the Microsoft Knowledge Base. Check out these articles:

- "NM: My Video Window Is Displayed Black Screen" at support.microsoft.com/support/kb/articles/q166/1/14.asp

- "NM: Poor Video Image Quality in NetMeeting" at support.microsoft.com/support/kb/articles/q165/7/78.asp

- "NM: Cannot Exchange Audio and Video at Start of Conference" at support.microsoft.com/support/kb/articles/q174/5/94.asp

No local audio or video when connected to your Internet service provider?

If you are connected to a local area network and you use your modem to call your Internet service provider, most likely you won't be able to contact anyone else with audio and video on your LAN using NetMeeting. This is because your local TCP/IP services are stopped automatically when you start using TCP/IP remotely. Microsoft does this to keep your Windows 98 computer from serving as an IP router.

At least that is what many others have experienced, and what happened when we tested NetMeeting under these circumstances. When our technical editor tested NetMeeting on her two-computer TCP/IP network, she was able to transmit audio locally while connected to her ISP. Go figure. Perhaps it will work for you.

Your local area network may consist of just a few computers at your home, and may use other networking protocols as well. These protocols are not affected when you connect to your Internet service provider. If your LAN uses other protocols in addition to TCP/IP, you will still be able to chat, use the whiteboard, and so on. But TCP/IP is required to share audio and video data.

I can't hear anyone through my router

NetMeeting requires a direct connection over a TCP/IP network for audio and video to work. Some routers incorporate a Network Address Translation (NAT) table to translate local IP addresses to an address that will work on the Internet at large. Some implementations of NAT don't pass dynamic UDP (Internet standard for a packet type used for audio and video) properly, and thus you're not able to get audio or video at all.

Make sure that you are not behind a firewall that uses a NAT if you want to have audio and video work when you're connected to someone on the other side. If you're running a NAT on a Windows 95 or Windows 98 server, you can switch over to SyGate (www.sygate.com), which can handle NetMeeting or WinGate (www.wingate.com). Versions 2.*x* of WinGate don't work with NetMeeting.

If you are running Windows NT and its proxy server, you'll want to learn how to configure it allow Windows 98 clients to receive NetMeeting calls. There is a web site dedicated to the proxy server at proxyfaq.networkgods.com/

downloads.htm. Here's the Windows NT Registry change that you want to make:

```
REGEDIT4
[HKEY_LOCAL_MACHINE\Software\Microsoft\Internet Audio\NacObject]
"DisableWinsock2"=dword:00000001
```

Thanks to Doug Thews for this secret. This is one that we haven't tested. The NT Registration file that includes the above text, NT Registry change for NetMeeting.reg, is provided on the CD-ROM that accompanies this book.

You can find out more about firewalls, port numbers for TCP/IP connections, and UDP in the *NetMeeting Resource Kit*, at www.microsoft.com/netmeeting/reskit/.

Connecting to other NetMeeting users

Unlike using a phone, you can't just call up anyone using NetMeeting. Your friend's computer must be turned on, and he or she must be connected to your network, or you both must be connected through the Internet for you to be able to connect at all. Even if your friend is connected to your network or the Internet, you have to know this person's current address (which may be just his or her computer name).

How do I find out the address of the person I want to talk to?

The short answer is that you should write an e-mail message and ask your friend for his or her Internet address or listing on a NetMeeting directory server (an ILS server).

The problem with Internet or IP addresses is that in many, if not most, cases they aren't static (that is, fixed). Most often, they are dynamically assigned when the user connects to his or her server or Internet service provider. It's hard to keep track of someone's address if it is always changing. You don't even necessarily know your own IP address after you connect to your Internet service provider, for example, unless you check.

NetMeeting directory servers are one way of dealing with this problem. If you log onto a directory, your current IP address is captured and associated with your fixed directory listing. All you have to do is notify your associates of this listing (which you may choose not to have displayed on the directory server), and whenever you are logged onto the directory, they can connect to you. If you'd prefer to solve this problem by getting a fixed IP address, see "Your own dynamic IP address and static domain name" in Chapter 11.

You may be wondering, if you can have a stable e-mail address, why can't you have a fixed IP address that NetMeeting can use? With a fixed e-mail address it is relatively easy to let others know how they can get hold of you by e-mail—just write them a note. Unfortunately, this is not always possible with a real-time communications package such as NetMeeting.

E-mail is a store-and-forward system. Messages are mailed to an e-mail server (POP3 or IMAP4 are the Internet standard e-mail server types) that is connected full time to the Internet. This server has a fixed address. When you want to get your e-mail, you use your e-mail client—Outlook Express, for example—to interrogate the e-mail server and have it download the messages.

NetMeeting creates a real-time connection among the various parties communicating with each other. In order to do this, it needs to know where to send the packets of voice, video, and data. It can't send these packets to a server and let you connect to the server at your convenience.

Computers on the Internet or an Intranet connect by using IP addresses. Every computer participating in a NetMeeting needs to know the IP address of all the other computers with which it is communicating. You can't connect to someone with NetMeeting unless that person is online and running NetMeeting also.

If you are using NetMeeting to connect to someone else over an Intranet (that is, a local or wide area network that uses the TCP/IP protocol), it is likely that the IP address for this person's computer is fixed. Once you know it (or the computer's name), you can keep a copy of this IP address (or computer name) in your NetMeeting SpeedDial list and connect to your associate's computer at any time. In this case, you have no need for a directory.

If you are NetMeeting with someone else, you can find out his or her IP address. Click Start, Run. Type **netstat -n 30** and press Enter. A DOS window opens and displays an updated network status every 30 seconds, including the IP addresses of those computers to which you are connected (see Figure 9-8). The IP address is on the left side of the colon. The TCP/IP port addresses that NetMeeting is using are to the right of the colon. Each TCP/IP application uses a different port address.

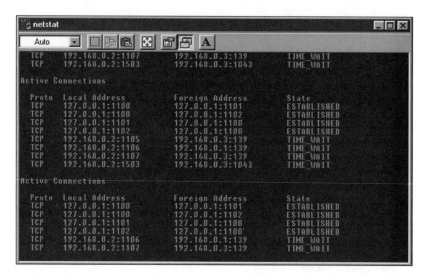

Figure 9-8: The netstat results are displayed in a DOS window.

To stop netstat, click the Close button in the upper-right corner of the DOS window, and then click Yes.

Create a SpeedDial listing to send to others

One convenient way to send people your address (and have them send their address to you) is to create a SpeedDial listing shortcut. You can create it using the following steps:

STEPS:

Creating Your Own SpeedDial Listing

Step 1. Click the Start button, Programs, NetMeeting.

Step 2. To open the Add SpeedDial dialog box shown in Figure 9-9, you have three options. Click the SpeedDial button on the NetMeeting toolbar (this button is available in all views except Current Call view). Choose SpeedDial, Add SpeedDial on the NetMeeting menu bar. Click Call, Create SpeedDial. (You would think that Microsoft could be consistent in naming these almost identical operations.)

Continued

STEPS

Creating Your Own SpeedDial Listing *(continued)*

Figure 9-9: The Add SpeedDial dialog box. Enter your address and the method used to find that address.

Step 3.   Type your address or directory listing in the Address field. If you clicked Call, Create SpeedDial, your default address will be the combination of your default NetMeeting directory server and your e-mail address.

If you have a fixed IP address, you can type it in — for example, **10.141.5.170**.

You can also type your computer's name (you'll find it in the Control Panel, Network icon, Identification tab).

You can type the name of a NetMeeting directory server that you want to use, followed by a slash and then your e-mail name, as shown in Figure 9-9.

Step 4.   Display the Call Using drop-down list and choose the method that NetMeeting will use to find the address.

If you are on an Intranet (any local network using the TCP/IP protocol) without a NetMeeting directory server, choose Network (TCP/IP).

If you are on the Internet and want to connect through a NetMeeting directory server, choose Directory Server.

Step 5.   Mark the Save on the Desktop option button. Click OK, and then click OK again. You've now created a NetMeeting shortcut on your Desktop. It is a file with a *cnf* extension.

Once you have created this SpeedDial listing, you can send it around to anyone who asks for it. If you send e-mail to someone asking for his or her SpeedDial listing, you might ask your associate to follow these steps and send the shortcut to you. To send a SpeedDial listing, right-click its icon on the Desktop, click Send To, Mail Recipient, type the e-mail address of the person to whom you're sending the listing in the To line of the New Message window, and send the message.

Tip

If you want to put the SpeedDial listing in an e-mail message as you create it, Choose Send to Mail Recipient in step 5 above. You can Ctrl-drag the SpeedDial listing from the Attach line of the e-mail message to the Desktop to place a copy of it there before you send the message.

To find out your IP address (whether you have a fixed one, or one that was just assigned to you), click Start, Run and type **Winipcfg**. In the IP Configuration dialog box that appears, your IP address is listed in the IP Autoconfiguration Address field. If you're asking for an IP address from someone on a Windows NT workstation, have him or her click Start, Run and type **Ipconfig**. (You can also see your address when you run netstat, as detailed in the previous section.)

You'll find Winipcfg in your \Windows folder. You can place a shortcut to it on your Desktop. You may have to choose the correct network adapter in the drop-down list at the top of the dialog box.

You can also open a DOS window by clicking Start, Run, and typing **ping** *yourcomputername* where *yourcomputername* is replaced by the name you have given your computer in the Identification tab of the Network dialog box (click the Network icon in the Control Panel).

If you use a fixed IP address in step 3, this address will become the name of the SpeedDial listing shortcut. It won't be very helpful to receive or send out such an attachment. You can change the name of the shortcut to your name (right-click it, click Rename). The IP address will still be used, but the listing will have a much friendlier name. If you use your computer's name in step 3, you might also want to rename the shortcut to your own name.

You can keep as many of these SpeedDial listing shortcuts on your Desktop as you like, but they may crowd out other icons that vie for that space. Drag them into another folder; better yet, drag them into the \Program Files\NetMeeting\SpeedDial folder in an Explorer window. If you do this, they will appear in SpeedDial view in the NetMeeting window. To drag and drop a SpeedDial listing to your NetMeeting SpeedDial folder, take these steps:

STEPS:

Adding a SpeedDial Shortcut to the List

Step 1. Click the Start button, Programs, Windows Explorer.

Step 2. Navigate to \Program Files\NetMeeting\SpeedDial.

Continued

STEPS

Adding a SpeedDial Shortcut to the List *(continued)*

Step 3. Drag and drop a SpeedDial listing shortcut from your Desktop to this folder in the Explorer window.

Step 4. Click the Start button, Programs, NetMeeting.

Step 5. Click View, SpeedDial. You'll see your new listing.

Step 6. If you don't see your new listing, press F5. If that doesn't work, exit NetMeeting and restart.

Tip

If, when you create a new SpeedDial entry, you click the Add to Speed Dial List option button in the Add SpeedDial dialog box, the new entry is automatically added to the \Program Files\NetMeeting\SpeedDial folder. If you receive a SpeedDial entry as a *cnf* file attachment in an e-mail message, you can just save it to this folder.

How do I know if someone is online?

In order to use NetMeeting, all of the participants in a meeting have to be online. This isn't a problem if you are connected together through an Intranet, or if your computer is always connected to the Internet and you are running NetMeeting (perhaps in the background).

If you are permanently online, you'll most likely have a fixed IP address, and it will be easy for your associates to contact you. They'll just click your name in their SpeedDial folders.

If you go online at irregular intervals, your associates will either have to contact you (say by e-mail) to make arrangements to NetMeet at a certain time, or wait to contact you when you do go online. One way to do this is to use a notification service such as ICQ that works with NetMeeting. ICQ provides the option of holding a NetMeeting whenever you find that one of your buddies (that is, someone on your buddy list) is online. You'll find ICQ at www.mirabilis.com.

If your correspondents register with a NetMeeting directory server (an ILS server), you can see if they are logged onto their server by keeping their name and address in your SpeedDial list. NetMeeting regularly checks your SpeedDial list to see if one of your buddies is online. You get to set the interval (Tools, Options, Calling tab, Automatically Refresh SpeedDial List Every [   ] Minutes).

They can also send you e-mail when they go online, telling you their IP address or sending you a SpeedDial listing.

Can NetMeeting act like an answering machine?

The problem with NetMeeting is that you have to be online and running the program for anyone to be able to connect to you using NetMeeting. It is possible to run NetMeeting in the background, so that it can recognize when someone is calling you and alert you to start a NetMeeting.

You can have NetMeeting start automatically, or only when you decide to start it. You can also have NetMeeting track who else has tried to contact you with NetMeeting while you were away or not responding for other reasons.

To set these options, take these steps:

STEPS:

Putting NetMeeting in the Background

Step 1.   Click the Start button, Programs, NetMeeting.

Step 2.   Choose Tools, Options, and click the General tab. The first three check boxes let you configure NetMeeting to work in the background (see Figure 9-10).

Figure 9-10: The General tab of the Options dialog box.

Continued

STEPS

Putting NetMeeting in the Background *(continued)*

Step 3. Mark Show Microsoft NetMeeting Icon on the Taskbar. This actually puts the NetMeeting icon in the system tray. If the icon is in the system tray, you can start NetMeeting by double-clicking the icon or by right-clicking it and clicking Open.

If NetMeeting is running (you'll know that this is the case because its button will appear on the Taskbar), you can also click the icon in the system tray and choose among four NetMeeting functions: Share Application, Start Collaborating, Chat, and Whiteboard.

Step 4. Mark Run When Windows Starts and Notify Me of Incoming Calls. This puts a command in your startup sequence that runs NetMeeting in background mode (it doesn't put a button on the Taskbar).

To get this mode to start, you'll need to click OK in the Options dialog box, and then choose Call, Exit to stop NetMeeting. To start NetMeeting again, double-click its icon in the system tray.

You can see that this option has in fact set up NetMeeting to start in background mode by taking clicking Start, Programs, Accessories, System Tools, System Information, Tools, System Configuration Utility, Startup. You'll find Microsoft NetMeeting in the list of startup items.

Step 5. Mark or clear Automatically Accept Incoming Calls. If this option is cleared, you will be notified by a little pop-up window when someone tries to connect to you with NetMeeting.

If you are not around or you click Ignore, the ignored incoming call is recorded in your history file as Ignored. When you come back later, you can call the person who tried to get hold of you by double-clicking his or her name in the History folder. This is your answering machine function.

In our tests, we were unable to double-click a name in the History folder and have our copy of NetMeeting call the person back. This apparently has worked for others, but we couldn't get it to work when we tested it over a couple of local area networks with TCP/IP.

Step 6. Click OK.

If you want to use NetMeeting to communicate with others on a regular basis, you'll need to have it running at least in background mode pretty much all the time. You'll also have to be connected to at least an Intranet as much as possible, if not continuously. Otherwise, you will have to send e-mail to your associates to arrange a time for your NetMeetings, or use a notification service such as ICQ.

How can I log on to a new NetMeeting directory server?

Secret

A list of NetMeeting directory servers is kept, where else, in your Registry, under HKEY_CURRENT_USER\Software\Microsoft\Conferencing\UI\ Directory. You can add or subtract servers from your list of directory servers either by editing the list in your Registry or by using the NetMeeting Super Enhancer shown in Figure 9-11. You'll find NetMeeting Super Enhancer at www.netmeet.net.

Figure 9-11: NetMeeting Super Enhancer.

You can add (but not subtract) a server listing in NetMeeting by typing its name in the Server Name field. Choose Call, Change My Information to display the Options dialog box, click the Calling tab, and type a server name in this field.

If you are on an Intranet with a directory server, you'll want to add it to your list. You may want to get rid of other directories from this list, especially if you are a system administrator and don't want users on your network trying to access outside servers.

To choose a directory to log onto, choose Tools, Options, click the Calling tab, and select a server name in the Server Name field, as shown in Figure 9-12.

Thanks to Tom Lake for pointing out where the list of servers is kept.

You can find a list of the NetMeeting directory servers available on the Internet at www.netmeet.net/ilslist.htm.

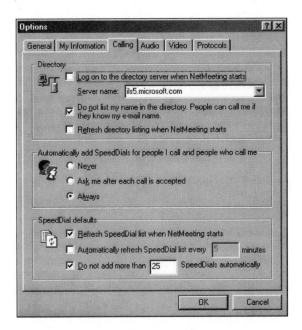

Figure 9-12: Use the Calling tab of the Options dialog box to choose a directory to log onto.

How can I use NetMeeting to contact others outside my corporate firewall?

James Rice helped us out with this one. Have your system administrator configure your firewall so that the ports listed in Table 9-1 are not blocked:

Table 9-1   Firewall Settings for NetMeeting Users

Port Number	*Protocol*
ULS server	(TCP)
1503	T.120 (TCP)
1720	H.323 call setup (TCP)
1731	Audio call control (TCP)
Dynamic	H.323 call control (TCP)
Dynamic	H.323 streaming (RTP over UDP)

The H.323 call setup protocol (over port 1720) dynamically negotiates a TCP port for use by the H.323 call control protocol. Both the audio call control protocol (over port 1731) and the H.323 call setup protocol (over port 1720) dynamically negotiate UDP ports for use by the H.323 streaming protocol, called the *real time protocol* (RTP). In NetMeeting, two ports are determined on each side of the firewall for audio and video streaming. These dynamically negotiated ports are selected arbitrarily from all ports that can be assigned dynamically.

Can I use NetMeeting to talk with AOL users?

You can if they have installed AOL 3.0 or later and are running Windows 95 or 98. They have to connect to AOL using a 32-bit version of TCP/IP. Earlier versions of the AOL client software used 16-bit connections.

Why can't my friend accept my NetMeeting calls?

There are several reasons why the person you are trying to contact may be unavailable even if both of you are logged onto the same NetMeeting directory server and see each other's name in the directory.

The directory server's list of names is not immediately updated if someone logs off. Therefore, while it may appear that the person is there, he or she may in fact have already left.

If the person you are trying to access is connecting to his or her Internet service provider through a non-standard protocol, perhaps a PPP emulator, NetMeeting won't be able to establish contact. If the person is behind a firewall or a server/router that converts IP addresses, NetMeeting won't be able to find its way through.

If your friend's computer has the TCP/IP protocol bound to the network card and the Dial-Up Adapter, the NetMeeting directory server may have associated the wrong IP address with your friend's directory listing. Your friend has to unbind the TCP/IP protocol from his or her network card temporarily. To do this, have your friend take these steps:

STEPS:

Releasing a Network Card's TCP/IP Address

Step 1. Click Start, Run, type **winipcfg**, and press Enter.

Step 2. Display the drop-down list at the top of the IP Configuration dialog box and choose the network card.

Step 3. Click the Release button, and click OK. (To later rebind the TCP/IP protocol to the network card, your friend will need to restart his or her computer.)

On the other hand, your friend may not want to be disturbed and may have clicked Call, Do Not Disturb.

Can I call into my computer at work and use NetMeeting?

You can configure your computer at work as a Dial-Up Networking Server. You can then call in from your computer at home, and as long as you are running the TCP/IP protocol over your Dial-Up Adapter, you can run NetMeeting and pass audio and video information.

You'll first need to install Dial-Up Networking on both computers. If you haven't done this already, you can follow the steps in Chapter 17 of *Windows 98 Secrets*. In particular, review the sections "Setting Up Your Windows 98 Computer at Work As a Host" and "Setting Up Your Computer at Home As a Guest." You can also follow the steps in the *Windows 98 Resource Kit* on your Windows 98 CD-ROM.

Once you have installed Dial-Up Networking and the Dial-Up Adapter, take these steps to configure your computers to allow a connection between them:

STEPS:

Setting Up Your Computers to Allow NetMeeting Calls

Step 1.   On your computer at work, click the Start button, Settings, Control Panel, Network, Configuration. Scroll down to and highlight TCP/IP -> Dial-Up Adapter, as shown in Figure 9-13. Click Properties.

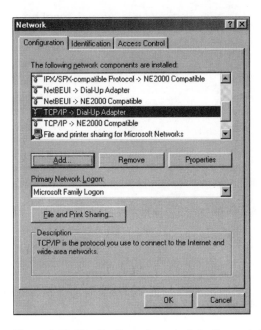

Figure 9-13: The Configuration tab of the Network dialog box.

Step 2. You will be warned that setting the TCP/IP properties in the Network dialog box is not a good idea, and that you should set them in the dial-up connectoid (see Figure 9-14). Click OK.

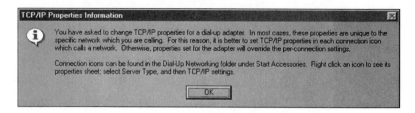

Figure 9-14: The TCP/IP Properties Information dialog box.

You are only going to set the IP address for the DUN Server. This will be overridden if you dial into the Internet with a DUN connectoid using the computer at work.

Step 3. In the TCP/IP Properties dialog box, click the IP Address tab, and mark Specify an IP Address. Type **192.168.0.1** for the IP address, and for the Subnet Mask, use **255.255.255.0**, as shown in Figure 9-15. Click OK, and OK. You will have to restart the computer when prompted.

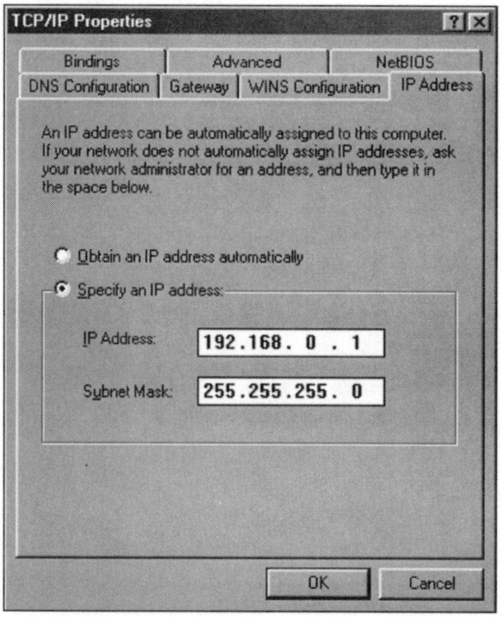

Figure 9-15: The IP Address tab of the TCP/IP Properties dialog box.

Continued

STEPS

Setting Up Your Computers to Allow NetMeeting Calls *(continued)*

Step 4. After your computer restarts, click Start, Programs, Accessories, Communications, Dial-Up Networking. In the Dial-Up Networking folder window, choose Connections, Dial-Up Server.

Step 5. In the Dial-Up Server dialog box, mark Allow Caller Access (see Figure 9-16). Click OK.

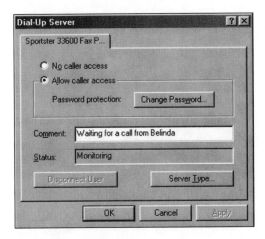

Figure 9-16: The Dial-Up Server dialog box.

Step 6. On your computer at home, click Start, Programs, Accessories, Communications, Dial-Up Networking. In the Dial-Up Networking folder window, click the Make New Connection icon.

Follow the steps in the Make New Connection Wizard, giving your DUN connectoid a new name, and entering the phone number for the phone line connected to the computer at work.

Step 7. Right-click this new connectoid. Click Properties, and click the Server Types tab.

Step 8. Under Allowed Network Protocols, clear NetBEUI and IPX/SPX Compatible, and leave TCP/IP marked (see Figure 9-17). Click the TCP/IP Settings button.

Step 9. In the TCP/IP Settings dialog box, mark Specify an IP Address, and type **192.168.0.2**, as shown in Figure 9-18. Click OK. Click OK.

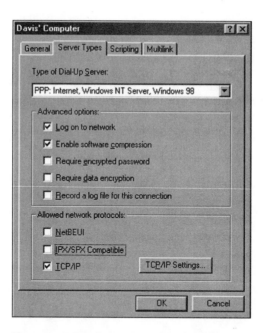

Figure 9-17: The Server Types tab of the Properties dialog box for your new DUN connectoid.

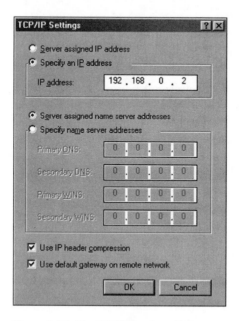

Figure 9-18: The TCP/IP Settings dialog box.

Continued

STEPS

Setting Up Your Computers to Allow NetMeeting Calls *(continued)*

Step 10. On both computers, in an Internet Explorer window click Tools, Internet Options. Click the Connections tab. Mark Never Dial a Connection. Click OK.

Step 11. On both computers, in a NetMeeting window, choose Tools, Options, and click the Calling tab. Clear Log On to the Directory Server When NetMeeting Starts. Click OK.

Step 12. On the computer at home, click the DUN connectoid that calls up and connects to the computer at work. When the connection is successful, click Call, New Call, and enter the TCP/IP address of the computer at work, as given in step 3.

Step 13. Choose Network (TCP/IP) in the Call Using field, and click the Call button.

Your NetMeeting session should now begin. Thanks to Mark Andres for tips on some of the more obscure steps.

Let people contact you through your web site

You can put a call button on your web site and ask folks to contact you by going to your web site and clicking the call button. If they have NetMeeting and they click the call button on your web site, their copy of NetMeeting will open. You have to be online to take the call, and they have to use Internet Explorer as their browser to be able to use the call button.

Here is an example of some HTML code that you could add to your web page to add a call button:

```
You can contact me using NetMeeting at <A
HREF="callto:ils5.microsoft.com/davis@davisstraub.com">
ils5.microsoft.com/davis@davisstraub.com</A>.
```

If you have a fixed IP address, you can substitute it for the NetMeeting directory server address. You can also use a graphical button if you like, instead of the text shown in the example.

Connect a few computers together to use NetMeeting

If you have a small local area network, you can configure your network in a very simple fashion to allow NetMeeting to work between computers. If you want to exchange audio and video, you will have to bind the TCP/IP protocol to your network card. You can see how to do this in Chapter 24 of *Windows 98 Secrets*.

Each computer on your local area network will have a unique name. To connect to any one of them, click Call and type the name of the computer. (You can assign a unique name to a computer in the Identification tab of the Network dialog box — see Chapter 24 of *Windows 98 Secrets* for more information.)

If you assign an IP address to each of the computers on the network, you can call that unique address just by including it in your SpeedDial. You can assign such an address by clicking the Network icon in your Control Panel, highlighting TCP/IP on your network card, clicking Properties, and then clicking the IP Address tab. Click Specify an IP Address, and type an IP address (mine is 10.141.5.170) and a submask (mine is 255.0.0.0).

Using NetMeeting to talk on the telephone

Here's an inappropriate use of technology. Use a $2500 computer as a $50 telephone. Well, it is almost worth it. Of course it's harder than just using the phone.

You can connect to other NetMeeting users who are online and talk to them. Your voice is carried as packages of data that are reassembled and played when they get to the person you're calling. You can also (theoretically) use NetMeeting to call a telephone number and speak to the person who answers the phone as though you were using a phone (sort of).

This is different than Microsoft Phone (or other H.324-compliant software). Microsoft Phone uses a voice capable modem (V.80) and/or sound card to turn your computer into a phone. You dial through your computer and it acts just like a phone.

To use NetMeeting as a phone, you need to connect to a server that will convert the NetMeeting data stream into a regular analog audio stream as well as place the call that you have dialed. What is cool about this capability is that you can use the cheap Internet backbone to get to a server close to the location that you want to call, and then have the server place a local call. It cuts down on the cost of long distance calls by using the Internet to get most of the way.

The problem is that you need to be able to connect to a server that provides this IP-to-audio switcheroo — an H.323 gateway. There may soon be publicly available servers that you can use to make these kinds of calls. We expect that they will figure out how to bill you.

There may be a couple in Australia. You can check them out at www.cst. com.au.

You have to provide the IP address of the H.323 gateway. In NetMeeting, choose Tools, Options, click the Audio tab, mark the Use H.323 Gateway check box, and type the IP address in the field on the right.

Want to learn more about H.323? A good primer is located at 205.181.113.18/pcmag/pclabs/nettools/1622/tools/tools2.htm. Also visit www.netmeet.net/.

Net Phone

Net Phone is not a part of NetMeeting, but an alternative to it for certain functions.

If you want a solution that is available now to use your computer as a phone and to call up a telephone, you can use Net Phone at www.net2phone.com. Net Phone turns your microphone, sound card, speakers, and computer into a telephone that can call any telephone in the world. You use the Net Phone software and Net Phone's Internet servers to place the telephone call. The advantage is that you may be able to make inexpensive long distance or international phone calls, partially through the Internet and partially over the local phone company at the receiving end.

You need to sign up with Net Phone after you download their client software in order to place phone calls. You can check out their rates and determine if they are any less expensive than using your regular telephone. The big advantage comes from calling back into the U.S. Your international call from China to the U.S. might only cost you the price of the local call to an Internet service provider in China, plus $0.10/minute for the long distance connection in the US.

You use Net Phone just like a regular phone, punching in the numbers on the keypad or using the speed dial (see Figure 9-19).

Figure 9-19: Net2Phone gives you a familiar user interface.

Connecting to other conferencing systems

You can use NetMeeting to connect to similar systems that exchange audio, video, and textual information. For example, you can connect to Pictel at an H.320/H.323 gateway. Check out www.picturetel.com/www.picturetel.com for more details.

A number of video conferencing software systems comply with the H.320 standard. They require high throughput to work at all and are often based on ISDN modems.

NetMeeting won't run?

Why can't the software all just get along? Even software from Microsoft has conflicts with other Microsoft software. It's a complex world out there.

NetMeeting makes a call to an invalid DLL

Secret

Installing Windows 98 over Windows 95 should update all dynamic link libraries to the latest versions — and if you have the latest version of NetMeeting, then all should be well. That said, time marches on, and things change. If you get the error message, "Program Error - Your program is making an invalid dynamic link call to a .DLL file," you may have an out-of-date video or Direct Sound driver.

You can update your Windows 98 NetMeeting setup by clicking Start, Settings, Windows Update.

NetMeeting freezes your computer when starting

Secret

There are a couple of reasons this might happen. NetMeeting enumerates and sorts all your fonts when it starts up so that they can be used for application sharing. If some of your font files are corrupted or you've previously installed Hewlett Packard's "Fonts for the Family," then NetMeeting will hang your computer. You can find out which fonts come with the HP set by reading the Microsoft Knowledge Base article "NM: NetMeeting Hangs When Starting" at support.microsoft.com/support/kb/articles/q156/0/94.asp.

NetMeeting may also be conflicting with a remote control application such as PC Anywhere, which installs a virtual display driver. When NetMeeting attempts to interact with the "real" display driver, the computer freezes. You may need to uninstall any remote control software. Check the manufacturer's web site first to see if they have a solution.

Thanks to Roman Deeds for this secret.

Going further with NetMeeting

Be sure that you add the right equipment so that you'll have a good experience with NetMeeting. You can check out the latest information on the newsgroups and web sites listed at the end of this chapter.

Cameras and video capture cards that work with NetMeeting

Purchase an inexpensive charged couple diode camera as an input device to the video card, or get a card that attaches to your existing video camera. You also have to buy a video card to process the video input. Without it, your computer's CPU would be bogged down processing the video signal.

You'll want to check out www.winnov.com. You'll find cards both for desktop and portable computers there.

You might find that NetMeeting incorrectly states that you have video capture hardware already installed. Some software, such as Microsoft Camcorder, emulates video devices and will be detected by NetMeeting. To eliminate this false video capture detection, click Start, Settings, Control Panel, Multimedia, Devices, Video Capture Devices. Disable any device found there. (Thanks to Bill Schneider for this secret.)

Want to create a videogram (an audio/video clip) and send it off as e-mail? Check out Videogram Creater at www.labtam.com.au. You can send out a recording that's accompanied by its own player.

Of course, you can do this directly with Outlook Express. Just insert the video clips in your e-mail and send them out. The Microsoft media player should play them.

NetMeeting web sites and newsgroups

NetMeeting is changing. Anything we say in this book could be out of date. New versions of NetMeeting are released all the time, sometimes even without a version number change.

If you are going to keep up with the changes, you need to visit the sites listed in Table 9-2 and browse the NetMeeting newsgroups every so often.

Table 9-2   Useful NetMeeting Web Sites

Description	URL
Video capture	www.winnov.com
Standard Scoble Advice	www.netmeet.net
NetMeeting FAQ	support.microsoft.com/support/netmeeting/faq/

Chapter 10

Chat

In This Chapter

Microsoft provides not one but two chat clients. Will they catch on? Will the chat room providers dominate with Java clients instead?

▶ Find the Microsoft chat clients, as well as the other clients that are available on the web.

▶ How to deal with a pest or worse.

▶ Build your own three dimensional V-Chat worlds.

▶ Finding the Chat Easter Egg.

Chatty Microsoft

"Embrace and extend." Embrace, extend, and extinguish. Since 1995, Microsoft has been in a panic to make sure that it doesn't miss any boat or even canoe that may be leaving the Internet dock. Therefore, they gave a few programmers in the backroom the task of providing an Internet chat client.

There were plenty of Internet Relay Chat (IRC) clients available when Microsoft first introduced Microsoft Comic Chat 1.0, so they added the twist of displaying little two dimensional characters that could express a limited array of "emotions." It took a special Comic Chat server, which Microsoft also developed, to display these different faces to the other comic chatters.

Microsoft has since renamed Comic Chat as Microsoft Chat. They were wondering if you were laughing with them or at them. Chat displays either text or cartoon characters with balloons containing your typed text.

Microsoft now provides Microsoft Chat, Microsoft V-Chat (a chat room client that allows two-dimensional characters in a three-dimensional space), and a chat server that comes with the Exchange Server and lets you set up your own Intranet chats. Microsoft also operates publicly available online Internet chat servers for both chat clients. You'll find these tools and services at the locations listed in Table 10-1:

Table 10-1 Microsoft Chat Services	
Tool or Service	*URL*
Chat	www.microsoft.com/ie/chat
V-Chat	www.microsoft.com/ie/chat/vchatmain.htm
Exchange Chat server	www.microsoft.com/exchange
Chat server	mschat.msn.com (access through Chat client)
V-Chat server	vchat://vchatsrv.microsoft.com (access through V-Chat client)

Microsoft operates other free chat servers at other URLs. They are all part of the irc.msn.com chat network. In addition, there are plenty of other chat servers, even V-chat servers, operated by other entities. See "Chat servers" later in this chapter for some of their addresses.

There are plenty of other IRC clients. You might try mIRC at www.mirc.co.uk, and Pirch at www.pirchat.com.

Starting a conversation

A *Secrets* book isn't designed to get you started. We're here to help you with more advanced issues. If you have installed Chat and/or V-Chat, you'll be able to connect to the Microsoft default chat servers as soon as you click these chat clients under Start, Programs. You may need to connect to the Internet first, perhaps using your DUN connectoid.

Once you're online and connected to a chat server, you can look around. You don't need to respond to anyone, and you can enter rooms that are open without having to chat, whisper, accept files, open NetMeeting chats, or interact in any fashion whatsoever.

You'll find all the basics covered in Microsoft's online help files for Chat and V-Chat. You can check these out offline before you enter any room populated by other chat users (as well as a few chat bots). There is usually a help room available for questions about the chat network or your chat client. Just ask a question of the host.

Microsoft maintains a FAQ about its chat network. You'll find it at computingcentral.msn.com/help/howtochat.asp. If you're a new chat user, we suggest that you check out a couple of introductions to chat at www.mirc.co.uk/irc.html and www.mirc.co.uk/ircintro.html.

Who are you?

Chat clients let you mask a bit of your identity. This is part of the appeal of chat. You get to pretend. Of course, if you are on an Intranet chat, there may be some restrictions on how much anonymity, if any, you are allowed.

Both Chat and V-Chat encourage you to enter some information about yourself — your real name and e-mail address for instance — but you are not required to do so. You can leave these fields blank, or make imaginary entries. You are required to enter a nickname (which can be your real name). A character (or *avatar*) is assigned to you, and you can choose another if you prefer. This is the limit of your identity, almost.

Others can find out this information about you by double-clicking your nickname when you are in a chat room. They also see your user ID. The user ID contains a *masked* version of your current IP address. For example, here are some representative user ID's from V-Chat and Chat, respectively: ~vchat@xxxxxxxxxxxx.dialup.online.no and ESPERANZA's identity: ~ESPERANZA@207.249.170.XX.

The V-Chat user in this example didn't enter an e-mail address or user name, so *vchat* was used instead. Notice that the last set of numbers in Esperanza's IP address is replaced with XX. The replacement of part of your IP address is referred to as *masking*. While your IP address is masked to other users in your chat room, the chat room's host gets to see the whole thing.

This comes in quite handy if you behave badly. The host can ban anyone using the miscreant's Internet service provider from entering his or her chat room. Because in most cases IP addresses are assigned dynamically, it would do no good to ban a given IP address. It would be a simple matter for the person who has behaved inappropriately to just log off his or her service provider and then log on again to receive a new IP address.

The host or system operator may therefore decide to ban the Internet service provider by choosing to disallow a range of IP addresses (those dynamically provided by the Internet service provider). The ban may occur for a few hours or days. It is then up to the service provider to deal with the user who has now inconvenienced all of the ISP's other users who may have wanted to enter that same chat room.

Given that we could be easily talking about America Online as the service provider, you can see how this could become a major hassle very quickly.

So even if you are playing the game of hiding your identity, it isn't hidden from all those who may be in a position to make your life a little bit harder. Hassle a chat room operator, and you may pay a heavy price (get kicked off your Internet service provider).

Is someone hassling you?

You go into a chat room to chat with someone else. It may turn out that you don't want to chat with a person who wants to talk to you, and he or she just can't take a hint. If you are using Chat or V-Chat, right-click the name of the offensive individual and click Ignore to ignore the pestering.

This works unless the person is persistent or obsessive — a modern fear, if there ever was one. When computer communication makes reaching out and touching someone so easy, the flip side is that it is realistic to fear getting hounded by one of the millions of thoughtless boors who inhabit the cyber planet.

Ignoring only works as long as the person doesn't change his or her name. Changing a nickname doesn't work because the chat server tracks users by their user IDs. Unfortunately, the person can easily change his or her user ID by briefly logging off the chat server and changing names.

You can ask the room host to ban the unpleasant individual. The host may do so, and he or she may ban all the users from that Internet service provider. You then have the opportunity to contact the service provider and ask them to take action against the offender. The service provider now has a definite interest in fixing the problem, because all of their users are being banned from the chat room.

If you are using V-Chat, you'll find the domain name of the miscreant's Internet service provider within his or her user ID. Send a message and your recording of the harassment to hostmaster@*serviceproviderdomainname.com* or support@*serviceproviderdomainname.com*. You can ask the room host to do the same.

If the harasser has decided to nuke you — that is, send ICMP packets to your computer with various error messages in them — you have arrived at the next level of Internet irritation. ICMP is the acronym for Internet Control Message Protocol. This protocol reports errors and provides other information relevant to IP packet processing. It's documented in RFC 792 (use a search engine on the Internet to find out more about this if you like). If the IP address and port numbers in the ICMP packets match your connection to the chat server, your connection will be terminated.

There are a number of ways to deal with the nuker. First, Windows 98 incorporates Winsock 2.2, an upgraded layer of the multi-layered Internet protocols. Winsock stands between your Internet application and the network. Winsock 2.2 successfully combats many of the ICMP attacks.

Second, you can contact the attacker's service provider to ask that this person be dropped as a customer. You can protect yourself by installing firewall software, even if you are a standalone computer.

You can find out more about these types of denial-of-service attacks at mirc.stealth.net/nuke/, www.irchelp.org/irchelp/nuke/, and www.microsoft.com/security/.

Chat commands

You're just chatting away until you enter a slash (/) as the first character, and then you are sending a command. Chat and V-Chat's friendly user interface make many of these commands unnecessary. In addition, these clients come with keyboard shortcuts that let you react quickly as you chat.

Still, the command interface is available to you, and you may use other IRC clients that use it exclusively. You can find out about the standard and extended IRC commands at www.mirc.co.uk/ircintro.html.

Chat clients may not implement all (or even most) of the commands. You can give each of them a try and see what's available.

If you are having trouble joining a chat room, you can use the /list command to what chat rooms meet your criteria. Table 10-2 lists some ways to use this command:

Table 10-2   Common /List Commands

Command	Type of Room
/listx R=1	Registered rooms
/listx R=0	Dynamic rooms
/listx N=*comic*	Rooms with the word *comic* anywhere in the name
/listx T=*help*	Rooms with *help* in the topic
/listx >25	Rooms with more than 25 members
/listx <20	Rooms with fewer than 20 members

You can then use the /join *roomname* command to join a chat room. An interested party makes up dynamic rooms on the spot. Registered rooms have a more permanent status.

V-Chat Angel Society

There may be people looking out for you when you enter the lobby of a V-Chat world. It depends on their schedule, so they're not always available, but if they're there, you can get some help.

The Angel Society is a group of volunteers who schedule time to help out at vchat://vchatsrv.microsoft.com/V-ChatLobby. You can find out more about them at the Angel Society home page at members.tripod.com/~AngelSociety/.

You'll often find Angel Robert Moir, members.xoom.com/Robert_Moir/ frames5a.htm, answering questions on the chat newsgroups listed in "Internet chat newsgroups and resources" later in this chapter.

Build your own V-Chat worlds

The V-Chat worlds are stored on your computer. You'll find them at C:\Program Files\Microsoft V-Chat\WORLDS.

You can find new worlds and instructions on how to change these worlds at Snow Angel's web site at www.grafton.net/~snowangel/roomhelp.htm. She also has an avatar web page that you can reach from her site.

Chat servers

In addition to the Microsoft irc.msn.com chat network, there are plenty of other chat servers out there on the Internet. You'll find an index at public.surfree.com/saint/.

The irc.msn.com network goes by many names and has many servers. You can connect to it using any of these server names:

mschat.msn.com
mschat2.msn.com
mschat3.msn.com
mschat4.msn.com

irc.msn.com
irc2.msn.com
irc3.msn.com
irc4.msn.com

comicsrv.microsoft.com
comicsrv2.microsoft.com
comicsrv3.microsoft.com
comicsrv4.microsoft.com

204.255.245.172:6667
204.255.245.173:6667
204.255.245.174:6667

MSN has its own chat server restricted to MSN users. You'll find it at chat.msn.com.

The Microsoft V-Chat server is at vchatsrv.microsoft.com. Other V-Chat servers are available. For example, go to www.info66.com/ircaccess/v-chat.html for more information about chat1.info66.com.

TalkCity at www.talkcity.com/ runs an extensive schedule of chats. You'll even find the authors of *MORE Windows 98 Secrets* chatting away over there from time to time. Check out the IDG Books Worldwide web site at www.idgbooks.com for more information and author chat schedules.

Tip

You can add a new server to your list of chat servers just by typing its name in the Server field of the Chat Connection dialog box, which appears when you start up Chat, or under Room, Connect in either chat client. You can remove names from the chat server list by editing your Registry. Find out more about how to do this in Chapter 15 of *Windows 98 Secrets*.

To change your personal list of chat servers, use the Registry editor to navigate to HKEY_CURRENT_USER\Software\Microsoft\Microsoft Comic Chat\ServerList. Double-click ServerList, and edit the entry.

Tip

If you are trying to connect to irc.msn.com from AOL, you might want to try irc.msn.com:7000 instead. The default is port 6667, but this address may work better for you.

Internet chat newsgroups and resources

It is a bit funny when you think about it, but there are newsgroups about chat. Of course, if you have a question, you can just go to the help room on your chat network and ask one of the system operators. Then, again, they really don't answer questions about the chat clients, so you'll have to check out the newsgroups.

Microsoft provides newsgroups for its chat clients and chat server, as well as for its chat network. Table 10-3 lists some of them.

Table 10-3   Newsgroups for Microsoft Chat

Newsgroup	URL
Help with Microsoft's chat network	news://publicnews.msn.com/msn.irc.support
Help on Chat	news://msnews.microsoft.com/microsoft.public.internet.mschat
Help on Chat	news://msnews.microsoft.com/microsoft.public.inetexplorer.ie4.mschat
Help on V-Chat	news://msnews.microsoft.com/microsoft.public.vchat
Help on the Exchange chat server	news://msnews.microsoft.com/microsoft.public.mcis.chatserver

You can find other newsgroups that focus on chat and IRC issues on Usenet. Use your newsgroup reader (Outlook Express, for example) to connect to your Internet service provider's news server and then search for *irc*. Complete instructions on how to use Outlook Express as a newsgroup reader can be found in Chapter 19 of *Windows 98 Secrets*.

You'll find a couple of FAQs about these two chat clients at the Microsoft chat newsgroups listed above.

Other web resources are available to supplement those provided by Microsoft. In addition to the Angel Society (people who help others use V-Chat) at members.tripod.com/~AngelSociety/, you might want to visit Steve Howland's Comic Chat Help site at members.tripod.com/ComicChat/ (for FAQs and more comic characters), and Timothy Akehurst's Avatar Zone at www.mad-web.net/avatarzone (for lots of additional V-Chat avatars).

Microsoft Chat 2.5 Easter Egg

Secret

Steve Howland, the super support person for the Microsoft Chat products (he doesn't work for Microsoft), gives us the instructions on how to activate the Easter Egg for Microsoft Chat 2.5. You can go to his site to get an update if you have a later version of Chat at members.tripod.com/ComicChat/.

STEPS:

Start the Dancing Chat Team

Step 1.   Click Start, Programs, Microsoft Chat.

Step 2.   Log on to a Microsoft chat server. You can stay offline if you like. Just click Cancel when the Chat Connection dialog box first appears and asks if you want to connect. Then click OK.

Step 3.   In the text box at the bottom of the Microsoft Chat window, type **WhoIsTheGenius?** Don't press Enter, and keep the case and spacing as shown.

Step 4.   Hold down the Ctrl and Shift keys and click the Open Favorites button on the main Chat toolbar.

Step 5.   You should now see characters in the comic chat space with balloons over their heads stating their names and dancing, as shown in Figure 10-1.

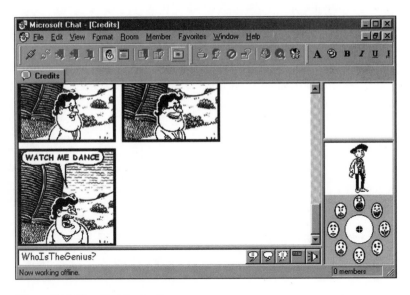

Figure 10-1: The Chat Easter Egg.

Summary

We show you how to get your chat client up and running, how to change your world, and how to keep from being pestered.

▶ How you are identified to others on the chat rooms.

▶ You can use some of the standard IRC chat commands with Microsoft Chat.

▶ You can get help in three dimensional chat rooms from the group of angels.

▶ You can find additional resources and help with Chat.

Chapter 11

Publishing on the Web

In This Chapter

Windows 98 comes with a web page editor and the ability to ship web pages and graphics to your web server. Having a web presence is actually pretty cool, and if you're a business, it can actually make you some money. We provide some add-ons and tweaks to make this a little more possible.

▶ Why not make it easier to get to Notepad when you want to edit an HTML file?

▶ Download a reference library for HTML development.

▶ Use FrontPage Express to create simple web pages.

▶ Use Microsoft's FTP built into Internet Explorer to copy your web pages up to your web server.

HTML

We've got a few little add-ons that help you get your HTML code up a bit more quickly.

Edit HTML files with Notepad

Secret

Sometimes Notepad can be the perfect little HTML editor, even if you usually use FrontPage Express or another fancy WYSIWYG editor. While it is always possible to use Send To to "send" an HTML page to Notepad, you can also just add a command to the HTML context menu that allows you to right-click the HTML file and edit it with Notepad.

One way to do this is to insert the following text into a text file, save the file and rename it Notepadhtml.reg, right-click the renamed file, and click Merge. This creates a new command called Notepad, which shows up on the HTML context menu when you right-click an HTML file.

```
REGEDIT4
[HKEY_CLASSES_ROOT\htmlfile\shell\notepad]
@="&Notepad"
[HKEY_CLASSES_ROOT\htmlfile\shell\notepad\command]
@="c:\\windows\\notepad.exe %1"
```

We've included Notepadhtml.reg on the accompanying CD-ROM. Thanks to Yannis Pantzis for this secret.

Change your text files to HTML

If you want a quick and dirty way to convert your text files into HTML format, you should check out Text2Web at www.virdi.demon.co.uk/. It's not beautiful, it's not sophisticated, and it's not real clever, but it will create tables and lists from your text.

You can insert text from the Clipboard or from a text file. You can set the font, font color, and background color of the resulting HTML page, as shown in Figure 11-1. Text2Web will convert HTML and mailto addresses to hyperlinks.

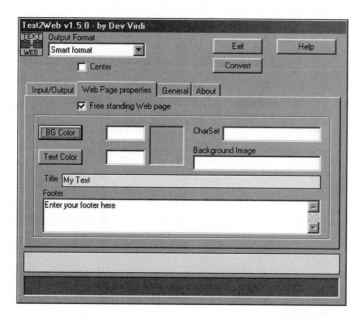

Figure 11-1: You need the Pro version of Text2Web to set the font, font color, and background color.

You can download Text2Web from www.geocities.com/SiliconValley/Heights/ 9709/txt2web/t2web150.zip.

Thanks to Chris Pirillo at www.lockergnome.com for the pointer to this site.

Prettify or compress your HTML code

If you use FrontPage Express, you'll notice that your underlying HTML source code doesn't look all that readable. The indents aren't in the right places, the line lengths can get pretty long, and you'll wonder why there aren't any carriage returns. This may even be true if you are editing your own code straight in Notepad.

<PRETTY>HTML (that's the name of the product) will read through your HTML source and put in the proper indents, add comments at the beginning of headers and tables, and set the line lengths so that you don't have to scroll to the right. We tried it on a number of our HTML files, and it did a beautiful job, as you can see in Figure 11-2. This makes it much easier to actually edit the HTML source document.

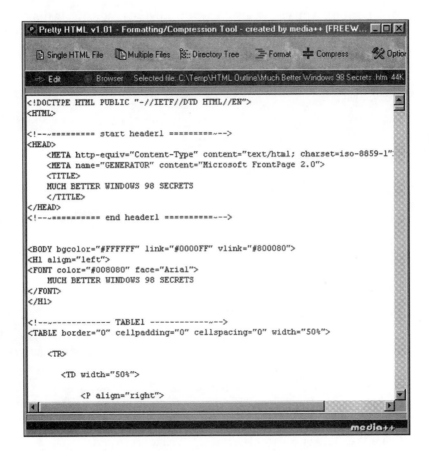

Figure 11-2: This HTML document has been processed by <PRETTY>HTML.

You can also use <PRETTY>HTML to compress HTML files, however they were produced. This actually uglifies the HTML file but makes for a quicker download. We saw about a 20 percent reduction in the size of HTML files. This will make your web site seem a bit zippier.

You'll find <PRETTY>HTML at www.mpp.at. There is a freeware version, and also a professional version with a few more features.

Buttonz! and Tilez!

These two programs, which work separately but come together in the same zipped package, are just as cute as can be. They do exactly what their titles say they do.

Buttonz! helps you make sophisticated button icons that you can activate on your web pages. Associate the button image with an action, a link to another web page, whatever.

With Buttonz!, you can easily create the bevels, gradients, textures, lighting, colors, captions, size, and shape of all kinds of buttons, as shown in Figure 11-3. Output your buttons as JPEGs, BMPs, or in a number of other standard graphical formats.

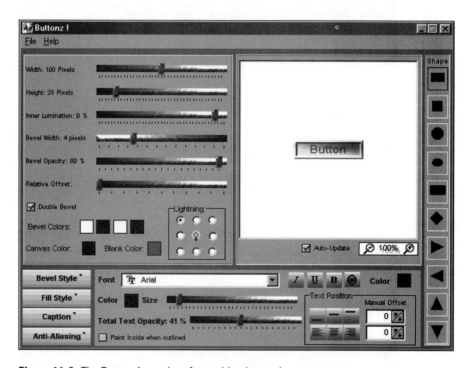

Figure 11-3: The Buttonz! user interface with a button in progress.

Tilez! is a dedicated tile painter. Put the tiles together to create a background for your web pages or folder views in your Explorer. Tilez! uses three layers to create its effects, as shown in Figure 11-4. You can insert various images into any of the layers.

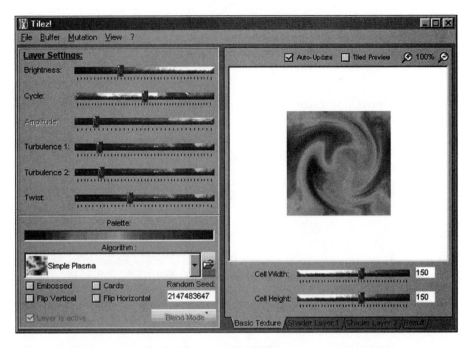

Figure 11-4: The Tilez! interface with one layer of a tile displayed. You switch to the other layers by clicking tabs along the bottom of the window. A fourth tab lets you see the result.

Both of these very cool programs are free, and you'll find them at www.b-ischo.horizont-is.net.

Special cursors for your web site

You can insert code into your web pages that will change the cursor displayed on the computer screens of the folks who visit your site. They'll need to download a little browser plug-in, but you can easily send them out to get it.

You'll find the plug-in and a set of cursors at LiveCursors at www.livecursors.com. When you select a cursor to use at your web site, you'll be presented with the HTML that you can then copy and paste into your web pages to display that cursor.

Thanks to Chris Pirillo at www.lockergnome.com.

Watermark your graphics files

If you'd like to put a unique mark in your graphics files to dissuade others from appropriating them and using them on other web sites, check out the freeware program Stash. You can use one of five data hiding techniques on GIF, PCX, BMP, PNG, and TIFF images (although not JPEG).

A number of programs allow you to do this, but this one is free. To watermark a graphics file, Stash simply encodes data (text from a text file) into the graphics file. If you are checking out a graphics file, it decodes the data from the graphics file (creates a text file from the text) .

In the Stash window (see Figure 11-5), you need to first browse to a graphics file, then to a text file, and finally to an output file. You have to actually browse to an existing output filename.

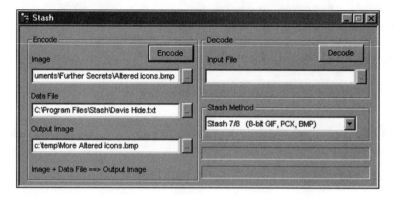

Figure 11-5: You have to enter the path and name of an existing output image file in the Output Image field.

You find Stash at www.smalleranimals.com/stash.htm.

Create HTML applications

If you can write HTML documents, you can write HTML applications that use underlying Internet Explorer functions to display and operate. They'll work on any computer running Internet Explorer version 5 and later.

Here's a sample of a very simple application:

```
<HTML>
<HEAD>
<TITLE>Simple HTML Application</TITLE>
<HTA:APPLICATION ICON=x.ico borderStyle=Raised sysMenu=no>
</HEAD>
<BODY>
This is a simple HTML application.
<BR>
<BUTTON onclick="self.close()">Exit</BUTTON>
</BODY>
</HTML>
```

Save this text in a text file. Rename the extension *hta*. Click it, and you'll have an open application window. All of the tags above are standard HTML tags, except <HTA:APPLICATION ICON> and <BUTTON>. These have been added to allow for HTML applications.

You can find out how easy this really is if you go to a Microsoft Site Builder article at www.microsoft.com/sitebuilder/magazine/ie5hta.asp.

FrontPage Express

Microsoft ships a WYSIWYG HTML editor with Internet Explorer (and Windows 98). It definitely isn't as good as many of the shareware options, but it's free. Use it until you can't stand it any more and then move up to a better editor (which Microsoft hopes will be FrontPage).

Where's the FrontPage Express help?

If you click the Help button in FrontPage Express, you'll get a total of four pages of HTML help, one of which is an advertisement to buy Microsoft FrontPage. One incentive to buy it, apparently, is that it comes with a real help file.

A review of Microsoft Knowledge Base articles about FrontPage Express provides a little more information, but nothing like what is available for other applications. Maybe no one called in with any questions.

Fortunately, FrontPage Express is a very straightforward WYSIWYG HTML editor. If you know how to use any Microsoft product, it will be clear how to use FrontPage Express. The universal issues of how to create web pages and how to make them look good are addressed very adequately by the many HTML help pages available on the web. For example, you might refer to "A Beginner's Guide to HTML" at www.ncsa.uiuc.edu/General/Internet/WWW/HTMLPrimerAll.html.

There is a FrontPage Express tutorial on the web. It's like any other tutorial on how to create a basic web page, with the added advantage that it uses FrontPage Express as the tool. We found it quite useful, and it looks as though the author is going to add more to it. You'll find it at members.aol.com/mcwebber/fpx/.

IDG Books Worldwide publishes a number of books on web page creation. You can browse through the titles at www.idgbooks.com. The CD-ROM that accompanies *Windows 98 Secrets* includes the outstanding HTML Reference Library in Windows help format (how ironic).

We've always really liked the HTML Reference Library, and now an update is available, as shown in Figure 11-6. It details the implementations of HTML 4.0 under Internet Explorer, Netscape Navigator, and NCSA Mosaic. It covers Cascading Style Sheets, Dynamic HTML, and the scripting object models supported by Netscape and Internet Explorer. It's not a tutorial, and it won't show you how to create web pages, but if you want to know how a specific HTML tag works, this is the place to go.

If you have trouble displaying the HTML Reference Library index, check out hot.virtual-pc.com/htmlib/faq.htm.

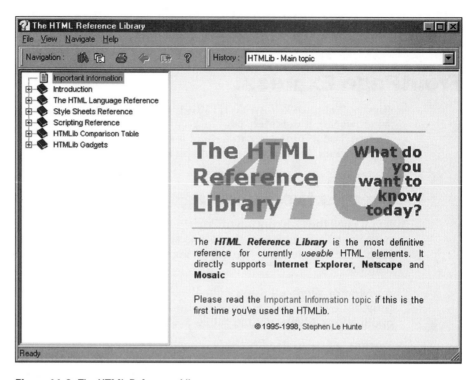

Figure 11-6: The HTML Reference Library.

You'll find the most recent version of the HTML Reference Library at hot.virtual-pc.com/htmlib/.

Steal that web page

One of the best ways to learn how to produce better web pages is to save a web page that you like (click File, Save As and choose Web Page, complete (*.htm, *.html)). The accompanying graphics files will be saved in a subfolder of the folder where you saved the web page. The saved web page will be changed to reference the graphics files in this subfolder, instead of in their original location.

Of course, we assume that you're not going to use the web page for anything other than to learn how to do it yourself. Web pages are copyrighted, but thankfully the web and the Internet are open media, so you can see how someone does something. You can then apply the author's tricks and understanding to your own projects.

Right-click the saved web page, and click Edit. If you've installed FrontPage Express, and haven't changed the default HTML editor to Word or some other editor, then FrontPage Express will start up. If you installed Word 2000 after you installed Windows 98 or Internet Explorer 5.0 with accessories, then the default editor for *htm* or *html* files may be Word. You can of course, change this file association using the various methods that we discuss in Chapter 13 of *Windows 98 Secrets*.

To start FrontPage Express directly, click Start, Programs, Internet Explorer, FrontPage Express.

If the web page that you've saved is quite complicated, it will take a while to be rendered in FrontPage Express. In Figure 11-7, Jesse Berst's Alert web page is displayed in FrontPage Express. This page takes several minutes to display, and any changes you make to it take several minutes more.

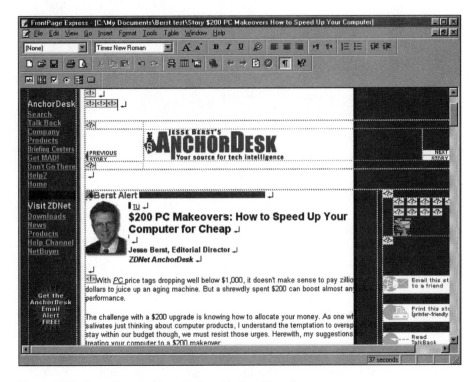

Figure 11-7: Jesse Berst's *Alert,* displayed in FrontPage Express.

You'll also notice the little exclamation points and question marks. FrontPage displays HTML comments of the form <—comment —> as exclamation marks. The question marks indicate <TBODY>, <STYLE>, or <INPUT> HTML tags. <TBODY> is specific to Internet Explorer. You've got to wonder about FrontPage Express if it can't display Microsoft-specific tags.

FrontPage Express won't display a web page that uses frames. Another incentive to move up to Office 2000 Professional.

What is FrontPage Express good for?

Outlook Express is a very capable Internet e-mail client. Those of us who use it don't really spend too much time thinking about the extra power available with Outlook.

On the other hand, FrontPage Express is a limited WYSIWYG web page editor (to say the least). It is not a web site manager like FrontPage, and it can't do all the web page editing that you might want. For example, you will find it difficult to cut and paste text from Word documents into FrontPage Express. Instead of formatted text, we got the RTF formatting tags and plain text, as shown in Figure 11-8. Our editor, on the other hand, got formatted text. Either Microsoft pulled the ability to do this translation automatically when they scaled back FrontPage to FrontPage Express, or there are some other glitches that we are not aware of.

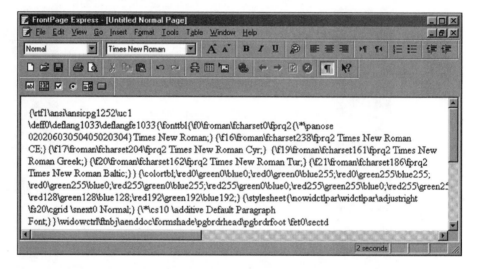

Figure 11-8: The contents of a Word document after being pasted into FrontPage Express. All you see at first are the RTF codes, until you scroll further down.

If you are having the problems that we had with cutting and pasting text from Microsoft Word into FrontPage Express, first copy the text into Notepad. This will eliminate the formatting, and banish all thoughts of RTF. Once you've got the plain text in Notepad, then copy and paste it into your FrontPage Express document.

An even better option is to save a file (a Word file or an Excel file, for example) as an HTML file and then copy the entire contents of the file. Next, click View, HTML in FrontPage Express and paste in the HTML text. This too has limits, though, as there appears to be a size restriction on how much text you can copy in this way.

Another option is to use FrontPage Express to save an empty target file. Next, open it as a plain text file in WordPad or Word, and cut and paste HTML text from a file previously saved in HTML format into it. Later you can open the file in FrontPage Express and continue editing from there.

Two different groups within Microsoft, each with its own agenda, developed Outlook and Outlook Express. Outlook Express didn't come out of Outlook, and the folks working on Outlook had to run hard just to keep up with the folks doing Outlook Express. This is not true for FrontPage Express, which has always been a crippled version of FrontPage. Microsoft wants you to move up.

FrontPage Express is a web page editor of limited means that works just fine to create small web pages. You can copy and paste HTML code directly into it with few problems, as long as the pages are not overly complex.

Get all your files in a row

Web pages go together. Web sites most often consist of a set of HTML files, associated graphics files, and script files. Web pages and their associated files are linked together by references in each web page to the associated files' filenames, including their pathnames. You want to be sure that these pathnames are correct so that when your web page is displayed it shows some pretty pictures and not a bunch of X's.

FrontPage Express keeps track of the pathnames of graphics files that you insert in your web pages. If you're dragging a graphics file from some god-awful corner of your hard disk, the whole absolute pathname is coming with it. If you later move your web pages and graphics files up to a web server, the pathname to this graphics file is going to be wildly inappropriate. If you're not planning to move your web pages, no problem.

A much better idea is to move the files associated with your web pages into the same folder with your web pages, or into a subfolder of the web pages folder. Later, if you move the web pages, you can move them and the subfolders together.

Once you've placed the associated files in the same folder as your web pages, or in a subfolder, then you can drag them into your web pages. The pathnames will work if you later move the web pages because they are relative to your web pages folder.

Any folder can serve as your web pages folder. There are no references in the web pages to the path to this folder unless you specifically enter them.

Tip

FrontPage Express defaults to saving your file in your \Windows folder. This little glitch is one sure sign that Microsoft hasn't placed a lot of emphasis on this program. You can fix this annoying little habit by clicking Start, Programs, Internet Explorer, FrontPage Express. Right-click FrontPage Express, click Properties, and then enter the pathname of your default web pages folder in the Start In field, as shown in Figure 11-9.

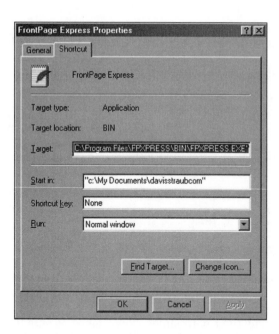

Figure 11-9: Enter the path and folder for saving web pages in the Start In field.

Edit locally or on the web server

FrontPage Express lets you edit your web pages on your own hard disk or on your web server. If you edit the files on your hard disk, you can later move them up to the web server. Web pages that you edit on the server are referenced by their URLs, in contrast to local files, which are accessed by their path and filenames.

The FrontPage Express File Open dialog box, shown in Figure 11-10, gives you the option of entering a filename and path or a URL. Opening a web page in FrontPage Express is the same as reading it, as far as the web server is concerned — so you can access any web page that you like, just as though FrontPage Express were a web browser.

If you click Browse in the Open File dialog box, and then display the Files of Type field (see Figure 11-11), you'll notice that there are a lot of file types listed that FrontPage Express can't actually open. FrontPage can. You just have to ignore anything other than the *txt*, *htt*, and HTML files.

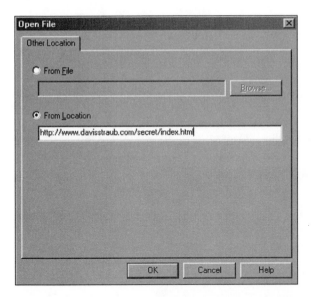

Figure 11-10: Type the document's URL to open it directly from the server.

Figure 11-11: The Files of Type list includes many file types that FrontPage Express cannot open.

Once you've edited or created your web page, you can save it to a file or to a URL on your web server, as shown in Figure 11-12. If you save it to your web server, you will be asked for a user name and password. FrontPage Express uses its underlying web publishing services (the same services that the Web Publishing Wizard uses) to copy the file to your web server.

The Microsoft Knowledge Base article, "Cannot Edit Web Pages on Internet Using FrontPage Express" at support.microsoft.com/support/kb/ articles/q174/9/74.asp states that you can't edit web pages on a web server that you access through a dial-up connection. This article only mentioned Windows 95 and Windows NT 4.0, so perhaps it never did apply to Windows 98. I've been able to edit files on my ISP's web server while connected to it over a 28.8 modem. I have had trouble saving some files to some folders, but perhaps that is due to an incorrect mapping of the URL to the actual path and filename on the server by the underlying web publishing services.

Figure 11-12: Enter a page title and URL to save (publish) your page on the server.

Tip

If you open a file, edit it, and then try to save it, only to get an error message, it may be because the file is marked as Read Only. If the error message is "An error occurred while attempting to write the file," then for sure that's the problem. Click File, Save As and save it to another name.

Edit hypertext templates with FrontPage Express

When you right-click the right-pane of your Explorer and click Customize This Folder, you start a little wizard. If you choose Create or Edit an HTML Document in the first wizard dialog box, the wizard invokes the Notepad editor, which lets you make any changes that you want in the folder.htt file that is about to be placed in the folder. See "Add hot links to your folders" in Chapter 13 for an example of why you might want to customize a folder.

Folder.htt is an HTML template file. This file, in combination with a desktop.ini, file mark a folder as customized. Any changes that you make to the folder.htt file change how the folder looks when viewed as a web page.

Once you've created a folder.htt file, you can change it at any time. Right-click it, click Open With, choose Notepad, and mark Always Use This Program to Open This Type of File. Click OK. These actions will associate Notepad with *htt* files.

Otherwise, you can also drag and drop the file into FrontPage Express, or click File, Open in FrontPage Express and navigate to it to open it.

You can specify FrontPage Express as the default editor for *htt* files. It doesn't
come up as fast as Notepad, but it might offer you a bit more power for
editing. If you've already specified Notepad as the editor of *htt* files, hold
down the Shift key while right-clicking a folder.htt file in your Explorer, click
Open With, mark Always Use This Program to Open This Type of File and
then search for the FrontPage Express executable. (If FrontPage Express isn't
included in the list of executable programs in the Open With dialog box, click
the Other button, and browse for Fpxpress.exe in \Programs Files\FrontPage
Express\bin.) While this will work to make FrontPage Express the default *htt*
file editor, it still won't be called when you start the Customize This Folder
Wizard. To make this association work, take these steps:

STEPS:

Making FrontPage Express the Customizing Folder Editor

Step 1.   In your Explorer, click View, Folder Options, and click the File
Types tab.

Step 2.   Press the H key, and then scroll down to HyperText Template in
the Registered File Types list, as shown in Figure 11-13.

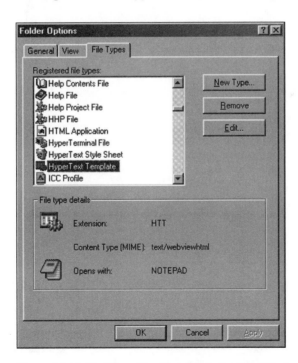

Figure 11-13: Find HyperText Template in the list of file types.

Continued

STEPS

Making FrontPage Express the Customizing Folder Editor

(continued)

Step 3. Highlight HyperText Template and click Edit. Click the New button in the Edit File Type dialog box (see Figure 11-14).

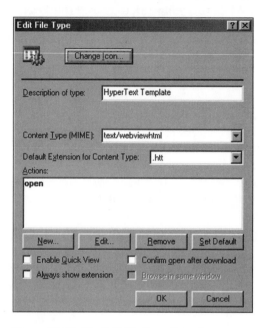

Figure 11-14: The Edit File Type dialog box.

Step 4. In the New Action dialog box, type the word **edit** in the Action field (see Figure 11-15).

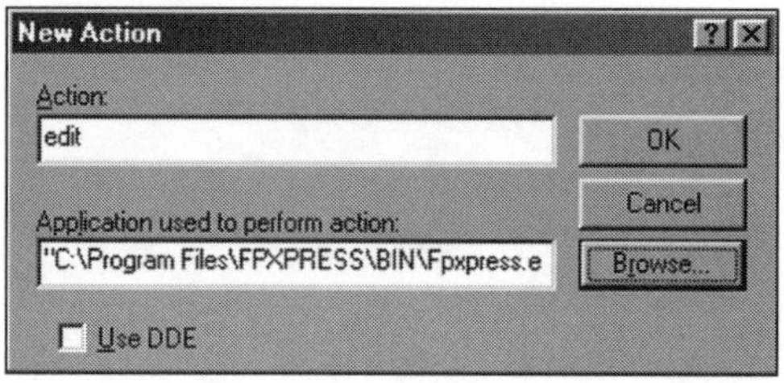

Figure 11-15: The New Action dialog box lets you specify what will happen when you click an *htt* file in the Explorer.

Step 5. Click the Browse button. In the Open With dialog box, browse to and select the FrontPage Express executable file. It's most likely at C:\Program Files\Fpxpress\Bin\Fpxpress.exe. Click Open.

Step 6. Click OK, and click Close twice.

Now when you click Customize This Folder, FrontPage Express will be the editor. In the past, we have experienced problems making FrontPage Express the default editor for *htt* files. However, it may work fine for you. You can always leave Notepad as the editor (or go back into the Edit File Type dialog box and remove *edit* as an action for *htt* files) and then edit these files by opening them with FrontPage Express after they are created.

Heavy duty web site development

FrontPage Express really isn't up to the task of developing sophisticated web sites, so if you're in the web master business you're using a different tool. If you'd like to get a good understanding of web page development tools, especially for sites that use backend relational databases, check out "The Web Tools Review." You'll find it at photo.net/wtr/.

Publishing your pages on the web

Windows 98 provides the tools necessary to get you a presence on the web—maybe not the best tools, but enough to get you going. We give you a few other options here (and there are many more).

Publish on your own web domain

On the web no one knows you're a dog, at least not unless you make it painfully obvious. You can publish all the painful details on your own web site.

Internet service providers have been providing web site hosting to their dial-in accounts for a number of years. It was quite easy for them to add your user name to the end of their World Wide Web address and give you a web address. For example, the Windows Secrets site, which has been up since the release of *Windows 95 Secrets* in August of 1995, was initially under the web address www.halcyon.com/davis/secrets.htm.

Not all Internet service providers offered a web hosting service. MSN was a conspicuous bad example of this lack of service. Other companies decided that there was a business in only providing web hosting (and POP3 e-mail receiving service on the side) without having to go to the considerable expense of providing direct dial-in access ports.

The companies who just wanted to provide web hosting services only needed to provide a web server connected to a fast Internet backbone; they left it up to you to find a way to get on the Internet.

There are now many companies providing web hosting services with all kinds of business models. You can get free web hosting services, which include the insertion of advertising sold by the web hosting company either into or on top of your web page. You can also get cheap web hosting that includes a link to the web hosting service in your web pages.

To find an index of sites that offer free web hosting, go to wsindex. hypermart.net/.

If you are willing to pay, you can get web hosting at all levels of sophistication, from mere HTML page serving to full e-commerce transaction processing, including credit card payment verification.

Web hosting can include a virtual domain name. As one of its services, a web hosting company may interface with InterNIC for you (InterNIC is the organization that provides domain names). Once it has secured your domain name, the web hosting company will make sure that your domain name is associated with your directory on its web server.

Now you'll find the Windows 98 Secrets site at www.davisstraub.com/secrets.

You can find out more about the various web hosting companies, where else, but on the web. Their presentation on the web gives you a pretty good idea of their capabilities. If their own web site is slow, yours will be, too.

You might check out www.pair.com or www.websolo.com, shown in Figure 11-16 — just two examples.

Your own Internet service provider may also be able to match the deals available from dedicated web hosting companies. Check the web page of your own service provider to see what they have available.

Your own dynamic IP address and static domain name

If you dial up your Internet service provider, chances are you are assigned a dynamic IP address from its pool of available addresses. That address is yours for the length of your connection, but as soon as you hang up, your service provider can give the address to someone else. Without a static address, you're a hard man (or woman) to find.

There are a number of ways around this problem. You can set up your web site on a web server that is permanently connected to the Internet with a static address. Your Internet service provider or a dedicated web hosting company can provide this service. Still, this is only an address for your web page, and doesn't give you a static address for NetMeeting, game playing, and other Internet applications. For example, you might need a static address to telnet into a server with a security firewall where you work.

Figure 11-16: The WebSOLO web site.

You can also sign up for DSL with your local telco. You are going to be on 24 hours/day, so they might as well assign you a static IP address.

Another option is to use a *dynamic DNS* service, which takes your current IP address and assigns it to your static domain name. You can then have your clients or friends contact you through the dynamic DNS server using your domain name, which doesn't change. Of course, you have to be online, and your computer has to use an applet to send the server your latest IP address.

Your domain name is unique to the dynamic DNS service, and is not part of the standard Internet domain naming service. The service charges a yearly fee to provide this static-domain-name-to-dynamic-IP address service. ICQ, MSN, and AOL, through their "buddy" systems, all provide the ability to associate your dynamic IP address with your registered name for their format, but they don't provide a domain name that is associated with your dynamic IP address.

You can find this service at TZO at www.tzo.com. Check out their FAQ at www.tzo.com/tzomanual.html.

Microsoft FTP

You can use an FTP client either to access FTP sites, or to access web sites using FTP protocols. This second function lets you see the files making up a web site instead of their HTML content. It is very handy if you are maintaining your own web site.

Microsoft has significantly enhanced the FTP (file transfer protocol) capabilities of the Internet Explorer and partially integrated FTP into the Explorer interface. This has been a long time coming, and we've long since gotten used to other FTP clients that provide much more power than what Microsoft has given us now. Still, we want to be fair about what Microsoft has offered, so that if it meets your needs you won't have to find a third party application.

We wrote about Microsoft FTP late in the process of writing this book, because we kept hoping that the bugs would be driven out of the FTP module and that the capabilities we sought would be added. In the end, we had to write about what was actually there. If you've discovered that Microsoft has made some improvements since we wrote this, please go to our web site to review the updates we've made to our discussion of this capability (www.davisstraub.com/secrets).

Type **ftp.microsoft.com** in your Address toolbar (you are using the Address toolbar, aren't you?), and press Enter or click the Go button. If you're not already online, you soon will be. Up will pop an Internet Explorer window that looks something like the one shown in Figure 11-17.

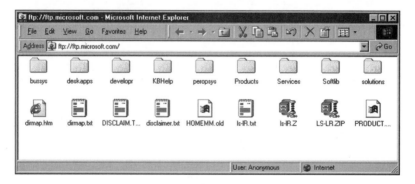

Figure 11-17: The Microsoft FTP window looks a lot like the Explorer.

The Microsoft FTP window gives you a single-pane view of the FTP site. Instead of a web site view, you get a folder view of a remote computer. It's sort of like the classic folder view associated with Windows 95, but now you get a classic view of a remote computer, perhaps even a Unix box.

Right-click the client area of this view and click View, As Web Page, and you'll be rewarded with the FTP server's notice, as shown in Figure 11-18.

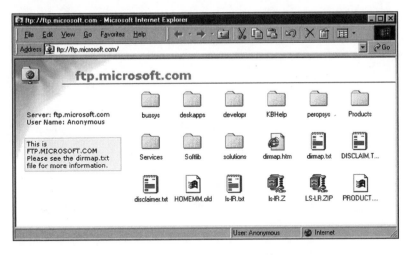

Figure 11-18: You can use web page view with an FTP window, too.

The names of FTP sites don't necessarily start with ftp, just as WWW site names don't necessarily start with www. If you want to invoke the FTP window on your computer, you might have to type **ftp://** before the name of the FTP site.

You can drag and drop files from your Explorer into the FTP folder window. You can't go the other way. You can right-click a file or folder in the FTP folder window, click Copy To Folder, and navigate to the folder that will be the repository of the file or folder you're downloading from the FTP site.

You can turn the FTP folder window into an Explorer view, just by clicking View, Explorer Bar, Folders. The FTP site is treated as a branch of the Internet Explorer, just as a web site would be. Folder icons with globes on them distinguish FTP sites from web sites, as shown in Figure 11-19.

Clicking View, Explorer Bar, Folders does seem to have a bit of a bug; we found that other windows such as My Computer would then open in Explorer view. This wasn't consistent, so it was hard to say what caused it.

The FTP site icons shown in Figure 11-18 are as transient as any web site icons attached to the Internet Explorer icon in the Explorer window. Open up another Explorer window, and you won't find them there at all. Close the first Explorer window and open a new one, and all visual indication of the web sites or FTP sites will be lost (except to the History folder).

If you've got FTP sites that you use all the time (such as your own web site), you won't be able to go back later and find them in the Explorer. To be able to repeatedly access an FTP site, you'll need to create a shortcut to it in the Favorites folder.

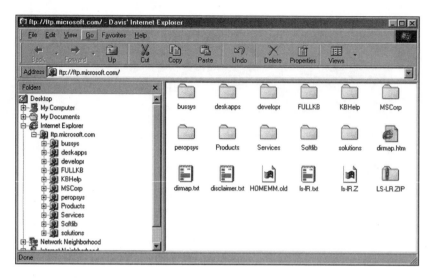

Figure 11-19: The Explorer view can be helpful for navigating around an FTP site.

There are thousands of FTP sites that allow you to download files. They are set up as file repositories, and anyone can log onto them to find the files that they want. Microsoft FTP assumes an anonymous logon when you type in an FTP address, so it will log you onto the site with the user name *anonymous* and the password *yourusername@yourisp.com*.

If you need a personal user name and password to log onto an FTP site, perhaps your own web site, and you try to log on to the site without providing this information, you will be prompted for it. If the FTP site has an area that allows anonymous logon, you will be logged onto that area without being prompted for your user name and password, which would allow you to go to your personal area.

Microsoft FTP will not, of its on accord, save your password for the selected site—although it will remember your user name. Your user name will then be appended to the FTP address and displayed in the Address field.

If you weren't prompted for your user name and password, you can force an FTP logon with your user name and password by choosing File, Login As in the FTP folder window.

Secret

If you want to save your user name and password for an FTP site, you'll need to click Favorites, Add to Favorites, and then save the FTP site in one of your Favorites folders. You might want to create a separate folder under Favorites for FTP sites. You can't right-click the FTP folder window and click Save as Shortcut to save a shortcut on the Desktop. But you can move the shortcut from the Favorites folder or subfolder to the Desktop or wherever you like.

You'll have to add the password to your shortcut. Right-click the shortcut to your FTP site, click Properties, type a colon right after your user name in the URL field, and follow that with your password, as shown in Figure 11-20. Click OK.

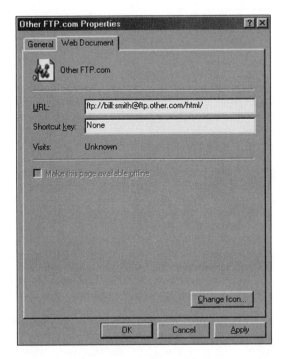

Figure 11-20: Insert your password right after your user name, and before the @ sign

Now whenever you click the shortcut icon, it will log on with your user name and password to the FTP site. Unfortunately, your user name and password are also now quite visible in the Address toolbar of the FTP window.

Internet Neighborhood, an FTP alternative

What's very good about Microsoft's FTP client is that it doesn't look like a client at all. It is integrated right into the Internet Explorer, which is integrated right into the Explorer. You have to learn how to use it, but you don't have to learn a lot.

Internet Neighborhood, from KnoWare, is an attractive alternative to Microsoft's FTP client for the very same reason: It is an extension of the Explorer. This means that the FTP sites hang as branches off the Internet Neighborhood icon in the Explorer, as shown in Figure 11-21. Internet Neighborhood and Microsoft FTP can happily coexist.

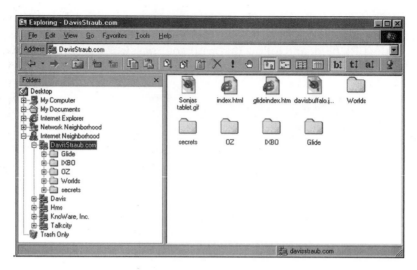

Figure 11-21: FTP sites are displayed under the Internet Neighborhood icon in the left pane; their contents are in the right pane.

Internet Neighborhood FTP icons are static. Once you create a connection to an FTP site, it remains a branch under the Internet Neighborhood icon until you delete it. While you can create shortcuts to the Internet Neighborhood, you can't create shortcuts to the FTP sites that branch off from it.

To access a new FTP site, highlight the Internet Neighborhood icon in the left pane of your Explorer and click FTP Site Wizard in the right pane. Type the name of the FTP site, as shown in Figure 11-22, and the user friendly site name and site description are created automatically. You can specify an initial directory on the remote computer.

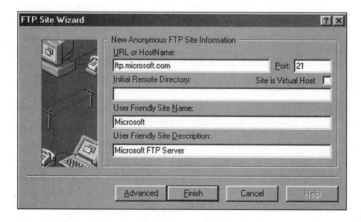

Figure 11-22: Fill out this dialog box in the FTP Site Wizard to add a new site.

You can enter all of the properties associated with an FTP site by clicking the Advanced button in the FTP Site Wizard. You can also change them by right-clicking an FTP site icon, and clicking Properties. The information about your FTP site is stored in the various tabs of the FTP Site Information dialog box, as shown in Figure 11-23.

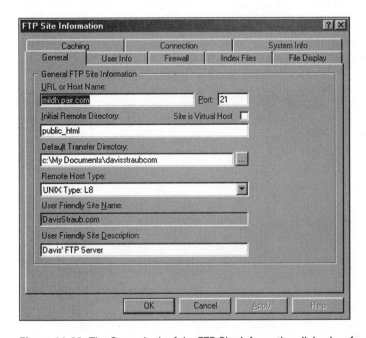

Figure 11-23: The General tab of the FTP Site Information dialog box for a particular web site.

You can drag and drop files and folders in either direction. Sites appear in the Explorer under their user friendly names (not necessarily the combination of FTP site name and initial remote directory). You can set a user name and password for a site, and the password will be hidden behind asterisks. If your FTP site requires an account name, you can enter that also.

If the FTP site maintains an index file of the files at the site, you can specify its filename; the file descriptions will then appear next to the filenames in the Internet Neighborhood Explorer window. You can cache FTP directory listings so that you don't have to go online again to check over the filenames and descriptions. This makes it quite a bit easier to see what files are on the FTP or web site without having to be online at all times.

Internet Neighborhood is also significantly faster then Microsoft's FTP client. Really, you've got to wonder about just who wrote this thing at Microsoft. It works, but it's a dog.

You can download Internet Neighborhood from www.knowareinc.com. Once you install it, be sure to right-click its icon in the Explorer and click Online Help. You can download the help file as a compiled Windows 98 help file. We wonder why this help file doesn't get downloaded in the original file.

Another popular shareware FTP package is WS_FTP. Frankly, we cannot figure out why this package is popular. It does work, which is more than we can say for the Microsoft Web Publishing Wizard (discussed later in this chapter). But relative to many other FTP clients, including Internet Neighborhood, its user interface is very clumsy and way out of date. Strangely, it is often listed as the most popular shareware FTP package, at least as far as the number of downloads are concerned. Hopefully, we can help put an end to that.

FTP between FTP sites

Neither Microsoft's FTP client nor Internet Neighborhood will let you crossload between FTP sites. You have to download to your hard disk first and then upload to another FTP site.

Not everyone needs to move files between FTP sites, but if you do need this ability it's great to have a tool that can accomplish the task. Flash FXP is just the tool for the job. In the example in Figure 11-24, we've copied disclaimer.txt from ftp.microsoft.com to davisstraub.com.

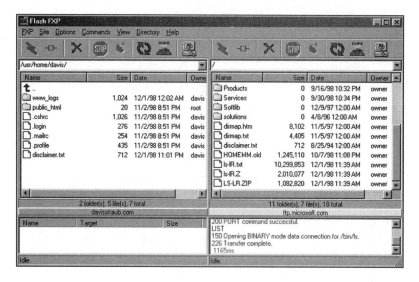

Figure 11-24: In this illustration, disclaimer.txt appears in the directories for both FTP sites.

To use Flash FXP, click Site, Site Manager, New. Enter the FTP site's name, address, your user name and password if necessary, the complete pathname of any folder on the remote computer in which you want to start, and the local folder for downloading. Click Save. Do this for two sites. Double-click each site name in the Site Manager, and you're connected to both.

You can download Flash FXP from free.prohosting.com/~flash/. It's donationware.

FTP here and there

We didn't get a chance to use this tool, unlike all the others that we've reviewed in this book, because we found out about it when our book was almost at the printer's. We wanted to mention it so that you could take a look at it. Why? Because it supports FTP both between your computer and FTP sites on the Internet, and between FTP sites.

You'll find Cupertino at members.xoom.com/CupertinoFTP/.

Thanks to Christopher Nye for finding it.

Web Publishing Wizard

The Web Publishing Wizard is a front end to some of the Windows 98 FTP functions (Start, Programs, Accessories, Internet Tools, Web Publishing Wizard). FrontPage Express uses these same functions to upload files to the web server. If you feel comfortable using the Microsoft FTP client or a third party FTP client, then we suggest ignoring the Web Publishing Wizard.

One function that the Web Publishing Wizard tries to carry out undercover is translation from an HTTP address to an FTP address. For example, to copy a file to your web site, you only have to give the HTTP address of the web site (see Figure 11-25), and the FTP address will be substituted. Sometimes this works, and sometimes it doesn't.

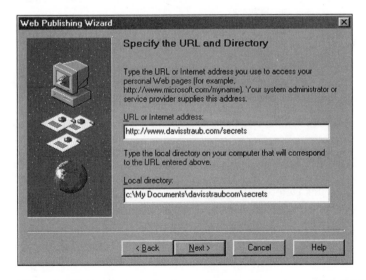

Figure 11-25: You don't need to know the FTP address to use Web Publishing Wizard.

Of course, the Web Publishing Wizard is a one way deal. You can't use it to delete files from your FTP site or web site. You also can't use it to see what files are up on the site. Sort of like the Wizard of OZ when it comes to packing much of a punch.

Once you've put in an address that doesn't work out, there is no user friendly way to get rid of it. You'll need to use your Registry editor if you want to get rid of an old or incorrect URL. Here's how:

STEPS:

Deleting Old URLs in Your Web Publishing Wizard

Step 1. Start your Registry editor.

Step 2. Navigate to HKEY_USERS\ .Default\ Software\ Microsoft\ WebPost\ Sites. Double-click this key in the left pane of your Registry editor.

Step 3. You'll notice a number of keys under this key. Each of these keys is a placeholder for an FTP or web site address (see Figure 11-26).

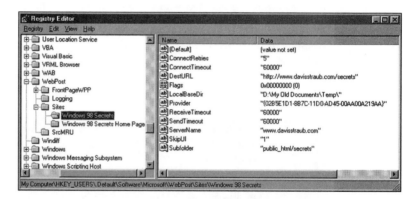

Figure 11-26: Navigate to the key for an FTP or web site, and you can see the URLs that the Web Publishing Wizard has associated with the site.

Step 4. To delete old or incorrect addresses, right-click the key corresponding to the old or incorrect address in the left pane and click Delete.

Step 5. To change the FTP or web server name, right-click the corresponding key and click Rename. To change a URL, double-click DestURL in the right pane. To change a subfolder of the URL, double-click Subfolder in the right pane.

The Web Publishing Wizard really is a weak sister, but it's usable once you get the addresses correctly entered and at least one file copied to the FTP site or web site. A major problem is that the wizard won't record your server setup information until you've successfully transferred at least one file. It can be quite frustrating restarting the wizard time after time, trying to figure out what went wrong.

One way around this, assuming that you've created at least one successful connection, is to export the key of the successful site from your Registry, and then re-import it under a new key name. You can then edit the key to try different addresses until you get it to work. All in all, it's not worth the effort given the power of other tools.

Tip

If you are using the Web Publishing Wizard and having problems, try not typing the name of a folder on the server when prompted to enter one. The server side software should be able to determine the correct folder name from your user name and password. If you are logging in as anonymous, then do enter a folder name if you want to navigate to that subfolder.

Web Folders

Starting with Internet Explorer 5, Microsoft added Web Folders as a special folder type in your Explorer. You can use this folder to store subfolders, which are connections to your web servers. Unfortunately, the web servers must support the FrontPage extensions if they are going to work with Web Folders. Web servers that are only accessible through FTP will not do it.

You can get the latest word about how to install and use these folders in "How to Install and Use Web Folders in Internet Explorer" at support.microsoft.com/support/kb/articles/q195/8/51.asp.

All in one Internet tool box

There is one nifty little tool that we use all the time to check up on our Internet and local TCP/IP connections. It's called NetInfo, and it's free.

NetInfo is a collection of standard Internet and TCP/IP utilities. You get Ping, Trace, Finger, and more, all in one window. Just click the tabs to switch among them (see Figure 11-27). In the Ping tab, type in the IP address or server name and click Start to ping a server.

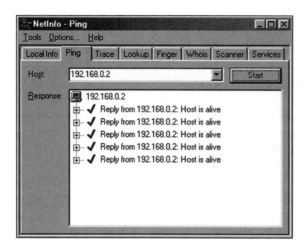

Figure 11-27: You can use NetInfo to ping a server and see if it responds.

You'll find NetInfo at www.netinfo.co.il. Be sure to check out its FAQ page.

Summary

Use Microsoft FTP to upload web pages to your web server.

▶ Prettify or compress your HTML files with third party add-on.

▶ Use FrontPage Express to edit files on your computer or directly on the web server, even if you only have dial-up access to the server.

▶ Set yourself up on the web with your own web domain name.

▶ Use Internet Neighborhood, a third party add-on, to turn your Explorer into an FTP client as well.

Part II

Local Secrets

Chapter 12

The Desktop

In This Chapter

Internet Explorer 5 brings new powers to the Desktop. This chapter is long, because the Desktop is the user interface for Windows, so there are lots of changes possible here. The Desktop includes the Desktop itself, the toolbars, the Taskbar, and the Start menu. We also discuss screen savers and sharing your Desktop with others.

▶ Remove the blocks of color behind the names of your Desktop icons.

▶ If you want to change just about anything on your Desktop or Start menu, use WinBoost. It's safer, easier, and more powerful than simple Registry edits.

▶ Make it easy to get to your Find by putting it in the Quick Launch toolbar.

▶ Hide Start menu items without using any shareware.

▶ Resort your Start menu items.

Make your Desktop yours

The Windows 98 Desktop is pretty darn flexible. We show you plenty of ways to change it in Chapters 6 and 28 of *Windows 98 Secrets*, and we show you a few more here. If you want to throw the whole thing out and start again, we show you how to replace the entire Desktop.

Change the automatic font color

Secret

One of the Desktop changes that we detail in Chapter 28 of *Windows 98 Secrets* also makes a change in your other programs. Right-click your Desktop, click Properties, and click the Appearance tab. In the Item field, scroll down to and highlight Window. You can now set the Fonts color. It is defaulted to black.

This item changes the color of the fonts used in windows. Since Windows uses windows all the time, this is a pretty major change. In addition to changing the font color used in the system windows (Windows 98 windows), programs that use the "automatic" font color use this setting to determine their default font color.

You can check this out by changing the Windows font color, and then opening WordPad (Start, Programs, Accessories, WordPad). You'll see that the default font color (that is, the color of the characters you type in the WordPad client window) is the color that you just chose. In WordPad, you can choose another color than the default. This is true in some other programs as well, but not in Notepad. In Notepad, the font in a new document automatically has the new color, and you can't change it.

Unstretch that wallpaper

Secret

Numerous Windows 98 users have reported trouble getting their wallpaper to stretch, center, or tile. Usually the Background tab of the Display Properties dialog box (right-click your Desktop, click Properties) has a Display drop-down list in the lower-right corner. Some users don't have this drop-down list.

Dialog boxes are often just user front ends to the Registry. If you don't have this particular front end, you can make the changes in the Registry yourself.

STEPS:

Setting Wallpaper to Center, Tile, or Stretch

Step 1. Start your Registry editor and navigate to HKEY_CURRENT_USER\ Control Panel\desktop, as shown in Figure 12-1.

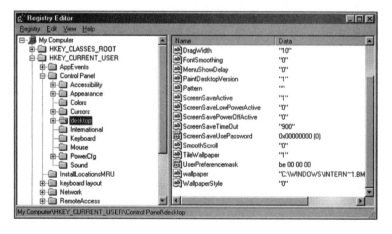

Figure 12-1: The Registry location for changing your wallpaper style.

Step 2. Double-click the WallpaperStyle variable in the right pane of the Registry editor.

Step 3. Change the value to 0 for centered nonstretched wallpaper, 1 for tiles, or 2 for stretched. Click OK, and then close the Registry editor.

Thanks to Penelope Baker for pointing us toward this secret.

Animate your Desktop

You can place animated *gif* files on your Desktop and let them play over and over and over again. Animated *gif* files are graphics files that contain multiple images that are displayed one after another to simulate motion. You can create animated *gif* files with Paint Shop Pro. You'll find the latest version at www.jasc.com. You can also use the GIF Construction Set found at www.mindworkshop.com/alchemy/gifcon.html.

To allow your Desktop to play animated *gif* files, you need to take the following steps:

STEPS:

Putting Animated GIFs on Your Desktop

Step 1. Right-click your Desktop, and choose Active Desktop, Customize My Desktop.

Step 2. In the Web tab, mark View My Active Desktop As a Web Page.

Step 3. Click the New button, and then click No.

Step 4. In the New Active Desktop Item dialog box, click the Browse button and navigate to an animated *gif* file, as shown in Figure 12-2. We're assuming that you have already stored this file on your computer or network. Click the Open button. Click OK. Click OK.

Step 5 Move your mouse pointer over the animated *gif*, and when the gray title bar appears, drag it to move the *gif* window to the desired spot on the Desktop.

Continued

STEPS

Putting Animated GIFs on Your Desktop *(continued)*

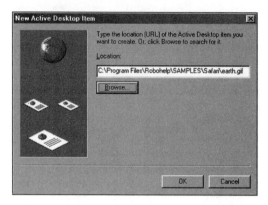

Figure 12-2: Type the name and path of the *gif* file that you want to put on your Desktop.

Thanks to Mike Adams for help with this tip.

Your Active Desktop doesn't find its content

Secret

If you're using the Active Desktop, and your ActiveX components or on-the-Desktop web page don't show up when you first turn on your computer, it's probably because they're waiting to see if there's an update. They want to go check on the Internet to see if newer information is available. If there isn't a connection to the Internet, they're standing around waiting.

You probably want them to update the Active Desktop based on what's stored in the Internet Explorer cache, since you haven't made the connection to the Internet yourself. You'll have to make a change in the Internet Explorer configuration to get the Explorer to find its Active Desktop content. Here's how:

STEPS:

Waking Up Your Active Desktop

Step 1.   Right-click the Internet Explorer icon on the Desktop, click Properties, and then click the Connections tab.

Step 2. Make sure the correct dial-up connection is highlighted as the default in the Dial-Up Settings list (see Figure 12-3). To change the default, click the name of the dial-up connection in the list, and then click the Set Default button.

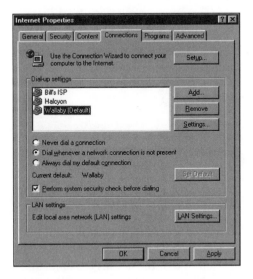

Figure 12-3: Set the dial-up connection that you want to use as the default, if necessary.

Step 3. Mark either Always Dial My Default Connection or Dial Whenever a Network Connection Is Not Present. Click OK.

Get rid of unattached Desktop icons

Secret

If you have icons on your Desktop that you can't get rid of, there is still hope for you yet. We're not talking about My Documents, My Computer, Network Neighborhood, and the Recycle Bin. You can use TweakUI, and click the My Desktop tab to take the Recycle Bin and the Network Neighborhood icons off the Desktop. We discuss how to deal with all of these icons in topics throughout this book and in *Windows 98 Secrets*.

No, we mean icons that got there when you installed a piece of software, and didn't go away when you deleted it. If right-clicking the icons and clicking Delete doesn't work, and you can't see what is creating them, then we've got a spot in the Registry where you might just find them.

Open up your Registry editor and navigate to HKEY_LOCAL_MACHINE\ SOFTWARE\ Microsoft\ Windows\ CurrentVersion\ explorer\ Desktop\ NameSpace. There you'll find a set of Class IDs, as shown in Figure 12-4.

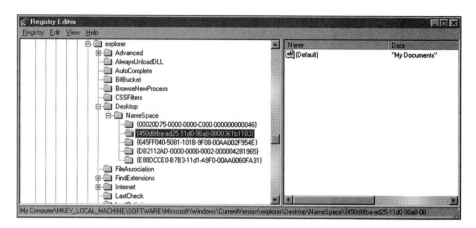

Figure 12-4: The Registry location of the NameSpace Class IDs.

Highlight NameSpace in the left pane, and click Registry, Export Registry File. Enter the name for this text backup of this branch, perhaps **NameSpace**, and click Save. If later you delete something that you'd rather not have deleted, you can get it back by importing this file.

You can highlight each one of these Class IDs and see if there is a corresponding application name displayed in the right pane. If there is a name that corresponds to the software that has been deleted from your computer, you can highlight the Class ID and then delete it.

If you have installed Outlook 98, it has a Class ID in the NameSpace for its Desktop icon (the Class ID starts with 00020D75) but no name in the right pane.

If you're considering deleting a Class ID and want to search first to see if there are other instances of it in the Registry, you can do that. If you want to find all the instances quickly, use Registry Crawler, as discussed in "Crawl through the Registry" in Chapter 14.

If you find other instances of this Class ID, you can see if they refer to program executables that are now deleted. If so, you can delete these branches of the Registry.

Deleting the Class IDs from the NameSpace will delete the icons from the Desktop.

Thanks to Alex Nichol for pointing out this secret.

Change My Documents

The My Documents folder (irrespective of its actual name) is a special folder used by Windows 98 as the likely target for storing your files when you open up a File Save dialog box. Of course, you can subdivide this folder into subfolders that reflect documents of particular types, subject matter, or whatever.

Windows 98 puts a My Documents folder icon on your Desktop, giving you a handy way to get to your documents. It's actually a special type of shortcut, called a *shell extension shortcut*, that points to the My Documents folder. Some of you may find this additional Desktop icon a bit annoying, and feel that Microsoft is pushing you to organize your documents in a manner that doesn't match your predilections.

You can do a few things to turn this capability into something more comfortable. It is cool that the operating system wants to help you get to your documents quickly. However, it would be nicer if it did it your way.

Secret

The first change you might make is to rename your My Documents folder. We discuss this more in the next section. Just right-click your C:\My Documents icon in your Explorer under your boot drive letter designator (not on the Desktop), click Rename, and give it a new name.

To check that the special folder once called My Documents has a new name, right-click the My Documents folder icon on your Desktop, click Properties, and find the new name of the folder in the Target field (see Figure 12-5). Now you can also change the name of the My Documents folder icon on the Desktop; just right-click it and click Rename, and enter a new name.

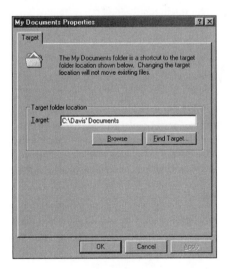

Figure 12-5: After renaming the My Documents folder, its new name appears in the Target field of the Properties dialog box for the My Documents icon on the Desktop.

You may find that some existing shortcuts to documents in your My Documents folder no longer work, but you can edit them to use the new path and filename. Also, previous document paths inside of Word won't work, so you'll have to browse for the previously opened files that were stored in the My Documents folder when it was named My Documents.

You may now want to remove the My Documents icon (or its renamed version) from your Desktop by right-clicking it and clicking Remove from Desktop. Once this icon is gone, you can still use TweakUI to change the name and/or location of your My Documents folder, as shown in Figure 12-6.

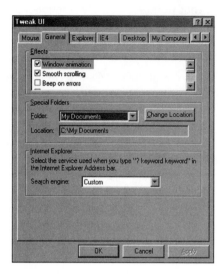

Figure 12-6: Use the Change Location button in the General tab of TweakUI to move My Documents.

Tip

Instead of renaming your existing My Documents folder, you can choose to designate another folder as your My Documents folder. Use either TweakUI or the My Documents folder icon on your Desktop. Just give either of them the name of your newly designated My Documents folder. (Use the Change Location button in TweakUI, or the Target field in the Properties dialog box for the My Documents folder icon.) You can then delete the former My Documents folder in your Explorer. Be sure to move any document files from it first and put them in your newly designated My Documents folder, whatever its actual name.

If you have a problem connecting the My Documents Desktop icon to your new My Documents folder, see the fix in "My Documents Desktop icon doesn't work" later in this chapter.

Rename the Recycle Bin

Secret

You can rename the Recycle Bin icon on your Desktop (although you can't rename the Recycle Bin icons in your Explorer). To change its name, take these steps, or see the end of this section if you want to accomplish the same thing with TweakUI:

STEPS:

Renaming the Recycle Bin

Step 1.   Start your Registry editor.

Step 2.   Press Ctrl+F and type **645FF040**. Click Find Next.

Step 3.   Click the plus sign next to 645FF040, and highlight ShellFolder in the left pane of the Registry editor.

Step 4.   Double-click Attributes in the right pane. In the Edit Binary Values dialog box, press the Delete key once, and type **7** (see Figure 12-7). Click OK.

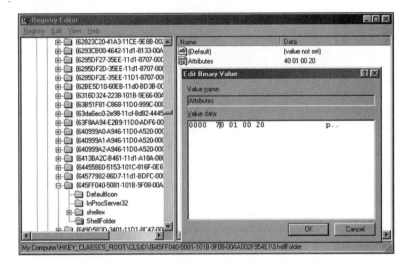

Figure 12-7: Add the numeral 7 to the other numerals in the Value Data box to match what you see here.

Step 5.   Highlight 645FF040, double-click Default in the left pane of your Registry editor, and type a new name for your Recycle Bin, as shown in Figure 12-8. Click OK.

Step 6.   Leaving the Registry editor open, click your Desktop, and press F5. Check to be sure that the new name appears under the trash can icon.

Continued

Renaming the Recycle Bin *(continued)*

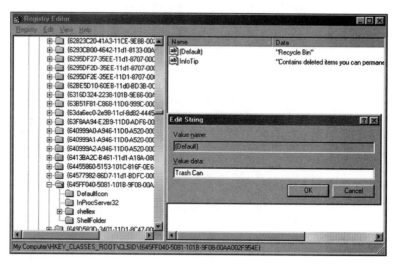

Figure 12-8: Type the new name for your Recycle Bin in the Value Data field of the Edit String dialog box.

Step 7. Highlight ShellFolder in the left pane of your Registry editor, double-click Attributes in the right pane, press the Delete key once, and type **4**. Click OK, and close the Registry editor.

You have to change the Attributes value to 70 01 00 20 to be allowed to rename the Recycle Bin. Once you've renamed it, you have to change the value back to 40 01 00 20 to keep it from being changed accidentally in the future.

Thanks to Roy Ballew for help with this secret.

You can also use TweakUI to rename the Recycle Bin. Click the TweakUI icon in your Control Panel, click the Desktop tab, scroll down to the Recycle Bin icon, right-click it, click Rename, and type a new name. Then click OK. The icon name will update as soon as you activate the Desktop.

Altered icons

Scrows Icons is a very cool web site for finding icons to replace those that come standard with Windows 98. We thought you'd get a kick out of the slightly altered standard icons, as shown in Figure 12-9.

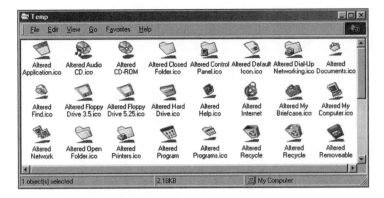

Figure 12-9: No need to use the same old boring icons.

You'll find these icons and many more at members.xoom.com/scrows/. You can edit the icons using a shareware program such as Microangelo (www.impactsoft.com) or Microsoft's Image Editor at msdn.microsoft.com/ developer/sdk/sdktools.htm (you'll have to download the whole set of SDK tools).

An icon library that includes Macintosh icon conversion

IconShop is a wonderful icon library generator that is free, small (only 31K to download), and fast. Better yet, it can convert Macintosh icons so that you can use them on Windows computers. To use IconShop, you can just drag and drop a file or folder onto its client window. The icons extracted from the file (or from the files within the folder) will be displayed, as shown in Figure 12-10. You can then save them to an icon library.

Like most icon library generators, IconShop can get bogged down if you try to extract thousands of icons at once. We suggest that you create only a few icon libraries by being selective about which folders you drop on the IconShop window.

You'll find Macintosh icons on the web, just search for *mac icons*. You also might try www.iconfactory.com.

Mac icons often come packed in StuffIt (*sit*) and/or BinHex (*hqx*) format. WinZip can handle *hqx* files, but not *sit* files. You'll need another expander for these. Download the free Aladdin Expander for Windows from www.aladdinsys.com/expander/expander_win.html. To expand your downloaded Mac icons, simply drop them in Expander's client window.

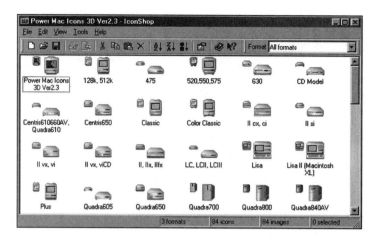

Figure 12-10: IconShop displaying Macintosh icons in All Formats mode, which displays both 16 x16 and 32 x 32 icons. Only if both sizes of icons are available in the source file are both formats displayed.

When you first run Aladdin, it asks if it should be the application associated with a number of extensions. You can clear all these extensions and still have it open *sit* files. The Aladdin Expander defaults don't work. Follow the instructions in the IconShop help file (found in the index under *mac icons*) to set up the Expander to correctly expand the Macintosh icons.

Tip

Aladdin also has a shareware product, Aladdin DropStuff, that makes it easy to compress and send files back and forth from a Windows computer to a Macintosh. You'll find it at www.digitalriver.com/AladdinDSWin10/Win. It's a mere $15.00.

Once you've expanded the Macintosh icon files, they show up as folders in your Explorer. Drag and drop the top folder to IconShop, and then save the icons in an icon library.

You can also use IconShop with the Mac icons found at iconJam 98. This web site represents collaboration among icon designers. It also contains lots of links to other Mac icon sites. You'll find iconJam 98 at www.iconplanet.com/iconjam98/. To download the icons, go to www.iconplanet.com/iconplaneticons/zip/iconJAM98.zip. Notice that they are compressed using the Zip format.

Thanks to Chris Pirillo at www.lockergnome.com for pointers to a few of these sites.

Remove the block of color behind the names of your Desktop icons

If you are using wallpaper as the background of your Desktop, you'll no doubt notice that there is a rectangular block of color behind the icon's name. Annoying, isn't it? Well, if you aren't using wallpaper, or if it doesn't annoy you, you might as well go onto the next section.

Not sure just what we are talking about? Check out Figure 12-11. Obviously, the Desktop icon on the left has the colored background, and the one on the right doesn't. You can change the appearance of your icons with a little (and we mean really little) freeware program called Transparent. This tool gives you a surprising amount of control over just how you want your icon names to look. It comes in four versions (all 25K in size). TransparentW.exe makes the icon text white, TransparentB.exe makes the text black, TransparentD.exe lets you set the icon text color, and Transparent.exe lets you use a slew of command line switches.

Figure 12-11: Transparent lets you make your Desktop icons look like the one on the right.

The easiest thing to do is extract the four files from the downloaded Transparent zip file into a temporary folder, move the one that you want to use to your \Program Files\Accessories folder, and then drag this file from the Accessories folder to your \Windows\Start Menu\Programs\StartUp folder. Because it's an *exe* file, you won't move the file to the StartUp folder; you'll create a shortcut there.

Click the Transparent file after you have moved it to your \Program Files\Accessories folder and it will immediately take effect. From now on, when you restart Windows it will be called from the StartUp folder. It takes up very little memory and CPU resources.

You'll find Transparent at www.pobox.com/~jayguerette/transparent.

Get rid of the ToolTips in caption buttons

The caption buttons are the three buttons in the upper-right corner of a window — minimize, maximize, close. So, if you already know what those buttons do, do you need to be reminded again?

If not, click TweakUI in your Control Panel, click the General tab, scroll down the Effects list, and clear the Mouse Hot Tracking Effects check box.

Write notes right on your Desktop (sort of)

Take a look at Figure 12-12 and see how the text and the surrounding blue line are right there on the Desktop. Well, it looks that way anyway.

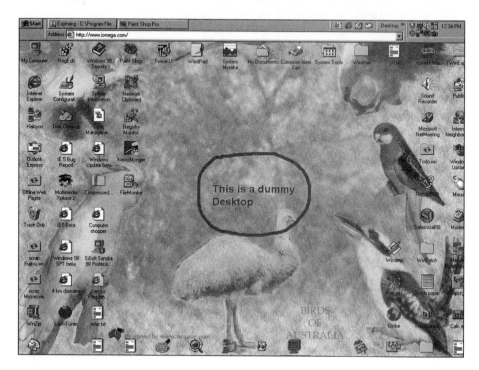

Figure 12-12: A sticky note without the paper.

Screeble (screen + scribble, get it?) takes a shot of your Desktop and then places it right over the Desktop. Now you can paint and type on the Screeble screen. Right-click and click Exit to get back to your Desktop.

You'll find Screeble at village.infoweb.ne.jp/~tek/

Tweaking the Windows 98 Desktop

We mentioned WinBoost in Chapter 2 because it allows you to change the name of the Internet Explorer (as displayed on its title bar) to whatever you like. WinBoost can do quite a bit more damage to your orthodox Windows 98 user interface, if you like things your way (see Figure 12-13).

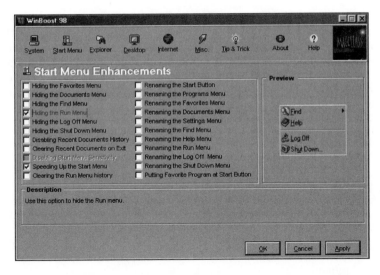

Figure 12-13: The Start Menu Enhancements screen in WinBoost gives you a good idea of its potential for changing things to suit yourself.

The enormous range of tricks the authors of WinBoost have found to tweak Windows 98 is too great to summarize, but here are a few examples of what you can do:

■ Hide, disable, or rename various parts of the Start menu, such as Recent Documents (if you don't want people to see the documents you've recently worked on), Favorites, Find, Run, Log Off, and Shut Down.

■ Rename the Start button.

■ Place a variety of cascading menus on your Start menu, including the contents of Control Panel, Printers, Network Neighborhood, Recycle Bin, My Computer, Fonts, and Briefcase.

■ Customize your CD-ROM cache memory (in ways you can't with the Control Panel).

■ Optimize your file system for running multimedia applications.

You can also make your Explorer refresh with each change, view non-associated files with Notepad, and change the Internet Explorer animated logo.

After you've experimented with WinBoost's various productivity improvements, you can play with one of its "non-productivity" enhancements, a way to cheat at the MS Hearts game included with Windows 98.

In the tips and tricks list, the authors of WinBoost show that Microsoft apparently started to implement something called a DeskBar, but then crippled the feature before shipping Windows 98. To see this undocumented feature, click Start, Settings. While holding down your Ctrl key, click Taskbar & Start Menu. In the Taskbar Properties dialog box that appears, you'll see a new DeskBar Options tab. If you click it, however, you'll see that the tab is empty and there is no way to change any settings.

WinBoost 1.24 is a 1.2MB download from the Magellass Corp. at www.magellass.com/main.html. It has a 10-day trial period, after which the product is $15 per user or $145 for a site license.

Yet another little tweaker can be found at www.windows-help.net/wtt/. Not as powerful or extensive as WinBoost, Tweaking Toolbox for Windows does give you a couple of extra options (see Figure 12-14). For example, you can get rid of some options in the Display Properties dialog box, remove the File System and Virtual Memory buttons from the Performance tab of the System Properties dialog box, edit MS-DOS mode options, and get rid of the Users control panel.

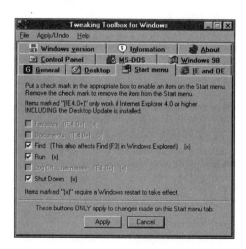

Figure 12-14: The Start Menu tab of Tweaking Toolbox for Windows. Compare its features with those of WinBoost in Figure 12-13.

Virtual desktops with Desktop Plus

It's hard to get everything on a 15-inch screen, especially when you have multiple applications open. You can press Alt+Tab, you can click the Taskbar buttons, or you can set up *virtual desktops* (as though yours wasn't virtual to begin with).

Desktop Plus lets you set up to nine virtual desktops (see Figure 12-15). You can switch between them via hot keys, the Desktop Plus floating toolbar, shortcuts (on the Desktop, Start menu, or Quick Launch toolbar), or icons in your system tray.

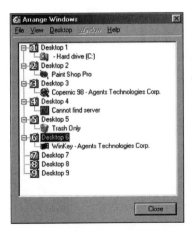

Figure 12-15: Use the Arrange Windows dialog box in Desktop Plus to determine what will be on each of the nine virtual desktops.

You'll find Desktop Plus, where else, but at www.desktopplus.com.

TweakUI, the Desktop, and the Control Panel

TweakUI allows you to eliminate extra icons from the Desktop and the Control Panel. It's not particularly hard to do this, and not particularly secret either. But, once you removed some items from these areas, you might forget about the functionality that you've lost. Just a warning.

There are plenty of good reasons to remove icons from the Desktop and Control Panel. For example, the Windows 98 Service Pack 1 adds the Universal Serial Bus icon to your Control Panel, even if you don't have USB installed on your computer. It's kind of irritating to have this useless icon reminding you of its uselessness every time you open up your Control Panel.

To remove any item from the Control Panel (and easily put it back), click the TweakUI icon (for example, in your Control Panel), and then scroll over to and click the Control Panel tab. Clear the check boxes next to any Control Panel items that you'd rather not see for now, as shown in Figure 12-16.

The Desktop icons get similar treatment. Click the Desktop tab to display a list of the icons that TweakUI thinks are available to the Desktop. The only problem is that TweakUI may find some that are out of date, or doubles of the same one (see Figure 12-17). Don't worry about these discrepancies. Just clear and mark the check boxes in this dialog box (and click the Apply button) until you see what you want on your Desktop. You can also use TweakUI to fiddle around a bit with the Desktop icons. Right-click any of the items in the Desktop tab to see what you can do. You might rename the Recycle Bin, for example.

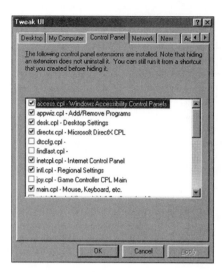

Figure 12-16: The Control Panel tab of TweakUI lets you easily remove and replace Control Panel icons.

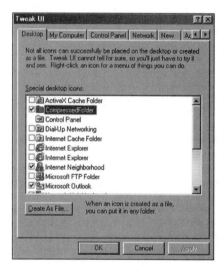

Figure 12-17: In this example, TweakUI displays two copies of Internet Explorer — we've cleared both.

Remember that removing the Network Neighborhood icon from the Desktop removes the associated functionality (why, Microsoft?) from the Explorer also.

Replace the Explorer shell

Would you like to try a different user interface? Something without shortcuts on the Desktop? Perhaps multiple Desktops? Maybe a pop-up Start menu? X mouse?

You can easily replace the Windows 98 Explorer shell (or Desktop or user interface) with any other shell that folks have a mind to create. The LiteStep development team developed a freeware shell that resembles AFTERSTEP, a Linux shell. It uses a vertical bar called the Wharf to dock your application icons (see Figure 12-18), and a Taskbar to hold your system tray and active task buttons (see Figure 12-19). By default, the Wharf is on the right side of the Desktop, and the Taskbar is at the bottom.

Figure 12-18: Litestep's Wharf holds application icons.

Figure 12-19: Litestep's Taskbar holds active tasks as well as the system tray.

Right-click one of the squares at the bottom of the Wharf to switch from virtual desktop to virtual desktop. Click an icon on the Wharf to reveal additional program icons. Right-click anywhere on the desktop to get an expanded version of the Start menu (called the PopUp menu).

All of your Windows 98 resources are available (other than the shell), so you can invoke an Explorer window, get to the Control Panel, call any of your applications, and so on. When you install LiteStep, it finds all of the shortcuts on your existing Start menu and puts them on its PopUp menu.

Unfortunately, LiteStep doesn't search your Desktop for shortcuts and add them to the Wharf. And the Wharf includes plenty of icons for software that you may not have on your computer. In addition, we found that the Wharf kept moving over to the left and not sticking to the right edge of the screen. To edit the Wharf, you need to edit the text file Step.rc, unless a user friendly utility has been developed recently.

To install LiteStep, extract the zip file that you download from www.litestep.net into the C:\litestep folder (you'll need to create this folder first). We tried to put it into C:\Program Files\litestep, but even after editing the LiteStep resource file (Step.rc) we couldn't get LiteStep to start from this folder.

You also need to edit your System.ini file in your \Windows folder. The required editing is simple. Just put a semicolon (;) at the beginning of the line *shell=Explorer.exe*, and type the following line after this line: **shell=c:\ litestep\litestep.exe**. Save your System.ini file and restart Windows.

If you get an error message that says you have to reinstall Windows, don't panic. Just click OK, and restart your computer. Hold down the Ctrl key during power-on self test to bring up the Windows 98 Startup menu, press 5, and then press Enter to go to the DOS command prompt. Change directories to your \Windows directory (type **cd\Windows** and press Enter). At the DOS prompt, type **edit system.ini** and press Enter. You can now remove the semicolon in front of the line *shell=Explorer.exe* and place one in front of *shell=c:\litestep\litestep.exe*. Save System.ini and restart Windows. This changes your user interface (shell) back to the Windows 98 Explorer interface.

Want to change the look of the Explorer title bar? You'll find eFX, which lets you do just that, at www.litestep.net. This site also offers lots of other utilities to change the look of your LiteStep (and standard) interface.

Turn your PC into a Mac over the Internet

Just for fun, check out www.yaromat.com/macos/index.htm. We don't tell you what to expect there because that would spoil the fun. It won't hurt.

If you really do want to make your Windows 98 computer look a lot more Mac-like (and why not), download some of the icons and other things that you'll find at members.xoom.com/macos98/. This will make those of you who have switched from the Mac to the dark side a bit more comfortable with your choice. Sort of like old home week.

Some folks didn't like the iMac, so they created the iHate iMac site. You can download their iMac Recycle Bin icon and Desktop from www.iamlost.com/ imac.

Replace the Explorer shell with the Macintosh interface

If you are interested in using the Macintosh user interface on your Windows 98 computer, you might want to give the freeware MacVision a try. It transforms your Desktop and your Taskbar into the Macintosh desktop and Finder bar. Here's what the MacVision web site claims:

The MacOS Finder Bar — MacVision is very useful, since it can replace your taskbar! Instead of using the old Windows Taskbar, you can use its fully functional MacOS Finder bar (The bar at the top of the screen on MacOS computers) that has dynamic menus that change with every application. Every aspect of the Finder Bar is emulated with great attention to detail — everything looks, works, and acts how it should in Macs, right down to the flickering of the menu items when selected on custom made MacOS-style menus!

That's just what it did. The author keeps improving it and is working on a MacOS 8.5 version.

You'll find MacVision at members.aol.com/JMB1984/MacVision. Thanks to Chris Pirillo at www.lockergnome.com for telling us about it.

Feeling frustrated?

Has Windows 98 got you down? Share it with others who are probably in the same mood at www.ihatewindows98.com/frames/.

Pretty much just a long list of rants from the little people, but there are some fun parts (and we wish there were more). Any site with the word *hate* in the name is going to have a tough time being "light." Then, for some folks this is a religious issue.

Toolbars and the Taskbar

The Taskbar and the little toolbars that sit on the Desktop can absorb quite a few of the Desktop functions. They give you a way to get things off the Desktop.

Move your toolbars quickly to the right or left

You'll notice the sizing bar (the vertical bar) at the left end of your toolbars. You can drag the sizing bar to move your toolbar around. If you double-click it, the toolbar will move for you. The sizing bar is a toggle, so keep double-clicking it.

Double-click the sizing bar once to move the toolbar to the left, so that it squeezes the Taskbar buttons. Double-click it again to move it back to the right. If you have multiple toolbars, you can get pretty elaborate with these double-clicks. Of course, this also works if you have a vertical Taskbar and toolbars.

Use a toolbar to quickly get to your files

It can be quite time consuming to navigate around with your Explorer to find the files that you are working on. That's why there is a My Documents shortcut on your Desktop, why you can create shortcuts to any of your documents, and why there is a list of recently opened documents on your Start menu and the File menu in your applications.

Another very clever way to get to your documents and programs, and to almost anything on your computer, is to use menus cascading from a toolbar. To see how this works, open up your Desktop toolbar by taking these steps:

STEPS:

Opening a My Desktop Toolbar

Step 1. Right-click your Taskbar, and choose Toolbars, Desktop.

Step 2. Drag the sizing bar at the left end of the toolbar to move the Desktop toolbar over to the right (assuming you have a horizontal Taskbar) so that only the word *Desktop* and a chevron arrow show.

Step 3. Click the arrow and notice that the Desktop contents are displayed in a menu, as shown in Figure 12-20.

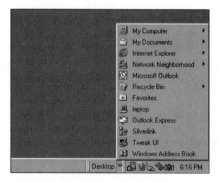

Figure 12-20: The toolbar you have created displays the contents of your Desktop as a menu.

Step 4. Click the My Computer icon in your Desktop menu. The contents of your computer are displayed in a new menu.

Step 5. Click your hard drive icon. You get a menu containing the items found in your root directory (except for the hidden files).

Step 6. Continue opening up menus of folders on your hard disk to get to any folder or file that you wish.

You can get to any application or file just by navigating down cascading menus. But there is a way to make this easier.

STEPS:

Opening Your Hard Disk Toolbar

Step 1. Right-click your Taskbar, and choose Toolbars, New Toolbar.

Step 2 In the New Toolbar dialog box, highlight your main hard disk, and click OK.

Step 3. Drag the sizing bar at the end of the new hard disk toolbar to the right to so that you see only the name of the hard disk and a chevron arrow.

Step 4. Click the arrow to display the contents of your root directory (minus the hidden files) in a menu, as shown in Figure 12-21.

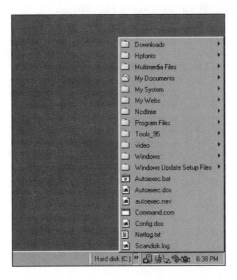

Figure 12-21: Display the contents of your root directory as a menu by creating a new toolbar.

Continued

STEPS

Opening Your Hard Disk Toolbar *(continued)*

Step 5.   Click a folder on your hard disk menu to display the contents of the folder as a menu.

Step 6.   Click subfolders to display their contents.

You can set up toolbars for multiple hard disks. You can create a toolbar using My Computer instead of your hard disk. In the My Computer toolbar, click Control Panel, Dial-Up Networking, Printers, Web Folders, or Scheduled Tasks; the items in these special folders are displayed as menu items.

You can also create toolbars for the Control Panel folder, the Dial-Up Networking folder, and so on. Pretty much any folder can become a menu. These menus are not menus of shortcuts, so you'll need to be careful not to delete items from the menus. If you do, you'll delete the actual thing itself and not just a shortcut to it. For example, if you make a menu of the Dial-Up Networking folder and delete a DUN connectoid from the menu, the actual connectoid is gone.

Thanks to James A. Boyce for his help with this secret.

New folders for new toolbars

When you create a new toolbar (right-click your Taskbar and choose Toolbars, New Toolbar) you are not given the opportunity to create a new empty folder, as you can see in Figure 12-22.

Figure 12-22: The New Toolbar dialog box does not include a new folder button.

A toolbar can be a convenient place to put shortcuts, especially if you move the toolbar all the way to the right and turn it into a menu of shortcuts. One approach that you might take is to group your shortcuts by common themes and send them to the appropriate toolbar. Then you can get to them easily even if they are also on the Desktop and currently covered up.

A good place to put your toolbar folders is the same location that Microsoft places the Quick Launch toolbar folder. Another option is to put them in your own \My System folder (which we suggest you create to store the files and folders you use to customize Windows 98).

Take these steps to create your own new toolbar folders and make them easy to get to when creating new shortcuts:

STEPS:
Creating New Folders for New Toolbars

Step 1. Using your Explorer, navigate to \Windows\Application Data\Microsoft\Internet Explorer\ as shown in Figure 12-23.

Figure 12-23: Your Quick Launch folder is stored in the location shown here. You could create your toolbar folders here or in the \My System folder.

Step 2. Right-click the Explorer client area, click New, Folder, and type a short name for the new folder/toolbar. Repeat this step as many times as needed to create the new folders.

Step 3. In the left pane of your Explorer, scroll down to \Windows\SendTo.

Continued

Creating New Folders for New Toolbars *(continued)*

Step 4. One by one, right-drag the folders that you just created to \Windows\SendTo, and click Create Shortcut(s) Here after you drop each one there.

Step 5. Right-click your Taskbar, and choose Toolbars, New Toolbar. Select the first of your new folders, and click OK. Repeat for each new folder.

Step 6. You can now move items off of your Desktop or Start menu just by right-clicking them, clicking Send To, and choosing the appropriate toolbar.

Tip

You don't have to do the SendTo portions of this procedure (steps 3, 4, and 6). Because the items on the Start menu are shortcuts, you can just drag them to any of the toolbars once you open the toolbars. This is part of the improvement of the Windows 98 interface. You can easily move the Start menu items to reflect how you want to work.

Thanks to Martijn Dekkers for pointing out this tip.

Put the Recycle Bin on a toolbar

If your Recycle Bin is on your Desktop, you can right-drag a Recycle Bin shortcut to a toolbar, and thereby see the Recycle Bin's contents more easily when your Desktop is cluttered up. If you have used TweakUI to take the Recycle Bin off the Desktop, then you won't be able to place a shortcut to it on a toolbar. If you are using the Norton Utilities Protected Recycle Bin, this won't work either.

If neither of those cases is true for you, just right-drag the Recycle Bin icon to a toolbar area and drop it there, and then click Create Shortcut(s) Here. If you don't have a toolbar showing, right-click the Taskbar, and choose Toolbars, Quick Launch. You can right-drag the Recycle Bin icon there to create a shortcut.

Thanks to Mike Brazil help with this tip.

Toolbars as web pages

Because the Windows 98 user shell is an object-oriented program, you'll find that certain items can take on the characteristics of other items even when it doesn't seem that useful. For example, check out the *Windows 98 Secrets* Home Page toolbar shown in Figure 12-24. You can view the whole web page through the little window in the toolbar.

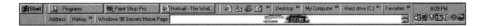

Figure 12-24: A toolbar can actually contain a whole web page.

At first glance, this looks rather silly. Indeed, the *Windows 98 Secrets* home page is so big that it is probably not a great choice for a toolbar, but there are other Internet web pages that may be just right — for example, a stock ticker.

To put a web page on a toolbar, take these steps:

STEPS:

Putting a Web Page on a Toolbar

Step 1. Right-click your Taskbar, and choose Toolbars, New Toolbar.

Step 2. Type the URL of a local or Internet resource, as shown in Figure 12-25.

Figure 12-25: Type the complete URL in the New Toolbar dialog box.

Step 3. Click OK.

Of course, you can resize the toolbar and drag it over to one of the other edges of your Desktop, as shown in Figure 12-26.

Figure 12-26: This toolbar has been resized so that it fits along the side of the Desktop.

Thanks to Roger Wolfson for mentioning this tip.

Tab through your Taskbar buttons

Hold down the Win key as you press the Tab key repeatedly. You'll see each button on your Taskbar appear to be pressed. Press Enter to bring the associated document or application to the foreground.

Use the Address bar to run your programs

Right-click your Taskbar, and choose Toolbars, Address to display an Address bar on your Desktop. The Address bar is a toolbar whose main purpose is to call up Internet Explorer when you type or paste in a URL. It looks and works just like the Internet Explorer Address bar, as you can see from Figure 12-27.

Figure 12-27: The Address bar is a toolbar on your Desktop.

Despite its name, the Address bar is also a command line processor (oops, here we go back to DOS). You can type a filename and the associated application will open and display the file. You have to type the complete pathname as well as the filename, and there is no Browse button, as there is in the Start, Run dialog box.

Thanks to Todd D. Perlmutter for this tip.

Put Find on the Quick Launch toolbar

You can easily put Find on your Quick Launch toolbar. Here's how:

STEPS:
Putting Find on the Quick Launch Toolbar

Step 1.   In Explorer, click Tools, Find, Files or Folder.

Step 2.   Make any changes to the Find dialog box necessary to make this your general Find.

Step 3.   Click File, Save Search. This saves the Find settings as a shortcut on the Desktop.

Step 4.   Change the name of the Find shortcut on the Desktop if you like. Otherwise, just drag and drop it onto the Quick Launch toolbar. Delete the shortcut from the Desktop.

Move the Quick Launch icons around

You can move the icons in the Quick Launch toolbar just by dragging them to a new location on the toolbar, and dropping them when the black line appears between icons. You can also do this with other toolbars as long as they are folders of shortcuts. You won't be able to do it for a My Computer toolbar. You can do it with a Favorites toolbar.

The order in which the toolbar items appear in these menus is kept in the Registry. This is why you can rearrange their order on the toolbar.

While we haven't experienced it, it appears as though toolbar icons can become garbled, especially if you change monitor resolutions. Right-click the sizing bar for any of the toolbars and click Refresh to redisplay the icons.

Thanks to Bo Bickley for pointing out some of these tips.

Restore the Quick Launch toolbar

Secret

The Quick Launch toolbar contains two icons that may get lost, but are easily restored: Show Desktop and View Channels. If you navigate to \Windows\ Application Data\Microsoft\Internet Explorer\Quick Launch, you'll see these two items. Right-click either of them, click Send To, Notepad, and you'll see that they are text files. (If you haven't put a shortcut to Notepad in your \Windows\SendTo folder, you can open these files by right-clicking them, clicking Open With, and then clicking Notepad.)

If you have accidentally deleted one of these files, you can restore it.

STEPS:

Restoring the Show Desktop File

Step 1. Navigate with your Explorer to \Windows\Application Data\Microsoft\Internet Explorer\Quick Launch.

Step 2. Right-click the right pane in Explorer, and choose New, Text Document.

Step 3. Insert this text into the new document:

```
[Shell]
Command=2
IconFile=explorer.exe,3
[Taskbar]
Command=ToggleDesktop
```

Step 4. Save the file as **Show Desktop.scf**.

STEPS:

Restoring the View Channels File

Step 1. Navigate with your Explorer to \Windows\Application Data\Microsoft\Internet Explorer\Quick Launch.

Step 2. Right-click the right pane in Explorer, and click New, Text Document.

Step 3.   Insert this text into the new document:

```
[Shell]
Command=3
IconFile=shdocvw.dll,-118
[IE]
Command=Channels
```

Step 4.   Save the file as **View Channels.scf**

Corrupted Taskbar icons

Bryan Rockwood reports that Windows 98 has a problem in which icons on the Taskbar and the toolbars display garbage icons. This is particularly known to happen when you have changed your display from one resolution to another.

The workaround is to right-click a toolbar and click Refresh in the context menu. (This doesn't work if you don't have a toolbar on your Taskbar.)

Increase the size of your icon cache

Secret

If you find that the icons on your Taskbar keep changing, it may be because your icon cache is too small to keep copies of all the icons.

You can increase the size of your icon cache by taking these steps:

STEPS:

Increasing Your Icon Cache Size

Step 1.   Click Start, Run, type **regedit**, and press Enter.

Step 2.   Navigate to HKEY_LOCAL_MACHINE\ SOFTWARE\ Microsoft\ Windows\ CurrentVersion\ explorer. Highlight this key in the left pane of your Registry editor.

Step 3.   Right-click the right pane, and choose New, String Value.

Step 4   Rename the string value **MaxCachedIcons**.

Step 5.   Double-click MaxCachedIcons in the right pane, type the value **2048**, and click OK.

Thanks to Tom Porterfield for this secret.

Keep running your system tray programs even after Explorer crashes

Linus Thorvald has wondered aloud if Windows users have grown inured to their computers crashing. Of course, Linus has a valid point, irrespective of whether his operating system (Linux), highly respected for its resistance to crashes, matches up to user demands in every area. Windows users are used to at least the Explorer crashing, if not the operating system.

Most often, an Explorer crash doesn't cause great harm because it automatically starts again — but you lose your system tray icons. These icons represent running applications, so it sure would be nice to have access to them.

WinResQ to the rescue, sort of. This application keeps a list of running processes, as shown in Figure 12-28. It also sits in the system tray (although its icon disappears). If Explorer crashes, you can invoke WinResQ again. Keep a shortcut to it on your Desktop and click it there. Double-click any process in the WinResQ window that is matched to a missing icon in the system tray to open up that process' main window. This may not always work.

Figure 12-28: A list of currently running processes, viewed using WinResQ.

You'll find this little helper at www.magnetiq.com.

You can also just put shortcuts to the applications that have icons in the system tray on your Desktop. Better still, create a shortcut to a batch file that restarts all the applications with system tray icons.

Foobar, not toolbar

Foobar is a launch bar with a series of little applets attached to it, as illustrated in Figure 12-29. *Quick* is the key word here — applets that start and end fast, and do a little bit well. Figure 12-30 shows the Reminders applet.

Figure 12-29: Foobar is a collection of helpful little applets that appear as buttons on the launch bar.

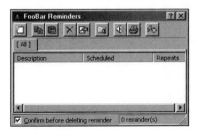

Figure 12-30: The Reminders applet lets you set up reminders that pop up on your screen.

You can keep your passwords (not integrated with Windows 98), write sticky notes, store a contact list (not integrated with the Windows address book), keep track of the time spent on various activities, keep a To Do list, open your favorite documents, run your favorite applications, and set some reminders.

You'll find Foobar at matrixsoftware.com.

Hide windows and Taskbar buttons

Hide Windows puts an icon in your system tray. Right-click the icon and you can choose which windows and their associated Taskbar buttons to hide. You can also click Show All or Hide All.

Hide Windows also uses command line switches that allow you to start windows hidden and hide multiple windows with batch files. There is no installation procedure. The program is reasonably small and works as advertised. We liked it.

You'll find this freeware program at www.nettworks.com. Thanks to Chris Pirillo at www.lockergnome.com.

Change any time zone city

You can change the name of the city that appears in any time zone in the Time Zone tab of the Date/Time Properties dialog box (see Figure 12-31). To display this dialog box, double-click the clock in the system tray. Display the drop-down list in the Time Zone tab to display other time zones.

Figure 12-31: The name of a city in the selected time zone appears above the top of the map.

Secret

In Chapter 6 of *Windows 98 Secrets*, we discuss how to download and use the Time Zone editor that is part of the Windows Kernel Toys. You can use that editor to make this change, but it's also easy to make it using the Registry editor. Here's how:

STEPS:
Changing Your Time Zone City

Step 1.   Click Start, Run, type **regedit**, and press Enter.

Step 2.   You can either search for the name of a city that you've seen displayed in the Time Zone tab, or you can navigate to HKEY_LOCAL_MACHINE\ SOFTWARE\ Microsoft\ Windows\ CurrentVersion\ TimeZones, and click the key indicating your time zone, as shown in Figure 12-32.

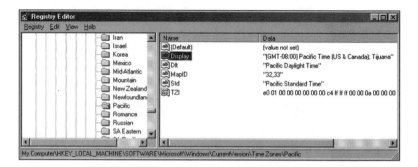

Figure 12-32: In this example, Tijuana is the city associated with Pacific Daylight Time.

Step 3.   Double-click Display in the right pane, and edit the city name as desired. Click OK, and close the Registry editor.

The Start menu

The Start menu is the main shortcut collection window. We give you a number of ways to keep this thing from growing out of control.

Hide menu items

Secret

The Start menu won't display folders, files, or shortcuts that have been marked as hidden. This is a nondestructive way of taking items off of your Start menu without deleting them or moving them. If you decide later that you want an item back on the menu, just unhide it.

STEPS:

Hiding Menu Items

Step 1.   Click Start, Programs.

Step 2.   Right-click any of the menu items in the Programs folder, click Properties, click the General tab if needed, mark the Hidden check box (see Figure 12-33), and click OK.

Step 3.   If you want to unhide a hidden Start menu item, open your Explorer and navigate to \Windows\Start Menu\Programs.

Step 4.   Right-click the item in the right pane of the Explorer, click Properties, clear the Hidden check box, and click OK.

Continued

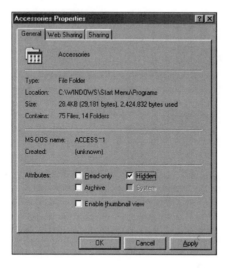

Figure 12-33: The General tab of the Properties dialog box lets you hide a menu item.

A number of Start menu items won't let you do this. For example, even if you use your Explorer to mark the Programs or Favorites folders as hidden, they will still show up on the Start menu. If you want to remove the Favorites folder from the Start menu, you can use TweakUI.

Thanks to Byron Hinson, MS-MVP, for help with this tip.

Resorting the Start menu

Secret

Windows 98 keeps track of the order of the items on your Start menu. This includes the items in the submenus Programs, Accessories, System Tools, and so on. It does this by creating a variable named *Order* in the Registry under the submenu's name whenever you first rearrange the menu from its default alphabetical order.

It's easy to see this in action. Start your Registry editor by clicking Start, Run, typing **regedit**, and pressing Enter. Navigate to HKEY_CURRENT_USER\ Software\ Microsoft\ Windows\ CurrentVersion\ Explorer\ MenuOrder\ Start Menu\ &Programs\ Menu. You'll see the Order variable in the right pane of the Registry editor, as shown in Figure 12-34.

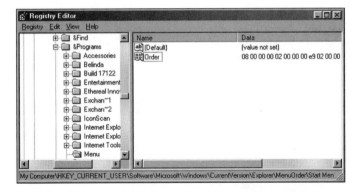

Figure 12-34: The Registry location of the menu order variable.

This Registry item is the menu order variable that remembers the order of the items in the Programs menu. To return the Programs menu to its default alphabetical order, right-click the Order variable in the right pane, and click Delete.

You don't need to worry about doing this, because Windows will create the variable again as soon as you reorder anything in the Programs menu. If you don't reorder any items in this menu, it will sort new entries alphabetically and will not create an Order variable.

We found that it was not possible to resort the Programs menu correctly without deleting the Order variable in the Registry. Right-clicking any of the submenus and clicking Sort By Name works fine. (This command is new to Internet Explorer 5.)

Other menus have their Order variable stored in a similar location in the Registry — under a Menu key under their name, or directly under their name. For example, on our computer, the Accessories menu has a Menu key, which holds its Order variable, but the System Tools key itself holds the System Tools' Order variable. Look around a bit in this area of the Registry and it's easy to see what's going on.

We'd like to thank Sky King for pointing this out to us.

Redecorate the Start menu

You can jazz up the Start menu by replacing the icons to the left of your menu items, including Programs, Favorites, Documents, Find, and so on. Not a big change in Windows 98, but yet another battle in the larger war of user control.

DecoMenu acts like a wizard to step you through the process of creating a graphic that fits in the slot where the icons now stand. It tries to figure out just how big the space is based on what you've still got left on your personalized version of the Start menu. We found that even when we didn't have quite the layout that DecoMenu thought we had, it still worked.

Click the Blank button in the DecoMenu window (see Figure 12-35) to create a blank *bmp* file and call the associated application. In our case it's Paint Shop Pro, but it could be MS Paint. Add to the blank *bmp* file and save it. Now click the Choose button, and then the Next button, and you'll have a new Start menu.

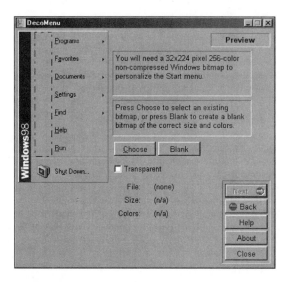

Figure 12-35: DecoMenu functions as a wizard to step you through the process of creating a new look for your Start menu.

If you don't like the effect, you can easily back out of it and go back to the original version of the Start menu icons.

Neil J. Rubenking of PC Magazine wrote DecoMenu, and you'll find it at www.zdnet.com/pcmag/pctech/content/17/13/ut1713.001.html.

The Start button is a window, too

Secret

Almost everything in Windows is a window. Some windows just look different than others. For example, click your Start button, and press Alt+Spacebar. You'll see the menu shown in Figure 12-36 appear next to the Start button. Click Close to bring up the Shut Down Windows dialog box.

Figure 12-36: Even the Start button contains the standard context menu for a Taskbar button.

A shortcut to a Windows restart

You can place a little shortcut on your Desktop (or wherever) that lets you quickly restart Windows 98 without going through the Start, Shut Down, Restart, OK routine. Unfortunately, it doesn't restart Windows as fast as this routine does if you also hold down the Shift key when you click OK.

STEPS:
Creating a Restart Shortcut

Step 1.   Right-click the Desktop, click New, and then click Shortcut.

Step 2.   Click the Browse button, browse to C:\Windows\Rundll.exe, and click Open.

Step 3   Add a space at the end of the path in the Command Line field, and then type **user.exe,ExitWindowsExec**.

Step 4.   Click Next, and type a new name for the shortcut. We suggest Restart.

Step 5.   Click Finish.

An easy shortcut

You can use your Start menu to create a hot key to any application without actually creating a new shortcut. The trick is to properly position the application on the Start menu. To see how to do this with a DOS window, take these steps:

STEPS:

Creating a Hot Key to DOS

Step 1.   Click Start, Programs.

Step 2.   Drag the MS-DOS Prompt shortcut all the way to the top of the Programs menu and drop it there.

Step 3.   Press the Win key (or Ctrl+Esc), then the P key, and finally the Enter key (not all together).

Yes, it's cheating, and a bit silly, by why not.

Thanks to Peter Lara for pointing out this trick.

Get rid of Log Off

If you are the only person using your computer, you can get rid of the Log Off option on your Start menu. Use TweakUI, click the IE tab, clear the Allow Logoff check box, Click OK, and reboot your computer.

Fun with Run

Click Start, Run, type a period (.), and click OK. A folder window containing the shortcuts on your Desktop opens.

Click Start, Run, type two periods (..), and click OK. A folder window focused on your Windows folder appears on the Desktop.

Click Start, Run, type a backslash (\ ), and click OK. A folder window focused on the root directory of your boot drive appears on the Desktop.

Thanks to Byron Hinson, MS-MVP, for help with these tips.

Shortcuts to anywhere

The Windows 98 shortcuts make it possible to quickly get to your programs and documents.

Drag a shortcut to the Desktop without clearing the Desktop

You can create a shortcut to anything just by right-dragging it to your Desktop. However, sometimes your Desktop is obscured. Not to worry.

STEPS:

Dragging Shortcuts to Your Covered Desktop

Step 1. Open your Explorer. Right-drag a folder icon from your Explorer to your Taskbar. Be sure that you hover it over a spot on your Taskbar that is not occupied by a button. You can hover it over your system tray if you like.

Step 2. Wait for a second, and all the windows on your Desktop will be closed.

Step 3. Drag the icon over the now clear Desktop and drop it there. Click Create Shortcut(s) Here.

You can also use this method to move or copy a file or folder to the Desktop. Remember that if you decide not to drop the item on the Desktop, you can just click the other mouse button while dragging. This cancels the command.

Thanks to Joe deSousa help with this tip.

Create a shortcut to a document

Secret

Using Microsoft Word, you can create a shortcut to a document that will open the document at a specific location in the text. Place the shortcut on your Desktop and you can invoke Word, open the document, and have it open at your designated location, all with one click.

STEPS:

Creating a Shortcut to a Word Document

Step 1. Open Microsoft Word, click File, Open, and open a Word document.

Step 2. Highlight a piece of text within the document.

Step 3. Right-drag the highlighted text to your Desktop and drop it there.

Step 4. Click Create Document Shortcut Here in the context menu, as shown in Figure 12-37.

Continued

STEPS

Creating a Shortcut to a Word Document *(continued)*

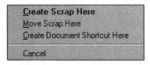

Figure 12-37: Click Create Document Shortcut Here in the context menu to create a new shortcut.

Step 5. Save and close your document.

You can now rename the shortcut to be the document name, if you like. When you click this shortcut, you will open the document and the text that you highlighted will be highlighted once again.

When you create this shortcut, an OLE link is created in your Word document in the form of a (non-printing) bookmark. If you should delete the shortcut, the link will remain. You can use Word's Go To command to find bookmarks called OLE_LINK. To delete a bookmark, click Insert, Bookmark, select the bookmark, click the Delete button, and then click Close.

Thanks to David C. Worthington for pointing out this tip.

Create a shortcut from a shell window

Open up your Internet Explorer, Explorer, My Computer, or any folder window. You can create a shortcut to any item that currently has the focus in the window (the item whose name is displayed in the title bar) by dragging the little control icon at the left end of the title bar to the Desktop.

For example, click the Internet Explorer icon on your Desktop, which will open to your home page, even if you are offline. Drag (or right-drag) the aforementioned icon to the Desktop, and you've created a shortcut to your home page. You can do this with any web page. You can create your own separate Favorites folder in this fashion by putting a shortcut to it on the Desktop and dragging the little control icon to the shortcut every time you open a favorite web page.

To try this in the Explorer, highlight any of your folders in the left pane, and drag the control icon to your Desktop. (Of course, you can also use the more general method of right-dragging a folder or a file icon from your Explorer to the Desktop and do the same thing.)

Thanks to Holland Rhodes for clueing us into this tip.

My Documents Desktop icon doesn't work

If you click your My Documents icon on your Desktop and you get an error message telling you that the program has performed an illegal operation and will be shut down, it's because the My Documents icon is pointing to nowhere. You need to be sure that it has somewhere to point to.

The My Documents icon on the Desktop is a special type of shortcut that points to the actual My Documents folder (whatever its actual name).

Secret

Click TweakUI in your Control Panel, click the General tab, display the Folder drop-down list, and highlight My Documents. Click the Change Location button and point My Documents to your My Documents folder, or to any folder that you want to designate as the My Documents folder. Click OK.

If that doesn't work, try this:

STEPS:
Fixing the My Documents Icon

Step 1.   Click Start, Run, type **regedit,** and press Enter.

Step 2.   Navigate to HKEY_CURRENT_USER\ Software\ Microsoft\ Windows\ CurrentVersion\ Explorer\ User Shell Folders.

Step 3.   Double-click Personal in the right pane of the Registry editor, and type **C:\My Documents**, or the path and name of another folder that you want to designate as the My Documents folder. Click OK, and then exit the Registry editor.

Kill dead links

Notice how some of the links on web pages send you off into HTTP error space when clicked? The same thing can happen to the shortcuts on your Start menu and Desktop. The target of the shortcut has moved or is no more.

The *Windows 98 Resource Sampler Kit* comes with a little link checker that will get rid of the links with no linkees. If you click setup.exe in the Windows 98 CD-ROM under \tools\reskit, you'll find the Checklinks program in the Management Console under Desktop Tools (expand the Tool Categories branch). Click Start, Programs, Windows 98 Resource Kit, Tools Management Console.

You can also just copy the executable from the Windows 98 CD-ROM or run it from there if you like. You'll find it at \tools\reskit\desktop\chklnks.exe.

Send it to the printer

In Chapter 29 of *Windows 98 Secrets*, we show you how to create a batch file that will print your print files (those files that contain the stuff that would go directly to the printer if you issued the Print command in your application). You would normally create such a print file if you set up your printer properties to print to a file instead of to the printer.

Now you can download a little freeware utility that does the same thing, with a bit more flair. You can use this utility to print your PostScript files, as well as any other print file (as long as you send it to the right printer).

Send To Printer, shown in Figure 12-38, is installed in the SendTo folder. To use it, right-click a print file and click Send To, A Printer. Send To Printer is available in French or English at www.essi.fr/~berger. You'll also find other freeware and shareware create by the author at this site.

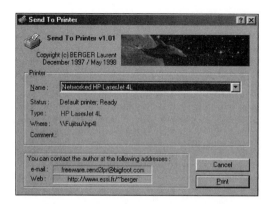

Figure 12-38: Send To Printer makes it easy to output print files such as *ps* or *prn* files.

Navigating on the Desktop

We give you a few quick ways to make it easier to deal with your Desktop.

Clear the Desktop

You can easily clear the Desktop to get at any of your Desktop shortcuts. Hold down the Win key and press D. This is a toggle, so all your open windows come back when you do it again.

The Win key plus M also works to clear the Desktop, but it isn't a toggle. You have to press Win+Shift+M to bring back the windows.

Quickly show the properties of Desktop and Explorer icons

You ordinarily right-click an icon and click Properties to display its properties. But you can do this even more quickly by pressing the Alt key as you click the icon.

Try this with your My Computer, Internet Explorer, My Documents, and other icons.

Choose where to save your file

The Windows 98 standard File, Save As dialog box contains a View Desktop toolbar button just to the right of the Up One Level button. Click the View Desktop button and you're ready to save your document on the Desktop.

The trick is to click the View Desktop button again. This redisplays the contents of the original folder that was displayed when you opened this dialog box, and allows you to save the file there (see Figure 12-39). You can use this toggle to switch between the Desktop and any folder to which you navigate.

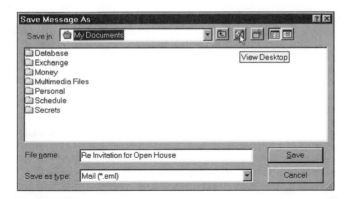

Figure 12-39: Click the View Desktop button to toggle between the Desktop and another folder.

Thanks to Sergio Esteva for help with this tip.

Screen savers

Screen savers can be fun and actually useful. Looking at PicSaver (see the next section) is like watching yourself and your friends on television.

Show your pictures on your screen saver

Wouldn't it be nice to have your screen saver display the pictures that you've stored on your hard disk or CD-ROM? One at a time for a few seconds, perhaps as a collage, or at random locations on the screen?

PicSaver is a little freeware applet that will do just that. It supports *jpg*, *gif*, *bmp*, *dib*, *jif*, *rle*, *pcx*, and *tga* picture files. It will show an unlimited number of pictures from multiple folders (see Figure 12-40). It loads them quite quickly and gives you options to change display style, size, and time viewed. You can display all the Desktop themes if you like, and put in a password.

Figure 12-40: The PicSaver user interface lets you designate multiple folders of images to view.

PicSaver consists of three files — a readme file, a screen saver file, and a dynamic link library. Here's how you set it up:

STEPS:
Configuring PicSaver

Step 1. Unzip PicSaver.zip and place the screen saver and *dll* file in your \Windows\System folder.

Step 2. Right-click your Desktop, click Properties, and then click Screen Saver tab.

Step 3. Display the Screen Saver drop-down list, and highlight PicSaver. Click the Settings button.

Step 4. Click the Add button (refer to Figure 12-40) to add folders containing graphics files to the Directories list. PicSaver will display all the graphics files in all the folders that you choose.

Step 5. Make any other changes that you like in the Options for PicSaver dialog box, and then click OK.

Step 6. Click the Preview button to see how your screen saver will look.

We had some trouble displaying some *jpg* files. Perhaps this is fixed by now. We received an error message stating that PicSaver was unable to load a given file. The workaround was to remove the offending files from the folders found in the list of directories. Another option is to remove the folder with the offending files from the list of directories in the Options for PicSaver dialog box.

Tip

One approach that worked for us was to use Paint Shop Pro to convert the *jpg* files to less-compressed *jpg* files. PicSaver then displayed them without a problem. Many of our pictures files had the same name, the name that the Nikon Color Pix 100 gave them. Using THE Rename (see "Rename your files en masse" in Chapter 13), we were able to rename all the photos in batch mode, put all the photos in one folder, and then have Paint Shop Pro convert them in batch mode. Very cool.

You'll find PicSaver at falcon.jmu.edu/~jenninms/apps/picsaver/.

Indoor rock climbing

We don't dwell on too many screen savers in this book. After all, our job is to provide the tools that make it easier for you to take charge of the Windows 98 operating system. That said, every once in a while we see something that is pretty darn neat. Maybe not extravagantly neat, but cool enough to merit a little bit of our readers' limited attention.

How about a screen saver that consists of a rock climber and his partner on belay? The rock climber appears to weigh the decisions required to make the next pitch, and even falls when he doesn't get it right.

You'll find the *scr* file compressed in climber.zip at ftp://ftp.download.com/ pub/win95/utilities/climber.zip. After you download the file, unzip it and click it to start. You can move it to your \Windows\System folder later.

Hot corners on screen savers doesn't work

According to the Microsoft Knowledge Base (support.microsoft.com/ support/kb/articles/q189/6/89.asp), the hot corners feature on your screen saver from Plus! 95 or Plus! 98 won't work if you've installed the Task Scheduler from Plus! 98. They may have fixed it by the time you read this, but then again, they may not.

You can find a ready substitute in Sleeper, a 17K freeware download from Paradigms Lost at www.netcom.com/~baren/.

Sharing your Desktop

If you're not alone, you can at least get along.

Put stuff on their Desktop

If you're on a network and you share your Desktop, you might come into the office one day to find it piled high with files and documents from your coworkers. Sure, this happens on your physical desk, and maybe that's what you want with your virtual desk, also.

If you share your Desktop, other users on the network can send you documents by copying them to an icon on their Desktop. All they have to do to create this icon is to drag your \Windows\Desktop folder to their Desktop and click Create Shortcut(s) Here.

You have to share your \Windows\Desktop folder and allow full or password-controlled access before anyone else can put something on your virtual Desktop. To share your Desktop, right-click your \Windows\Desktop folder and choose Sharing. Then mark Shared As, and mark Full or Depends on Password.

While this might not be a good idea in a large office that may contain a few unruly individuals, hopefully you can trust the people in a small office, or at your home.

Thanks to Fred Diether for pointing out this tip.

User profiles and My Documents

Secret

If you have set up your Windows 98 computer to enable multiple user profiles, you'll find that a My Documents folder gets created for each user under his or her user profile folder — in other words, C:\Windows\Profiles\ *username*\My Documents. This can be a bit irritating because it makes it somewhat hard to back up everything in the My Documents folder. Fortunately, you can undo the damage that Microsoft has done here.

You'll want to create a folder that will act as a central repository of all the users' My Documents folders. Here's how:

STEPS:
Dealing with User Profiles and My Documents

Step 1. Using your Explorer, navigate to your root directory or the root directory of a secondary partition.

Step 2. Right-click the right pane of your Explorer, click New, Folder, and rename the folder **Documents**.

Step 3. Right-click the Documents folder, and click Explore.

Step 4. Right-click the right pane of your Explorer, click New, Folder, and rename the new folder after the name of one of the users.

Step 5. Repeat step 4 as many times as needed for all the current users (including yourself).

Step 6. Right-click the My Documents icon on the Desktop, click Properties, click the Browse button, and navigate to the folder that corresponds to your profile (C:\My Documents*username*). Click OK.

Step 7. Click Start, Log Off, and log on as one of the other users. Repeat step 6 for each user, selecting the folder that corresponds to his or her profile.

Step 8. Use your Explorer to copy any files and folders stored in the older My Documents folders into the appropriate new folders under each user's name.

Step 9. Delete the My Document folders under the user names in the C:\Windows\Profiles folder.

There seems to be a problem if one user's folder that is treated as the My Documents folder is a subfolder of another user's folder. Be sure to put all of the folders on the same level.

Thanks to Chuck Rizzio, MS-MVP, for pointing us toward this tip.

Summary

Your Desktop, Start menu, Taskbar, and toolbars are major components of the Windows 98 user interface. There is a lot you can do to revise these elements to be a bit friendlier.

▶ Replace your Desktop and user interface with a completely different shell.

▶ If you don't have multiple people using your computer, get rid of the superfluous Log Off option.

▶ Use the *Windows 98 Resource Sampler Kit* to kill dead links in your Start menu.

▶ Clear the Desktop with one keystroke.

▶ Set up your screen saver to allow you to view all of your digital photos.

▶ Move everyone's My Documents folder to someplace other than a location under the \Windows folder.

Chapter 13

The Explorer

In This Chapter

The Explorer may not be the most powerful user interface to your files, but it does have a certain charm. Instead of replacing it with a completely different file management system, we suggest a few tweaks and a few add-ons.

▶ You can turn your folder views into web pages, so why not add a few of your more important links to the appropriate folders.

▶ If you've always wondered about the case of filenames, we give you the definitive scoop.

▶ If you have a folder that stores graphics files, then activate the Thumbnails view to create a database of small views of the files.

▶ Right-click to a context menu, but make it be the context menu that you want. We show you how to edit the various context menus.

▶ Configure Compressed Folders and WinZip so that they can work together.

Files and folders

You can rename a collection of files, create a bunch of folders all at once, print a folder directory, control the case of your filenames, and more.

Add hot links to your folders

If you view your folders as web pages, you can easily add links that show up in the web page view of any folder. The links can show up in all folders, or just in customized folders. You can create links to files, folders, or Internet resources.

If you want to put your links in all your folders, you'll need to edit the file folder.htt (a hidden file) in your \Windows\Web folder. If you want to put them in a specific folder, you can edit a file of the same name in that folder. Here's how:

STEPS:

Adding Links

Step 1. Use your Explorer to navigate to a folder that you are willing to view as a web page.

Step 2. If you're not viewing the folder as a web page, right-click the right pane of your Explorer window, and click View, As Web Page. If you want to make web page view the default, choose View, Folder Options, and mark the Web Style option button — or click the Settings button and mark For All Folders with HTML Content. Click OK.

Step 3. Right-click the right pane of your Explorer window, and click Customize This Folder to open the Customize This Folder Wizard, as shown in Figure 13-1.

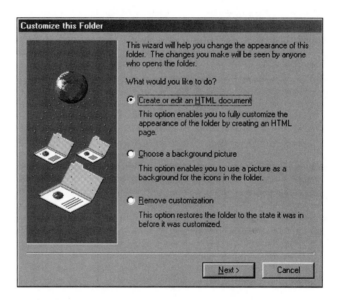

Figure 13-1: The first dialog box of the Customize This Folder Wizard. You should mark the first option button.

Step 4. Click Next, and Next again. This will create a file named folder.htt in your current folder. It will also open up Notepad as your HTML editor and display the contents of the folder.htt file.

Step 5. Scroll down to one page up from the bottom of the file, as shown in Figure 13-2.

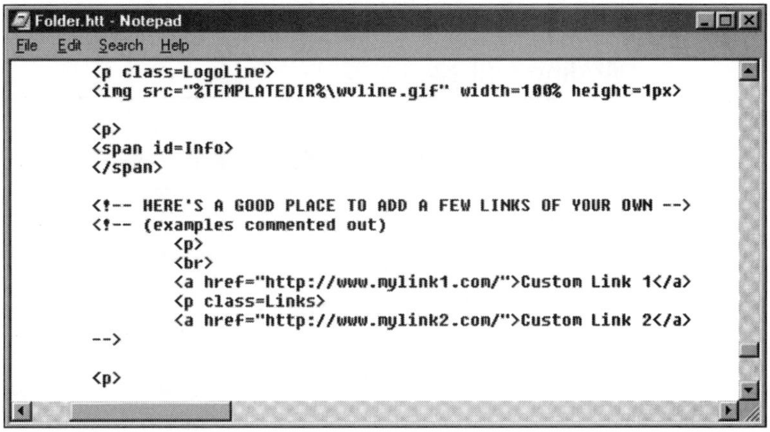

Figure 13-2: Look for this text near the end of folder.htt telling you where to add links of your own.

Step 6. Make the changes as shown in Figure 13-3. That is, delete the entire "examples commented out" line and the –> below the "Custom Link 2" line to uncomment out the links. Change the links to your own links. We've put in a link to the root directory and a link to a web site as examples.

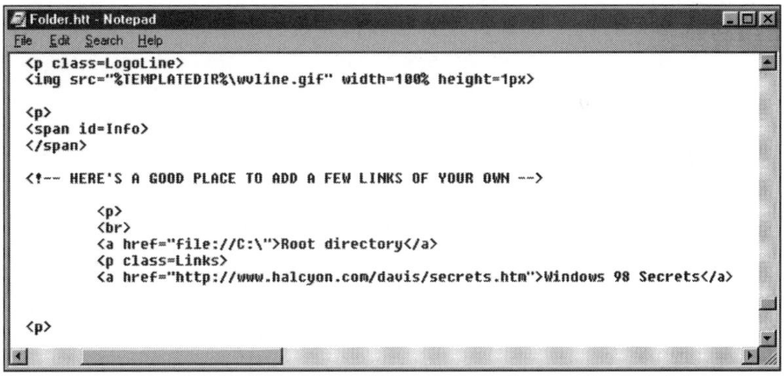

Figure 13-3: This folder.htt file has been edited to add two links.

Step 7. Click File, Save, and exit Notepad. Click the Finish button to close the wizard. Your folder, when displayed in web page view, will change to something like that shown in Figure 13-4.

Continued

STEPS

Adding Links *(continued)*

Figure 13-4: You can see the two new links to the left of the file list in the Explorer.

You can use these same steps to edit the folder.htt file in your \Windows\Web folder. Your edits will then be applied to all folders that don't have their own folder.htt files. In other words, if you have followed these steps to edit the folder.htt file for specific folder, that folder will use its own folder.htt and not the one in the \Windows\Web folder.

FrontPage Express is not associated with *htt* files. When we associated it with the *htt* file type using the Open With command after right-clicking folder.htt, we found that it crashed when attempting to edit the file. Still, it might work for you; see "Edit hypertext templates with FrontPage Express" in Chapter 11 for more on creating the association. We use FrontPage 2000 and have used it successfully with *htt* files.

Tip

You can associate *htt* files with Notepad and easily edit them. Once you've created a folder.htt file, you'll want to open it and edit it to revise it, instead of using the Customize This Folder menu item.

If you can't find folder.htt, be sure that you can view hidden files by choosing View, Folder Options in your Explorer window, clicking the View tab, and marking Show All Files (see Figure 13-5).

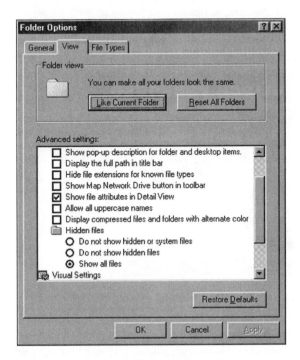

Figure 13-5: Set your folder options so that you can view hidden files.

Tip

This is just one example of how you can customize your folder view when viewing folders as web pages in Explorer or My Computer windows. Microsoft uses scripting and ActiveX controls to create these effects, and depending on your level of familiarity with these programming tools, you can add additional features to your folder views.

Select all files and folders within a folder

If you want to copy, move, or delete all files (or all files and folders) within a folder, use your Explorer to focus on a folder in the left pane and display its contents in the right pane, and then press Ctrl+A.

This selects the entire contents of the folder. You can now right-click the highlighted files, drag and drop them, or whatever. If you want to select all items except for a few, hold down the Ctrl key and click (or hover) over the ones that you want to remove from the selection. (The hovering works if you have single-clicking enabled — View, Folder Options, Custom, Settings, Single-click to Open an Item (Point to Select).)

Get rid of the warning about viewing the Windows folder

If you have folder options set to display windows as web pages, you may find that when you click your \Windows folder, you get a display something like that shown in Figure 13-6. This warning tells you to be careful with this folder.

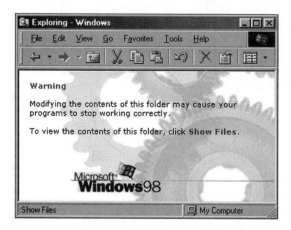

Figure 13-6: The web page view of the \Windows folder in the Explorer.

We assume that anyone who is reading this book is capable of viewing and messing with the files in the \Windows folder and all of its subfolders. Not gratuitously mind you, but with a good idea of what you're doing. Therefore, it seems a bit much to ask you to put up with such a warning, at least after you've seen it once.

We also assume that you've chosen to view all file types, by choosing View, Folder Options, clicking the View tab, marking Show All Files, and clearing Hide File Extensions for Known File Types.

Secret

If you now scroll through your \Windows folder, you'll find the folder.htt file. Its Hidden attribute is marked, but it is still visible to your Explorer. (If you don't see the Attributes column in Details view, choose View, Folder Options, View, Show File Attributes in Detail View.) This HTML template file contains the code that displays the original warning message and then lets you into the \Windows folder when you click Show Files.

You can either delete this file, or, if that seems too drastic, rename it. Now you'll be able to view your \Windows folder without being asked if you really want to.

Print a directory of files in a folder

In Chapter 34 of *Windows 98 Secrets*, we tell you how to print a filename listing for any folder. You can use a little freeware package to make the task even easier. Directory-2-HTML, shown in Figure 13-7, creates an HTML page from the filename listings for a folder. You can then print out the new HTML page.

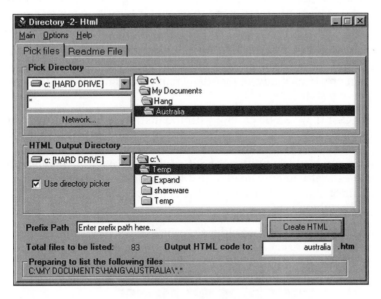

Figure 13-7: The user interface for Directory-2-HTML.

You'll find Directory-2-HTML at home1.gte.net/billyb99/dir2html/.

While Directory-2-HTML does a nice job, you might want to try something a little more austere. PrintFolder adds an item to your folder's context menu that lets you print (or copy) a directory listing for any folder, including subfolders if you like. It looks a lot like a DOS directory printout, as shown in Figure 13-8.

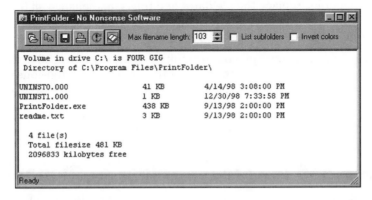

Figure 13-8: PrintFolder is ready to print the directory of files in the PrintFolder folder. You can copy the filename listing to a file, print it, or both.

You'll find this freeware package at no-nonsense-software.com/.

Create a bunch of folders

If you use the Explorer to create a folder, you get to create one folder at a time. If you want to create more than one or two, it becomes a pain in the neck.

Mathew Boxall in West Sussex, England, apparently had to create more than one or two, because he created instead the Sequential Folder Creator. With it, you can create as many sequentially named and numbered folders as you like, in one step.

Tip

We suggest that you be careful with the install on this one. We also suggest that you do not merge Mathew's Registration file into your Registry unless you want to add yet another command to your context menus for folders. You can run his little utility without adding all this "convenience," the very few times that you may need it, just by making a shortcut to the executable. Read his Sfc.txt file after you run the self-unzipping executable, but before you do anything else.

You'll find the Sequential Folder Creator at www.mboxall.demon.co.uk/ freeware/SFC10.exe.

Rename your files en masse

Windows 98 has a very limited file rename capability. Users who want to change the names of a bunch of files usually need to open a DOS window and use the REN command. Even this command is limited.

Another option is to use a freeware package, THE Rename, which provides you with plenty of renaming power, as shown in Figure 13-9.

You can use THE Rename to replace filenames with up to the first 25 characters of the file contents, rename files using consecutive alphanumerics, replace the file dates and times, and change all the extensions. You can have THE Rename create a DOS batch file to do the renaming after you decide what results you want.

THE Rename lets you type your own filter — say, to choose all of the files that start with *Belinda*. You can change just the prefixes or extensions, change the case of either, do freeform changes, and see your results before making the changes.

You'll find THE Rename at freeware95.atnet.at/file1.html.

Upper- and lowercase folder or filenames

The default action when you type a new name for a folder or a file in the Explorer is to capitalize the first letter and make all the rest of the letters lowercase. So, even if you type all of the letters in uppercase, you only get one uppercase letter. Now for the exceptions.

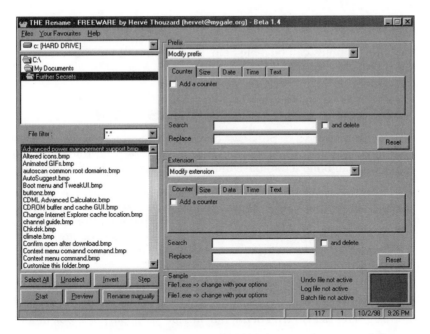

Figure 13-9: THE Rename gives you lots of options for renaming groups of files.

If you type only lowercase letters, the first letter isn't capitalized. If you type more than eight characters in uppercase or mixed case, they retain their individual cases.

If you include characters that are not allowed in the DOS 8.3 format for file or folder names (such as a space followed by a character, or a comma), the case of the individual letters is retained. Typing long file or folder names — anything over eight characters — retains the name as you typed it.

Tip It's possible to force Explorer to retain the case of letters as you type them for names of fewer than nine characters. You can make this change in either Explorer or TweakUI. To use Explorer, choose View, Folder Options, click the View tab, and mark Allow All Uppercase Names. To use TweakUI, click the Explorer tab, and mark the Adjust Case of 8.3 Filenames check box.

The problem with choosing Allow All Uppercase Names is that all filenames that are stored as uppercase names will now appear that way in your Explorer. Names that you thought were nicely subdued with a first letter in uppercase and the rest in lowercase will now be shouting at you.

For the purposes of identifying files and folder names, the Explorer treats uppercase and lowercase letters as though they were the same. For example, the Explorer will not let you create two subfolders within one folder and give them the same name except for the case. To test this, first turn on Allow All Uppercase Names, and then try creating two subfolders in the same folder, one called New and one called NEW.

Thumbnails

Little graphics can be a big help. Be sure to turn on Thumbnails view for the appropriate folders.

Activate your Thumbnails view

You get two ways to preview your graphics and HTML files with Windows 98. You can preview them one at a time if you view your folders as web pages, or you can build a database of thumbnail views in each folder.

To preview your files one at a time, right-click the client area of your Explorer, and mark View, As Web Page. You may have already configured your Explorer to display all folders as web pages (View, Folder Options, Custom, Settings, For All Folders with HTML Settings), in which case you don't need to choose View, As Web Page. This is also true if you've chosen Web style as your Explorer viewing option.

You can now highlight any *gif*, *bmp*, *jpg*, or HTML file in your folder and view its contents in the preview area to the left of the file list, as shown in Figure 13-10. This is also true of *art*, *dib*, *jfif*, *jpe*, *jpeg*, *png*, *ocx*, *ppt*, *tif* and *wmf* files.

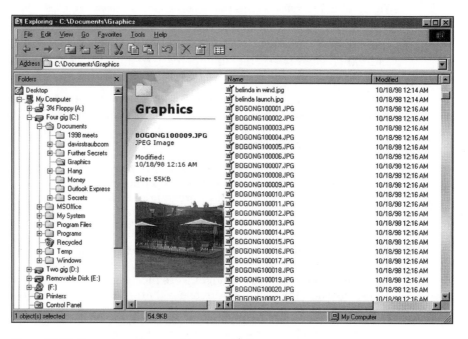

Figure 13-10: You can preview graphics one at a time.

You can also view the files themselves as thumbnails instead of using one of the other views (Large Icons, Small Icons, List, or Details). With Thumbnails view, the thumbnails are the same size as in the preview, but Explorer saves

them so you can go back to them quickly, and you can see thumbnails of all
the files in the folder at once, as shown in Figure 13-11.

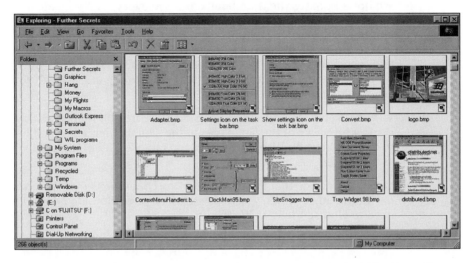

Figure 13-11: Thumbnails view lets you display thumbnails of an entire folder of graphics.

Thumbnails view is designed for folders that contain only or predominantly
graphics or HTML files. Windows constructs a database of thumbnails
(Thumbs.db) in each folder that you have set to show thumbnails. It does
this by creating a hidden desktop.ini file in the folder that specifies which
Explorer extension resource is required to display the thumbnails.

To display a folder's contents in Thumbnails view, right-click the folder's icon
in your Explorer, click Properties, mark the Enable Thumbnail View check
box, and click OK. This action creates the desktop.ini file in the folder. Now
right-click the folder's client area in your Explorer, and click View,
Thumbnails, as shown in Figure 13-12.

Figure 13-12: Select Thumbnails in the View context menu.

The files that Explorer can display as thumbnails will start to appear as
Windows builds a thumbnail database from the files currently visible in the
Explorer client area for this folder. As you scroll down, Windows creates
additional thumbnails and adds them to the folder's Thumbs.db file.
Thumbs.db will only contain thumbnails of *all* the files in the folder if you
bring all of the files into view. This allows Windows to forgo the long process

of creating a complete database of thumbnails if you just take a look at a couple of the first ones and then switch to another folder.

Tip

Windows updates the thumbnail database every time you add a file to the folder and view that file in the folder's Thumbnails view. If you move to view another folder in your Explorer and then move back, the icons in the folder will no longer be displayed in Thumbnails view. This speeds the display of folder contents within the Explorer. You'll need to right-click the client area for the folder in your Explorer (or folder window) and click View, Thumbnails again to switch back to this view.

View As Web Page and Thumbnails view are in a bit of a conflict. They both display previews of the same files in the same folder. Microsoft has decided to turn off View As Web Page when you choose Thumbnails view, and vice versa.

You'll also notice that if you switch from Thumbnails view to Details, or to one of the other views, you'll lose the web page view. If you want it back, you need to choose View, As Web Page.

The Explorer's Thumbnails view may not be the best thumbnail viewer for your needs. It appears to have difficulty when there are a lot of graphics files in a folder. It also seems quite a bit slower than dedicated thumbnail databases. We used Paint Shop Pro to manage all of the figures for this book, and we can create thumbnail databases quite easily, and more robustly with it. Other shareware packages are available as well.

Troubles with the thumbnail database

When Microsoft added an extension to the Explorer to handle the display of thumbnails, they opened themselves up to a little bit of trouble. They needed a database file that could be stored in the same folders as the graphics files. Once they created that file, any problems with it would cause problems with the Explorer.

Microsoft did this before when they introduced desktop.ini and folder.htt as add-on helper files that are stored in the affected folders. Everything is fine until something happens to these files, or someone erases them.

Secret

If you get one of these error messages when you try to view a folder in Thumbnails view, it's because the Thumb.db file is corrupt:

```
EXPLORER caused an invalid page fault in module THUMBVW.DLL at
015f:799eaee4
EXPLORER caused an invalid page fault in module KERNEL32.DLL at
015f:bff9d709
```

The solution is to delete the Thumbs.db file.

Secret

If you try to empty the Recycle Bin when it contains the contents of a folder that was enabled for Thumbnails view, and you are viewing the contents of the folder (now empty) in Explorer, you'll get another error message:

```
Can not delete Thumbs: Access is denied.
```

While you might be happy that your thumbnails aren't going to be deleted, you can click another folder icon and then empty the Recycle Bin.

Bring back your thumbnails and previews

Secret

If you are unable to view thumbnails or previews of some of the file types that you previously viewed, it may be because the particular file type is no longer associated with the function that displays the previews and thumbnails.

STEPS:

Restoring Previews

Step 1. Click Start, Run.

Step 2. Type **regsvr32 /i shdocvw.dll** and press Enter.

If this doesn't work, check in the Registry to see if the shell extension that points to this thumbnail and preview display function is properly associated with your graphics file type. Open your Registry editor and navigate down HKEY_CLASSES_ROOT to .bmp. You should have the same entries as those shown in Figure 13-13.

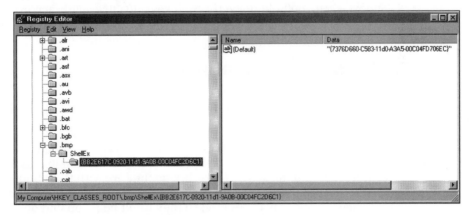

Figure 13-13: The correct Registry entries for the shell extension of the *bmp* file type. Both the right and left panes should match this figure.

You can also check any further graphics file extensions that are not being correctly displayed to make sure that they contain this same entry (the same exact alphanumeric codes). All of the following graphics file types should contain this Registry entry: *gif, bmp, jpg, art, dib, jfif, jpe, jpeg, png,* and *wmf.* If they don't, you can manually add it to them.

You may find that you are unable to see previews or thumbnails of some *jpg* files, although you can view them when you open the files in MS Paint, Paint Shop Pro, Internet Explorer, or other applications. The functions that display preview and thumbnail views can't handle *jpg* files that use the CMYK format instead of the RGB format. CMYK files are normally created by desktop publishing packages to prepare a file for production on color printing presses. If your *jpg* file is CMYK formatted, it just won't show up in the preview.

If you still can't get previews to work, you can take these steps:

STEPS:

Restoring Previews (the Alternate Method)

Step 1.   Click Start, Run.

Step 2.   Type **regsvr32 actxprxy.dll** and press Enter.

Step 3.   Click Start, Shut Down. Mark the Restart option button, and click OK.

Thanks to Adam Vujic for his help with this secret.

This last fix should also restore your ability to open a new Internet Explorer window when you hold down the Shift key and click a link, according to James Geater at Microsoft.

Make actual thumbnail files

Big graphic files in, little graphic files out. This is the way programs used to work. Give them an input folder and wait for the output, as shown in Figure 13-14.

Thumbnailer reads your graphics files and converts them into thumbnails — by default, 100 x 100 pixel *jpg* files at about 3K. These thumbnails are all separate files, not images in a browser, as they are with Paint Shop Pro. You can use them as thumbnails on your web pages. Because they are separate files, they are not easy to browse, so they won't help you find out what's in your graphics files.

You'll find Thumbnailer at www.smalleranimals.com.

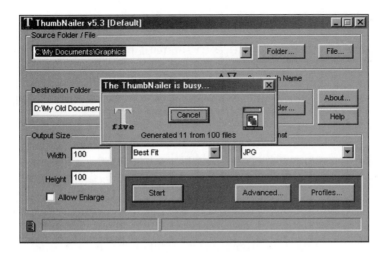

Figure 13-14: Waiting for a thumbnail to generate.

Navigating

The Explorer is for exploring after all.

My Computer now has a Folders pane

Earlier versions of Windows 98 wouldn't let you go from My Computer to My Explorer. If you opened My Computer, you didn't get the View, Explorer Bar, Folders option. You could get rid of the left pane if you opened in Explorer mode, but you couldn't add it if you opened in My Computer mode. Happily, that's no longer the case with Internet Explorer 5.

Explore from here

In Chapter 8 of *Windows 98 Secrets*, we show you how to use the Explorer command line switches to change the Explorer's behavior. One way that you can use switches is to set the top of the Explorer folder list at your current folder and just display the branches shooting out from there.

Secret

If you want to do the same thing without command line switches, you can add Explore from Here to the context menu that appears when you right-click a folder icon in your Explorer or My Computer window. Selecting it brings up a new Explorer window displaying just the subfolders of the folder you right-clicked. Follow these steps to make this change yourself. Alternatively, you can download PowerToys and use one of its utilities, as described at the end of this section.

STEPS:

Adding Explore from Here to All Your Folders

Step 1. Click Start, Run, type **regedit**, and press Enter.

Step 2. Navigate in the left pane to HKEY_CLASSES_ROOT\Folder\shell.

Step 3. Right-click the right pane of your Registry editor, and click New, Key.

Step 4. Rename the key something like **fromhere**.

Step 5. Highlight the fromhere key, double-click Default in the right pane, and type **E&xplore from Here** in the Value Data field. The ampersand allows you to use the X key to select this item in the context menu. Click OK.

Step 6. Highlight the fromhere key, right-click the right pane, and click New, Key.

Step 7. Rename the new key **command**.

Step 8. Highlight the command key, double-click Default, type **Explorer.exe /e,/root,/idlist,%i** in the Value Data field, and click OK.

Step 9. Close the Registry editor.

You'll now have a new context menu item whenever you right-click a folder icon.

Windows 95 PowerToys includes an Explore.inf file that does exactly what we have shown you how to do here. You can find it at www.microsoft.com/windows/downloads/contents/PowerToys/W95PwrToysSet/. Extract the PowerToys utilities to a temporary folder, and install Explore from Here by right-clicking Explore.inf and clicking Install.

To find out other ways to modify your context menus, see the "Tweaking your context menus" section later in this chapter.

The left pane of your Explorer is missing?

Wow, where did it go? Are you sure that you just didn't click View, Explorer Bar, and clear the check mark next to Folders? If you did, just click it again. If not, right-click the Explorer title bar and click Maximize. Is the divider between the two Explorer panes hiding on either the right or left side?

Secret

If these suggestions don't work, you can always edit the Registry to return the Folders pane to its default position. Here's how:

STEPS:

Recovering the Folders Pane

Step 1.   Click Start, Run, type **regedit**, and press Enter.

Step 2.   Navigate to HKEY_CURRENT_USER\Software\Microsoft\Internet Explorer\Main.

Step 3.   Scroll down until you see the ExplorerBar value in the right pane of the Registry editor.

Step 4.   Right-click ExplorerBar, click Delete, and then click Yes. It will revert to its default value.

Step 5.   Close the Registry editor.

Put two Explorers next to each other

TWinExplorer is a standalone Explorer that combines two Explorers in one window (see Figure 13-15). It's easy to drag and drop files from one folder to another when you can view the source and the target in one window.

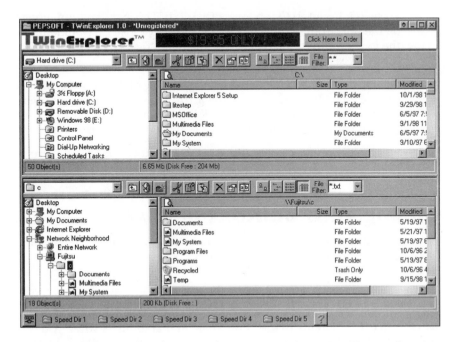

Figure 13-15: TWinExplorer gives you two connected Explorer views for easy dragging and dropping.

TWinExplorer doesn't replace your Windows Explorer; it is a separate application that gives you most of the Windows Explorer functionality while providing two connected Explorer-like views. Those of you who remember Windows 3.1 with its ability to put up two windows or more in the File Manager will recognize what TWinExplorer is trying to accomplish.

While it can't display HTML pages like the regular Windows Explorer and it doesn't have right-click functionality in the right pane, TWinExplorer can still do some things that the Windows Explorer can't. For example, you can highlight a folder icon in the left pane and click the New Folder toolbar button to create a new folder in the right pane. You can also use the File Filter drop-down list to select which file types to display. And you can define up to five buttons on the status bar that allow you to quickly jump to the assigned folder.

Easy to install and uninstall, you'll find TWinExplorer at www.pepsoft.com.

Moving around multi-tabbed dialog boxes

In Chapter 27 of *Windows 98 Secrets*, we provide a long list of keyboard shortcuts that work with the Windows 98 user interface. Chris Pirillo reminded us of a couple that we discussed generally, but not specifically, that are very useful when working with multi-tabbed dialog boxes.

To switch from tab to tab, press Ctrl+Tab. This combination moves the focus on the tabs from left to right. To move it back, use Ctrl+Shift+Tab. To change the focus within the tab, use Tab and Shift+Tab. To mark and clear check boxes, press the Spacebar.

To display drop-down lists, use Alt+up arrow or Alt+down arrow. To then choose an item in the list, use the arrow keys to select it and press Enter. Pressing Enter sends an overall OK if the focus isn't on any other button (even if you aren't focused on the OK button), and closes the dialog box.

It's actually pretty easy to use Windows without a mouse, but you do have to learn quite a few different (and not always consistent) keystrokes.

Tweaking your context menus

Lots of programs add their own contributions to the various context menus. You can delete theirs and add yours.

Add items to the context menu

Secret

You can add items to the context menu that appears when you right-click your My Computer icon, Start button, or any folder icon. Sometimes software manufacturers use this simple and simple-minded method to add their commands to your context menu. You can use these steps to find out if they did, and remove their commands if you so choose.

STEPS:

Adding New Commands to the Context Menu

Step 1.   Open your Registry editor, and click Edit, Find.

Step 2.   Type **{20D04FE0** in the Find What field to search for {20D04FE0-3AEA-1069-A2D8-08002B30309D} (the Resource ID for My Computer). Click Find Next.

Step 3.   Click the plus sign next to {20D04FE0, and highlight the *shell* key in the left pane of the Registry editor.

Step 4.   Right-click the right pane of the Registry editor, click New, Key (see Figure 13-16). Type a short descriptive name for the command you are about to add to the context menu.

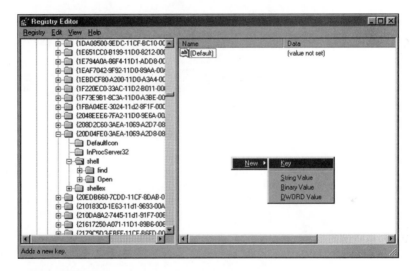

Figure 13-16: Click Key to create a new Registry key containing your new context menu command.

Step 5.   Double-click Default in the right pane of the Registry editor, and type the new context menu command as it will appear in the context menu. Put an ampersand in front of the letter that you want to designate as the hot key, as shown in Figure 13-17. Click OK.

Step 6.   Highlight the new key in the left pane of your Registry editor, right-click the right pane, and click New, Key. Rename the key **command**.

Continued

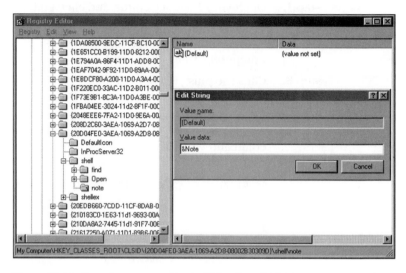

Figure 13-17: Type the command in the Value Data field. Use an ampersand to designate a hot key for your command.

Step 7. Highlight your new *command* key in the left pane, double-click Default in the right pane, and type the actual program that you want to call when you click this context menu item, including its pathname (see Figure 13-18). Click OK.

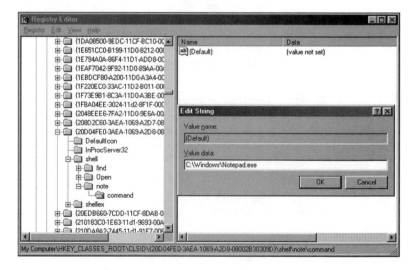

Figure 13-18: Type the program that your command will run, along with its path.

Step 8. Close the Registry editor, and then right-click the My Computer icon on the Desktop to see your new command.

Thanks to Stephen Charles Rea help with this secret.

Secret

Software authors can also use this method to add a menu item to the context menu for all files: Add a key under HKEY_CLASSES_ROOT/*/shellex/ ContextMenuHandlers. You can see a context menu handler for WinZip in Figure 13-19 because WinZip is installed.

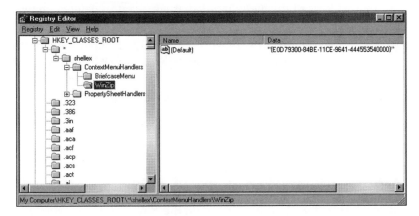

Figure 13-19: The ContextMenuHandlers Registry key lists some applications that have added their commands to the context menus for all files.

If you want to delete the context menu items associated with the indicated application (in this case, WinZip), just delete the key under ContextMenuHanders. You might first highlight the key and click Registry, Export Registry File to save this Registry entry in case you want to put it back in later.

Clear your hard drive context menu

When you right-click your hard disk icon, you may discover that the context menu items are adding up. Plus! 98 adds the McAfee scanning for viruses and Windows Backup. Icon Wizard adds a call, as does Sandra. WinZip adds one, too (although it doesn't go into the same place in the Registry—see the previous section.

Secret

To remove items that get stuck to your hard drive's context menu, you'll need to edit your Registry, as described in these steps:

STEPS:

Clearing the Hard Drive's Context Menu

Step 1. Click Start, Run, type **regedit**, and press Enter.

Step 2. Navigate to HKEY_CLASSES_ROOT\Drive. Click the plus signs next to Drive and next to *shell*. This displays the keys representing the context menu items that have been added to the drive's context menu. Open each of the menu items, highlight the *command* key, and see which applications are called.

Step 3. After viewing the context menu items under *shell*, right-click the keys of the menu items that you want to delete one by one, and click Delete.

If you are not sure, you can save the Drive branch of the Registry first; just highlight the Drive key in the left pane, click Registry, Export Registry File, and name this file **Drive.reg**.

Step 4. When you are done, close the Registry editor.

Missing New from your context menu?

Secret

If your context menu doesn't contain the New menu item when you right-click the Desktop or the right pane of your Explorer, it may be because there is a damaged key in your Registry. We've included a file, New.reg, on the accompanying CD-ROM that will fix this problem. It includes this text:

```
REGEDIT4
[HKEY_CLASSES_ROOT\Directory\Background\shellex\ContextMenuHandlers\Ne
w]
@="{D969A300-E7FF-11d0-A93B-00A0C90F2719}"
```

Right-click the file and click Merge. You can also open your Registry editor, and navigate to the New key to see what the default value is in the right pane of your Registry editor. If it is different than the value given in New.reg, you can edit it to match this value.

Find

You can fix up your find so that it doesn't fill up with less useful items. You can also get to your previous finds quickly.

Find your Finds

Press F3 while your Explorer window has the focus, and up pops the Find dialog box. Press F4 now and the previous finds (those that you did after the last time you started Windows) are displayed in the Named drop-down list. It's just the same as clicking the down arrow to the right of the list.

Find menu items

Secret

After installing a piece of software, you may find that the Find menu (on the Start menu or the Explorer's Tools menu) has grown a bit. If you want to pare it back, you'll have to edit your Registry.

STEPS:

Deleting Find Menu Items

Step 1. Start your Registry editor.

Step 2. Navigate to HKEY_LOCAL_MACHINE\SOFTWARE\Microsoft\ Windows\CurrentVersion\explorer\FindExtensions\Static (see Figure 13-20). You won't have CopernicFind and OutlookFind in your Registry unless you've installed these programs.

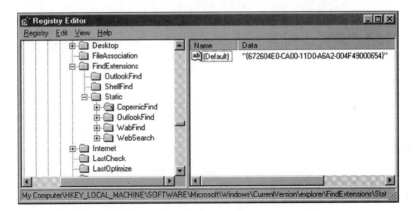

Figure 13-20: The Registry editor focused on CopernicFind. Copernic is a third party program that searches search engines.

Step 3. To save your existing settings before making any changes, highlight Static in the left pane of the Registry editor. Click Registry, Export Registry File, and save the selected branch as **Static**.

Continued

Deleting Find Menu Items *(continued)*

Step 4. Double-click any of the keys under Static, and click the 0 key under any of them. If the menu item that is displayed as the Default in the right pane of the Registry is the item that you want to delete, highlight the associated key under Static, and press Delete.

Step 5. Continue until you have removed all of the items that you want to remove from the Find menu, and then exit your Registry editor.

Managing Explorer icons

You can fix a few problems that arise with icons displayed in your Explorer.

Change your disk drive icons in the Explorer

If you don't like the icons that represent your hard disks, you can change them quite easily. All you need to do is add a small text file to the root directory of the hard disk whose icon you want to change. Both the D and F drive (which is a CD-ROM drive) icons have been changed in Figure 13-21.

Figure 13-21: You can use different icons for your drives, as in this example.

To change the icon for a disk drive, take these steps:

STEPS:

Changing a Disk Drive Icon

Step 1. In your Explorer, highlight the disk drive icon in the left pane.

Step 2. Right-click the right pane of the Explorer, and click New, Text Document.

Step 3. Rename the text document **autorun.inf**.

Step 4. Click the new text document to open it. Type:

[autorun]
icon=d:\otherfolder\youricon.ico

Step 5. Save the new text file and exit Notepad.

Step 6. Press F5 to refresh the Explorer.

Be sure that the pathname and filename of your icon are correct. We had a problem with the names of some icons that had capital letters near the ends of the prefix. Also, you can reference icons in *exe*, *dll* and other files. You just have to add a comma after the filename, and then the icon's index number.

WinBoost will help you do this also (see "Tweaking the Windows 98 Desktop" in Chapter 12).

Stray icons in your Explorer

If you find stray, perhaps blank icons in your Explorer near the Dial-Up Networking, Control Panel, Printers, and Scheduled Tasks icons, you can get rid of them fairly easily. They are left over from some program that stuck them in this unlikely spot.

Secret

As we discussed in "Get rid of unattached Desktop icons" in Chapter 12, these folders are attached to Class IDs found under the NameSpace key. Open your Registry editor and navigate to HKEY_LOCAL_MACHINE\SOFTWARE\ Microsoft\Windows\CurrentVersion\explorer\mycomputer\NameSpace.

Highlight each of the Class IDs under NameSpace in the left pane of the Registry editor and see if there is an associated application name in the right pane. If not, you can use Registry Crawler, as discussed in "Crawl through the Registry" in Chapter 14, (or just use the Registry editor itself) to search for other instances of the Class ID. Use the information found in these other branches to determine whether you should delete the Class ID from the NameSpace.

If the Class ID is not associated with any application, or is associated with a deleted application, then you can remove it. You can also export the NameSpace branch as a *reg* file before you delete any Class IDs, so that you can re-import the *reg* file later if it turns out you got carried away.

Zipping along

We discuss using WinZip with Windows 98, especially using it along with Plus! 98, which includes a similar file compression capability.

Zip (compress) your files

WinZip has been one of the most downloaded shareware programs of all time. It probably continues to be to this day. If you have Plus! 98, you'll notice that the basic functionality of WinZip is now built right into Windows 98, in its Compressed Folders feature.

We wonder why Microsoft hasn't trumpeted this particular feature for the Plus! 98 package. It works well and seamlessly, and Microsoft certainly has had a history of adding basic functionality to the operating system, thereby undercutting the competition. Maybe it is because WinZip is so popular and is a shareware package that they didn't want to be seen as destroying the little guy — in this case, Nico Mak.

When you install Plus! 98, Windows 98 automatically takes over the zip function from WinZip by changing the action taken on files with *zip* extensions. But the Add to Zip item is still on your context menu (or in a WinZip submenu of your context menu as Add To), and you can reassociate WinZip with zip files just by right-clicking a file in your Explorer and clicking Add to Zip. You will be given the chance to make WinZip the default compression program, as shown in Figure 13-22. (This also works with Extract To.)

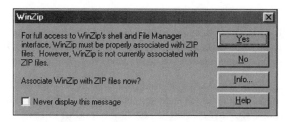

Figure 13-22: To reassociate WinZip with your zip files, click Yes when you see this message box.

If you have installed Plus! 98's Compressed Folders feature and *zip* files are associated with this Explorer shell extension, you can right-click a file with a *zip* extension and click Explore to see an Explorer-like view of the contents of the zip file, as shown in Figure 13-23.

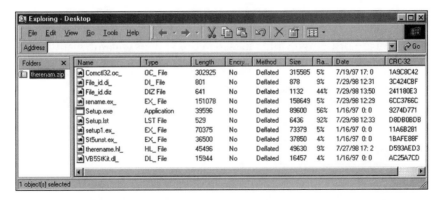

Figure 13-23: The Explorer view of a zip file.

Instead of using WinZip's Add to Zip context menu item, you can move files into a compressed zip file (known by Windows 98 as a *compressed folder*) by right-clicking the file, and clicking Send To, Compressed Folder. A zip file with the same filename is created in the same folder as the original file. You can then drag and drop other files to the compressed folder.

You can extract compressed files from a compressed folder by clicking the zip file in your Explorer to open it, and then dragging icons from the compressed folder window into another Explorer window.

To create a new empty compressed folder on your Desktop, right-click the Desktop, and click New, Compressed Folder. Type a new name (with the *zip* extension), and then drag files to the folder on the Desktop. Of course, you can do this in any folder in your Explorer, not just on your Desktop.

WinZip takes over my Compressed Folders

WinZip is a wonderful compression/decompression program with lots of extra features that are not available from Microsoft's Compressed Folders. Compressed Folders is included in Microsoft Plus! 98 and integrates *zip* files into your Explorer as a version of folders. Compressed Folders does the basic job of compressing and decompressing files while appearing to be just a part of Windows.

If you install WinZip after you've installed Compressed Folders, it takes over the function of handling *zip* files, and Compressed Folders just seems to disappear. We'll show you how to get it back.

If you installed WinZip before you installed Plus! 98 and Compressed Folders, you may find that it tries to take over for Compressed Folders, and often succeeds without your express permission. You've suffered from a Niko Mak attack!

Older versions of WinZip win back control by rewriting a setting in the Registry even as you try to tell them not to. For example, if you right-drag a

Compressed Folder icon in your Explorer to a new folder, the context menu shown in Figure 13-24 appears. The first option invokes WinZip. Click it and you are presented with a message box that asks if you want to use WinZip as the application that is associated with *zip* files.

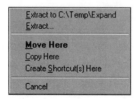

Extract to C:\Temp\Expand
Extract...

Move Here
Copy Here
Create Shortcut(s) Here

Cancel

Figure 13-24: Choose the first option in this context menu to make WinZip your default.

The Yes button has the focus, and if you don't click No in time, or if you click No but the dialog box never gets the focus, older versions of WinZip go ahead and overwrite the Compressed Folders setting in the Registry and take charge of zip files.

No matter what version of WinZip you have, you can re-associate Compressed Folders with zip files by taking one of the following two sets of steps. The first is the recommended Microsoft method found in the Microsoft Knowledge Base article "Plus! 98: Cannot Use Compressed Folders After Installing WinZip" at support.microsoft.com/support/kb/articles/q189/7/86.asp.

This method basically has you uninstall and then reinstall Compressed Folders. Given that all you really want to do is make a change in the Registry, this seems a bit much. But it goes quickly, and as long as you have the Plus! 98 CD-ROM, you're all set.

Secret

The second method changes the Registry to point the zip files back to the Compressed Folders application. It merges a *reg* file into the Registry, so that you don't have to make this change yourself.

STEPS:

Reinstalling Compressed Folders (from Microsoft KB)

Step 1. Insert the Microsoft Plus! 98 CD-ROM into the CD-ROM drive. Press and hold down the Shift key when you insert the Plus! 98 CD-ROM to prevent it from starting automatically.

Step 2. Click Start, Settings, Control Panel.

Step 3. Click Add/Remove Programs, click Microsoft Plus! 98, and then click Add/Remove.

Step 4. Click Add/Remove, and then click Next. If the Compressed Folders check box is cleared, skip to step 9. If the Compressed Folders check box is marked, continue to the next step.

Step 5. Clear the Compressed Folders check box, and then click Next.

Step 6. Click Next, click Finish, and then click OK.

Step 7. Click Microsoft Plus! 98, and then click Add/Remove.

Step 8. Click Add/Remove, and then click Next.

Step 9. Mark the Compressed Folders check box, and then click Next.

Step 10. Click Next, and click Finish.

Step 11. Click OK to restart your computer.

STEPS:

Changing the Registry to Re-associate Compressed Folders

Step 1. Right-click the Compressed Folders Zip.reg file on the *MORE Windows 98 Secrets* CD-ROM, and click Merge. You're done.

Step 2. If you don't have this CD-ROM, right-click your Desktop, click New, Text Document, and rename the document **Compressed Folders Zip.reg**. Click Yes to accept the file type change.

Step 3. Click the new text file to open it and insert the following text:

```
REGEDIT4

[HKEY_CLASSES_ROOT\.ZIP]
@="CompressedFolder"
"Content Type"="application/x-zip-compressed"
```

Step 4. Click File, Save.

Step 5. Right-click the new Compressed Folders Zip.reg file, and click Merge. Click Yes to confirm that you want to add the information to your Registry, and then click OK.

Tip

This second set of steps works by associating files with the *zip* extension with the Compressed Folders application. If you open your Registry editor before you take these steps and focus it on HKEY_CLASSES_ROOT\.zip, you can watch the change taking place.

WinZip takes over the Cabinet view

Secret

Installing WinZip 7.0 also gets rid of the View context menu item that appears when you right-click a *cab* file. To restore this handy menu item (without taking away any WinZip functionality or ease of use), take these steps:

STEPS:

Restoring the Cabinet View

Step 1. Open your Registry editor. Navigate to HKEY_CLASSES_ROOT\ .cab.

Step 2. Double-click the Default variable in the right pane of the Registry editor and replace "WinZip" in the Value Data field with:

CLSID\{0CD7A5C0-9F37-11CE-AE65-08002B2E1262}

Step 3. Click OK, and then close the Registry editor.

Step 4. Now when you right-click a *cab* file, you should see the View menu item in boldface at the top of the context menu (see Figure 13-25). If you don't, proceed to step 5.

Figure 13-25: The *cab* file context menu after WinZip is installed and the View menu item restored.

Step 5. If the fix in step 2 didn't work, open your Registry editor to navigate to HKEY_CLASSES_ROOT\CLSID\{0CD7A5C0-9F37-11CE-AE65-08002B2E1262}\shell\open\command.

Step 6. Double-click the Default variable in the right pane of the Registry editor and be sure that it states:

explorer /root,{0CD7A5C0-9F37-11CE-AE65-08002B2E1262},%1

If it doesn't, enter this value in the Value Data field.

Step 7. Click OK, and close the Registry editor.

Thanks to Don Lebow for pointing out this Microsoft Knowledge Base article to us.

Using WinZip with Compressed Folders

Just because you've installed Compressed Folders from Plus! 98 doesn't mean that you can't use WinZip. Maybe you'll want to use it anyway and ignore Compressed Folders. You can also use it in conjunction with Compressed Folders.

The WinZip setup adds a number of items to your context menus. You have some choices about how these menu items are displayed when you configure WinZip, either during its setup or any time later.

You can compress a file by right-clicking it and clicking WinZip, Add To. Or, you can click Send To instead and choose Compressed Folder to compress it to a file of the same name, in the same path, with a *zip* extension.

Right-click a zip file, and you'll see a combination of WinZip and Compressed Folder options.

The fact that WinZip and Compressed Folder get along makes for peace on the Desktop. It allows you to choose either one and see which one you like best without having to worry about the conflicts.

Crashing down and backing up

You might as well be safe.

Explorer crashes but you're still running

It's not all that hard to crash the Explorer, we say with typical understatement, but it is a bit more difficult to understand just what went wrong. We're inclined to leave the whys to certain subbranches of philosophical inquiry. What we want is our system tray icons back—that is, assuming that the system is well enough to teeter onward.

To force the Explorer to refresh these icons, click Start, Log Off *username* and then click Yes. Of course, this assumes that there is someone else that you can log in as, and then log back in as yourself.

Keep a second copy

Not all backup programs are the same or even similar. We often think of a backup program as something that allows us to restore our hard disk if it crashes, or something that runs overnight.

Second Copy 97 is a bit different. You set it up to run on a schedule to copy files from one device to another, making a second copy. The copied files can be compressed as they are copied. The previous versions of the files to be copied are deleted on the target device, or you can set how many versions deep to keep. You can copy to a floppy diskette, to a Zip drive, to another hard disk, to a network drive, or to another folder on the same hard disk.

You can create multiple sets of Second Copy instructions, called *profiles*, that determine which files are copied, how often, to what folder, and how many versions are kept. See the example in Figure 13-26. You can keep folders in sync, or just copy from source to target. You do all of this through wizards just like the Windows wizards.

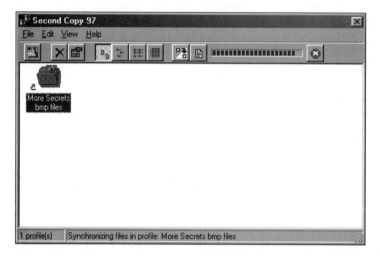

Figure 13-26: In this example, the icon called More Secrets Bmp Files represents a *profile*, or set of instructions for making copies of specific files.

Second Copy 97 runs as an icon in your system tray. You can set it to start when you start Windows, and make the first backup at a set time after Windows starts. You can also just use it to backup whenever you tell it to. Even if a file is in use, Second Copy 97 can most likely back it up.

We highly recommend Second Copy 97. It is available for a 30-day trial at www.centered.com.

Summary

Add power to your Explorer with third party extensions and applications.

▶ Clear out the warning in web page view about viewing the Windows folder.

▶ The Twin Explorer gives you two Explorers side-by-side.

▶ Explorer can barely rename files. When you need a massive rename, use THE Rename.

▶ Set up Second Copy 97 to make copies of your most important files, even as you work on them.

▶ It's easy to print a directory of files with Directory-2-HTML, a freeware application that creates an HTML version of your filenames.

Chapter 14

The Registry

In This Chapter

In *Windows 98 Secrets* we called the Registry the real user interface. Of course, that was a bit of a joke, but the Registry editor continues to prove so useful that we just can't get away from it.

▶ A safe and easy way to interact with the Registry is to use Registration files (text files with a *reg* extension) that can be merged into the Registry.

▶ The Registry editor is way too slow in search mode. You absolutely need the Registry Crawler, which doesn't crawl at all.

▶ The Registry monitor tells you what is happening with your Registry at any moment. Use it to record the changes that are made when you install new software.

▶ Did you get the scary message that your Registry is damaged? Maybe it is just bad memory.

Editing the Registry

We want you to be able to keep some of your Registry entries safe. You'll also appreciate the ability to speed through your Registry.

Editing the Registry with *reg* files

When you upgrade to Windows 98, you lose some of the little fixes to the Registry that we've outlined in *Windows 95 Secrets*, as well as in *Windows 98 Secrets*. You can get them back if you create Registration files (*reg* files) that save these changes before upgrading, and then merge them back into your Registry after your upgrade. Is it too late for you? Well, you can still save any important personal settings you defined after your upgrade to Windows 98 so that they will be available when you upgrade your operating system the next time.

Tip

Most often, you edit the Registry by changing settings in dialog boxes, without being directly aware that the changes you make are being recorded in the Registry. Another way that you can switch between Registry settings is to create and use *reg* files. With this method, you first choose one of the settings you want in a dialog box. You then export the small branch of the Registry that contains this setting to a text file and save the file with the *reg* extension. Next, you use the dialog box to switch to another setting, and then export the updated Registry branch to a second *reg* file. If you now place shortcuts to these two *reg* files on your Desktop, you can quickly switch back and forth between the settings by clicking these files instead of by interacting with a dialog box.

Crawl through the Registry

On the CD-ROM that comes with *Windows 98 Secrets*, we provide you with a tool called Registry Search and Replace that you can use to search and replace any given string in your Registry.

Registry Crawler is a somewhat different tool that works with the Windows 98 Registry editor to search for all the instances of a given string, as shown in Figure 14-1. It consolidates all the branches within which the string occurs and lets you more easily edit each of the branches. You'll find it at www.4developers.com/regc.

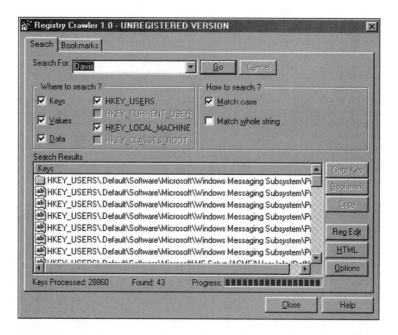

Figure 14-1: In this example, Registry Crawler displays all the places where the string *Davis* appears in Davis' Registry.

What we really like about the Registry Crawler is that it is very fast, much faster than searching through the Registry with the Registry editor. And while it is still searching you can click any found branches to open up the Registry editor to the indicated location.

Help with Registry edits

You can download a help file (Regedit.hlp) that provides a bit of help with Registry edits for Windows 95, Windows 98, and Windows NT (2000?). It includes a Registry FAQ, plus lots of little Registry edits that help out.

It is not a comprehensive Registry help file that thoroughly explains the Registry and its deeper branches (well, many of them do depend on what software you've loaded), so we were a little disappointed. We'd hoped to provide you with a cheap way to get more information about your Registry. Something like what is available in our *Windows 98 Secrets* book.

You can download this help file from www.regedit.com. Check out the web site for more information about Registry edits.

Little fixes to the Registry

Here are a few important Registry edits that can easily be overwritten.

Open My Computer in Explorer view

In "Turning My Computer into the Explorer" in Chapter 8 of *Windows 98 Secrets*, we told you how to change My Computer so that it opens with a Folders pane (the two-pane Explorer view). If you've made this change, you can keep it safe by exporting the proper branch of your Registry to a *reg* file. This is the branch you'll want to export:

HKEY_CLASSES_ROOT\CLSID\{20D04FE0-3AEA-1069-A2D8-08002B30309D}\shell\Open

If you haven't made this change yet, or it was overwritten when you upgraded to Windows 98, you can import the following text into your Registry. We make this easy by supplying the Explorer.reg file on the accompanying CD-ROM.

```
REGEDIT4

[HKEY_CLASSES_ROOT\CLSID\{20D04FE0-3AEA-1069-
A2D8-08002B30309D}\shell\Open]

[HKEY_CLASSES_ROOT\CLSID\{20D04FE0-3AEA-1069-
A2D8-08002B30309D}\shell\Open\command]

@="Explorer.exe"
```

Changing the default action for *reg* files

We find it a bit unnerving that the default option when clicking a file with the *reg* extension is Merge (into the Registry). This used to be a real problem with Windows 95, because the merge just took place without a question. Now, Windows 98 asks if you want to merge the file contents into the Registry.

Still, we'd like a little more deliberation before such a drastic action is taken. We'd like the user to have to right-click the file, and then click Merge. Therefore, we change the default action for *reg* files to Edit. Put the following text in a file called Regedit.reg and store it in your My System folder:

```
REGEDIT4

[HKEY_CLASSES_ROOT\regfile\shell]
@="edit"
```

You'll find the Regedit.reg file on the accompanying CD-ROM. Merge it into your Registry to make this change.

Make sure you're the owner

When you install a new version of Windows, it seems to forget who the computer's owner is. You can restore your rightful ownership by placing this text in a file named Owner.reg and merging it into your Registry.

```
REGEDIT4

[HKEY_LOCAL_MACHINE\SOFTWARE\Microsoft\Windows\CurrentVersion]
"InstallType"=hex:01,00

"RegisteredOwner"="Davis Straub"

"RegisteredOrganization"="Windows 98 Secrets"
```

You'll find Owner.reg file on the accompanying CD-ROM.

Oh yes, be sure to replace "Davis Straub" with your name in quotes, and "Windows 98 Secrets" with your company or organization name, if any.

Your own colors

You can keep track of your own Desktop colors and pass them on to friends. Here's an example of one color scheme that we use (a bit greenish). Before you import this color scheme, you'll want to save your present color scheme if it isn't a standard scheme. Right-click your Desktop, click Properties, Appearance, Save As, and enter a name for your present color scheme.

```
REGEDIT4

[HKEY_CURRENT_USER\Control Panel\Colors]

"ActiveTitle"="0 0 128"
"Background"="166 202 240"
"Hilight"="0 0 255"
"HilightText"="255 255 255"
"TitleText"="255 255 255"
"Window"="192 220 192"
"WindowText"="0 0 0"
"Scrollbar"="192 220 192"
"InactiveTitle"="192 220 192"
"Menu"="192 220 192"
"WindowFrame"="0 0 0"
"MenuText"="0 0 0"
"ActiveBorder"="0 0 0"
"InactiveBorder"="192 192 192"
"AppWorkspace"="255 255 128"
"ButtonFace"="0 128 128"
"ButtonShadow"="128 0 128"
"GrayText"="0 0 128"
"ButtonText"="0 0 0"
"InactiveTitleText"="0 0 0"
"ButtonHilight"="192 220 192"
"ButtonDkShadow"="0 0 0"
"ButtonLight"="192 192 192"
"InfoText"="0 0 0"
"InfoWindow"="255 255 225"
"MessageBoxText"="0 0 0"
"MessageBox"="0 128 128"
@="255 255 192"
"ButtonAlternateFace"="184 180 184"
"HotTrackingColor"="0 0 255"
"GradientActiveTitle"="0 128 128"
"GradientInactiveTitle"="128 128 128"
```

You'll find this particular color scheme in the Colors.reg file on the accompanying CD-ROM. To merge it into your Registry, right-click the file and click Merge.

Tip You can also make up your own color scheme (right-click the Desktop, click Properties, click Appearance), and then export the HKEY_CURRENT_USER\ Control Panel\Colors key. Name the file Colors.reg.

Dealing with file associations

Windows uses file extensions to associate files with applications.

Set your own file associations

We're always on the lookout for tools that give you more power over the Windows 98 operating system. One of the most difficult areas to manage — because it is such a massive data structure — is the Registry. We've found a few tools that help. One, Freedom of Association, lets you delete orphaned file extensions, re-associate extensions with the applications you prefer, and add extensions to existing file types.

None of your deletions are lost. You can undelete any of them at any time. You can restore any file association that you've changed.

When you first start Freedom of Association, it searches your Registry, finds all the file extensions and file types, and displays them as shown in Figure 14-2. If you see a red or yellow mark next to a file extension, you most likely can delete it.

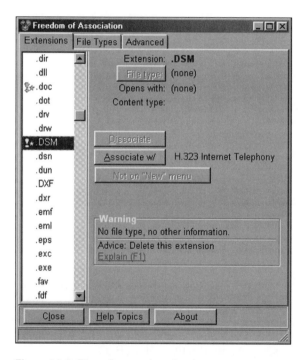

Figure 14-2: The yellow mark makes it easy to see an unassociated file extension.

To re-associate a file extension with another file type, highlight the extension in the Extensions tab, click the File Type button, scroll to the file type with which you want to associate this extension, highlight it, click the Extensions tab, and click the Associate W/ button.

Neil J. Rubenking of *PC Magazine* wrote Freedom of Association, and you'll find it at www.zdnet.com/pcmag/pctech/content/17/12/ut1712.001.html.

What extension goes with what application?

If you've forgotten which obscure file extension goes with which long forgotten application, check out the PC Web Encyclopedia, file extension section, at www.pcwebopaedia.com/file_extension.htm. There is a lot of other useful computer information here as well, especially computer terminology.

Watching your Registry

Changes to the Registry take place behind your back. Here's how to look around the corner.

Follow the Registry

The Registry Monitor will record and display every read or write to your Registry. You can use it to track Registry writes during the installation of new software, or to see what might be going wrong when you use a specific piece of software (see Figure 14-3).

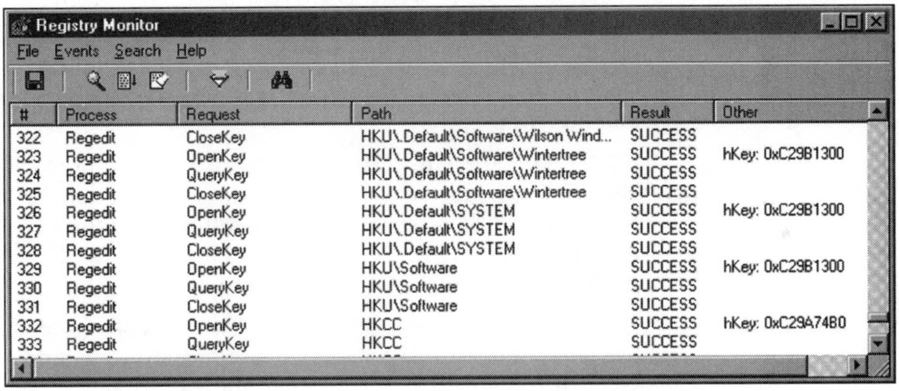

Figure 14-3: The Regmon window lists every process that has called the Registry, in the order it occurred.

You'll find a section devoted to the Registry Monitor in Chapter 15 of *Windows 98 Secrets*. We mention it here to advise you that there is a new version. You can now filter the output so that the Registry Monitor will only display reads and writes that meet your criteria. You can also limit the number of lines that will be kept in its history. And you can now search the output for a specific string.

You'll find the Registry Monitor at www.sysinternals.com.

Compare your Registry before and after

When you install software, your Registry is changed to record its location and to keep a central repository of the software's vital parameters. You can track just what changes are made to your Registry by taking these steps:

STEPS:

Tracking Your Registry Changes

Step 1. Click your shortcut to your Registry editor (\Windows\ regedit. exe). Highlight My Computer in the left pane of your Registry editor.

Step 2. Click Registry, Export Registry File, navigate to a scratch folder, enter a name for the exported text file, something like **Before**, and click Save.

Step 3. Install the new software. If you have SafeInstall98, be sure that it is running first before you install the software. It will determine if you are overwriting any system files with previous versions.

Step 4. After you have completed the new software installation, again click your shortcut to your Registry editor, highlight My Computer, and export the new Registry to a new file, perhaps named **After**.

Step 5. Click your shortcut to the Microsoft Management Console (you'll also find it in Start, Programs, Windows 98 Resource Kit, Tools Management Console). You did install the Windows 98 Resource Kit didn't you? If not, check out how in "Windows 98 Resource Kit Online" in Chapter 16.

Step 6. Expand the Windows 98 Resource Kit Tools Sampler branch in the left pane of the Management Console window, expand Tool Categories, click File Tools, and double-click WinDiff in the right pane (see Figure 14-4).

Step 7. In WinDiff, click File, Compare Files. Select the first file (Before.reg) in the Select First File dialog box, and click Open. Select the second file (After.reg) in the Select Second File dialog box, and click Open.

Step 8. Highlight the first line in the WinDiff client window (see Figure 14-5) and click the Expand button.

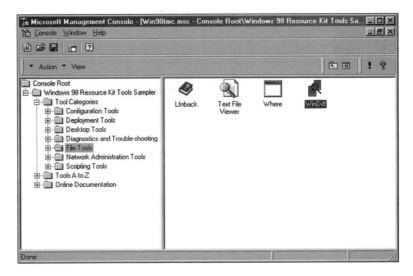

Figure 14-4: The WinDiff icon appears in the right pane when the File Tools folder is selected.

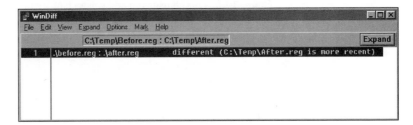

Figure 14-5: The WinDiff client window lists file comparisons. The Expand button is on the far right.

Step 9.   Be prepared to wait for a few minutes while WinDiff reads the two files. Mine were 6MB each, so it took a while.

Step 10.   Press Ctrl+Home, and choose View, Next Change to move to the first difference between the two files (see Figure 14-6). Lines that are present in the second file but not in the first (in this case, indicating new portions of the Registry) are highlighted in yellow. Lines that are present in the first file but not in the second (indicating portions of the Registry that have been altered) are highlighted in red. Continue pressing F8 to move from change to change, and then close WinDiff when you're finished comparing the files.

Continued

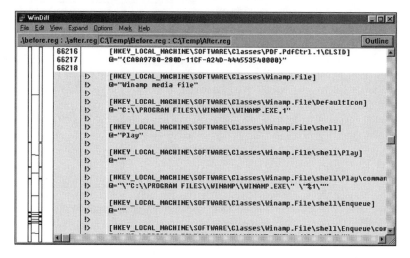

Figure 14-6: WinDiff uses red and yellow highlights to draw your attention to the areas that have changed.

Monitoring the files

File Monitor displays any file activity, whether in memory or from the hard disk. You can see how your applications use files or DLLs, as shown in Figure 14-7.

#	Time	Process	Request	Path	Result	Other
52	6:30:04 PM	Rcrawler	Read	0x20A	SUCCESS	Offset: 62976 Length: 4096
53	6:30:04 PM	Rcrawler	Read	0x200	SUCCESS	Offset: 29061120 Length: 4096
54	6:30:04 PM	Rcrawler	Read	0x200	SUCCESS	Offset: 27963392 Length: 4096
55	6:30:04 PM	Rcrawler	Read	0x20A	SUCCESS	Offset: 103936 Length: 4096
56	6:30:04 PM	Rcrawler	Read	0x200	SUCCESS	Offset: 29044736 Length: 4096
57	6:30:04 PM	Rcrawler	Read	0x200	SUCCESS	Offset: 29065216 Length: 4096
58	6:30:04 PM	KERNEL32	Close	0x33C	SUCCESS	CLOSE_FINAL
59	6:30:04 PM	KERNEL32	Close	0x340	SUCCESS	CLOSE_FINAL
60	6:30:04 PM	KERNEL32	Close	0x344	SUCCESS	CLOSE_FINAL
61	6:30:10 PM	Waterfal	Read	0x200	SUCCESS	Offset: 9854976 Length: 4096
62	6:30:10 PM	Waterfal	Read	0x200	SUCCESS	Offset: 16269312 Length: 4096

Figure 14-7: The File Monitor user interface.

Written by the same folks who wrote Registry Monitor, it provides a similar display of activity, and you get the same kinds of functions for controlling output display and searching.

You'll find the File Monitor at www.sysinternals.com.

Safeguarding your Registry

Bad things happen.

Is your Registry damaged?

Have you started up Windows 98 only to receive this scary message?

```
Windows registry is damaged. Windows will restart and try to fix the
problem.
```

While Registry damage is indeed a scary proposition, that may not be the problem at all. You may have a faulty memory chip, and because the Registry is read into memory during startup, it may fail to be written correctly. When ScanRegistry (Scanregw.exe) scans the Registry — it does so automatically at startup unless you configure Windows to skip this step — it finds the badly written part of the Registry. The copy of the Registry on your hard disk is still just fine. (We discuss how to turn off Scanregw.exe in the "AutoScan" section of Chapter 5 in *Windows 98 Secrets*.)

Once Scanregw.exe discovers that the Registry in memory is damaged because of bad memory, it marks the Registry as damaged and runs the real-mode version of Scanreg.exe when it restarts Windows. This may or may not restart Windows normally, because the real-mode version of Scanreg.exe may not find the bad memory location.

You can put new memory chips in your computer to see if that solves the problem, run a memory tester, or limit the amount of memory Windows 98 sees in the hope that the bad chip is beyond your imposed limit.

To test for damage by limiting the amount of memory used to start Windows, take these steps:

STEPS:

Limiting the Amount of Memory Used By Windows

Step 1. Restart your computer. Hold down the Ctrl key during the power-on self test, and when you see the Windows 98 Startup menu, choose to start in Safe mode.

Continued

STEPS

Limiting the Amount of Memory Used By Windows *(continued)*

Step 2.   Click Start, Programs, Accessories, System Tools, System Information. Then choose Tools, System Configuration Utility.

Step 3.   Click the Advanced button to display the Advanced Troubleshooting Settings dialog box shown in Figure 14-8.

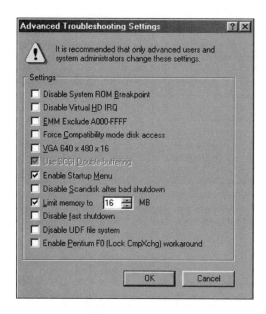

Figure 14-8: Use the Advanced Troubleshooting Settings dialog box to limit memory use for troubleshooting.

Step 4.   Mark the Limit Memory to [   ] MB check box, and enter **16**.

Step 5.   Click OK. Click OK. Restart Windows.

If your computer restarts Windows and you don't get the error message shown at the beginning of this section, then your Registry isn't damaged and you probably have a bad memory chip above the 16MB boundary. If you get the same error message, your bad memory chip may be below the 16MB boundary (if that is the problem). Download the memory test program RAMexam and check.

RAMexam runs in DOS and does a very thorough job of testing your memory. There is a demo version of it, which we found useless, on the company's web site. The demo is also not a good representation of the program's capabilities. The full version costs $24 and you can download it from the web, so you're not taking much of a financial risk.

You'll find RAMexam at www.qualitas.com.

Back up your Registry once a day

The Windows 98 ScanRegistry applet scans your Registry every time you restart Windows. If you use the Startup tab of your System Configuration Utility (Start, Programs, Accessories, System Information, Tools, System Configuration Utility, Startup), you'll see how it is called up when Windows starts.

ScanRegistry is configured to back up your Registry once a day, no matter how many times it is called during the day. However, if you don't shut down your computer at night, ScanRegistry won't run and you won't have a daily backup (for the last five days).

You can add a call to your Task Scheduler to run ScanRegistry at night, so that each day you will have a new Registry backup.

STEPS:

Calling ScanRegistry at Night

Step 1. Open your Explorer, and click Scheduled Tasks in the left pane. Click Add Scheduled Task in the right pane.

Step 2. In the Scheduled Task Wizard, click Next and wait while your computer goes out and finds registered programs.

Step 3. Click the Browse button (see Figure 14-9), and navigate to Scanregw.exe in your \Windows folder.

Step 4. Highlight Scanregw.exe and click Open.

Step 5. Click Daily, as shown in Figure 14-10. Click Next.

Continued

STEPS

Calling ScanRegistry at Night *(continued)*

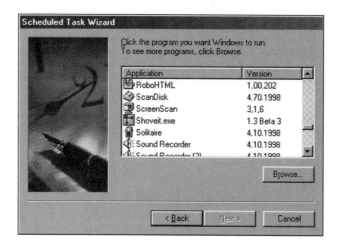

Figure 14-9: You won't find ScanRegistry in the application list, so use the Browse button to navigate to Scanregw.exe.

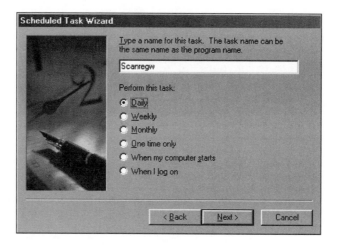

Figure 14-10: Mark the Daily option button.

Step 6. Set a time in the Start time field. Click Next.

Step 7. Mark the Open Advanced Properties for This Task When I Click Finish check box, as shown in Figure 14-11. Click Finish.

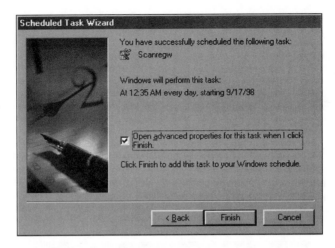

Figure 14-11: Mark the check box in the last wizard dialog box before clicking Finish.

Step 8.   Add a space and **/autorun** to the Run field, as shown in Figure 14-12. Click OK.

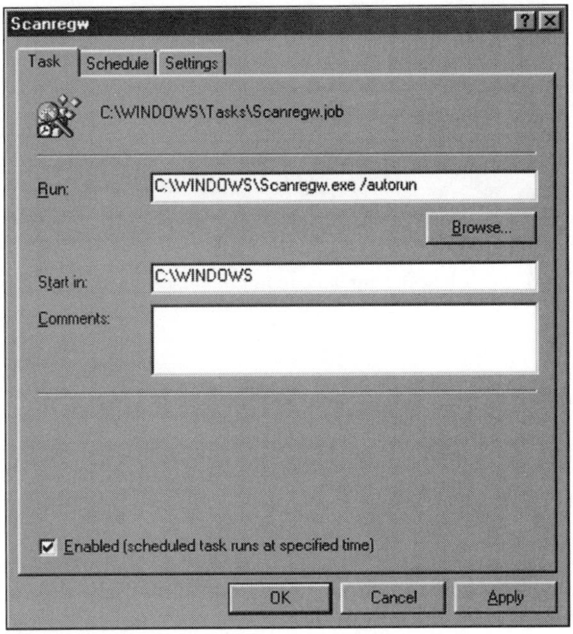

Figure 14-12: Edit the Run field as shown.

Your Registry will now be backed up once a day at the scheduled time, presumably when you are not working on the computer.

Thanks to Daniel E. Germann for this tip.

Back up your Registry, plus other settings and files

The Windows 98 Registry backup program, Scanregw.exe, does an admirable job creating five daily backups of your Registry automatically. If you want to create more backups and add additional settings and files to the backup file, check out WinRescue 98 (see Figure 14-13). You can download this shareware from www.superwin.com.

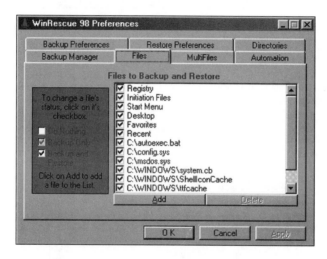

Figure 14-13: Use WinRescue's Files tab to select which files to back up and restore.

Emergency Recovery Utility doesn't come with Windows 98

We talk at length in Chapter 15 of *Windows 98 Secrets* about backing up and recovering your Registry. We also discuss a tool called Emergency Recovery Utility (ERU), which Microsoft included on the Windows 95 CD-ROM. The ERU utility creates an emergency boot diskette with a copy of your Registry and several other configuration files, such as Config.sys. Although in general we recommend using ScanRegistry instead of ERU, there may be times that ERU comes in handy.

Unfortunately, while Microsoft included both ScanRegistry and ERU on the Windows 98 beta CD-ROM, it dropped ERU from the final product — after

Windows 98 Secrets had gone to press. We apologize for any difficulty this may have caused.

You can still use ERU if you have access to a Windows 95 CD-ROM. Read the Eru.txt file found in the \Tools\Misc\Eru folder of your Windows 95 CD-ROM for details. Copy the four files you find in that folder to your \Windows folder, and then create a shortcut for Eru.exe and run it. If you don't have an ERU emergency boot diskette, make one right now. If your hard disk won't boot up (it's only a matter of time), boot from the floppy and you may be able to get your system back to normal.

Registry Key Backup

You can export any branch of your Registry to a text file just by opening the Registry editor, highlighting a key, clicking Registry, Export Registry File, and typing the name of the *reg* file that will contain the text version of the branch. Simple, but not that powerful.

Suppose you want to export multiple branches into one *reg* file? Or, you want to repeatedly export the same set of branches as you make changes? What you need is a little utility that lets you define different sets of branches to be exported, and then saves these definitions for later use.

This is exactly what Registry Key Backup, a little freeware package, does for you. Click the Add button to open a new blank branches set, and then click the plus (+) button to navigate the Registry and add branches to the set, as shown in Figure 14-14.

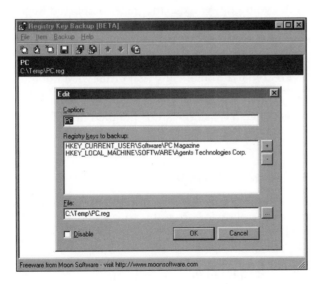

Figure 14-14: Use the + and − buttons along the right side of the Edit dialog box to navigate the Registry.

You'll find this handy little tool at www.moonsoftware.com.

Don't back up your Registry!

Every time Microsoft shows a Registry edit in their Knowledge Base, which is plenty of times, they include a disclaimer asking you to back up your Registry. They are not the only ones. We see this everywhere, and after a while it begins to look to us like the warning tags on pillows and mattresses that say *do not remove this tag*.

We've edited the Registry for over five years, and not once have we backed it up before a Registry edit! We've never had a problem.

We'll just bet that if you've done a number of Registry edits, you've rarely backed up your Registry (other than the automatic backups that happen when you start your computer for the first time each day). Therefore, all the warning messages aside, you're going bare, just like us. A fat lot of good the warning messages did!

There's a reason for this. The warning messages are too extreme. They tell you to do a bunch of work for the slight chance of something going wrong. One of the reasons they do this is to protect their authors' backsides. Just to be clear, we are not telling you to not back up your Registry (in spite of the title of this section).

We think that you might want to take a little precaution if you are unfamiliar with Registry edits, but this doesn't mean that you should back up the whole blessed thing. Before you make an edit that you are not sure about, export the little branch of the Registry that you are working on. To do this, highlight a key above the one you are editing, and click Registry, Export Registry File.

If you decide to undo your edit, you can merge the exported Registry branch back in. If you've added keys to your Registry, you'll have to delete them, because the merge function doesn't take anything out of the Registry.

Of course, you still have a complete Registry backup available to you at any time. Windows 98 created it automatically (isn't that what computers are supposed to do?) and you can access it if you get in over your head.

To restore a previous Registry, use the steps detailed in "Registry recovery" in Chapter 15 of *Windows 98 Secrets*.

Cleaning your Registry

If you didn't uninstall a program correctly, or if the programmer didn't write the uninstall routines correctly for programs that you uninstalled, you left behind dead branches in your Registry tree. It is possible for a utility program to check your Registry against programs available on your computer (just by going through the folders and seeing if they are there) and determine if it can do a bit of Registry pruning.

You have a couple of options. You can download either Perfect Companion, shown in Figure 14-15, from members.aol.com/easydesk, or Microsoft RegClean from support.microsoft.com/support/kb/articles/q147/7/69.asp. Both utilities work with Windows 98.

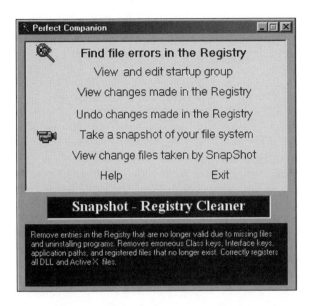

Figure 14-15: The Perfect Companion user interface.

Summary

Your Registry can grow to an unmanageable size if you don't use additional tools to help you keep it in check.

▶ Compare your Registry before and after you make changes to it.

▶ Set the Registry scanner to create a new backup of your Registry every day, even if you don't turn off your computer at night.

▶ Save Registry backup configurations to make it easier to export branches of your Registry.

▶ Prune the dead branches of your Registry left over from incorrectly uninstalled programs.

Chapter 15

The Task Scheduler

In This Chapter

The Task Scheduler has improved quite a bit since it was first introduced in the Windows 95 Plus! package. There are a few little gotchas, but we show you how to get around most of them.

▶ Change the default maintenance schedule so that it works for you, especially if you don't leave your computer on all night, every night.

▶ If you can't add tasks to the Task Scheduler, it may be because you've labeled your boot partition *Windows*.

▶ Stop the Task Scheduler so that you can clear out its log file.

▶ You can run programs when you quit Windows, you just can't do it with Task Scheduler.

Reschedule maintenance if your computer doesn't stay up all night

The Windows 98 and Plus! 98 installation routines automatically set up your Task Scheduler to accomplish various useful tasks while your computer is idle. When you install Plus! 98, you have the option of running the Maintenance Wizard, which lets you configure your maintenance tasks to run during the day or at night. The default is to run most of your tasks at night.

If you don't keep your computer on at night, then your Task Scheduler will never have a chance to run, and you'll miss out on the opportunity to have your computer's hard disk scanned and defragmented automatically. Fortunately, you can rework the schedule so that these useful tasks do get accomplished while you're not at the computer.

If you would rather not leave your computer on every night, you might want to reschedule most of the tasks to take place once a month, and then remind yourself to leave the computer on that night only. To take this approach, follow these steps:

STEPS:

Running Your Tasks Once a Month

Step 1. Open your Explorer, and highlight Scheduled Tasks in the left pane. Your scheduled tasks will appear in the right pane, as shown in Figure 15-1.

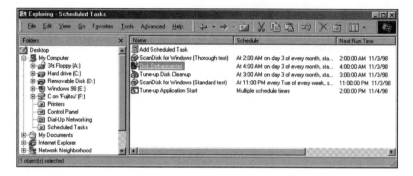

Figure 15-1: The Scheduled Tasks folder contains a list of scheduled tasks.

Step 2. Look for the ScanDisk for Windows item. (You might have two ScanDisk tasks, one labeled Standard Test and one labeled Thorough Test. If so, right-click the Thorough one.) Your item may also be named ScanDisk or Maintenance-ScanDisk. If you don't have any ScanDisk item, go on to the next step. Otherwise, skip to step 4.

Step 3. Click Add Scheduled Task, and wait a few minutes while the Scheduled Task Wizard searches your Registry for registered applications, as shown in Figure 15-2. Highlight ScanDisk, and click the Next button. Continue using the wizard to define the task, and click Finish when done.

Step 4. Right-click your ScanDisk item, and click Properties. Click the Settings button (not the tab), and make sure that Thorough and Automatically Fix Errors are marked, as shown in Figure 15-3.

Step 5. Click the Schedule tab, display the Schedule Task drop-down list, and select Monthly. Click the Day option button, and then choose a start time for this first task, as shown in Figure 15-4. Click OK.

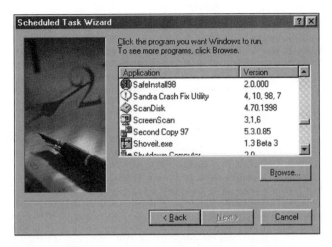

Figure 15-2: The wizard lists applications that you might add to your schedule.

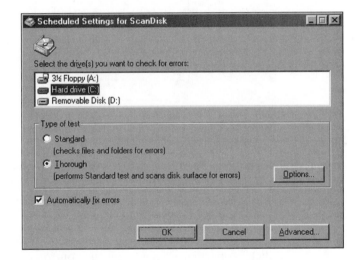

Figure 15-3: Mark the Thorough option button and the Automatically Fix Errors check box.

Continued

STEPS

Running Your Tasks Once a Month *(continued)*

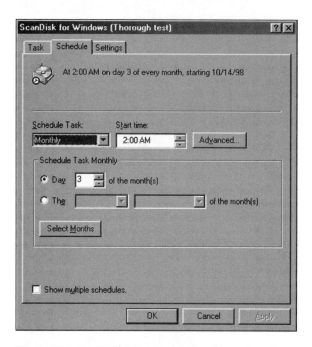

Figure 15-4: The Schedule tab, showing the settings for our example.

Step 6. Right-click the Maintenance-Disk Cleanup item in the Task Scheduler. It will be there if you've installed Plus! 98. This task might be called Tune-up Disk Cleanup on your computer — if you're in doubt, check that the Run field on the Task tab says C:\WINDOWS\CLEANMGR.EXE. (If you don't see any Disk Cleanup item, follow step 3 again, this time adding the Disk Cleanup task.) Click Properties. Click the Settings button on the Task tab, and make sure you've selected the files to be deleted automatically, as shown in Figure 15-5. Click OK.

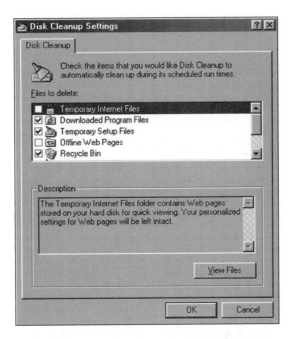

Figure 15-5: The Disk Cleanup tab provides a brief description of each item to help you decide whether to include it for deletion.

Step 7. Click the Schedule tab, and set Disk Cleanup to run an hour later than ScanDisk, but on the same night. Click OK.

Step 8. Right-click the Disk Defragmenter task in the Task Scheduler. (It may also be called Maintenance-Defragment Programs. If you don't see any Disk Defragmenter item, follow step 3, this time adding the Disk Defragmenter task.) Click Properties. Click the Schedule tab and schedule the Defragmenter to occur on the same day of the month as ScanDisk and Disk Cleanup, but an hour after the cleanup. Click OK.

Tip

Now that you've set up your Task Scheduler to perform these tasks on one day of the month, you'll want to be sure that there are no conflicts between the Disk Defragmenter and your screen savers, power management, or any other applications. At the end of your workday on the day that you are going to have these tasks performed overnight, you might want to run through the steps that we've detailed in "Stop everything else to run the Defragmenter" in Chapter 20.

Did the scheduled tasks get done?

Your scheduled tasks are supposed to happen in the background, but your computer may have been turned off when they were supposed to take place. You can keep track of what happened to your scheduled tasks by clicking the Scheduled Tasks icon in the left pane of your Explorer.

Switch to Details view (View, Details) and scroll the right pane to the right until you can see the Status column, as shown in Figure 15-6. If a task was missed, it will say so in this column.

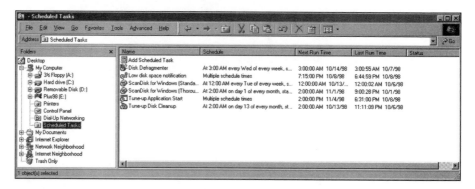

Figure 15-6: The Status column is empty, so in this case all of the tasks were completed. The Last Run Time column tells you when.

If you want to be notified of a missed task when you restart Windows, choose Advanced, Notify Me of Missed Tasks. This can become a bit bothersome because some tasks, such as Low Disk Space Notification, happen every hour or so and you'll get a notice of a missed task every time you restart Windows.

The Task Scheduler doesn't always appear to be aware of whether the tasks got completed. You can interrupt Defrag for example, and the Task Scheduler log shows that nothing was amiss. If the task ended on its own with an error, the Task Scheduler log displays this problem.

Can't add tasks to the Scheduled Tasks?

If you can't add tasks to the Task Scheduler, or if the Task Scheduler will not run at all, it may be because your boot drive is labeled with the same name as your \Windows folder. Weird, huh?

Assuming that your \Windows folder is in fact called Windows, then you want to be darn sure your C drive is not called Windows. In your Explorer, right-click your boot drive hard disk icon, and click Properties. If the drive is labeled Windows, as shown in Figure 15-7, rename it in the Label field. Click OK.

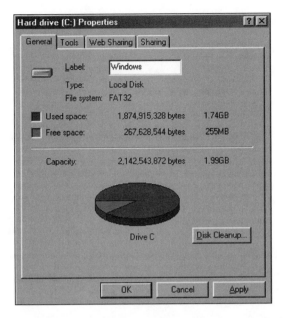

Figure 15-7: Look in the Label field to make sure your C drive is not labeled Windows, as this one is.

Run the Maintenance Wizard to schedule maintenance tasks

The Task Scheduler has a wizard front end, the Maintenance Wizard, as well as the Scheduled Task Wizard, which we discussed earlier in this chapter. The Maintenance Wizard singles out a few of the more important computer maintenance tasks (ScanDisk, Defrag, WinAlign, virus checking, and temporary file erasing) and sets them up in the Task Scheduler. (For a description of WinAlign, check out "WinAlign makes Microsoft applications load faster" in Chapter 16.)

You can invoke the Maintenance Wizard by clicking Start, Programs, Microsoft Plus! 98, Maintenance Wizard. Yes, that means you get it with Plus! 98. (Of course, you need to install Plus! 98 first if you want this little wizard on your Start menu.) Mark the option Change My Maintenance Settings Or Schedule in the dialog box shown in Figure 15-8, and click OK.

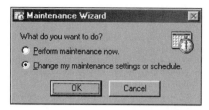

Figure 15-8: Choose the second option button to modify your Maintenance Wizard settings.

The first dialog box of the Maintenance Wizard appears (see Figure 15-9). You definitely don't want to use the wizard in Express mode if you have already set up a list and schedule of tasks that you like, because they will all be written right over.

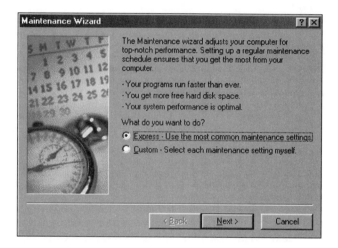

Figure 15-9: The first dialog box of the Maintenance Wizard.

The Maintenance Wizard runs when you first install Plus! 98. It is this wizard that sets up your initial task schedule. If you run the wizard (or if it is run for you by the Plus! 98 installation procedures) and you choose the Custom option, then you get to determine which tasks are going to be run. Otherwise, the default Express option gives you what some of the good folks and Microsoft think you should be running as your maintenance tasks.

If you choose the Custom option in the first wizard dialog box, you get to use the current Task Scheduler settings, if any (see Figure 15-10) in the second wizard dialog box. That way you don't wipe out the existing, perhaps somewhat complex schedules.

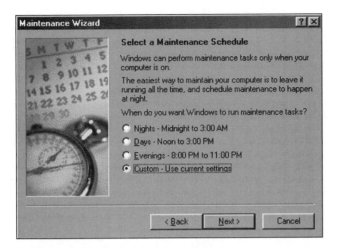

Figure 15-10: Mark the Custom – Use Current Settings option button to keep your other Task Scheduler settings.

The third wizard dialog box reminds you that you have a number of programs that are run at startup time, as shown in Figure 15-11, and it lets you decide whether to have them run or not. This is not nearly as comprehensive as the System Configuration Utility, which we discuss in "Manage how Windows 98 Startup files start up" in Chapter 18, as well as in lots of other places in this book. With the System Configuration Utility, you can choose from the much larger list of programs that actually start at Windows 98 startup. The Maintenance Wizard only lets you choose from the programs whose shortcuts are found in the \Windows\Start Menu\Programs\StartUp folder.

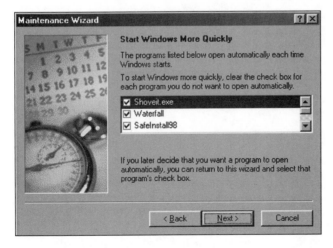

Figure 15-11: This Maintenance Wizard dialog box only lists applications in the StartUp folder.

After you run through the Maintenance Wizard, be sure to click each of the scheduled tasks in the Scheduled Tasks folder, and click the Settings button in the Task tab of the dialog box that appears to make sure that the settings for that task are the ones that you actually want.

Add anti-virus checking to the Task Scheduler

Plus! 98 installs McAfee VirusScan on your computer, and by default it will be added to your list of scheduled tasks. If you don't find Maintenance-Anti-Virus in the list of scheduled tasks, you can add it in two ways.

The first is to invoke the Maintenance Wizard, as discussed in the previous section. Choose the Custom option, and step through each possible task without making any changes, until you get to the Scan for Viruses dialog box (see Figure 15-12). Here, mark Yes, and click the Reschedule button to set up a schedule for scanning for viruses.

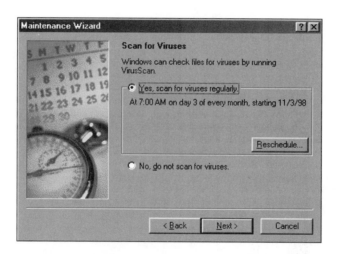

Figure 15-12: Mark the first option button to schedule automatic scanning for viruses.

Keep stepping through the Maintenance Wizard until you finish.

The other way is to take these steps:

STEPS:

Creating an Anti-Virus Scanning Scheduled Task

Step 1.   Open your Explorer and highlight Scheduled Tasks in the left pane.

Step 2.   Right-click an existing scheduled task, and click Copy.

Step 3.   Right-click your Desktop and click Paste.

Step 4.   Press F2 (while the new item on your Desktop is highlighted) and type Maintenance-Anti-Virus and press Enter.

Step 5.   Drag the new icon from your Desktop back into your Task Scheduler.

Step 6.   Right-click the Maintenance-Anti-Virus task icon, and click Properties.

Step 7.   Change the Run field to read c:\Progra~1\Plus!\Viruscan\ sched.vsc, as shown in Figure 15-13. You may have this file in another folder, so you might want to check with another copy of your Explorer to make sure that it is where we say it is.

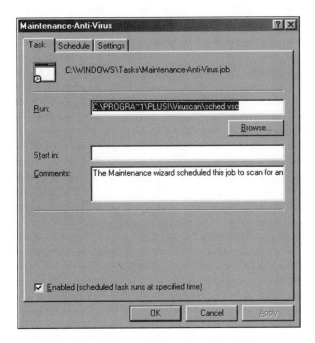

Figure 15-13: This Run field shows the normal path to the VirusScan configuration file.

Step 8.   Change the Comments field to reflect the current application.

Step 9.   Click the Schedule tab to make any changes to the virus scanning schedule that you deem necessary. Click OK.

Task Scheduler and Critical Update Notification conflicts

As we write this chapter in early 1999, there continue to be conflicts between the Critical Update Notification applet and the Task Scheduler. Even if you turn off Scheduled Tasks, the Critical Update Notification applet keeps it on so that it can use the timing functions to access the Microsoft Windows Update site on a regular schedule.

You have the option of uninstalling the Critical Update Notification applet using Add/Remove Programs in your Control Panel. You can also stop it from running by using the System Configuration Utility and clearing the Critical Update Notification check box in the Startup tab.

To check on the latest fixes for this problem, check "Cannot Disable Task Scheduler" in the Microsoft Knowledge Base at support.microsoft.com /support/kb/articles/q195/9/33.asp.

Clear out the Task Scheduler log

If you open your Explorer to the Task Scheduler (highlight Scheduled Tasks in the left pane) and click Advanced, View Log, you'll open a text file (\Windows \SchedLog.txt) in Notepad. This file lists the times and application names for applications that have been run by the Task Scheduler.

After a few months, this log file can get a bit long and hard to read. Because it's just a text file, you might get the idea that you can choose Edit, Select All, press Delete, and then choose File, Save to clear out the file. Unfortunately, that probably won't work. If you delete the text and then attempt to save the changes with File, Save, you'll find that the Save As dialog box appears and you're asked to come up with a filename to save the changes to. In other words, you won't be able to save the changes to the SchedLog.txt file.

If Task Scheduler is running, and that means Mstask.exe is loaded in memory and running, you won't be able to delete the contents of the SchedLog.txt file. What you have to do is stop Task Scheduler. You could use the processor killer, WinKill (see "Quickly kill any process or application" in Chapter 16), but there is an easier way.

In the Explorer while you are focused on Scheduled Tasks, choose Advanced, Stop Using Task Scheduler. You can now save the newly empty SchedLog.txt file back onto its former self. Once you've done this, click Advanced, Start Using Task Scheduler to load Mstask.exe back into memory and start running Task Scheduler.

Can't view the Scheduled Tasks log file

If you open up your Explorer to Scheduled Tasks, click Advanced, View Log, and find that you can't view the log file, this may be because your plain text files are associated with an application other than Notepad. Notepad, unlike other text editors, can open files that are currently in use by other applications (in this case, the Task Scheduler). If you have files with the *txt* extension associated with a different application, say WordPad, that application won't be able to open the log file as long as the Task Scheduler is running.

The easiest way to deal with this little glitch is to stop the Task Scheduler by clicking Advanced, Stop Using Task Scheduler. You can then click Advanced, View Log to display the log file. Be sure to restart the Task Scheduler after you are done viewing the log file by clicking Advanced, Start Using Task Scheduler.

You can also re-associate plain text files with Notepad. We explain how to do this in great detail in Chapter 13 of *Windows 98 Secrets*.

Run programs when you shut down Windows

There are many tasks you might want to run in Windows at a certain time. For example, you might want to automatically log off a network connection, synchronize your desktop PC with a laptop or palmtop, scan for viruses, run Defrag, or backup your entire system — but only at a certain time of day, such as late at night.

Oddly enough, the Task Scheduler can't schedule a program for the time when you're most likely not to be using your system — when you're quitting for the day and are shutting down. Usually, shutting down means you won't need your computer until the next morning. It's a perfect time to run lengthy processes, but the Task Scheduler can't help you. Fortunately, there are some tools that can take care of this.

WrapUp is a completely updated version of a tool that runs on Windows 98 and 95, Windows NT, and earlier versions of Windows. It's produced by Tessler's Nifty Tools, and you can order it from www.NiftyTools.com. It's not shareware, but you can download a free evaluation version, and a single user license of the registered version costs $39 plus shipping and tax.

Running a program with WrapUp is as easy as dragging a shortcut into the ShutDown folder that WrapUp creates in your \Windows\Start Menu \Programs folder during installation. The program could be a system tool such as ScanDisk, or it could be a batch file or Visual Basic routine that you've written. If there are command line switches for your program, right-click the shortcut in the Start menu, select Properties, and edit the Target field to add a switch. For example, you can tell ScanDisk to run without user input by adding /n at the end of this field. In addition, you can add a number of command line switches that help control WrapUp, and these are well documented in its online help. Unfortunately, you can't add or change them from within WrapUp.

WrapUp works best if it has a shortcut in your StartUp folder, so you don't have to remember to start it. It appears on your Taskbar (not your system tray, unfortunately) unless you use the /i switch to make it invisible. When you shut down Windows, WrapUp asks you if you want to close all programs and run the items in the ShutDown folder, unless you have configured it to run without asking you for confirmation. If you ever want to shut down Windows and not have the programs in the ShutDown folder execute (for example, when you just want to restart Windows), it's a simple matter to cancel WrapUp and shut down normally. You can disable WrapUp by pressing its toggle button, as shown in Figure 15-14.

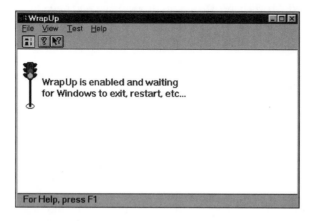

Figure 15-14: The WrapUp user interface. To toggle it on and off, use the button on the left end of the toolbar.

A different approach to this same problem is taken by ShutdownPlus, available from WMSoftware at www.wmsoftware.com. Again, it's not shareware; the free evaluation version times out after 30 days, after which you must register ($24.95 for a single license).

ShutdownPlus replaces the Shut Down Windows dialog box with the one shown in Figure 15-15. As you can see, it allows you to set programs to run on particular days of the week, or to only run once a day. You can use a handy wizard to add standard utilities such as ScanDisk and Defrag or browse to add whatever other programs you like. All of ShutdownPlus' settings are available in its detailed Options dialog box, which you access by right-clicking the icon in your system tray, so there's no messing around with command line switches.

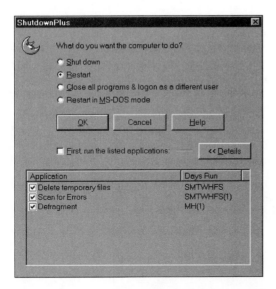

Figure 15-15: The ShutdownPlus Shut Down dialog box.

If you don't need to get too fancy, you might be just as satisfied running a simple batch file. Type the text into an empty Notepad file, and save it in your My System folder (which we recommend you create) as something like Shutdown.bat. The batch file shown here, written by Jeff Kushen, runs ScanDisk and Defrag on your C and D drives, and then exits Windows.

```
START /W C:\Windows\Scandskw.exe /sagerun:0 C: D:
START /W C:\Windows\Defrag.exe /f c: d:
C:\WINDOWS\RUNDLL.EXE user.exe,ExitWindows
```

Tip

No matter which of these automated methods you use, your computer will not shut down when you exit Windows unless you have power management enabled. See "Get Stand By back in your Shut Down Windows dialog box" in Chapter 22 to see how to turn it back on if necessary.

None of the programs described in this section can help you with the most obvious maintenance task, backing up your files with Microsoft Backup. This is because you can't specify an individual backup job to run. See the next section for more on this.

Microsoft Backup doesn't work with the Task Scheduler

The big problem with a program like Task Scheduler is that it has to run applications on an operating system that is designed to be interactive. If the human isn't there to do something, will these applications perform any useful work?

In most cases the answer is no. Of course, there are plenty of tasks that could be done with no user interaction if they were just designed to operate that way. The standard way around this is to run programs from the command line and include a few command line switches that stand in for user input. Obviously, this is just what you do with a program like ScanDisk, which requires no user input as long as it can use its default settings or you can configure it to use the ones you want.

The Task Scheduler makes this process somewhat easier by including the Settings button. The tasks that you can define via the Settings button previously required that you enter command line switches in the Run field of Task tab in the Properties dialog box for the scheduled task.

The key input that Microsoft Backup requires in order to run a backup is the name of the backup job. Backup jobs are the specifications that tell Backup which files to back up when and where (see Figure 15-16).

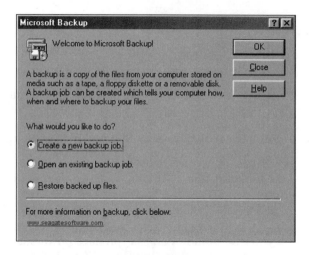

Figure 15-16: The initial screen of Microsoft Backup.

Unfortunately, Microsoft and Seagate decided to take out the capability of specifying a backup job name in the Task Scheduler. Therefore, you can't use Microsoft Backup for unattended backup. You have to be there to run it.

Seagate would rather that you buy an upgrade of this basically good program to get this additional feature. You'll find the upgrade at www.seagatesoftware.com.

A replacement for the Task Scheduler

If you want a task scheduler that can much more effectively replace you as an input unit (we're smiling here), you'll want to check out ClockMan95 or similar shareware packages. What ClockMan95 brings to the party is the ability to send keystrokes to the programs that it calls. Now you have a way to automate the Microsoft/Seagate Backup program that is too crippled to work with Task Scheduler.

ClockMan95 also comes with a version of the Windows Interface Language that allows much greater control over hundreds of Windows functions. The batch files that you can create using this language can only be run in ClockMan95, unless you have WinBatch (see "Windows Interface Language" in Chapter 16).

ClockMan95 doesn't have all the finely tuned schedule manipulation power of Task Scheduler, as you can see from Figure 15-17. It also is about as ugly as a Windows program gets, but there is power under the hood.

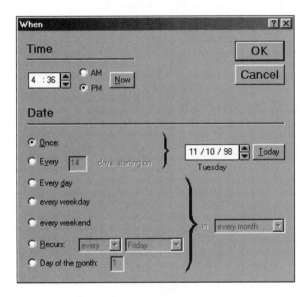

Figure 15-17: ClockMan's scheduling dialog box.

You'll find it at www.graphicaldynamics.com.

Scheduling with VBScript and JScript

If you install the Windows Scripting Host, you can run VBScript and JScript programs directly from Windows. To do this, click Start, Run, type the name of the script file, and press Enter, or click the script in the Explorer. You can also create a shortcut to the script and include all the command line parameters that you want to use with the script.

You can download the Windows Scripting Host from msdn.microsoft.com/ scripting/default.htm?/scripting/windowshost.

You can also have the Task Scheduler, ClockMan95, or Alarm++ run a script at an appointed time. Alarm++ comes with a couple of sample scripts that you can run with it. Alarm++ doesn't have its own scripting language, as ClockMan95 does, but it can easily use JScript and VBScript. Unlike ClockMan95, it doesn't internally support sending keystrokes. It will send e-mail directly through Windows Messaging, but not directly through Outlook Express. You'd have to call Outlook Express as you would any other program.

You'll find Alarm++ at www.skst.com/perpetualmotion/.

Summary

Task Scheduler can run maintenance programs without your intervention. You might want a more powerful option though.

▶ If anti-virus scanning didn't get added to your Scheduled Tasks, we show you how to put it there.

▶ If you can't see the Scheduled Task log file, you'll need to re-associate *txt* files with Notepad.

▶ The basic backup program that comes with Windows 98 won't work with the Task Scheduler. You'll need to upgrade.

▶ With VBScript and JScript, you can write scripting programs that carry out many Windows and browser functions, and you can set them to run at an appointed time.

Chapter 16

My System

In This Chapter

This extensive chapter deals with many different system issues, including installing Windows with other operating systems, Windows scripting, and password control. Windows can be complex, and this chapter reflects this.

▶ The Windows Upgrade web site is supposed to solve problems. It can have a few of its own.

▶ Your Windows programs run faster if you have configured your computer to make your most frequently used programs the most accessible on your hard disk.

▶ You can set up your hard disk to accommodate multiple versions of Windows as well as other operating systems. We show you how.

▶ Wouldn't it be great if Windows came with a powerful and easy to use scripting or batch language and recorder? It doesn't, but we tell you what's there.

▶ If you want to clear out your user profiles, you'll learn how.

▶ Put your information in where your computer manufacturer did previously.

Setting up your system

It's not just one operating system, which is all most of us need. Variants and competitors are out there, just like the truth.

The different versions of Windows 98

You can the purchase the Windows 98 CD-ROM in three versions: the complete retail version, the upgrade version, or (with a new computer) the OEM version. The full retail version allows you to format and install Windows 98 on a new hard disk without any reference to an existing copy of Windows or DOS. This version can also upgrade your previous version of Windows — it just costs more than the upgrade version.

The OEM version that comes with new systems cannot upgrade previous versions of Windows. Microsoft would rather that you didn't try to use it for that function. If you try to use this CD-ROM to upgrade your neighbor's system, you will get an error message.

The next section shows you how to circumvent some of these restrictions.

Undocumented Windows 98 setup switches

Secret

You can find out about the documented setup switches in Chapter 2 of *Windows 98 Secrets* or online in the Microsoft Knowledge Base. Look for these articles: "Windows 95 Setup Switches" (support.microsoft.com/support/kb/articles/Q128/4/00.asp) and "Description of the Windows 98 Setup Switches" (support.microsoft.com/support/kb/articles/Q186/1/11.asp). Table 16-1 lists three undocumented setup switches.

Table 16-1	Undocumented Switches for Windows 98 Setup
Switch	**Resulting Action**
setup /NTLDR	Bypasses any detection of a previously installed operating system. By default, OEM/VAR versions of the Windows 98 full releases can be installed only on a new computer without any previously installed operating system. This switch allows the Windows 98 setup program to circumvent this restriction.
setup /Pf	Creates a new Windows 98 Registry. All existing settings found in your Registry will be lost. You would only want to use this if you are unable to load Windows 98 because of a corrupted Registry and you are unable to copy a previously saved version of the Registry over your corrupted version.
setup /nm	Bypasses the detection of your computer's processor. Allows Windows 98 to be installed on computers that do not meet Microsoft minimum requirements (in other words, 386, 486SX, and so on). Also skips the check for the math coprocessor.

Thanks to Anthony Kinyon for pointing out these undocumented features.

Save your Windows 98 uninstall information

Remember back when you installed Windows 98 over your previous operating system? You had the option to save system files. If you said yes, then you can uninstall Windows 98 later and go back to Windows 3.1 or Windows 95.

Tip

If you've forgotten whether you saved this information or not, you can check it out by clicking Start, Settings, Control Panel, Add/Remove Programs. If you can find Uninstall Windows 98 in your Install/Uninstall program list, then you in fact did save the system files for your previous operating system.

If you should reinstall Windows 98 (for whatever reason), these saved system files from your previous operating system are going to be lost, and you won't be able to get back to your previous operating system.

Secret

Before you reinstall Windows 98, you'll want to move the files that contain the backed up system files for your previous operating system to another folder. We suggest that you use your own My System folder.

These files — Winundo.dat, Winundo.ini, and Winlfn.ini — are marked Read-only, Hidden, and System. You'll find them in the root directory of the drive that contains your \Windows folder. You can drag and drop them into the My System folder. After you've moved the files, you can reinstall Windows 98.

If you want to uninstall Windows 98, you'll need to copy these files back to the root directory. To uninstall Windows 98, follow the directions in the Microsoft Knowledge Base article "How to Uninstall Windows 98" at support.microsoft.com/support/kb/articles/Q186/1/02.asp.

Check your Readme files to avoid problems

When most software developers release a product that has last-minute changes — or incompatibilities that appeared after the manual was written — they include a Readme.txt file with the program. When Microsoft releases a new operating system, it includes a *dozen* or so of these text files, all with different names.

It's a good idea to read these files, whether you are responsible for maintaining only your own computer or hundreds. A few lines in one of these last-minute files can describe a fix to a problem that could take you hours to figure out yourself.

To find these files, open your \Windows folder in the Explorer, and click View, Arrange Icons, By Type (or click the Type column heading button in Details view). All the *txt* files should appear together.

If you are running Windows 98, you should examine at least these major files:

- General.txt — for problems that affect all computers
- Hardware.txt — for specific computers and peripherals
- Network.txt — if you have a network
- Printers.txt
- Display.txt

These files offer a fascinating look at the difficulties that can occur when Microsoft and independent hardware and software developers try to make all of their stuff work together. Here are a few gems:

- USB hubs. Numerous Universal Serial Bus (USB) hubs have problems when powered by a PC bus (rather than a power adapter), or when certain USB devices are plugged in. See Hardware.txt for Microsoft's comments on Belkin, CATC, Unixtar, and Samsung hubs; Toshiba and Hitachi laptops; and other devices.

■ PCI video. Some PCI-based video adapters (Microsoft doesn't say which ones) crash Windows 98 upon first startup, or in 16-color VGA mode, or in Safe mode, because they need different Vga.drv and Vga.vxd files. Copy these files from the Windows 98 CD-ROM at \Drivers\Display\Vga\ Vga.drv and \Drivers\Display\Oldvga\Vga.vxd to your \Windows\System folder, as described in General.txt.

■ Briefcase. A problem that affects all Windows 98 users is that when user profiles is enabled, the Briefcase does not copy files to each profile correctly. The fix is to right-click the Briefcase icon on the Desktop, delete it, right-click an unoccupied space on the Desktop, and then click New, Briefcase.

■ Update your BIOS. You can avoid numerous problems running Windows 98 by upgrading your computer to the latest version of its BIOS firmware. See Hardware.txt for Microsoft's recommendations on the Digital HiNote, Compaq Presario, IBM ThinkPad, Micron, NEC Versa, and other PCs.

■ PC Card modems. If you get Modem Not Found or Modem Not Ready messages from your PC Card modem with Windows 98 power management enabled, you may need to add a short delay to the Registry. Click Start, Run, type **Regedit.exe**, and when Regedit opens, navigate to \HKEY_LOCAL_MACHINE\System\CurrentControlSet\Services\Class\ Modem. Select the key for your PC Card modem. (Click 0000, 0001, or a similar key number and read the modem description in the right pane to determine which modem is your PC Card modem if you have more than one.) Right-click the right pane, and choose New, DWORD Value. Rename this value **ConfigDelay**. Double-click ConfigDisplay. In the Edit DWORD Value dialog box, mark the Decimal option button and type **3000** (for a 3-second delay) in the Value Data field. Click OK and close the Registry editor.

WinAlign makes Microsoft applications load faster

One of Windows 98's biggest performance improvements is that it *aligns* programs. Microsoft has demonstrated that aligned programs load an average of 30 to 40 percent faster than ordinary programs. They also run faster and consume less memory.

When you install Windows 98, its setup routine automatically runs a utility called WinAlign.dll. This utility rewrites application programs so that their executable sections begin on 4K boundaries. WinAlign is automatically placed in your Task Scheduler (it's labeled Tune Up Application Start). You should definitely let it run as part of your regular maintenance. (See "Reschedule maintenance if your computer doesn't stay up all night" and other topics in Chapter 15 for more on scheduling your maintenance.)

Aligned programs benefit from Windows' support of *mapped memory I/O out of cache*. This means that Windows 98 can run a program from cache memory without also copying the program to an equal amount of main memory. This saves RAM and reduces the use of a much slower swap file.

WinAlign gives programs the greatest benefit after you have converted your hard drive to FAT 32, a more efficient method of storing information than the File Allocation Table used by older versions of Windows, FAT 16. We discuss the pros and cons of converting to FAT 32 in Chapter 33 of *Windows 98 Secrets*, and in the section "To FAT 32 or not to" in Chapter 20 of this book.

Oddly, the WinAlign.dll utility currently aligns only Microsoft programs, including Windows 98 executables and Microsoft Office 95 and 97 applications. Shawn Sanford, a product manager for Windows 98, says this is because Microsoft didn't want to disrupt other vendors' programs.

To see a list of which programs have been aligned, open the Winali.ini file in the \Windows\System folder (see Figure 16-1).

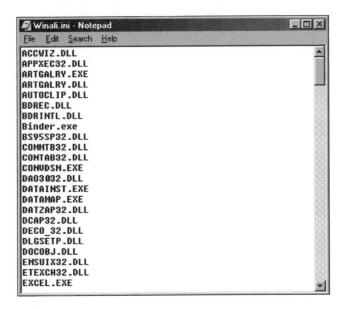

Figure 16-1: A portion of one computer's Winali.ini file, opened in Notepad.

Take advantage of Windows 98 performance improvements

Unfortunately, applications don't load more quickly as soon as you install them. To make this happen, you have to do four things:

■ You must convert your hard drive to FAT 32.

■ You must run the WinAlign utility to convert your installed applications to work with the new optimization methods. (See the previous section for more about WinAlign.)

■ You must run each of your favorite applications at least four times. This allows a small background process called Taskmon to monitor your applications and log the files they need and the order in which they load.

Taskmon logs each application the second time you run it and every third time after that. Programs you've run eight times will be optimized first, then programs you've run five times, and so on. You can see Taskmon's logs (*lgc* files) by using Notepad to open them from the hidden \Windows\Applog folder. Figure 16-2 shows the contents of Winword.lgc, the log file for Microsoft Word.

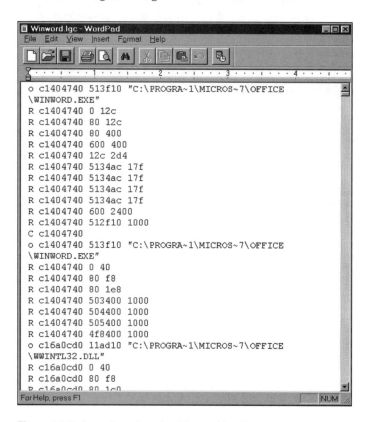

Figure 16-2: A small portion of a Winword.lgc file.

■ You must run Defrag. Defrag uses Taskmon's logs to write your program files to disk in the order in which they load fastest.

Microsoft has designed the optimization process to happen over a period of time for all Windows 98 users who convert to FAT 32. Eventually, every user will run every installed application four times or more. And eventually every user will run Defrag (or schedule it to be run automatically, a process that the

Task Scheduler makes easy). This causes the new, more efficient loading patterns to be written to disk.

But why wait for all of this to take place gradually? If you have just installed Windows 98, and if you decide to convert to FAT 32, you might as well get its benefits sooner rather than later by running WinAlign, opening your favorite applications more than four times each, and running Defrag.

Before you implement these features, however, you may want to know how much of a speedup you've gained. To document this, you can perform a simple test using your existing configuration.

STEPS:
Measuring Speedup in Opening Applications

Step 1. Create a shortcut in your \Windows\Start Menu\Programs\StartUp folder for each of your major applications. To do this, find the executable file that launches each application. Right-drag each *exe* file into the StartUp folder, and click Create Shortcut(s) Here.

Step 2. Shut down Windows, and then turn off the power and restart the system. Clock the launch time required by Windows and your suite of applications. You can do this before or after converting to FAT 32, which by itself has little or no performance benefit.

Step 3. Now open each of the applications in your test, four or more times apiece, and run Defrag. You may want to do this at the end of your work day, because Defrag can take several hours.

Step 4. Repeat step 2, noting the difference in time to launch your suite of applications. After the test, delete the shortcuts from your StartUp folder.

Running multiple versions of Windows (and other operating systems)

You can configure your computer in a number of ways to run multiple operating systems or multiple versions of Windows 98. One method is built into Windows 98 and Windows NT; another requires only the use of batch files; others require additional software.

Rename the boot files

Originally, Microsoft made it somewhat easy to switch between DOS (or Windows 3.1) and Windows 95. They thought that this allowed people who worried about their transition to Windows 95 a way to get back to their older applications.

With the release of FAT 32, the 32-bit disk file system, Microsoft pulled this dual boot capability from the OSR 2 version of Windows 95 because DOS couldn't handle FAT-32 formatted hard disk partitions. But you can dual boot between Windows 98 and DOS using only the capability that comes with Windows 98 if your boot partition is formatted as FAT 16. (You can find out more about this capability in *Windows 98 Secrets*, in the "Dual-Boot Configuration" section of Chapter 5.)

Microsoft accomplishes the feat of dual booting by renaming certain files in the root directory. For example, when dual booting between DOS (or Windows 3.1) and Windows 98, the Autoexec.bat, Config.sys, Io.sys, Msdos.sys, and Command.com files are given either the *dos* or *w40* extensions, depending on which operating system you are booting to. If you are booting to DOS, the files with the *dos* extension are renamed.

Use the Windows NT, or other boot loader

If your primary partition is FAT 16, you can put Windows NT and Windows 98 on the same computer and boot to either one using the Windows NT boot loader. Install Windows 98 first and then Windows NT. Be sure to install each of them in its default folder, and not in the same folder as the other.

Tip

If you've already installed Windows NT, you can still make this work. Check out the Microsoft Knowledge Base article "Setting Up Dual Boot After Installing Windows NT" at support.microsoft.com/support/kb/articles/q153/7/62.asp.

We discuss OS/2, NT, and other boot loaders in Chapter 2 of *Windows 98 Secrets*.

Batch files that copy boot files to the root directory

You can use a number of variations on the method described in "Rename the boot files" earlier in this chapter to store as many different versions of Windows 95 or 98 as you have room for. You can then switch among them after running a batch file and rebooting your computer. The batch file will copy the appropriate versions of the Autoexec.bat, Io.sys, and other files to your root directory from a folder associated with each version of Windows. You'll find instructions and examples on how to do this at Lee Chapell's site: www.webdev.net/orca/.

This method works best when you have two completely different operating systems, such as DOS and Windows 98, or Windows NT and Windows 98. Both DOS and Windows NT require a FAT-16 boot partition if they are going to be dual booted with Windows 98.

If you want to run Windows 95 and Windows 98, you'll need to also track the Program Files folder. For example, installing Windows 98 after Windows 95 would install the newer version of Outlook Express over the Windows 95 version, unless you used batch files to rename the Program Files folder.

Using this method, you can install two different language versions of Windows 98. This allows you to develop and test programs in two different languages on the same computer.

Partition your hard disk

If you use additional software, it is possible to completely hide one operating system from the other (or multiple others). For example, Partition Magic (www.powerquest.com/product/pm/PMdescription.html) lets you partition your hard disk, switch between active partitions (booting first off one and then the other), and hide partitions from each other. With this method, you can install completely different operating systems in different partitions.

Partition Magic lets you decide which partition is the active partition—the C drive. You can install one version of Windows 98 on drive C, change the active partition to another partition, and install another version of Windows 98 on that partition, which also is seen as drive C.

You'll find details about how disk partitioning works at www.users.intercom. com/~ranish/part/primer.htm.

For complete instructions on how to set up Partition Magic to run multiple operating systems, check out support.powerquest.com/multios.html. Descriptions of other issues concerning the IBM boot manager that comes with Partition Magic can be found at support.powerquest.com/pm/ pm1035.html and support.powerquest.com/pm/pm5221.html.

Partition Magic is not the only software that is available to partition your hard disk and allow for multiple operating systems. There is a freeware program, Ranish Partition Manager, available at www.users.intercom.com/ ~ranish/part/. You can see how it works by going to www.users.intercom. com/~ranish/part/faq.htm.

Partitioning the hard disk and making first one partition active, then another, can cause lots of problems if you want to keep one e-mail folder, one set of favorites, one set of documents, and so on. You'll probably want to move your My Documents folder, your Favorites folder, your e-mail and newsgroups folders, and even all of your program folders to another partition that can be viewed by both operating systems.

You can use TweakUI to change the location of the My Documents, Favorites, and Program Files folders. Click the General tab, and then click the Change Location button. To see how to move your e-mail, newsgroups, and Windows address book, turn to "Save all your documents" in Chapter 3.

Boot from different hard disks

Usually the switch settings on your hard disks determine which physical hard disk can be used as your boot drive. Some BIOSes allow you to switch between hard drives, but not many. You can, however, use software to switch between hard drives, making one or the other your boot drive.

The program that allows this is BootIt, and it is available at www. terabyteunlimited.com/DIF.HTM.

Linux boot manager

Linux and Windows 98 can coexist on the same hard drive, although in different partitions. You can use the DOS FDISK tool to create the partitions without buying any third party disk partitioning tools. If you use the Linux boot manager, you have the option of exiting to DOS and then starting Windows 98, or just continuing on with Linux. You can find out more about how to do this at visar.csustan.edu:8000/HyperNews/get/giveaway/10/3.html and listas.conectiva.com.br/LDP/HOWTO/mini/Multiboot-with-LILO-1.html.

Numerous other sites mirror the Multiboot-with-LILO-1.html document. You can receive these and other Linux HowTo documents via e-mail if you fill out a form at any of these mirror sites. Use a web search engine to find "LDP/ HOWTO". (LDP stands for the Linux Documentation Project.)

Swap in the Windows 95 Explorer

If you'd rather not have an integrated Internet Explorer as part of the user interface sitting on top of your operating system, Shane Brooks has a different answer for you. His utilities allow you to swap in the Windows 95 Explorer in place of the Windows 98 Explorer/Internet Explorer.

Shane Brooks is an Australian who is currently studying at the University of Maryland. His web site also shows you step by step how to remove Internet Explorer in the comfort of your own home or Fortune 500 company. He lists these benefits:

- You get back about 35MB of hard disk space

- Windows 98 runs much faster

- Netscape Navigator doesn't crash under Windows 98 any more (what a *coincidence!*)

Brian has interviewed several people who've followed Brooks' methods and confirm they work under different conditions. Here are the basic steps:

STEPS:

Disentangling Internet Explorer and Windows 98

Step 1.   Use a test system. Do this on a PC you can easily reformat and reconfigure if need be after your test.

Step 2.   Replace the Windows shell. On a computer with Windows 98 installed, boot to DOS (hold down the Ctrl key during the power-on self test and select Command Prompt Only in the Windows 98

Startup menu). Move Explorer.exe from the C:\Windows folder to a floppy. Move Shell32.dll and ComDlg32.dll from C:\Windows\System to floppies. Copy the Windows 95 versions of these three files into the correct locations and reboot.

At this point, Brooks states that you have a smaller, faster Windows shell. You can run Internet Explorer at any time by switching these three files back. But let's continue to remove Internet Explorer itself.

Step 3.   Delete folders. In Windows 98, delete the following folders (including all files they contain) from the C:\Windows folder: Catroot, Cookies, Downloaded Program Files, History, Java, Temporary Internet Files, and Web. From the C:\Windows\Application Data\Microsoft folder, delete Internet Explorer and Welcome. From the C:\Program Files folder, delete Internet Explorer and Uninstall Information. Search for and delete all desktop.ini and *htt* files (used for the web page view of folders). Finally, if you are the sole user of the computer, delete C:\Windows\All Users.

Step 4.   Delete favorites. Exit to DOS and delete the C:\Windows\Favorites folder.

On the down side, you lose the Windows Update feature, but you can get the same thing at www.microsoft.com/windows98/downloads/corporate.asp. Notepad and WordPad also won't work, but you can copy the Windows 95 versions if you need these editors.

Brooks' web site names many other files you can delete, Registry entries you can remove, and so forth.

By the time that you read this, his utilities will all be integrated. As we write this, they come in three parts, so we really can't tell you how to use the integrated utilities. Check out his web site at www.98lite.net (see Figure 16-3), and if you feel comfortable with what he is doing, you might give it a try.

Brian asked readers of his InfoWorld column to write in about their experiences with Shane's methods. Within five days after his first column, he received more than 200 detailed responses. Overwhelmingly, readers who ran Brooks' method to remove Internet Explorer from Windows 98 reported that their systems ran faster and with fewer crashes.

Here is what some of them had to say:

Reader James Yan of Hong Kong sent in a typical response: "I have 64MB of RAM in my Celeron-A 333 system, which ran like a 32MB system with Win 98 and IE installed. Now I've got my full 64MB back with the removal of IE! All my MS Office applications now load and close much faster than before, with a huge improvement in games."

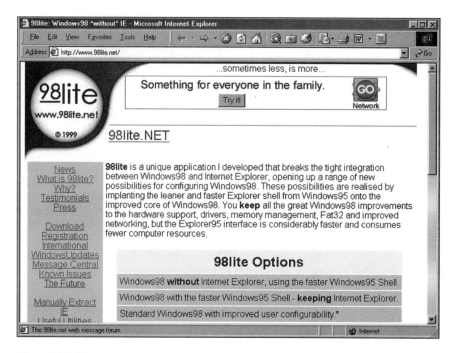

Figure 16-3: The 98lite web site offers latest information on Brooks' utilities.

Michael Conner was one reader who quantified his findings after Internet Explorer removal: "With CDEX ripping a CD and encoding it into MP3, Netscape 4.5 running, Notepad open, and other things running, including the ATI taskbar, my system resources were at 80%. If I were doing this pre-IE4 uninstall, it would be down in the neighborhood of 50% to 65%. There's something *seriously* wrong with the Win 98/IE integration combo."

Marc Boulware, the owner of a technical firm in Charlotte, North Carolina, conducted extensive benchmark testing on an old Pentium: "Excell Computer Systems performed the given instructions, and noticed that after step 2 [switching three shell files], there was a 15% to 25% improvement in speed in the machine. After applying steps 3 and 4 [removal of other files], our Pentium 75 with cache disabled showed a 25% to 35% improvement in performance."

Several critical messages came from readers who thought the process merely reverted a Win 98 machine to Win 95. Actually, Brooks gives a lot of detail on his web site about Win 98 benefits that remain after IE removal (click the "Why?" link on his home page). These include the FAT-32 file system, native USB/AGP support, better right-mouse behavior, and several other features.

A more salient problem is that Microsoft is building more and more applications that require components of IE. Chuck Thompson said, "The problem stems from the new (to Visual C++ 6.0) MS requirement that IE 4.0 be installed to do the Developer installation."

David Hecksel cites SQL/Server and Site Server as other applications with Internet Explorer requirements. He adds, "Office 2000 won't install without Internet Explorer on the machine. I think they call this a 'Trojan Horse' strategy where I got my MBA (Duke)."

Thanks to Chris Pirillo at www.lockergnome.com for telling us about the 98lite site.

How about another operating system?

While you might be able to go for another word processor, spreadsheet, or database, getting a completely different operating system is a whole other story. Not to mention all the religious issues involved, there are the questions of how to install it, where to put it, how to make it work with your existing operating system, and how to read your existing files and hard disks. Oh, and did we mention, what's the point of all this pain?

Other operating system vendors want to have a life after Microsoft, so those that provide operating systems on Intel hardware have had to accommodate the huge installed base of Windows 95/98 by providing ways for users to use both their operating system and Windows. For the most part, they have done so only grudgingly, which has only hurt their case and their sales.

On the other hand, if you think of another operating system as just another application that's working in its own unique environment, then it doesn't seem quite so quirky — especially if that operating system has been tuned to provide particular advantages in a well defined niche.

Linux and BeOS are two operating systems that could find a home on your (large) hard disk, and still let you boot into Windows. There are lots of reasons to use these other operating systems, most of which don't apply to the vast majority of computer users. But since you're reading this book, you can't necessarily count yourself out.

BeOS is aimed at people producing multimedia, whether they be rock bands, video artists, wedding photographers, or the weekend artist. BeOS supports FAT-16 and FAT-32 hard drives — always a good first start — and can network on the Microsoft Network (we're talking the local area network, not MSN, although BeOS has a browser that will let you do that, too).

BeOS supports a wide range of hardware (although nothing like Windows 98), so if you're on its hardware support list, you at least have a fighting chance of getting it up and running. You can find out more about BeOS at its web site at www.be.com, and at www.bedepot.com.

Why not Linux?

Linux has a great reputation among its supporters for reliability. It doesn't have much of a reputation for ease of use, ease of installation, or a consistent, universally supported standard graphical user interface (it doesn't have one).

Linux appeals to the folks who are interested in a very clean implementation of Unix on Intel hardware. While that isn't everyone, it certainly is a market. It benefits from the fact that you don't have to feel that you are supporting a monopolist when you purchase or download the software. You're rooting for the little guy, the underdog. All the ambivalent feeling of envy and desire can be set aside.

Linux is supported by anyone and everyone who is interested in supporting it. It's a community as opposed to a corporate support network. Since everyone hates the kind of software support they're used to receiving (although I must admit I've been getting great support lately from corporate support groups), this has definite appeal.

Linux is open source code; anyone who has a very good grasp of C can modify the code to his or her own specifications. This turns a large portion of the geek world into your development department. Many souls can take pride in a shared product.

So combine its socially redeeming characteristics, its techno-geek pastiche, and its undoubted technically solid base, and you've got an operating system that is at the very least a competitive product. You need the worldwide support of a community the size of the Linux community to compete against a company the size of Microsoft.

You can read the gospel from the prophet's mouth at www.linux.org.

An excellent Linux 101 primer can be found at www.wugnet.com/wininfo/win2000/not_nt/981203.html.

Transfer files from Windows to Linux

If you run Samba using the latest versions of Linux, you can mount a FAT-32 volume. You can also access the Linux file system from another Windows 98 computer by running Samba under Linux. Because Windows 98 sends an encrypted password by default, you'll need to either configure Samba for CHAP or PAP password authentication protocols or change the Windows 98 Registry to send unencrypted passwords. You can see how to do this by reading "Unable to Connect to a Samba Server with Windows 98" at support.microsoft.com/support/kb/articles/Q187/2/28.asp.

Making your system my system

By far one of the biggest holes in the Windows operating system has been its lack of a command driven interface. Users could benefit by gaining the ability to automate repeated tasks.

Windows 98 scripting

Windows 98 comes with a scripting engine (the Windows Scripting Host) that allows software developers to write little programs, known as *scripts*, to automate various tasks. It is sort of a Windows macro language, but at a higher level, with a longer learning curve, and without the built-in capability for macro recording. Scripts can be written in JScript and VBScript.

You can find scripts written with browsing in mind at www.javascriptsource. com/ and www.scriptsearch.com/. Some of these may be applicable to your Windows 98 Desktop. If you are a developer, you can learn more about how to use scripting languages at msdn.microsoft.com/ scripting/default.htm?/ scripting/vbscript/ and msdn.microsoft.com/ scripting/default.htm?/scripting/ jscript/.

One very cool site with a long list of FAQs about scripting is located at wsh. glazier.co.nz/frame.htm. You'll find a chat area there with an archive and links to newsgroups. Also, the PC Tech area of the *PC Magazine* web site, an excellent source of information on deeper Windows 98 issues, has an article on scripting at www.zdnet.com/pcmag/pctech/content/solutions/uu1714a.htm.

Chris Pirillo recommends www.infohiway.com/javascript/indexf.htm. He says, "...this particular site covers JavaScript, Perl, CSS and various Plug-ins — and they've got a monthly newsletter, so you shouldn't be more than a few weeks away from getting the latest JavaScript scoop."

Another obvious scripting web site is www.scripting.com. It's not really devoted only to scripting, but has plenty of other material regarding web site development.

If you want a Windows macro program that lets you record not only keystrokes but also mouse movements and clicks, then check out Macro Magic at www.iolo.com. You can use this macro development program, shown in Figure 16-4, to automate repeated tasks that are carried out while you use either Windows 98 itself or Windows 98 applications.

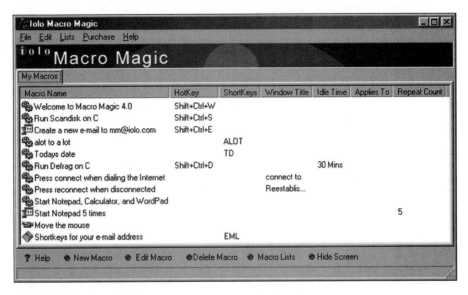

Figure 16-4: Macro Magic lists your macros for quick reference.

While Macro Magic can't automate every Windows task, it does enough to automate many of the simpler functions. The only trouble we found in our tests was that shortcuts created from the macros didn't carry out all of the steps.

Windows Interface Language

WinBatch has been around forever, and it just keeps growing (at least in the number of Windows functions that it includes). While Microsoft has opened up the Windows scripting market with the ability to use JScript and VBScript, WinBatch uses its own Windows Interface Language (WIL).

WIL is basically a set of function names specific to Windows, along with the associated standard program flow control names. It is a very straightforward language, requiring only that you search for a function in the WIL help file to learn how to use that function. Did you really want to turn into a programmer?

WinBatch doesn't include a recorder to allow you to create a program by just performing the tasks that you want the program to automate. If you just want to send keystrokes to a Windows dialog box, this is essentially a three-line program. Your program can grow from there.

Here is a sample of a WIL program that opens up the Power Management control panel and changes the power scheme setting to the last one in the list of schemes:

```
;Open Power Management Control Panel
Run("C:\Windows\Control.exe", "powercfg.cpl")
;Wait 5 seconds until the Power Management window displays
WinWaitExist("Power Management Properties", 5)
;Change Power Management setting to the last one on the list and then
close the dialog box
SendKey("{PgDn}{Tab}{Tab}{Tab}{Tab}{Tab}{Enter}")
```

The WinBatch installation has a very nasty habit of adding a massive number of commands to your file context menu. You can get these items out of your context menu by editing the Registry as follows:

STEPS:

Pulling WinBatch Out of Your Context Menu

Step 1. Click Start, Run, type **regedit**, and press Enter.

Step 2. Click the plus sign to the left of HKEY_CLASSES_ROOT*.

Step 3. Continue opening up branches to ContextMenuHandlers.

Step 4. Highlight FileMenu under ContextMenuHandlers in the left pane of your Registry editor.

Step 5. Click Registry, Export Registry File. Type **WinBatch FileMenu**, and click Save. This saves this small branch of the Registry in case you decide that you want these context menu items later.

Step 6. With FileMenu still highlighted, click Edit, Delete, Yes. Then close the Registry editor.

Now all of the context menu items associated with WinBatch will be gone from your file context menus.

WinBatch is a shareware program and you can download it from www.windowware.com.

AutoMate

If you're willing to pay for a macro/scripting/recording tool whose basic version costs almost as much as the operating system to begin with, then AutoMate is the program of choice. The $180 professional version lets you write VBA-compatible scripts. AutoMate also works as a scheduler, which allows you to set up tasks to be run at night.

We found that its keystroke and mouse movement recorder worked without any glitches, but AutoMate isn't restricted to just simple tasks. Its front end, shown in Figure 16-5, was a delight to use. An enterprise version of AutoMate sends task instructions over a TCP/IP network.

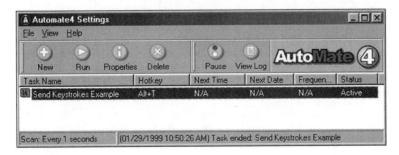

Figure 16-5: The main AutoMate window with one task highlighted.

You can order or download AutoMate from www.unisyn.com/automate/.

Thanks to Chris Pirillo at www.lockergnome.com for telling us about this program.

Change your password when you don't have one

If you use a blank password, you have the happy fortune of not having to enter a password when you start Windows, or even to see the password dialog box. But if you'd like to get this dialog box back, it's easy to do.

Click Start, Settings, Control Panel, Passwords, and click the Change Windows Password button (see Figure 16-6). Press Tab to shift from the Old Password field to the New Password field, leaving the Old Password field blank. Enter the new password twice, the second time in the Confirm New Password field. Click OK.

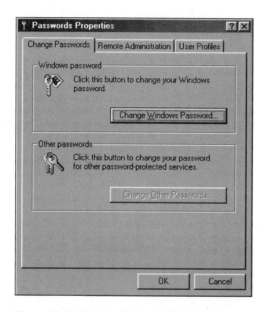

Figure 16-6: Click the Change Windows Password button to enter a new password.

To change your password back to blank, type your existing password in the Old Password field, Tab through the other fields to the OK button, and press Enter.

Manage your passwords

Windows creates a file that stores various passwords, in an encrypted format, as you accumulate them. The key to this cache of passwords is the password that you use when you start Windows. If you have a blank password, then you don't see the opening user name and password dialog box.

In this case, all your other passwords are available to you (and anyone else) without the bother of going through a password logon sequence.

A password cache is very powerful because it trades multiple passwords for just one (or, with a blank password, none). As passwords proliferate, especially on web sites, it would be very inconvenient to keep track of them all manually. The password cache is a *pwl* file, and you'll find it in your \Windows folder.

Windows 98 comes with a limited password management tool, the Password List Editor. You'll find it on your Windows 98 CD-ROM at \tools\reskit\ netadmin\pwledit. It is a standalone application; you can run it from the CD-ROM by clicking the executable. The installation file, pwledit.inf, just puts a shortcut to it in the System Tools menu on your Start menu and installs it in the \Windows folder.

All that the Password List Editor will let you do is delete previously stored passwords, as shown in Figure 16-7. You can't see what the passwords or user names are. (See the next section to find out about tools that reveal passwords.)

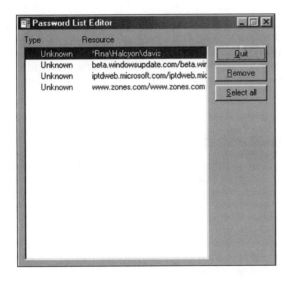

Figure 16-7: The Password List Editor doesn't let you edit, just delete.

Internet Explorer 5's AutoComplete feature lets you save passwords on the fly as you create them at various web sites. You can clear the passwords if you like: In the Internet Explorer window, choose Tools, Internet Options, click the Content tab, click AutoComplete, and click Clear Passwords. The AutoComplete Settings dialog box, shown in Figure 16-8, also lets you decide whether to cache your user names and passwords as you create them.

Figure 16-8: You access the AutoComplete Settings dialog box through Internet Explorer's Tools menu.

You can find much more sophisticated password management tools at www.winfiles.com/apps/98/password.html. The problem with the tools displayed on this web page is that they are standalone; they don't interact with the powerful and convenient features of the Windows 98 password caching system.

Passwords revealed

Password Revealer is a little utility that displays your passwords when you move a special mouse pointer over the asterisks in the password field of a dialog box (for example, the DUN Connection dialog box).

You'll find it at user.online.be/jos.branders/revealer.exe.

Password Revealer comes ready to go; there is no install procedure. The executable you download is the program. Run Revealer.exe, and hold down your left mouse button over the Track button. Then drag over any button or field to display its contents. When you move your pointer over a field of asterisks, the underlying password appears.

Thanks to Chris Pirillo at www.lockergnome.com.

Another freeware package that reveals passwords is appropriately named Revelation. Drag Revelation's little cross, shown in Figure 16-9, across the asterisks in a password field, and the password behind the asterisks is revealed.

You'll find Revelation at www.snadboy.com.

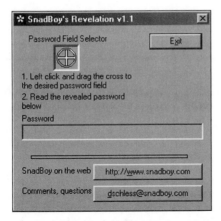

Figure 16-9: Revelation reveals the password behind the asterisks.

Get rid of the users and their profiles

Once you start allowing other folks to use your computer, you'll find that their "stuff" is lying all over the place. You'll be wondering what happened to "one person = one computer." We discuss how to set up your computer for multiple users in Chapter 12 of *Windows 98 Secrets*.

Of course, there are lots of situations where it isn't *your* computer, but rather a shared resource — a family or business computer. If each person has his or her own user profile, then Windows keeps track of all sorts of individual settings for each user. User profiles aren't required, however, because a large group of people can choose to use the computer with the same settings.

Outlook Express 5 can manage *user identities*, which are different than *user profiles*. One of the main reasons to set up user profiles prior to Outlook Express 5 was to separate everyone's e-mail, but you had to reinstall Outlook Express every time you added a profile. Now that identities are available, however, e-mail is no longer much of a reason to use profiles. Outlook Express handles identities in a completely different manner than user profiles — see "Using identities" in Chapter 3 for a discussion of how to use them.

To delete one or more user profiles, take these steps:

STEPS:

Deleting User Profiles

Step 1.   Restart Windows, and click Cancel at the Windows logon dialog box. You'll have a Windows logon dialog box if you have set up user profiles.

Continued

STEPS

Deleting User Profiles *(continued)*

To remove a user profile, you need to log in to Windows as either another user or by clicking Cancel at the logon dialog box. You can't delete a user profile if you are logged on as that user.

If you click Cancel, you aren't logged in as anyone. If you have a previous default user name that isn't used in the user profiles, you can log on as that user later.

Step 2.   Click Start, Settings, Control Panel, and click Users to display the User Settings dialog box. If you have user profiles enabled and you have set up some users, they will be listed here, as shown in Figure 16-10. Highlight the user that you want to delete, and click Delete.

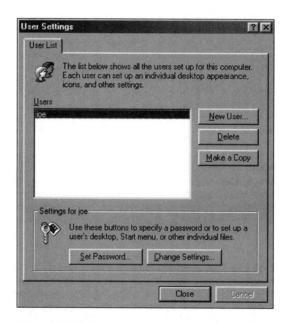

Figure 16-10: Joe is currently the only user enabled on this computer.

Step 3.   Continue deleting users until you have deleted all that you want. Click Close.

Deleting a user in this manner does three things. It deletes the user's entry in the profile list in the Registry, it deletes the user's profile folder in the

\Windows\Profiles folder, and it deletes the user's password cache file, *username*.pwl. You can check to be sure that these actions have taken place, or you can actually perform manually what the User Settings dialog box lets you do automatically by taking these steps:

STEPS:

Deleting User Profiles Manually

Step 1. Open your Explorer and navigate to \Windows\Profiles. Delete any subfolders that have the same name as the user profile that you want to delete.

Step 2. Open your Registry editor, navigate to HKEY_LOCAL_MACHINE\ SOFTWARE\Microsoft\Windows\CurrentVersion\ProfileList. Delete any keys under ProfileList that have the same name as the user profile you want to delete. If you want to delete all user profiles, delete the ProfileList key. Close the Registry editor.

Step 3. In your Explorer, right-click the Windows folder icon, click Find, type the name of the user profile that you want to delete, and press Enter. If and when it appears in the find results, delete the *pwl* file whose prefix is the same as user profile name.

This will delete the user's password cache. All of the passwords in the cache will be lost. Users whose *pwl* files you've deleted will need to know their user names and passwords if they want to access the same resources later. (This does not include the Outlook Express passwords.)

Step 4. The Find command used in step 3 may turn up cookie files associated with the user profile. You can delete these cookies in the Find dialog box by highlighting them there and pressing the Delete key.

All of the unique user settings will be eliminated. This includes all unique Favorites lists, Desktop shortcuts, and so on. Be sure to save these beforehand if you don't want them deleted.

If you've deleted all the user profiles, and checked to make sure that all traces of them are gone, you can now disable user profiles. You could have disabled user profiles first, but then you wouldn't have been able to delete user profiles automatically because the user list wouldn't have shown up in the Users control panel. You can delete user profiles manually even after you have disabled user profiles.

To disable the user profiles capability altogether, take these steps:

STEPS:

Disabling User Profiles

Step 1.   Restart Windows, and click Cancel at the Windows logon dialog box. You'll have a Windows logon dialog box if you have set up user profiles.

You don't need to take this step if you have already started Windows in this fashion when you deleted the user profiles.

Step 2.   Click Start, Settings, Control Panel. Click Passwords, and click the User Profiles tab.

Step 3.   Mark All Users of This PC Use the Same Preferences and Desktop Settings, as shown in Figure 16-11. Click OK.

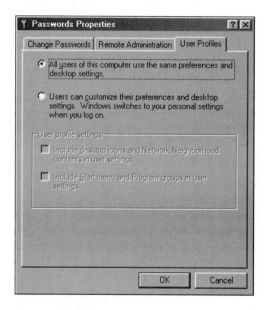

Figure 16-11: Mark the top option button on the User Profiles tab.

Step 4.   Restart Windows when prompted.

You will now be prompted to enter your password, and will be provided the user name of the last user that logged on. If you have an original user name that you used before you started adding user profiles, enter this name in the User Name field (see Figure 16-12). Enter the password associated with this user name, or tab to the OK button and press Enter if the password was blank.

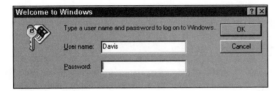

Figure 16-12: If you don't use a password, leave that field blank and click OK.

Windows will restart and use the password cache file associated with the user name that you just entered, *username*.pwl.

On the other hand, you may want to keep and later use a specific user's settings as the default user settings, while you get rid of all the other users and disable user profiles. In this case, you shouldn't delete this user profile from the user list. You can delete all the other user profiles using the Deleting User Profiles or Deleting User Profiles Manually steps earlier in this section.

Once you've deleted all of the other user profiles and disabled user profiles using the Disabling User Profiles steps earlier in this section, you can manually make the other changes required to make this user the default and only user as follows:

STEPS:
Changing a User Profile to the Default User

Step 1.   Open your Explorer. Navigate to \Windows\Profiles*username*. Move any of the files in the subfolders found under the user name to their corresponding location under the \Windows folder.

   For example, copy any of the shortcuts in the user's Favorites folder to the \Windows\Favorites folder. You may want to delete the files and subfolders in the \Windows\Favorites folder first, or just add these favorites to them.

Step 2.   Open your Registry editor, and navigate to HKEY_LOCAL_ MACHINE\SOFTWARE\Microsoft\Windows\CurrentVersion\ ProfileList. Delete the ProfileList key. Close the Registry editor.

Step 3.   Restart Windows and log in under this user name.

Get your Quarterdeck QuickBoot back

Installing Windows 98 disables Quarterdeck QuickBoot. You can get it back by taking these steps:

STEPS:

Re-enabling QuickBoot

Step 1. Click Start, Programs, Accessories, System Tools, System Information.

Step 2. Click Tools, System Configuration Utility.

Step 3. Click the Advanced button, and then mark the Disable Fast Shutdown check box in the Advanced Troubleshooting Settings dialog box (see Figure 16-13).

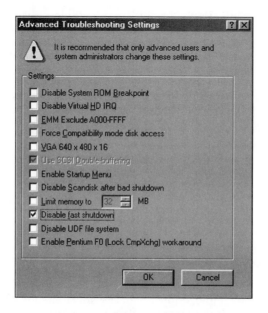

Figure 16-13: The Advanced Troubleshooting Settings dialog box.

Step 4. Click OK. Do not restart your computer when asked.

Step 5. Click Start, Shut Down, mark the Shut Down option button, and click OK.

Step 6. Restart Windows 98. QuickBoot will now work normally.

Thanks to Michael James Grey for pointing out this secret.

Take over the General tab of the System Properties dialog box

Microsoft lets computer manufacturers (OEMs) have access to the General tab of the Systems Properties dialog box, so that they can provide a bit of labeling and some support information. It comes about through the magic of the Oeminfo.ini file in your \Windows\System folder.

You can take over this space for yourself. All you have to do is edit the Oeminfo.ini file and add an Oeminfo.bmp file to your \Windows\System folder, or replace the one that's already there.

STEPS:

Editing the Oeminfo.ini File

Step 1. Using your Explorer, navigate to your \Windows\System folder and find the Oeminfo.ini file.

If you don't have one, right-click in the \Windows\System folder in your Explorer, and click New, Text Document. Give the new document the name **Oeminfo.ini**.

Step 2. Open the Oeminfo.ini file in Notepad by right-clicking it and clicking Open. You'll notice that it looks something like Figure 16-14, if you haven't just created it.

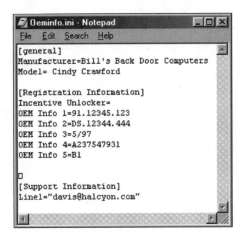

Figure 16-14: A sample Oeminfo.ini file.

Continued

STEPS

Editing the Oeminfo.ini File *(continued)*

Step 3. Change the string after "Manufactuer=" to whatever you like. Do the same after "Model=". If you are creating a new Oeminfo.ini, copy Figure 16-14, adding your own information.

Step 4. Under [Support Information], add as many lines as you like, starting with **Line1=**, and continuing with **Line2=**, and so on. Put double-quote marks around the text that you are typing in here.

Step 5. When you're done, click File, Save.

Step 6. Open up your System Properties dialog box with Win+Pause/Break (or right-click the My Computer icon on your Desktop and click Properties). You'll notice that the manufacturer and model information you entered is displayed in the General tab. Click the Support Information button to see what you entered in the support information section of Oeminfo.ini.

Now it's time to add a logo.

STEPS:

Adding an Oeminfo.bmp File

Step 1. Open up Microsoft Paint or any other paint package that can create a *bmp* image file. You can start Microsoft Paint by clicking Start, Programs, Accessories, Paint.

Step 2. Create an image 210 pixels wide and 120 pixel high. You can set the height and width of your image in Paint by clicking Image, Attributes.

Step 3. Save the image as Oemlogo.bmp in the \Windows\System folder.

Open up your System Properties dialog box (right-click the My Computer icon on your Desktop and click Properties). It will now contain your logo, as shown in Figure 16-15.

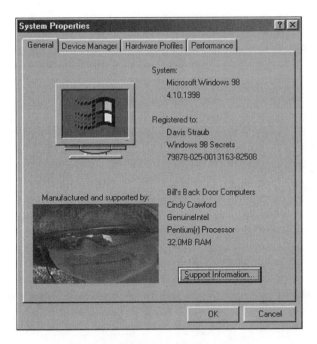

Figure 16-15: Our modified System Properties dialog box includes a photo.

Control the Control Panel

In Chapter 16 of *Windows 98 Secrets*, we show you how to create shortcuts to any of the Control Panel applications, and how to display specific tabs in multi-tabbed dialog boxes. Microsoft covers some of the same ground in their Knowledge Base article "How to Run Control Panel Tools by Typing a Command" at support.microsoft.com/support/kb/articles/q192/8/06.asp.

Help!

Perhaps, like us, you've found that Windows Help is often not as useful as you would like. We don't mean just the Windows 98 help files, but all the help files associated with all applications.

There are a number of obvious problems. For example, often the help file doesn't contain any information about the problems that you are experiencing. Also, help files are often poorly organized, and it is difficult to know where to find what you're looking for.

One particular irritant is the use of a character like "Clippy" in Microsoft Office, who is supposed to help you find your answer. We find it hard to imagine a less helpful entity.

Now Microsoft has two help systems. One is the familiar Winhelp and the other is the new compiled HTML-based help. Both help display engines come with Windows 98, so you can view help files written in either version. The fact that we now have two help systems doesn't make things any easier.

Once you get Clippy and the Answer Wizard out of the way, you can interact with a help file in three ways: through the table of contents, the index, or a full text search. While there will almost always be a table of contents tab and an index tab in the help file window, there may not be a search or find tab. This is unfortunate, because it is the full text search (which lies behind the Search or Find button) that we find most useful.

The full text search is available with both help systems. With full text search, you can display a list of all the topics that include the word that you type in the search field. You can then click a topic heading to see if the contents of the topic are helpful. HTML help adds a nice feature. It highlights each occurrence in the displayed topic of the word that you have typed in the search field, as shown in Figure 16-16.

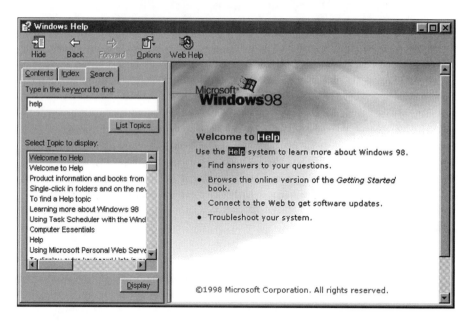

Figure 16-16: With HTML help, all instances of the word that you type in the search field are highlighted in all the displayed topics.

The Winhelp full text search is also powerful. You can create a full text search index file that allows you to search for topics that contain the words that you typed, in the exact order that you typed them. You can also search for all topics that contain all the words you typed (an AND condition) or all topics that contain at least one word you typed (an OR condition).

To obtain these powerful full text search features with Winhelp-formatted help files, you need to click the Find tab (see Figure 16-17) or Find button (see Figure 16-18) in the associated help file. If a particular help file doesn't have a Find tab or a Find button, you are out of luck.

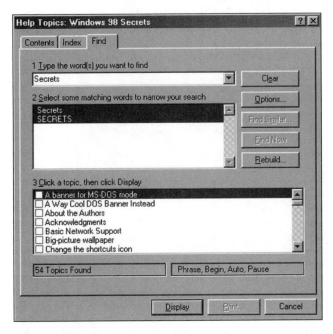

Figure 16-17: Click the Find tab the first time you open a new help file to create a full text search index.

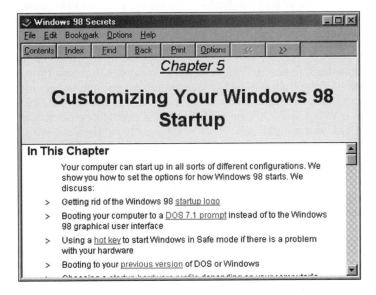

Figure 16-18: It is up to the help file author to include a Find tab or Find button.

Once you click the Find tab or button, you will be prompted by the Find Setup Wizard to create a full text search index, as shown in Figure 16-19. Click the Maximize Search Capabilities option button to produce the most powerful and flexible search index. This index file will be larger than the minimum produced if you don't click the Maximize button (which is why Microsoft doesn't make it the default choice), but if you have a hard disk whose size is measured in gigabytes, you'll have plenty of room for help file indices.

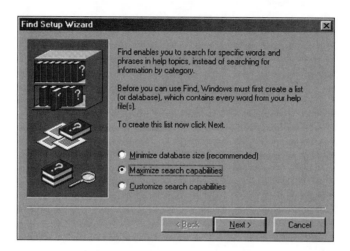

Figure 16-19: Microsoft used to be concerned about creating big help index files. Choose to maximize search capabilities unless you have a very small hard disk.

Once you have created a full text search index, you can determine how help will search the topics by clicking the Options button (see Figure 16-17 earlier in this section). Clicking this button displays the Find Options dialog box, shown in Figure 16-20.

You can customize how HTML help uses the words that you type in the search field if the help file author has been kind enough to include this capability. Click the right arrow at the right end of the search field. You can then click AND, OR, NEAR, or NOT. If there is no right arrow to the right of the search field, you are out of luck. This appears to be the case with Windows 98 help (as shown earlier in Figure 16-16), although the *Windows 98 Resource Kit Book Online* includes this capability, as shown in Figure 16-21.

Not only does Microsoft Office 2000 make it quite difficult to get to the Microsoft Office help file, it also doesn't include full text search in its HTML help. Now to be fair, the index is very extensive, as shown in Figure 16-22, so you may be okay using the index to find help. Unfortunately, in most cases we've found that the indexer didn't have in mind what we had in mind.

Figure 16-20: I usually search a help file using the option The Word You Typed in Exact Order.

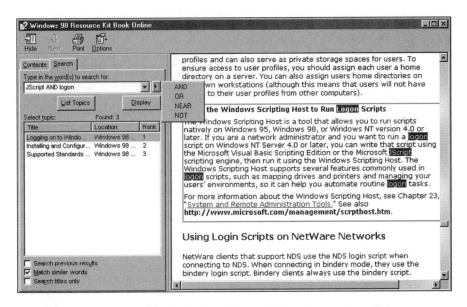

Figure 16-21: Note the pop up AND, OR, NEAR, and NOT options in this help file.

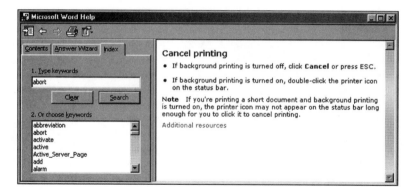

Figure 16-22: The word *abort* isn't actually in the topic, but it is a synonym for the actions described in the help topic.

The Clippy character gets in the way in Office 2000 especially, but you can turn off the little monster.

STEPS:

Turning Off the Office Assistant

Step 1.   Click Start, Programs, Accessories, Systems Tools, System Information, Tools, System Configuration Utility, Startup.

Step 2.   Clear the check box next to Microsoft Office StartUp. Click OK.

Step 3.   Click Start, Programs, Microsoft Word.

Step 4.   Click Help, Hide the Office Assistant.

You've turned off the call to start up Office Assistant so that it doesn't start up each time you restart Windows. It is still running in memory until you restart Windows.

Shortly after I wrote this, Peter Deegan, the editor of Woody's Office Watch (www.woodyswatch.com/) and Woody's Windows Watch (www.mcc.com.au/www/index.htm), wrote his "Kill Clippy!" article for ZDNet. It provides a number of ways to seriously injure (but not actually kill) Clippy. We recommend it to all of our friends, and you'll find it at www.zdnet.com/zdhelp/howto_help/killclippy/clippy_1.html. It includes some great replacement art for damaged Clippies.

Staying out of trouble

Windows 98 provides more ways to help yourself when things go bad.

Dr. Watson returns

Dr. Watson can be of some help in figuring out why you are having General Protection Fault errors. He is available if you click Start, Programs, Accessories, System Tools, System Information, Tools, Dr. Watson. Dr. Watson runs minimized in your system tray until you need him.

You can also get him to come to the office whenever you start your computer by putting a shortcut to him in the StartUp group. Here is one way to do this:

STEPS:
Adding Dr. Watson to Your StartUp Group

Step 1. Right-click your Taskbar, click Properties, and click the Start Menu Programs tab.

Step 2. Click the Add button, and enter C:\Windows\Drwatson.exe in the Create Shortcut dialog box, as shown in Figure 16-23. Click Next.

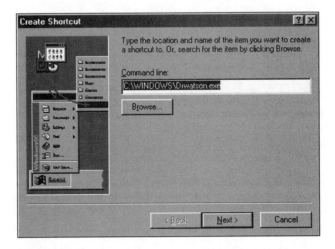

Figure 16-23: Type the path to Dr. Watson in the Command Line field.

Step 3. Choose the StartUp folder, as shown in Figure 16-24. Click Next and then Finish. Dr. Watson will start the next time you restart Windows.

Continued

Adding Dr. Watson to Your StartUp Group *(continued)*

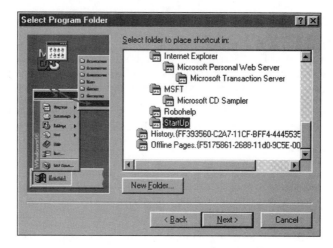

Figure 16-24: The StartUp folder is toward the bottom of the folder list.

Thanks to Daniel P. Cayea for pointing out this tip.

Windows 98 boot diskette

When you install Windows 98, you are given the option of creating an emergency startup disk, sometimes referred to as the Windows Startup diskette. You can also create it after installing Windows 98 by clicking Add/Remove Programs in your Control Panel and following the instructions in the Startup Disk tab.

In addition, you can create a slightly different Windows 98 emergency boot diskette without attempting to install Windows 98, or without having Windows 98 installed. All you need is the ability to read the Windows 98 CD-ROM.

If you can read the Windows 98 CD-ROM, which only requires a real-mode CD-ROM driver, you can create a Windows 98 boot diskette. You can do this from DOS, from Windows 3.1, or from Windows 95.

Tip

The Windows 98 boot diskette will include the generic CD-ROM drivers, so you should be able to boot from it and have access to the CD-ROM drive on your computer. If not, and if you have access to the real-mode CD-ROM driver for your specific CD-ROM, you should copy this driver onto the diskette and edit your Config.sys to call it.

To create this version of a Windows 98 boot diskette, you need to run the program fat32ebd.exe. You'll find it on your Windows 98 CD-ROM in the \tools\mtsutil\fat32ebd folder. Just click it and insert a diskette in drive A.

This Windows 98 boot diskette will let you boot your computer, access FAT-16 and FAT-32 formatted drives, and create FAT-32 partitions with the Windows 98 version of FDISK. It doesn't have all the utilities that you'll find on the Windows 98 Startup diskette, and it doesn't get fancy and create a RAM drive and extract compressed utilities onto the RAM drive.

We found that we needed to edit Config.sys to free up enough memory to run ScanDisk on this floppy when we were accessing compressed drives (drvspace.bin was stored in conventional DOS memory otherwise). We also copied Emm386.exe to the floppy diskette. The edits were minor; we essentially just added the call to emm386.exe and moved the call to himem. sys. You can compare our edited Config.sys with the one that Windows 98 automatically creates:

```
device=himem.sys /TESTMEM:OFF
device=emm386.exe noems
dos=high,umb

[menu]
menuitem=CD, Start computer with CD-ROM support.
menuitem=NOCD, Start computer without CD-ROM support.
menudefault=CD,30
menucolor=7,0

[CD]

;device=himem.sys /testmem:off
devicehigh=oakcdrom.sys /D:mscd001
devicehigh=btdosm.sys
devicehigh=flashpt.sys
devicehigh=btcdrom.sys /D:mscd001
devicehigh=aspi2dos.sys
devicehigh=aspi8dos.sys
devicehigh=aspi4dos.sys
devicehigh=aspi8u2.sys
devicehigh=aspicd.sys /D:mscd001

[NOCD]

;device=himem.sys /testmem:off

[COMMON]
files=10
buffers=10
stacks=9,256
lastdrive=z
```

CD-ROM God boot diskette

Here's what its own web site has to say about the CD-ROM God:

The CD-ROM God Ver 5.5 is a boot disk that has 50+ CD-ROM drivers. It has basic ATAPI drivers, and model specific drivers. This version unzips drivers to a ramdrive! It has a better — sleeker — shareware free menu. This version continues to use DEVICE.COM to load. This way you won't have to re-boot a million times! ISO-9660 CD Support and SMARTDRV.EXE!

If you want to create a Windows 98 boot diskette that includes all the known (to the author) CD-ROM drivers (not just the ATAPI drivers that Microsoft supplies), then the CD-ROM God is the software for you. This solves the very real problem of creating a boot diskette that can give you access to your CD-ROM drive in real mode.

You'll find it at members.xoom.com/cdromgod/start.html. John Staker told Chris Pirillo about this site, and we got it from Chris at www.lockergnome.com.

Trouble creating a Startup diskette

BugNet has found that you can't create a Startup diskette if the diskette has ten or more bad sectors. This is a good thing, but it sure would be nice to know what was going on.

You can put in a new diskette, or you can check the diskette with ScanDisk and see if the sectors really are bad. If it turns out that this isn't the problem, then turn off any virus scanning software that may be running. The McAfee virus checker that comes with Plus! 98 doesn't cause any problems.

If this doesn't do it, BugNet says either you've got a tape drive hooked to that floppy controller, you've got a bad floppy drive, or the BIOS setting for your floppy doesn't show a floppy drive.

BugNet actually got this information from the Microsoft Knowledge Base, as they freely admit. You can check out more bugs on BugNet at www.zdnet. com/chkpt/bugnet/www.bugnet.com/.

Get crash recovery help from your Zip drive

The Windows 98 setup routines strongly encourage you to create an emergency Startup diskette. You can also go back and create one later from your Control Panel (use Add/Remove Programs).

Iomega and Symantec Corporation provide you with a much-enhanced ability to recover from problems with Windows 98 by offering Zip drive users a free copy of the Norton Zip Rescue program, shown in Figure 16-25. Here's how they describe it:

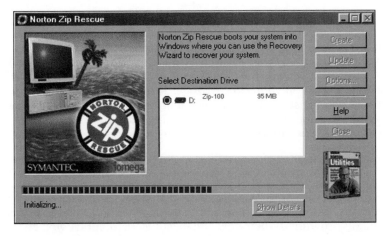

Figure 16-25: Norton Zip Rescue lets you make a Zip cartridge that will allow you to recover from a system crash.

Norton Zip Rescue is designed to help you keep running in the event of a system crash. Norton Zip Rescue can help you and your computer recover from almost any failure that keeps a PC from starting including:

- Viruses that keep a PC from starting (boot sector and system viruses)
- Windows Registry corruption
- CMOS corruption
- Deleted files
- Disk failures
- Boot sector failures

Norton Zip Rescue does not address applications problems, nor can it fix physical hardware damage, such as a broken hard drive head. However, in the event of a hard drive failure, you may be able to use your Zip Rescue Disk to get into Windows and retrieve undamaged files that have been created or changed since your last backup.

When the user experiences a PC failure where the PC doesn't start Windows properly; the user simply turns off the PC, inserts the Zip Rescue Disk and floppy, turns the PC on, and Windows will load automatically from the Zip Rescue Disk. The Rescue Wizard guides the user through the rescue, and has the ability to find and fix many problems. Finally, the user is instructed to turn off the PC, remove the Rescue Disk and turn on the PC. From that point, in many instances, the PC should run properly.

The program creates a bootable floppy in addition to copying a significant portion of your Windows operating system and configuration files onto the Zip drive. This includes your profile files, SendTo folder, Start Menu folder, Favorites folder, system web pages (found in Windows\Web), and Desktop shortcuts. You can add files, but this is not a backup program, and you can run out of room on your Zip cartridge. This program is meant to allow you to recover your existing Windows 98 configuration, but you may have to use it to copy your important files (such as additional fonts) from your hard disk to be used on a new computer, for example.

To keep the Zip recovery cartridge current with your latest hardware and software installations, updates to your Desktop, Favorites, and so on, you'll need to update it as often as you can manage using Norton Zip Recovery.

Of course, Iomega has enhanced the value of their Zip drives by providing this 8MB program to their new and existing customers. If you currently have a Zip drive, you can profitably download the latest version of this free program from www.iomega.com/software or www.symantec.com.

How the Recycle Bin stores files

If you're curious about how Windows 98 keeps track of the files that you've deleted into the Recycle Bin, you can find out by reading the Microsoft Knowledge Base article "How the Recycle Bin Stores Files" at support. microsoft.com/support/kb/articles/q136/5/17.asp. Essentially, Windows renames files using their source drive letter and the order of their deletion, and it keeps a separate file that links the new name to the old.

This Knowledge Base article also provides a couple of ways to deal with problems that you may encounter with the Recycle Bin.

Stop a malicious program

If you happen to run a program that sends a maliciously designed sequence of instructions to your Pentium processor, it can freeze your computer. Windows 98 lets you guard against this particular problem.

STEPS:
Enabling the Pentium F0 Workaround

Step 1.   Click Start, Accessories, System Tools, System Information.

Step 2.   Click Tools, System Configuration Utility.

Step 3.   Click the Advanced button in the General tab, and mark Enable
             Pentium F0 (CmpXchg) Workaround, as shown in Figure 16-26.

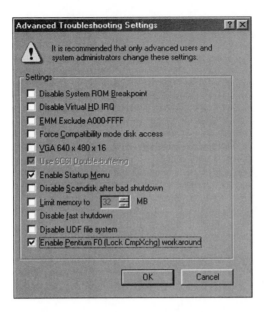

Figure 16-26: Mark the last check box to enable a protective workaround for
Pentiums.

Step 4.   Click OK. Click OK.

Quickly kill any process or application

WinKill sits in your system tray waiting for you to decide to close an application or kill any process. It will also perform a fast Windows shut down
that fails to notify any ongoing processes that Windows is shutting down,
and simply shuts Windows down quickly. Documents whose contents have
changed and haven't been saved recently are not updated. You probably
don't want to use this capability unless you know that you've saved all
your changes, and you just want to quickly close Windows and turn off
your computer.

Right-click the WinKill icon, click Kill, and you are presented with a list of
current processes, as shown in Figure 16-27. Click a process to kill it.

ddhelp.exe
explorer.exe
kernel32.dll
mmtask.tsk
mprexe.exe
msgsrv32.exe
msimn.exe
mstask.exe
psp.exe
rundll.exe
safeinstall.exe
sc97.exe
shoveit.exe
spool32.exe
systray.exe
tapisrv.exe
taskmon.exe
transparentb.exe
vshwin32.exe
waterfall.exe
winhlp32.exe
winkill.exe

Figure 16-27: The WinKill context menu lists the current processes.

WinKill is a freeware applet, and you'll find it at ftp://ftp.download.com/ pub/win95/utilities/WinKill.exe.

If you click the WinKill icon, the mouse pointer turns into a cross. You can then click a window to close it and terminate the underlying task.

Use Chkdsk to check for viruses

Plus! 98 comes with a virus checker. But you can do a quick and dirty virus check with an old DOS tool. All you need to do is open a DOS window and run Chkdsk to see how much lower memory it sees.

STEPS:

Checking for Viruses

Step 1. Click Start, Programs, MS-DOS Prompt.

Step 2. Type **Chkdsk** and press Enter.

Step 3. If the value for Total Bytes Memory is 655,360 (see Figure 16-28), you probably don't have a virus.

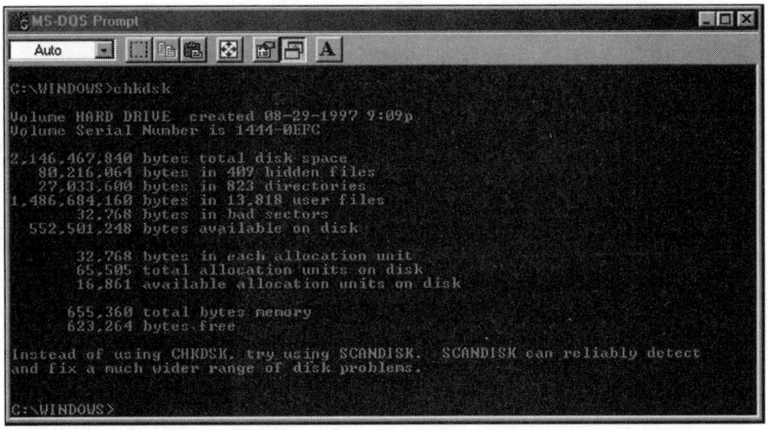

Figure 16-28: Total Bytes Memory is listed next-to-last. In this case, it is the expected number.

On some Packard Bell systems, Chkdsk will return 655,264, which is normal. If you get a different value, you might want to try Chkdsk again after rebooting Windows to the Windows 98 Startup menu and choosing Safe Mode Command Prompt Only. If you get 655,360, then all is okay.

To get to the Windows 98 Startup menu, click Start, Shut Down, Shut Down, OK. Restart your computer, and hold down the Ctrl key during power-on self test.

You might get a different value if you are using a hard disk utility such as Ontrack or EZ drive.

Thanks to Anthony Kinyon for help with this tip.

Imm32.dll error message

Secret

If you receive this error message when you install or run a program, it may be because you have a corrupted Mfc42.dll or Imm32.dll file. Your program installation might also have overwritten Mfc42.dll with an older version.

Don't panic. This is easy to fix if you have your original source files. Microsoft could have placed copies of these files in the \Windows\Sysbckup folder, but they missed the fact that these might be susceptible files. You can place copies there later, after you fix the problem.

You'll find these files in the \Windows\System folder. To extract the original versions from the Windows 98 cabinet files, follow the steps detailed in the next section, "Extracting files from cabinets in Windows 98."

Extracting files from cabinets in Windows 98

Even on the Windows 98 CD-ROM, the files that make up the Windows source files are packed into cabinet files, which use the *cab* extension. Other programs come packed into cabinet files, too, including updates to Internet Explorer downloaded from the Microsoft web site. This format was originally used to compress Windows 95 onto diskettes.

Most of the time, you let the accompanying setup routines extract files from cabinet files. However, you may want to extract files manually when a file is corrupted, or when you want to retrieve a specific file that the installation program didn't extract. Windows 98 adds a couple of new ways to extract files from your cabinets.

The System File Checker has a built-in option that lets you extract one file at a time from a set of cabinet files. Mark the Extract One File from Installation Disk check box, as shown in Figure 16-29.

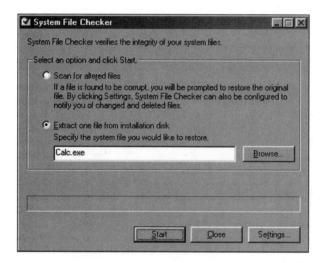

Figure 16-29: The System File Checker.

Open the System File Checker by clicking Start, Run, typing **SFC**, and clicking OK. Another alternative is to click Start, Programs, Accessories, System Tools, System Information, Tools, System File Checker. Or you may want to put a shortcut to the System Information Utility on your Desktop, and click Tools, System File Checker.

While the option button in the System File Checker refers to the *installation disk*, you can extract a file from any folder of cabinet files. You can browse for the file that you want to extract if that file is already installed on your hard disk outside of the cabinet files, but you would do this only if you are trying to replace a corrupted version with a new one from the cabinet.

Otherwise, just type the name of the file you want extracted, since you can't browse *within* a *cab* file.

Click the Start button and wait while the System File Checker checks the files in your system. After a moment, it displays the Extract File dialog box shown in Figure 16-30.

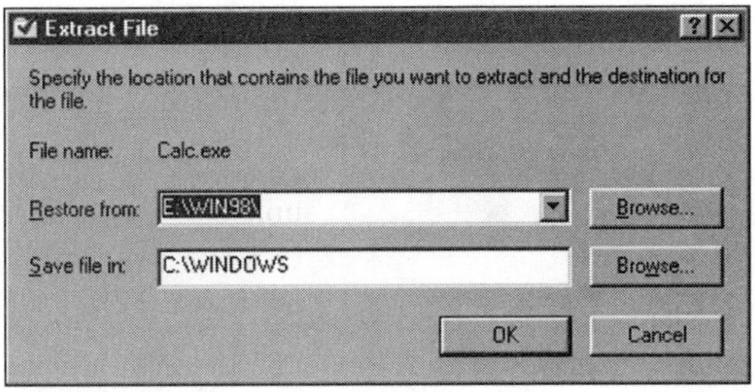

Figure 16-30: The Extract File dialog box.

You can use the Browse buttons to locate the folder that contains the cabinet files. As you can see in Figure 16-29, you can search for them on your CD-ROM (drive E, in this case) or on your hard disk, perhaps where you downloaded your new Internet Explorer files. You can also tell the System File Checker where to place the extracted file.

Click OK, and you'll be asked if you want to make a backup of the existing file (if there is one). The default location shown in Figure 16-31 should be fine. Click OK. Your file will be extracted.

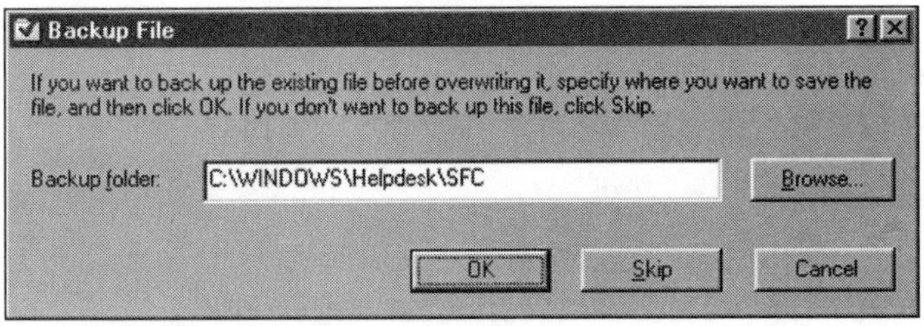

Figure 16-31: The Backup Folder field shows where your backup file will be saved.

This method only gets you one file at a time. If you'd like to extract more of them, you might want to use the DOS-based Extract.exe program, or its little command line helper, Ext.exe. Extract.exe is a command line driven DOS program. Ext works as a friendly intermediary between you and Extract.exe, prompting you for the commands and then sending them along as a command line string to Extract.exe.

Windows 98 places Ext.exe on the Windows Startup diskette when you create it, either when you first install Windows 98 or later from the Control Panel, Add/Remove Programs icon. (To create this diskette, click Start, Settings, Control Panel, Add/Remove Programs, the Startup Disk tab, and the Create Disk button).

When you run Ext.exe, you'll be prompted for input for the Extract.exe command line, as shown in Figure 16-32.

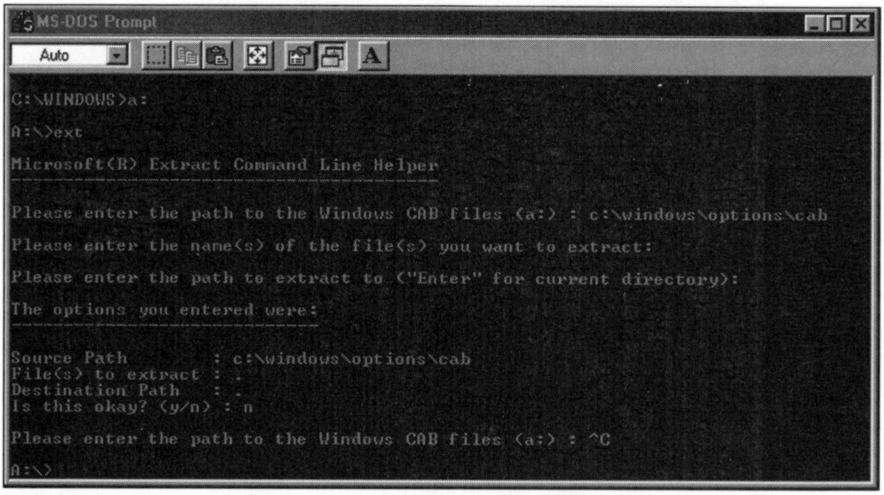

Figure 16-32: Ext.exe prompts you for paths and filenames.

You can see how Extract.exe works by opening a DOS window (Start, Programs, MS-DOS Prompt), typing **Extract /?**, and pressing Enter.

Keeping current

We help you get a little bit of control when it comes to updating Windows.

Use the Windows Update Wizard without having to register

You'll find the Windows Update Wizard on your Start menu. If it is no longer there, check out Start, Settings, Windows Update. When you run the wizard, it checks Microsoft's web site for new versions of drivers and other Windows components. If it finds newer versions than the ones you have, it offers to update your system for you.

There's a problem that can keep you from using the Windows Update Wizard, however. If you skipped Microsoft's Registration Wizard when you installed Windows 98, the Windows Update Wizard won't run. Larry Passo of Newport Beach, CA was the first to send Brian a workaround for this foolishness.

Secret

Passo points out that running the Registration Wizard changes two lines in the Registry. You can easily make these changes yourself by creating and merging this *reg* file, which you might name Register.reg:

```
REGEDIT4

[HKEY_LOCAL_MACHINE\SOFTWARE\Microsoft\Windows\CurrentVersion]
"RegDone"="1"
[HKEY_LOCAL_MACHINE\SOFTWARE\Microsoft\Windows\CurrentVersion\Welcome\
RegWiz]
"@"="1"
```

After you have merged this file into your Registry, you can run the Windows Update Wizard without complaint. Brian asked Rob Bennett, group product manager for Windows 98, if there was anything else readers should know about this trick. He said, "There is actually some value in registration. It's not just about Microsoft getting name and address info, it's really about helping Windows Update grow over time, so we can learn more about what people are actually doing out there."

Brian also asked whether Passo's patches would have any side effects. Bennett replied, "For now we're going to leave it as-is, but we may do some more stringent checking in the future." If a later version of Windows 98 does turn out to actually check to see if the Registration Wizard was run, you can always run it for real — but we hope that won't be necessary.

Trouble with Windows Update

The Microsoft Windows Update web site (and command in your Start menu) is supposed to make it easy to upgrade your current Windows 98 installation. Well, two steps forward and one step back. The address for this site, in case you've lost it, is windowsupdate.microsoft.com/.

You may run into problems (and as beta testers for the site we've run into and reported most of them). For example, instead of seeing the Windows Update web page, you may see a blank page, or you may receive an error message, or, the horror of it all, Windows may hang as it tries to download a file.

Microsoft has identified a number of problems that cause these symptoms. You can check out the latest list in the Knowledge Base article "Troubleshooting Windows Update Connection and Download Problems" at support.microsoft. com/support/kb/articles/q193/6/57.asp.

Track Windows 98 system updates

Microsoft wants to update your computer without bothering to tell you what is going on. Some folks like it this way, others don't. If you're in the second category, check out Windows 98 System Updates before you go to the Windows Update site. You'll find a listing of the recent updates, a description of what they do, a list of all the files, and additional information that will help you decide whether to update.

We think this is a great service to the Windows community. Check it out at www.walbeehm.com/win98upd.html.

Keep Windows updates

The Windows Update feature of Windows 98 is a great example of the power of Windows/Internet integration. When it works, it's wonderful to be able to go to one web site, have it check out your computer, and provide the latest updates of Windows software and drivers.

The only problem is the time it takes to download the new software. If you have a couple of computers that you would like to update and you know that they all need the same update, it is a needless pain to have to repeatedly download the same updates. Or, if you wipe your hard disk clean and reinstall Windows 98, you won't have these updates. Of course, if you have a DSL, cable, or T1 line connected to your computer or network, who cares?

Tip

After a great number of complaints from Windows users, Microsoft added a web site that allows you to download the Windows 98 updates for later installation. You'll find it at www.microsoft.com/windows98/downloads/corporate.asp. Download these updates and put them on a server (or in your My System folder). Then, every time you install Windows 98 anew, or get a new computer with the old version of Windows 98, just go to these updates and install them.

Thanks to Chris Pirillo at www.lockergnome.com.

If you use the Windows Update site, you can also save the updates as they are downloaded behind the scenes with a little help from Tom Porterfield, a regular contributor to the Microsoft support newsgroups. You don't need to do this if you download from the web site just mentioned.

Secret

Windows Update doesn't just download a compressed file for you and assume that you know how to install it. It goes ahead and does the actual system update. But to accomplish this task, it must first download the files needed for the update. These files are most likely installed in your \Windows\Temporary Internet Files\Content.IE5 folder, although they may perhaps have been sent to the \Windows\msdownload.tmp folder (yes, the folder name has an extension, but it's a folder, not a file). Microsoft could even store them in your \Windows\Temp folder, but apparently doesn't.

Tom recommends that you clear out your Temporary Internet Files\Content. IE5 folder first, so that you can see exactly what Windows Update is downloading. To do this, choose Tools, Internet Options in Internet Explorer, and click the Delete Files button.

You don't have to clear out this folder, though, because you can monitor which files are downloaded to interact with the Windows Update web site. Just leave your Explorer focused on your \Windows\Temporary Internet Files\Content.IE5 folder and watch as the files are downloaded. You can also use the time stamp for these files to determine which files were downloaded from this site. The files will be stamped with the time that they were downloaded (not the time that they were created by Microsoft).

One way to make this a bit easier is to view the \Windows\Temporary Internet Files\Content.IE5 folder in Details view and drag the Last Accessed column over to the left so that it appears to the right of the Type column, as shown in Figure 16-33.

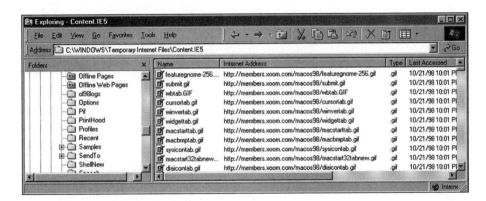

Figure 16-33: Move the Last Accessed column closer to the filename so that you can see it more easily.

Once the files have been downloaded (and the upgrade accomplished), copy all the files to another folder. We like to keep a folder called Temp where we store files that can be deleted later. You might even create a subfolder of the Temp folder and store the files for a particular upgrade there.

The files will most likely have an *exe* extension (that is, they are executable files) or a *cab* extension (if they are cabinet files). If the upgrade consists solely of an executable file, then you can easily ship that off to another computer and run it there by clicking it. If it consists of an executable with associated cabinet files, copy the whole lot to another computer and run the executable. The executable should search the cabinet files for the additional files that it needs.

If the download consists of only cabinet files, then you'll need to extract the files from the cabinet files in a temporary folder. Right-click each cabinet file, and click View. When the files contained in the cabinet file are displayed, drag all of them back into the temporary folder to extract them. Follow this procedure to extract all of the files from all of the cabinet files that were downloaded.

You're looking for an install file — one that has the *inf* extension. If you find one, right-click it and click Install. This will not work on the newer type of install file. If this is the case for you, you'll need to run another command to install these files.

You'll need to click Start, Run, type **RunDll32 advpack.dll,LaunchINFSection** *theinstallfilename.inf* and press Enter. If you are using just a section of the install file, you can place a comma after the install filename, and enter the name of the section. You'll only do this if you know just exactly what is going on inside the install file.

Tom recommends that you create a little DOS batch file and run the command in a DOS window. The batch file will extract everything from the cabinet files and then run the advanced install routine. You'll need to copy the following two lines into an empty batch file, which you can easily create with Notepad:

```
for %%1 in (*.cab) do extract %%1 /E
for %%2 in (*.inf) do RunDll32 advpack.dll,LaunchINFSection %%2
```

Place the batch file in the same temporary folder as the cabinet files and run it from there.

You can save the downloaded Windows Update files for future installation instead of installing them when Microsoft wants you to. You'll find a long discussion on how to do this at Arie Slob's Windows tips site at www.windows-help.net/windows98/troub-22.shtml.

Windows 98 Resource Kit Online

There is a compiled HTML help file version of the *Windows 98 Resource Kit* on your Windows 98 CD-ROM. This wonderful resource, shown in Figure 16-34, is available to you free of charge. You don't get all of the utilities that come with the printed book and CD-ROM, but you do get 26 applets.

Microsoft Press sells the *Windows 98 Resource Kit* separately as a book and CD-ROM, but if you can get by with the e-version (Windows HTML help format) of the book, then you can get it for free by installing it from your Windows 98 CD-ROM. Here's how:

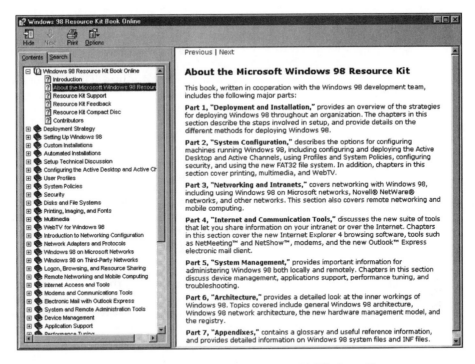

Figure 16-34: The *Windows 98 Resource Kit* that comes with Windows 98.

STEPS:

Installing and Starting the *Windows 98 Resource Kit*

Step 1. Insert your Windows 98 CD-ROM into your CD-ROM drive, and use your Explorer to navigate to \tools\reskit.

Step 2. Click setup.exe.

Step 3. The *Resource Kit* and all of its applets will be installed under your \Program Files folder in the folder Win98RK. The setup won't tell you that a shortcut has been added to your Start menu.

Step 4. Click Start, Programs, Windows 98 Resource Kit, Resource Kit Online Book.

There are a few documented errors in the *Windows 98 Resource Kit*. You can find a listing of these errors at the Microsoft Knowledge Base at support. microsoft.com/support/kb/articles/Q198/3/07.asp.

A web-page style index is available for the *Resource Kit*. You can put the index wherever you like, and it will access the *Resource Kit* help file in the default folder /Program Files/Win98RK. The index was created by the pseudonymous MrScary, Attila Szabo (a Microsoft MVP), and it is on the accompanying CD-ROM under the filename Resource Kit Index.htm. This type of index is great because it shows you all of the subheadings without having to open each heading.

It's possible to just read the *Windows 98 Resource Kit* document as a Windows 98 HTML help file right on the Windows 98 CD-ROM. You don't even need to install it on your computer or load any of the associated applets. Just click the \tools\reskit\help\rk98book.chm file on the CD-ROM.

For even easier access to the *Windows 98 Resource Kit Book Online*, drag this file to your \Windows\Help folder. Then right-drag it to your Desktop or Start menu, and create a shortcut there for easy access. You don't have to install the whole *Resource Kit* just to get the *Book Online*.

You need only install those *Resource Kit* applets that you want to use, without installing them all. You can simply drag some of the applets to new folders. Others include setup executables or install files. You'll have to go through each subfolder of the \tools\reskit folder on your Windows 98 CD-ROM and decide for yourself what you want to do with these various applets.

Quick support from Microsoft

Why doesn't Microsoft make it easier for you to get to the Knowledge Base? You won't find a quick link to the Microsoft Support Online web page on the Links toolbar. If you click the Support button at the top of the page at the Microsoft web site (www.microsoft.com, for example), it doesn't take you to the Knowledge Base.

We suggest that you create a shortcut to this URL and put it on your Quick Launch toolbar.

STEPS:

Putting the Microsoft Knowledge Base on Your Desktop

Step 1.   Click the Internet Explorer icon on your Desktop, type **http://support.microsoft.com/support/search/c.asp** in the Address toolbar, and press Enter.

Step 2.   When the Microsoft Personal Support Center, Advanced View web page appears, right-click the Internet Explorer client area, click Create Shortcut, and click OK. A shortcut will appear on your Desktop.

Step 3.   Hold down the Win key and press D to clear the Desktop.

Step 4. Drag the Microsoft Personal Support Center, Advanced View shortcut to your Quick Launch toolbar.

Thanks to Edward Stonich for providing this tip.

Keep tabs on the latest Windows 98 updates

You can use the Microsoft Knowledge Base to keep track of ongoing changes to Windows 98.

STEPS:

Checking for the Latest Windows 98 News

Step 1. Click your Microsoft Personal Support Center shortcut in your Quick Launch toolbar. (See the previous section if you haven't created this shortcut yet.)

Step 2. Select Windows 98 or Plus! 98 in the My Search Is About field of the Microsoft Personal Support Center page, as shown in Figure 16-35.

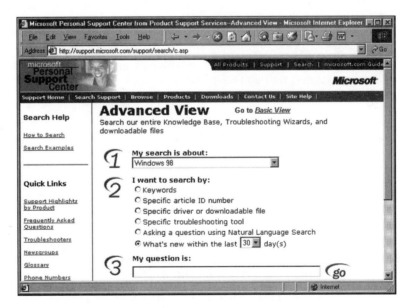

Figure 16-35: The Microsoft Personal Support Center web site.

Continued

Step 3.   Mark What's New Within the Last [   ] Day(s) and specify 30 days.

Step 4.   Leave the My Question Is field blank, and click the Go button.

Internet Explorer will display a list of articles about Windows 98 or Plus! 98. Click the title of any of the articles to read more details.

Keep aware of the latest Windows betas

You'll find news about the latest beta tests at www.betanews.com.

Keep up on Windows 98 bugs and solutions

This is the best list of bugs and solutions that we've found on the web. Most of the bugs are esoteric. That is, they will only affect a few thousand users, but if you're among that group you will appreciate this site: Bug Alert at www.zdnet.com/zdhelp/bug_help/bugs/bugalert_win98.html.

Inside Windows 98

If you'd like an overview of the core architecture of Windows 98, we'd strongly suggest that you have a look at *Inside Windows 98* by Keith Pleas. Here's a sample of what Keith has to say:

> The Windows 98 operating system, like Windows 95 before it, provides a complete 32-bit base system that includes a Virtual Machine Manager (VMM), an Installable File System Manager, configuration management for Plug and Play, and other necessary system services. The VMM creates and manages a single virtual machine (VM) that contains all Win32 applications (and the Win32 subsystem) as well as additional VMs for DOS applications that require exclusive access to machine resources.

We found his articles to be understandable, succinct, and jargon free. If this appeals to you, you can read it online at www.zdnet.com/pcmag/pctech/content/17/14/tf1714.001.html.

The Ziff Davis web sites provide a significant amount of good information about Windows 98, although most of it (other than the PC Tech area) is quite a bit lighter than the material that you'll find in this book. By "lighter" we mean more restricted to the level of beginner tips and tricks. They don't include anything that requires you to edit the Registry, for example. While this is not always true, this is their general approach.

You can check out some of their Windows 98 tips at search.zdnet.com/ cgi-bin/ texis/zdhelp/zdhelp/search.html?Uprod=Windows+98%2520&Utiptype=tip and www.zdnet.com/zdhelp/howto_help/win98tips/win98tips_1.html.

You might want to also check their help center for Windows 98 at www.zdnet. com/zdhelp/filters/windows/windows98/.

While there are a number of sites that handle Windows 98 shareware, Ziff-Davis does a good job of providing you with longer descriptions of the shareware products. You'll find plenty of links to their shareware at the sites we just mentioned, or you can go directly to www.zdnet.com/swlib/.

Microsoft's "Miscellaneous FAQ About Windows 98"

You can find out what Microsoft thinks are the random questions about Windows 98 by reading "Miscellaneous Frequently Asked Questions About Windows 98" at support.microsoft.com/support/windows/faq/98/misc.asp.

Desktop Engineer's Junk Drawer

This web site and associated list server provides a little help to those who maintain Windows systems in the corporate environment. It offers tools, techniques, and clues.

Check it out and subscribe at www.info-evolution.com/dejd/.

The Year 2000 is coming, the Year 2000 is coming!

One if by land, two if by sea, but four numbers if you need to keep track of the date.

Microsoft has a web page where you can get Year 2000 information. You'll find it at www.microsoft.com/technet/year2k/. Computer vendors also have Year 2000 web sites. You can check out a particularly good one at www.ibm.com/ ibm/year2000. This site also lets you download BIOS updates for all IBM personal computers, starting with the IBM PC AT bus.

Windows 98 solves Year 2000 problems that Windows 95 didn't. You can learn more about this in the Microsoft Knowledge Base article "Windows 95 Year 2000 Problems with DATE and DIR Commands" at support.microsoft.com/ support/kb/articles/q182/9/67.asp.

Windows 98 will also overcome Year 2000 bugs found in various BIOSes. You can see four-digit dates in a DOS directory listing (see Figure 16-36), or when you boot up DOS and type **dir /4** at the DOS prompt.

Figure 16-36: In this DOS directory, the file creation dates use four digits.

In December 1998, Microsoft released an update to Windows 98 that fixed some additional Year 2000 problems. You can easily update your Windows 98 system to include this update by clicking Windows Update on your Start menu (or Start, Settings, Windows Update).

Another interesting Year 2000 site: www.y2kcertified.com/index.shtml.

Other sources of Windows information

Sometimes it seems as though all we talk about are further sources of information. There must be thousands of URLs throughout this book. At least you can be assured of finding some backup to the statements that we make here.

We track Windows information every day by following the discussions on newsgroups, visiting web sites, and receiving e-zines from knowledgeable sources. One example is WinInfo, from Paul Thurott. This is mostly a sampling of news stories about Windows. It very rarely includes any tricks or secrets, but it is always interesting. You'll find it at www.wugnet.com/wininfo.

Then there is Woody's Windows Watch (WWW). Woody Leonard, Barry Simon, and especially Peter Deegan started up this follow-on to the successful Woody's Office Watch (WOW) in November of 1998. Woody and Barry are the co-authors of *The Mother of All Windows 98 Books*. The working title for this very book was *Not Your Mother's Windows 98 Secrets* — our little joke.

WWW is a power-packed bundle of Windows information in a beautiful HTML format. It is jam packed with Windows tips and tricks as well as interesting news and links to other web sites. I love that fact that it comes from Australia, my favorite country. WOW is also full of Office tips and tricks. You can sign up for WWW at www.wopr.com/www/ and WOW at www.wopr.com/wow.

We've mentioned Chris Pirillo's Lockergnome in various places throughout this book. It is a guide to Windows shareware in a good-looking HTML newsletter delivered every working day, with a roundup at the end of the week for the folks with HTML-challenged e-mail clients. Check it out at www.lockergnome.com.

The CNET Shareware dispatch comes out about once a week and gives you a heads up on the latest shareware for both Windows and the Mac. You can of course go to their web site and search through the archives, but it is nice to have someone looking out for good shareware. You'll find them at www. shareware.com/?dd.sw.

The Berst Alert provides daily news about personal computing, Windows, and the computing industry. There is almost always a link to some specific highlighted shareware for the day. You'll also find information on web site construction, the latest news about Microsoft and its enemies, links to ZDNet's TipZone, and Windows-specific advise. You'll find it at www.anchordesk.com.

Windows 98 Central is updated several times daily with the latest Windows 98 news. You'll find it at www.activecomputing.com/. It includes lots of help, troubleshooting, and the latest downloads.

Bud's Windows 9x Troubleshooter is just a great site. He offers wonderful material on setting up multiple monitors, for example. You can download an anti-nuke device, stop Windows from searching for a floppy, and fix power management for PC Cards. The site deals with Windows 95 and 98, as the title should tell you, so you'll have to weed out the older material.

You'll find it at www.geocities.com/~budallen/. Thanks to Mark McClure via Chris Pirillo at www.lockergnome.com.

WinReviews claims to be the number one site for hardware reviews. It actually collects and organizes links to the various reviews and to the latest Windows news. WinReviews comes with a chat room and a search engine. It looked quite strong to us in early 1999.

You'll find it at www.winreviews.com.

Note to shareware/freeware developers

We tested a great deal of freeware and shareware as we wrote this book (and all of our previous books). After a while, you get to know what works regarding software installs and what doesn't. If you install software, you might be on the lookout for some of the things that we've noticed. Here's our advice to the developers:

■ If you install a shortcut to your software in the \Windows\Start Menu\ Programs\StartUp folder, open a small folder window next to it at the end of the install to allow us to remove your program from this folder. This is a lot easier than using the System Configuration Utility.

■ If you install system files — most likely DLLs in the \Windows or \Windows\System folder — be sure to check the version numbers of possible duplicates of your DLLs. Only install the latest version.

■ Better yet, don't install anything in \Windows\System.

■ Create a log file of everything that setup does and place it in your folder.

■ Ask the user where he or she wants your program to be placed, and don't make the default something two layers deep inside of \Program Files with your company name as the first subfolder. We don't care about putting all your company programs together.

■ Ask if we want a shortcut in the Start menu, or on the Desktop, or neither.

■ Why don't any of you let us put the shortcut on the Start menu anywhere but in the Programs menu at the top level? It never ends up there.

■ Don't install a CPL without asking first. Don't install any context menu items without asking first.

■ Don't package your program in an executable that just unzips everything to the current folder in a DOS window.

■ If you put your install executable in a zip file, this is cool because you can include a readme.txt file, which we can read before we decide to install the software. In the readme.txt file, tell us what the program does and why, list your web site (which may be different from where we down-loaded it), tell us if the install program deposits files to any folder other than its own folder, mention whether your software can be uninstalled easily, and tell us who the author is.

■ Always include an uninstall program unless it is really trivial (no Registry entries), and then include explicit instructions on how to uninstall.

■ Open a small folder window focused on the new folder at the end of the install. There's no need for a check box about the readme.txt file at the end, because we can click it in the folder window if we like.

■ Use a Windows 95/98 install program that adds an entry to the Add/ Remove Programs Registry branch.

■ How about displaying your help file before we have to commit to installing your software? We've seen it done, so we know it can be done. This is possible with the standard software installation programs.

Summary

This is a large and diverse chapter that covers many different system elements. From system configuration, to dealing with bugs, to keeping up to date.

▶ Create an emergency boot diskette.

▶ Kill any ongoing Windows process.

▶ Install or at least access the *Windows 98 Resource Kit* from your Windows 98 CD-ROM.

▶ Keep current with the latest list of Windows 98 bugs.

▶ Is the Year 2000 here yet?

▶ Are you a freeware or shareware developer? If so, check out our note to shareware/freeware developers.

Chapter 17

Communications

In This Chapter

Faxing, dialing, and dealing with your modem. We could have put these topics in the hardware chapter, but there were so many that dealt just with these kinds of communication problems that we felt they stood alone.

▶ Windows 98 dropped (for the most part) the fax capabilities that came with Windows 95. You can still add these exact same functions back in.

▶ Is your computer always starting up your modem without warning? We show you how to put a stop to this obnoxious behavior.

▶ Just because you're moving to another computer doesn't mean that you have to leave your DUN connectoids behind. We show you how to take them along.

▶ How about speeding up downloads on a cable modem?

Install Microsoft Fax

Windows 95 included Microsoft Exchange client and Microsoft Fax. This combo allowed you to keep a fax phone number list and send and receive faxes.

Windows 98 includes an older update to Microsoft Exchange client, called Windows Messaging, and Microsoft Fax. If you haven't installed Outlook 98, you might want to install Windows Messaging and Microsoft Fax. Windows Messaging isn't installed automatically when you install Windows 98. If you have installed Outlook 98, you can combine Outlook with Microsoft Fax. You can't use Microsoft Fax alone; it requires a full MAPI messaging client such as Exchange (Windows Messaging) or Outlook. Outlook Express doesn't work with Microsoft Fax.

If you want to combine Outlook with Microsoft Fax, check out the instructions at the Exchange Center at www.slipstick.com/exchange. You'll need to install the corporate version of Outlook to connect to Microsoft Fax (even if you're not a corporation).

You can install Windows Messaging and Microsoft Fax from your Windows 98 CD-ROM. Use your Explorer to navigate to \tools\oldwin95\message\us (or intl for the international version). First click wms.exe to install Windows Messaging. Restart Windows after it is done installing. Next, click awfax.exe to install Microsoft Fax. You can read more about this in the wms-fax.txt file, which you'll find in the same folder as these other two files.

We detail how to use Windows Messaging for e-mail and faxes in Chapter 20 of *Windows 98 Secrets*. Better still, use the Outlook client in place of Windows Messaging (although Microsoft charges for Outlook now).

There are third-party fax programs that you can use with Windows applications. Unfortunately, we don't know of any at present that use the Windows address book. You might check out MightyFAX at www.rks-software.com. This is a shareware package that you can try out for a limited number of times. It basically runs as a printer driver.

Stop dialing!

You may find that your computer wants to dial into your Internet service provider unbidden. This may happen when your computer first starts up, on a regular schedule, or at odd hours during the day and night. It can be quite annoying, especially if it is running up costs on its own, without accomplishing any useful work.

Add in the irritating sound of the modem at work, and the fact that you feel yourself at war with your computer, and the annoyance factor of this behavior can get quite high. We'll show you how to put the computer in its place.

In the section "Stop your modem from dialing when you start Windows 98" in Chapter 18, we discuss how to get the Personal Web Server to stop dialing in when you first start Windows. You've also got to be on the lookout for other software that will try to dial the modem.

Synchronizing offline web pages

If you have configured offline web pages to update on a schedule, possibly on a schedule determined by the channel publisher, then Internet Explorer will, if properly configured, cause your modem to dial into your Internet service provider. You need to get to your offline web pages to stop this behavior. We show you how to set up easy access to them in "Easy access to your Offline Web Pages folder" in Chapter 2.

Once you've opened the Offline Web Pages folder window on your Desktop, right-click an offline web page name and click Properties. Click the Schedule tab to see if the offline web page has been scheduled for updating, as shown in Figure 17-1.

You need to add a schedule if there aren't any listed and you do want your offline web sites updated. If there aren't any schedules listed in the Schedule dialog box (whether marked or unmarked), you know that none of your offline web pages have been updated automatically and your modem hasn't been invoked to call up your Internet service provider.

If you see a marked schedule, highlight it and click the Edit button. Click the Synchronization Items tab. You get to see a list of offline web pages, as shown in Figure 17-2. Notice the check box at the bottom of the dialog box (If My Computer Is Not Connected...).

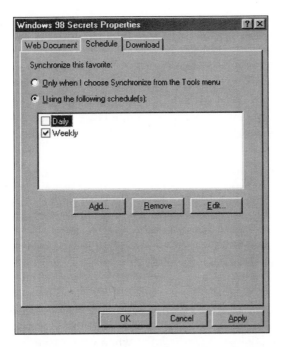

Figure 17-1: The Schedule tab for this offline web page is set to synchronize weekly.

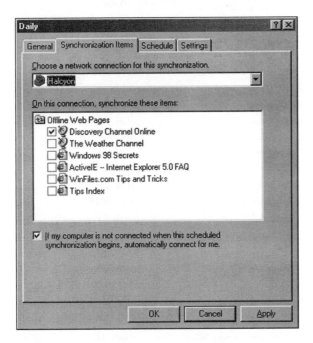

Figure 17-2: The Synchronization Items tab for this schedule shows which offline web pages will be updated.

If this check box is marked, it is pretty clear what is going to happen. Whenever the schedule calls for a specific web page to be updated, Internet Explorer will invoke its Dial-Up Connection dialog box (a connection manager), which will in turn send the command to your modem to dial up your service provider.

You can either clear this check box or click the Schedule tab and reschedule the offline web page updates to a time less bothersome to you. Also, you can decide to synchronize the offline web pages upon your command by marking the Only When I Choose to Synchronize from the Tools menu check box (refer back to Figure 17-1).

You can also turn off the capability to synchronize offline web pages on a schedule. In the Internet Explorer, click Tools, Internet Options, click the Advanced tab, and clear the Enable Offline Items to Be Synchronized on a Schedule check box.

Outlook Express dials in to gather your e-mail

If it turns out that offline web page synchronization isn't causing your computer to dial up, perhaps it's dialing because Outlook Express is trying to download your e-mail. Click your Outlook Express icon on your Desktop. Click Tools, Options, and see if you've marked Check for New Messages Every [   ] Minute(s) in the General tab, as shown in Figure 17-3.

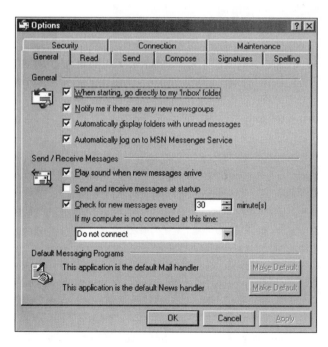

Figure 17-3: In this example, the computer will dial up every 30 minutes if necessary to send and receive mail.

If you have selected Connect Only When Not Working Offline or Connect Even When Working Offline in the drop-down list under Send/Receive Messages, then Outlook Express will dial up your Internet service provider based on the interval you've chosen.

Outlook Express will also try to connect to your service provider if you have marked Send Messages Immediately in the Send tab, as shown in Figure 17-4.

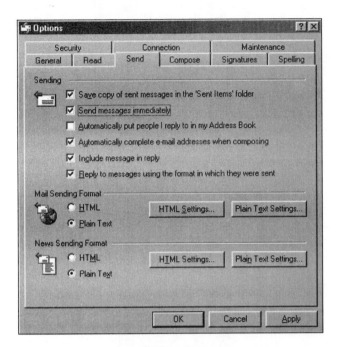

Figure 17-4: The Send Messages Immediately check box is marked, so Outlook Express will dial a connection every time you send a message.

When you start Outlook Express, it will also ask if you want to connect to your service provider if you have marked the Send and Receive Messages at Startup check box in the General tab (see Figure 17-5).

Click the Change button in the Connection tab of the Options dialog box to see if Internet Explorer and Outlook Express are configured to always dial your default connection, as shown in Figure 17-6. If they are, then they will in fact dial into your service provider.

You can stop Internet Explorer from dialing into your Internet service provider by marking Never Dial a Connection. This will stop the offline web page synchronization feature and the Task Scheduler from forcing Internet Explorer to dial into your service provider.

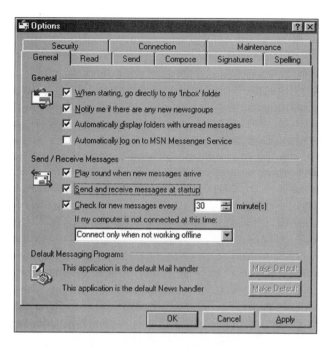

Figure 17-5: Because the Send and Receive Messages at Startup check box is marked, Outlook Express will ask whether to dial up every time it starts.

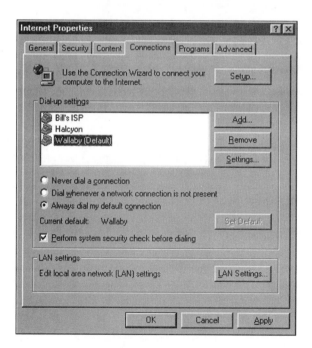

Figure 17-6: When you click the Change button on the Connection tab, the Internet Properties dialog box appears, set to its own Connections tab.

The Task Scheduler schedules a task that dials your modem

The Task Scheduler uses the same scheduling functions as offline web page synchronization. If you have a scheduled task that dials up your modem, that could be the source of your problem. You can easily check this out.

Open your Explorer, and highlight Scheduled Tasks in the left pane. Check the Next Run Time column to see if there are any tasks that appear to call your modem. Right-click such a task, and click Run. See if it does dial or not. If so, you can remove it from your Scheduled Tasks folder, or set a less bothersome schedule.

Traveling connections

You can copy your DUN connectoid settings and your calling card settings from one computer to another.

Take your DUN connectoids with you

Windows 98 provides Dial-Up Networking services that allow you to connect your computer to your Internet service provider, to a Dial-Up Server on another Windows 98 computer, to a Windows NT RAS server, or to another communications server.

You can create a new connection by clicking Start, Programs, Accessories, Communications, Dial-Up Networking, Make New Connection. You can also just click the Dial-Up Networking icon in your Explorer and then click Make New Connection.

Your existing dial-up connections are displayed as icons in the Dial-Up Networking folder. To activate a connection — that is, to dial into your server — just click any of your connection icons (DUN connectoids).

Each DUN connectoid maintains the settings required to successfully make a modem-to-modem connection with a particular server. It's easy to transfer your connectoids to other folders on your computer or to other computers. Here are some situations in which you might want to do this:

- You use multiple computers
- You travel to different locations and use other people's computers
- You want to install the e-mail connection on a department full of computers
- You want to e-mail your connection information to someone else
- You want to save your DUN connectoids in your My System or other folder so that you can recover them if you have to reinstall Windows or you lose your Windows installation

The DUN connectoids are front ends for Registry settings. Right-click a connectoid and click Properties. You'll find the server's phone number and, in the Server Types tab, various server connection settings.

To transfer these Registry settings as a package, all you have to do is drag and drop the DUN connectoid, just as though it were a file (it has a *DUN* extension). You can drop it onto your Desktop, into any (real) folder on a computer on your network, onto a diskette, into an e-mail message, into a document, whatever. You won't be able to drop it on another computer's Dial-Up Networking folder (although it will in fact show up there later), Control Panel folder, Printers folder, or Scheduled Tasks folder, because these aren't actually folders.

If you carry your DUN connectoids with you on a diskette, you can drag and drop them onto the Desktop of any Windows 98 computer. Click the connectoid, and the computer will dial up your server. You'll notice that the DUN connectoid also shows up in the Dial-Up Networking folder after you click it once.

There are some caveats. Your user name and password are not included with the connectoid. You'll have to type these in yourself. If the computer's Dial-Up Networking connection settings are set to not prompt you for information before dialing, you won't have an opportunity to enter these values. To get that opportunity, click the Dial-Up Networking icon in the left pane of the computer's Explorer window, and choose Connections, Settings. Mark the Prompt for Information Before Dialing check box, and click OK.

The DUN connectoid includes the name of the modem on the source computer. This points to all the parameters that define the modem and its serial connection. If the target computer doesn't have the same modem, you can change the modem that your connectoid uses. To do so, right-click the connection and click Properties. Then display the Connect Using drop-down list, and choose the installed modem.

You may not have to do this. Just click the connectoid and see if it dials the target computer's modem. It may work just fine. If you right-click your transferred connectoid on the target computer in the Dial-Up Networking folder and click Properties, you will be notified if the modem it names isn't installed. Follow the steps in the previous paragraph to associate the installed modem with this connectoid. There are numerous pieces of shareware that allow you to do what we've just detailed. You couldn't do this using earlier versions of Windows 95 with the earlier version of Dial-Up Networking. Windows 98 solves these problems, and renders the shareware unnecessary.

Take your calling card or long distance provider with you

We have to confess that we think that Windows has the weirdest telecom interface. If we knew of a way to access the Dialing Properties dialog box directly, we would tack a little icon on it and put it on our Quick Launch toolbar. Barring this, you can choose between clicking the Modems icon in your Control Panel and clicking Dialing Properties, opening the Phone Dialer (Start, Programs, Accessories, Communications, Phone Dialer) and clicking Tools, Dialing Properties, or any of a myriad of other indirect ways. We just wish there were one overall console that let you deal with all the Windows communication issues.

The Calling Card button in the Dialing Properties dialog box brings you to the calling card creation interface shown in Figure 17-7. We extensively discuss how to set up specific long distance carriers and other calling cards in Chapter 32 of *Windows 98 Secrets*.

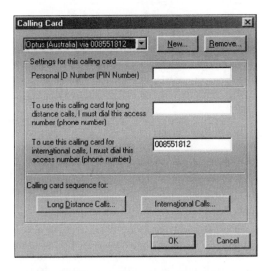

Figure 17-7: Click the New button to begin creating a new calling card. Click the Long Distance button to set up the dialing rules for the card.

Secret

Once you set up a new calling card, you will want to make a copy of this vital information so that you can take it to other computers, or restore it if you ever lose your Windows configuration. You can do this by exporting the relevant portion of your Registry.

STEPS:

Saving Your Calling Card

Step 1. After you have set up a card using the steps in Chapter 32 of *Windows 98 Secrets,* use Registry Crawler (see "Crawl through the Registry" in Chapter 14) to search your Registry for your calling card name or long distance provider name. You can also just use your Registry editor to navigate to the following branch of your Registry (see Figure 17-8):

Continued

STEPS

Saving Your Calling Card *(continued)*

HKEY_CURRENT_USER\Software\Microsoft\Windows\
CurrentVersion\Telephony\Cards

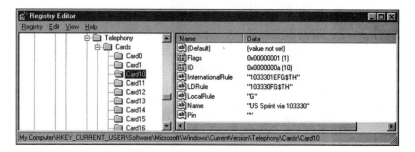

Figure 17-8: Each card has a card number as shown in the left pane. Your latest entry will be the highest card number.

Step 2.   If you've just entered a new card, it will have the highest number. Highlight the card you want to save in the left pane of your Registry editor, click Registry, Export Registry File. Give the file the same name as your calling card, and save it in your My System folder or another appropriate folder.

In the exported card's *reg* file, your PIN number will be encrypted and the phone number will be phony. You'll have to reenter your PIN and phone number after you merge this information to another Registry.

Step 3.   To import this calling card entry into another Registry, you have to make sure that you don't overwrite an existing entry. Navigate to the location shown in step 1 in the new Registry, and check and see what the highest Card# is in the left pane.

Step 4.   Edit the following line in your exported card *reg* file so that the Card# shown at the end of the line is one higher than the highest card number in the new Registry:

[HKEY_CURRENT_USER\Software\Microsoft\Windows\
CurrentVersion\Telephony\Cards\Card24]

Step 5.   Right-click your exported card *reg* file, and click Merge to merge it into the new Registry.

Step 6.   Highlight the Cards key in the new Registry. It's just above the Card# keys (refer back to Figure 17-8).

Step 7.   Double-click NextID in the right pane of your Registry editor. Click the Decimal option button (see Figure 17-9) and increase the number in the Value Data field by 1. Click OK. You have to do this because in step 5, you just added one card to the list of cards stored in the Registry.

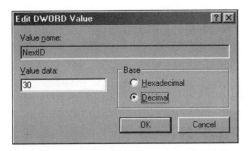

Figure 17-9: You've inserted one calling card, so you need to increase the NextID data value by one.

Step 8. Double-click the NumEntries variable in the right pane of your Registry editor, click the Decimal option button, increase the number in the Value Data field by 1, and click OK. You've added one card to the number of cards stored in the Registry.

Step 9. Highlight your card number key in the left pane of your Registry editor. Double-click the ID variable in the right pane. Click the Decimal option button. In the Value Data field, enter a value that's one less than the current NextID value, which you set in step 7. Close the Registry editor.

Step 10. Click Start, Settings, Modems, Dialing Properties, Calling Card. Enter the correct value for this card's PIN in the Personal ID Number (PIN Number) field. Click OK.

This would all be too much work if it weren't for the fact that remembering the dialing rules and the calling card dial-in numbers is even more work.

Tip

You don't have to merge the exported card *reg* file. You can just keep it for reference, and look at it if and when you have to create a new entry using the standard user interface. If you follow the discussion in Chapter 32 of *Windows 98 Secrets*, you may even be able to figure out the abbreviations for the dialing rules stored in the Registry file.

Tip

Here's another option. Instead of just exporting the branch for your particular calling card, export the whole Cards branch. When you want to merge it into another Registry, just be sure that the number of cards in the new Registry is equal to or less than the number in the saved branch. The entries in the Registry of the target computer will be overwritten.

Speed is everything

We provide you with a few tricks to speed up your modem.

Speed up modem dialing

Ever notice how fast your modem dials into your Internet service provider? Just turn up the volume on your system tray a bit and listen to the touch-tone tones as your modem spits them out. You may have to click the Modems icon in your Control Panel, highlight your modem, click Properties, and move the Speaker Volume slider over to the right to hear the modem.

The phone company's equipment can interpret the tones much faster than your modem is likely putting them out. If you want to speed up your dialing, you can send a command to your modem.

STEPS:
Speed Up Your Modem Dialing

Step 1.   Click Start, Settings, Control Panel, and click the modems icon.

Step 2.   Highlight your modem and click the Properties button.

Step 3.   Click the Connection tab, and then click the Advanced button.

Step 4.   In the Extra Settings field, type **S11=35** (see Figure 17-10). Click OK, click OK, and click Close.

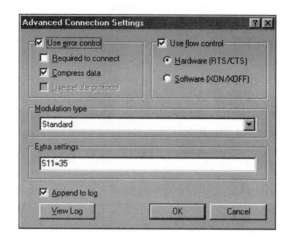

Figure 17-10: The Extra Settings field in this figure contains the setting for modem dial speed.

Secret

The S11 setting is the setting for modem dial speed. Some modems can't go this fast, so you can drop back to S11=50. With your volume up, you should be able to hear the difference before and after you make these changes.

If your modem can't dial this fast, you may get the error message shown in Figure 17-11. If you do, then you'll know that you have to either back off on the dialing speed or not use this setting at all.

Figure 17-11: You may get this error message if your modem can't dial the phone number as fast as you want it to.

Some modems are not fully Hayes compatible, and for them this modem string will have no effect. You can hear the difference quite clearly if the modem string does take effect, so you'll know right away whether or not your modem supports it.

Thanks to Greg Miller for pointing out this tip.

Don't let your modem fall back too far

Modems fall back to lower communication speeds if they encounter line noise that is too intense. But they can fall back too far without making additional efforts at maintaining the higher speed. While your modem manufacturer may claim that your modem is Hayes compatible, it may not set certain modem registries to the correct default values that allow for these more aggressive efforts at maintaining high speeds.

Secret

If you have your modem manual handy, you can check the default values for the crucial modem registries. You'll want to check the S10 and S36 registry default values, which should be 50 and 7, respectively. If these are not the default settings, you can add these values to the modem initialization string:

STEPS:

Keeping Your Modem from Slowing Down Prematurely

Step 1. Click Start, Settings, Control Panel, and click the Modems icon.

Step 2. Highlight your modem and click the Properties button.

Step 3. Click the Connection tab and then click the Advanced button.

Continued

Step 4. In the Extra Settings field, type **S10=50** and **S36=7** (see Figure 17-12). Click OK, click OK, and then click Close.

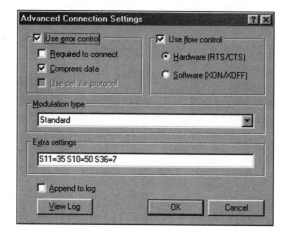

Figure 17-12: Add these modem settings to the Extra Settings field.

Thanks to Anthony Kinyon for help with this tip.

STAC compression

Microsoft has added the STAC (www.stac.com) compression algorithm to its modem communication drivers. You may remember back in ancient history when Microsoft added disk compression to Windows that competed with STAC's disk compression algorithm. Later, it paid STAC a bunch of money and bought a chunk of stock in the company.

Secret

If your Internet service provider supports STAC compression on their end, you could get dramatically increased performance. One Internet service provider claims up to 4 times the download speed, or 13 Kbytes/second with a 33.6 modem.

You can check with your Internet service provider to see if they support the STAC protocol. Perhaps they advertise this feature on their web page. Service providers who use Livingston PM3 units and support 56K access are likely candidates.

You have to configure your Dial-Up Networking connectoid and your modem driver to take advantage of this capability. Here's how:

STEPS:

Configuring Your DUN Connectoid and Modem Driver to Use STAC

Step 1. Click your My Computer icon, and then click the Dial-Up Networking icon.

Step 2. Right-click the connection icon for your Internet service provider, click Properties, and then click the Server Types tab.

Step 3. Mark Enable Software Compression. The other check boxes under Advanced Options can be cleared, as illustrated in Figure 17-13.

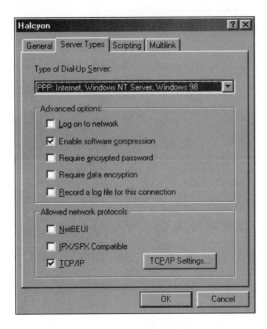

Figure 17-13: Mark the Enable Software Compression check box on the Server Types tab of the Properties dialog box for your DUN connectoid.

Step 4. Click the General tab, and click the Configure button to open the Properties dialog box for the modem associated with this connectoid. Go to its Connection tab, and click the Advanced button.

Step 5. Clear the Compress Data check box, as shown in Figure 17-14. Make sure that you have marked Use Flow Control and Hardware (RTS/CTS). Click OK, click OK, and click Close.

Continued

STEPS

Configuring Your DUN Connectoid and Modem Driver to Use STAC *(continued)*

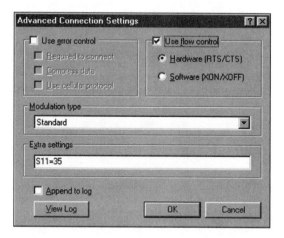

Figure 17-14: The Advanced Connection Settings dialog box for the modem associated with this DUN connectoid.

To check whether STAC compression is being used, connect to your Internet service provider by clicking its DUN connectoid. After the connection is made, double-click the modem icon in your system tray, and click the Details button to expand the Connected To dialog box (see Figure 17-15). This dialog box indicates whether you are using STAC compression.

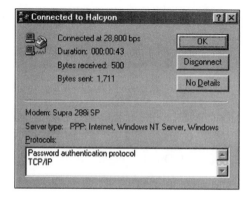

Figure 17-15: If you are using STAC compression, it will be listed under Protocols in the Connected To dialog box. In this example, there is no STAC compression.

If you are sure that your service provider supports STAC, and you don't see it in this dialog box, go once again to the Advanced Connection Settings dialog box and mark Use Error Control.

Thanks to Penelope Baker for help with this secret.

Speed up download on cable or DSL modems

Unlike Windows 95, Windows 98 has an automatic mode that is supposed to reset your IP packet size depending on the speed of your Internet connection. You can read more about this in the Microsoft Knowledge Base article "Description of the Internet Protocol Packet Size Setting" at support. microsoft.com/support/kb/articles/Q183/4/37.asp, or in Chapter 18 of *Windows 98 Secrets*.

If you've got a fast and noise-free connection to your ISP, you can enjoy the benefits of cutting down on the overhead of continuous error detection and correction. If you increase the size of your IP packets, you will decrease the percentage of extra error checking characters that are sent with your data.

Secret

If you are using a cable or DSL modem, you might check to see if the automatic mode is right for you. One user we heard from found that changing the IP packet size from Automatic to Large sped up large file downloads by a factor of three.

STEPS:

Changing Your IP Packet Size

Step 1.   Click Start, Settings, Control Panel, and click the Network Icon.

Step 2.   Highlight Dial-Up Adapter, click Properties, and click the Advanced tab.

Step 3.   Select IP Packet Size, display the Value drop-down list, and highlight Large (see Figure 17-16).

Step 4.   Click OK, and click OK again.

Continued

STEPS

Changing Your IP Packet Size *(continued)*

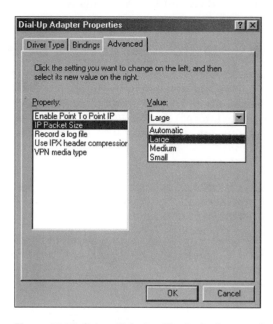

Figure 17-16: Select IP Packet Size in the Property list, and then display the Value drop-down list and select Large.

This is the same as increasing the MTU size to 1,500.

Thanks to Scott Sizemore and Dustin Miller for insights on this issue.

Test your download rate

A number of variables affect your file download speed from your Internet service provider. All of these values get set in the Registry, pretty much behind the scenes or at best in Advanced dialog boxes, as shown in the previous section. A clear view of these variables and their effects on the speed of communication would be helpful.

A perfect little piece of freeware for doing just that is iSpeed. It displays all of the relevant variables and lets you adjust their values, either one at a time or as a set based on your connection type (see Figure 17-17). You can then test the settings and decide for yourself which ones provide the best file download rates. You'll find iSpeed at www.hms.com.

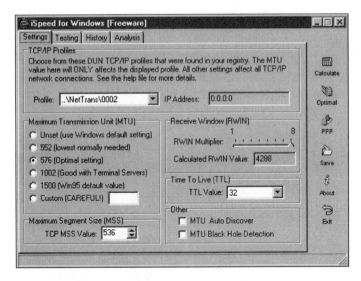

Figure 17-17: The Settings tab in the iSpeed window lets you test different combinations of communications settings.

All of the Windows 98 TCP/IP settings that you can add to the Registry are listed in the Microsoft Knowledge Base article "Windows TCP/IP Registry Entries" at support.microsoft.com/support/kb/articles/Q158/4/74.asp. Don't make these additions unless you are thoroughly familiar with TCP/IP protocol issues.

The Microsoft Knowledge Base also contains an interesting article on a Winsock bug that was not fixed until Winsock 2.0 was released for Windows 95. Windows 98 comes with Winsock 2.0. The bug kept a Registry entry that modified the search order for DNS servers and kept them from making any difference. You'll find the article, "Windows 95 Service Provider Priority Values Not Applied," at support.microsoft.com/support/kb/articles/Q170/6/19.asp. This article contains links to many other Knowledge Base articles that pertain to Winsock, DUN, and TCP/IP issues.

Medical care for your modem

Modem Doctor, shown in Figure 17-18, is one neat little shareware package for checking over your modem and learning a little bit about how it operates. The shareware version doesn't do all of the tests, but it does enough. Register it and you get the rest of the tests.

Modem Doctor checks all of your serial ports for modems, and tests your serial ports and modems by sending out commands and waiting for answers. You can do loopback tests with the registered version. Modem Doctor also works with Windows 98 to call up the modem, Dial-Up Networking, and Internet configuration dialog boxes.

You'll find it at www.modemdoctor.com.

Figure 17-18: The Modem Doctor user interface.

Can't save your Dial-Up Networking password

Of all Windows 95/98 problems, this one has probably plagued the largest number of people. You are unable to save the password that you use to log on to your Internet service provider, or to any other network that you dial into.

A number of different factors can cause the DUN connectoid or the connection manager not to display your password in asterisks in the Password field, and to dim the Save Password check box. We discuss these factors and how to fix the problem in "Saving your DUN connectoid passwords" in Chapter 18 of *Windows 98 Secrets*.

Additional information is available in the article "Dial-Up Networking Password Is Not Saved" at support.microsoft.com/support/kb/articles/q148/9/25.asp.

You can follow the steps detailed in these documents, or you can download a shareware package that saves the password for you. Affirmative Action DUN saves the password itself and integrates with the Windows 98 dialer. We recommend that you just solve the problem, but if you want a quick fix, this is it.

You'll find AA DUN at www.nadalia.com/aadun.

HyperTerminal update

HyperTerminal, a smart terminal communications program, comes with Windows 98 — but Microsoft doesn't have it on the Windows Update web site. You can get the latest version of HyperTerminal, updated since the release of Windows 98, at the Hilgraeve HyperTerminal Private Edition web site: www.hilgraeve.com/htpe.html.

Summary

It really pays to get your modem in order and up to speed. We give you the clues on how to help it out.

▶ Enter a character string to get your modem to dial a lot faster.

▶ If your Internet service provider has the right stack of modems, you can speed up your access.

▶ The freeware program iSpeed tells you how to get optimum performance from your Internet connections.

▶ The doctor is in for medical care for your modem.

Chapter 18

Starting Up

In This Chapter

With the System Configuration Utility, Windows 98 makes it much easier to determine what starts up when you start up Windows.

▶ Use TweakUI to give yourself a little time before Windows starts up.

▶ If Explorer won't start, you can still get to Windows.

▶ Use the Boot Log Analyzer to see where you might have a problem.

▶ Stop Windows from dialing up your Internet service provider when it starts up.

Starting up

Lots of bad things can happen when you start up Windows 98. We show you how to solve a number of startup problems.

Get to the Startup menu

The Windows 95 startup procedures gave you a two-second window between the message "Starting Windows 95" and the actual startup of Windows 95. During these two seconds, you could press the F8 key to bring up the Windows Startup menu, which allowed you to boot to DOS, open Windows in Safe mode, and so on. You can read more about it and other startup procedures in Chapter 5 of *Windows 98 Secrets*.

The two-second delay has been eliminated in Windows 98, and to get to the Windows Startup menu you must now hold down the Ctrl key during your computer's power-on self test. You can use TweakUI to get the two-second (or more) delay back, which will make it easier to get to the Startup menu.

If you haven't yet installed TweakUI, follow steps 1 and 2. Otherwise, begin with step 3.

STEPS:

Using TweakUI to Bring up the Windows Startup Menu

Step 1. Insert your Windows 98 CD-ROM in your CD-ROM drive and the Explorer to navigate to \tools\reskit\powertoy.

Step 2. Right-click tweakui.inf and click Install.

Step 3. Click Start, Settings, Control Panel, and click the TweakUI icon.

Step 4. Click the right arrow in the upper-right corner of the TweakUI dialog box until the Boot tab scrolls into view (see Figure 18-1), and then click it.

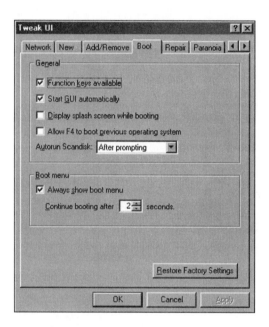

Figure 18-1: The Boot tab in TweakUI.

Step 5. Mark the Always Show Boot Menu check box, and enter **2** in the Continue Booting After [   ] Seconds field. Click OK.

The next time you start Windows, the Windows Startup menu will appear for two seconds, giving you a chance to press one of the Startup keys. You can make the startup delay longer if you like.

The Boot tab also lets you turn off Autorun Scandisk. This would prevent Windows from automatically running ScanDisk after an improper shut down.

Thanks to Phil Leonard for help with this tip.

Get to Windows when the Explorer won't start

Ah, that agonizing feeling. You start your computer and a few seconds after the Desktop appears (with no icons yet), you get an error message stating that your Explorer has just crashed. There you are with a perfectly nice Desktop, but no way to access your computer. There is no steering wheel on this runaway car.

If you're on a network, someone can likely access your computer through the network. If you've shared your boot drive, perhaps someone can look at it and at least reassure you that your files are still there. Might not be a bad time to back up all your data over the network.

If you've recently installed a piece of software, check its Install.log file (hopefully, it has one). You'll find this file in the same folder with the new software (probably under \Program Files*thesoftwarepackagename*). You may find that the software installation process has overwritten a newer system file with an older one.

"How to Access Your CD-ROM Drive when Windows Hangs at Startup," a Microsoft Knowledge Base article, indicates that Shlwapi.dll may have been the unfortunate victim. You can find this article at support.microsoft.com/support/kb/articles/q182/0/90.asp.

If you have a later version of this file, you can copy it from one computer over the network onto the computer that couldn't bring up the Explorer. Then reboot the computer and see if that solves the problem.

If that doesn't work, or if the computer isn't on a network, you can reboot to the DOS prompt. (You might try Safe mode, but that probably won't work because the Explorer still won't start.) Once you're in DOS mode, you can check the folder of any newly-installed software for an Install.log file and see what damage has been done to the \Windows\System folder — in other words, which system files have been overwritten by the new software. You can also check the date of the Shlwapi.dll file, and see if it matches the dates shown on most of your system files.

To be able to boot into Windows, you'll need to edit the System.ini file in your \Windows directory. Change directories with the cd\Windows command, and then type **Edit System.ini** and press Enter. Replace the line shell=Explorer.exe with **shell=winfile.exe** (or **shell=c:\litestep\litestep.exe** if you've previously installed this alternate Windows shell). Save the file and restart Windows, or just type **win** and press Enter at the DOS prompt. (For more on the LiteStep shell, see "Replace the Explorer shell" in Chapter 12.)

This will start Windows with an alternate shell and let you at least get to your computer, even if you still can't run the Explorer or My Computer to manipulate the files.

If you've previously installed SafeInstall98 (see "Dealing with DLL hell" in Chapter 19), you may find the aggrieved newer DLLs in the \Programs Files\ SafeInstall\Backup folder. If this is the case, you may be able to run SafeInstall98 and copy the newer DLLs over the older ones. Or, you can just copy them over the older DLLs in a DOS window.

If none of this works, you may need to reinstall Windows 98 (always the last ditch effort). Your Registry should be intact, and given that there are at least five Registry backups, you shouldn't have a problem. Of course, if your Windows 98 CD-ROM is hopelessly out of date because you've updated with Internet Explorer 5, you'll want to try reinstalling Internet Explorer first to see if that fixes the problem.

Troubleshoot Windows 98 startup problems

Microsoft provides a reasonably comprehensive troubleshooting guide to startup and shut down problems that you might encounter with Windows 98. You can read the HTML version online, or download it from the Microsoft Knowledge Base site. You'll find the Knowledge Base article "Troubleshooting Windows 98 Startup Problems and Error Messages" at support.microsoft. com/support/kb/articles/q188/8/67.asp. The downloadable version is at support.microsoft.com/support/tshoot/default.asp.

Manage how Windows 98 Startup files start up

The Windows 98 System Configuration Utility lets you decide whether or no t to run any one of the programs in your StartUp group when you start Windows 98. Click Start, Programs, Accessories, System Tools, System Information, Tools, System Configuration Utility, and Startup to see how.

If you want to set the order in which the programs run, you can use a batch file, or a little program called DoWinStartup. Download it from www.mrdo. com/dowinstartup/. It's free.

Pause during power-on self test

Sometimes you'd like to be able to read the messages that your BIOS is displaying on your screen. While we show you how to get the basic BIOS information from your Registry (see "Basic BIOS info from your Registry" in Chapter 21), the POST screen is still a convenient place to find some information about your computer.

Some computers allow you to pause during POST. To do so, just press the Pause/Break key.

Keep a bootlog

Your root directory contains a file that records the steps your computer went through when it booted up. But it won't be a record of the last time that you started your computer, because it isn't created every time.

If you'd like to create a new bootlog.txt file that records your next reboot, you can edit the Msdos.sys file in your root directory. Because this is a read-only file, you'll need to clear that file attribute first (right-click Msdos.sys in your Explorer, click Properties, and clear the Read-only check box), edit the file, and then set it again.

The change you need to make to Msdos.sys is to add the line BootMenu-Default=2. We discuss editing this file in greater depth in Chapter 5 of *Windows 98 Secrets*. You can also read more about it in the electronic version of the *Windows 98 Resource Kit* under the topic System Startup Files. Just click the \tools\reskit\help\rk98book.chm file on your Windows 98 CD-ROM.

Once you've added this line to the Msdos.sys file and you've changed the file attribute back to read-only, you can restart your computer. A bootlog.txt file will be created.

A handy little freeware utility called the Boot Log Analyzer will display failures or delays in your bootlog.txt file (see Figure 18-2). You can download it from www.vision4.co.uk/vision4. It doesn't tell you much about how to read the bootlog, but it does point out the problems.

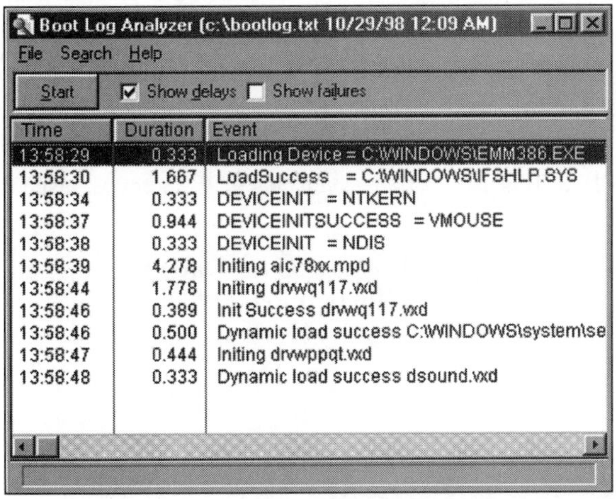

Figure 18-2: Boot Log Analyzer lists the events of this computer's last boot process and their duration. Note that we have marked Show Delays.

You can use Boot Log Analyzer in combination with the *Windows 98 Resource Kit*.

STEPS:

Learning About Bootlog in the *Windows 98 Resource Kit*

Step 1.   Click the \tools\reskit\help\rk98book.chm file on your Windows 98 CD-ROM.

Step 2.   Click the Search tab. Type **bootlog** in the Search window, and click List Topics.

Step 3.   Double-click System Startup Files in the left pane.

Step 4.   Scroll down the right pane to *Bootlog.txt: The Startup Process Log*, as shown in Figure 18-3.

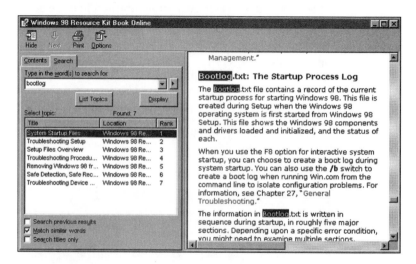

Figure 18-3: This section of the Windows 98 Resource Kit discusses bootlog.

Step 5.   In this section of the *Windows 98 Resource Kit*, you can read more about how to interpret the bootlog.txt file.

Stop your modem from dialing when you start Windows 98

It can be quite annoying if every time you start up Windows 98, a DUN connectoid or a dial-up connection dialog box pops up and you hear your modem dialing your Internet service provider. This annoyance can be caused by a couple of things.

First, if you've installed the Personal Web Server (PWS) that comes on the Windows 98 CD-ROM, its default setting is to connect to the Internet. After all, its job is to publish all these web pages that you've placed on it.

You can stop this behavior and only connect to the Internet when you desire by running the System Configuration Utility and clearing the MSDTC check box in the Startup tab, as described in these steps:

STEPS:

Stopping PWS from Dialing

Step 1.   Click Start, Programs, Accessories, System Tools, System Information.

Step 2.   Choose Tools, System Configuration Utility.

Step 3.   Click the Startup tab, and clear the MSDTC (msdtcw-start) check box, as shown in Figure 18-4.

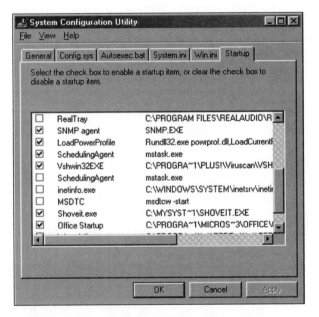

Figure 18-4: Your list on the Startup tab will not be in the same order as this one. Scroll down and look for MSDTC in the middle column.

Step 4.   Click OK. Click Yes when asked to restart Windows.

Thanks to Lance T. Pfeifer for pointing out this tip.

Another possibility is that you have a shortcut to Internet Explorer in your StartUp group. When you restart Windows, Internet Explorer wants to connect to display a web page. This can happen if you have not marked File,

Work Offline in the Internet Explorer window, or if you have marked Tools, Internet Options, Connections, Always Dial My Default Connection or Dial Whenever a Network Connection Is Not Present.

To prevent your modem from dialing, you can mark Never Dial a Connection, pull the shortcut out of the StartUp group, or mark File, Work Offline. There are yet other reasons why your modem could be dialing when you start up Windows 98. If you've installed Symantec's WinFAX, you may need to make a change in your Registry. Or, you may have a Trojan Horse virus.

You can check out the various possibilities using the Microsoft Knowledge Base article "Modem Attempts to Dial When Windows Starts" at support.microsoft.com/support/kb/articles/q175/3/12.asp.

Quit searching for floppy disks

Lots of portable computers don't have floppy disk drives permanently installed. Often, you just plug them in when you need one — which, we are happy to say, isn't that often. You can speed up the Windows startup process by telling Windows not to bother looking for a floppy drive.

STEPS:

Ignoring the Floppy Drive

Step 1.   Hold down your Alt key as you click My Computer.

Step 2.   In the System Properties dialog box, click the Performance tab, and click the File System button.

Step 3.   Click the Floppy Disk tab, and clear Search for New Floppy Disk Drives Each Time Your Computer Starts, as shown in Figure 18-5.

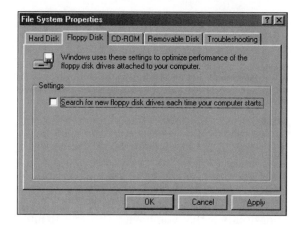

Figure 18-5: Clear the Search for New Floppy Disk Drives Each Time Your Computer Starts check box.

Step 4.   Click OK. Click OK.

Thanks to Jamie Sanchez for help on this tip.

Replace the Windows 98 logo screens

In Chapter 5 of *Windows 98 Secrets*, we show you how to replace the startup and shut down (logo) screens that come with Windows 98 and Plus! 98. We also direct you to a web site where you can download additional animated logos or download a tool that will help you make your own.

There are lots of web sites where you can find other logo screens. Just search the web for them and you'll have more than you can deal with. We found some nice 3D screens for Windows 95 at mall.lnd.com/Galitsky/tweaks/tweak24.html (see Figure 18-6).

Figure 18-6: An oblique view of your logon screen.

Start up your computer with a dialog box

If you don't have a blank password, Windows 98 starts up with a password dialog box. You can add another dialog box if you like (whether or not you have a password dialog box), although this is not very useful if the computer is your personal computer.

You might want to use this startup dialog box to display a standard message whenever the computer starts, perhaps reminding people to log in as themselves.

To create this message and dialog box, merge the following text into your Registry. We've placed this text in a file called Logon.reg on the accompanying CD-ROM. You can merge it into your Registry (right-click its name in your Explorer and click Merge) and then edit the text using your Registry editor (navigate to the branch indicated below).

```
REGEDIT4

[HKEY_LOCAL_MACHINE\Software\Microsoft\Windows\CurrentVersion\Winlogon]
"LegalNoticeText"="Your Message"
"LegalNoticeCaption"="Legal Notice"
```

You'll want to edit the "Your Message" and "Legal Notice" text to reflect your message and the name of the dialog box that you want to use. For example, replace "Your Message" with "Bill's Computer," and "Legal Notice" with "Keep Your Hands Off."

Thanks to Mark Dormer for pointing out this secret.

Windows 98 logs on nobody

Do you find that when Windows 98 starts up you are logged on as ...? You can tell if you click the Start button and check out Log Off at the bottom of the menu. If three dots follow Off, you aren't logged on. Nobody is logged on.

This is not a good thing. Windows won't remember your passwords, for example. You'll have to log off and log on as yourself—time consuming.

Secret

There is an errant entry in your Registry that is automatically logging on nobody when you start Windows. You need to take these steps to clear up this matter:

STEPS:

Stopping AutoLogon

Step 1. Click Start, Run, type **regedit**, and press Enter.

Step 2. Navigate to HKEY_LOCAL_MACHINE\ SOFTWARE\ Microsoft\ Windows\ Current Version\ Network\ Real Mode Net\.

Step 3. You can delete the AutoLogon variable in the right pane or rename it xAutoLogn. Either way will work. Close the Registry editor.

Step 4. The next time you restart Windows, you won't log on as nobody.

Thanks to Bill Greening who came up with the problem and asked us to find an answer (and to the person on the Windows 98 support newsgroup who actually solved it for him).

Shutting down

Shutting down can have its problems also.

Don't wait around for shut down

It's not such a speedy thing to shut down your computer these days. Not only does it require four mouse clicks (Start, Shut Down, Shut Down, OK), but waiting for Windows 98 to run through its shut down routine can take quite a while. Here are some products designed to make the process faster and more convenient.

CloseFast 5 is designed to work in a network environment and includes such features as Internet Based Shutdown, Remote NT Shutdown, and Timed Shutdown. You can also use CloseFast to close all open applications without shutting down, and to manage the windows you have open. You can run it as a small or large toolbar (the large one is shown in Figure 18-7), or in your system tray. CloseFast is very polished and feature-rich freeware. It's available at www.thrustpack.com/ CloseFast.

Figure 18-7: The large CloseFast toolbar.

Windows Restart 98 is a fraction of the size of CloseFast at only 350K. It gives you the basic quick shut down and restart functions shown in Figure 18-8, plus some nice features for managing windows and opening various folders. It runs in your system tray with a spare but functional menu. Windows Restart is freeware. It was created by Jeffrey Carlyle and is available at his web site, spruce.evansville.edu/ ~jc82/ wr.

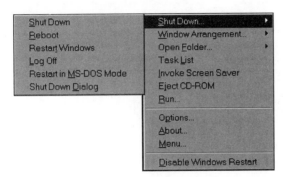

Figure 18-8: The system tray menu for Windows Restart 98.

If you'd like more options for shutting down your laptop, ejecting removable media, or emptying files and folders before shut down, ShutDown NOW! by Carsten Stratz may be for you. It runs in your system tray and can also run from a command line. The 1MB download is available from http://www.arco.de/~cstratz.

Windows 98 shut down problems

There are a number of different reasons why your computer might have trouble shutting down. You can disable Fast Shutdown and Fast Find (if you have it) to see if these measures clear up the problem. To disable Fast Shutdown, take these steps:

STEPS:

Disabling Fast Shutdown

Step 1. Click Start, Programs, Accessories, System Tools, System Information.

Step 2. Click Tools, System Configuration Utility.

Step 3. Click the Advanced button and mark the Disable Fast Shutdown check box in the Advanced Troubleshooting Settings dialog box, as shown in Figure 18-9.

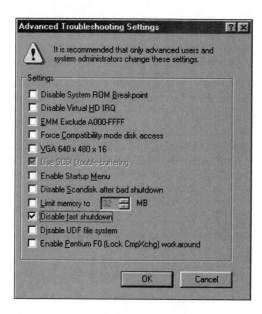

Figure 18-9: The Disable Fast Shutdown check box is near the bottom of the dialog box.

Step 4. Click OK. Restart your computer when prompted.

Thanks to Dustin Miller for pointing this out. Dustin responded to an IDG Books Secrets contest at the IDG Books Worldwide web site, www.idgbooks.com.

You can also check out these Microsoft Knowledge Base articles:

- "How to Disable Fast Shutdown in Windows 98" at support.microsoft.com/support/kb/articles/q187/6/07.asp
- "Computer Stops Responding When Shutting Down Windows 98" at support.microsoft.com/support/kb/articles/q189/8/80.asp
- "Norton AntiVirus causes window to hang on shutdown" at support.microsoft.com/support/kb/articles/q187/3/24

To disable Fast Find, take these steps:

STEPS:
Disabling Fast Find

Step 1. Click Start, Programs, Accessories, System Tools, System Information.

Step 2. Click Tools, System Configuration Utility.

Step 3. Click the Startup tab.

Step 4. Clear the check box to the left of Microsoft Find Fast, and click OK.

Step 5. Click Yes when you are prompted to restart your computer.

You can find out more about Fast Find at "OFF97: Overview of Find Fast Indexer" at support.microsoft.com/support/kb/articles/q166/3/02.asp.

Your computer may have other problems that cause Windows shut down to malfunction. You may have a virus scanner that is looking for a floppy diskette on shut down. You'll have to track down any virus scanning software that you've loaded.

Your computer may be trying unsuccessfully to disconnect from the network. You'll need to restart the computer without the network to see if this is the source of the problem.

You may have a corrupted Windows swap file. You'll need to restart Windows in Safe mode and then shut down and restart in normal mode. If that doesn't work, start in DOS mode and delete the Win386.swp file in your \Windows folder. Restart your computer and reboot normally into Windows. Windows will rebuild the swap file.

You may have more than one Windows swap file. Use the Find command to search all your local hard disks for files with the *swp* extension. Boot to DOS and delete any swap files that are not in the \Windows folder.

Summary

Windows 98 has problems getting going and shutting down. We give you the fixes to deal with these problems.

▶ Start the startup applets in the order that you want.

▶ Pause before Windows starts.

▶ Disable Fast Shutdown and Fast Find.

Chapter 19

DLL Hell

In This Chapter

Dynamic link libraries are compiled libraries of functions that are called by other programs to carry out various tasks. Because it's hard to keep track of which version of which library is used by any program, users get thrown into DLL hell.

▶ Windows 98 installs some older versions of the basic system DLLs.

▶ You can use the Version Conflict Manager to see if this has caused a problem.

▶ If you have a program that is having a problem, let the Process Viewer show you which DLLs the program is using.

▶ If you want to protect yourself against software that overwrites newer DLLs with older ones, use SafeInstall98.

Windows 98 may disable other software

The setup routine for Windows 98 disables shared library files used by other software and installs the versions of these files that it needs.

These changed files include dynamic link libraries, as well as other shared files. If the Windows 98 setup routine detects that a competitor's program has installed a newer shared file than the version that comes with Windows 98, the setup routine moves the file to a new location, disabling it. Windows 98 then installs an older version of the same file into the proper location. The application that depends on the newer version of that file may no longer work properly or at all.

Windows 98 includes a utility, the Version Conflict Manager (VCM), that tracks the disabled files and provides a way for users to switch the files back. However, the Windows 98 setup routine does not tell you that it is changing the files or suggest that you consult the VCM if some of your other software no longer operates properly.

The VCM lets you select a file and trade the older version for the newer version. However, many Windows 98 users have no way of knowing what applications call each shared file or which version of the file would be "better." Moreover, you're not likely to come across the VCM routinely, because it is buried deep within Windows 98's menu structure (see the next section).

As an example of what we're talking about, on one test machine the VCM showed that the Windows 98 setup routine had disabled three shared files: Twain.dll 1.6.0.3 (which supports numerous scanners and other devices), Msconv97.dll 1997.4.2, and W95inf32.dll 4.71.17. The files were replaced with these older versions: Twain.dll 1.6.0.1, Msconv97.dll 1997.3.12, and W95inf32.dll 4.71.16. These files originated with Microsoft and were distributed to developers for use with their products. But Windows 98 appears to rely on earlier versions, and it swaps the files whether or not this has a negative effect on installed applications.

Readers of Brian's *Infoworld* column have experienced similar DLL problems. For example, reader Ed Barnett says that Windows 98 will not run the Hewlett-Packard ScanJet 4/c, likely a result of the Twain.dll incompatibility. This was also a problem for Michael Spagnuola, who found that Windows overwrote Twain.dll version 1.6.0.3, used by Microsoft Picture-It version 2, with an earlier version, and prevented Picture-It from working properly. Dennis Wingo found he was unable to use his HP 7200i internal CD writer after installing Windows 98.

Microsoft strongly emphasizes that Windows 98 does nothing to harm any competitor. Shawn Sanford, a Windows 98 product manager, says Microsoft's extensive beta testing did not reveal a single application that was harmed by Windows 98 switching to an older version of a shared file. He explained that the decision to have the setup routine change files was made to ensure that users had a stable, working copy of Windows 98 after installation. One of the biggest complaints Microsoft received from Windows 95 users was that the system crashed or would not boot due to conflicts between Windows and other programs.

In the worst case, according to Sanford, a video driver or other shared file could make Windows 98 fail to boot. If such a problem occurred, a user would have no way to reconfigure Windows to fix the error. To prevent this, Windows 98 installs file versions known to work.

Sanford admitted, "There is a very, very small possibility that a sequence of DLLs could hurt Windows 98." But even a small possibility could affect thousands of users, so it was better to have Windows 98 establish a known set of shared files, even if some of those files were older than ones installed by other applications. "By down-leveling in that situation," he said, "the user can get into the operating system and adjust the drivers they need."

We agree with Microsoft officials regarding an overall goal for Windows stability. Ironically, the origin of the Version Conflict Manager may have been a series of four magazine columns written by Brian in 1996. The columns complained that Windows 95 allowed applications to install older versions of shared files over newer ones, causing programs to crash. Brian urged Microsoft to have Windows catch such conflicts and prevent them, while letting users switch between shared files later, if necessary.

Rather than make the VCM available to all applications, however, the VCM mechanism is only turned on during Windows 98 installation. After Windows 98 setup is over, VCM disables itself. If the installation of a third party application subsequently causes a problem, the VCM will have no information about the situation. You can, however, use SafeInstall98 to remedy this (see "Dealing with DLL Hell" later in this chapter).

Ideally, Windows would prevent any applications from adding or changing files in the \Windows or \Windows\System folders. This way, the functions of all system files would be predictable and applications could not change a DLL, possibly breaking Windows or another program.

In fact, Sanford indicated that since the release of Windows 95, Microsoft's policy has been that third party vendors should not install updated, shared files into the System folder. Developers have continued to do so, however.

Using the Version Conflict Manager

If you install Windows 98 on a system that was using Windows 95, and then have trouble when you try to use one of your software applications, you may see an error message indicating that a DLL or other shared file is missing or damaged. You can check the Version Control Manager to see what might have happened to this file.

This little utility shows you the version numbers of files that were backed up by the installation of Windows 98 and lets you compare them with the version numbers of the same-named files that are currently installed. If you didn't install Windows 98 over Windows 95, there won't be any backed up files. The Windows 98 installation only backs up those files that it overwrites with an earlier version.

You can get to the Version Conflict Manager by clicking Starting, Programs, Accessories, System Tools, System Information, Tools, Version Conflict Manager. Or click Start, Run, type **vcmui**, and press Enter.

The files are backed up into the \Windows\Vcm folder. If you've updated Windows 98, the version numbers of the current files may be later than the backed up files, as shown in Figure 19-1.

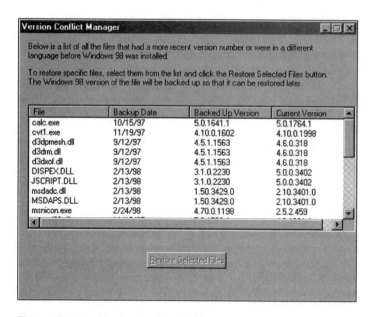

Figure 19-1: The Version Conflict Manager compares the version numbers of current files to those of backed up files.

The Version Conflict Manager lets you restore the backup files (and then re-restore the current files if you like). Unlike the files detected by SafeInstall, these backup files are probably best left in the \Windows\Vcm folder unless you really do need the backed up version.

Check your DLL dependencies

DLL Show, shown in Figure 19-2, displays the DLL files that are called by the applications and utilities currently running on your computer. You'll find it at www.execpc.com/~sbd.

You can also use Process Viewer, a freeware utility that not only shows you each running program, the DLLs used by the program, the threads used, and the memory allocated, but also lets you kill any process.

Right-click any of the processes and click Modules in the context menu (see Figure 19-3) to see which DLLs are used by the running application.

You'll find Process Viewer at www.teamcti.com/pview/. You can just extract the contents of the zipped file to a folder and run the executable file without having to install the software.

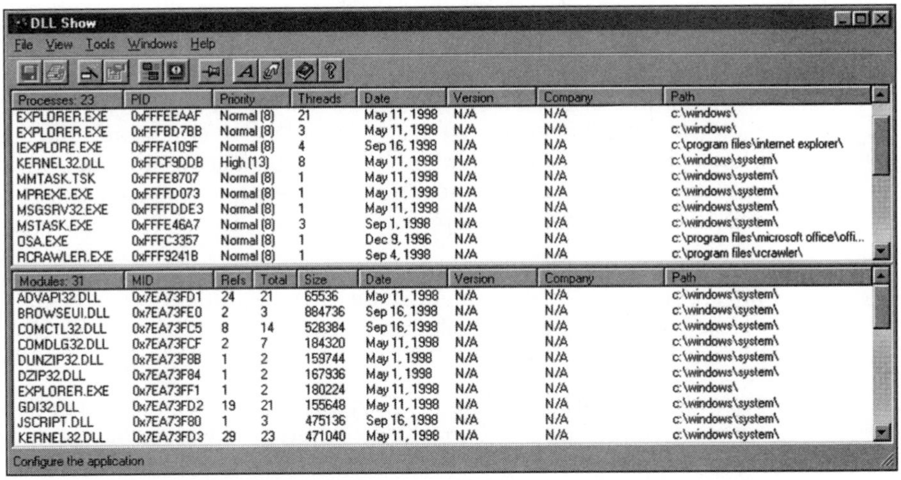

Figure 19-2: DLL Show lists all your DLLs.

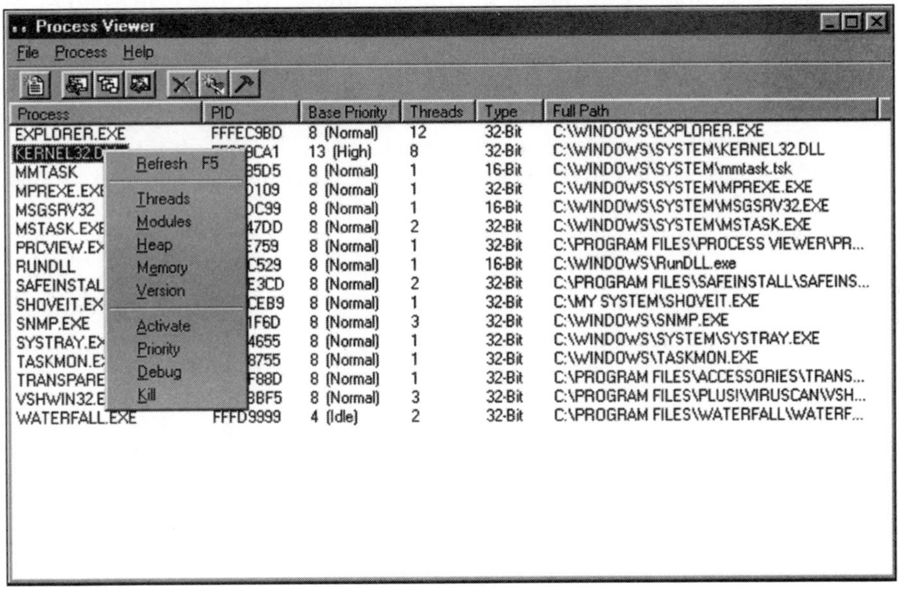

Figure 19-3: Select Modules in the context menu.

Readers pray for deliverance from DLL Hell

"DLL Hell" occurs when one program disables others by installing an incompatible DLL. This corrupts your system in one of two ways. In the first instance, an application installs an older DLL over a newer one, failing to check the internal version number first. This causes applications that require the newer DLL to fail. The second instance occurs when a newer DLL is properly installed, but an application requires an older version and won't work with the newer one.

Microsoft's own applications can be the worst offenders in both types of errors. For example, Office 4.3c required version 2.01 of Ole2nls.dll, and wouldn't work with version 2.02.

When Brian invited readers of his magazine column to send in their solutions, he received well over 100 proposals. Many of them contained genuinely good ideas that Microsoft could use to get us out of purgatory. The overwhelming sentiment among those who responded was that Microsoft should completely abandon the idea of applications sharing DLLs at all.

"Application vendors should be prohibited from distributing parts of the operating system with their applications," wrote Kevin Klein of Millennium Partners Inc. "It ought to be Microsoft's responsibility to provide a stable, tested, and certified platform for running applications (that's what an OS is, after all). The whole Windows\System32 subdirectory should be write-protected to applications as far as I'm concerned. All of the interim bug fixes and API upgrades should be packaged by Microsoft into clearly identifiable units, similar to the current service packs but with finer granularity and released much more frequently."

Many readers prescribed that all DLLs should be installed into the applications' own folders. "All application vendors, including Microsoft, should put DLLs, even 'shared' ones like Ctl3d32.dll, in the home directory of the application, not in the Windows directory," said Thornton Rose. "Some of my favorite applications already do this — WS_FTP, Programmer's File Editor (PFE), and WinZip, to name a few."

If two applications require different versions of the same DLL, moving the correct version into each application's folder can sometimes cure the conflict. One problem with this is that Windows does not allow two DLLs with the same name to run at the same time — and this extends to ActiveX OCX components, such as those used by Visual Basic. Mark Thrailkill wrote, "Microsoft released VB 5 with newer versions of VB 4 controls, but did not provide backward compatibility. As a result, a VB 5 application could disable a VB 4 application that uses the same controls — do they care?"

A reader with the handle Jon B. had a solution for such conflicts: "In the illustrious Microsoft tradition, add a 'thunk' (software routine) to the DLL-handling routines (such as 'LoadLibrary' and 'Load Module'). The 'thunk' would check the Registry and redirect DLL calls to the correct version of the DLL. Of course, this implies that the kernel would be modified to manage (and allow) multiple versions of a given DLL simultaneously into memory."

Unix, OS/2, and Apple's Rhapsody accomplish this kind of compatibility as a built-in feature.

Dealing with DLL Hell

One of the key problems with installing software is that the setup routines copy DLL, OCX, VBX, and other "system" files into the Windows\System folder, whether these files actually "belong" there or not. A problem can arise if they copy an older (or newer) version of a DLL over a newer (or older) version. SafeInstall98 monitors your software installations and checks the version numbers of any files that overwrite or delete existing system files, comparing them against the version numbers of the files that are overwritten or deleted (see Figure 19-4).

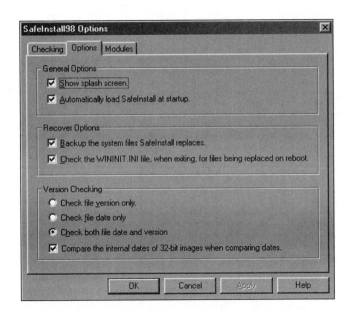

Figure 19-4: The Version Checking area on SafeInstall98's Options tab gives you some flexibility in how you monitor file versions.

SafeInstall98 backs up newer system files before older versions overwrite them, so that you can get back to where you started. It also checks your Winint.ini file to see if any files are going to be replaced after a reboot. (Winint.ini is a temporary file that is created when a software install requires that Windows be rebooted to finish the installation. The steps required to finish the installation are placed in the file.)

SafeInstall stores any newer system files that were overwritten in the \Programs Files\SafeInstall\Backup folder. When you restart your computer after installing the software, SafeInstall prompts you to reinstall the original files from this folder. In general, it's a good idea to do this.

When you install SafeInstall98, it puts a shortcut to itself in the StartUp folder, thereby assuring you that it is operating at all times and is monitoring any of your installs. Of course, you can take this shortcut out of the StartUp folder and only start SafeInstall98 just before you install new software.

You'll find SafeInstall98 at www.iwinsoftware.com.

Summary

We are all in DLL Hell. We show you how to fix some of the problems you may have experienced because of it and suggest ways to keep it from causing even more problems.

▶ Windows 98 tracks the DLLs it replaced and keeps the newer versions so that you can restore them.

▶ Show DLL and Process Viewer let you see your program's dependencies.

▶ SafeInstall98 is your best bet to keep from suffering at the hands of thoughtless programmers.

Chapter 20

The Hard Disk

Bigger and better

Hard disks always get bigger, and the operating system and BIOSes have to catch up with them.

What's a gigabyte?

In the physical world, a kilo is 1000. But in the computer world, a kilo is 1024, or 2 to the 10th power. Still, it doesn't stop there. The mega, as in a megabyte, is 2 to the 20th power, or 1,048,576 — a bit more than a million. To keep things straight, we use this convention: KB is kilobytes in the sense of 1024 bytes. And MB is megabytes in the sense of 1,048,576 bytes.

When it comes to gigabytes and hard disk sizes, things may be not quite as they seem. Windows 98 uses this convention: A gigabyte, GB, is 1,073,741,824 bytes. You can see this in Figure 20-1 if you compare the two capacity figures for the hard drive. (Actually, the GB amount shown should have been rounded up to 2.00GB, because it is equal to 1.995GB.)

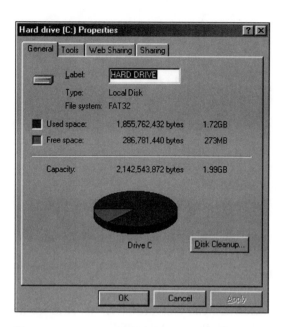

Figure 20-1: The Properties dialog box for this 2GB hard disk illustrates the convention that a GB equals 1,073,741,824 bytes.

We've summarized all of this in Table 20-1:

Table 20-1   Size Designations

Physical World	*Computer World*
k=1000	K=1024
m=1000000	M=1048576 (1024 x 1024)
g=1000000000	G=1073741824 (1024 x 1024 x 1024)

Hard disk manufacturers, on the other hand, like to make their gargantuan hard disks look even bigger. They declare that one billion bytes equals a gigabyte. So what do we care?

Windows 98 using FAT 32 can handle 2 terabytes (2 times 1024 times a gigabyte, or 2 to the 41st power) of hard disk space, but many older computer BIOSes can only handle 7.8GB hard disk drive partitions. This is due to an incorrect implementation of their Interrupt 13 (INT 13) extensions. To purchase a drive that fits just right at 7.8GB (as all but the hard disk manufacturers define it), you'll want to buy an 8.4GB drive.

Of course, you can buy bigger drives, but you'll need to partition the drive into partitions no larger than 7.8GB partitions unless you have a more recent BIOS.

FDISK

Microsoft provides FDISK, a utility that partitions hard disks into logical volumes that can then be formatted. It also writes the master boot record.

We discuss using FDISK quite a bit in this chapter. If you want to learn a bit more about how it works and some of its version history, check out "Notes on DOS FDISK Command" at www.firmware.com/support/bios/fdisk.htm and "Undocumented FDISK" at www.lyngsoe.com/fdisk.

Windows 98 takes on the big drives

Windows 98 can handle a single hard disk partition of 2 terabytes (2 to the 41st power bytes). Even with hard disk storage values doubling every year, this book will be out of print by the time (2005) you can purchase such a drive for your personal computer.

However, it is quite possible to purchase hard disks that are greater than 8.455GB (decimal GB, as used by hard disk manufactures), which translates to 7.874GB (binary) under Windows 98. If your computer's BIOS "fully" supports the Interrupt 13 extensions, you can install a drive bigger than 8.455GB (decimal) and create a primary partition on it greater than 7.874GB (binary). The Microsoft Knowledge Base article that pertains to this issue is "Hard Disk Limited to 8-GB Partition," found at support.microsoft.com/support/kb/articles/q153/5/50.asp.

When you start your computer, Io.sys tests your BIOS to make sure that it has all the Interrupt 13 extensions required to support drives larger than 8.455GB. If it doesn't find them, then that is the limit.

The next three sections outline what three disk drive manufacturers have to say about this issue.

Seagate

This quote comes from the Seagate web site at www.seagate.com/support/disc/faq/8point4.shtml:

> The 8.4-Gbyte constraint is based on an obscure method of causing the PC to perform a disc drive operation called an interrupt (INT). When the BIOS wants to get data onto or off of the hard disc, it must send a software interrupt. The key storage interrupt is INT 13h. Older versions of BIOS do not support this interrupt on disc drives larger than 8.4 Gbytes. Like the rest of PC architecture, this interrupt has been enhanced to accommodate the larger capacities required in today's systems.
>
> There are three solutions for adding INT 13h Extensions to existing systems: upgrade system BIOS, add an intelligent host adapter card with new BIOS on the board, or use Seagate's DiscWizard software. The new BIOS is a hardware solution that will allow the system to recognize greater than 8.4-Gbyte capacity as a native function, and the DiscWizard software bundle, utilizing Disk Manager, will create a new layer of software that will translate to accommodate greater than 8.4-Gbyte capacity.

Continue reading the Seagate web page for more clues on how to set up your BIOS and get a correct reading on your hard disk capacity.

Maxtor

This quote comes from the Maxtor web site at www.maxtor.com/technology/q&a/qa610017.html:

> The maximum parameters at the 8.4 GB barrier are 16,383 cylinders, 16 heads and 63 sectors for a capacity of 8.455 GB. To go beyond this boundary, a new extended INT 13 function is needed from the BIOS as a support feature for the drives. The BIOS listed below are all "CORE" BIOS. Even though a BIOS is dated correctly or is the current version, it may not be able to support extended interrupt 13 because of modification done to the "CORE" of the BIOS from the motherboard manufacturer.
>
> If the BIOS is believed to fall within the following guidelines but does not support the drive, contact the system or motherboard manufacturer for a potential upgrade to their product.

- **American Megatrends INC. (AMI):** BIOS versions with a date of January 1, 1998 or newer.

- **Award:** BIOS versions dated November 1997 or newer. Award recommends Unicore (800-800-2467 or www.unicore.com) for BIOS upgrades.

- **Phoenix:** Version 4 Revision 6 or newer. If the BIOS is revision 5.12, it does not support extended interrupt 13. All Phoenix BIOS are Version 4, so 5.12 is an older release than 6. Phoenix recommends Micro Firmware (877-629-2467 or www.firmware.com/support/index.htm) for BIOS upgrades.

End quoteQuantum

This quote comes from the Quantum web site at www.quantum.com/src/whitepapers/8.4barrier.html:

> Addressing more than 8.4GB of capacity on a hard disk drive is a problem for most PCs because of BIOS limitations. The best way to solve the problem is to use a BIOS that utilizes Interrupt 13 extensions and an LBA (logical block address) method of addressing. If a system's BIOS can't be upgraded, OnTrack Disk Manager driver software (available on Quantum's World Wide Web) can be used to move beyond the 8.4GB limitation.

Check if your BIOS "fully" supports the INT 13 extensions

You can use Sandra, a shareware package discussed in "Add to your system info" in Chapter 26, to check to see if your BIOS "fully" supports the Interrupt 13 extensions. Double-click CPU & BIOS Information. Scroll down to System BIOS Properties. If Supports Enhanced Disk Drive has a green check mark (it does not in Figure 20-2), your BIOS "fully" supports Interrupt 13 extensions.

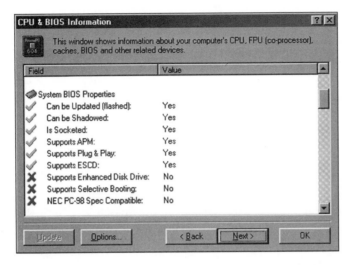

Figure 20-2: Sandra shows that this computer's BIOS does not support hard disks larger than 8.4GB.

ExtBios, a small freeware utility, can also provide some help. You'll find it at "The BIOS IDE Harddisk Limitations" page at web.inter.nl.net/hcc/J.Steunebrink/bioslim.htm.

The version we used was out of date, but hopefully the author will have updated it by the time you read this. ExtBios interrogates your BIOS and uses a couple of functions from the Interrupt 13 extensions to provide version information and drive parameters, as shown in Figure 20-3.

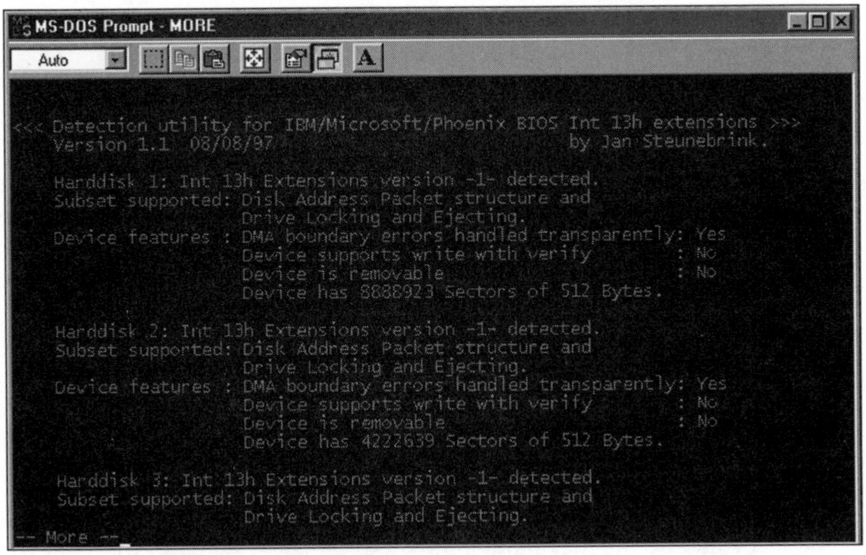

Figure 20-3: Some of the results from running ExtBios.

An easy way to use this utility is described in these steps:

Running ExtBios

Step 1. After your have downloaded Extbio11.zip, extract its contents to a new folder. (You can either use the Compressed Folders feature of Plus! 98 or WinZip.)

Step 2. Display the contents of the folder that contains the extracted files.

Step 3. Click Start, Programs, MS-DOS Prompt.

Step 4. Drag the file Extbios.exe from the open folder to the DOS window and drop it there.

Step 5. In the DOS window, at the end of the command line type | **more** and press Enter.

If the results displayed by Extbios indicate only version 1 support for Interrupt 13 extensions (as shown in Figure 20-3), your BIOS doesn't "fully" support the extensions. You won't be able to create a hard disk partition greater than 7.8GB unless you take some additional steps.

You can choose one of these solutions:

■ Upgrade your system BIOS, if possible

■ Install a new hard disk controller card, assuming that your card isn't built into your motherboard, or that if it is, you can disable it

■ Upgrade the BIOS on your hard disk controller card

■ Use one of the translation packages offered by the hard disk manufacturers

The version of FDISK that comes with Windows 98 can partition a drive bigger than 8.4GB. You can limit the size partitioned to 8.4GB by using the /x switch. You can run FDISK from a DOS window or from the real-mode DOS command line.

The Format command that comes with Windows 98 will not give the correct disk size.

FAT32X for drives over 8GB

On a FAT-32 hard drive larger than 8GB, Microsoft uses FAT32X (X as in *extended*). A FAT32X partition supports hard drives with more than 1024 cylinders, the maximum number supported by many computers' BIOS routines.

Disk utilities are beginning to adapt to FAT32X partitions. For example, version 4.0 of Partition Magic, the premium third-party partitioning software, supports FAT32X drives. Partition Magic supports conversions both ways between FAT 32 and FAT 16. It also includes the Boot Magic utility, which allows a single drive to multi-boot between Windows, Windows NT, Linux, and so on. For more information, see www.powerquest.com/press/ pm4available.html. (Boot Magic is described further in the "Boot Magic doesn't handle the big drives" section later in this chapter.)

Does your hard disk have overlay software installed?

Disk drive manufacturers include overlay software with their big hard disks just in case your BIOS can't handle the large hard drive. If your hard disk came bundled with the computer, the odds are that the BIOS can address all of the hard disk, but that isn't always true.

Computers whose BIOSes cannot handle hard disks greater than 7.8GB can be made to work with bigger drives using EZ Drive, DiscWizard, Disk Manager, or one of the other overlay packages. If you later upgrade your BIOS to handle larger drives, or if you move this drive to a new computer, you'll want to remove this overlay software.

Tip

If you didn't set up your computer, or if you've forgotten whether or not you loaded overlay software, you can check if it's there. Microsoft provides a Knowledge Base article that gives you a number of ways to do this. You'll find "How to Tell If Drive Overlay Program Is Installed in Windows" at support. microsoft.com/support/kb/articles/q186/0/57.asp.

Boot Magic doesn't handle the big drives

While Windows 98 can handle the big partitions (over 7.8GB), Boot Magic, the boot manager that comes with Partition Magic 4.0, apparently can't. While this may have changed by the time that you read this, if you have an older version, you might want to update if you're moving to drives bigger than 7.8GB.

The partition that includes Boot Magic must be completely within the first 1024 cylinders on the hard drive if you want to see the graphical Boot Magic menu. That means the first 7.8GB. If the partition crosses the 1024 cylinder boundary, you can still boot with Boot Magic into the current active partition as long as the boot files are within the first 1024 cylinders.

The reason for this is that Boot Magic replaces the Windows 98-generated master boot record with its own. This master boot record only understands the traditional BIOS Interrupt 13 values, not the extensions.

You can use Boot Magic to boot to other partitions even if they cross the 1024 cylinder boundary, as long as their boot files are within it. If you have a partition that is beyond the 1024 cylinder boundary, Boot Magic won't find it.

Thanks to Tom Pfeifer for testing this out.

Add a new hard drive

In Chapter 2 of *Windows 98 Secrets*, we tell you how to copy all your Windows 98 files to a new hard disk. It involves a great many steps, but no additional software purchases.

If you'd like to install a new hard disk in your computer and move Windows 98 to the new, hopefully bigger and faster drive, then you might check out John Hildrum's Add A New Hard Drive web site. He'll take you through each step, and when you're done installing your new hard drive, he'll show you how to transfer Windows 98 onto it (no need to buy our other book just to get these steps).

There is software that makes this process easier, and Microsoft includes a batch installation wizard in its *Windows 98 Resource Sampler Kit*, which you'll find on the Windows 98 CD-ROM. You can find out more about the other software packages at John's site.

You'll find John's instructions at www.hildrum.com/harddriveadd.html.

You should also check out Seagate's "Installing a Second ATA (IDE) Hard Disk" at www.seagate.com/support/disc/faq/www96009.shtml. You also might review "Adding a second hard drive" at 204.191.245.9/1996/Feb96/HardDriv/2ndHD/2ndHD.html.

Add a second SCSI hard drive

If you've got a SCSI hard drive in your computer, it is a simple process to add a second hard drive—or at least it can be. In the previous section, we pointed you to a number of articles that discuss how to add a second hard drive, transfer the Windows 98 operating system to the second drive, and make this the boot drive. These articles concentrate on EDI drives, which are more common and also a bit more difficult to reconfigure than SCSI drives.

If you buy a second drive, it is most likely going to be bigger than the first drive, if only because the price per megabyte of the new drive will be much less than the previous drive. If the new drive is bigger, it makes it that much easier to copy everything, or almost everything, from the old drive.

Tip   Adding a new drive increases the power draw on the power supply and adds to the heat load of your cabinet. Most computer manufacturers supply a power supply that is adequate to handle the hard disk addition. But to keep the new hard disk cool enough to be within specs, you'll want to make sure that there is adequate air flow over it. Most cases are designed to allow airflow over two hard disk drives. You can always put a temperature probe on your new hard disk after the fact and make sure that the temperature of the air around it is within spec.

Get ready to plug in your new drive

You only have to do two things before you plug the new SCSI drive in. First, pull off the jumper that activates the terminator. We're assuming, at least for now, that this drive won't be the last drive on your SCSI cable. You may have to move a jumper (instead of just pull it) to accomplish this task, or even pull the terminator. Bare SCSI drives come configured as if they were going to be the only drive in the computer (true in most cases), and as if they were going to be at the end of the SCSI cable (also true in most cases). In your case, you don't want the SCSI cable to be terminated before it reaches the existing SCSI drive at the end of the cable.

Second, arrange the jumpers on the drive so that this drive gets identified as number 1 — or perhaps another number between 1 and 6, but some number that is not being used to identify another SCSI device. SCSI ID 0 is normally used for the boot drive, which is usually at the end of the SCSI cable. SCSI ID 7 is normally used for the SCSI adapter, which is at the other end of the SCSI cable. There may be other devices on the SCSI cable (a CD-ROM and/or Zip drive perhaps). If you know those SCSI IDs, be sure to set the SCSI ID of the new hard disk to a different number.

You can find out the SCSI ID numbers of the other devices (and the boot device) using the Device Manager. Navigate to the Disk Drives branch, highlight each hard disk or Zip drive, click Properties, and then click the Settings tab. You'll see the SCSI ID in the Target ID field, as shown in Figure 20-4. Also check in the CD-ROM branch.

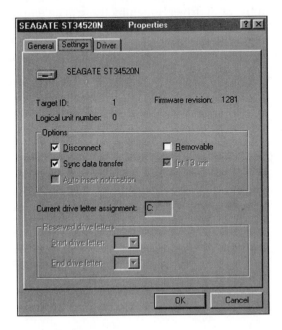

Figure 20-4: The Target ID for this SCSI drive appears on the first line under its name.

If your SCSI adapter has been set to use SCAM (SCSI Configured Auto Magically), you don't even have to set the SCSI ID number on the new hard disk — but at this point you may not know whether this is the case or not. To find out, boot your computer, and during power-on self test, you may be given the opportunity to access the SCSI BIOS. The Adaptec AHA 2940 SCSI controller is accessed by pressing Ctrl+A, for example.

If you are able to access the SCSI card's BIOS, you may be able to set the SCSI adapter to SCAM mode, or at least determine if it is already in this mode. You may also be able to later change the boot drive's SCSI ID — if so, this will come in quite handy, because you will be able to easily designate which drive is the boot drive.

Plug in your new drive

Now you're ready to turn off your computer and plug in your drive. Most consumer personal computers that include SCSI drives use the standard 50-pin SCSI cable. When you purchase a SCSI drive, make sure that it has this interface. Narrow SCSI drives use the 50-pin interface.

There are a couple of other interfaces — 68-pin and SCA 80-pin. Unless you're building servers and doing hot plug and play with hard disks, you won't need to purchase these types of SCSI drives. It is possible to buy small adapter cards that let you plug drives of this type into 50-pin cables, but unless you get a real good deal, this is not the best choice.

You hope that your computer manufacturer has laid out the SCSI cable so that you can just plug in the SCSI drive. Hopefully there is an empty 3 1/2-inch bay just above the last drive that has a 50-pin connector. If so, you're in luck because you can just attach the new hard disk to the metal clamp built into the bay, plug in the SCSI cable, and then plug in the 4-line power cable.

Turn on your computer and let it restart Windows. If your computer hangs trying to identify your new hard disk, you've probably set the SCSI ID of the new hard disk to a value that is already being used. Turn off the computer, and reset the SCSI ID to your new drive.

Use FDISK to partition your new drive

Once you are up in Windows, click Start, Programs, MS-DOS Prompt. Type **fdisk** at the DOS prompt and press Enter. Press Enter again to allow the hard disk to be formatted (later) in 32-bit FAT format, as shown in Figure 20-5.

Press **5** to change the current fixed disk drive (see Figure 20-6), and then press Enter. You are going to format the second drive, your new drive, and you want to be sure that you don't format the first drive. Then press **2** (to format the new drive) and press Enter.

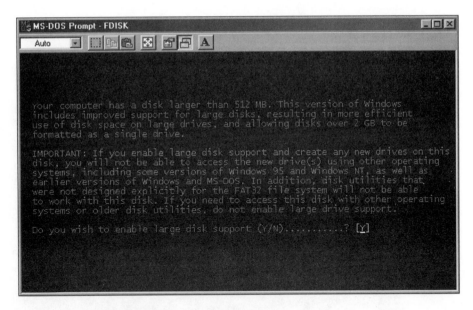

Figure 20-5: Press Enter to answer Yes to this question.

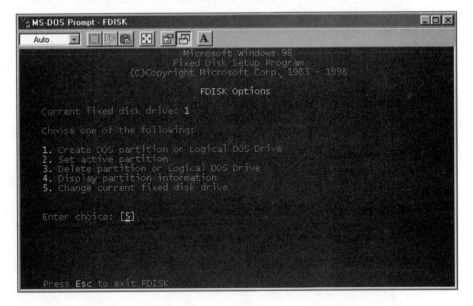

Figure 20-6: Enter **5** to choose the last option.

Press **1** and then Enter to create a DOS partition on drive 2, as shown in
Figure 20-7.

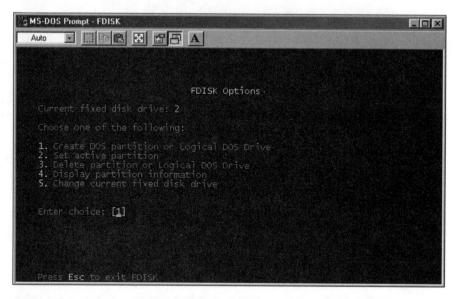

Figure 20-7: Press **1** to select the first option here.

Press **1** again, and then Enter to create a primary DOS partition, as shown in
Figure 20-8. You want to create a primary DOS partition to allow this partition
to become the bootable volume, the C drive.

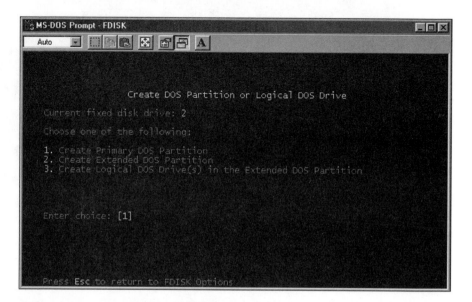

Figure 20-8: Your choice here should be **1**.

Press Enter to use the maximum available size of your new hard disk for the primary DOS partition. All drives less than 8GB will use 4K clusters for file storage. You might as well format the whole drive as one primary partition unless you have criteria other than optimal file storage space efficiency for dividing the drive. Press Esc to end FDISK.

Now restart Windows, and your new hard disk will be recognized as drive D. The second primary partition is assigned the drive letter D.

Format your new drive

You now need to format the new drive. Right-click the D drive icon in your Explorer, select Format, mark the Full and Copy System Files options in the Format dialog box (see Figure 20-9), and click the Start button. Alternatively, you can click Start, Programs, MS-DOS Prompt, type **Format D:/s**, and press Enter.

Figure 20-9: Select the Full and Copy System Files options.

Copy files onto your new drive

After the formatting is complete, you now have a hard disk that is ready to accept files. You can click its icon in your Explorer and see that there are currently no files on it.

It's quite easy to copy everything over to your new hard disk from the old hard disk. If you are going to make the new hard disk the boot drive, you'll definitely want to do this.

Using your Explorer, drag all the files in the root directory on C to D. We assume that you've set Explorer to display all files (View, Folder Options, View, Show All Files). Drag and drop all of the folder icons that branch off the root directory of your C drive to your D drive, except your C:\Windows folder.

Highlight your D drive icon in the left pane of your Explorer, right-click the right pane, and click New, Folder. Change the name of this new folder to Windows, assuming that is the name of your Windows 98 folder on your C drive.

Drag and drop all the subfolders of your C:\Windows folder onto your D:\Windows folder. Drag and drop all the files in your C:\Windows folder onto your D:\Windows folder *except*, and this is crucial, your Win386.swp file. This is the Windows swap file; it is dynamically created and sized when you run Windows. It will be created automatically when you reboot later.

Swap drive assignments and designate active partition

Now that you have copied everything other than the Windows swap file from C drive to D drive, you are ready to turn the D drive into the C drive, and vice versa. If you can use your SCSI adapter BIOS to specify which SCSI ID number is associated with the boot drive, then you'll be able to leave the drives alone and switch them around logically.

If your SCSI adapter does not have this capability, you'll have to change the SCSI ID values for the drives by pulling them out of their bays and moving jumpers. You'll want to change the SCSI ID of your new disk to 0 and the SCSI ID of your older disk to 1 (or whatever the new disk was previously).

You are going to need a Windows 98 Startup diskette for the next few steps. You may have created one when you first installed Windows 98. You can create one now by clicking Start, Settings, Control Panel, Add/Remove Programs, Startup Disk. You can also create one by using the method we discuss in "Windows 98 boot diskette" in Chapter 16. If you don't have one, create one now.

Insert your Windows 98 boot diskette in drive A.

If you can change the boot disk assignment in the SCSI BIOS, click Start, Shut Down, Restart, OK. Go into your SCSI BIOS during the power-on self test, and change the designation of the boot drive from 0 to the current SCSI ID for your new drive. Escape from your SCSI BIOS, and continue your power-on self test. If you can't change the boot disk assignment in the SCSI BIOS, click Start, Shut Down, Shut Down, OK. Make the changes in the drives while the computer is off, and then turn it back on.

Your computer will boot up to the MS-DOS prompt on drive A. Type **fdisk** and press Enter. You are now going to designate the primary DOS partition on your new hard disk as the active or bootable partition. Press **2** and Enter, as shown in Figure 20-10.

Press Esc, and remove the Windows 98 boot diskette from your floppy disk drive. Restart your computer. It should now bring up Windows 98 on your new hard disk. You can erase the now-redundant files on your D partition at any time.

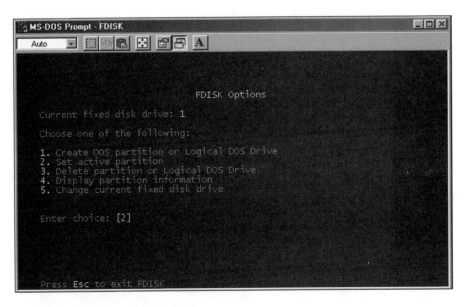

Figure 20-10: Select option 2 in this list.

Get Internet Explorer straightened out on your new drive

Secret

You will find that Internet Explorer doesn't seem to know where the Internet Explorer executable file is, even though logically it is in the same place, C:\Program Files\Internet Explorer. Click the Internet Explorer icon on your Desktop, click the Locate button in the Program Not Found dialog box (see Figure 20-11), and then browse down to C:\Program Files\Internet Explorer\ Iexplore.exe.

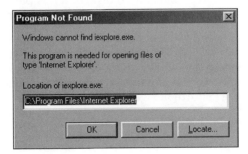

Figure 20-11: Click the Locate button to point to Internet Explorer's executable file.

Internet Explorer won't be able to remember what's in the Temporary Internet Files folder. Your history web page names will still be there, but they won't know that the associated files are still stored on your hard disk. The same is true for your offline web pages. You'll have to synchronize again.

You may also find that when you click a link in your e-mail client, it doesn't always bring up your Internet Explorer window and access the indicated site. You can always right-click the link, click Copy Shortcut, and then paste the URL into your Address field, either in the Internet Explorer window or in the Address toolbar.

You might reinstall Internet Explorer and Outlook Express, if you have downloaded these from the Microsoft web site, or have a separate setup file for them.

Secret

You may also find that you can no longer invoke Internet Neighborhood (a third party FTP client) in the Explorer. You'll have to reinstall it. The FTP sites that you've configured under Internet Neighborhood will still be there after you reinstall. You can use the Registry Crawler or the Registry editor to go to HKEY_USERS\.Default\Software\KnoWare\Internet Neighborhood\FTP-Sites to see which FTP sites you've registered.

Where can you purchase a bare drive to install in your computer? There are lots of places to buy them. We recommend Dirt Cheap Drives at dirtcheapdrives.com. They treated us right.

To FAT 32 or not to

Windows 98 comes with a new file system. You can upgrade your existing file system, but you should know about all the pitfalls first.

Convert to FAT 32?

Converting your hard drive from a FAT volume to a FAT-32 volume can really decrease the amount of wasted space you currently have and free it up for more documents and programs. Still, it seems like quite a drastic step to make for an uncertain benefit. If you have a small hard disk, or if it is partitioned into small logical volumes, it probably will not be worthwhile to convert.

To see how much additional space you'll gain by converting your existing drive to the FAT-32 file format, you should check out diskSpace Explorer. It not only shows you what percentage of disk space each of your folders and files currently consumes, it also lets you compare wasted space under multiple formatting options, as shown in Figure 20-12.

You'll find diskSpace Explorer at www.east-tec.com.

A freeware disk statistics program, Stats '99, shown in Figure 20-13, is available at www.contactplus.com/index2.htm. It gives you a different set of measures of your hard disk space usage, such as use by file type, date, modification date, and so on.

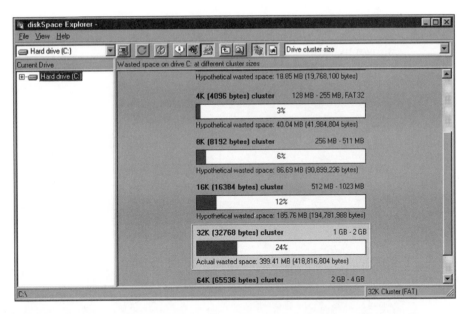

Figure 20-12: Comparisons of wasted space for a hard disk, as performed by diskSpace Explorer.

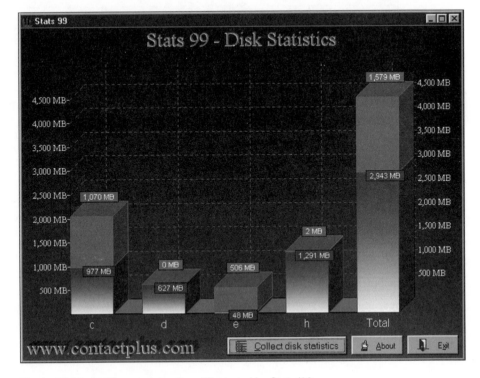

Figure 20-13: A different comparison, illustrated by Stats '99.

Like diskSpace Explorer, Stats 99 can give you an idea of how much you would gain by converting your FAT-16 formatted hard drive to FAT 32, as shown in Figure 20-14.

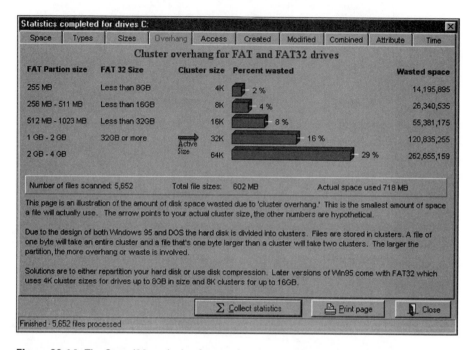

Figure 20-14: The Stats '99 analysis of wasted space on the same disk.

Yet a third tool, one that gives somewhat different results, is available right on your Windows 98 CD-ROM. You'll find it in \tools\reskit\config. It's fat32win.exe. If you run the setup program in \tools\reskit, you'll install this program and all the rest of the 26 *Windows 98 Resource Sampler Kit* programs. You can then access them by clicking Start, Programs, Windows 98 Resource Kit, Tools Management Console.

The Tools Management Console, shown in Figure 20-15, is a common interface that consolidates a bunch of utilities and network management functions, helping you remember where all these little critters are hiding out.

Fat 32 Conversion Information Tool gives quite a bit higher number than the two previous tools, but in our test, its estimate appeared to be just about right.

If you'd like to learn more about FAT 32, you can read the Microsoft Knowledge Base article "Description of the FAT32 File System" at support.microsoft.com/support/kb/articles/q154/9/97.asp.

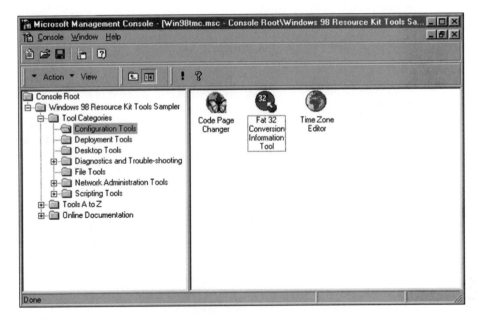

Figure 20-15: The Tools Management Console. Look in the Configuration Tools folder to find the Fat 32 Conversion Information Tool.

Also, the Seagate FAQs are quite good. Check out these two:

- "FAT32 Basics" at www.seagate.com/support/disc/faq/win98_fat32_light_faq.shtml

- "Windows 98 and FAT 32 File systems" at www.seagate.com/support/disc/faq/win98_fat32_faq.shtml

FAT32 Converter won't?

The FAT32 Converter will choke if things aren't quite right. Fortunately there are ways around these problems.

Bad sector problems

You may have tried to convert your FAT-16 volume to FAT 32, only to find that the Microsoft FAT32 Converter refused to do the job because your hard disk had a bad sector. It appears that Microsoft has erred on the side of caution with respect to whether to convert a hard disk when ScanDisk reports a bad sector. Here is what Don Lebow, a Microsoft MVP, had to say about the matter on the *Windows98 disk general* newsgroup:

> Piecing together some conversations I've had with MS folks, I think it goes something like this...

Their approach is conservative. The thinking seems to be that if a bad cluster is spotted, there may be problems with the disk (may or may not be true, as we know). And such a problem could farkle up something else in the data conversion process. Data loss is the Big Scary. They wanted to cut the possibility of that happening to the absolute bare minimum. So they felt that since this is a basic OS tool, they'd rather "err" on the side of caution.

The same thinking went into why they don't offer a FAT32-FAT16 conversion, which again Partition Magic does. The process itself is more complicated than converting the other way, due to disk space considerations and such. Their internal testing indicated that it couldn't be made as bulletproof as they wanted. So they decided not to offer it.

If you think about it, from their point of view it's probably better to have some "issues" with the conversion program not working, rather than a big splash box on www.news.com saying "Windows 98 Users report Scrambled Disks."

So what do you do if you want to convert a hard disk to FAT 32 and you've got a bad sector or two? You can do a number of things, according to Attila Szabo (aka MrScary) also a Microsoft MVP.

First, you can check out "How to Cause ScanDisk for Windows to Retest Bad Cluster" at support.microsoft.com/support/kb/articles/q127/0/55.asp.

Be aware that the method detailed in the Knowledge Base article does nothing more than tell ScanDisk to ignore the bad sector mark and recheck this area to determine if it really is bad or not. If it is bad (pretty likely), ScanDisk will leave it marked as bad, and you will have made zero progress.

Also, the method described states that you should change the fourth value found at HKEY_CURRENT_USER\Software\Microsoft\Windows\CurrentVersion\Applets\Check Drive\Settings from 00 to 04. Other users have stated that this is incorrect — you should instead add 4 to whatever value you find there. Then run ScanDisk.

Second, use a third party application that converts with the errors present (such as Partition Magic).

The Partition Magic web site (www.powerquest.com) doesn't give any indication that Partition Magic can indeed convert a hard drive with bad sectors from FAT16 to FAT32, but Don Lebow mentions:

> As far as Partition Magic goes, the evidence I've seen has been anecdotal (i.e. "CVT.EXE wouldn't do it, but Partition Magic would"). I suspect that the program just takes note of any (presumably mapped) bad clusters and ignores them.

Seems reasonable to us.

Finally, use a third party package that reliably recovers the bad clusters, such as Gibson Research Center's SpinRite 5.0. Attila states, "Personally, SpinRite has been my choice and it has had a perfect record (so far) in recovering the clusters, allowing the intended MS Converter to run successfully."

SpinRite is the ticket. It can determine what spare sectors are available from the hard disk spare sector table and remap them to remove the bad clusters from the purview of Windows 98 ScanDisk and FAT-32 disk drivers. Here's what Steve Gibson, the author of SpinRite, had to say, after following our little discussion on the *Windows98 disk general* newsgroup:

> Question: After upgrading my Windows 95 system to Windows 98, when I tried to convert to Fat 32, it said I had bad cluster marks and it refused to do it. Sure enough, when I did a thorough ScanDisk, it said I had 32,768 bytes in bad sectors, and when I was defragging my hard drive I saw a bad cluster in the details. When I wrote the Windows 98 newsgroup with this problem, a bunch of people there suggested SpinRite. But since I'm not a computer expert, I have a few questions I would like to ask before I try it out: (1) What potential negatives could SpinRite do to my hard drive? (2) Is it easy to use? (3) Is this the right product to fix this problem?
>
> 1. What potential negatives could SpinRite do to my hard drive? SpinRite is more than ten years old, and it's been used with complete safety in every imaginable situation and configuration. It's bullet proof and is the most widely known and recommended hard drive utility in the PC industry. You can use it with total confidence.
>
> 2. Is it easy to use? Yes, embarrassingly so. Sometimes "techie folks" who LOVE SpinRite's power want more options and features and more "power stuff" ...but we have always steadfastly refused to do that since we believe that such "power features" would bog it down and make it more complex. We really did write SpinRite for YOU, not for some propeller head (even though we very much appreciate their support!)
>
> 3. Is this the right product to fix this problem? Apparently so, since we're selling many copies to people for exactly this reason. Since SpinRite is able to inter-operate with the drive's internal defect systems, it's able to "unmark" bad sectors in the system's FAT, and then have the drive replace those bad sectors with brand new spare sectors (from the drive's internal spare sector pool). It thus gives Windows and its FAT32 Converter a "perfect" drive to convert after having moved the defects from "external" management to "internal" management. It works like a charm!"

SpinRite 5.0 worked just fine for us. You'll find it at www.grc.com.

SpinRite is able to replace the bad sector with a good one from the drive's spare sector table. It remaps the new sector to appear as though the new sector is in the same location as the bad sector. You should run SpinRite at level 5 the first time you use it to repair bad sectors, which can easily be the first time you run it on your computer. It defaults to a lower level to test the disk and recover data, but it doesn't do bad sector remapping at the lower level. Because this process can take many hours (let it run overnight), you'll want to go to level 5 first if bad sectors are your problem.

SpinRite doesn't indicate in its onscreen messages that it is repairing the bad sectors by using good sectors from the spare sector table. In fact, it indicates that it is testing the bad sector at a very deep level and checking if it is okay, and if it is, then unmarking the sector as bad.

Well, this wouldn't cut it, because if the sector is bad it needs to be replaced in order for the Microsoft FAT 32 conversion to work. This replacement is in fact what is going on, so realize that SpinRite is not telling you the whole story.

Memory shortage problems

FAT32 Converter may refuse to work because it doesn't have enough DOS or conventional memory. The drive converter restarts in real-mode DOS (it is in fact a DOS program), so it has to have enough DOS memory to carry out its tasks. If it finds that there isn't enough memory, it complains with an error message in a dialog box, and gives up.

The error message asks you to edit your Config.sys and Autoexec.bat files to remark out real-mode drivers or applications that may be loading and taking up conventional memory. This may be the ticket for you. You might also add the following lines to your Config.sys file to allow some of DOS to be loaded in the upper memory blocks:

```
DEVICE=C:\WINDOWS\HIMEM.SYS /TESTMEM:OFF
DEVICE=C:\Windows\Emm386.exe noems
DOS=HIGH,UMB
```

Then make sure that any drives loaded in Config.sys are using the DEVICEHIGH command instead of DEVICE so that they will attempt to load them into high memory. Programs loaded by your Autoexec.bat should use LOADHIGH.

Unless it is obvious from looking at your Autoexec.bat and Config.sys files that you can free up a lot of conventional memory, you might check to see whether Windows 98 is in fact causing the problem behind the scenes before you make any changes.

Secret

Windows may be loading its DoubleSpace/DriveSpace compression driver in conventional memory, even if you don't have a compressed hard drive. Windows does this so that it can read compressed floppy drives (not a very good reason in our opinion).

The DriveSpace 3 compressed drive driver that came with Plus! for Windows 95 was quite large at 100K, and couldn't load itself into the upper memory blocks to free up conventional DOS memory. If DriveSpace 3 is getting loaded, you won't have enough DOS memory to run the FAT32 Converter.

DriveSpace 3 is loaded by Io.sys, the program that underlies real-mode DOS. Io.sys starts up before Windows and is also operating whenever you are in real-mode DOS (or MS-DOS mode). Io.sys reads the contents of the hidden text file Msdos.sys in your root directory to determine whether it should load Dblspace.bin and DrvSpace.bin.

You can determine if DriveSpace 3 has eaten a good chunk of your conventional memory by taking the the following steps. If it is, we'll show you how to make sure that it isn't loaded into memory. You'll then be able to run the FAT32 Converter.

STEPS:

Checking Your Memory to See If DriveSpace 3 Is There

Step 1. Click Start, Shut Down, Restart in MS-DOS Mode, and OK.

Step 2. At the DOS prompt, type **mem /d/p** and press Enter.

Step 3. Press Enter once, and check column two, just above the line that ends in BUFFERS=12, to see whether DriveSpace 3 has been loaded into memory and whether a good chunk of memory is being used.

Step 4. Press Enter again, and in the column labeled Free on the right side of the screen, see if you have more than 523,000 bytes of free conventional memory. Press Enter one last time to end the mem program.

Step 5. Type **exit** and press Enter to exit MS-DOS mode and restart Windows.

If DriveSpace 3 has been loaded into conventional memory and you have less than 523,000 bytes of free conventional memory, you can easily stop it from loading.

If you have a compressed hard drive, you don't want to do this, so be sure to check first in Windows. Right-click all of your local hard disk icons in your Explorer, click Properties, and if there is a Compression tab, click it to see if your disk is compressed. You can't convert a compressed drive to a FAT-32 drive—and you really wouldn't want to anyway—but you sure don't want to disable compression if you already have a compressed drive. If you do, you won't be able to access it.

To keep DriveSpace/DoubleSpace from loading into conventional memory (or even into the upper memory blocks), you can either move the driver files out of your root directory or edit your Msdos.sys file. If you edit this file, then you can tell Io.sys not to load these drivers. Later, if you decide you need them, you can go back and re-edit Msdos.sys to have them loaded the next time you restart Windows.

To edit the Msdos.sys file, take these steps:

STEPS:

Editing Msdos.sys

Step 1. Right-click the Msdos.sys file in the root directory of your boot partition (C drive) and click Properties. If you can't see Msdos.sys, click View, Folder Options in your Explorer, click the View tab, clear Hide File Extensions for Known File Types, and mark Show All Files (see Figure 20-16).

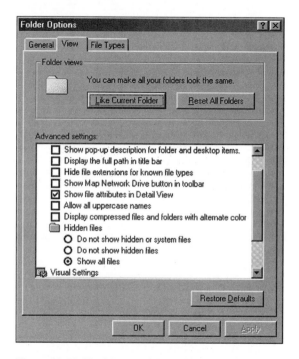

Figure 20-16: The View tab of the Folder Options dialog box.

Step 2. In the Msdos.sys Properties dialog box, clear the Read-only check box, as shown in Figure 20-17. Click OK. You can re-mark this check box after you have finished editing Msdos.sys.

Step 3. Right-click the Msdos.sys icon in your Explorer again, and click Send To, Notepad (or WordPad). If you don't have a shortcut to Notepad.exe in your \Windows\SendTo folder, click Open With after right-clicking Msdos.sys, select Notepad in the Open With dialog box, and click OK.

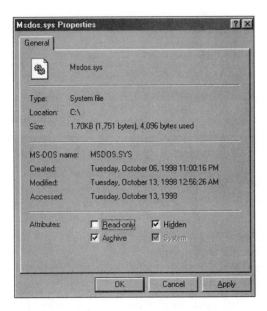

Figure 20-17: Msdos.sys Properties dialog box.

Step 4.   Enter these two lines right under the [Options] line in your
Msdos.sys file, as shown in Figure 20-18:

```
Drvspace=0
Dblspace=0
```

Figure 20-18: The [Options] section of the Msdos.sys file, with the new lines
added.

Continued

Editing Msdos.sys *(continued)*

Step 5. In Notepad or WordPad, click File, Save to save these changes to your Msdos.sys file. Then click File, Exit.

Step 6. Restart Windows by clicking Start, Shut Down, Restart, OK.

Instead of editing the Msdos.sys file, you could just move the Dblspace.ini, Dblspace.bin, and Drvspace.bin files into a folder other than the root directory.

If DriveSpace 3 caused your conventional memory problem, this will solve that problem and FAT32 Converter will work just fine. You can run it either from Windows (Start, Programs, Accessories, System Tools, Drive Converter (FAT32)) or from real-mode DOS.

To run it from DOS, click Start, Shut Down, Restart in MS-DOS Mode. At the DOS prompt, type **CVT *C:* /CVT32** and press Enter, where C is the drive letter for the disk partition that you want to convert to FAT 32. Running the FAT32 Converter from DOS has the advantage of allowing you to quickly (without restarting Windows every time) make changes to your Autoexec.bat and Config.sys files.

You may find it more convenient to start in DOS by holding down the Ctrl key during power-on self test, instead of restarting in MS-DOS mode from Windows.

BIOS problems

If you still have problems, it may be because you have a setting in your BIOS that protects the boot sector on your hard disk. This feature keeps viruses from editing these files and corrupting your computer.

You'll need to press the indicated key during the power-on self test to go to your BIOS setup and turn off this feature.

Don't let the help confuse you

The FAT32 Converter help file (click the Details button in the FAT32 Conversion Wizard) states the following:

> Once you convert your hard drive to FAT32 format using Drive Converter, you cannot return to using the FAT16 format unless you repartition and reformat the FAT32 drive. If you converted the drive on which Windows 98 is installed, then you must reinstall Windows 98 after repartitioning the drive.

Secret

Don't be confused by the poor wording here. You don't have to reinstall Windows 98 if you convert your drive to FAT 32. Also, you can use Partition Magic (www.powerquest.com) to convert a FAT-32 partition back to a FAT-16 partition without having to reformat the partition. All your data, including Windows 98, will be saved.

Wasted space

Secret

You can use DOS to give you an idea of how much space you might be wasting by putting small files into large clusters. This method will also tell you how much less you're wasting after you move up to FAT 32 with 4K clusters.

Click Start, Programs, MS-DOS Prompt. At the DOS prompt, type **cd** and press Enter. Then type **dir /a/s/v** and press Enter. You'll see your whole hard disk flash before your eyes.

After a minute or so, you'll see something like what we show in Figure 20-19. The difference between the value for Bytes and the value for Bytes Allocated is the amount of space not used by the files, but allocated to the clusters that store those files. To convert this to megabytes, divide the difference by 2 to the 20th power.

```
MS-DOS Prompt                                                    _ □ ×

Auto ▾  [] [] [] [] [] [] A

SWENUM   SYS         9,488         12,288  08-15-98  7:21p  11-15-98        A
swenum.sys
        23 file(s)     3,130,736 bytes
         2 dir(s)      3,186,688 bytes allocated

Directory of C:\WINDOWS\WORDVIEW
File Name         Size        Allocated      Modified      Accessed  Attrib

              <DIR>                        06-05-97  7:48a              D
              <DIR>                        06-05-97  7:48a              D

ADDWV    INF       1,415         4,096  01-16-96  5:03a  08-19-97        A
ADDWV.INF
         1 file(s)      1,415 bytes
         2 dir(s)       4,096 bytes allocated

Total files listed:
    15,922 file(s)  1,625,027,916 bytes
     2,894 dir(s)   1,661,476,864 bytes allocated
                      251,150,336 bytes free
                    2,142,543,872 bytes total disk space,  88% in use

C:\>_
```

Figure 20-19: Subtract Bytes from Bytes Allocated to determine your wasted space.

In the example shown in Figure 20-19, 1,661,476,864 bytes allocated minus 1,625,027,916 bytes equals 36,448,948 bytes, or 34.76MB wasted.

You can't compress your FAT-32 volume

While you can create a compressed volume file (CVF) on a FAT-16 formatted hard disk, you can't do this on a FAT-32 formatted drive. Microsoft felt that there was no good reason to offer the DriveSpace 3 compression on FAT 32, because while DriveSpace 3 stores files in virtual clusters as small as 512 bytes, FAT 32 already stores files reasonably well in 4K clusters.

DriveSpace 3 compression found a ready audience with Windows 95 users who had 1GB and 2GB drives. One of our options was to divide up our hard disks into small, arbitrarily-named partitions to reduce cluster size and thereby minimize the space taken up by any file, no matter how small. Another was to live with a significant amount of wasted space, with minimum cluster size at 32K. Or, we could use DriveSpace 3 to get a lot closer file packing on small virtual clusters as well as actual file compression.

DriveSpace 3 has a maximum size of two gigabytes. Therefore, it doesn't allow you to create a CVF that would encompass a complete volume on a hard disk of greater than one gigabyte in original size. With standard hard disks greatly exceeding that value now, there is little use for DriveSpace 3.

Storing files in 4K clusters, as FAT 32 does, captures most of the benefit of DriveSpace 3. However, if you have highly compressible files that you would like to store on a compressed volume, you may still want to partition your hard disk in a manner that allows for a FAT-16 formatted partition. You can then create a CVF on this partition. See Chapter 33 in *Windows 98 Secrets* for instructions on how to do this.

Another way to store highly compressible files efficiently is to create a zip file(or multiple zip files) that will be viewed by Windows 98 as a folder, and to store the files there. You'll need Microsoft Plus! 98. Be sure to install the Compressed Folders portion of the program.

Once you have installed Plus! 98, right-click the Desktop, and click New, Compressed Folder. Rename this folder and drag and drop it to any useful place. You may want to place a shortcut to it on your Desktop. Now you can just drag and drop files that you feel are highly compressible into the compressed folder.

What if your computer hangs after you convert to FAT 32?

Secret

If you have a SCSI drive and your computer won't boot once you've converted your hard disk to FAT 32, it may be because the BIOS on your SCSI card does not fully implement the Interrupt 13 extensions. You need to update your SCSI card's BIOS.

If you have an Adaptec 2940 or 3940 series SCSI card with a BIOS version prior to 1.23, you'll need a new BIOS. You can determine the version of your Adaptec BIOS by pressing Ctrl+A when prompted to do so during the power-on self test.

To upgrade your Adaptec SCSI BIOS, contact Adaptec at www.adaptec.com/advisor/index1.html. You can download the latest BIOS and update your onboard SCSI BIOS yourself.

If you are updating your BIOS to version 1.34.3, you'll probably be downloading the file afu1343a.exe, although there may be a newer version of the BIOS update by the time you read this.

After you update your SCSI BIOS (following the instructions from Adaptec) you'll want to reset your SCSI parameters (press Ctrl+A when prompted during the power-on self test) to their defaults. This gets rid of previous erroneous values for the hard disk size. You can then change the values to the ones that are right for you.

You'll also want to update your SCSI driver, as discussed in the next section.

Thanks to Bill Drake for help with this secret.

Upgrade your Adaptec 29XX and 394X series SCSI driver

If you are experiencing any problems with your Adaptec SCSI cards, you might want to download the latest drivers for these cards. You'll find them at www.adaptec.com/support/overview/windows98.html. Download the 7800w9x.exe file. This file includes all of the drivers for the 29XX and 394X cards, and they supercede the ones that came on the original Windows 98 CD-ROM.

After you have downloaded the file, click it to unzip the drivers.

Thanks to Attila Szabo for this update.

FAT32 for Windows NT 4.0

While Windows 2000 (Windows NT 5.0) supports FAT-32 formatted partitions, Windows NT 4.0 does not. Fortunately, there is a shareware program that lets Windows NT 4.0 read from and write to FAT-32 drives.

It won't create a FAT-32 partition, nor will it convert existing FAT-16 or HTFS-formatted partitions to FAT 32. You'll need Windows 98 or Partition Magic to accomplish that task. Also, the Windows NT 4.0 boot drive cannot be formatted as a FAT-32 partition.

You'll find FAT32 for Windows NT at www.winternals.com/products/fat32.shtml.

Better performance from your hard disk

So many things can keep your hard disks from doing their best.

Stop thrashing!

Almost as annoying as your computer dialing your modem on its own is your computer thrashing about without any input from you. The hard disk just takes off, and after a while the racket gets a bit unbearable. Besides the noise, you'd rather the computer waited patiently for your commands, and didn't find something irritating to do on its own.

Actually, if the computer did some useful things on its own, but did them unobtrusively, it wouldn't nearly so bad. But hard disk thrashing can be a signal that the computer is having a difficult time handling its memory, and this can be a cause for alarm.

If you're off the computer and you hear the hard disk start up and continue, it's probably because a background application has started. These applications are meant to do useful work while you're not demanding all of the computer's resources through your interactions. Unfortunately, some of them can be installed without you ever being aware of their existence. Not a pleasant thought, actually.

Stop indexing

If you've installed Microsoft Office 97, you'll find that it likes to maintain an index of all the words in your Word document files. While you're not at the computer, a program called Find Fast starts up and searches through your hard disk to find your Word documents and build or update its index based on what it finds. It's out there on its own reading and writing. (Microsoft Office 2000 sets up Find Fast as an "install on demand" component. You'll find its icon in the Control Panel. When you click the Find Fast icon for the first time, the feature is installed.)

The System Configuration Utility lets you prevent Find Fast from loading when you first start Windows. It won't build an index for you if it never loads, so that's the trade off. Personally, I only used the results of Find Fast a couple of times, and after that I turned it off.

STEPS:

Turning Off Find Fast

Step 1. Click Start, Programs, Accessories, System Tools, System Information, Tools, System Configuration Utility.

Step 2. Click the Startup tab. Clear the check box next to Microsoft Fast Find.

Step 3. Click OK.

You'll need to restart Windows if you want this setting to take effect immediately. You can get the indexing to stop in the short term by clicking Start, Settings, Control Panel, Find Fast, Index, Pause Indexing.

Your screen saver

If you have a screen saver activated, the screen saver may be reading files from your hard disk. This would be especially true if it displays lots of different graphics files.

You can check this by right-clicking your Desktop, clicking Properties, Screen Saver, and Preview. Listen to your hard disk to see if it is making a racket.

Scheduled tasks are being performed

Your Task Scheduler may be scheduled to perform its maintenance chores whenever you leave the computer for a while, or at certain times whether you are working on the computer or not. The Task Scheduler has plenty of flexibility built in, and if you, or someone who has access to your computer, have used this flexibility to schedule tasks at inopportune times, you'll hear about it.

Open your Explorer and highlight Scheduled Tasks in the left pane. Review the schedule of tasks in the right pane. If you see one that might be the cause of the problem, double-click the offending task.

You can click the Schedule tab to rearrange the task schedule for a more appropriate hour or day. Click the Settings tab and see if the task is told to begin only if there is a break in your use of the computer. See if Only Start the Scheduled Task If Computer Is Idle for [ ] Minutes is marked (see Figure 20-20).

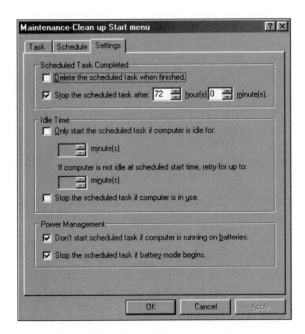

Figure 20-20: Because the check boxes in the Idle Time area are cleared, the Clean Up Start Menu task will start whether or not the computer is in use.

If this check box is cleared, then the scheduled task could start up as you use the computer. If that's what is happening to you, mark this check box.

Swapping from memory to disk

Windows 98 includes a virtual memory manager that makes its own decisions about when it should write the contents of memory to the hard disk and free up space to be used for other purposes. Usually this happens when you load a program, so you're not going to notice that Windows 98 is both reading and writing to the hard disk within the same short time interval. There will be times, though, when the memory manager moves stuff out of memory onto the hard disk by itself.

The amount of memory swapping and writing to the hard disk is minor at these times, so it should not be a major source of irritation.

In Chapter 33 of *Windows 98 Secrets*, we show you how to reduce the amount of paging to the cache by fixing the size of your cache at 2.5 times the size of your memory.

Quit checking for a CD-ROM

If you have enabled the Auto Insert Notification option in the Properties dialog box for your CD-ROM drive, Windows looks for a CD-ROM in the drive every few seconds. You're not going to notice any disk thrashing, but you may at least notice the CD-ROM light flashing every couple of seconds. The hard disk light may also flash on if both devices are on the SCSI bus.

You can turn off Auto Insert Notification by taking these steps:

STEPS:

Turning Off Auto Insert Notification

Step 1.   Press Win+Pause/Break (or right-click the My Computer icon and click Properties), and click the Device Manager tab.

Step 2.   Double-click the CD-ROM (right at the top of the devices list), and then double-click your installed CD-ROM device.

Step 3.   Click the Settings tab and clear the Auto Insert Notification check box, as shown in Figure 20-21.

Step 4.   Click OK. Click Close. Restart your computer when prompted.

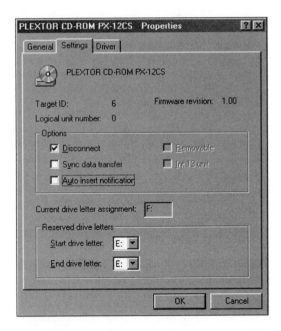

Figure 20-21: The Auto Insert Notification check box is selected, but has been cleared.

Hitting the disk lightly

Do you notice that even after you've done everything we've discussed here, your hard disk light flickers on briefly every half second? The disk is being hit ever so lightly. If so, it's because you have a SCSI hard disk. The disk (or maybe just the SCSI bus) is being interrogated to make sure that everything is still there.

Prevent stop-and-go defragmenting

The Windows 98 Disk Defragmenter has a lot of problems dealing with other programs. You'll basically have to stop everything else to get it to run correctly.

Defrag before anything else runs

The Disk Defragmenter utility is very picky. If any other application changes the contents of the hard drive while it is running, it restarts. Sure, you can use your computer while Defrag is running, but just don't write a file to the hard disk. Also, screen savers are a constant irritant. Defrag stops as soon as they come on.

You may have programs in your StartUp folder that interfere with the operation of Defrag. You can force Defrag to start before anything else. In your \tools\mtsutil folder on your Windows 98 CD-ROM, you'll find the defrag.inf file. Right-click it and click Install. The next time you restart Windows 98, it will run Disk Defragmenter before anything else starts.

If you want this to happen again, you'll need to right-click this file and install it again. You won't need to issue any command when you restart Windows to start Defrag.

You can find out more about this utility, and lots of other handy utilities, by reading the mtsutil.txt file in the same folder.

Unfortunately, while Defrag starts first, all of the other applets that normally run at startup also get started. Because Defrag can have problems when other programs are running, it is best to close down everything that you can before you run Defrag.

You can start Disk Defragmenter in two ways: Start, Programs, Accessories, System Tools, Disk Defragmenter, or right-click a hard disk icon in your Explorer, click Properties, click the Tools tab, and then click the Defragment Now button. When you use the first method, the Disk Defragmenter begins by displaying the Select Drive dialog box. Clicking the Settings button in this dialog box brings up the Disk Defragmenter Settings dialog box (see Figure 20-22), which lets you change the way Defrag works. When you use the second method, the Select Drive dialog box doesn't appear automatically. To get to it, click Stop, Select Drive, Settings.

Figure 20-22: Whether the Disk Defragmenter Settings dialog box appears automatically depends on the method you use to start the Defragmenter.

The first check box optimizes your hard disk so that your most heavily and recently used programs start faster. You probably want to leave this setting marked, but defragmenting can take significantly longer when it's enabled, especially if you haven't defragmented in a while.

Stop everything else to run the Drefragmenter

You can set up the Disk Defragmenter to run before anything else gets a chance, as we detailed in the previous section. Another option is to stop everything else and let it run by itself.

The Disk Defragmenter restarts when something is written to the disk. When this happens, it quickly sees that a bunch of the hard disk has been defragmented and soon catches up with itself and continues defragmenting. Unfortunately, if some application keeps writing to the disk, the Defragmenter starts over and over again, and ends up getting nowhere fast. If this is happening to you, then it's best to stop everything else and let the Disk Defragmenter run the show.

To ensure that everything has stopped, take these steps:

STEPS:

Quieting Down the Computer to Run the Defragmenter

Step 1. Close all running programs. Right-click any Taskbar buttons and click Close. Right-click any icons in the system tray, and click Close, Exit, or an equivalent command. Press Ctrl+Alt+Delete, highlight a task other than Systray and Explorer, and click End Task. Repeat this process until only Systray and Explorer are left open.

You can ignore system tray icons that don't have Close, Exit, or equivalent commands.

Step 2. Right-click the Desktop and click Properties, and then click the Screen Saver tab. Display the Screen Saver field, scroll up to the top, and highlight (None). Click OK.

Step 3. Click Start, Settings, Control Panel, and Power Management. For both System Standby (if you have it) and Turn Off Hard Disks, choose Never. Don't worry about Turn Off Monitor. Click OK. If you want to save these settings, click Save As, and name the settings **Defrag**. Click OK.

Step 4. Click Start, Programs, Accessories, System Tools, Disk Cleanup. Choose which disk, and click OK. Mark the check boxes for the files that you will delete, and click OK.

Step 5. Right-click your Recycle Bin, click Empty Recycle Bin, and Yes. You don't need to do this if you emptied the Recycle Bin as part of the disk cleanup.

Continued

> **STEPS**
>
> Quieting Down the Computer to Run the Defragmenter *(continued)*
>
> **Step 6.**   Click Start, Programs, Accessories, System Tools, Disk
> Defragmenter, and OK. Let 'er run.

If you have installed Microsoft Office, you might find that the background program Find Fast, which builds an index of words in Word documents, is running without being obvious about it. Find Fast interferes with the Disk Defragmenter and makes it restart when it updates its index.

Before you run the Disk Defragmenter, you'll want to stop Find Fast. To do so, click Start, Settings, Control Panel, Find Fast. Click Index, Pause Indexing, and then OK.

Tip

If you have a power management setup in your BIOS, you may need to disable it there so that your computer doesn't go into Standby mode or wind down the hard disk. See "Let Windows do power management" in Chapter 22.

Turn off your screen saver automatically before defragmentation

While you still have to deal with your power management settings, you can run an applet that will automatically stop your screen saver if it notices that a disk maintenance utility has started up. If you run ScanDisk and Disk Defragmenter from the Task Scheduler, it is nice to be able to automatically close down your screen saver so that it doesn't interfere.

Tray Widget 98 has this automatic feature. Run it when you start up, and it sits in your system tray. Double-click it to bring up the menu shown in Figure 20-23. This menu lets you suspend your screen saver, disable it, or let Tray Widget stop it automatically.

Figure 20-23: The Tray Widget menu gives you several options for suspending your screen saver.

You'll find this shareware utility at www.windowspc.com/TrayWidget98/.

Take advantage of new hard drive technology

Progress marches on, and progress brings us new technologies. One technology that keeps changing is hard drives. As computers have gotten faster, hard drive controller manufacturers have tried to keep up by supporting ever-newer standards.

In the old days, when the IBM PC/AT sported a 16-bit bus, manufacturers developed the 16-bit ATA (or AT Attachment) standard for hard drive controllers. This standard is better known today as IDE (or Integrated Drive Electronics).

A new standard, ATA-2 — also known as Fast ATA or Enhanced IDE — introduced better Direct Memory Access (DMA) modes. These modes speed up disk reads and writes.

The latest IDE drive standard is variously called Ultra ATA, ATA-33, DMA-33, Ultra DMA, or simply UDMA. Ultra DMA theoretically can support a maximum burst mode transfer of 33.3 megabits per second (Mbps). (*Burst mode* is a non-sustained transfer rate over a very short period of time.)

This is an improvement over the 16.6 Mbps maximum rate for DMA transfers under the original IDE standard, although you won't actually hit these ideal speeds in real-life usage. For more information on these standards, see www.pcguide.com/ref/hdd/if/ide/std-c.html.

We used HD Tach, a utility that reports on hard disk performance, to test two hard drives, both with and without DMA enabled. One drive improved its read burst speed from 8.4 Mbps to 11.9. The other improved from 8.3 Mbps to 11.2. More important, the CPU utilization dropped from 83 percent to 29 percent on one drive, and from 61 percent to 20 percent on the other. Lowering the CPU utilization of a drive allows a computer to process more data or serve more users at the same time as disk files are being transferred.

HD Tach is available at tcdlabs.simplenet.com/hdtach.htm. The trial version of HD Tach tests your drives' read performance; the $49.95 registered version also tests write performance.

If your system's BIOS, chipset, and hard disk support UDMA, Windows 98 is supposed to automatically load driver support and enable bus-mastering DMA transfers when it is installed. If your system is DMA/UDMA capable but has not been configured to take advantage of DMA/UDMA, you may be able to improve your hard disk performance by enabling it.

We asked Microsoft for a definitive answer about whether Windows 98 does or does not automatically enable DMA. It turns out that the Windows DMA drivers, when installed for the first time, do *try* to enable DMA but may disable it if your system fails certain tests. Specifically, the drivers query the motherboard chipset, query the drive itself, and then test a short pattern of disk reads and writes to see if they are reliable at DMA speeds.

Microsoft spokesman Frank Kane put it this way:

> On a machine that is upgraded to Windows 98, we retain the DMA settings (or lack thereof) of the previous state. If it was Windows 95 Gold, DMA will be off. But if a user had an OSR2 [Windows 95B] machine and had turned on DMA, it will remain on in Windows 98...
>
> When users check the DMA box in Device Manager, sometimes it appears unchecked after the system reboot. In such a case, we have determined that at least one of the three criteria mentioned above have not been met, so the system is not suitable for DMA.

To test for yourself whether a drive supports DMA, see "Does your system support DMA?" later in this chapter. You can also run \tools\reskit\help\ rk98book.chm on the Windows 98 CD-ROM. Search on **PIO mode 4** and read the resulting topic.

Remove your Intel IDE driver

While Windows 98 comes with the drivers to support DMA capability, Windows 95 did not. If you downloaded an Intel Bus Master IDE driver from the Intel web site and installed it under Windows 95, when you update your computer to Windows 98, you'll probably run into problems. You'll find corrupted files due to improper timing of the DMA transfers. The Intel Bus Master IDE driver is not needed and doesn't work under Windows 98. You'll want to use the one supplied by Microsoft.

If you did install the Intel Bus Master IDE driver, you'll find that you can't remove it under Windows 98. In order to remove it, you'll need to download the latest version of the Intel Bus Master IDE driver. The installer program that comes with it allows you to uninstall the older version and replace it with the Microsoft driver. You'll find version 3.02 at developer.intel.com/ design/chipsets/drivers/busmastr/index.htm. You can find a discussion of this issue at www2.ldd.net/scribers/griz/intelbus.htm.

You'll also find drivers and an overview of the bus master problem at www.bmdrivers.com.

Does your system support DMA?

How can you tell if your computer will support DMA transfers to the hard disk? Intel claims that their 430 and 440 chipsets support DMA transfers via bus mastering of the IDE drives. Of course, if you have SCSI hard disks (as opposed to IDE drives), this doesn't apply to you.

You can check to see if you have this chipset by using a system information program such as Sandra. We discuss Sandra in "Add to your system info" in Chapter 26. If you have installed it, just double-click the Mainboard Information icon, as shown in Figure 20-24.

Scroll down in Mainboard Information window to display Chipset Information, as shown in Figure 20-25. If you find a listing under System Chipset whose last three numbers start with 43 or 44, then you have an Intel 430 or 440 chipset.

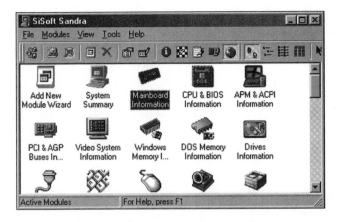

Figure 20-24: The Sandra user interface, with the Mainboard Information icon highlighted.

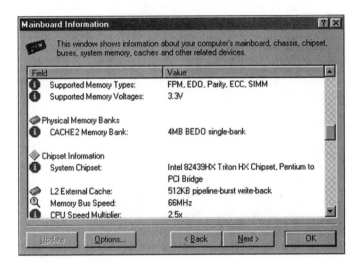

Figure 20-25: The chipset information appears about halfway down Sandra's Mainboard Information window.

One knowledgeable writer on the Microsoft support newsgroups, Jain Sandeep, claims that Intel 430TX or later chipsets are required to support DMA transfers, but this conflicts with Intel statements. We didn't resolve the conflict in our limited tests.

You'll need IDE hard disks that support DMA. If you have the manuals for your drives, you can see if the manufacturers bothered to inform you of this capability. You can check whether your drives support the *multiple-word DMA protocol* (that's what Microsoft calls it) by following the steps in the Microsoft Knowledge Base article "DMA Check Box Does Not Remain Checked" at support.microsoft.com/support/kb/articles/q159/5/60.asp.

You'll also need a computer BIOS that is Bus Master IDE aware. The BIOS should be in sync with the Intel chipset, and if the chipset supports bus mastering, so should the BIOS. You can check your BIOS settings to see if there is any indication of Bus Master or DMA support for IDE.

You can mark the DMA check box if you have one, as shown in Figure 20-26. To find it, press Win+Pause/Break (or right-click the My Computer icon and click Properties) to open the System Properties dialog box, click the Device Manager tab, click the plus sign next to Disk Drives, highlight your hard disk name, click the Properties button, and click the Settings tab. After you mark the check box and click OK, restart Windows.

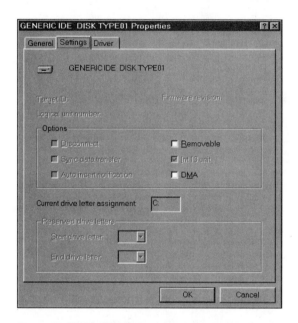

Figure 20-26: The DMA check box is in the Options area of the Settings tab in your hard disk's Properties dialog box.

You can look for one more reassuring sign that your computer can do DMA transfers to IDE devices. Open up your Device Manager, click the plus sign next to Hard Disk Controllers, and look for Intel 82371XX Bus Master IDE Controller, where XX is replaced by AB, EB, SB, and so on, as shown in Figure 20-27. If you find this, then you know your computer can do DMA transfers. If you see an entry such as Intel 82371AB/EB PCI Bus-Master IDE Controller, you have a UDMA-capable system. The entry Standard Dual PCI IDE Controller means you do *not* have bus-mastering drivers loaded.

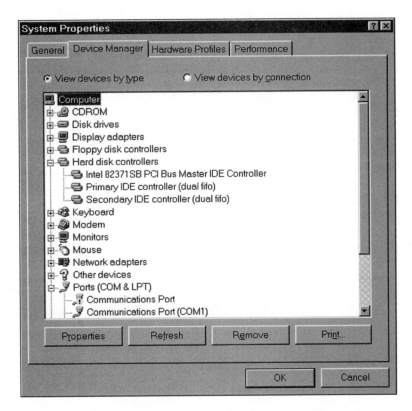

Figure 20-27: This computer is equipped with a UDMA-capable hard disk controller.

To mark or not mark the DMA check box

If you want to reduce the load on your processor due to hard disk reads and writes, then you want your hard disks operating in UDMA or DMA mode. Of course, you have to have hard disks, BIOSes, and hard disk controllers that support this.

While there seems to be continuing disagreement over whether marking the DMA check box is necessary to activate UDMA or DMA operation, given that your computer has this capability, you can test it yourself. When you install Windows 98, it is supposed to test your computer to see if it can use DMA, and implement it if it can. Windows 98 is supposed to leave the DMA check box cleared if your computer can't do it.

If Windows correctly identifies your IDE hard disks, and determines that they can't support DMA, you may find that you do not have a DMA check box at all.

If you press Win+Pause/Beak (or right-click the My Computer icon and click Properties), click Device Manager, double-click Hard Disk Controllers, and see that you have bus mastering installed, then Windows 98 should set up the drivers to handle UDMA and DMA. You can mark the DMA check box by double-clicking Disk Drives in the Device Manager, highlighting a hard disk drive, clicking Properties, clicking the Settings tab, and then marking the DMA check box.

You'll want to use a hard disk performance testing program such as HD Tach to compare how much of your processor is used when the DMA check box is marked versus cleared.

Microsoft's take on enabling IDE DMA

Microsoft provides a few paragraphs of help regarding implementing DMA with IDE drives under Windows 95 and Windows 98. Their method calls upon the user or OEM to edit an *inf* file, remove the enumerated and detected IDE devices from the Device Manager, and then mark the DMA check box. You are supposed to do this after you determine that your computer and hard disks can manage DMA. You'll find "Enabling IDE DMA on Windows-based Systems" at www.microsoft.com/hwdev/devdes/idedma.htm.

Bill Drake, a regular contributor to the Microsoft technical support newsgroups, looked further into the issue of updating *inf* files and the subsequent changes to the Registry. He concluded that revising the *inf* file is not enough to change the Registry, and that redetection of the hardware is required. Here is what he had to say:

> If the entries detailed in the "Enabling IDE DMA on Windows-based Systems" article properly exist in mshdc.inf — with the proper values to enable DMA/UDMA mode — then the file is correct as is. However, if the value-data has changed (for whatever reason), the actual info is not incorporated into the Registry until the hard disk controller entries are removed from the hardware tree and redetected.
>
> *Inf* info is not used by Windows 98 directly. When an *inf* entry is updated, the only way to make Windows 98 aware of the change is to delete/redetect that item.
>
> When you update a hardware item in Window 98, that change often results in changes to that particular hardware device's *inf* file entries. The changes to the *inf* file usually occur as part of a device driver update. However, to make the *inf* changes effective, the modifications must be incorporated into the Windows 98 Registry itself.
>
> To incorporate the change, Windows 98 must be forced to "see" that the hardware has changed. This will ensure the *inf* database is updated — and then the new data in the *inf* database will be consulted when the new piece of hardware is actually incorporated into the Registry.
>
> When you change an item in the hardware tree, and an *inf* file has been updated, you will see a dialog box with a progress-bar that says "Building Driver Information Database." At that point, you are building (or rebuilding) two files called DRVDATA.BIN and DRVIDX.BIN, which live in your C:\WINDOWS\INF folder along with most of your Windows 98 *inf* files.

The *bin* files are what Windows 98 actually consults when fiddling with hardware. The *inf* files are simply the raw "input" files that are compiled into the *bin* data files. If you have updated something, and you do not see the "Building Driver Information Database" item, then as far as Windows 98 is concerned, the *inf* entries have not changed since the last time the *bin* files were compiled/updated.

Consequently, if you know that something has changed, and you don't see the "Building" dialog, that update will not be reflected in your Windows 98 hardware tree until such time as the "Building" dialog is forced to appear.

Updating the *bin* files is normally driven by an "Add New Hardware" request — either manually through Control Panel or automatically through PnP. However, if you are not sure whether the *bin* files have been properly updated or not — you can go to the *inf* folder and manually delete the DRVDATA.BIN and DRVIDX.BIN files. This will force Windows 98 to recompile those files in their entirety the next time a request to update any driver is made.

Once you are sure you have a current copy of the *bin* data files, then the way you move the data from the *bin* files into the W9x Registry itself is to remove/redetect the piece(s) of hardware whose *inf* files were changed. This is the only way that improvements which require *inf* changes can be incorporated into the Windows 98 Registry itself.

Changing the *inf* or recompiling the *bin* files does not update the Registry, and only the Registry changes actually result in changes to the operation of that particular driver.

Bill goes on to say:

I puzzled out the *inf* methodology originally by zeroing the archive attributes in the *inf* folder and seeing what happened when an *inf* update went in. This was years ago, shortly after the W95 Gold release — when I was investigating just exactly what goes on during one of US Robotics' notorious modem *inf* updates.

Since then, I have investigated the methodology used for the various Intel chipset *inf*-compatibility updates for Windows 95, the various Adaptec SCSI Host Adapter *inf* updates for the 154x, 284x and 294x DMA bus master Host Adapters. Also, I've investigated the continuing US Robotics Sportster and Courier Modem *inf* updates, which have occurred through the development of X2 and now V.90, and finally the Intel and Microsoft DMA bus master updates for EIDE hard disk controller chipsets.

By comparing the similarities and differences between the various manufacturers' approaches — along with each manufacturer's specific installation instructions, I was eventually able to narrow down the common threads in each update procedure, and figure out what I thought was really going on. I then did a bunch of tests on my own system to establish what *inf* changes are reflected in the Registry, and when.

Since then, info released by US Robotics Technical Support has confirmed the specific methodology required to ensure an update is actually propagated into the Registry, but this was common knowledge in my technical support community long before USR posted their details.

Furthermore, continuing improvements to the algorithm used to detect changes to *inf* file contents in the *inf* and INF/OTHER folders has removed the necessity to manually delete the DRVDATA.BIN and DRVIDX.BIN files to "force" an update in the vast majority of cases.

However, when Microsoft is having a problem with compatibility (and the Windows 98 hard disk drivers are having a problem with this) it is common to find uncrossed t's and undotted i's in install procedures, which force the need for manual housekeeping of stuff that should be automatic.

There were similar compatibility problems with the early Windows 95 hard disk drivers. Microsoft went through several versions of the REMIDEUP.EXE patch as they found and fixed problems with the Windows 95 hard disk drivers, which eluded the original beta testers.

Furthermore, my experience has also shown me that the current Windows 95 REMIDEUP.EXE patch fixes many more problems than Microsoft officially admits in the Knowledge Base.

I expect a similar evolution for the Windows 98 hard disk drivers. We'll see this as developments in the DMA/UDMA implementation by hard disk manufacturers make it obvious that there is a need for better "bulletproofing" in the Windows 98 drivers to catch sloppy DMA/UDMA/ATAPI implementation in hard disk/CD-ROM/tape drive/Zip/LS-120 hardware.

Add to the above the relative "youth" of the Windows 98/NT driver model as well as the ACPI specification — and the three issues mentioned combine to create interactions the original driver designers could not anticipate (or find and fix) without extending the beta testing period into infinity.

Personally, I think Microsoft should have waited until they got the ACPI support working properly before releasing Windows 98. In my opinion, then they would have had time to find and bulletproof against the vast majority of the DMA/UDMA hard disk and EIDE controller bugs which are plaguing so many Windows 98 users. However, the above is not an absolute guarantee that the Windows 98 hard disk drivers would have been bulletproof from the get-go.

Microsoft admits that there is a problem with getting the information in *inf* files incorporated into the Registry, at least for Windows 95, in the Knowledge Base article "Hardware List Not Updated After Installing New .inf File" at support.microsoft.com/support/kb/articles/q139/2/06.asp.

Ultra DMA drives may have difficulties with Windows

Most UDMA drives, perhaps the great majority, work fine under Windows 98. But there seems to be a discernable minority of UDMA drives that have been installed in systems that aren't quite capable of supporting the maximum speeds that UDMA can produce. Problems can be caused by electromagnetic interference on the system bus, poor flow control in hardware or firmware, or inferior circuitry on the drive itself. In such cases, a drive can "time out," slowing the system and/or corrupting data files.

If you have a UDMA drive in a system that isn't quite up to speed (so to speak), you may experience one or more of the following difficulties when upgrading to Windows 98:

- Windows 98 fails during the plug and play process and won't complete the installation.

- After a successful installation, Windows 98 will only start in its very limited Safe mode.

- When transferring files, a drive appears to slow way down, and then speed up again. This may also pause or hang software or your keyboard and mouse.

- You start missing perfectly good files, or you lose the ability to access your hard drive at all.

- Windows 98 shut down takes much, much longer than normal.

Of course, these symptoms can be caused by many other problems. One of the frustrating things about UDMA difficulties is that they may be intermittent and hard to diagnose.

If your hard disk controller identifies itself as an Intel Bus Master IDE Controller, you should read developer.intel.com/design/chipsets/drivers/busmastr/dwnlod.htm. You may need to switch drivers — see "Remove your Intel IDE driver" earlier in this chapter.

Seagate Technology has prepared a fix for three early production versions of its Medalist Pro 7200 RPM hard drives. If a drive controller has been configured for UDMA support with these drives in Windows 95 and NT, and then Windows 98 is installed, the Windows 98 installation crashes. This also occurs with some other manufacturers' drives, and Seagate is to be commended for publicly posting on its web site the exact model numbers affected, and for offering a fix. See www.seagate.com/support/disc/faq/medpro_dma.shtml or call Seagate technical support at 405-936-1200.

Microsoft reports that a Windows 95 driver can cause computers to crash while accessing a hard drive using UDMA if a hardware error is encountered. The driver may also read or write incorrect data when a hard drive is recovering from a "suspend" state. You can correct both of these problems and others with an updated driver, available from support.microsoft.com/support/kb/articles/q171/3/53.asp.

Mark Stapleton, a mechanical engineer with Georgia Tech Research Institute, has done extensive research on this subject. By far the most frustrating problems, according to Stapleton, are intermittent crashes or data errors caused by UDMA transfers at speeds that are not quite reliable. He and others point to the old IDE cable that many PC manufacturers still use to connect drives to the motherboard. The cable is not shielded against electrical interference, which can be a problem at high transfer rates. The Circuit Assembly Corp. sells a special ATAS cable for $12.99 plus shipping that is well grounded and may solve this kind of trouble. See www.ultracable.com.

Trouble with IDE

Some Windows 98 users have noted performance problems with their IDE hard drives after they have installed new motherboards in their computers.

Windows 98 apparently doesn't detect the presence of some of the new hardware correctly, and could use a little help.

Check your IDE drive interface by pressing Win+Pause/Break (or by right-clicking the My Computer icon and clicking Properties). Click the Device Manager tab. Under Hard Disk Controllers, check if there is an exclamation point in a yellow circle for the primary and secondary IDE channels (if they are listed). If there is, click the Performance tab, and check if File System and Virtual Memory might be set to something other than 32-bit (see Figure 20-28).

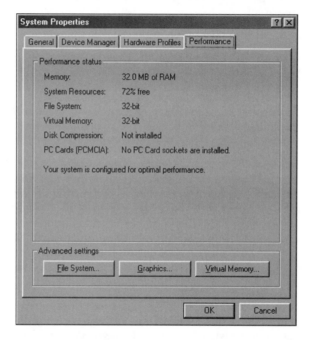

Figure 20-28: On this computer, the Performance tab indicates 32-bit for both File System and Virtual Memory. If you have different settings, it could indicate an erroneous Registry entry.

Secret

If you are experiencing both of the symptoms discussed in the previous paragraph, and you have IDE hard disk drives, it is likely the case that a NOIDE drive entry was placed in your Registry when Windows first unsuccessfully attempted to initialize the 32-bit hard disk driver.

To remove this entry, use your Registry editor to navigate to HKEY_LOCAL_MACHINE\System\CurrentControlset\Services\VxD\IOS. Remove the "NOIDE" string in the right pane, exit the Registry editor, and restart Windows.

You can learn more about this issue in these three Knowledge Base articles:

■ "Compatibility Mode Problems with PCI-IDE Controllers" at support/microsoft.com/support/kb/articles/q159/5/60.asp

■ "Troubleshooting MS-DOS Compatibility Mode on Hard Disks" at
support.microsoft.com/support/kb/articles/Q130/1/79.asp

■ "Secondary CMD Controller Not Recognized at Startup" at
support.microsoft.com/support/kb/articles/q159/5/56.asp

Fine-tune your caching and swapping

You can go beyond the defaults and limitations of the standard front ends to
customize your caching settings. You may also find a better place for your
swap file.

Front end for disk, file, and directory caching

Windows 98 sets aside chunks of memory for saving the current list of file
and directory names. As we describe in Chapter 33 of *Windows 98 Secrets*,
you can set how much memory is used for these tasks by pressing
Win+Pause/Break (or right-clicking the My Computer icon and clicking
Properties), clicking Performance, File System, and then choosing one of the
options in the Typical Role of This Computer drop-down list. The Network
Server option uses the largest amounts of memory (about 40K) for this task.

There is another tool you can use to set these values and cache an even
larger number of file and directory names. Cacheman, a disk and filename
cache utility, lets you incrementally determine the number of filenames and
directory names you will cache.

You use the lower two sliders to set the Name and Directory Cache values, as
shown in Figure 20-29.

The Cacheman settings are not displayed in the File System Properties dialog
box (see the first paragraph in this section), but the fact that the Cacheman
settings are being used is. Cacheman adds its key to the HKEY_LOCAL_
MACHINE\SOFTWARE\Microsoft\Windows\CurrentVersion\FS Templates
branch of your Registry so that it can tell Windows to set different values for
these cache settings.

You can also use Cacheman to set disk cache or vcache settings that are
normally set in System.ini, if you set them at all. Windows 98 normally uses
its dynamic memory to cache its disk reads. When this memory fills up, it
swaps the oldest disk reads out to the hard disk swap file.

You can limit how much memory Windows 98 uses for disk caching so that all
of the rest of your dynamic memory is managed by Windows 98 for its other
functions without bothering about disk caching. Depending on your usage,
this can increase your computer's performance.

The top three sliders in Cacheman allow you to set the disk cache minimum
and maximum size, as well as a memory chunk size, which has a minor
effect on system performance. Cacheman lets you choose from a list of
performance settings based on your usage, and then sets the slider values
for you. You can then manually move the sliders if you don't care for these
values.

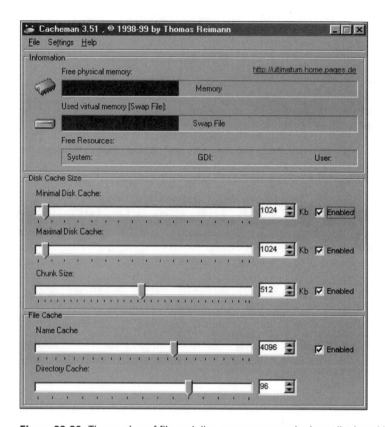

Figure 20-29: The number of file and directory names cached are displayed in the lower two right-hand boxes.

Cacheman writes the results of your changes (if you click File, Save) to the System.ini file. They take effect the next time you restart Windows.

We found a number of little bugs in Cacheman as well as in its help file. It also doesn't explain what is going on with the program, and why you would choose certain values. Nonetheless, it works and makes the correct changes in your System.ini file and Registry—changes that you could make manually, if you so desired.

You'll find this freeware program at members.xoom.com/ultimatum. Thanks again to Chris Pirillo at www.lockergnome.com.

Speeding up caching and swapping

The best way to speed up the performance of your computer is to add memory. This allows you to switch among already loaded programs and data much more quickly, because they will be more likely to be in the memory cache if they have been swapped out to the hard disk. Windows uses additional memory for caching what it swaps out, so with more memory, Windows 98 will find your programs and data in the memory cache and won't have to go to the hard disk to find them.

If you have two or more physical hard disks (not hard disk partitions or logical drives), you can get some additional performance by moving your Windows 98 swap file and your Internet Explorer cache folder to the other drive. This assumes that the other drive is little used, and pretty much dedicated to swapping and caching. The additional performance comes about because the other hard drive circuitry can handle some of the data transfer independently and not interfere with those data transfers happening on the primary drive.

To change the Windows 98 swap file location, follow these steps:

STEPS:

Managing Your Swap Space

Step 1. Right-click My Computer, choose Properties, and click the Performance tab.

Step 2. Click the Virtual Memory button to display the Virtual Memory dialog box.

Step 3. Choose Let Me Specify My Own Virtual Memory Settings, as shown in Figure 20-30.

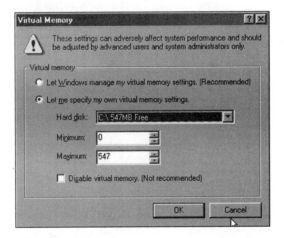

Figure 20-30: After you mark the second option button, you will be able to change the settings below it.

Continued

STEPS

Managing Your Swap Space *(continued)*

Step 4. Choose volume and size parameters. Click OK, click Yes when you see the warning about not letting Windows 98 manage virtual memory automatically, and click Close.

Step 5. Restart Windows 98.

To change your Internet Explorer cache location, follow these steps:

STEPS:

Changing Your Internet Explorer Cache Location

Step 1. Right-click the Internet Explorer icon on your Desktop, click Properties, and click the Settings button.

Step 2. Click the Move Folder button shown in Figure 20-31. This lets you specify a new folder on the second hard disk. You will lose all of your temporary Internet files and all of your offline web pages. You'll need to resynchronize your offline web pages again later.

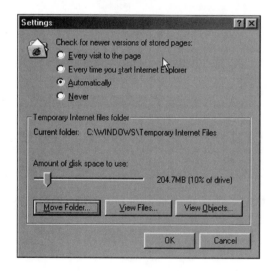

Figure 20-31: The Move Folder button lets you move your Internet Explorer cache.

Step 3. Choose a new folder on your secondary hard disk. Click OK, click OK, and then click Yes when asked if you want Windows to restart and finish moving your Temporary Internet Files folder.

Setting aside the swap file and the Temporary Internet Files folder

Windows 98 is quite happy to manage your swap file and your Temporary Internet Files folder without any interference or guidance from you. The only recommendation that Microsoft makes is that if you have a spare drive that is faster than your main drive and you aren't using it for anything else, you might think of putting the swap file there. We'll just bet that not too many of you are in this situation.

One option for speeding up Windows 98 and its associated applications is to cut down on the hard disk fragmentation that develops between defragmenting sessions. One way to do this is to stick the swap file in its own partition and put the Temporary Internet Files folder in another partition. If each of these folders is in its own partition, they won't place parts of themselves in every momentarily free portion of your main hard disk.

It's not worth the effort to repartition your hard disk with FDISK because it wipes out everything, but you can use Partition Magic to set up a couple of 200MB partitions that you can use to store these files. If you're setting up a new computer with a multi-gigabyte hard disk, you might consider setting aside a mere 400MB for these files.

You'll need to configure Windows 98 to use these additional partitions. To set the location of your swap file in the Virtual Memory dialog box, press Win+Pause/Break (or right-click the My Computer icon and click Properties), click the Performance tab, and click the Virtual Memory button. Mark Let Me Choose My Own Virtual Memory Settings, and then select the hard drive partition by volume name in the Hard Disk drop-down list (see Figure 20-32). Click OK, click Yes, click Close, and restart Windows.

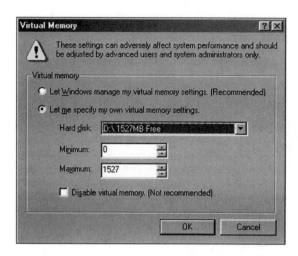

Figure 20-32: Select a partition from the Hard Disk drop-down list.

To change the location of the Temporary Internet Files folder, follow the Changing Your Internet Explorer Cache Location steps in the previous section.

Not enough room on a hidden or host drive?

You may receive messages that you are running out of space on a host or hidden drive, but when you run the Disk Cleanup utility, there are no files to clean up. Makes you wonder just what is going on.

You'll have a host drive if you've used disk compression (say DriveSpace 3) to create a compressed drive or a compressed volume file (CVF). The host drive, which can be and often is hidden, can be sized so that it has only a couple of megabytes free at most. The rest of its space is used by the CVF, and is given a different drive designator. You can read more about this in Chapter 33 of *Windows 98 Secrets*.

Secret

The Windows 98 Disk Cleanup utility may incorrectly and automatically find that the available space on the host drive is below a certainly threshold percentage and ask you to run the utility to delete certain files. When you run Disk Cleanup, you'll see that there are no files marked for deletion. And after you run it, you'll find that the free space on the drive hasn't changed.

This often happens after you install new software. What we think is going on here is that Disk Cleanup is incorrectly calculating the space that the temporary setup files used, and is assigning that space to the host drive instead of to the CVF. This reduces the amount of the free space on the host drive as seen by Disk Cleanup, and as a result it is automatically triggered to run.

You can stop this erroneous behavior by taking these steps:

STEPS:

Taming Disk Cleanup

Step 1.   Click Start, Programs, Accessories, System Tools, Disk Cleanup.

Step 2.   In the Select Drive dialog box, select the host drive in the Drives drop-down list (see Figure 20-33), and then click OK.

Step 3.   Click the Settings tab, and clear the check box (see Figure 20-34).

Step 4.   Click OK, and click Yes.

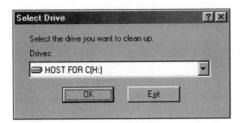

Figure 20-33: Select the host drive in the Drives field.

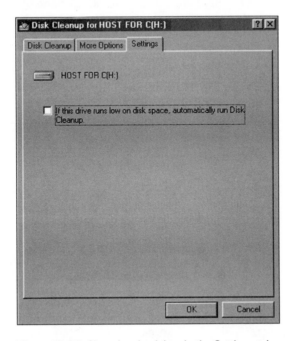

Figure 20-34: Clear the check box in the Settings tab.

Now you won't get any spurious messages about low disk space on a drive to which, in fact, you don't actually add any software or files.

About a month after I discovered how to solve this little problem, Microsoft posted a Knowledge Base article that gave the same answer. Always nice to have them come in second and back up my original idea.

Disable low disk space notification

You can disable low disk space notification altogether by eliminating the broadcasting of the message. You can do this for one drive or for a set of specific drives. You'll need to edit the Registry by taking these steps:

STEPS:
Stopping the Low Disk Space Message

Step 1. Click Start, Run, type **regedit**, and press Enter.

Step 2. Navigate to HKEY_LOCAL_MACHINE\System\CurrentControlSet\control\FileSystem. Highlight this key in the left pane of your Registry editor.

Step 3. Right-click the right pane, and click New, DWORD Value.

Step 4 Rename the DWORD value **DisableLowDiskSpaceBroadcast**.

Step 5. Double-click DisableLowDiskSpaceBroadcast, and enter a value from the following table to correspond with the disk drive whose low disk space message you want to stop:

Drive Letter	Data Value
A	1
B	2
C	4
D	8
E	16
F	32
G	64
H	128
I	256
J	512
K	1024
L	2048
M	4096
N	8192
O	16384

Drive Letter	Data Value
P	32768
Q	65536
R	131072
S	262144
T	524288
U	1048576
V	2097152
W	4194304
X	8388608
Y	16777216
Z	33554432

You can add the values to come up with a unique value for a set of drives. For example, a value to turn off the low disk space warning for drives C and D would be 12.

Step 6. Exit the Registry editor.

Completely clear your hard disk

Secret

Apparently the DOS command FDISK, used to partition your hard disk, does not completely update a disk partition after the first time it is used. You can force FDISK to completely start over. This is useful in removing Disk Manager, EZ Drive, or other non-standard disk partitioning schemes. You can also use it to remove any rr viruses.

You'll need to run a little debug script or a compiled program that incorporates the script. You can find the script at www.firmware.com/pb4ts/hdclear.htm. You can find the program, clearhd.com, on the accompanying CD-ROM. It is documented in clearhd.txt.

Thanks to Attila Szabo for getting this program written and Robert M. Whitworth for writing it.

You can completely clear the partition information in other ways as well. After further discussions with Attila, he came up with a list of web sites that speak to these issues and a list of URLs for other programs that provide this kind of service. Attila states, "I've used these three programs before, and they produce the same results in a roundabout way as the debug script or clearhd.com. I included the start web pages just for reference."

- IBM hard drive support at www.storage.ibm.com/techsup/hddtech/hddtech.htm. The Utilities link on this page leads to Zap at index.storsys.ibm.com/hddtech/utility/ZAP.ZIP.

- Western Digital hard drive support at www.wdc.com/support/. The WD Diagnostics link on this page leads to Wd_Diag (which replaced Wd_clear, it seems) at www.wdc.com/support/ftp/wddiag/wd_diag.exe.

- Quantum hard drive support at support.quantum.com/. The Software and Utilities link on this page leads to Zero Fill Utility at support.quantum.com/software/ZDISK101.EXE.

Summary

Help Windows run the big drives, convert to FAT 32, use UDMA, speed up your programs, defrag your drive, and cut down on wasted space.

▶ Fix Windows configuration problems with UDMA, DMA, and IDE drives.

▶ Put your swap file and Internet cache files in other partitions to cut down on fragmentation.

▶ Get rid of the bogus low disk space notification.

▶ Run a program to completely clear your old partition information.

Chapter 21

Managing Hardware

In This Chapter

We placed all sorts of secrets about pieces of your computer here, including ones related to input devices, the display, the CD-ROM drive, and so on. Most importantly, we discuss how to deal with interrupts, the bane of any Windows power user.

▶ Remap your keyboard to add a Win key and then add macros.

▶ Make it easier on your wrists by turning your mouse into a left-handed mouse. Add some left-handed mouse pointers.

▶ Add a power control to your display and video card.

▶ Increase the buffering on your fast CD-ROM drive.

▶ The Click of Death — trouble with Zip drives.

▶ Get more interrupts for your plug in cards.

Keyboards, mice, joysticks

They are near at hand, and they can be so much more useful.

Add a Windows key to your Windowless keyboard

The Windows keyboards are pretty cool because they give you two very useful keys that are well integrated with Windows 98. If you don't have a Windows keyboard (heck, they're only about $15), you can remap your existing keyboard to include a Windows key and a context menu key.

To do this, use the Keyboard Remap applet, one of a collection of applets in Microsoft's Kernel Toys. You can download Kernel Toys from chipsetwww. microsoft.com/windows95/downloads/default.asp. (Click the link for the Windows 95 Kernel Toys Set.)

STEPS:

Remapping Your Keyboard

Step 1. Download the executable file for Kernel Toys (W95krnltoys.exe) into a folder where you store files temporarily (we create our own permanent Temp folder). Click the file to extract its contents into the temporary folder.

Step 2. Right-click the Keyremap.inf file, and click Install. (If you see the Insert Disk dialog message box, click OK. Then in the Copying Files dialog box, click the Browse button, navigate to the folder that contains the downloaded files, click OK, and click OK.)

Step 3. Click Start, Settings, Control Panel, and click the Keyboard icon.

Step 4. Click the Remap tab, as shown in Figure 21-1.

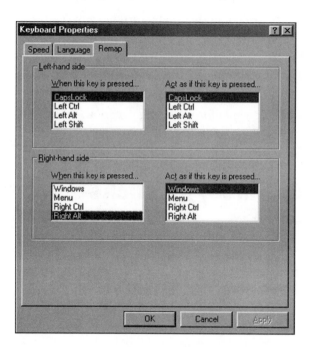

Figure 21-1: The Remap tab of the Keyboard Properties dialog box.

Step 5. In the Right-Hand Side area, select Right Alt in the When This Key Is Pressed list, and select Windows in the Act As If This Key Is Pressed list. Click Apply.

Step 6. Select Right Ctrl in the When This Key Is Pressed list, and select Menu in the Act As If This Key Is Pressed list. Click OK.

You have now created a Windows key and a context-menu key for your Windowless keyboard.

Thanks to Anthony Kinyon for pointing out this tip.

More Win key keyboard shortcuts

Microsoft defines a small set of useful shortcuts that use the Win key. In the previous section, we showed you how to use Microsoft's keyboard remapper to turn your right Alt key or Ctrl key into a Win key (or context-menu key).

Winkey! is a keyboard macro programmer that lets you define up to 200 macros that work with the Win key (combined with other keys), as shown in Figure 21-2. It takes 2MB of RAM, but RAM is cheap these days, so if you have plenty, and you'd like to use the Win key to speed things up, this freeware package may be your ticket.

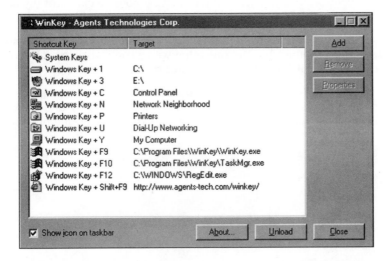

Figure 21-2: Winkey! lets you take full advantage of your keyboard's Win key.

Tip

Winkey! works fine with the Microsoft keyboard remapper, so you can define a Ctrl or Alt key as your Win key and then define key combinations with Winkey!

You'll find this not-so-little utility at chipsetwww.agents-tech.com/winkey/.

Scrolling with a three-button mouse

Windows 98 supports a two-button mouse and a two-button mouse with a scrolling wheel. It also supports a three-button mouse, turning the middle button into the equivalent of a scrolling wheel.

Move your mouse so that your pointer is near the middle of your screen. Click the middle mouse button once. A special panning pointer appears and remains at this original spot.

Now move your mouse up or down and the screen scrolls in the direction that you have moved your mouse. The further away from the panning pointer you move the mouse pointer, the faster the screen scrolls.

Thanks to Randy Linden for telling us about this tip.

Mouse left-handed

Have you ever thought of switching? We did, and have never looked back. You can imagine that it takes a bit of mousing around to write four books, plus respond to lots of e-mail from our readers. The old right hand gets plenty sore, and way overworked. Switching to left-handed mousing completely cleared up all of our repetitive stress problems. It took about two days to get used to using the left hand, but it soon became totally natural. Of course, if you're left-handed, you'll have even less trouble switching.

So you say that you have a mouse that is designed for the right hand? No worries, we've found that the ones that we've tried work great in your left hand. Check it out for a few days and see for yourself.

To switch to a left-handed mouse, click Start, Settings, Control Panel, Mouse, go to the Buttons tab, mark Left-Handed (see Figure 21-3), and click OK. Your index finger on your left hand will now click the number-one button.

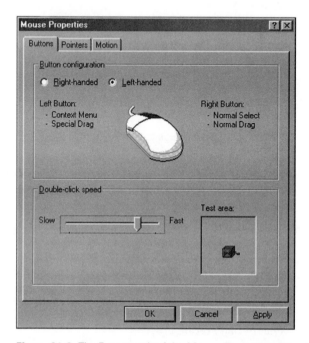

Figure 21-3: The Buttons tab of the Mouse Properties dialog box makes it easy to switch the "handedness" of your mouse, and tells you what each button does.

Use number-pad mouse keys together with the mouse

Under Accessibility Options in your Control Panel, Microsoft offers the option of using the numeric keypad to control your mouse pointer. What's cool about this is that you can use it in conjunction with your mouse. Turn your mouse into a left-handed mouse, and now you're controlling the mouse pointer with two hands.

If you don't find the Accessibility Options in your Control Panel, click Add/Remove Programs in the Control Panel. Click the Windows Setup tab, double-click Accessibility, and mark Accessibility Options to install them.

You can choose whether the numeric keypad controls the mouse pointer when NumLock is on or off. You can also turn this capability on or off using the MouseKeys shortcut, which appears in your system tray (see Figure 21-4).

Figure 21-4: The options at the bottom of the Settings for MouseKeys dialog box let you change the way the numeric keypad interacts with the mouse pointer.

Click Start, Settings, Control Panel, click the Accessibility Options icon, and click the Mouse tab. Mark the Use MouseKeys check box, and click the Settings button to display the dialog box shown in Figure 21-4. You can now use the slider bars to set the pointer speeds. If you use your numeric keypad for data entry, mark the Off option button. If you use it for navigation keys, mark the On option button.

Now you can use the mouse keys and your mouse at the same time to control the mouse pointer.

Left-handed mouse pointers

We use the left-handed mouse all the time. It really helps keep the work spread evenly between both hands.

Ever notice that the arrow mouse pointers point to the upper-left corner? Left-handed pointers would point to the upper-right corner. You could edit your pointers to point in the right direction, or you can download some from chipsetwww.stanback.net/.

These pointers at this web site are very basic. If you are interested in editing pointers, animated pointers, or icons, then an icon editor and a library program are the answer. We include a couple of them on our *Windows 98 Secrets* CD-ROM. The library programs search through all of your files that contain icons, including pointers, and create a library so that the icons are easy to get to (see the next section).

Animated pointers are made up a series of individual frames, each of which must be edited. Changing a pointer from right-handed to left-handed just involves a mirrored flip. This is a simple one-step operation in an icon and pointer editor. For example, we used IconEdit Pro to flip the pointer arrow shown in Figure 21-5.

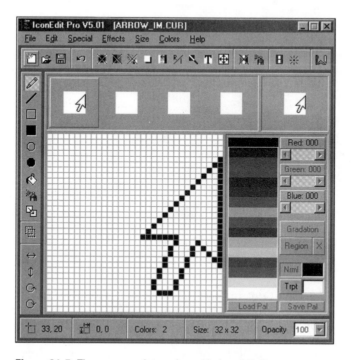

Figure 21-5: The mouse pointer, viewed in IconEdit Pro.

You'll find IconEdit Pro at chipsetrainbowpcm.com/icon_edit_pro.html.

Icon library generator

If you are going to edit icons as well as pointers, you will need an icon library generator that can gather up all of the existing icons on your hard disk and place them in an easily accessible library or libraries. Pointers, both static and animated, are much easier to find than icons because they exist in standalone files with recognizable extensions.

EasyIcons 98 generates icon libraries and includes Icon Easel, which you can use to edit icons, static pointers, and animated pointers. You can drag and drop a folder onto EasyIcons, and it will search all of the files in the folder and subfolders for icons. It then places the icons in a library, as shown in Figure 21-6.

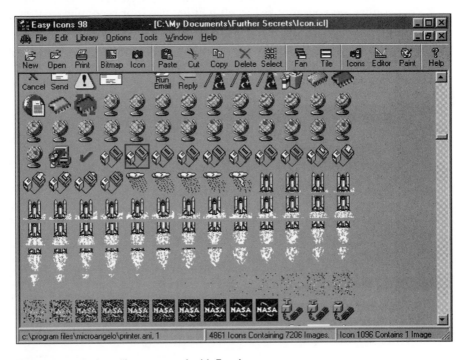

Figure 21-6: An icon library created with EasyIcons.

You'll find EasyIcons 98 at chipsetwww.easyapps.com. If you put a few thousand icons into one library, it will take a while to save them — quite a while. You might think about breaking up the libraries into smaller chunks.

Left-handed PenPartner

Wacom makes a wonderful and inexpensive digital tablet, the PenPartner, which lets you draw (and mouse) with a stylus. I find it very difficult to drag with a mouse, and I much prefer using the stylus. The stylus acts as a mouse also, so you can run any program with it (although not as easily as with a mouse).

The PenPartner is powered off a PS/2 or keyboard port, but it also connects to a serial port. If you have a portable computer, it may not put out enough power to power both the PenPartner and the keyboard. Other more expensive tablets are available from Wacom that have their own power supplies.

The PenPartner can work in conjunction with a mouse, and you can plug in both at the same time, using the stylus in one hand and the mouse in the other. Well, almost. The PenPartner driver won't let you run the mouse in left-hand mode and the PenPartner in right-hand mode. This is crucial for a stylus, because the left-mouse button on a stylus is the pen point. If you have configured your mouse for left-handed use (our recommendation), the stylus works as a right mouse button. Not good.

Wacom provides drivers for some of its other, more expensive, tablets that allow for left-handed mice and right-handed pens, but not for the PenPartner. This seems a bit shortsighted to us. Of course, they don't tell you about this in any of their literature or on their support web site.

You can check out the PenPartner at chipsetwww.wacom.com.

No joy from your joy stick

If you're getting no response from your joystick, you might check out the Microsoft Knowledge Base article "How to Troubleshoot a GamePort Joystick" at chipsetsupport.microsoft.com/support/kb/articles/q141/8/54.asp.

The display

Microsoft provides some tools for manipulating your display, but they are pretty limited. We give you access to quite a few more.

Getting a bigger picture

We include a couple of freeware screen magnifiers on the *Windows 98 Secrets* CD-ROM. Microsoft also provides a nifty little magnifier with Windows 98 that has the unfortunate habit of moving your Desktop icons. Takes forever to get them back into place.

You can get to the Microsoft Magnifier by clicking Start, Programs, Accessories, Accessibility, Magnifier. You may not have installed it, so it may not be there. If it's not, click Start, Settings, Control Panel, Add/Remove Programs, Windows Setup, Accessibility, Details, and then mark Accessibility Tools in the Accessibility dialog box, as shown in Figure 21-7.

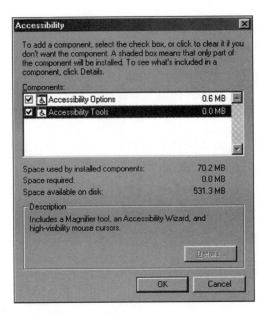

Figure 21-7: Mark the Accessibility Tools check box to install Microsoft Magnifier.

To start the Magnifier, click Start, Accessories, Accessibility, Magnifier. If you don't have this Start menu item, you can also start the Magnifier this way: In your Explorer click Help, Help Topics, Index, type **mag**, double-click Magnification level, and click Click Here. Up comes the Magnifier.

One thing that is neat about the Microsoft Magnifier is that it shows the mouse pointer. Sure would be nice if it didn't take up the whole top of the screen though.

Screen Loupe is a shareware screen magnifier that is quite a bit more advanced, although it doesn't show the mouse pointer, as you can see in Figure 21-8.

With lots of options, as shown in Figure 21-9, this clever and well-programmed little goody is for Windows spies who want to see exactly what is going on in those pixels.

Screen Loupe will let you capture a view to the Clipboard so that you can save it as a graphic, it displays your mouse pointer position even while minimized, and you can lock a view so that it is displayed while you still move the mouse pointer.

Figure 21-8: A sample Screen Loupe view, magnified to 2x.

Figure 21-9: The General tab of Screen Loupe's Options dialog box shows some of its capabilities.

You can display horizontal and vertical pixel rulers at any position and length across your Desktop (see Figure 21-10) to determine the size of any visual element. You can also pop up a window of ASCII codes or Windows error codes, and display the current level of resources.

Figure 21-10: Screen Loupe lets you display a ruler like this one on your Desktop.

You'll find Screen Loupe at chipsetwww.execpc.com/~sbd.

Quickly change your display resolution and color depth

The Quick Res utility that came with the Windows 95 PowerToys has been incorporated into the standard Windows 98 package. Now you can quickly change your display resolution and color depth by clicking a system tray icon and choosing from among the values shown in Figure 21-11.

Figure 21-11: You access this context menu via the Display Settings icon.

What if you don't see this icon in your system tray? You can turn it on by taking these steps:

STEPS:

Turning on the Display Settings Icon

Step 1. Right-click the Desktop, click Properties, and click the Settings tab.

Step 2. Click the Advanced button to display the Display Properties dialog box, shown in Figure 21-12.

Continued

STEPS

Turning on the Display Settings Icon *(continued)*

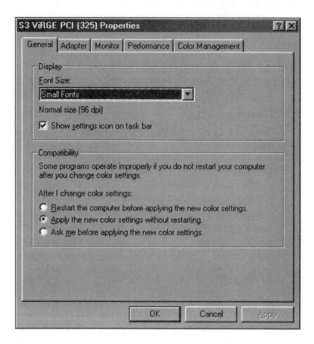

Figure 21-12: The Display Properties dialog box.

Step 3. Mark the Show Settings Icon on Task Bar check box. Click OK.

Set your display/video adapter refresh rate

If you have a plug and play video adapter and monitor, then Windows 98 can set the optimum video refresh rate for your combination of card and display. You may be able to check what Windows has selected and choose from a limited range of other options. To do so, take these steps:

STEPS:

Changing the Video Refresh Rate

Step 1. Right-click the Desktop, click Properties, and click the Settings tab.

Step 2. Click the Advanced button to display the Properties dialog box for your display, and click the Adapter tab, as shown in Figure 21-13.

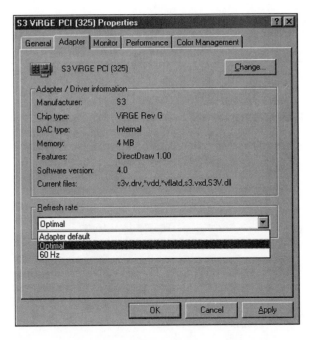

Figure 21-13: The Adapter tab shows the settings for your display adapter.

Step 3. See if you have a Refresh Rate drop-down list. If you do, you can continue on to step 4. If you don't, you won't be able to adjust this setting.

Step 4. Display the Refresh Rate drop-down list and pick a refresh rate. Click Apply. Your screen will now go black and then come back as the refresh rate is adjusted. You can choose to keep the new refresh rate if your Desktop looks good.

As you'll notice in Figure 21-13, the Adapter tab may not give you any indication of what your actual refresh rate is. Since the refresh rate of a monitor is a big selling point, it might be nice to know if you are getting what you paid for.

PowerStrip, described later in this chapter in "Get control of your monitor and video card," tells you what your current refresh rate is and lets you choose a specific value for the refresh rate. If PowerStrip correctly detects your video card and monitor model, it will display the supported refresh rates. To choose a specific refresh rate with PowerStrip, take these steps:

STEPS:

Changing the Video Refresh Rate with PowerStrip

Step 1.   Click the PowerStrip icon in the system tray, and then click PowerStrip Configuration.

Step 2.   Check the Refresh rate displayed at the bottom of the PowerStrip Configuration dialog box, as shown in Figure 21-14. This is your current refresh rate. Click Cancel.

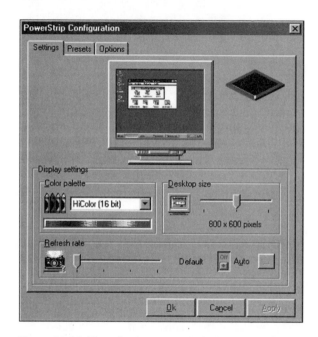

Figure 21-14: The refresh rate area is in the lower part of PowerStrip's Settings tab.

Step 3.   Click the PowerStrip icon in the system tray, and choose Advanced Options, Graphics System Information.

Step 4.   Scroll down the Display Modes Supported list to see a complete list of the display modes supported by your video card/monitor combination (see Figure 21-15). Choose a supported refresh rate, resolution, and color depth by double-clicking one of the values in this list. Click Close.

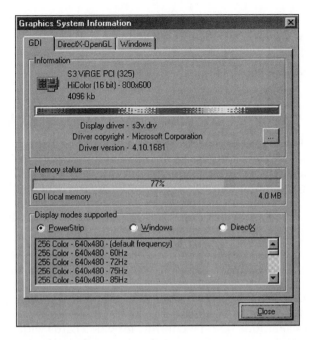

Figure 21-15: Select a display mode from the list in the Graphics System Information dialog box.

Don't restart Windows when you change your monitor properties

Some changes in screen properties request a restart of Windows before the changes take effect. You may be able to get your computer to make the changes without restarting Windows.

STEPS:

Making Monitor Changes without Restarting Windows

Step 1. Right-click your Desktop, click Properties, Settings, Advanced, and Performance.

Step 2. Mark the Apply the Changes Without Restarting check box.

Step 3. Click OK. Click OK.

You may not have this check box in your Performance tab. If you don't, you won't be able to make this change. Also, older analog monitors do not support this capability.

Thanks to Penelope Baker for help with this tip.

Get control of your monitor and video card

Sometimes the Display Properties dialog boxes just don't provide enough control and feedback about the capabilities of your video card and monitor combination. EnTech Taiwan produces a truly super utility that lets you control your monitor and video card from the Desktop. It appears that most of EnTech's income is from sales to video card and monitor manufacturers who want to give customers a powerful tool for controlling their products.

PowerStrip is a very professional package with a great online overview that runs automatically the first time you start it. The overview highlights PowerStrip's capabilities — easy access to resolution, font size, and refresh rates settings. PowerStrip's features include display power management for Windows NT 4.0, hot keys to switch display resolutions, screen adjustment controls (such as those under your monitor bezel), custom refresh rates, color calibration, and TV controls for video cards with NTSC/PAL codecs on the chip. In addition, PowerStrip offers optimization of DirectX and OpenGL parameters, 3D accelerator support, multi-monitor support, and PCI diagnostics. And that isn't all.

PowerStrip sits in your system tray. Right-click it and click Show PowerStrip to display the toolbar shown in Figure 21-16.

Figure 21-16: The PowerStrip toolbar.

PowerStrip is not limited to the buttons in the toolbar. It offers numerous other functions as well, including screen adjustments, redefining the mouse pointer, and power management (see Figure 21-17).

You'll find PowerStrip at chipsetwww.entechtaiwan.com/.

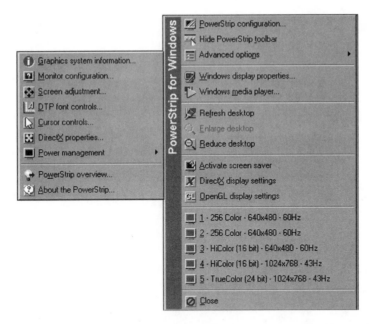

Figure 21-17: Double-click the PowerStrip icon in your system tray to select from this menu.

Newer video drivers for the Acer video chipsets

Video card manufacturers update their drivers frequently to clear up reported bugs and take advantage of new Direct Video software from Microsoft. You can normally update your video card or chipset by clicking Start, Settings, Windows Update, and downloading the latest video driver from the Microsoft Windows Update support site.

You can also check with your video card/chipset manufacturer to see if they have the latest video driver.

The standard Windows 98 drivers on the Windows 98 CD-ROM do not correctly support video cards that use the 1740 AGP chipset if the computer's motherboard uses the Ali M1541 AGP system controller. With the standard Windows 98 video drivers, the video card can't display its full resolution and color depth. This affects the Addonics card from Acer Group.

You can download the latest AGP driver from Acer labs at chipsetwww. acerlabs.com or chipsetwww.ali.com.tw.

STEPS:

Upgrading Your AGP Driver

Step 1.   Right-click your My Computer icon, click Properties, and click the Device Manager tab. Double-click Display Adapters.

Step 2.   Highlight your existing video driver, and click the Remove button.

Step 3.   Drag the new video driver executable file that you have downloaded to a temporary folder. Click the file.

Step 4.   Click Start, Shut Down, Restart, and OK.

Step 5.   Let Windows 98 automatically detect your video card as a standard VGA card.

Step 6.   Right-click the Desktop, click Properties, and click the Settings tab.

Step 7.   Click the Advanced button, and click the Adapter tab. Click the Change button and use the Update Device Driver Wizard to select the Ali driver.

Thanks to Daniel Song for help with this tip.

What's the point of two monitors?

Somebody must want this feature, because Microsoft used an awful lot of resources to make it available. Here's something you can do with the second monitor if you have a constant connection to the Internet.

Use the second monitor as a real-time monitor. Right-click the Desktop on the second monitor, click Active Desktop, and View As Web Page. Place active components on the Desktop, such as stock tickers, timely updated news web pages, and so on.

Drag over your e-mail client and have it check for e-mail periodically. You'll be able to read your e-mail or check the stocks while you are working on your other monitor.

If you are doing development work, set the resolution of the second monitor at a different resolution than your primary monitor. You can check your web pages or dialog boxes on the lower or higher resolution monitor to see how they look.

Thanks to Jamie Sanchez for pointing us toward these tips.

Which monitor is which

Once you spread your Desktop across multiple monitors and hook them up to various video cards (which actually determine which is which), you might forget what's connected to what. Here's how to get back to where you started:

STEPS:

Make the Monitors Identify Themselves

Step 1.   Right-click the Desktop, click Properties, and click the Settings tab.

Step 2.   You'll see icons representing multiple monitors. You can move these icons around to reflect the physical location of the actual monitors. But, that is what you are trying to remember. So...

Step 3.   Right-click one of the monitor icons, and click Identify. A number will appear on the monitor.

Thanks to Steve Ellmore for help on this tip.

CD-ROMS and removable drives

These types of drives have been slowly integrated into the Windows world, but often with a few rough edges. We show you how to tweak some of the unlisted settings.

Increase your look-ahead buffer for fast CD-ROM drives

Secret

If you use your CD-ROM drive extensively, it could be worth it to increase the amount of RAM memory that you allocate to the buffer (often referred to as the *pre-fetch buffer* or *look-ahead buffer*) for reading data from the drive. Windows 98 lets you indirectly set the size of the buffer, but you can edit your Registry to increase the size of the cache and the buffer to correspond to faster CD-ROM drives.

Your CD-ROM drive needs to use the Windows 98 CDFS (32-bit Compact Disc File System) for this to be worthwhile. If your drive runs in MS-DOS compatibility mode, none of these changes will do anything useful. To determine whether your CD-ROM drive is using the CDFS driver, right-click your My Computer icon, click Properties, and click the Device Manager tab. If *CD-ROM* is listed directly below *Computer* at the top of the device list, then Windows is using the CDFS driver.

To see how you normally change the size of the CD-ROM cache and pre-fetch buffer, take these steps:

STEPS:

Changing the CD-ROM Cache and Pre-Fetch Buffer Size

Step 1. Right-click your My Computer icon and click Properties (or press Win+Pause/Break), and click the Performance tab.

Step 2. Click the File System button, and click the CD-ROM tab.

Step 3. Move the Supplemental Cache slider to the left and right, and read off the amount of cache that corresponds to each position, as shown in Figure 21-18.

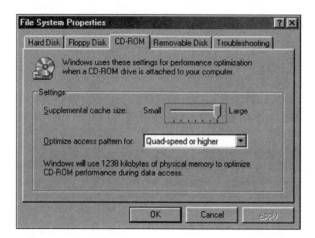

Figure 21-18: As you move the slider bar from Small to Large, the corresponding cache size is listed at the bottom of the Settings area.

Step 4. Display the Optimize Access Pattern For drop-down list to change the size of the pre-fetch buffer corresponding to the speed of your CD-ROM drive. Notice that it doesn't go any higher than quad speed. Newer CD-ROM drives are 32x speed.

Step 5. Click Cancel twice to close the dialog boxes.

While the File System Properties dialog box allows you to change these values within a restricted range, you can edit your Registry (or merge in a *reg* file) to directly change the values to correspond to your hardware. Larger values for the buffer and cache will take larger chunks of memory, so make sure that you have plenty to start with, and then test your configuration after restarting Windows.

STEPS:

Editing CD-ROM Cache and Pre-Fetch Buffer Size in Your Registry

Step 1. Start your Registry editor. Navigate to HKEY_LOCAL_MACHINE\ System\CurrentControlSet\Control\FileSystem\CDFS.

Step 2. Double-click the value in the right pane of your Registry editor that you want to change, and then edit the value in the Edit DWORD Value dialog box.

Step 3. Depending on whether you upgraded Windows 95 to Windows 98 or started with a clean or new computer, you will have either hexidecimally formatted or decimally formatted DWORD values (see Figure 21-19). Notice that the decimal value is in parenthesis.

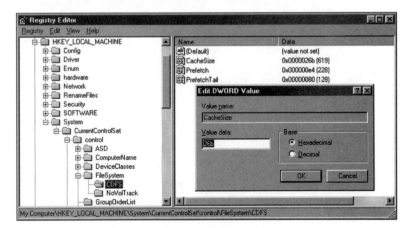

Figure 21-19: The Edit DWORD Value dialog box shows whether the data is in hexadecimal or decimal format.

Continued

STEPS

Editing CD-ROM Cache and Pre-Fetch
Buffer Size in Your Registry *(continued)*

Step 4. To change your cache value, double-click CacheSize and type the value in the Value Data field of the Edit DWORD Value dialog box, using Table 21-1 as a reference:

Table 21-1   CacheSize Registry Values

Cache Size	Decimal	Actual Cache Size (KB)	Hex
[Default]	619	1238	26b
Medium	1238	2476	4d6
Large	2476	4952	9ac

Step 5. To edit the value for your pre-fetch buffer, double-click Prefetch and make the change, using Table 21-2 as a reference:

Table 21-2   Pre-Fetch Buffer Registry Values

CD-ROM Speed	Decimal	Hex	DWORD
4x [Default]	228	e4	000000e4
8x	448	1c0	000001c0
16x	896	380	00000380
24x	1344	540	00000540
32x	1792	700	00000700

Step 6. Click OK to close the Edit DWORD Value dialog box, close the Registry editor, and restart Windows to see how the changes affect your CD-ROM speed and memory use

You may find speed improvement when playing video clips (*avi, mov, mpeg*), running multimedia apps, or copying large files from your CD-ROM. This may not be the case with graphics-intensive games because most games use their own disk read-ahead technologies, which work independently from the Windows pre-fetch buffer and cache values.

Thanks to Anthony Kinyon for pointers on this secret.

DMA, UDMA, and CD-ROM

DMA, direct memory access, allows quicker access to hard drives and CD-ROM drives. Not all hard disk or CD-ROM controllers support DMA.

Secret

UDMA CD-ROM drives seem to conflict with DMA. Users have reported that with both UDMA and DMA operating, UDMA CD-ROM drives work but cannot play audio CDs.

If you turn off either DMA or UDMA, the problems disappear. To turn off DMA, right-click your My Computer icon, click Properties, click the Device Manager tab, double-click your CD-ROM driver, click the Settings tab, and clear the DMA check box if you have one (see Figure 21-20).

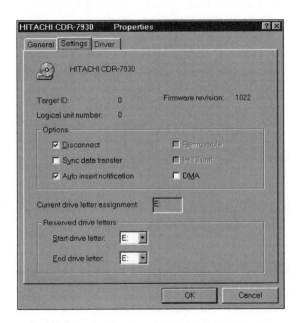

Figure 21-20: The DMA check box in the Settings tab has been cleared.

Thanks to Don Lebow for giving us guidance on this secret.

Copy files from "foreign" CD-ROMs

Secret

It is possible to read files on CD-ROMs that were written by other operating systems, as long as they were written to the ISO standard. Some of the filenames on the CD-ROM may not be compatible with the Windows or DOS standard. However, even if this is the case, you can still copy the files from the CD-ROM to your hard disk.

Using the method detailed in these steps, you can copy all the files whose names comply with the standard using one command. Then go back and individually copy those files whose names don't comply, one at a time.

STEPS:

Copying Files with Xcopy

Step 1. Click Start, Programs, MS-DOS Prompt.

Step 2. Type the following command, making changes to match your CD-ROM letter designator and the target folder on your hard disk:

```
Xcopy /c d:\*.* c:\targetfolder
```

The /c switch allows Xcopy to continue after encountering a bad filename.

Step 3. Copy individual files from the CD-ROM using the Copy command to rename them one at a time. For example:

```
Copy d:\badfilename c:\targetfolder\goodfilename
```

Thanks to Matthew Berryman for pointing out this tip.

Learn about CD-ROM drives

Would you like to know more about CD-ROMs before you purchase a computer or CD-ROM drive? If so, check out "18 Questions to Ask Before Purchasing a CD-ROM" at the Plextor site (see Figure 21-21). You'll find the page at chipsetwww.plextor.be/english/18qie.htm.

Windows 98 and real-mode CD-ROM drivers

The issue of accessing the CD-ROM drive when in MS-DOS mode or Safe mode has been a bugaboo right from the beginning with Windows 95. Microsoft supplanted the real-mode CD-ROM drivers that came with Windows 3.1 and DOS with 32-bit drivers that worked great when Windows 95 or 98 started up, but couldn't help you when you went to DOS before or after Windows.

We have covered quite a bit of this territory in *Windows 98 Secrets*, and we discuss it in this book in "Windows 98 boot diskette" in Chapter 16, so it doesn't make sense to cover it again here. We just want to point you toward a set of Microsoft Knowledge Base articles that discuss this matter in great detail.

The main issue is that you have to call the real-mode CD-ROM driver from your Config.sys file, and you must also call the Mscdex.exe file from your Autoexec.bat file. As long as you have the correct CD-ROM driver for your CD-ROM, or a semi-universal driver supplied by Microsoft, and you have made the correct switch settings, you'll be able to access your CD-ROM drive. It's getting to that point that's the hard part.

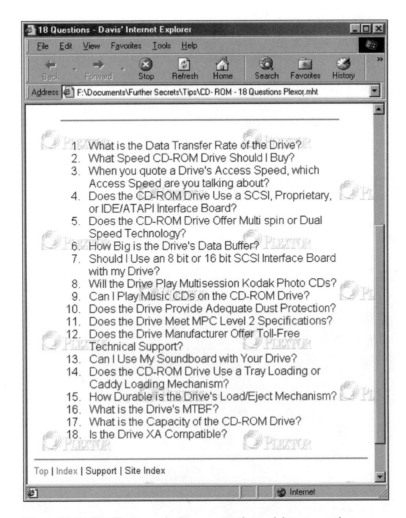

Figure 21-21: The Plextor web site answers these eighteen questions.

You can start with "Cannot Access CD-ROM Drive from MS-DOS Mode or Command Prompt" at chipsetsupport.microsoft.com/support/kb/articles/ q135/1/74.asp. This article shows you how to install both your real-mode driver and Mscdex.exe.

To see whether you can just use the real-mode CD-ROM drivers off the Windows 98 CD-ROM, check out "How to Use Real-Mode CD-ROM Drivers from Windows 98 Startup Disk," which you'll find at chipsetsupport. microsoft.com/support/kb/articles/q190/3/03.asp.

For a discussion about specific hardware that requires real-mode CD-ROM drivers, you can follow a link in the above article to "CD-ROM Drives Requiring Real-Mode Drivers," at chipsetsupport.microsoft.com/support/ kb/articles/q131/4/99.asp. Other links in the previous article provide additional guidance.

If you can't access your CD-ROM when in Windows Safe mode, you'll need to first configure your Config.sys and Autoexec.bat files as described in the article "How to Use Real-Mode CD-ROM Drivers from Windows 98 Startup Disk."

Next, you'll need to boot your computer to the DOS prompt. Hold down the Ctrl key after you restart your computer until the Windows Startup menu appears, and choose Command Prompt Only. Start Windows in Safe mode by typing **win /d:m** at the DOS prompt and pressing Enter.

Test your CD-ROM drive

If you have a CD-ROM drive, why not test it to be sure that you're getting all the performance that you've paid for? You can download a very nifty testing tool, the CD-ROM Drive Analyzer, shown in Figure 21-22.

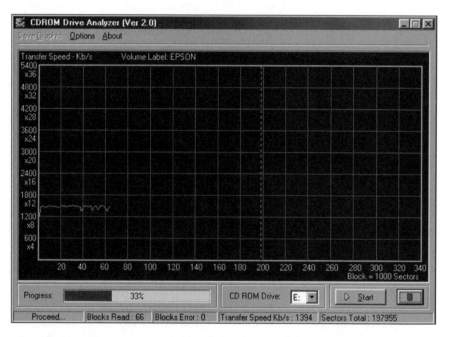

Figure 21-22: This chart displays the results of the CD-ROM Analyzer's performance tests.

Let the CD-ROM Analyzer run for a few minutes to build up a graphical record of its results. You'll find it at chipsetwww.geocities.com/ResearchTriangle/ Lab/1228/cdan_e.html.

Trouble with Zip and Jaz cartridges and drives?

Secret

Does your Zip or Jaz drive emit a series of clicking sounds when you first insert a cartridge or when you attempt to read or write data? If so, you may be experiencing the "Click of Death," a symptom of future serious problems with your drive and/or cartridge.

According to Steve Gibson:

> Iomega Zip and Jaz drives cause Click of Death by incorrectly writing to their removable media. This miswriting can damage the user's data, the factory-written low-level formatting, the head's positioning servo information, and the proprietary "Z-Tracks" that are used internally to manage and maintain the Zip and Jaz drive's cartridge data.
>
> The clicking sound itself is nothing more than the sound of the heads being retracted from the cartridge into the drive and then immediately reinserted. This deliberate strategy is employed by the drive when it is having trouble locating, reading, or writing any of the cartridge's data. This removal and reinsertion of the heads recalibrates the head positioning mechanism, "scrubs" the heads to remove excessive oxide deposits, and eliminates electrostatic charge build-up on the heads.

There have been extensive discussions of this problem. You can follow them and check out many of the web sites dedicated to the subject by first going to Steve's site at chipsetwww.grc.com/clickdeath.htm and following the links to "What Else Has Been Written About the Click of Death?"

If you are experiencing this problem, Steve has a couple of answers for you. You can download a freeware Zip and Jaz drive and cartridge-testing program with a cute name, Trouble In Paradise (TIP), from his site. Use this program to see if your drive is damaging your cartridges (see Figure 21-23). If it is, you'll need to replace your drive before you can attempt to recover lost data. (Apparently Iomega will replace your drive even if it is not under warranty if you are experiencing these problems.)

Trouble In Paradise will also check to see if you have the latest ASPI (Advanced SCSI Programming Interface) driver. These drivers are used by Zip and Jaz drives, as well as SCSI CD-ROMs, tapes, scanners, and other devices.

If Trouble In Paradise finds that you don't have this driver, it provides you with a link to download the latest version from Steve's site. You can get there yourself by going to chipsetwww.grc.com/freestuff.htm.

Unfortunately, you will find that Adaptec has forced Steve to quit offering this service, as you will see at his site. However, Steve is attempting to come up with a new way to address the issue of providing ASPI drivers, and he may have found a solution by the time you visit his site.

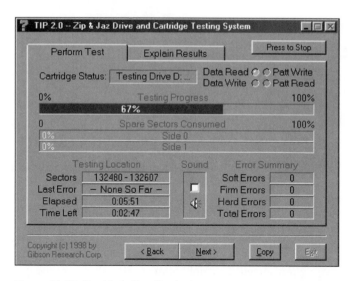

Figure 21-23: Trouble In Paradise in the process of testing a Zip drive.

If you have damaged Jaz or Zip cartridges, and you've replaced your malfunctioning drive, you can use SpinRite 5.0 (here's where the money comes in) to recover the data from the damaged cartridges. This is all discussed at Steve's site, and you can decide for yourself whether this is what you need to do.

Upgrade to Windows 98 around the Zip drive programs

Secret

The Windows 98 upgrade from Windows 3.1 doesn't catch everything that might be in your Autoexec.bat file that could negatively affect the performance of Windows 98. You need to go through the Autoexec.bat and Config.sys files and make sure to remark out or remove outdated drivers if the Windows 98 upgrade has not correctly done so.

One program that the upgrade appears to miss is the Iomega Zip Tools Guest.exe program. This program is called by the Windows 3.1 Autoexec.bat file to allow the use of a parallel port Zip drive. The call only appears in your Autoexec.bat file if you have a Zip drive.

The call to Guest.exe forces all of your hard drives to work in MS-DOS compatibility mode, thereby reducing their performance. You can solve this problem by first remarking out the call to Guest.exe in your Autoexec.bat file before you upgrade to Windows 98.

If you upgraded before noticing the problem, remark out the call in your Autoexec.bat and restart Windows. To make sure that Windows 98 is now using 32-bit disk drivers, right-click your My Computer icon, click Properties,

Performance, File System, Troubleshooting, and make sure that all the check boxes are clear, as shown in Figure 21-24.

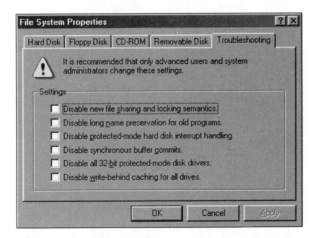

Figure 21-24: The Troubleshooting tab of the File System Properties dialog box. All the check boxes should be clear if you are using the 32-bit disk drivers.

Thanks to Jim Stark for pointing us toward this tip.

DVD support in Windows 98

Wondering about DVD support in Windows 98? Check out a too-small article from Microsoft, "DVD Support in Windows 98," in the Knowledge Base at chipsetsupport.microsoft.com/support/kb/articles/q188/5/13.asp.

Did you get a DVD drive for Christmas? Are you still trying to make it work? Isn't it great how Microsoft and the DVD manufacturers put out crummy drivers when the new equipment first comes out?

If you are looking for a much better driver, check out Power DVD (thanks to Chris Pirillo at chipsetwww.lockergnome.com for this tip) at chipsetwww. cyberlink.com.tw/. As we write about this driver in early 1999, there are still some legal issues. Hopefully this will be cleared up by the time you read this.

Managing printers

Just a few paperwork items here.

Windows 98 Setup changes the values for your print spooler

Secret

The Windows 98 Setup program can change the values of your print spooler settings if they are different than the Windows 98 defaults. If you have more than one printer defined, you'll need to change back the spooler values for each one.

Windows 98 Setup changes the spooler settings for data format to EMF, and for communications support to bidirectional. If those are the settings that you used previously, there is no need to check your current settings. But, if you set your data format to RAW and your communications support to disable bidirectional, you'll want to change them back.

STEPS:

Setting Your Print Spooler Values

Step 1.   Click Start, Settings, and click the Printers icon.

Step 2.   Right-click a printer icon, click Properties, and go to the Details tab.

Step 3.   Click the Spool Settings button to display the Spool Settings dialog box, shown in Figure 21-25.

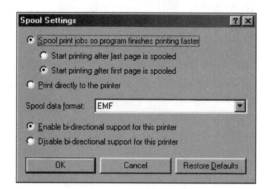

Figure 21-25: The Spool Settings dialog box lets you change the Windows 98 defaults if your printer doesn't support them.

Step 4.   Display the Spool Data Format drop-down list to switch to RAW if you so desire.

Step 5.   Mark the Disable Bi-directional Support for This Printer option button.

Step 6. Click OK. Click OK.

Step 7. Right-click the next printer icon and repeat steps 2 through 6 until you have completed them for all of your printers.

Thanks to Dale Grant for help with this secret.

No fonts in your text editor?

If one day you open up Microsoft Word or another text editor and find that you can't type anything, that the font list only contains one font repeated many times, that most of your fonts are missing, that your characters are scattered all over the page, or that the formatting has gone haywire, don't despair. You could either have a corrupted printer driver, or you may have accidentally chosen a printer driver for a printer that doesn't support your normal array of fonts.

Choose File, Print in your editor, and see what printer you are defaulted to use. If you normally use another printer, choose it instead. You can also click Start, Settings, Printers. The default printer has a check mark next to it, as shown in Figure 21-26.

Figure 21-26: In this example, the Networked HP LaserJet is marked as the default printer.

Right-click another printer and set it as the default instead. See if your fonts return.

It may be that all of the printer icons in your Printers folder are dim. If this is the case, check to see if you have two different hardware profiles. (Press Win+Pause/Break or right-click your My Computer icon and click Properties, and then click the Hardware Profiles tab.) You may have booted your computer into a hardware profile that doesn't have any printers configured for it. This might happen, for example, if you have docked and undocked hardware profiles for a portable computer. Reboot to a hardware profile that contains printers or add printers to the hardware profile without them (click Start, Settings, Printers, Add Printer).

If this doesn't solve your problem, install a new printer, or remove an existing printer and install the same printer again. Click the Add Printer icon in the Printers folder (see Figure 21-26) and follow the steps in the Add Printer Wizard. When asked if you want to set the new printer as the default printer for Windows-based programs, mark the Yes option button.

Complex graphics on Hewlett Packard printers

Hewlett Packard LaserJet 4 and 5 models may not print your complex graphical image due to lack of memory installed in the printer. The best way around this problem is to force your computer to use its processor and memory to do the work that the printer can't do.

You can force the computer to get busy (and slow) by taking these steps:

STEPS:
Helping Out the Hewlett Packard Printer

Step 1. Click Start, Settings, Printers. Right-click your HP LaserJet icon, and click Properties.

Step 2. Click the Details tab, and click the Spool Settings button. Then display the Spool Data Format drop-down list, and select RAW (see Figure 21-27). Click OK.

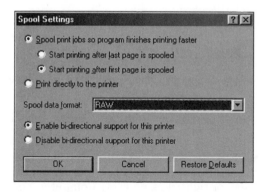

Figure 21-27: The Spool Settings dialog box. RAW has been selected in the drop-down list.

Step 3. Click the Graphics tab. Mark the Use Raster Graphics option button, as shown in Figure 21-28.

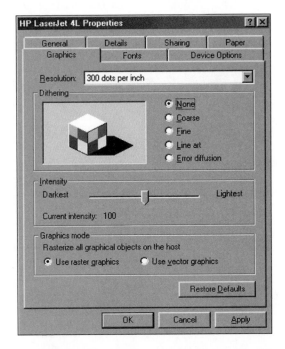

Figure 21-28: The Graphics tab of the Properties dialog box for an HP LaserJet 4 or 5 printer. Mark the Use Raster Graphics option button.

Step 4. Click the Fonts tab, and mark Print True Type As Graphics.

Step 5. Click the Device Options tab, and move the Printer Memory Tracking slider all the way to the right for Aggressive memory tracking, as shown in Figure 21-29.

Continued

Helping Out the Hewlett Packard Printer *(continued)*

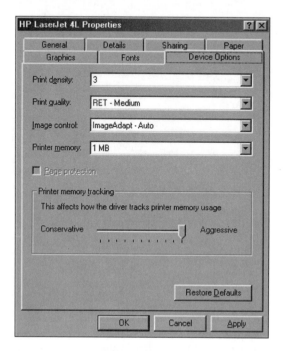

Figure 21-29: The Device Options tab for the same printer's Properties. Adjust the Printer Memory Tracking slider bar.

Step 6. See whether the Page Protection check box is dim. If it isn't, clear it if it is marked, and mark it if it is cleared. Click OK.

For a more detailed discussion of how printer memory is managed, see "Spooling EMF, not RAW printer codes" in Chapter 29 of *Windows 98 Secrets*.

Different printers for different papers

If you want to quickly switch between different settings for your printer driver, you can create different printer icons in the Printers folder for the same printer. Assign different names and settings for each printer icon and then print to the printer with the appropriate settings.

Click the Add Printer icon (Start, Settings, Printers) to create a new printer icon. In the Add Printer Wizard, mark Keep Existing Driver to use the same driver that you have already installed for your printer. Give the new printer a name that describes what its settings will be.

Right-click the new printer icon, click Properties, and change its properties to reflect the settings you desire. For example, if you have an Epson Stylus Color 800, you might want to change the settings for different resolutions and paper type. You might name three printer icons as follows:

Normal paper (360 and 720 dpi)
Photo quality Inkjet paper (720 and 1440 dpi)
Glossy paper (720 and 1440 dpi)

Thanks to Marc Arts for help with this tip.

Interrupts

There are never enough of them.

Grab interrupts for new peripherals

It is most unfortunate that we still have only the 16 defined interrupts that came with the IBM AT hardware. PCI architecture does add interrupt sharing, and Windows 98 supports IRQ steering, which allows the interrupts to be shared. Still, there may be times when you could use a few free interrupts.

It is possible to free up hardwired interrupts with a bit of rewiring, or at least reconfiguring, on your part.

If your computer has COM2 enabled, but you are not using this port for a modem or a serial connection, you can disable it. You can do this either in your computer's BIOS, or by rearranging jumper connectors on your computer's motherboard or peripheral card. The same is true of any other COM port that is available to be freed up.

Newer computers allow you to disable the serial device in the computer's BIOS. You'll need to restart Windows and press the designated key during power-on self test to enter the BIOS setup program. Then navigate within the setup menus to find the menu in which you can disable the serial ports. The designated key and the menu structure are different for every BIOS.

If you have an older computer or a card that is configured with jumpers, you'll need to refer to the manual to correctly change the jumper settings.

After you disable the serial port, you'll want to remove it from your Device Manager. Restart Windows after making the changes in your BIOS or jumpers, and press Win+Pause/Break (or right-click the My Computer icon and click Properties). Click the Device Manager, highlight the disabled Communications Port under the Ports (COM & LPT) branch, and click the Remove button (see Figure 21-30). The port that you have disabled should be marked with a yellow exclamation point.

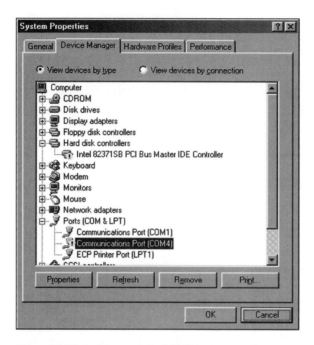

Figure 21-30: In this example, COM4 is the one we want to remove. Note the yellow exclamation point.

Some motherboards and BIOSes (in particular AMI BIOSes) still let Windows 98 see the serial ports even if they have been disabled in the BIOS. In these cases, our recommendations won't work.

If your computer has a dual PCI IDE controller used to control only one device (most likely your hard disk), then it is possible to free up one half of the dual controller and thereby free up Interrupt 15. You will need to do this in your computer's BIOS.

Be sure that your computer isn't using the second IDE controller. While your hard disk may be on the first controller, your CD-ROM drive could be on the second. If it is, don't do this. The Device Manager won't tell you directly, nor will Microsoft System Information. You'll have to check in your computer's BIOS and use your hardware manuals.

After you disable the second controller in your computer's BIOS, restart Windows and go to your Device Manager. The Secondary IDE controller will be marked with a yellow exclamation point. Highlight the device and click the Remove button. Click OK.

Finally, you can free up Interrupt 7 (or perhaps Interrupt 5) by disabling LPT1, your parallel port (again, in your computer's BIOS or with jumpers), and then removing it from the Device Manager. You'll be able to do that and still print to your printer if your parallel port hardware supports ECP (see the following steps).

STEPS:

Freeing Up IRQ 7 Or IRQ 5

Step 1. Start your computer. During the power-on self test, press the designated key to enter your BIOS setup. Disable your LPT1 parallel port. Exit the BIOS setup, saving your changes.

Step 2. Start Windows. Press Win+Pause/Break (or right-click My Computer and click Properties). Click the Device Manager tab. Click the plus sign next to Ports (COM & LPT) and highlight your LPT1 port. Click the Remove button, and click OK.

Step 3. Click Start, Shut Down, Shut Down, OK.

Step 4. Turn off your computer and install the device that is configured to use IRQ 7 (or IRQ 5).

Step 5. Turn on your computer, and let Windows install the new device, using drivers either from the Windows 98 CD-ROM or from the device manufacturer's diskettes. Go to the Device Manager and make sure that the device is installed. If it is, shut down Windows.

Step 6. Re-enable LPT1 in your BIOS before restarting Windows. Windows should automatically find the LPT port when it restarts.

Step 7. Check in the Device Manager to see if Windows indicates a conflict. Even if there is an exclamation mark next to the LPT1 device, it may work fine.

Step 8. If your parallel port can operate as an ECP port, you can define it to take advantage of these characteristics, and then remove the conflicting LPT1 port. Use the Add New Hardware control panel applet to manually add the ECP port, and then follow the remaining steps.

Step 9. Using the Device Manager, click the LPT1 port, click the Properties button, click the Resources tab, and write down the Input/Output Range memory values. Click Cancel, and then remove the original LPT1 device by clicking the Remove button and OK while the LPT1 port is highlighted.

Step 10. Click the ECP port in the Device Manager, click the Properties button, and click the Resources tab. Clear the Use Automatic Settings check box, and display the Setting Based On field. Choose a setting (if possible), that matches the previous LPT1 Input/Output Range with no Interrupt Request. Click OK.

Step 11. Shut down Windows and restart. Windows may redetect the LPT1 port. If this happens, you can most likely ignore the yellow exclamation point in your Device Manager regarding the LPT1 port.

With plug and play BIOSes, other devices may grab interrupts before your newly-installed device has a chance to get the ones that you just freed up. That's fine; there should then be others available and you can use them.

Thanks to John Helms for help with many of these steps.

Need to share an interrupt, but can't?

Secret

If you find that you can't get your IRQ steering to work with your PCI bus, it may be because you don't have the latest patch for your VIA chipset. Of course, this is only true if your motherboard uses the VIA chipset.

The symptom: IRQ steering is disabled, even though the Use IRQ Steering check box is marked in the PCI Bus Properties dialog box (see Figure 21-31). To get to this dialog box, press Win+Pause/Break (or right-click My Computer and click Properties), click the Device Manager tab, scroll down to System Devices, open up this branch, double-click PCI Bus, and click the IRQ Steering tab.

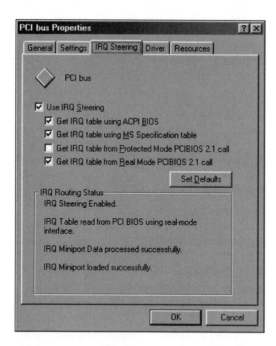

Figure 21-31: The IRQ Steering tab of the PCI Bus Properties dialog box. Use IRQ Steering has been marked.

If the Get IRQ Table from Real Mode PCIBIOS 2.1 Call check box is dim and clear (it is not in this figure), you may be able to fix this with the patch that corrects the IRQ routing table. You can use Sandra (see "Add to your system info" in Chapter 26) to check if you have the VIA chipset. Click the Mainboard Information icon, and then scroll down to Chipset Information.

Download the VIA IRQ routing miniport driver from chipsetwww.via.com.tw/drivers/.

Thanks to Atilla Szabo for pointing out this secret.

Disable PCI interrupt steering

You'll find an extensive discussion of interrupts and PCI steering in Chapter 25 of *Windows 98 Secrets*. In that chapter, we discuss both ISA interrupts and enabling PCI interrupt steering. If you have two PCI devices that are having a conflict, you may have to disable PCI interrupt steering to work out the problem. To do this, take these steps:

STEPS:
Disabling PCI Interrupt Steering

Step 1.   Press Win+Pause/Break (or right-click My Computer and click Properties). Click the Device Manager tab.

Step 2.   Double-click System Devices at the bottom of the Device Manager and then double-click PCI Bus. Click the IRQ Steering tab.

Step 3.   Clear the Use IRQ Steering check box (see Figure 21-32).

Step 4.   Click OK, and then click Yes to restart your computer and have this new setting take hold.

Continued

STEPS

Disabling PCI Interrupt Steering *(continued)*

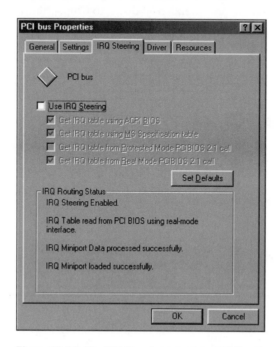

Figure 21-32: The IRQ Steering tab of the PCI Bus Properties dialog box. The first check box is the one to clear in this instance.

You may find that you also have to disable PCI steering in your computer's BIOS. Press the indicated key during the power-on self test to enter your BIOS setup program, and then hunt around for the option that lets you disable it (this will vary depending on your BIOS).

PCI steering only works if you have a mixture of PCI devices — some plug and play, and some not. PCI steering sits in front of the non-plug and play PCI device and handles requests for device configuration values. This stops a plug and play PCI device from stealing an interrupt that a non-plug and play PCI device must use. It sort of makes non-plug and play devices look like plug and play devices to the lower-level Windows device drivers.

PCI steering doesn't affect interrupt sharing. If the PCI devices can share interrupts, PCI steering supports it.

You still have to have a sufficient number of interrupts in your computer to support all of your devices, PCI or not. You'll need to check the Device Manager to determine what available interrupts you have, and then make changes in your BIOS or other areas, as described in the previous section.

You can find out more about this issue by viewing "How to Disable PCI BIS IRQ Steering in Windows" at chipsetsupport.microsoft.com/support/kb/articles/q182/6/28.asp. Also, click *Interrupts* or *Interrupt sharing on PCI-devices* in the "Windows 95/98 Networking FAQ" at chipsetwww.helmig.com/j_helmig/faq.htm.

Thanks to Jeff Richards for insights on these issues.

Get enough interrupts for your PCI cards

Secret

If you have only PCI cards, and not ISA cards, you want to be sure that all the interrupts are available to your PCI bus. If you have only plug and play PCI cards, you'll have no need for PCI steering. Make sure that your BIOS allocates all of the available interrupts to your PCI bus. This prevents them from being used by plug and play ISA cards (we are assuming you don't have any).

You'll have to go to your plug and play BIOS setup by pressing the indicated key during the power-on self test. Navigate through the menus until you find the interrupt setup screen that allows you to nominate which interrupts are assigned to the PCI bus.

Secret

After you have configured your plug and play BIOS, install one PCI card at a time, and then confirm in the Device Manager that an interrupt has been assigned to the card. If you have two PCI cards that allow for interrupt sharing, install them last if you have only one interrupt left.

Secret

If any of your PCI cards are not plug and play, you may need to enable PCI steering. Use the steps in the previous section to enable PCI steering, marking the Use IRQ Steering check box instead of clearing it. If none of your PCI cards will share an interrupt, install your non-plug and play PCI cards last, and you won't have to enable PCI steering. If you have PCI cards that can share interrupts, and you have non-plug and play PCI cards, you will have to enable PCI steering.

Thanks to Jeff Richards for help with these secrets.

USB

The Universal Serial Bus isn't universal yet, but it's available on most new computers.

Turn off USB if you don't use it

If you don't have a USB (Universal Serial Bus) device attached to your computer, you can turn off USB support in your BIOS and save the time required to load the USB drivers in Windows 98. You'll have to get to your BIOS setup menu before Windows 98 starts (hold down the indicated key during the power-on self test), and then find the USB IRQ setup and disable it.

If later you decide to install a USB device, enable this feature in your computer's BIOS. Windows 98 will then automatically detect and install USB functionality.

To see if you have a USB port, open your Device Manager and see if the Universal Serial Bus Controller is listed under Computer.

Thanks to David Bradford for pointing us toward this tip.

Want to know more about the Universal Serial Bus? Check out the USB web site at chipsetwww.usb.org.

USB – adding on to get add-ons

Most computers produced since late in 1998 include a Universal Serial Bus port. Some include two. These ports provide a new way to connect a device to your computer, and may allow you to connect a device without having to use one of the limited IRQs.

The USB port will probably allow you to connect only one device, not the vaunted 127. If you want to connect more than one device to the USB port, the device either has to incorporate a USB hub (most don't), or you'll have to purchase a USB hub.

The power provided from the computer's USB port will probably not be enough to support more than one device. If you want to add multiple devices, make sure that the hub you purchase can be powered by an AC adapter.

You'll find an example of such a hub at chipsetusb.belkin.com/html/products.html.

Tip

You should also confirm that your computer's BIOS fully supports USB peripherals. Some computers that include USB ports don't have a BIOS that recognizes USB peripherals — including keyboards and mice — on startup. You can go to the support area of your computer manufacturer's web site to check on its BIOS updates.

Thanks to Bob O'Donnell at InfoWorld for these words of caution.

Debug your Universal Serial Bus

The Universal Serial Bus Viewer is a part of the *Windows 98 Resource Sampler Kit*, which you'll find on your Windows 98 CD-ROM. If you've followed the steps in "Windows 98 Resource Kit Online" in Chapter 16 to install all the applets, then you can go to the Microsoft Management Console to find the Universal Serial Bus Viewer.

Click Start, Programs, Windows 98 Resource Kit, Tools Management Console. In the left pane of the Microsoft Management Console, expand Windows 98 Resource Kit Tools Sampler, then Tool Categories, and then Diagnostics and Trouble-shooting. Double-click USB Viewer in the right pane.

Otherwise, you'll find the Universal Serial Bus Viewer under \tools\reskit\diagnose\usbview.exe on the Windows 98 CD-ROM. You can run it from there or right-drag and drop a copy of it to wherever you like.

If you have an early version of the Intel 82371SB PCI to USB universal host controller chipset, you may have problems with your USB port. If this is the case, you're going to need an update to your motherboard.

STEPS:

Determining Whether You Have an Early Chipset

Step 1. Press Win+Pause/Break (or right-click My Computer and click Properties). Click the Device Manager tab.

Step 2. Double-click the Universal Serial Bus Controller.

Step 3. Double-click Intel 82371SB PCI to USB Universal Host Controller, and then click the General tab.

Step 4. If the Hardware Version field states that the USB controller is 000, then you definitely have the early version of the chipset. Problems have also been noted with version 001.

Other hardware issues

We came up with a few other hardware issues that deserve mention.

Is your computer compatible with Windows 98?

To find out, turn to the Windows compatibility list at Microsoft's web site at chipsetwww.microsoft.com/hwtest/hcl/. Click the Advanced link, clear all of the check boxes under Operating System but the one for Windows 98, and click the Search button.

Thanks to Scott Schnoll for pointing us toward this site.

GenuineIntel?

Secret

Ever wonder what was up with the single word *GenuineIntel* in the General tab of your System Properties dialog box (right-click My Computer, click Properties)? Couldn't they have put a space between *Genuine* and *Intel*? Maybe there is a secret code?

To find out if there is, take these steps:

STEPS:

Checking Out Your Processor

Step 1. Open your Registry editor and navigate to HKEY_LOCAL_MACHINE\hardware\DESCRIPTION\ System\CentralProcessor\0.

Step 2. Double-click VendorIdentifier in the right pane of the Registry editor to display the Edit String dialog box and put a space between *Genuine* and *Intel*, as shown in Figure 21-33. Click OK, and close the Registry editor.

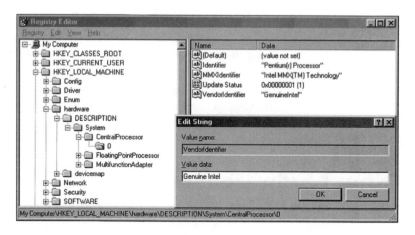

Figure 21-33: Edit the Value Data field to add a space.

Step 3. Right-click My Computer, click Properties, and notice that if you have an Intel processor (something similar appears for other processors), you will see additional information under Genuine Intel, such as "x86 Family 5 Model 12 Stepping 12."

The next time you restart Windows 98, this reverts to GenuineIntel, and the additional information disappears. Strange.

Thanks to Anthony Kinyon for help with this secret.

Basic BIOS info from your Registry

Secret

Windows 98 stores your BIOS name, version, and date in your Registry. If you don't see this information during the power-on self test, you can get to it by opening your Registry editor and navigating to HKEY_LOCAL_MACHINE\ Enum\Root*PNP0C01\0000, as shown in Figure 21-34.

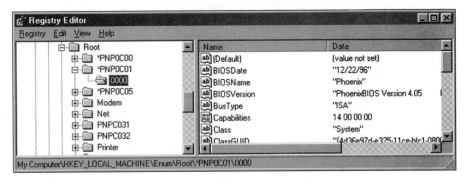

Figure 21-34: This branch of the Registry lists basic information about your BIOS in the right pane.

Add more memory

If you have empty memory sockets on your motherboard, you can add additional memory—SIMMs or DIMMs—to your computer. The first thing you want to do is take a peek at your motherboard and confirm that you do have some empty memory sockets. If you don't know what they look like, pull out the manual for your computer (or any computer's manual) or check out the support pages at your computer manufacturer's web site. If neither of these resources is available, review the diagram of a (typical) motherboard at chipsetsupport.micronpc.com/faq/mbdfaq/images/ts00838.html. (The memory sockets are labeled SIMM BANKS in the diagram.)

Most computers built in the last few years use either SIMM modules (single in-line memory modules) or DIMM modules (dual in-line memory modules). Check out your computer's manual to see which kind of memory modules you have in your computer.

You also need to know what type of memory chips you have on the modules—EDO, FPM, and so on—and whether they are non-parity-checking (very likely) or parity-checking (maybe in a server). You can use Sandra (see "Add to your system info" in Chapter 16) if you can't find out from your manuals. In Sandra, click Mainboard Information, and scroll down to

Supported Memory Types to see if you have SIMM or DIMM modules, as shown in Figure 21-35. Scroll further down to Logical Memory Banks to see what type of memory you have installed.

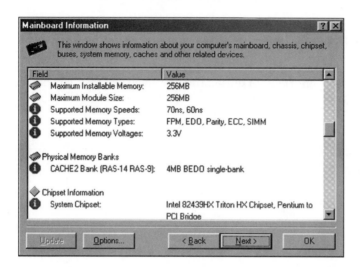

Figure 21-35: The computer in this example uses SIMM modules.

Your computer may also display your memory chip type during the power-on self test. You may be able to see it then, and you might be able to press the Pause/Break key to pause the display and confirm what it says.

Next, you need to know how much memory you can install and how much you are willing to pay for. If you have a couple of banks for SIMM sockets available, you will probably be able to install anywhere from 8MB (what's the point) to 64MB (whoa, big fella) of memory. Check your computer manual for a chart of possible memory sizes and combinations.

Now, if you have a couple of banks of memory sockets available, you know your memory type and module type, and you know how much you can install, it's time to spec out the memory modules to purchase. You don't necessarily need to purchase the memory from your computer vendor, unless you want to put a little extra change in their pocket.

For example, SIMMs are for the most part packaged in 72-pin modules (although older computers may use 30-pin SIMMs) using EDO non-parity-checking chips. A single module at 16MB would be labeled 4x32. The 4 stands for 4x4, in other words 16MB. The 32 means non-parity-checking memory. The other option would be 36, which stands for parity-checking memory. You can read more about this nomenclature as it is applied to SIMMs and DIMMs at Micron's general memory explanation site, chipsetsupport.micronpc.com/faq/topissues/ts16531.html.

It is a rare personal computer that uses parity-checking memory. If, for example, you want to add 32MB to your computer, and you have two banks of SIMMs available, you'll want to purchase two 16MB modules (two 4x32 72-pin SIMMs), as shown in Figure 21-36.

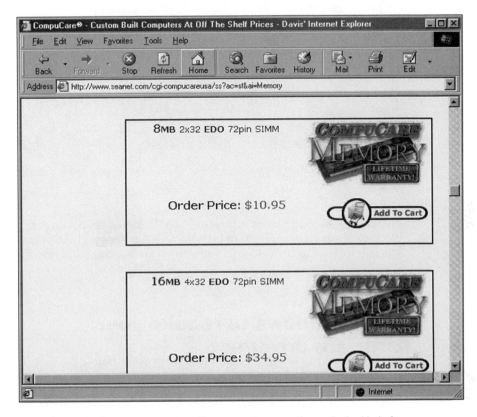

Figure 21-36: In this page from an online store, the second entry is the kind of memory we want. We want to purchase two of these.

Once you've purchased the memory modules, putting them in couldn't be easier. The main issue is keep your hands off of anything but the insulated material. Your computer manual should supply you with instructions on how to push in the new modules. If not, you can check out Micron's support site at chipsetsupport.micronpc.com/faq/mbdfaq/specs/ts00315.html.

Cool down your CPU

You can send software commands to your CPU to shut down portions of it that aren't doing any useful work. If those portions are idled, then they aren't producing heat. This cuts down on the overall heat production of your CPU, thereby putting less stress on the components. Laptop users may find it simply makes working with the computer in your lap more comfortable.

Waterfall Pro is a little shareware utility, shown in Figure 21-37, that sends HLT commands to idle portions of your CPU. You can find it at chipsetcpu. simplenet.com/leading_wintech.

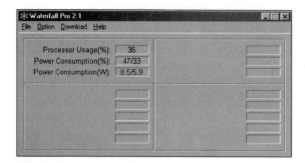

Figure 21-37: The Waterfall window tells you how much of your system is shut down to cool off.

Installing Waterfall places it in your StartUp folder. After you restart Windows 98, its appears in your system tray. Waterfall comes with an uninstaller. Just click Setup.exe in the folder where you've installed the utility.

Thanks to Robert Sullivan for telling us about this software.

Force Windows to rebuild your hardware driver set

Secret

Windows 98 may have detected your hardware incorrectly and installed the wrong driver. You may find that you have a "ghost" driver for a piece of hardware that isn't installed. You can often remove these bad hardware drivers using the Device Manager. Right-click My Computer and click Properties, click the Device Manager tab, highlight the offending hardware driver, and click the Remove button.

If this doesn't work, you can force Windows 98 to reinstall all of your hardware drivers. This secret is for advanced users only. Don't use it unless you are willing to reinstall Windows 98 and all of your software and drivers if it doesn't work for you.

STEPS:

Reinstalling Your Hardware Drivers

Step 1. Restart your computer and hold down the Ctrl key during the power-on self test.

Step 2. In the Windows 98 Startup menu, choose the third menu item, Safe mode.

Step 3.   Click Start, Run, type **regedit**, and press Enter.

Step 4.   Navigate in your Registry to HKEY_LOCAL_MACHINE, right-click the Enum folder as shown in Figure 21-38, and click Delete. Close the Registry editor.

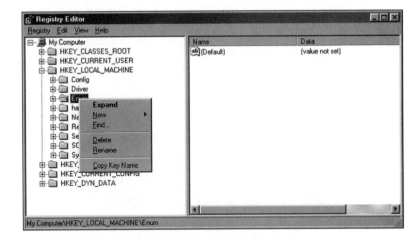

Figure 21-38: Delete the Enum folder from the Registry editor.

Step 5.   Click Start, Shut Down, Restart, OK.

Step 6.   Windows 98 should automatically detect your hardware and rebuild the Enumeration tables. If it does not, click Start, Settings, Control Panel, Add New Hardware, Next, Next. Let Windows 98 search for all the hardware and install the correct drivers.

Thanks to Serge Paquin for help with this secret.

Wake up your SCSI devices

If you forget to turn on SCSI devices such as your scanner or Zip drive before you start Windows 98, there's no need to do a restart to get Windows to detect the devices. After you turn them on, hold down the Alt key as you click My Computer, click the Device Manager tab, and click the Refresh button. Windows will now detect your devices.

Thanks to Bill Schneider for pointing out this tip.

Real information online about computer hardware and software

No web site does it all, and you have to search around the web to get answers to your specific questions. We did find one site though, PC Mechanic, which concentrates on the kinds of questions that people building or buying personal computers need to ask. The site contains lots of good information about drive types (buy EDI and forget SCSI), memory, motherboards, video cards, networking, and monitors. It's definitely geared toward the buyer who wants to specify every component in his or her new purchase.

PC Mechanic also has a nice section on setting up a small network and connecting the network to the Internet. You'll find it at chipsetwww. pcmech.com. The networking article starts at chipsetwww.pcmech.com/ networking.htm.

Behind the Dell Inspiron

One of the great things about the web is that computer users can put up their own sites and tell the world about the computers that they use. If there is a newsgroup to help gather the impressions of a wide range of users of a particular model, the web site author can provide a great resource to everyone using that computer by interacting frequently with the newsgroup. Turns out, this kind of web site is also very useful for people looking to buy a computer.

If you are looking at a particular model, use the search engines to find web sites that specialize in the computer model that you are interested in. Chris Pirillo at chipsetwww.lockergnome.com pointed out a great site that deals with the Dell Inspiron portable. You'll find it at chipsetwww.edgeworld.com/ notebook/i7main.htm.

Summary

There is hardware, and then there are hardware drivers. Sometimes they just don't get along.

▶ How to get the fonts back when they've all gone away.

▶ Install only plug and play PCI cards — dealing with PCI steering and interrupt sharing.

▶ USB, still on the bleeding edge.

▶ Figure out what kind of memory to add to your computer.

▶ Force Windows 98 to recognize your hardware.

▶ Find out more about your computer online.

Chapter 22

Power Management

In This Chapter

Power management has always been a hit and miss item, with Windows and BIOSes not quite on the same page. You can come to a provisional détente, but don't expect total victory.

▶ If you want to schedule a task to run when your computer is suspended (it has to wake up), you might be able to.

▶ Windows and the BIOS fight to see who is in charge of power management. You can put Windows in charge, most of the time.

▶ If you've set your BIOS to enable power management, you can force Windows to reinstall power management.

▶ Will it all work out in the future? Maybe.

Schedule tasks to start when your computer's asleep

When you install Microsoft Plus! 98, it automatically runs the Maintenance Wizard and sets up a schedule of tasks to be run during the night. It assumes that this is when you'd like these housekeeping tasks to occur. But if you turn your computer off at night, none of the essential mopping and dusting ever gets done, until you are forced by system slowdowns to do it yourself during billable hours.

To check your existing schedule of tasks, open your Explorer and click Scheduled Tasks under My Computer. You'll see a list of tasks and their scheduled times and dates, as shown in Figure 22-1.

You can reschedule any task for a more appropriate date and time by right-clicking it, clicking Properties, and clicking the Schedule tab.

You'll want to make sure that at least the tasks originally scheduled by the Maintenance Wizard are carried out. If you let your computer run WinAlign (referred to in Scheduled Tasks as Tune-Up Application Start) and Defrag, your most heavily used applications will load faster and your data files will also load more quickly because they are more likely to be contiguous. Again, this is only going to happen if you let it.

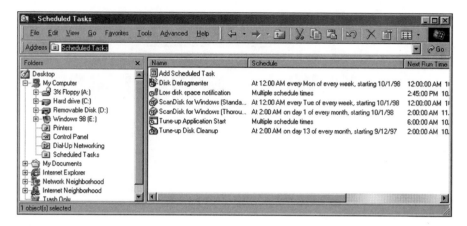

Figure 22-1: Scheduled Tasks is a special Explorer folder that keeps track of all the tasks you have scheduled.

If you have a computer whose BIOS supports at least Advanced Power Management (APM) 1.2, you'll be able to let your computer go to sleep at night, and it will wake up at the scheduled times to carry out the scheduled tasks. We often turn off our computers because they are wasting electrical power, because the fan is noisy, or because turning it off creates less wear on the hard disk. Letting the computer go to sleep solves these problems. As long as it will wake up to take care of its night time duties, then we've got the best of both worlds.

To check what level of power management your computer can support, take these steps:

STEPS:

Checking Your Level of Power Management Support

Step 1. Press Win+Pause/Break (or right-click My Computer and click Properties).

Step 2. Click the Device Manager tab.

Step 3. Scroll down to System Devices, and click the plus sign.

Step 4. Click Advanced Power Management Support, and click the Properties button.

Step 5. Click the Settings tab to see your level of Advanced Power Management support, as illustrated in Figure 22-2.

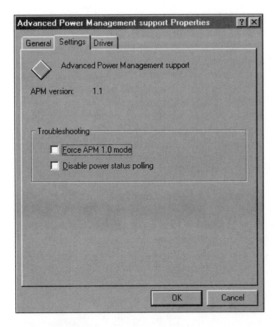

Figure 22-2: The computer in this example can support only APM 1.1 or lower.

If your computer can support at least APM 1.2, you'll find the Wake the Computer to Run This Task check box in the Settings tab for each individual task, as shown in Figure 22-3. (Click the Scheduled Tasks icon in your Explorer, right-click a task, click Properties, and click the Settings tab.)

Mark this check box if you want the computer to be woken up to carry out this task. This is the default action.

A Microsoft Knowledge Base article that states that this check box may exist even if your computer doesn't support at least APM 1.2. However, it won't work unless your computer does support APM 1.2. You'll find the article "'Wake the Computer to Run This Task' Feature May Not Work," at support.microsoft.com/support/kb/articles/q188/6/24.asp.

Tip

If your computer doesn't support APM 1.2, you might think about letting it stay on overnight once a week or once a month. Schedule all of the tasks for that night, in order (ScanDisk first) and about an hour apart (see "Reschedule maintenance if your computer doesn't stay up all night" in Chapter 15).

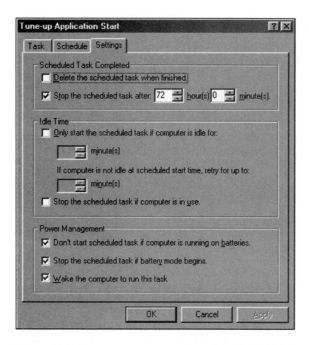

Figure 22-3: The power management settings for APM 1.2 or higher include the additional setting Wake the Computer to Run This Task.

Let Windows do power management

If you have a new computer that fully and completely supports the Microsoft-defined Advanced Configuration and Power Interface (ACPI), then you can fully control your computer's standby, disk spin down, monitor turnoff, and power management features. All you have to do is go to your Control Panel and click the Power Management icon.

If you have an older computer whose BIOS supports Advanced Power Management, either APM 1.1 or APM 1.2, you may find that controlling the power management settings is not quite so easy. Your computer's BIOS and the Windows Power Management control panel are fighting to see whose settings should be used. Because you can set the power management features in either location, your computer doesn't know whom to believe.

If you want to control your computer's power management features through the Windows 98 Power Management control panel, you'll need to reset the values for power management in your BIOS. To do this, click Start, Shut Down, Restart, OK.

When your computer restarts (reboots), press the indicated key that allows you to set up your BIOS. Sometimes computers are configured so that you aren't given any indication on the screen of what this key is. You'll need help from the person that set up your computer in this case. Try Esc or F2 during the power-on self test.

In the BIOS setup window, go to the power management features menu. Make sure that APM is enabled. Now, disable the power management mode—not power management itself, but all the timing settings, if you have any. If there are timing settings in the BIOS that are not reflected in similar settings in your Windows Power Management control panel, do not disable power management mode for them. Instead, customize the values for each of these settings.

For those BIOS power management settings that are replicated in the Window Power Management control panel, either disable their settings in the BIOS, or set them to the largest value available. You can then use the control panel to set these values. The unfortunate consideration here is that the terminology used in these BIOS settings may not be reflected in the control panel, so it is sometimes difficult to understand which setting is which.

The Power Management control panel for APM 1.1, shown in Figure 22-4, has only two settings: initiate system standby and turn off monitor. APM 1.2 has an additional setting for spinning down the hard disk. When you configure your power management settings in your BIOS, be aware that these are the only settings that you can control in the Windows Power Management control panel, if your BIOS only supports APM and not ACPI.

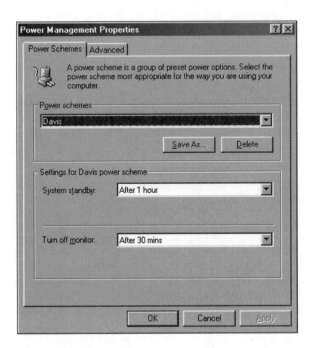

Figure 22-4: The Power Management Properties dialog box for APM version 1.1 has only two settings. If you have version 1.2, you'll see an additional setting.

Advanced Configuration and Power Interface

When you set up Windows 98, ACPI is installed only on those systems that Microsoft had certified as ACPI compliant at the time of the release of Windows 98. This list was updated in early 1999, but your computer may not have been on the list when Windows 98 was installed.

Secret

If you are sure that your computer is ACPI compliant and you want to give this version of power management a try, you can force the ACPI driver to be installed. Here's how:

STEPS:

Forcing ACPI Installation

Step 1.   Click Start, Run, type **regedit**, and press Enter.

Step 2.   Navigate to HKEY_LOCAL_MACHINE\SOFTWARE\Microsoft\Windows\CurrentVersion\Detect. Highlight this key in the left pane of your Registry editor.

Step 3.   Right-click the right pane, and click New, String Value.

Step 4   Rename the string value **ACPIOption**.

Step 5.   Double-click ACPIOption in the right pane, type the value **1**, and click OK. Exit the Registry editor.

Step 6.   Click Start, Settings, Control Panel, Add New Hardware. Click Next twice, and have the wizard search for new hardware.

You can remove ACPI support by changing this value to **2** and running the Add New Hardware Wizard again.

A more detailed discussion of this process can be found in the Microsoft Knowledge Base article "How to Enable ACPI Support in Windows 98" at support.microsoft.com/support/kb/articles/q195/2/18.asp. You can also keep track of the latest developments in the slow progress toward OnNow technology by reviewing Microsoft's "Update on Windows 98 Retail Upgrade for ACPI System" at www.microsoft.com/hwdev/desinit/retailup.htm. (OnNow is a Microsoft initiative that is supposed to provide standards that let computer manufacturers put their computers into a sleep state, and then restore your last configuration and state of your work almost instantly when the computers are revived.)

Get Stand By back in your Shut Down Windows dialog box

You'll find the Stand By option in your Shut Down Windows dialog box if your computer supports Automated Power Management (APM) or the Advanced Configuration and Power Interface (ACPI). It's possible to lose this option if there are some problems with your Standby mode.

You will lose the Stand By option if you received the following message in a dialog box and answered yes: "The last few times your computer went on standby it stopped responding. Would you like to prevent your computer from going on standby in the future?" You will also lose this option if your computer stopped responding while in Standby mode two times in a row.

If you have changed the APM configuration in your BIOS, or if you never had it properly configured, you will not have the Stand By option in your Shut Down Windows dialog box.

Secret

If you previously had the Stand By option and now it is gone, and if you haven't changed your BIOS, you can take these steps to get it back:

STEPS:

Retrieving Your Stand By Option

Step 1. Start your Registry editor (\Windows\regedit.exe).

Step 2. Navigate to HKEY_LOCAL_MACHINE\System\CurrentControlSet\Services\VxD\VPOWERD.

Step 3. In the right pane of your Registry editor, you should see entries for Flags and SuspendFlag, as shown in Figure 22-5.

Step 4. Double-click the Flags value and verify that its value is greater than or equal to 200. If it is, subtract 200 from its current value and type the new value. Click OK.

Step 5. If the SuspendFlag value is not already 0, double-click SuspendFlag, and enter the value **0**. Click OK.

Step 6. Exit the Registry editor and restart Windows 98.

Continued

STEPS

Retrieving Your Stand By Option *(continued)*

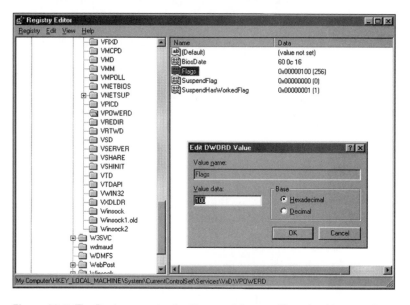

Figure 22-5: The Registry entries for Flags and SuspendFlag should appear in the right pane.

If you never had the Stand By option or if you lost it after making changes to your computer's BIOS, you need to make sure that you have some form of power management built into your computer and operating. Otherwise, you can't go into Standby mode.

Reinstalling power management

You can restore Standby without editing your Registry by removing Advanced Power Management from your Device Manager and then forcing Windows 98 to autodetect all of your hardware once again (thereby reinstalling APM). You may need to use this method if you lost APM after making changes in the power management area of your BIOS.

STEPS:

Reinstalling Advanced Power Management

Step 1. Re-enable power management in your computer's BIOS if you have disabled it.

Step 2. Right-click your My Computer icon, click Properties, and click the Device Manager tab.

Step 3. Click the plus sign next to System Devices, as shown in Figure 22-6, highlight Advanced Power Management Support, and click Remove. Click OK.

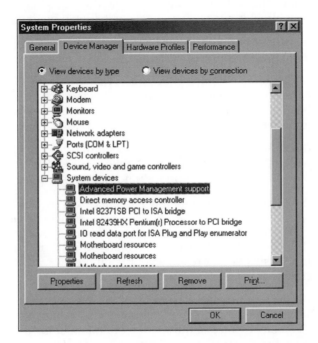

Figure 22-6: The Device Manager tab of System Properties. Click the plus sign to expand the list of system devices, and then remove Advanced Power Management Support.

Step 4. Click Start, Shut Down, Restart, and OK.

Step 5. Click Start, Settings, Control Panel, Add New Hardware, Next, and Next.

Step 6. Assuming that power management is enabled in your BIOS, Windows 98 will find it and reinstall it.

You should now have a Stand By option in your Shut Down Windows dialog box. If this is not the case, then there are probably incompatibilities between your computer's BIOS and Windows 98. See the next section, and look for further details in this Microsoft support article: "Standby Missing From Windows Shutdown Dialog Box" at support.microsoft.com/support/kb/articles/q188/1/34.asp.

Problems with power management

Windows 98 support for power management is not 100 percent foolproof, to say the least. Microsoft has had to write code that interfaces with code written by the BIOS manufacturers, and there has been little agreement in the past about how power management should be implemented.

You may have to update your BIOS to get it to work with the Windows 98 power management features.

One of the more common problems is that Windows 98 power management may prevent a PC from going into Standby mode because some driver or application is not ready. A different problem you may encounter is that your computer enters Standby mode normally, but you can't get out of Standby.

Microsoft has a web page to help you troubleshoot such problems. The Advanced Power Management Troubleshooter for Windows 98 is at support.microsoft.com/support/windows/tshoot/apm98.

The tool that is most commonly recommended by this page to determine the source of driver conflicts with power management is called Pmtshoot.exe. Download this 161K file from Microsoft into a temporary folder, and then run it once to install a background monitor. This monitor analyzes your next attempt to suspend or resume your computer. It can detect a driver or other program that is interfering with Standby.

Windows 98 ships with version 1.0 of this file on its CD-ROM. You can run the file \tools\mtsutil\pmtshoot\pmtshoot.exe to install the monitor. However, we recommend you use the version of Pmtshoot downloadable from the web because it is a later version with the ability to fix some problems by itself.

You can get Pmtshoot.exe from the Knowledge Base article "Description of the Power Management Troubleshooter Tool" at support.microsoft.com/support/kb/articles/q185/9/49.asp. Anyone who has questions about power management under Windows 98 should read this article.

The following PC manufacturers have special issues with Windows 98 power management. If you've upgraded or may be upgrading to Windows 98 and own one of these machines, you should read the relevant information on the web:

- **Toshiba**. With some Toshiba notebooks, you need to update the BIOS before you install Windows 98. Although Windows 98 will work, installing it before your laptop has a BIOS that explicitly supports ACPI makes it problematic to update the BIOS later. If Windows 98 does see the updated Toshiba BIOS when installing, it will record a variety of Registry settings that it would not write if you hadn't yet updated the BIOS. See www.csd.toshiba.com/tais/csd/support/issues/98070001.htm for details.

- **Gateway**. SoundBlaster audio may cause Gateway computers to lock up after resuming from Standby. Go to www.gateway.com/support/techdocs/software/windows/30682.html#PM.

- **Dell**. A variety of Dell models should have a BIOS upgrade before installing Windows 98. See www.dell.com/98upgrade, and then click the name of the Dell product you have.

- **Compaq**. A document describing a number of quirks with Compaq hardware can be found at www.compaq.com/athome/international/en/win98/1215.html.

Continuing problems with power management

If your computer's BIOS only supports APM, and not ACPI, then you may continue to have power management difficulties if you are unable to get a BIOS update. Computer manufacturers will volunteer the fact that earlier models don't completely support Windows 98 because of this very problem. While 99.99 percent of Windows 98 works just fine, power management may not.

The problems occur when your computer goes into Standby mode. It may not return from Standby, or it may return but with "flaky" behavior. Even if the Advanced Power Management Troubleshooter does not indicate a problem, that doesn't mean that there isn't one. You can follow the troubleshooting methods detailed at the Microsoft web site given in the previous section, but they may not pertain to your problem.

If you have installed Windows 98 on a computer that doesn't support ACPI, be cautious about using Standby and other power features. If they don't work for you, chalk that up to a bit of system incompatibility, and just assume that you don't have that feature (in spite of what the Windows dialog boxes indicate).

USB and Standby mode

Users have reported that their computers won't go into Standby mode if a peripheral device is plugged into their USB port. The USB port is supposed to be integrated with Windows 98 power management. If the device is causing the problem, it may be because the device driver is not written to account for the power management modes.

You'll need to get on the web and track down the device manufacturer's home page and see if you can download a new driver.

OnNow, ACPI, and Smart Batteries

Power management has definitely been a bear, as you can see from some of the topics discussed earlier in this chapter. The solutions to power management problems have been around for a while, but it takes time for everyone to implement them. Successful implementation requires support from the operating system (Windows 98 does), the drivers (some do, some don't), and the BIOSes.

Tip

If you are looking for a new computer, especially if it is a portable, make sure that it supports the OnNow, ACPI, and Smart Batteries power-management features. To learn more about them, start at www.microsoft.com/hwdev/ desinit/ONNOW1.HTM and www.microsoft.com/hwdev/desinit/wakeup.htm.

FAT 32 and suspend to disk

Some computers have a suspend to disk function that allows the computer to write the current contents of memory to the hard disk and go into a suspend mode. When the computer wakes up, it writes the previously written memory content back into memory. This function can be handled by the computer's BIOS, independently of the operating system's power management facilities.

The BIOS can write the current contents of memory to the disk and recover it without using any operating system resources. Unless the BIOS is of recent origin, though, it most likely won't be able to write to a FAT-32 formatted hard drive. The BIOS expects to find a FAT-16 formatted drive.

If you find that your computer can't suspend to disk after you've converted your hard disk to FAT 32, you may be able to get a BIOS upgrade from your computer manufacturer — but the odds aren't good. Navigate to the manufacturer's support web page and see what their story is.

Summary

First there was Advanced Power Management, but that relied on the BIOS to manage power. Then there was ACPI, but that relied on the BIOS to support it. Someday we'll have the operating system, the drivers, and the BIOS in sync.

▶ If your computer is ACPI compliant, you can force it to be installed.

▶ If you lose the Stand By option in your Shut Down Windows dialog box, you can get it back.

▶ Each computer manufacturer has its own unique problems with power management.

▶ Your computer may have a suspend to disk feature, but it may not understand FAT 32.

Chapter 23

Home and Small Office Networking

Why a network?

Sharing is cheaper and more fun (games), uses fewer phone lines for Internet access, and makes life easier when it comes to using peripherals. Sharing used to be too hard to make it worth the trouble. Sharing used to be expensive. Sharing used to use too many resources and degrade the performance of individual machines. Sharing used to cause difficult-to-diagnose problems. Sharing used to mean too much dependence on others or on some expert. Sharing doesn't mean any of those things any more.

A small network is much cheaper than a second printer. A small network is much cheaper than a second phone line and a second Internet service provider. A small network lets you share an expensive DSL or cable modem connection.

You can share information much easier over a network than by copying it onto a floppy diskette. Floppy diskettes are soon to be all-but-gone. Many portable computers have floppy drives that are external and rarely, if ever, connected.

Printers can be automatically configured over the network, so that any computer can use any printer on the network. No more wheeling the thing around on a cart and then trying to find the driver.

Sharing means that your files can be anywhere. You can use those large hard disks for backup, for making second copies in the background, and for organizing your documents using the whole network as a resource.

All of the software that you need to run a nifty little network comes with Windows 98, so why not use it? The Service Pack 1 release of Windows 98 provides Internet access through one computer on your small network to every computer on the network. You can also use other third party software to connect your computer to the Internet. Before Service Pack 1, Microsoft's only solution was to sell you Windows NT as a server. No more.

Setting up a small network quickly and cheaply

Given the low cost and ease of installation provided by Windows 98, it makes a lot of sense to connect two or more computers together in a workgroup with inexpensive networking hardware. If you purchase plug and play networking cards (adapters) and install them in computers with plug and play BIOSes, Windows 98 will install its networking software and drivers for you.

What's the easiest and cheapest way to set up a network? Buy an Ethernet starter kit and, if you have more computers than there are network cards in the starter kit, a few extra network cards and cables.

Are you going to be able to install it and set it up yourself? Yes — just follow the instructions in this chapter, perhaps backed up with Chapter 24 of *Windows 98 Secrets* and the web sites that we recommend.

What's it going to cost? Fast enough — $85; really fast — $130; more for additional cards and cables. To find a 100 Mbps (megabits per second) Ethernet starter kit, check out the kit available from Linksys at www.linksys.com. You can also visit the homePCnetwork at www.homepcnetwork.com to read their latest recommendations and reviews.

Installing a small network on the cheap requires nothing more than buying an Ethernet starter kit that includes a couple of ISA plug and play NE2000-compatible 10 Mbps Ethernet cards, some Class 3 cable with RJ-45 connectors, and a small hub. If you have a portable computer with a Type II PCMCIA slot and card and socket drivers, you need to purchase a separate 10 Mbps Ethernet PC Card for it (the kits don't include these PC cards). Plug everything together, turn on the computers, and the network installs itself. (If you want more detailed guidance on setting up your network, see the steps later in this section.)

The incremental cost of going to 100 Mbps Ethernet is now so small that the benefits don't have to be very great to justify the additional expense. The major difference you'll see is that applications and files stored on other computers appear to be stored on your own. When you're using 10 Mbps Ethernet, you notice that it takes a while to pump 100MB of data over to another computer. This might discourage you from backing up as often as you would with 100 Mbps Ethernet.

If your network consists of a portable with the docking station and a desktop computer, make sure that the docking station has a PCI interface and can handle the 100 Mbps Ethernet PCI cards. Otherwise there is no need to go to the faster network.

Buying a 100 Mbps Ethernet network means buying an Ethernet starter kit with a 100 Mbps hub, PCI network cards, and Class 5 cable with RJ-45 connectors (see the steps below for more about these hardware options). Your network starter kit should come with a manual on how to install the network. Use it.

If you have older equipment, you'll need to give Windows 98 some help in implementing the network. We intermix the details of setting up older equipment with our general networking setup steps:

STEPS:

Setting Up a Small Ethernet Network for Home Or Business

Step 1. Purchase an Ethernet starter kit, either 10 Mbps or 100 Mbps. This will include a hub, a couple of network cards, and the twisted pair (10BaseT) cables needed to hook two computers or more together.

If you need extra cards, buy NE2000-compatible plug and play network cards. (There is no need these days to purchase cards that aren't plug and play.) If you are setting up a small network with light networking tasks, you only need 10 Mbps Ethernet cards (at about $19 each) that comply with the IEEE 802.3 and 10BASE-T Ethernet standards.

These are very standard cards, and they are widely available. Most come with both BNC and RJ-45 connectors. They'll most likely include BNC T connectors. If you are going with 100 Mbps Ethernet, get Fast Ethernet (100 BASE-TX) cards, which handle both 10 and 100 Mbps at about $35.

Cards are available for ISA slots as well as PCI slots. The ISA-slot cards are less expensive and perfectly fine for small networks. In the future, computers will not come with ISA slots, so this option will not be available. If you are going to use 100 Mbps, use PCI network cards (your only choice, really).

Continued

STEPS

Setting Up a Small Ethernet Network for Home Or Business

(continued)

If you need a card that can connect to a portable, you can purchase a PCMCIA 10 Mbps Ethernet card for about $60. One place to look for this type of card is www.zdnet.com. Be sure that the connector cable that goes from the card to the RJ-45 and/or BNC jacks is included. PCMCIA cards that handle both 10 and 100 Mbps cost about $100.

If your portable connects to the network through a docking station, be sure that it either includes a networking card or purchase a ISA or PCI card that works with the bus in the docking station.

Install the cards in available slots in both of the computers.

Step 2.   If you need additional cables, purchase ready-made 25-foot Class 3 cables for 10 Mbps Ethernet. They are available for about $4. One place to check out is http://www.computergate.com. Class 5 cables, required for 100 Mbps Ethernet, cost about $7 for 25-foot lengths with the connectors already installed. Connect the hub and Ethernet cards by plugging in the cables.

Ethernet hubs used to be expensive. If you were just hooking two computers together, it was cheaper to go with a coaxial cable. (The problem with using a coaxial cable is that if one computer connection goes down, the whole network goes down, although with two computers, this doesn't matter.)

Now you can buy five-port 10 Mbps hubs for around $40. It makes sense to just purchase a hub and plug in Class 3 unshielded twisted-pair wire with RJ-45 jacks. This is a star configuration, with each computer plugged into the hub. If one leg goes down, it doesn't affect the other legs.

Hubs that handle 100 Mbps Ethernet cost a bit less than $100, standalone. If you purchased the Ethernet starter kit, you've got the hub.

If you are never going to have more than two computers networked to each other, you can use a *crossover* Class 3 or 5 twisted pair cable.

Step 3.   T-connectors and terminators come with the cards; use them to connect coxial cable to the T-connectors, the T-connectors to the cards, and the terminators to the other end of the T-connectors.

If you are using a hub, you don't need to worry about this. Use a hub.

Step 4. If your network cards are plug and play, turn off your computer, plug in the cards, plug in the hub, plug the cables into the cards and the hub, turn on the computers, and let your Windows 98 machines find the cards and install the network. Jump down to step 6.

If the cards aren't plug and play compatible, run the DOS-based configuration software first to set up their interrupts and I/O addresses. The default values for the cards may be okay, depending on what hardware you have installed in your computers.

To find out which interrupts and I/O addresses are available on your computers, boot them up, click the System icon in the Control Panel, click the Device Manager tab, highlight Computer, and click the Properties button. Click the Interrupt Request (IRQ) option button to see which addresses are already used, as shown in Figure 23-1; used interrupts are listed first.

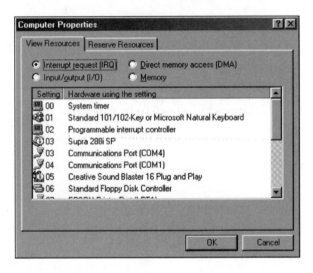

Figure 23-1: The Interrupt Request listing on the View Resources tab of the Computer Properties dialog box.

Click Start, Programs, MS-DOS Prompt, and run the DOS-based configuration software from the DOS prompt.

Step 5. Click the Add New Hardware icon in the Control Panel on both computers. You can have the Add New Hardware Wizard search for your new adapters, or you can specify what you have. The wizard will load and configure the 32-bit protected-mode NDIS 5 driver for your adapters.

Continued

STEPS

Setting Up a Small Ethernet Network for Home Or Business
(continued)

You can check which resources (interrupts and memory) your network card uses. Press Win+Pause/Break (or right-click My Computer and click Properties), click the Device Manager tab, double-click Network Adapters, double-click your network card name, and click the Resources tab, as shown in Figure 23-2.

If there are conflicts with other interrupts, you will need to free up interrupts. See "Grab interrupts for new peripherals" in Chapter 21.

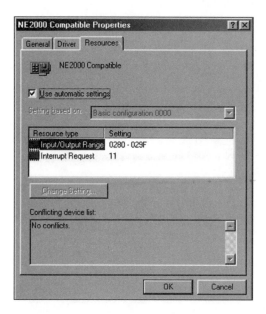

Figure 23-2: The network resources listing.

Step 6. If you have a PCMCIA network card, it will undoubtedly be plug and play. Be sure that your portable computer supports at least Card and Socket services. You may have a portable that supports CardBus, a 32-bit connection to the PC Card. If so, you can purchase a CardBus-compatible PC Card that allows for a 100 Mbps Ethernet connection.

You will be asked for your network card drivers after you turn on your computer. Windows may automatically find them on your Windows 98 CD-ROM and install them, although you can direct it toward driver files on diskettes or a CD-ROM supplied by the card manufacturer. There is no need to use the drivers from the manufacturer unless you are sure that they are newer than the ones on the Windows 98 CD-ROM. You can update these drivers later by going to the Windows Update site on the web.

After you restart your computer (when directed to do so), click the Network icon in the Control Panel. Click the Identification tab in the Network dialog box. Make sure that the two computers have different names, but the same workgroup name, as illustrated in Figure 23-3. Click OK.

Step 7. Click the Network icon in the Control Panel. Highlight your network adapter in the list of networking components. To see which networking protocols have been bound to the adapter, click the Properties button and then click the Bindings tab, as shown in Figure 23-4.

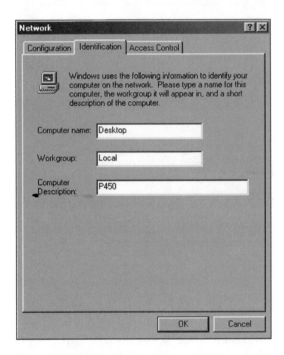

Figure 23-3: This computer is named Desktop, and it shares the Local workgroup with one or more computers.

For a small computer network, if you are not going to hook up to the Internet, you'll most likely want to bind NetBEUI and/or IPX/SPX (for playing games). Windows 95 automatically binds these two protocols.

The TCP/IP protocol (and only TCP/IP) is bound to your network card automatically by Windows 98. This works fine for a small network. There are lots of little software packages that work with it, and you'll need it if you're going to connect to the Internet.

Continued

STEPS

Setting Up a Small Ethernet Network for Home Or Business

(continued)

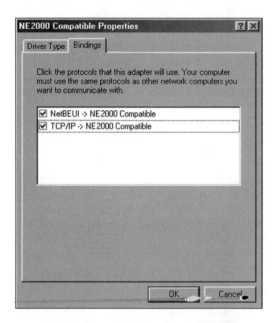

Figure 23-4: In this figure, both the NetBEUI and the TCP/IP protocols have been bound to the network adapter.

If you need to bind a protocol to the list, click OK to close the Properties dialog box, and then click the Add button in the Configuration tab of the Network dialog box. Highlight Protocol in the Select Network Component Type dialog box, click the next Add button, and select the protocol in the Select Network Protocol dialog box (see Figure 23-5). Click OK.

Step 8. Client for Microsoft Networks is added by default during the initial Windows 98 network setup. It is necessary if you want to allow sharing of your resources so that each of the computers can be a peer server to the others. If it isn't listed in the Network dialog box, you need to add it, as well as File and Printer Sharing for Microsoft Networks.

To add Client for Microsoft Networks, click Add in the Configuration tab of the Network dialog box, click Client in the Select Network Component Type dialog box, and click Add again. In the Select Network Client dialog box, highlight Microsoft on the left, and click Client for Microsoft Networks on the right. Click OK.

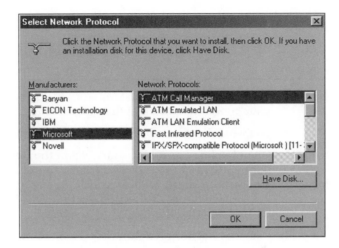

Figure 23-5: Select the manufacturer and the protocol that you want to add in the Select Network Protocol dialog box.

To add File and Printer Sharing for Microsoft Networks, click Add in the Configuration tab of the Network dialog box, click Service in the Select Network Component Type dialog box, and click Add again. In the Select Network Service dialog box, highlight Microsoft on the left, and click File and Printer Sharing for Microsoft Networks on the right. Click OK.

You probably don't want to be file and printer sharing over the Internet, so you can remove this binding to your Dial-Up Adapter. If you forget, you will be reminded the first time you try to access your Internet service provider, and you can remove it then.

To remove it manually, highlight TCP/IP -> Dial-Up Adapter in the Configuration tab of your Network dialog box, click Properties, and click OK when you see the warning shown in Figure 23-6 not to configure your TCP/IP properties for a dial-up connection here. Click Bindings, clear the File and Printer Sharing for Microsoft Networks check box, and click OK.

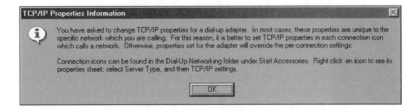

Figure 23-6: Click OK when you see this warning.

Continued

STEPS

Setting Up a Small Ethernet Network for Home Or Business
(continued)

Step 9. Click the OK button in the Network dialog box, and then reboot your computers for all of this to take effect.

You won't have to reboot if you are using plug and play cards.

Step 10. Open Explorer or folder windows on the Desktops of both computers. Right-click resources (disk drives and/or folders) that you want to share, click Sharing in the context menu, and configure the sharing properties. Do the same in the Printers folder for printers that you are going to share.

Step 11. Click the Network Neighborhood icon on the Desktop of one of the computers. You should see the name of the workgroup in the Network Neighborhood folder window; if not, click the Entire Network icon. Click the workgroup name to see the names of all the network computers. Click their names to see the shared resources.

Using these steps, you can install the NetBEUI, IPX/SPX, and/or TCP/IP protocols and bind them to your network cards. If you are running a small network, you don't have to run all three protocols. You can just use NetBEUI if you are just sharing printers, disks, and folders, and not accessing the Internet. You can remove the other protocols in the Network dialog box.

If you want to set up a local web server or share a modem on the network to contact your Internet service provider, you can get rid of all the protocols other than TCP/IP. TCP/IP is, after all, the default networking protocol for Windows 98.

IP address auto assignment

Windows 98, unlike Windows 95, automatically assigns each computer on your local network an IP address. This allows TCP/IP to be the default networking protocol for Windows 98 without further user configuration. Windows 98 goes out on the network when you first start Windows and checks if there is a Dynamic Host Configuration Protocol (DHCP) server. If not, it assigns an IP address to the local computer. It then checks to make sure that this is a unique address by checking all the IP addresses of the other computers on the local network. There is no need for a DHCP server locally.

To see for yourself how the auto assignment works, click Start, Settings, Control Panel, and Network. Highlight the TCP/IP bound to your network card (TCP/IP -> *network card name*), as shown in Figure 23-7, and click Properties.

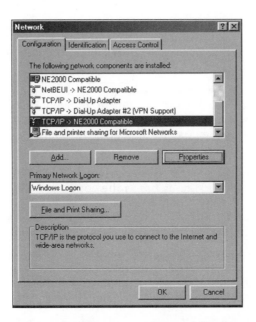

Figure 23-7: Select the TCP/IP bound to your network card in the Configuration tab of the Network dialog box.

Click the IP Address tab, and notice that Obtain an IP Address Automatically is marked by default, as shown in Figure 23-8.

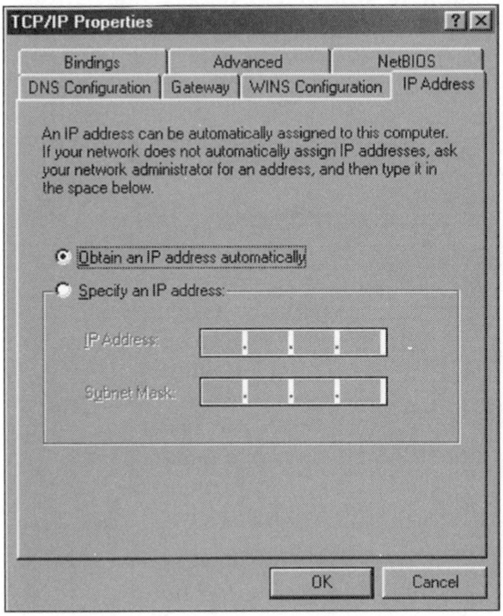

Figure 23-8: The first option is marked by default.

This setting allows Windows 98 to automatically assign each of the computers on your network a unique IP address. If you have a DHCP server on the network, this setting allows the DHCP server to assign each computer its unique IP address.

If you install Sygate, WinGate, or other Internet access software on one of your computers, it will include a limited implementation of a DHCP server that can assign IP addresses to the computers on your network. You should leave Obtain an IP Address Automatically marked if you want to use these mini-DHCP servers.

Without a DHCP server, Windows 98 takes a bit of time to assign IP addresses to the computers on your network every time you start up. It has to go out and make sure that each computer has a unique IP address, and assign addresses that don't conflict. You can cut out this automated bit of checking (and reduce the time that it takes to start Windows) by assigning the IP addresses manually.

One way to do this is to let them be assigned automatically at first. Then follow these steps:

STEPS:

Setting a Permanent IP Address

Step 1. Find out what IP address and subnet mask have been assigned to your computer by clicking Start, Run, typing **winipcfg**, and pressing Enter. Display the drop-down list at the top of the dialog box and highlight your network card name. Your computer's IP address will be displayed in the IP Autoconfiguration Address field, as shown in Figure 23-9. Write it down, or keep this window open.

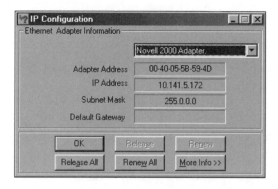

Figure 23-9: The IP Configuration dialog box. The first field should contain your network card name.

Step 2. Click Start, Settings, Control Panel, Network.

Step 3.   Scroll down the components list until you see the listing for TCP/IP and your network card, written thusly: TCP/IP -> *network card name*. Highlight this entry and click Properties.

Step 4.   Click the IP Address tab if it isn't already displayed. Mark the Specify an IP Address option button, as shown in Figure 23-10.

Step 5.   You can now manually enter an IP address and subnet mask. Type the IP address that you just saw in the IP Configuration dialog box. Enter a submask of **255.0.0.0**. Click OK, click OK.

Step 6.   You may be prompted to insert your Windows 98 CD-ROM and asked to restart your computer. Follow the prompts.

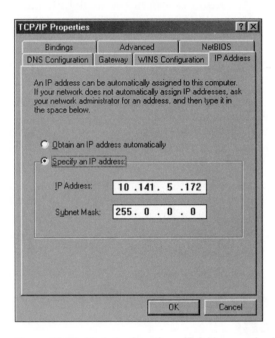

Figure 23-10: Mark the Specify an IP Address option button.

To get each computer on the network to recognize these changes on all the computers on your network, you may need to open your Explorer and press F5 to refresh its view.

You've now taken the automatically assigned IP address for your computer and permanently assigned it to your computer. All computers on the same local network should use IP addresses that start with the same first three numbers.

You can find out more about IP address autoconfiguration in the Microsoft Knowledge Base article at support.microsoft.com/support/kb/articles/q188/4/80.asp.

If you'd like to understand the nature of IP addresses and subnet masks, Microsoft provides a thorough explanation in "Understanding TCP/IP Addressing and Subnetting Basics," which you can find at support.microsoft.com/support/kb/articles/q164/0/15.asp.

Make the network resources local

You can get to the resources on the network by using the Network Neighborhood, or by entering the UNC (universal naming convention) name of another computer in the Start, Run dialog box or in the Address bar of the Explorer — but this gets old quick. If you had to do this every time you sent a document to a printer connected to another computer, you'd soon be shopping for your own printer.

You'll want to map the available hard disks and folders on other computers as though they were local drives. Of course, this is trivially easy to do. In your Explorer, click Tools, Map Network Drive. If you want this connection to persist (be there the next time you restart your computer), mark the Reconnect on Logon check box in the Map Network Drive dialog box.

If you find yourself doing this a bunch because new network resources keep being added, click View, Folder Options, click the View tab, and mark Show Map Network Drive Button in Toolbar (see Figure 23-11).

Even better, put shortcuts to shared hard disks and folders right on your Desktop or in your toolbars.

Going online with a small office/ home network

If you have a small office or home network using the TCP/IP protocol (automatically installed with Windows 98), it is quite easy to provide a single connection to the Internet through one computer on the network. This means that you only need to have one outside telephone or cable line that will be used to connect everyone on the network to the Internet. You only need to have one account at your Internet service provider. You only need one modem to service the whole network.

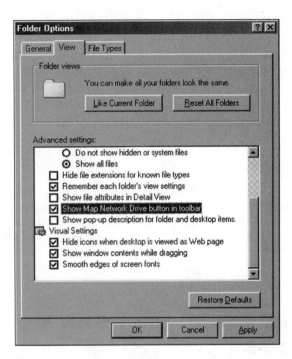

Figure 23-11: In the View tab of the Folder Options dialog box, mark Show Map Network Drive Button in Toolbar.

There are a couple of downsides. First, the computer that has the modem has to be up and running for everyone else to be able to connect to the Internet. If every computer on the network had its own modem, it would be each user's responsibility to make his or her own connection. If your Internet connection didn't work, well, no skin off anyone else's nose.

Second, all the traffic to the Internet service provider is going to go through one computer and over the local network. As you add client workstations, this can turn the network or the modem server into a bottleneck. You may need to go to a higher speed Ethernet and/or larger bandwidth access to the service provider.

The computer connection to the Internet service provider can be an analog modem (even a slow one), a cable modem, or a DSL connection through a network adapter (other options are available). With DSL, you'll need two network adapters — one for the local network, and the other for the DSL modem.

If you have the Service Pack 1 or OEM Service Release 1 version of Windows 98, you have the Internet Connection Sharing software that allows you to connect your network to the Internet. In early February 1999, Microsoft bought Nevod, Inc and its product NAT 1000, and turned it into Internet Connection Sharing.

If you don't have the service pack, there are numerous other ways to make one computer on the network the connecting node to the Internet. A simple solution is provided by SyberGen, Inc. Their Sygate software runs on one Windows 98 computer and turns it into the gateway to the Internet for the network.

Sygate is very simple to install and operates transparently. It has its own mini-DHCP that automatically assigns IP addresses to the rest of the computers on your network and enters a DNS and gateway address in each of the computer's network settings. This actually didn't work for us, but it was pretty easy to enter these values ourselves.

Our version of the software didn't come with a help file, but you can download online help by right-clicking the Sygate Manager icon in your system tray and clicking On-line Help. The PDF file that we could then download was out of date. Check the What's New icon on the Sygate web site to get a better idea of the current configuration.

You'll find Sygate at www.sygate.com.

WinGate, the pioneer Internet gateway for small networks

In addition to Internet Connection Sharing and Sygate, discussed in the previous section, you also have other options for getting your small network online. WinGate is the pioneer in this field, and at the end of 1998 they released a brand new version of their software, version 3.0. This version represents a big change in WinGate's architecture, which now includes client software at each computer.

The previous version allowed you to connect two computers to the Internet for no cost, certainly the deal of the year. It didn't have the ability to allow NetMeeting traffic, although no one seemed to be able to understand why.

WinGate 2.x is quite difficult to set up relative to Sygate. It requires modifications to your settings in Outlook Express (or other e-mail package) as well as to Internet Explorer. Sygate does not require any changes to your Internet application settings.

Furthermore, the WinGate 2.x help system, while extensive, is poorly organized. It is quite difficult to find and follow the setup procedures, especially because they are generally out of date with respect to the applications that have to be modified.

WinGate 3.0 is quite a bit of an improvement, although now it costs $40 to have two computers share a modem. You don't have to configure your applications, and your TCP/IP settings are configured automatically for you. You can check out WinGate and download a trial version at www.wingate.com.

Online network resources

Before you purchase a small business or home network, you'll want to check in with the homePCnetwork at www.homepcnetwork.com. Not only will you find instructions on how to set up a small network, but you'll also find the latest reviews and tests of Ethernet starter kits, network cards, Internet access software, and so on. This site is tightly organized and easy to understand. It concentrates on the small network, so you don't have to wander through lots of extraneous material.

At the other end of the spectrum, with respect to organization, you can check out the sprawling "Windows 95/98 Networking FAQ" at www.helmig .com/j_helmig/faq.htm. Presenting a much wider focus and drawing on the developer's history with Windows 95, this site provides the next level of network understanding as well as a jump up to bigger networks. You can learn about how networks and protocols operate, and explore all the little twists of connecting peer-to-peer networks with computers that aren't running Windows 98.

Be sure to check out "Workgroups have Limitations" if your network is getting bigger than 15 computers, "Browsing the Network" to see how the Network Neighborhood knows where the resources are, "Your Own Personal Web Server" to learn how to set up Microsoft Personal Web Server, and "Sharing and Mapping a Drive via the Internet" to learn how to use the Internet as though it were a local area network. The FAQ also includes lots of information on connecting to a Novell network, Direct Cable Connection, TCP/IP routing, troubleshooting, and on and on.

We do think that Mr. Helmig gets it wrong with his recommendations about pulling the TCP/IP protocol on a small network, but other than that, it's good stuff.

The *Windows 98 Resource Kit* has plenty of material on Windows networking. This is a main focus of the book and online manual. We suggest using it as a networking resource, especially for larger network installations. You'll find out how to install it in "Windows 98 Resource Kit Online" in Chapter 16.

The articles in the Microsoft Knowledge Base update the *Resource Kit*. Go to support.microsoft.com/support/search/c.asp. Then select Windows 98 in the My Search Is About field, type **Network** in the My Question Is field, click Go, and choose among the networking articles that appear.

xDSL

You can connect one of the computers on your local network to a DSL modem and get a super fast 24-hour-a-day digital connection to your Internet service provider for an additional $40/month. That is, you can if you are lucky enough to be close enough to a central (actually dispersed) telephone office, and if there is an available port at the office for you.

Exposed on the Internet

If you are about to connect to the Internet and you have bound File and Printer Sharing for Microsoft Networks to your TCP/IP protocol (the default setting), you will be warned that your TCP/IP is in turn bound to your Dial-Up Adapter. If you don't disable this setting when warned, you should be aware that you are about to turn your computer and printer into servers that anyone on the Internet can access.

It's just as though you were treating the Internet as a small local area network. You might share your C drive locally, but do you want everyone on the Internet to have access to it?

You can immediately disable this setting when warned, or you can disable it manually at another time. To do this, click Start, Settings, Control Panel, Network, TCP/IP -> Dial-Up Adapter, Properties, OK, Bindings, and clear the check box next to File And Printer Sharing For Microsoft Networks. You can also do this for TCP/IP -> Dial-Up Adapter #2 if you don't want to share your computer or printer on your virtual private network (VPN). (You won't be using VPN on a home network because you need at least a Windows NT server.)

If you want to see if you are reasonably secure when calling your Internet service provider, point Internet Explorer at www.rootshell.com/smbcheck.cgi. This will tell you your level of security. You can find out more about Internet hacking at www.rootshell.com.

Hackers on the Internet can use any of a number of IP address-scanning or port-scanning programs to scan a particular IP address or range of addresses. This process is called *strobing*. If you have File and Printer Sharing for Microsoft Networks bound to your TCP/IP protocol, this scanning software will display the share names of resources on your network and/or computer.

A hacker can type the command **nbtstat –a *yourIPaddress*** to display your computer name, your workgroup name, and any user account names on your computer. If you open a DOS window on your computer and type this command, replacing *yourIPaddress* with the IP address of a computer on your local area network, you'll see this information. By the way, the *nb* in the DOS command *nbtstat* stands for NetBIOS.

If you open a DOS window and type **netstat –a –n** and press Enter, you'll get a listing of your current IP address and the ports that are listening. Ports 137, 138, and 139 should be recorded as listening. Password cracking programs direct their attacks at these ports.

The "forgetting the password" problem

The most common problem that people have with Windows 95 or Windows 98 is that Windows won't allow them to store their passwords in the password cache. We discuss all the aspects of this problem in *Windows 98 Secrets*. We've saved a bunch of folks from the agony of re-installing Windows 95 and 98 by providing them with solutions.

You can also check out "The Windows 95/98 Network FAQ" at www.helmig .com/j_helmig/faq.htm and click "Dialup Networking Does NOT Save the Password." It's cheaper than buying our book. Also, see "Can't save your Dial-Up Networking password" in Chapter 17. PC Magazine has a long and useful article on passwords (that also deals with Windows 95) at www .zdnet.com/pcmag/pctech/content/16/21/os1621.002.html. You can find plenty of information in the *Windows 98 Resource Kit* compiled HTML help file on your Windows 98 CD-ROM. Just search on the word *password*. To see how to install it, refer to "Windows 98 Resource Kit Online" in Chapter 16.

Synchronize the clocks on your network

We use the little network utility Socket Watch to find the correct time every time we connect to the Internet. You can easily download it from a shareware site such as Tucows at www.tucows.com.

Once you've got the correct time on one machine, you might as well share it with the rest of them.

Use Notepad to create a little batch file called something like time.bat. You only need to put one line in the batch file: **net time \\\thenameofthecomputerwithsocketwatch**. Save the time.bat file in your \My System folder. Drag and drop a shortcut to it into your \Windows\Start Menu\Programs\StartUp folder. Do this for each of the computers (other than the one with Socket Watch) on your network.

Right-click the time.bat file in your Explorer, click Properties, click Program, and mark the Close on Exit check box.

Get rid of the hand under the shared resource icon

If you share a resource, a hand icon appears under the icon of the shared resource. You can eliminate this hand icon by taking these steps:

STEPS:

Ridding Yourself of the Blue-Sleeved Hand

Step 1. Click Start, Run, type **regedit**, and press Enter.

Step 2. Navigate to HKEY_CLASSES_ROOT\Network.

Step 3. Highlight the SharingHandler key in the left pane of your Registry editor, as shown in Figure 23-12.

Step 4. Double-click the Default value in the right pane.

Step 5. Delete the value **msshrui.dll** in the Value Data field in the Edit String dialog box. Click OK, and exit the Registry editor.

Step 6. Restart Windows for this to take effect.

To restore the hand, repeat these steps, but in step 5, define the Default value as **msshrui.dll**.

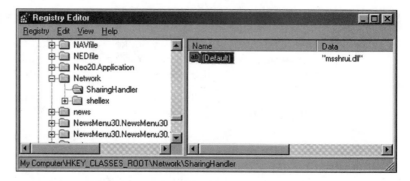

Figure 23-12: Highlight the SharingHandler Registry key.

Let me see those DHCP errors again

Windows gives you plenty of opportunities to never again see certain dialog boxes. If you received a DHCP error message and marked the check box in the DHCP error dialog box requesting not to see these error messages again, that's it, you won't. But in case you change your mind, you can take these steps:

STEPS:

Seeing DHCP Errors Once Again

Step 1.   Click Start, Run, type **regedit**, and press Enter.

Step 2.   Navigate to HKEY_LOCAL_MACHINE\System\CurrentControlSet \Services\VxD\DHCP.

Step 3.   Double-click PopupFlag in the right pane of the Registry editor, and press Delete.

Step 4.   Type **01**.

Step 5.   Click OK, and exit the Registry editor.

See the other players in a multiplayer game

Lots of multiuser games use the IPX/SPX networking protocol to support communication among players. Sometimes one player can't see the other players. What's missing is a commonly agreed *frame type*. To get everyone in sync, take these steps:

STEPS:

Setting the IPX/SPX Frame Type

Step 1.   Click Start, Settings, Control Panel, and click the Network icon.

Step 2.   Highlight IPX/SPX-compatible Protocol -> *your network adapter or modem.*

Step 3.   Click the Properties button, click the Advanced tab, and highlight Frame Type, as shown in Figure 23-13.

Step 4.   Display the Value drop-down list, select Ethernet 802.2 or Ethernet 802.3 (whichever is used on your network), and click OK.

Continued

STEPS

Setting the IPX/SPX Frame Type *(continued)*

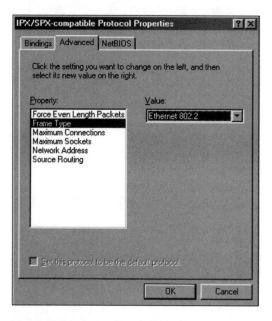

Figure 23-13: Frame Type is in the Property list. Use the Value drop-down list to set the type.

All of the other players should also do this with their computers.

Copy from machine A to machine B

I'm sitting at one computer typing away on this book. To my left I've got another computer that I use to test beta software, install and test shareware, and capture screen images. Across the room, Belinda sits in front of her computer working on the Outlook Express chapters or editing some of my previous work. I want to ship paragraphs and bits of documents or graphics between computers on our small network. What should someone like me do?

One option is to create Desktop or Start menu shortcuts to documents stored on another computer. Then I can copy and paste text to and from those documents by invoking the shortcuts and saving my edits. It works, but it isn't always that convenient to get to the shortcuts, the shortcuts can easily proliferate, and you've got to have the document on your own computer as well as one on the other one, in case the other computer isn't on.

Another option is to use NetMeeting. NetMeeting is nice as a communications tool, but it is a bit of overkill for just sending little pieces of documents.

What we need is a Clipbook that actually works. A clipboard that lets you share your Windows Clipboard with other users — a network clipboard.

That's just what you get with Network Clipboard. Install Network Clipboard on a few computers that are connected together with a local area TCP/IP network (basically the default for Windows 98), click its icon on the Desktop, and the other computers will show up in your Active Users list, as shown in Figure 23-14.

Figure 23-14: The Active Users list on a three-computer network. (The computer you are using isn't listed).

If your network consists of one person with two computers, and you log on as yourself on both computers, you won't be able to copy between computers. You need to use two slightly different logon names.

The Network Clipboard lets you send your Windows Clipboard to one of the listed users. He or she can choose to accept it or not. There is no provision for multiple Clipboards. Users can assign their own hot keys to bring up the Network Clipboard window (right-click the icon in the system tray and click Options), and can decide whether they want a beep when a Clipboard comes their way. By default, Network Clipboard places itself in each user's StartUp group.

You use your regular Copy command (Ctrl+C or Ctrl+Ins) to copy something to your Windows Clipboard. You then use the Network Clipboard to send whatever is in your Clipboard to another computer. It overwrites the material in the other computer's Clipboard.

One problem that we had with Network Clipboard was that it wouldn't work when we were connected to the Internet. The author knows about this problem and has promised to fix it. However, it hasn't been fixed yet, and we expected it to be fixed by early 1999. Check on this problem before you send in the money.

Network Clipboard is shareware, but it's pretty cheap at $15 for five users. You'll find it at www.geocities.com/SiliconValley/Network/7846/netclip.html.

Another option is the Polar NetworkClipboard. It appears to let you share multiple Clipboards, as indicated by the tab shown in Figure 23-15, although we were unable to test that feature. Actually, we weren't able to test any of its features. Unfortunately, Polar Clipboard didn't recognize any of the users on our network, not even one other one.

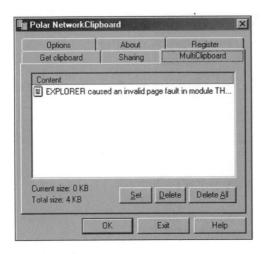

Figure 23-15: Polar NetworkClipboard's MultiClipboard tab.

We include Polar NetworkClipboard because, if it works for you, it adds that extra dimension of multiple Clipboards (we think). Multiple Clipboards were not actually mentioned in the help file (which is the only documentation).

Polar NetworkClipboard, unlike Network Clipboard, works on the Get model as opposed to the Put model. If you want something from someone's Clipboard, they have to be willing to share it with you first.

You'll find Polar NetworkClipboard at www.polarsoftware.com/products.asp.

Direct Cable Connection with TCP/IP only

When you install Dial-Up Networking with Windows 98, TCP/IP is the only networking protocol installed (unless you are installing Windows 98 over Windows 95). You can also install Direct Cable Connection (DCC) if you want to connect your portable to your desktop computer with a serial or parallel cable. You may find that when you start DCC, you will be asked for the host computer's name. If the host computer is on a network, its name, as far as DCC is concerned, is its IP address.

After you start DCC, you may see a dialog box such as the one shown in Figure 23-16, which asks for the host's name after it can't find the shared files and folders. DCC has already made the connection from the guest to the host. The host will verify that the guest has the correct name and password, if any, and then the guest will display this dialog box to prompt for the host name.

Figure 23-16: Enter the host's IP address.

Our experience is that if the host computer has a network card installed, and TCP/IP is the network protocol configured for the network card, DCC will not accept the host's name (its UNC name, otherwise known as the computer name) as its name, but only the host's IP address.

If you are using TCP/IP as your only networking protocol, then that is what DCC also uses. If the host doesn't have a network card installed (and therefore doesn't have an IP address), DCC will accept the host's.

Summary

Networking couldn't be easier and cheaper, so it's time to jump in.

▶ Connect your network to the Internet to save money and speed up access.

▶ Find online networking help resources.

▶ Synchronize the clocks on all your computers on the network.

▶ Get rid of that little sharing icon if it bothers you.

▶ Share your Windows Clipboard to copy and paste across the network.

Chapter 24

DOS

In This Chapter

Still using DOS? If you are, we've got a few tricks to help you out.

▶ Start DOSKEY when you open a DOS window.

▶ DOS handles UNC names over your network.

▶ If you use DOS a lot, you might want to load the real-mode disk cache.

Use DOSKEY when you open a DOS window

DOSKEY keeps track of the DOS commands you have entered so that you can scroll back and repeat a previous command. It also has lots of other uses in a DOS window. If you want to see what DOSKEY can do click Start, Programs, MS-DOS Prompt. Type **doskey /?** and press Enter.

You can put DOSKEY in your Autoexec.bat and it will always be there when you open a DOS window. The downside to this is that loading it in your Autoexec.bat means it will occupy a certain amount of conventional memory, with only a small benefit.

It is possible to load and unload DOSKEY every time you open a DOS window. This option gives you the benefits of DOSKEY without the conventional memory cost. DOSKEY is small and loads quite quickly.

STEPS:

Adding DOSKEY to Your DOS Prompt

Step 1. Click Start, Programs.

Step 2. Right-click MS-DOS Prompt, click Properties, and click the Program tab.

Step 3. In the Batch File field, type **DOSKEY > NUL**.

Step 4. Click OK.

You can add other DOSKEY switches to this command if you like.

Check the DOS filenames

There is one option in the ScanDisk Advanced Options dialog box that is not explained when you click the Help button (the question mark in the upper-right corner of the dialog box) and then click the option Report MS-DOS Mode Name Length Errors. To display this dialog box, shown in Figure 24-1, click Start, Programs, Accessories, System Tools, ScanDisk, Advanced. Windows 98 saves filenames in both long and DOS-compatible versions. The DOS-compatible version consists of eight characters and a three-character extension. Marking this option tells ScanDisk to check this 8.3-format version of the filenames and report any problems.

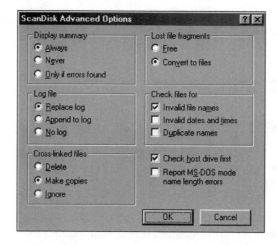

Figure 24-1: The ScanDisk Advanced Options dialog box. The check box for reporting name length errors is in the lower-right corner.

DOS understands server names on the network

You can use UNC-style server names with DOS commands in a DOS window. For example, if there is a server called Brian on the network, typing **dir\\Brian\C** and pressing Enter will display the contents of the C drive on the Brian computer, if the C drive is shared.

Tip

Not all of the DOS commands work. DIR, MD, RD, COPY, MOVE and REN do, while CD does not.

Run DOS batch files with long filenames

Windows 98 DOS includes an internal DOS command that allows you to use long filenames in DOS batch files. In particular, you can use long filenames with the IF, FOR, DO, ERRORLEVEL, and GOTO commands.

The command LFNFOR sets a mode switch to permit the use of long file-names. At the DOS prompt, type **lfnfor** and press Enter to see the current state of LFNFOR mode, as shown in Figure 24-2. You can use the command in a batch file to turn on this mode, or put it in your Autoexec.bat to turn it on automatically. By default, it is turned off.

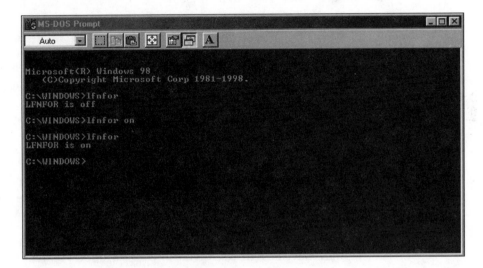

Figure 24-2: Type **lfnfor** at the DOS prompt to see its current state.

Thanks to Anthony Kinyon for help with this tip.

Disk caching in DOS

In *Windows 98 Secrets*, Chapters 34 and 35, we take great pains to discuss all the various aspects of DOS 7.1, the version of DOS that comes with Windows 98. Using our step-by-step guides in that book, you can configure your DOS Program Information Files to start up a DOS session with just the right configuration.

A simple trick that can do much to improve your DOS performance may have been lost amidst the wealth of information about DOS in *Windows 98 Secrets*. We want to take this opportunity to highlight this feature.

When you restart in MS-DOS mode (Start, Shut Down, Restart in MS-DOS Mode, OK), you may want to start the real-mode disk caching software, SmartDrive (Smartdrv.exe). This software speeds up access to programs and data stored on your hard disk, and may speed up your DOS application if it is disk access-intensive.

You have to weigh the benefit of faster access against the slower initial access to DOS and slower return to Windows. The default action of the Restart in MS-DOS Mode option in the Shut Down Windows dialog box is to start MS-DOS without rebooting your computer. A small stub of Windows is left in memory, and Windows will restart quickly without having to reboot your computer when you exit MS-DOS mode.

If you want to load the DOS disk cache program, you will have to configure your Restart in MS-DOS Mode command to reboot your computer when you go to DOS, and reboot it again to get back to Windows. Depending on your computer and the DOS application, this may be more trouble than it is worth.

To load SmartDrive with your Shut Down, Restart in MS-DOS Mode command, take these steps:

STEPS:

Loading SmartDrive When You Exit to DOS

Step 1. Use your Explorer to find the Exit To Dos file in your \Windows folder. If it isn't there, click Start, Shut Down, Restart in MS-DOS Mode, OK. Type **exit** and press Enter at the DOS prompt. You will now have an Exit To DOS file in your \Windows folder.

Step 2. Right-click your Exit To DOS file, select Properties, click the Program tab, and click the Advanced button. The MS-DOS Mode check box is marked, as shown in Figure 24-3. This means that marking the Restart in MS-DOS Mode command in the Shut Down Windows dialog box and clicking OK will restart your computer in MS-DOS mode without rebooting it. A stub of Windows will be left in memory and used to restart Windows when you exit MS-DOS mode.

Your computer will also read the \Windows\DOSStart.bat file and perform any commands in this batch file when it restarts in MS-DOS mode. This is not true if you make the changes detailed in the remaining steps.

Step 3. Mark the Specify a New MS-DOS Configuration option button. Config.sys and Autoexec.bat files for MS-DOS mode are created and filled with lines from your existing Autoexec.bat and Config. sys files (see Figure 24-4).

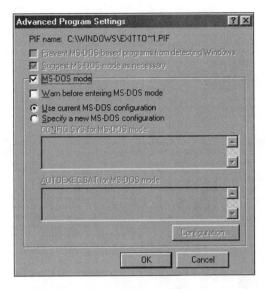

Figure 24-3: The Advanced Program Settings dialog box for the Exit To DOS program.

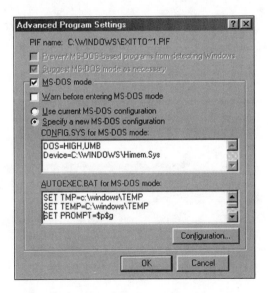

Figure 24-4: When activated, the Config.sys box and the Autoexec.bat box display editable lines from these programs.

Continued

STEPS

Loading SmartDrive When You Exit to DOS *(continued)*

Step 4. Click the Configuration button. The Select MS-DOS Configuration Options dialog box appears. Mark the Disk Cache check box (see Figure 24-5). Click OK.

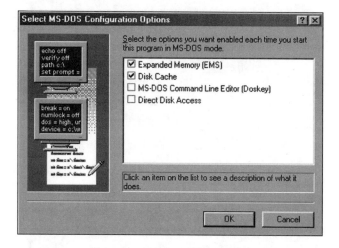

Figure 24-5: The Select MS-DOS Configuration Options dialog box.

Step 5. You will be warned by the message box shown in Figure 24-6 that the lines currently in your Autoexec.bat and Config.sys files for MS-DOS mode (only) will be replaced by a new configuration. Click Yes.

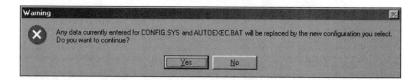

Figure 24-6: This warning lets you know that you are about to change your Config.sys and Autoexec.bat files for MS-DOS mode.

Step 6. Click OK in the Advanced Program Settings dialog box, and click OK in the Exit To DOS Properties dialog box.

If you now click Start, Shut Down, Restart in MS-DOS Mode, OK, you'll notice that your computer reboots to go to DOS. If you exit DOS, it will reboot to restart Windows. SmartDrive will be loaded when you exit to DOS.

You can configure any shortcut to any of your DOS programs using the same method described in these steps. There is nothing particularly special about the Restart in MS-DOS Mode command, other than the one issue discussed in the next paragraph.

You might wonder why you can't just load SmartDrive in DOSStart.bat and not have to reboot your computer to get to MS-DOS mode and later reboot it to get to Windows. This will in fact work, but there is a downside. When you exit DOS and go back to Windows, Windows will take note of the fact that SmartDrive has been loaded, and will drop you back to MS-DOS compatibility mode for disk access. Say goodbye to 32-bit disk access and its speed. Your computer is now using a 16-bit DOS driver to access your hard disk. You'll have to fully restart Windows to regain your 32-bit hard disk access.

If you are really tricky, you might think that you can load SmartDrive in your Autoexec.bat file and have it sitting there waiting for you to shut down Windows and go to MS-DOS mode. Unfortunately, Windows won't load SmartDrive from your normal Autoexec.bat file. If Windows sees SmartDrive in your Autoexec.bat file, it just ignores it. Besides, if it didn't, Windows would start up in MS-DOS compatibility mode and you wouldn't have 32-bit disk access.

You need to decide whether the tradeoff of disk caching versus rebooting to access MS-DOS mode and return to Windows is worth it.

You can read about these issues in much greater detail in *Windows 98 Secrets*.

Not enough memory for DOS programs in a DOS window

If you don't have enough memory to run a DOS program in a DOS window, it may be because Windows didn't unload the real-mode DriveSpace compressed disk driver when it started. When Windows loads, it is supposed to replace the real-mode version of DriveSpace and DoubleSpace with its own 32-bit protected-mode version that doesn't use conventional memory.

You can find out if this is your problem by checking the amount of memory available in the DOS window. Click Start, Programs, MS-DOS Prompt. At the DOS prompt, type **mem /d/p** and press Enter. Press Enter again. Check the output of mem to see if Drvspace.bin is loaded into conventional memory (see Figure 24-7). If it is loaded, it should be listed right above BUFFERS=12 in the rightmost column.

Figure 24-7: If Drvspace.bin is loaded, it will appear in the rightmost column, just above the line BUFFERS=12. In this example, it's not there.

If you find DriveSpace loaded in conventional memory in a DOS window, you can take a number of steps to make sure that it is unloaded when Windows starts. The steps are detailed in the Microsoft Knowledge Base article "DriveSpace Real-Mode Driver May Not Be Removed from Memory." You'll find it at support.microsoft.com/support/kb/articles/q134/3/64.asp.

Can't get out of DOS

You may find yourself in an odd predicament: You are unable to get to Windows because your computer keeps booting to DOS. Now you can certainly force this behavior by editing your Msdos.sys file and setting BootGUI=0, but this is unlikely to be the cause of your problem if no one else has had access to your computer and you have a reasonably good memory.

It is quite possible to get stuck in MS-DOS mode if you crashed your computer while running a program in MS-DOS mode. If you configured the MS-DOS program to work in MS-DOS mode and you specified that it use a new MS-DOS configuration (right-click the DOS program icon, click Properties, click Program, click the Advanced button), as illustrated earlier in Figure 24-4, you could be stuck with bogus Autoexec.bat and Config.sys files.

These private system files were created when you went into MS-DOS mode, and the regular Autoexec.bat and Config.sys files, if any, were renamed with the *wos* extension. They are still there if you crashed the DOS program and Windows didn't have a chance to delete them and rename the regular system files back to their, well, regular names.

If your computer boots to a DOS prompt when you start it, hold down the Ctrl key during the power-on self test, and then choose Safe Command Prompt Only in the Windows Startup menu. When you get to the DOS prompt, type **win /wx** and press Enter.

If you start the DOS program every time your restart your computer, exit the program normally and see if you are returned to Windows. If not, restart your computer and hold down the Ctrl key during power-on self test, and then choose Safe Mode Command Prompt Only from the Windows Startup menu. At the DOS command prompt, type **cd ** and press Enter to make sure that you are at the root directory.

Type these lines, pressing Enter after each one:

```
ren config.sys config.app
ren config.wos config.sys
ren autoexec.bat autoexec.app
ren autoexec.wos autoexec.bat
```

Restart your computer.

To find out more about MS-DOS and MS-DOS mode, read Chapter 34 of *Windows 98 Secrets*.

Summary

DOS is still with us, so we might as well make it easier.

▶ ScanDisk can check for correct DOS filenames.

▶ You can get DOS batch files to work with long filenames.

▶ DOS has memory limitations (as always), but we can help.

▶ If you get stuck in DOS and can't go back to Windows, here's how to get unstuck.

Chapter 25

Accessories

Find a Windows 98 file description

If you want to know more about a particular file, right-click it, click Properties, and see if it has a Version tab. If it does, click it and look for any information under Comments.

The Windows 98 File Information tool on your Windows 98 CD-ROM can also provide a wealth of information about your Windows 98 files (those that come on the Windows 98 CD-ROM), whether you have installed them or not. It displays the information found in a database (Access format) describing the purpose of each of the Windows 98 files. We assume someone at Microsoft has to keep track of this.

You'll find FileInfo.exe in the \tools\reskit\diagnose folder on your Windows 98 CD-ROM. It displays a list of Windows 98 files by name or extension, as shown in Figure 25-1. You'll need to at least copy this folder to your hard disk before you can read the contents of the database that contains the file information.

Tip

If you have a problem reading the database, right-click the Win98.mfi file in the copy of the diagnose folder on your hard disk. Click Properties, clear the Read-only check box, and click OK. Try again.

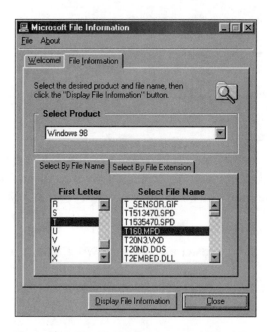

Figure 25-1: The File Information tab of Microsoft File Information dialog box lets you select a file by name or by file extension.

Double-click a filename (or select it and click the Display File Information button). The file's description, which can contain some pretty useful information, appears in the File Information dialog box (see Figure 25-2).

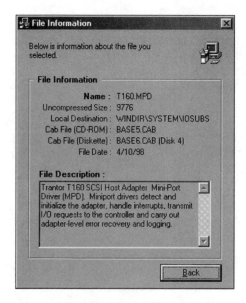

Figure 25-2: The file information for this *mpd* file shows, among other things, what the file does and which *cab* file contains it on the Windows 98 CD-ROM.

If you have installed the Windows 98 Resource Sampler Kit (by clicking the setup file in \tools\reskit on the Windows 98 CD-ROM), you can use it as another way to get to the Microsoft File Information tool. Click Start, Programs, Windows 98 Resource Kit, Tools Management Console. In the left pane of the Microsoft Management Console window, expand Windows 98 Resource Kit Tools Sampler, then Tool Categories, and then select Diagnostics and Trouble-shooting. Finally, double-click Microsoft File Information in the right pane.

The file information is stored in the Win98.mfi file, which is an Access database (as well it should be). You can open it with Access if you rename it to Win98.mdb.

Text Editors

Chances are, you use a text editor more than any other application on your computer. It sure is nice to tweak them so that they work the way you want them to.

Open Word 97 and Word 2000 documents in WordPad

The Windows 98 version of WordPad (Start, Programs, Accessories, WordPad) has been upgraded to allow it to read Word 97 documents (and because Word 2000 uses the same format, WordPad can read its files also). WordPad doesn't necessarily read files correctly if they use lots of Word's more esoteric features, but it at least gives you a good chance of seeing the text in Word files even if you don't have Word.

Tip

If you don't have Word and need to read Word documents, you can also download the latest Word reader from the Microsoft web site at www.microsoft.com/office.

Thanks to Adam Vujic for pointing this out.

A little Word 97 secret

We usually don't give out a lot of Word secrets, leaving that to authors, such as Woody Leonard, who concentrate on that particular piece of software. However, we received one secret from Galah Nuga, via Chris Pirillo at www.lockergnome.com, that we thought was too cool not to share.

Have you noticed that dragging the scroll box in the vertical scroll bar on the right side of your document in Word 97 doesn't actually scroll the document until you release your mouse button? Give it a try. Notice that this is not the behavior exhibited by Notepad or WordPad. Word 2000 also doesn't do this.

Now the nice thing about dragging the scroll box is that Word 97 does display the page number that you have scrolled to if you are viewing a multi-page document. Still, it would be nice to actually see the text as you scroll.

Secret

You can force the text to scroll as you drag the scroll box by making this change to your Registry:

STEPS:

Forcing the Scroll Bar in Word 97 to Scroll

Step 1.   Click Start, Run, type **regedit**, and press Enter.

Step 2.   Navigate to HKEY_CURRENT_USER\Software\Microsoft\Office\ 8.0\Word\Options.

Step 3.   Right-click the right pane of your Registry editor, click New, String Value.

Step 4.   Type the name **LiveScrolling** for the string value, and press Enter.

Step 5.   Double-click LiveScrolling. Type **1** in the Data Value field. Click OK. Exit the Registry editor.

Step 6.   Start up Word 97 and see if this works for you.

Make WordPad Write

In *Windows 98 Secrets*, we show you how to restore Windows Write so that you can use it as a very quick little editor for short notes, and so on. We did this because it is fast and its screen is uncluttered. Write does simple jobs without a lot of unnecessary frou-frou.

WordPad has improved quite a bit since its initial release in Windows 95, and maybe we were a bit hasty in dismissing it in *Windows 98 Secrets*. It is now quite fast, and you can make it look very much like Windows Write and even save files with *wri* extensions. This last feature is important if you want to invoke WordPad instead of Word when you click a file.

You'll also want to change some of the other default settings for WordPad, and you can do this by creating a template file on which new documents will be based. We'll show you how to do this, also.

STEPS:

A WordPad-to-Write Makeover

Step 1.   To do a Write makeover of WordPad, click Start, Programs, Accessories, WordPad. You'll see a program that looks a lot like a stripped down version of Word, as shown in Figure 25-3.

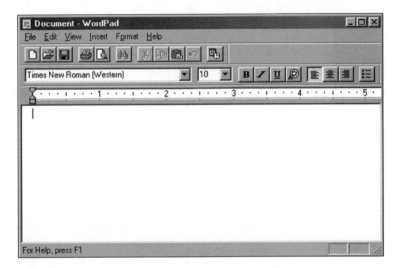

Figure 25-3: WordPad looks a lot like Word.

Step 2.   Click View, and clear the check marks next to Toolbar, Format Bar, and Ruler.

Step 3.   Click View, Options. Click the Word tab, clear the Toolbar, Format Bar, and Ruler check boxes, and mark the Wrap to Window option button. Take these same steps in the Write tab, and then click OK.

Step 4.   Now, with WordPad looking pretty much like it does in Figure 25-4, choose File, Save.

Step 5.   As you can see from Figure 25-5, WordPad will save the document in Word format by default. Click the Up One Level toolbar button a few times until Desktop appears in the Save In field (or simply display the Save In drop-down list and click Desktop).

Step 6.   In the File Name field, replace the default filename Document.doc with the name **WordPad.wri**. Click the Save button.

Continued

STEPS

A WordPad-to-Write Makeover *(continued)*

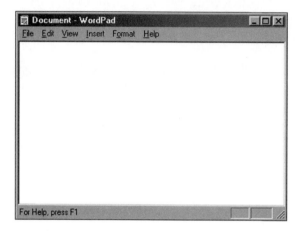

Figure 25-4: After your changes, WordPad should look more like Write.

Figure 25-5: Save your document to the Desktop.

Step 7. To exit WordPad, choose File, Exit.

Step 8. Click the TweakUI icon on your Desktop (assuming you put it there—if you haven't, click it in the Control Panel). Click the right arrow in the upper-right corner of the dialog box until the New tab appears. Click the New tab.

Step 9. Drag and drop the WordPad.wri icon from your Desktop to the middle of the TweakUI dialog box to add the Write Document file type to the New tab, as shown in Figure 25-6. You will now have a new item on your New menu. Click OK to close TweakUI.

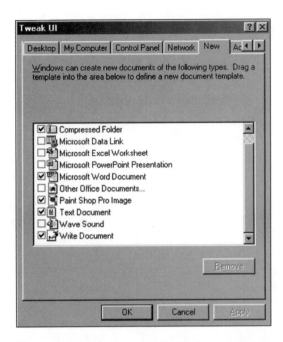

Figure 25-6: It's easy to put WordPad on your New menu.

Step 10. To create a new Write document that opens with WordPad, right-click your Desktop, click New, and then click Write Document. You can delete the WordPad.wri file from your Desktop, although you might want to use it in the next set of steps.

While these steps get you a blank WordPad document with the minimal settings for the Format Bar, Toolbar, and so on, they don't change the default font to something other than Times New Roman. To do this, you need to make a slight change in WordPad.wri (or to any other new file with a *wri* extension).

STEPS:

Setting a New Default Font for WordPad

Step 1. Click WordPad.wri on your Desktop. Type a period in the blank document.

Step 2. Press the Home key, and then press Shift+End to highlight the period.

Continued

STEPS

Setting a New Default Font for WordPad *(continued)*

Step 3.   Click Format, Font. Choose a font, font style, size, color, and script in the Font dialog box. Click OK.

Step 4.   Choose File, Save, and exit WordPad.

Step 5.   Drag the newly edited WordPad.wri file to the New tab of TweakUI (see step 8 in the preceding set of steps if you need help getting there). You will be asked if you want to replace your existing file. Click Yes, and click OK.

Now when you right-click your Desktop, click New, choose Write Document, and then click the new Write Document.wri, WordPad's client area defaults to Times New Roman, but then gets the message that it should type a period using your selected font style, and so on.

You may find that the New menu says WRI Document and not Write Document. If this is the case, or if you click the new document that you just saved and WordPad doesn't open it, you can fix this problem. You can also use this next set of steps to create another file type that WordPad will open.

STEPS:

New Document Types Associated with WordPad

Step 1.   Click Start, Programs, Accessories, WordPad.

Step 2.   Click File, Save As. Choose Text Document in the Save As Type field. Give the file a new name with the extension that you want (perhaps *wri*). Navigate in the Save In field to the Desktop.

Step 3.   Click the Save button. Click Yes if warned that you will lose any formatting when you save this file as a text document. Close WordPad.

Step 4.   Right-click the new document on your Desktop. Click Rename, and remove the *txt* extension if it is added. Press Enter.

Step 5.   Shift+right-click the new document. Click Open With, and scroll down to WordPad. Highlight WordPad and click OK.

You can make any other changes that you like in the File Types tab of the Folder Options dialog box. In your Explorer, click View, Folder Options, and click the File Types tab. Scroll down to your new file extension (or to *wri*).

Highlight the file type, and click the Edit button. You can change the description of the file type, and make other changes as well. We go into more depth about this in Chapter 13 of *Windows 98 Secrets*.

Use fonts with Notepad

While it is quite hard to believe, Microsoft has updated Notepad (click Start, Programs, Accessories, Notepad) to be able to display and print its text using a font. You wonder why they would modify this venerable and rickety plain-text editor, but there you have it. Perhaps they decided to make it easier for all of those users who had edited their Registries to choose a new font for Notepad.

To set the default font for all documents, just click Edit, Set Font.

Thanks to Adam Vujic for pointing this out.

Replace Notepad

The easiest way to increase the power of Notepad is to replace it with Notepad+, written by Roger Muers. This program has been around since 1996, and it is still a winner. It includes a multiple document interface, bigger files, search and replace, and fonts. It uses the same filename as Notepad.exe, so you just copy it over Notepad.exe.

You'll find it at lelystad.flnet.nl/~0meurs01/. If this site doesn't work, click the Search toolbar button in your Internet Explorer and look for *npplus.zip*. This file is available at a number of download sites.

Use Notepad as an unformatter

Notepad just doesn't remember formatting (except its default font), so you can strip formatting out of a document by cutting and pasting it to Notepad first. Next, cut it out of the Notepad document and paste it into your target message or document. The formatting that your text had in the original document will be gone.

Thanks to Carmen Knowles for helping us with this tip.

MS Paint

MS Paint is pretty basic, but you can use it for a number of graphics file types that you wouldn't likely guess it could handle.

Convert graphics files with MS Paint

The Windows 98 version of MS Paint (Start, Programs, Accessories, Paint) has been upgraded to allow you to convert among *bmp*, *gif*, and *jpeg* file formats if you have Microsoft Office installed. Just open a *bmp*, *gif*, or *jpeg* graphics file, and click File, Save As. Display the Save As Type field (see Figure 25-7), and choose the desired file type.

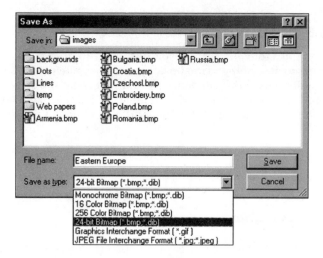

Figure 25-7: Use the Save As Type field to choose a different file type for the document you're saving.

Thanks to Adam Vujic for this tip.

Icons from MS Paint

In Chapter 6 of *Windows 98 Secrets*, we show you how to use MS Paint to create your own icons. If you set the image size to 32 by 32 pixels and save the file as a *bmp* file, you're all set.

Secret

You don't have to give the file the *bmp* extension. You can give it the *ico* extension so that it can be recognized as an icon file. You can still drag and drop this file into MS Paint, or associate the *ico* extension with MS Paint, and Paint will have no trouble opening it.

Let'r rip

Screen Rip32 is a freeware screen capture program that may turn out to be just right. When we tested it, it was a bit undone and in beta, but it had the makings of a nice little package.

We captured a shot of Screen Rip32 using Paint Shop Pro, while it was capturing a shot of Paint Shop Pro which was capturing a screen shot itself (not of itself), as you can see in Figure 25-8.

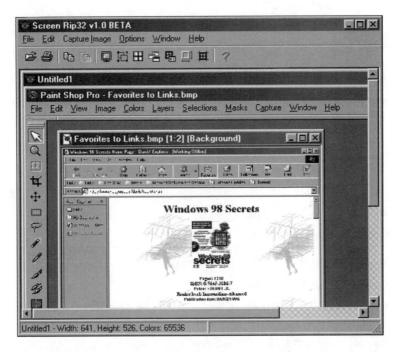

Figure 25-8: Screen Rip32 could be just what you need for screen captures.

Unlike Paint Shop Pro, but like SnagIt (see "Stealing text from dialog boxes" in the next chapter), Screen Rip lets you set the color depth that you want to use for capturing screen shots. Unfortunately it doesn't do a great job mapping down to the nearest color from High Color to 256 colors, and it doesn't let you capture an object the way Paint Shop Pro does. Screen Rip does make it easy to switch between capturing a window, client area, rectangle, and the whole screen, just by using different hot key combinations.

We hope to see more of this freeware ripper. You'll find the latest version at members.aol.com/progency/.

Use Quick View for files it didn't know you had

Windows 95 introduced a convenient file viewer named Quick View, but this utility is not well known to users and hasn't been promoted consistently by Microsoft since its inception. For example, if you install Windows 98 from the Windows 98 CD-ROM and select Typical Install, Quick View isn't even loaded onto your hard disk.

By default, Quick View supports almost 30 file types, determined by file extension. But it can support a lot more than 30 extensions if you ask it to.

And if you need more power than what the freebie offers, you can install its big brother under Windows 95, 98, and NT, as described at the end of this section.

To see if Quick View is installed, click Start, Programs, Windows Explorer. Right-click any *txt* file. If the resulting context menu contains Quick View, it's installed. If you click this menu item, a Quick View window displays the contents of the selected text file.

If you don't see Quick View on your context menu, you can install it from your Windows 98 CD-ROM:

STEPS:

Installing Quick View

Step 1.   Click Start, Settings, Control Panel.

Step 2.   Run Add/Remove Programs.

Step 3.   Click the Windows Setup tab, click Accessories, and then click the Details button.

Step 4.   Mark the Quick View check box, and then click OK twice. Windows may ask you to insert the Windows 98 CD-ROM.

To expand Quick View's capabilities, click View, Folder Options in your Explorer, and click the File Types tab. This tab lists every file type that's been registered by applications on your system. For example, your system may contain *diz* files. These are listed as Description Text Files in the File Types tab. They are often used by shareware authors, but they're just plain old text files. Even so, Quick View doesn't know by default that it can display them.

To turn on Quick View's ability to view a particular file type, select the file type in the Registered File Types list, and click the Edit button. In the Edit File Type dialog box, mark the Enable Quick View check box. Click OK twice.

Now when you right-click a file of this type, you will see Quick View on the context menu. If you ever do want to edit such a file, you can still click Open to run it within an editor.

Turning on Enable Quick View doesn't guarantee that Quick View can read a given file format. But keeping it turned off guarantees that Quick View won't even try to read the file.

To support every word processing and database file you're ever likely to encounter, you may want Quick View Plus. This commercial product supports about 175 more file types than Quick View and runs under Windows 95/98/NT. It's $59 through its distributor, JASC Inc (www.jasc.com). But we've seen it for $46.95 at Beyond.com (www.beyond.com).

PowerToys work with Windows 98

Secret

Some of the Windows 95 PowerToys can be used with Windows 98 to good effect. The most powerful toy, a new version of TweakUI, is found on your Windows 98 CD-ROM at \tools\reskit\powertoy. We discuss the many uses of TweakUI in this book and throughout *Windows 98 Secrets*. It is an absolutely essential component of Windows 98.

The other PowerToys aren't on the Windows 98 CD-ROM, but you can download them from www.microsoft.com/windows/downloads/contents/ PowerToys/W95PwrToysSet/. A number of these utilities have been superceded — they were essentially incorporated into Windows 98. Nevertheless, you may want to install the others. They come as a package, but once you extract them, you can install one at a time.

You can find out more about the Microsoft Windows 98 PowerToys at www.skwc.com/Beyond/powertoy.html and goinside.com/96/power.html.

Send To X

Send To X, version 1.4 (labeled 1.2 in some places) adds a number of items to the Send To menu, as shown in Figure 25-9. These include Any Folder, Clipboard As Contents, Clipboard As Name, and Command Line. To get to this menu, right-click any file or folder and click Send To in the context menu.

Figure 25-9: A Send To menu, with additional items courtesy of Send To X.

The Send To, Any Folder item lets you build a history of folders. Clicking Any Folder displays the Other Folder dialog box (see Figure 25-10). To add items to the history, click the Browse button.

Send To X also includes Mail Recipient CMC and Mail Recipient MAPI. You may already have a Send To, MAPI item, so you can delete this new one. They both work, although they use different DLLs. The Mail Recipient CMC command is supposed to send mail to an Exchange Server or other mail server that handles the Common Messaging Calls protocol. Unfortunately, this item adds a bug, which you'll probably want to fix.

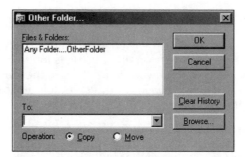

Figure 25-10: The Other Folder dialog box lists the previous folders to which you have copied or moved files, and lets you add more by browsing. In this example, there is no history yet.

Download the PowerToys executable and place it by itself in a temporary folder. When you click the executable file, it opens up a DOS window and extracts all the files that make up the PowerToys into the same folder. To install any of the PowerToys, right-click the associated *inf* file in the Explorer, and click Install in the context menu.

Installing Send To X overwrites a Registry entry that associates the Send To, Desktop (Create Shortcut) menu item with the DLL containing the function that actually does create a shortcut and place it on the Desktop. Instead, Send To X associates the Desktop (Create Shortcut) menu item with the Sendtox.dll file. You lose the ability to create shortcuts to items on the Desktop through the Send To menu. The icon for this item also changes to become a little yellow envelope.

Secret

Fortunately, you can get this functionality back after you install Send To X. All you have to do is merge the *reg* file Sendto Desktop shortcut.reg (on the accompanying CD-ROM) into your Registry. The Desktop (Create Shortcut) menu item will be back functioning correctly.

If you prefer, you can create this *reg* file yourself. Start a new text file and insert these commands into it:

```
REGEDIT4

[HKEY_CLASSES_ROOT\CLSID\{9E56BE61-C50F-11CF-9A2C-00A0C90A90CE}]
@=""

[HKEY_CLASSES_ROOT\CLSID\{9E56BE61-C50F-11CF-9A2C-
00A0C90A90CE}\InProcServer32]
@="C:\\WINDOWS\\SYSTEM\\SENDMAIL.DLL"
"ThreadingModel"="Apartment"

[HKEY_CLASSES_ROOT\CLSID\{9E56BE61-C50F-11CF-9A2C-
00A0C90A90CE}\DefaultIcon]
@="C:\\WINDOWS\\explorer.exe,-103"
```

Rename the file to give it a *reg* extension, and then right-click it in the Explorer and click Merge.

The Desktop (Create Shortcut) icon will also change back to the Desktop icon, as shown in Figure 25-11. If it doesn't, click your TweakUI icon on your Desktop (or in the Control Panel), scroll the Repair tab into view, and click Repair Now.

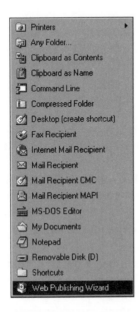

Figure 25-11: The Desktop (Create Shortcut) icon has been restored in this sample Send To menu. It is the seventh item from the top.

Unfortunately, you lose the functionality of the Mail Recipient CMC item. We haven't tested it, but perhaps this functionality can be retrieved by merging the CMC *reg* file from our CD-ROM (CMC.reg) into your Registry. It can't hurt.

All the CMC.reg file does is associate the CMCSend extension with the Sendtox.dll, and thereby associate the Mail Recipient CMC menu item with the functions in this dynamic link library.

Other PowerToys that are still useful

Round Clock, DOS Prompt Here, Explore from Here, Shortcut Target Menu, Telephone Location Selector, and Fast Folder Contents all work in Windows 98 as they did in Windows 95.

PowerToys that are no longer needed

DeskMenu is a system tray item that displays the icons on the Desktop as a menu when you click it. Of course, the Desktop toolbar does the same thing. In addition, the Show Desktop button in the Quick Launch toolbar clears the Desktop of windows (or redisplays them). Therefore, DeskMenu is not as necessary as it once was. However, you may still want to use it if you don't use the Quick Launch or Desktop toolbar.

Cabfile Viewer and QuickRes are now built into Windows 98, and X mouse is built into Windows 98 TweakUI.

Summary

There's life in these standard accessories, if you just put them to use — no need to download shareware alternatives and learn new programs. Microsoft has upgraded MS Paint and Notepad.

▶ WordPad is actually a very useful editor, and is small enough to load quickly. It is flexible enough to take on different file formats, and you can set it up to work with a range of file extensions.

▶ You can create icons with MS Paint. Just save the files in *bmp* format, and then rename them with the *ico* extension.

▶ With Screen Rip32, you get a freeware screen capture program that adds to the capabilities built into Windows 98.

Chapter 26

System Tools

In This Chapter

Windows 98 adds a number of system tools to those available with Windows 95. We show you how to make them easier to get to and how to get around a couple of problems.

▶ Put your System Configuration Utility on your Desktop.

▶ Fix some problems that get in the way of using System Information Utility.

▶ You'll want to know more about your computer than your System Information Utility tells you.

▶ Clear Type — where did it come from?

Access system configuration on the Desktop

Windows 98 comes with a utility that lets you see what programs are loaded when you start up Windows 98, and makes it easy for you to stop them from loading the next time you start Windows. You'll find the System Configuration Utility (Msconfig.exe) in your \Windows\System folder.

To get easy access to it, drag Msconfig.exe to your Desktop to create a shortcut to it. You can also find it by clicking Start, Programs, Accessories, System Tools, System Information, and then choosing Tools, System Configuration Utility. Microsoft decided to put it in a galaxy far, far away, but we find it so useful that we've put a shortcut to it on our Desktop.

When you install new software, you'll often find a new utility is loaded without your permission. The System Configuration Utility can help you find out what is loaded, and then you can decide whether or not you want that to happen.

Click your new System Configuration Utility shortcut, and then click the Startup tab to see what programs are loaded when Windows starts (see Figure 26-1). Clear the check boxes next to any programs that you'd rather not start. You can also check out your Autoexec.bat and Config.sys files by clicking the tab related to each.

Figure 26-1: Look on the Startup tab to see and control what will be loaded at Startup. Note also the tabs for Autoexec.bat and Config.sys.

While you're at it, you might as well drag some other useful programs onto the Desktop to create shortcuts to them. If you've installed the *Windows 98 Resource Kit*, drag the Tools Management Console to the Desktop. One way to do this is as follows:

STEPS:

Dragging the Tools Management Console to the Desktop

Step 1. Click Start, Programs, Windows 98 Resource Kit.

Step 2. Right-click Tools Management Console, and click Create Shortcut. A shortcut appears in the Windows 98 Resource Kit menu.

Step 3. Drag the new shortcut onto the Desktop. Select it, press F2, and get rid of the (2) in the name.

You can also place the System Information Utility (Msinfo32.exe) and the System Tools folder on your Desktop. The Tools menu in the System Information Utility is a gateway to a bunch of other utilities, including Dr. Watson and Version Conflict Manager. One easy way to get access to all of these utilities is to put the System Information Utility on the Desktop.

STEPS:

Putting the System Information Utility on the Desktop

Step 1.   Click Start, Programs, Accessories, and System Tools.

Step 2.   Right-click System Information. Click Copy.

Step 3.   Right-click your Desktop. Click Paste Shortcut.

To put a shortcut to the System Tools folder on your Desktop, take these steps:

STEPS:

Putting the System Tools Folder on the Desktop

Step 1.   Click Start, Programs, Accessories.

Step 2.   Right-click System Tools. Click Copy.

Step 3.   Right-click your Desktop. Click Paste Shortcut.

You'll notice that the System Tools icon that you just created on your Desktop is a Start menu folder icon. It is a shortcut to the Start menu folder \Windows\Start Menu\Programs\Accessories\System Tools. This folder is a folder of shortcuts.

Use the advanced features of System Configuration Utility

The Advanced button of the System Configuration Utility provides access to a variety of troubleshooting settings that previously required detailed knowledge of System.ini or the Registry.

Within the Advanced Troubleshooting Settings dialog box, shown in Figure 26-2, you can configure Windows to boot up in a variety of Safe, Safer, and Safest modes to eliminate potential startup problems. For example, you can force Windows to start up in plain-vanilla 640 x 480 VGA mode or disable the automatic ScanDisk routine to avoid delays if you need to reboot frequently to test your system. You can limit the amount of memory available to Windows to test for faulty memory chips. You can also disable Windows 98's fast shut down features to determine whether they conflict with your software.

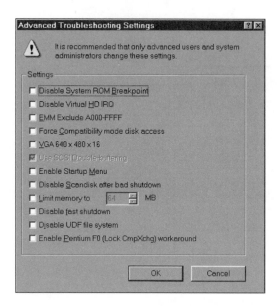

Figure 26-2: The Advanced Troubleshooting Settings dialog box of the System Configuration Utility.

Unfortunately, the help available within the System Configuration Utility provides even less information about the Advanced options than you get by simply looking at the dialog box itself. We don't propose that you start changing the Advanced Troubleshooting Settings at random to see if they improve Windows. But if you manage several Windows computers — or even if you just have to keep your own computer working — knowledge of these options may be a lifesaver some day.

You can find Microsoft's explanation of the options in the Advanced Troubleshooting Settings dialog box at support.microsoft.com/support/kb/ articles/q181/9/66.asp. This document explains the symptoms of problems you may experience with Windows 98 and why you might change various settings to troubleshoot the situation. The page also links to descriptions of little-known Win.com and Msdos.sys options that let you start Windows in troubleshooting modes.

Disabled startups

If you use the System Configuration Utility to clear some of the check boxes next to the startup applets that you don't want to run on startup, you might want to know just how this bit of magic is achieved. Also, the list of unused startup applets can get pretty long if, like us, you install hundreds of pieces of shareware. If you're in this situation, you will want to clean up this list.

Secret

You'll find part of the secret in the Registry. The System Configuration Utility moves the calls to many of the startup applets to a new key whose name is the same as the old key, but now followed by a minus sign. The three keys are:

```
HKEY_CURRENT_USER\Software\Microsoft\Windows\CurrentVersion\
RunHKEY_LOCAL_MACHINE\SOFTWARE\Microsoft\Windows\CurrentVersion\
RunHKEY_LOCAL_MACHINE\SOFTWARE\Microsoft\Windows\CurrentVersion\
RunServices-
```

If you compare the cleared boxes under the Startup tab in the System Configuration Utility with the variables stored under these keys in your Registry, you'll find a number of your applets. You can clear out old startup calls to old applets by deleting their values in the Registry. Right-click a variable name in the right pane of your Registry editor while you are focused on one of these three keys, and click Delete.

The rest of the startup applets are found in the \Windows\Start Menu\Programs\StartUp folder. Usually, you'll just find shortcuts to startup applets here. You can use the System Configuration Utility to move these shortcuts to the Disable Startup Items menu folder.

You can delete from the Disabled Startup Items folder any items that you no longer want. You can also delete the complete Disabled Startup Items menu item if you like. You'll have to create your own startup menu shortcuts if you later restore some calls to startup applets.

Check all your system files with the System File Checker

The System File Checker (Sfc.exe) that comes with Windows 98 is supposed to check for any corrupted or replaced "system" files. It will prompt you to replace any files that do not match the original files that came with Windows 98 (if you mark the right check boxes), and will replace them from the *cab* files on the Windows 98 CD-ROM.

You can use the System File Checker to check more than just the few files that are set in the defaults — files that you might consider to be "system" files. To do this, you need to change a few settings.

STEPS:

Changing the System File Checker Settings

Step 1.   Click Start, Programs, Accessories, System Tools, System Information.

Step 2.   Click Tools, System File Checker, and click the Settings button.

Continued

STEPS

Changing the System File Checker Settings *(continued)*

Step 3.   Mark the Check for Changed Files and Check for Deleted Files check boxes, as shown in Figure 26-3.

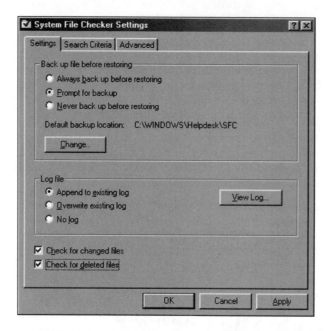

Figure 26-3: Mark the two check boxes at the bottom of the System File Checker Settings dialog box.

Step 4.   Click the Search Criteria tab.

Step 5.   Select C:\Program Files in the Select the Folders You Want to Check list, and click the Include Subfolders button shown in Figure 26-4.

Step 6.   Select C:\Windows in the Select the Folders You Want to Check list, and click the Include Subfolders button.

Step 7.   Click OK. Click Start to scan for altered files.

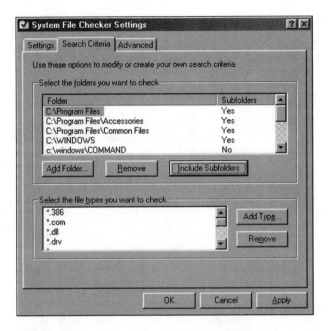

Figure 26-4: When you click the Include Subfolders button, a Yes appears to the right of the folder you have selected.

Trouble with the System Information Utility

If you find that your System Information Utility (Start, Programs, Accessories, System Tools, System Information) is not providing much information, it may be because some driver is blocking it. Navigate to the System Information Utility, double-click Components in the left pane, and click Multimedia. The default level of detail that will appear in the right pane is Advanced Information (see Figure 26-5), and it will take a minute for all the information to be gathered. If you only get a date and time for the driver, you've got trouble.

Click the Basic Information option button. If no information is displayed, and none is displayed when you click the History option button, then something is blocking your System Information Utility.

Secret

Ironically, it could be Microsoft's Intellimouse software that is getting in the way. Here's how you can figure out what it is. Use the WinKill freeware utility or the Close Program dialog box (displayed by pressing Ctrl+Alt+Del) to kill any ongoing processes you think might be interfering with the System Information Utility. You'll find information about WinKill in "Quickly kill any process or application" in Chapter 16.

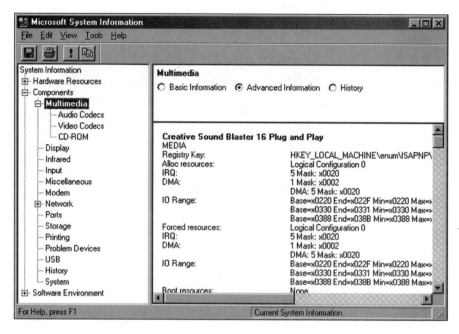

Figure 26-5: The Advanced Information option button is at the top of the right pane.

If you are running an IntelliMouse, you can kill the Point32 process. Press Ctrl+Alt+Del, highlight Point32, and click End Task.

Now, close down and run the System Information Utility again. See if that solves the problem. If not, kill other processes, or stop other programs from running. You will want to keep Explorer and Systray running, but you can close down everything else. Keep checking to see what is getting in the way of the System Information Utility.

Thanks to Don Lebow for this secret.

Microsoft System Information Utility isn't working

Secret

If you can't run the Microsoft System Information Utility (Start, Programs, Accessories, System Tools, System Information), it may be because you don't have WordPad installed, or maybe because you do. If it's installed, uninstall it and reinstall it. If it's not, install it. Here's how:

STEPS:

Installing or Reinstalling WordPad

Step 1.   Click Start, Settings, Control Panel, Add/Remove Programs, and click Windows Setup tab.

Step 2.   In the Components list, double-click Accessories (the word itself, not its check box), and then scroll down to the bottom of the Components list to display WordPad, as shown in Figure 26-6.

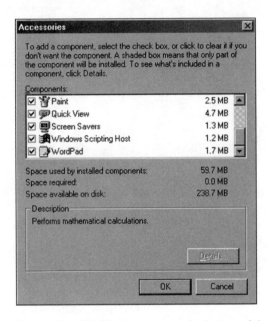

Figure 26-6: WordPad is at or near the bottom of the Components list.

Step 3.   If the check box next to WordPad is cleared, mark it to install WordPad, and click OK and OK again. If the check box is marked (meaning WordPad is installed), clear it and click OK and OK again. Then repeat steps 1 through 3 to reinstall WordPad.

So you've got to wonder, what does WordPad have to do with the System Information Utility?

Add to your system info

The Microsoft System Information Utility just doesn't quite do it when it comes to providing information about your computer. For example, try to get it to tell you how much video memory you have. You can improve on this utility with many others out there. One that we liked was InfoPro. The display information is shown in Figure 26-7. You can download this utility from www.dnttm.ro/edc.

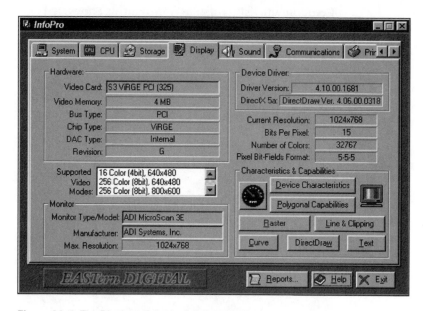

Figure 26-7: The Display tab in the InfoPro window.

Another full-fledged utility that we couldn't quite make up our minds about was SiSoft's Sandra (see Figure 26-8). This is a very professional package from a programming outfit that definitely knows its way around Windows. The standard version is free, but it is really just a way to get you to buy the whole package. Nothing wrong with that, mind you, but it was always disappointing to click one of Sandra's icons only to be told that you needed to buy the professional package to get the capability behind the icon.

When the Basic version of Sandra is installed, it not only finds its way onto your Start menu and Desktop, but also into the Control Panel, and onto various context menus. Makes it pretty convenient to use; still, this program puts itself in more places than any other we've ever used. Perhaps there should be a switch that lets you tell it to be a little less aggressive.

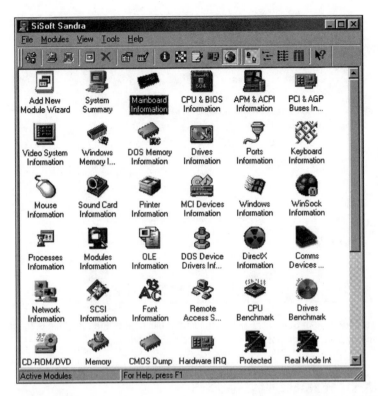

Figure 26-8: The Sandra user interface includes icons for features in both the Basic and the Professional versions.

There is a lot to like about Sandra. It provides detailed information about your hardware and software settings, in addition to a number of useful benchmarks that compare your computer against others. The authors include a plethora of useful hints, and the help is quite extensive. For example, the memory information module, shown in Figure 26-9, warns you if your swap file is too big.

One question we've had of all add-on system information utilities: Can they tell us which device is on which IDE controller? Sandra didn't answer that question (and none of the others we've checked have). So far, none of these utilities is perfect, but Sandra provides a lot of power, even at the cost of a bit of aggravation.

You'll find Sandra at www.sisoftware.demon.co.uk/sandra.

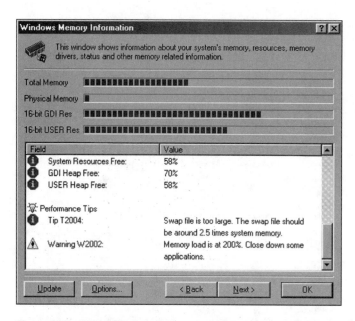

Figure 26-9: One of Sandra's Performance Tips tells us that the swap file is too large, while the yellow exclamation point warns us of memory overload.

Stop the critical update

Some users have reported that the Critical Update Notification feature of Windows Update (which advises users whenever they go on the Internet of updates to Windows and Internet Explorer that Microsoft considers critical) causes their Task Scheduler to go into start mode. They want to keep it in stop mode, thank you very much.

Secret

You can disable Critical Update Notification by using the System Configuration Utility and clearing the check box next to Critical Update in the Startup tab. Click Start, Programs, Accessories, System Tools, System Information, and choose Tools, System Configuration Utility to find it.

Undo your policy mistakes

Don't our political leaders wish they had this option? While they don't, you do. If you chose the option Only Run Allowed Windows Applications, and then forgot to place all your applications on the list of allowed applications, you'll want to go into the Policy Editor and add to the list. Oops. What if you forgot to put the Policy Editor on the list of allowed applications?

You've got a couple of options. If you have multiple user profiles, and you haven't set this option for everyone or for the Default User, log in as one of the users that isn't restricted and reset the option.

If you set this option for the Default User, you can also restart your computer, hold down the Ctrl key during the power-on self test, and choose Safe mode when the Windows 98 Startup menu comes up. When the Safe mode Desktop is displayed, click Start, Run, type **poledit**, and press Enter. You can then change this option.

Secret

If you happen to have put the Registry editor on the allowed applications list, you can navigate in your Registry to HKEY_CURRENT_USER\Software\ Microsoft\Windows\CurrentVersion\Policies\Explorer. You can then delete the Explorer key to get rid of all your policies, and then start again.

If you can get to the User Profiles tab in the Passwords Properties dialog box in your Control Panel, mark All Users of This Computer Use the Same Preferences and Desktop Settings and click OK. Then restart your computer, run the Policy Editor (Start, Programs, Accessories, System Tools, Policy Editor), and change the setting for allowed applications. You'll have to go back to your Passwords Properties dialog box, mark Users Can Customize Their Preferences and Desktop Settings, and click OK.

The *Windows 98 Resource Kit* has other options. Search for *Only Run Allowed*.

Stealing text from dialog boxes

If you happen to be writing a book about Windows 98 or doing beta testing for Microsoft Internet Explorer, there will be plenty of times when you'll want to do a screen capture to take a "photo" of the latest error message. SnagIt is the screen capture program that we use for *MORE Windows 98 Secrets*, and it is slick and easy to work with. SnagIt can also often capture the text displayed on your screen; you just have to set it for text capture, as shown in Figure 26-10.

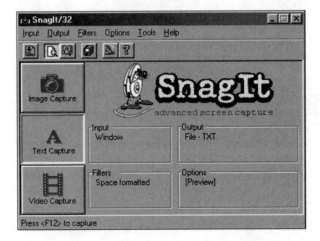

Figure 26-10: Click the Text Capture button to switch capture modes. SnagIt maintains separate settings for each mode.

In some cases (with the text in the Internet Explorer About dialog box, for example) SnagIt cannot capture text, and you're left wondering what to do. Kleptomania is a powerful text capture package that uses OCR technology, as well as a constructed database of your installed fonts, to capture text on your screen and place it on the Clipboard as text. You can then paste the text into any text editor. This is yet another way to print out a directory listing, for example.

You'll find SnagIt at www.techsmith.com. Kleptomania is available at www.structurise.com/kleptomania.

Fonts

Fonts can be a lot of fun, especially if you have the right tools to view them and they are up to date.

FontLister

The font display windows in Windows 98 are pretty rudimentary. If you have a lot of fonts, it's nice to have an applet that will display them for you, and maybe do a bit more. FontLister, at $5.00, is just the basic step up for the right price. It doesn't manage thousands of fonts, but if you have a hundred or two, it will help you manage them. You can display a few fonts at once for a comparison, as shown in Figure 26-11.

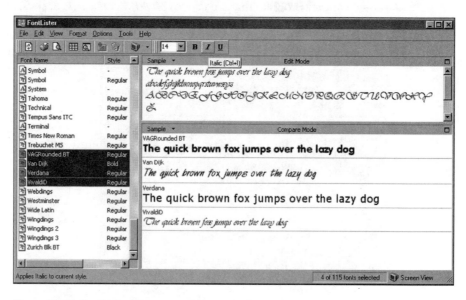

Figure 26-11: FontLister lets you easily compare fonts.

One thing especially nice about FontLister is that you get a character map that you can resize to display the characters in a much bigger window than the character map that comes with Windows. When you click a character, it gets even bigger (see Figure 26-12).

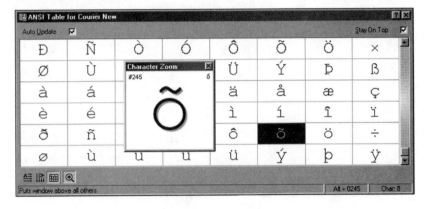

Figure 26-12: You can really magnify a character.

You'll find FontLister at www.conquerware.dk/fl.htm. You can register it online.

All the characters, all the time

We've been looking for a tool like this for a long time, and were amazed to find ourselves unsuccessful. Perhaps you've found such a tool, and wonder what took us so long. Yes, we've wanted to find a font lister that shows *all* of the characters in a font. We want to see not just the western character set, but all the characters in the Unicode fonts as well.

Microsoft has supported Unicode for a long time. They ship out plenty of fonts that use the Unicode character sets. So what's the problem?

With the help of Windows Office Watch (www.woodyswatch.com/wow/), we finally had our wishes answered. We can now see the complete set of characters in the extended fonts, as shown in Figure 26-13.

Choose a character set in the Character Set field in ListFont, and all of the fonts that you have installed that include that character set are displayed. Click the Show Unicode Font button to display a complete list of all characters in a given font.

You'll find Heiner Eichmann's freeware ListFont at sun1.rrzn.uni-hannover.de/nhbieich/software.htm. It's very small and very fast.

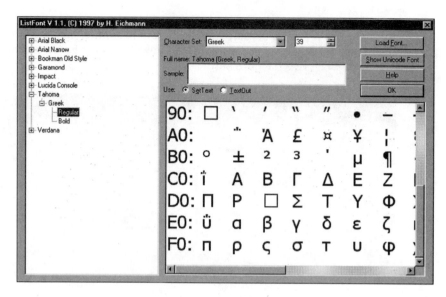

Figure 26-13: You can open up a font in the left pane, and pick a language and a style within it.

There's a euro in the fonts

The fonts that come with Windows 98 already include the euro currency symbol in the 128th slot. If you have Windows NT or Windows 95, you'll need to update your fonts to include the euro.

What does the symbol for the euro look like? As specified by the European Commission, it looks like a lower-case *e*, but with two horizontal bars similar to an equals sign, as shown in Figure 26-14.

You can download the original euro symbol file in Windows Metafile format at europa.eu.int/euro/html/dossiers/00203/html/index-EN.html. Click *Download of a vector image without constructions* to get the euro symbol shown in Figure 26-14. If you have trouble opening this file, try starting a blank Word document and inserting the file by clicking Insert, Picture, From File, *filename.*

Microsoft has placed free, updated font files for Windows 95 users that contain the euro symbol on its "Fonts for the Web" page, at www.microsoft. com/typography/fontpack/default.htm. This page offers the "core fonts" — Arial, Times New Roman, and Courier New — as well as several sophisticated new free fonts that display well on Web pages, such as Georgia, Verdana, and Trebuchet. Windows 98 users will want to download these web fonts.

Figure 26-14: The euro symbol adopted by the European Commission.

Microsoft's interpretations of the euro symbol are shown in Figures 26-15 through 26-17. Their type designers have made an excellent translation of the symbol into Arial, shown in Figure 26-15. The symbol is slightly condensed from its original, circular design. This is desirable, because it allows the symbol to align with numerals in spreadsheet columns.

Figure 26-15: The euro as rendered by Microsoft in Arial.

Microsoft's versions of the symbol in Times, Figure 26-16 and Courier, Figure 26-17, however, are pathetic. The horizontal lines are too light and will disappear at small point sizes. The euro in these two typefaces looks like an uppercase *C* with superimposed faint lines. The result hardly resembles an *e* at all.

Figure 26-16: The euro as rendered by Microsoft in Times New Roman.

Figure 26-17: The euro as rendered by Microsoft in Courier.

Details on Microsoft's euro symbol downloads — and a FAQ on application support for the euro symbol — are available at www.microsoft.com/typography/faq/faq12.htm. This page also contains numerous links to other free fonts, such as three free type families from Adobe.

Once you've installed the updates, users of U.S. keyboards can insert the euro character in their documents by typing Alt+0128. (Use Alt+0163 for pounds [£], and Alt+0165 for yen [¥].) Microsoft's FAQ describes several ways to insert a euro on most other countries' keyboards, usually RightAlt+e. Try it — impress your friends!

The Windows 98 Service Pack 1 and the Windows 98 OSR1 come with new euro fonts, which update existing Windows fonts.

Eurolater

Now that you've got the euro currency symbol figured out, how about the ability to convert between European currencies? The program took a day to write, but then it doesn't have to do much to be useful.

The Eurolater comes ready to display in four languages. This is the first program we've seen that quickly and easily flips between languages.

You can download the 160K Eurolater in a few seconds from www.stack.nl/ ~roelf/eurolator/.

Thanks to Chris Pirillo at www.lockergnome.com.

Completely ClearType?

As we write this, there is plenty of controversy about whether Microsoft has invented anything new with its ClearType font rendering technology. Many font technophiles are claiming that the basic idea has been around since the start of the Apple II.

Our old buddy, Steve Gibson, is right in the thick of things. He's making very substantial claims that Microsoft has no right to patent this technology. You can check out his web page on the topic at grc.com/cleartype.htm.

To get the other side of the story, consult Microsoft's ClearType web page at www.microsoft.com/typography/cleartype/default.htm.

Summary

The system tools do help out some, and if you add a couple more, things get even better. You can't ever have too much control over your system.

▶ Use the advanced features of the System Configuration Utility.

▶ Keep the Critical Update Notification at bay.

▶ Fix your Policy Editor mistakes.

▶ How about a $5.00 FontLister with a sizeable character map?

Chapter 27

Multimedia

In This Chapter

Sounds, video, CD-ROM players, MP3 players, and worldwide radio tuners. The computer is an entertainment machine.

▶ Make sure you can get the full range of 3D sounds.

▶ Find the *wav* file you are looking for.

▶ Microsoft provides a cool CD player with Plus! 98.

▶ Surround yourself in 3D video on the web.

▶ Web-TV and the web are integrated, so you can type channels in your Address bar.

▶ Make sure that you have the right driver for your ATI card.

▶ Use handy shortcuts for Web-TV.

▶ MP3 and Winamp—play that downloadable CD-ROM music.

Enable surround sound

Just because you have the speakers set up for surround sound doesn't mean that your computer is set up to deliver it. You can check to make sure it is by using the Multimedia icon in your Control Panel.

STEPS:
Enabling Surround Sound

Step 1. Click Start, Settings, Control Panel, Multimedia.

Step 2. Click the Advanced Properties button in the Playback section of the Audio tab.

Continued

STEPS

Enabling Surround Sound *(continued)*

Step 3. Display the Speaker Setup drop-down list, scroll down to the bottom, and select Surround Sound Speakers, as shown in Figure 27-1. Click OK.

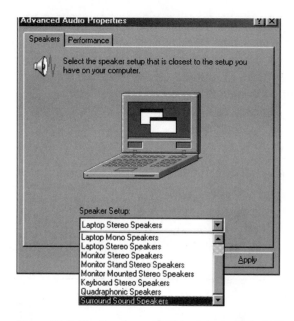

Figure 27-1: The Speakers tab of the Advanced Audio Properties dialog box lets you select the kind of speakers you're using.

Thanks to Adam Vujic for pointing out this tip.

Find that special sound file

Now that you have 3D surround sound and a 45-watt sub woofer, maybe you should have the coolest wave files to attach to each and every Windows "event." One of the earliest uses of the web, after it became accessible to ordinary people, was to swap *wav* files. Now that the web is all grown up, you can still use it to download *wav* files.

Check out the king of all *wav* sites, The Daily WAV at www.dailywav.com.

Microsoft's very cool audio CD player

There are plenty of CD and music front ends available as freeware and shareware. Later in this chapter we discuss several of these. Microsoft ships its Media Player, and you can download Real Networks' streaming audio and video player over the Internet.

Plus! 98 comes with a very nice little audio CD player that can add to your musical enjoyment. The first time you play an audio CD, it automatically downloads the album, artist, and track names from Tunes.com or the Music Boulevard web site.

Just to prove that not all Microsoft products (even if they do come from outside contractors) have to have Microsoft's standardized look and feel (like their ads, functional but not much fun) — and to squash all memory of the old chunking-looking CD Player — they've released an applet that feels neat when you use it. Compare the two versions in Figures 16-2 and 16-3.

Figure 27-2: Microsoft's new Deluxe CD Player.

Figure 27-3: Microsoft's original CD Player.

As an aside, Microsoft's Windows Media Player looks a lot more like the CD Player than it does the Deluxe CD Player (see Figure 27-4). Shouldn't computers be fun to use? Microsoft should involve artful designers more in the development of their software, like those who did the Deluxe CD Player. That's right, Windows is ugly.

Figure 27-4: Microsoft's Windows Media Player.

To test out Deluxe CD Player, I put in a CD that I bought from a group of Andean Indians who were playing on the street at the Pike Place Market in Seattle, Washington. What I knew about this group of six musicians consisted of what I had heard that day and listened to later on their CD.

As soon as the audio CD was inserted, I was asked if I wanted to download their album information. Sure, I thought, fat chance of that. A few seconds later, after Deluxe CD Player called up my Internet service provider, downloaded all of the track names, and Quichua Mashis were happily playing Alpa Maya from their El Caminante album. My jaw was on the floor. I was jumping up and down.

Since a later search on both www.tunes.com and www.musicblvd.com didn't turn up any listing for the album or artists, I've been reduced to magical explanations. Perhaps the fact that the album was recorded in Redmond, Washington (home of Microsoft) had something to do with it.

I really like the CD volume control in the lower-right corner of the Deluxe CD Player. Your mouse pointer becomes a hand when you point to the knob, and when you rotate it, the volume level is graphically displayed. You can also build a playlist by choosing Options, Playlist. You can search the Internet for the artist, album, or Billboard reviews by clicking Internet, Search the Internet. Quite a cool front end to the Internet.

So what's so secret about this little applet? It seems that lots of folks have dismissed the Plus! 98 CD-ROM as not so plus. Well, 'taint so. We don't want you to miss some things that we found to be quite cool.

Windows software may render audio CDs increasingly obsolete

Windows software is making big changes in the way we buy, store, and play back music in our offices and homes. The force behind this change is a music compression standard known as MP3 (Moving Pictures Experts Group 1 Layer 3). With the growth of the Internet, musicians around the world who haven't negotiated a contract with a recording label are converting their best tunes to the digital MP3 format and distributing them free as a method of promotion.

Thousands of such songs are now available on the web. Anyone can play these selections on any multimedia computer equipped with speakers and software such as the Windows Media Player that comes with Windows 98.

This underground music movement might have remained unknown to most consumers if it weren't for a lawsuit filed by the Recording Industry Association of America (RIAA). The suit, filed against Diamond Multimedia Inc. of San Jose, California, was an attempt to stop Diamond from distributing a $200 pager-sized MP3 player called Rio.

Using a parallel port adapter (with a pass-through for a printer), you download MP3 files from a PC into Rio's memory. The device then plays an hour or two of music through headphones or speakers. It's the ultimate in portable music enjoyment. Unlike portable audio CD players, vibration has little or no effect on the Rio's playback. It's a lot smaller than portable CD players, too.

At the time this chapter was written, the RIAA suit had been denied in Federal Court. The RIAA has appealed, but it appears that MP3 music is an unstoppable force that will shape our listening habits for years to come. Even if the RIAA suit were ultimately successful, Diamond would only have to pay a 2 percent royalty on all Rio devices and add anti-copying circuitry to discourage piracy of copyrighted songs. Two percent seems to be a small increment that wouldn't significantly harm Rio's market.

Special Windows software bundled with Rio units is a major factor in MP3's popularity. MusicMatch Jukebox is a shareware program that enables users to convert tracks from any audio CD into the MP3 format. The free version plays MP3 files and converts up to five tracks from your CD collection; the $29.99 registered version is unlimited. Once you've converted your audio CD collection, you can use Jukebox to play songs in any specified order (or in random order) on your multimedia PC. Or you can download the songs you want onto your Rio and go anywhere with them.

Brian recently interviewed the owners of MusicMatch, husband and wife Dennis Mudd and Pamela Evans, at their office in a Portland, Oregon suburb. They see an explosion of new music that multimedia PCs have made available. Their web site, www.musicmatch.com, is a haven for international musicians who have contributed one or more songs in exchange for the ability to sell their home-grown CDs through MusicMatch.

The "fair use" provisions of copyright law allow any buyer of copyrighted music or other media to make a copy for his or her own personal use. For example, you can copy a chapter of a book to read on the bus. But what about sharing songs with others who aren't buyers of the original CD? Many of the songs found on "pirate" web sites are pure copyright violations.

Mudd and Evans say pirate sites are quickly shut down by music-industry lawyers — and in any event there's plenty of good music to choose from that bands *want* you to share. There are now thousands of MP3 tracks to download, and lots of places to look for them.

To find music to suit your personal taste, start at www.mp3.com, a Grand Central Station for digital music. You'll also find a collection of software there, including the Nad MP3 Player (free) and the popular Winamp (see more on Winamp in the next section).

Audiofind is a useful index of music sorted by title, artist, and genre, found at www.audiofind.com. There are 30 different genres listed, so you're bound to find something that suits your tastes. If the alphabetical listings don't meet your needs, you can search on any word in a title or name. Audiofind also helps you buy regular audio CDs.

If you ever wondered what the artists were actually saying in their songs, you can try www.lyrics.ch. This Swiss site links to the lyrics of more than 100,000 songs. MusicMatch Jukebox can download lyrics from this site to display while playing the songs. As this book goes to press, this site has been shut down. Perhaps it will come back to life.

For a listing of dozens of other music sites, go to www.hot100.com/music. This web page sorts music sites by popularity, leading you to commercial and independent sources of audio CDs, MP3 files, and much more.

If you're noticing that it's a lot of work to download all these songs one by one, you'll want to automate the process. You can do this with MP3-Wolf, a shareware program that searches the web and downloads the type of music you like. MP3-Wolf — available from Trellian Australia, which makes several good Internet search tools — starts from a site such as Audiofind and a keyword you enter, perhaps **rock** or **jazz**. It then downloads from links that point to MP3 files with your particular emphasis.

MP3-Wolf can't listen to the songs for you and pick out the ones you'll like, of course. But it's a lot easier to choose music by listening to the files the program has downloaded for you than by downloading them individually. You can obtain MP3-Wolf from www.trellian.com. The free version is limited in the number of links it can index. The $25 registered version has unlimited indexing and it can download from 20 different web sites simultaneously.

Winamp — computer as music box

Winamp is a nag-free shareware music player. It will play a wide variety of sound files, but its raison d'être is its ability to play CD-quality MP3 files. This is not the only MP3 player out there, but it is definitely one of the most sought after and respected.

The MP3 sound format is a standard used to compress and replay CD-quality sound. Microsoft has built it into its Service Pack 1 upgrade of Windows 98 (in its Windows Media Player). So you can already play MP3 sound files without Winamp. It's just not as much fun.

Winamp comes with a CD player user interface, as you can see from Figure 27-5. You can download an MP3 music file from their site, or from one of the many provided as links within Winamp (click the icon in the upper-left corner of the Winamp player, and choose Winamp, Links). Winamp is a music front end to the MP3 portions of the Internet.

Figure 27-5: Winamp looks like a CD player on your screen.

After you download an MP3 file, click the play button and you're playing CD-quality audio recordings. Click the EQ button on the right side of the Winamp CD player to display the equalizer and control it with a slider bar.

Want to put a new face on Winamp? Download a new "skin." For example, you might like the Earth Tone version shown in Figure 27-6. The "skin" sites are all linked in Winamp. Need an updated list of "skin" and "music" sites? Click the Update button on your Winamp CD player, and the list will be downloaded from the Winamp site.

Figure 27-6: Give your CD player a different look by changing its "skin."

Want to have a visual display of the music, as shown in Figure 27-7? Download a visual plug-in, and then download a visual plug-in player.

Figure 27-7: One of Winamp's visual plug-ins.

All of this and more is available at www.winamp.com. Winamp is a portal to the world of Internet music.

If you develop an interest in encoding MP3 files from your music CDs or other sources, you will find shareware encoders as well as commercial converters at www.mp3.com and other linked sites. They also offer a CD-ROM containing a wealth of players, utilities, and the astounding number of 1,175 freeware Winamp skins. (Some Web users have too much time on their hands.)

Because MP3-formatted music files are downloaded over the Internet (this is not a streaming audio format unless you've got a fast connection), recording companies are concerned that their copyrighted material may be stolen. You can read more about this issue at www.mp3.com.

EarthTuner

As I write this, I'm listening over a 28K modem to Australian Broadcasting System's Triple J Radio, originating in Sydney, Australia. I found Triple J by rotating the globe shown in Figure 27-8 and clicking New South Wales. Up popped a list of Australian radio and TV stations broadcasting on the web and organized by format.

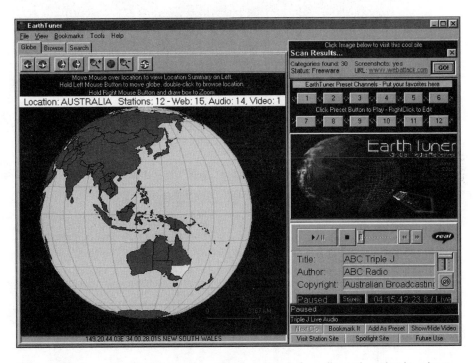

Figure 27-8: Rotate the EarthTuner globe to select a locale for radio stations that broadcast on the web.

EarthTuner keeps a database of available broadcasting sites and gives you easy access around the world to the stations' web sites (if available) and their streaming audio and video servers. With twelve preset push buttons, you can store your favorite Internet radio channels for easy retrieval.

EarthTuner uses the Real Networks RealPlayer streaming audio and video control, no doubt causing Microsoft a bit of heartburn. It will ask if you want to make it the default media player when you install it.

You'll find EarthTuner at www.earthtuner.com.

Built-in radio toolbar

Internet Explorer 5 comes with its own radio toolbar, as shown in Figure 27-9. To access Internet Explorer's radio features, invoke the toolbar by right-clicking the Internet Explorer or Explorer toolbar and marking Radio. To display Microsoft's radio station guide, click the Radio Stations toolbar button and click Radio Station Guide.

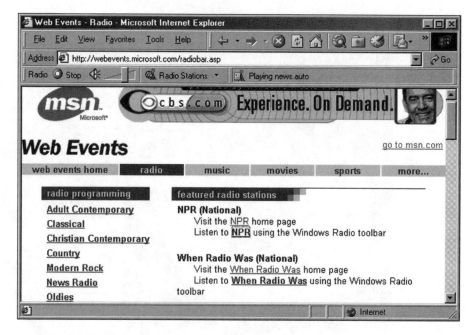

Figure 27-9: To listen to a radio station, click its call letters after *Listen to* in the radio station guide.

The speaker icon on the Radio toolbar is a general mute button. The radio volume control adds another volume control to the six already available. It appears to act as an additional control on the volume at which *wav* files are played.

Because the radio volume control and the wave volume control are configured so that radio volume is on top of wave volume, you'll find it quite difficult to keep the volume of Windows events low, but the volume of the radio up. To check this out for yourself, right-click your volume control icon in your system tray (or click Start, Programs, Accessories, Entertainment, Volume Control), and click Open Volume Controls. Then adjust the radio volume control in the Radio toolbar in your Internet Explorer and the wave volume control in the Volume Control dialog box (see Figure 27-10).

Figure 27-10: The Vol and Wave controls in the Volume Control dialog box control the volume of the radio, as does the radio volume control in the Radio toolbar. Are three volume controls enough? As it turns out, they aren't. You can't set the wave volume separately from the radio volume.

Find your video, sound, image, icon, midi, wave, and mouse pointer files

Your multimedia files are spread all over your computer. Wouldn't it be great to have a multimedia explorer that would seek them all out and give you quick access? Multimedia Xplorer does just that, and a lot more. This is great Estonian software.

Open Multimedia Xplorer and you'll see a version of the familiar Windows Explorer interface (see Figure 27-11). Click a filename in the lower-right pane to view the image or images or play the sound within it.

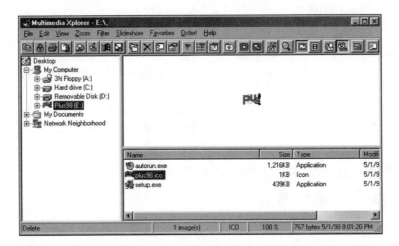

Figure 27-11: Multimedia Xplorer looks similar to the Windows Explorer, but it lets you view or play the multimedia files as you browse.

Click the Multimedia Detective toolbar button (the eighth from the left) to gather up a hierarchical list of all the files that contain images, sounds, videos, midi music, icons, or mouse pointers, as shown in Figure 27-12. Click any of the filenames listed in the Multimedia Detective to display or play its multimedia content.

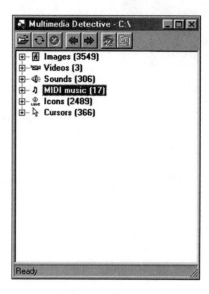

Figure 27-12: Multimedia Detective organizes your multimedia files hierarchically for easy previewing.

With Multimedia Xplorer, you can convert bitmap images (*bmp*, *jpeg*, *gif*, *png*, *tiff*, *pcx*), play sound files (*wav*, *mid*, *rmi*, *aiff*, *au*, *snd*, *mp2*, mp3, *mpa*, *ra*), play video (*avi*, *mpeg*, *mov*, *rm*), extract icons, display animated mouse pointers, change your startup, shut down, and power off Windows 98 logos, produce slide shows, and set up wallpaper. It uses the Windows Media Player to display all the files that it finds.

It is great to have this much power over your multimedia files. Multimedia Xplorer is shareware, and you'll find it at www.moonsoftware.com/.

Extract sound schemes from Desktop Themes

Desktop Themes usually come with a whole set of sounds that are assigned to various Windows events, such as Maximize, Minimize, Close Window, Exit Windows, and so on. All of the sounds taken together, along with their assignments to these Windows events, constitute a Windows sound scheme.

Secret

You can save sound schemes from Desktop Themes and invoke them whenever you like, even if you don't care for the rest of the Desktop Theme. You can edit any set of sounds and their assignments to create sound schemes.

If you haven't already loaded some Desktop Themes from the Windows 98 CD-ROM, or from various sites on the Internet, you'll need to get them first. To copy some themes from the Windows 98 CD-ROM, click the Start button, Settings, Control Panel, Add/Remove Programs, Windows Setup, Desktop Themes. You can pick which themes you want to install.

If you copy a zipped theme file down from a site on the Internet, just extract the files into your \Program Files\Plus!\Themes folder. Click Start, Settings, Control Panel, Desktop Themes, and there they are.

To use only the sounds from a theme, clear all of the check boxes except the Sound Events check box, as shown in Figure 27-13. Click OK to make those sounds the current sounds.

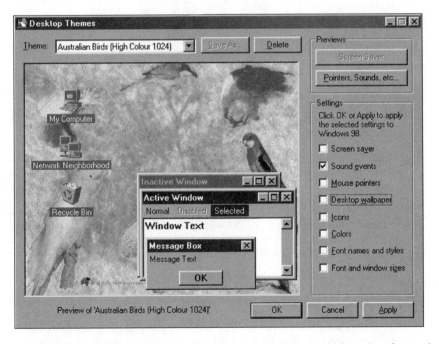

Figure 27-13: The Desktop Themes dialog box lets you choose which settings from a theme you will use. In this example, only the sounds are selected.

Now that you have a set of current sounds taken from a theme, click Start, Settings, Control Panel, Sounds. Click any of the Windows events, as shown in Figure 27-14. To hear the sound, click the play arrow to the right of the Preview box.

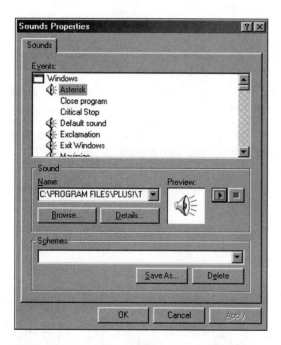

Figure 27-14: The Sounds Properties dialog box lets you hear a sound.

To save the current sounds as a sound scheme, click the Save As button, enter a name in the Save This Sound Scheme As field, and click OK.

You can use the Browse button to browse for any other *wav* files that you want to assign to Windows events. Other programs that use sounds will also appear in the Events list, so you can scroll down to them and assign new sounds to their events.

A good way to find *wav* files and other multimedia files is to use the Multimedia Xplorer. We discuss it in the previous section, "Find your video, sound, image, icon, midi, wav, and mouse pointer files."

Panoramic views

The Surround video viewer is seamlessly installed when you install Internet Explorer and/or Windows 98. It provides the user with a way of viewing properly formatted panoramic and rotating object views. To get an idea of what this means, you can check out a couple of web sites that use Surround video.

A good place to start is Black Diamond Consulting, the original authors of Surround video. They have a number of links to web sites that use this technology. You'll find the links at www.bdiamond.com/products/live.htm.

The MSN Carpoint site makes good use of Surround video, both for 360-degree interior panoramic shots of new cars and trucks, as well as for walk-around views of new cars (actually, the car appears to rotate). These are the two modes for Surround video, so you get a good idea of how to use this technology. You'll find the gallery of car panoramas at carpoint.msn.com/gallery. To see the Toyota Tacoma interior, visit carpoint.msn.com/Gallery/Inside/142800.

A particularly interesting site is Strolling.com at strolling.com/. You'll be able to click a map to get a number of views of London, Paris and New York.

Surround video is not the only format used to view panoramic and object pictures. Many producers use the Apple QuickTime VR format, and sometimes combine it with QuickTime movie to allow you to walk between panoramic views. You can check out a 360-degree panoramic view of a hang gliding launch site on Maui at www.maui.net/~drex/sixmile.html. We've included a sample of the view in Figure 27-15.

Figure 27-15: A portion of the 360-degree pan of the hang gliding launch half way up Haleakala. The complete pan took 18 shots.

In order to view this panoramic picture, you'll need to download the 7MB Apple QuickTime viewer (www.apple.com/quicktime/).

To see how you can integrate panoramic views with pseudo walkthroughs, go to Apple's campus for a virtual tour at www.apple.com/quicktime/samples/interactive-mm/vac/vacdemo.html. QuickTime movie is used to simulate walking from one panoramic viewpoint to the next.

As you will see from these sites, this video format is not actually a form of VR (virtual reality), in spite of Apple's hyped up name for it. Both Surround video and QTVR do essentially the same thing—allow the author to create and you to view panoramic and surround-object pictures.

I wrote to the author of the Maui panoramic view, cartographer Bob Franklin, and asked him what he thought about this technology. Here's what he had to say:

> Creating a view from one position is a file size and production issue. QTVR also has a mode for object views such as those in the rotating car. These are more difficult to produce, and file size resources are costly.
>
> There are pseudo walkthroughs available in QTVR, either as teleportation or a streaming view, as you move from one panorama

node to another. VRML would choke at the resources and production required to give an immersive experience in a real scene.

QTVR is a subset of QuickTime, arguably far more sophisticated and powerful than any other media format. The metaphors can easily mix with other aspects of QuickTime (straight audio, straight video, sprites, and so on), so the sky's the limit to create any level of virtual experience. Most people deploy panoramas, mainly to give a better sense of being somewhere else — academia, real estate, entertainment, interactive games, and so on. The object part of QTVR is used less frequently, due to production and file size issues, but it is typically used to show products in online catalogs.

Production issues are very complex, storage file size can go ballistic very quickly, and download bandwidth can go exponential. The ability to present "seamless" viewing experiences is more related to decompression technologies than to processor speeds.

The "one viewer position" issue is actually driven by the need to "stitch" multiple images together, because lenses just won't go beyond about 160 degrees. Most of the software designed to process these multiple images focus on automating the process. In fact, if you begin to put these images together, you'll discover that you need to keep the camera exactly centered vertically on the horizon and exactly aligned with the horizon. Furthermore, you need to make the shots centered at compass increments evenly divisible into 360 degrees.

To that end, a mini industry has developed to produce tripod heads with detented positions, some automated by electric motors, and universal leveling mechanisms. Look at www.kaidan.com. Bogen also makes them. Other issues related to creating these images have to do with lens focal lengths vis a vis number of shots, and maintaining exposures to a constant standard — in other words, a manual camera set to a fixed aperture and shutter speed.

My scene was done with a Polaroid PCD 2000 digital camera with no built-in compression (artifacts), but I had to correct the exposures after the fact (in PhotoShop), so that color and contrast matched. The lens was a 38mm, so it required 18 shots. A 20mm lens might only need 10. The best shots with an automatic camera would be done with the sun directly overhead. This is not usually possible. Also, you don't have to take shots sequentially. You can wait for part of the scene to get more interesting before shooting it. Doing this with a digital camera would require some expertise in PhotoShop or the like.

The concept and viewing technology was introduced by Apple through QuickTime four years ago. Since then, there have been a number of players in on it and, as you pointed out, there are a few technologies that can be implemented as browser plug-ins, or standalone apps, including viewers based on Java. There are many composing programs as well. IPIX at www.ipix.com is another major player on the technology end.

IPEX has an image format that is infinitely zoomable (well, almost) and serves the portion of the image that the viewer requires on the fly.

I believe they also have a Java player. Some other companies have various proprietary cameras and such, all aimed at making production easy. The Surround video technology is not available for Mac. In general, I disdain any technology that is not cross-platform—my major beef with Microsoft. User share on other platforms is still quite high, and ah, well, I'm one of them.

One of the issues with the technology of this "viewing experience" is that the image is not displayed pixel for pixel as it is stored. The idea is that at each point of view (360 per zoom level), whatever is displayed in the window is displayed in a perspective consistent with the viewing window's command. This requires compression for storage and a very rapid decompression on the fly as the viewer pans around, zooming in and out. There are quite a few licensors of codecs (compression/decompression) out there who have algorithms that do a fair to excellent job in this vein, *jpeg* being the most famous.

You can create a panorama in two ways, no matter which technology you use to store and display it. First, you can manually "blend" the collected frames together in a raster image editor such as PhotoShop. Second, you can use software that is "smart" enough to do the blending for you, assuming that the photographer has given the software mathematically consistent images to start with (hence the specialized tripod heads). If you use this second method, you also need a software tool to store the resultant data in a form easily reassembled. There are many, and fortunately for me, most use QuickTime.

Thinking about this then, one could imagine that "looking out" from a central position to a surrounding environment is fundamentally different than "looking in" at an object. "Looking out" has the potential for "interpreting" raw raster data in an infinite way, because the data are "stitched" together so that there is no start or finish. For each microscopically incremented viewing position, there is a version of the data that can be viewed and made sense of, visually.

My scene of the six mile launch is infinitely interpreted from data that are (roughly) 300 pixels high by 2800 pixels wide, or 840,000 total pixels. Let's take a finite example of "looking in" where, say, we look at a car from 360 positions. Extrapolating, my window for viewing the scene was 300 pixels high by 400 wide (120,000 pixels). To look in at an object from a finite 360 compass points would require a storage source file containing 43,200,000 pixels. Quite a difference. As a result, *object views*, as they are called, are often sampled from 15 to 30 degree compass points, and they often don't have that smooth look.

To carry the extrapolation a little farther, imagine the production, storage requirements, and access speeds necessary to "move" the panorama a finite distance in some singular direction, let alone give the viewer an infinite choice of directions! What would the "grain" of the movement have to be so that the movement would seem at least a little bit "seamless"? You can see this would be impossible under today's technology, except for some small demonstration project.

VRML has tried to address this issue by "re-creating" the environment as data, rather than "recording" it, as QuickTime has. Obviously this has its own limitations, but as rendering speeds increase, I would imagine that sophisticated production techniques will allow some pretty cool viewer experiences.

Meanwhile, the technologists in the immersive video world have deemed the "scene" to be the lowest common denominator. A scene is a collection of nodes. (The term *node* refers to the place where the user "stands.") Each node can consist of a panoramic view (looking out) or an object view (looking in). The user moves from node to node within a scene by clicking hotspots within his or her current view. This leads to an experience not unlike some interactive games, such as Riven or Myst, as opposed to Tomb Raider, which is really VRML. Thus the rudiments of a VRML experience can be approached in immersive video, but not duplicated.

For me, I find the interaction to be the fascination here. We do not experience the world in real life as the viewer of a movie being directed and shown by another, but as something we glance at, do double takes on, stop and focus on, return to and move on, and so on. This technology allows this type of interaction, and the net experience is one of being there.

I have found that producers of this sort of content do panoramas. Object movies (looking in) require a quantum leap in production effort to produce a good quality result. Ironically, automobiles have been a big exception to this. It turns out that auto shows often have the cars on giant turntables, which allows for very exact image sampling.

Some more ambitious attempts at scenes produce linear video between different panorama or object nodes. You are here, click on this hotspot, and you are transported (as on a moving sidewalk) to the next viewing spot, all the while watching your progress, as opposed to the usual "teleportation" metaphor.

When Voyager landed on Mars, a QuickTime VR was produced from the telemetry, showing a 360-degree view. It is posted on NASA's site (mars.jpl.nasa.gov/MPF/vrml/qtvr.html). I have found that academia is a big user of this technology, archeology (panoramas) and medicine (objects) in particular. Real estate is a big market too, as are travel, destination resorts, and so on.

I have seen an object movie (looking in) that was produced with 3 degrees of freedom. Imagine an object in motion as a loop (repeating movement, as a piston cycling). There is a user-selectable viewpoint, which not only moved around the object, but also moved around it from multiple views in the Y-axis. And all the while the object was in temporal movement. The limitation here was bandwidth. Only 8 percent of the possible three axis views were produced, with two seconds of temporal dimension, but it took 2.3MB of compressed data at 180 x 240 pixels to view in real time!

The real attraction is that quite a lot of information (in its larger sense) is storable in pretty low bandwidth data. While other developers have been attacking this venue in a strong way, Apple's QuickTime has a big head start in many aspects, probably due to its longevity in multimedia playback in general.

I use QuickTime because it has more production tools available; it is cross platform; it supports all media formats; and, in one technology, it will read virtually any audio or video format (including streaming with 4.0). On top of that, it licenses and distributes all major (and minor) audio and video codecs as part of QuickTime. This means that quality is extremely high. It is the only media player that mixes media, supports multinode scenes, and offers advanced animation and infographic tools.

Web-TV

Will the computer and the TV merge? Our feeling is that the computer/Internet experience will overpower TV within ten years.

Web-TV through URLs

Your Web-TV channels are accessible from your Address bar. You can use the Address bar in an Internet Explorer, Explorer, or My Computer window, or the Address toolbar on your Desktop. Simply type the TV prefix and enter the channel number type — for example, **tv://12**. This is just like entering **http://** to get to a web address or **file://** to get to a folder or file.

If Web-TV isn't running, you can launch it and go right to your desired channel by clicking Start, Run, and entering the TV URL. If you type the TV URL in the Address bar and Web-TV isn't already running, it will start up.

You can also create a Start menu folder and insert shortcuts for your favorite TV channels:

STEPS:
Creating a Folder of TV URLs for Your Start Menu

Step 1.   Navigate with your Explorer to your My System folder (hopefully you created one previously). Right-click the right pane of the Explorer, click New, Folder, and rename the new folder **TV Channels.**

Step 2.   Right-click the TV Channels folder and click Explore.

Step 3.   Right-click the right pane of the Explorer, and click New, Shortcut.

Continued

STEPS

Creating a Folder of TV URLs for Your Start Menu *(continued)*

Step 4.   Type **tv://12**, or whatever channel you want, in the Command Line field (see Figure 27-16). Click Next.

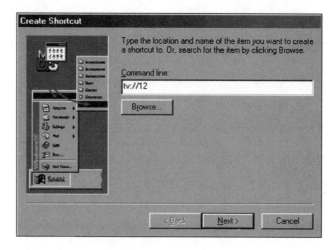

Figure 27-16: Type the "address" of the channel in the Command Line field.

Step 5   Rename the shortcut to a familiar name for the TV channel. Click Finish.

Step 6.   Drag the TV Channels folder to the Start button and drop it there. A shortcut will appear on the Start menu.

Web-TV with ATI All In Wonder cards

If you have the ATI All In Wonder card (which includes a TV Tuner) you might run into trouble when you set up Web-TV. If you find that Web-TV appears to be configured correctly, but you still aren't able to set up your TV channels — and hence cannot watch TV on your computer — you'll want to check out your video drivers.

Windows 98 may misidentify your display adapter as the ATI Rage II+ [mach_64]. This setting allows you to run your All In Wonder card at various color depths including up to True Color. This may mislead you into thinking that your display adapter is set up properly.

While the Mach_64 drivers correctly drive the ATI display adapter for most everyday tasks, these drivers don't include the files required to view Web-TV. To install the proper video driver, take the following steps:

STEPS:
Installing the Proper Video Driver for the ATI Card

Step 1. Right-click your Desktop, click Properties, click the Settings tab, and click the Advanced button.

Step 2. Click the Adapter tab, and click the Change button. In the Update Device Driver Wizard, click Next.

Step 3. Mark the option to display a list of all the drivers in a specific location, and click Next.

Step 4. Mark the Show All Hardware option button. Select ATI Technologies under Manufacturers, and the All-In-Wonder [ati_m64] driver under Models. Click Next.

Step 5. Restart Windows when asked.

Thanks to Dave Adams for help with this tip.

Web-TV control keys

It's not a remote control, but you can use the keyboard shortcuts listed in Table 27-1 to control Web-TV.

Table 27-1 Web-TV Keyboard Controls

Key	Action/Result
F10	Displays the Web-TV menu
F6	Toggles between full-screen and windowed display
0-9	Changes channels (cannot use keypad numbers)
Windows+Ctrl+Shift+Z	Program Guide (starts Web-TV if not running)
Windows+Ctrl+Z	Starts Web-TV or toggles between windowed and full screen display if running
Windows+Crtl+V	Turns volume up (this works even if Web-TV isn't running)

Continued

Key	Action/Result
	Table 27-1 *(continued)*
Windows+Shift+V	Turns volume down (this works even if Web-TV isn't running)
Windows+V	Mutes Master Volume (this works even if Web-TV isn't running)
Windows+Crtl+Alt+Z	Increases channel by one
Windows+Crtl+Alt+Shift+Z	Decreases channel by one

Thanks to Michael Grant for pointing out these tips.

Summary

Let's hear and see and feel it for Windows 98 multimedia. Make that ugly computer do something a lot more fun.

▶ MP3 audio threatens the music Industry. Download the threat to your computer.

▶ Tune into radio stations around the world and bring back audio memories of your vacations abroad.

▶ Search for all your multimedia files and only multimedia files.

▶ Mine the themes for sounds.

▶ Find panoramic views on the web.

▶ Create your own folder of Web-TV shortcuts.

▶ Use keyboard shortcuts to control your Web-TV.

▶ Watch CNN and read www.cnn.com at the same time.

Chapter 28

Fun

In This Chapter

Here's where we put all the stuff that didn't fit anywhere else, but then it turned out that this stuff was pretty cool. We can't always be serious, so we thought we'd let you in on some neat things we've found.

▶ Metric versus English, and all sorts of other conversions.

▶ Print your own graph paper.

▶ Keep track of the weather without going to the weather channel.

▶ Not creative? Download these answering machine greetings.

Unit conversion

Until we found Convert, we had not been impressed with the many unit conversion programs available as shareware or freeware. They've all been way too weak, with silly front ends. Convert converted us.

Convert has an extensive array of unit conversion ratios and can convert just about anything, as you can tell from Figure 28-1. As long as we live in the worst of all possible worlds (that is, one in which there are two widely used measurement systems), Convert is an absolute necessity.

Convert is freeware, and you'll find the latest version at www.joshmadison.com/software.

Lo and behold, we did find another conversion program that we liked, not that its shareware nag screens were all that pleasant. Tek Converter II uses a cute version of the Explorer interface to let you choose the units that you'll convert between. Just drag and drop each unit from the right pane of the Tek Explorer down to the boxes at the bottom of the window, as shown in Figure 28-2.

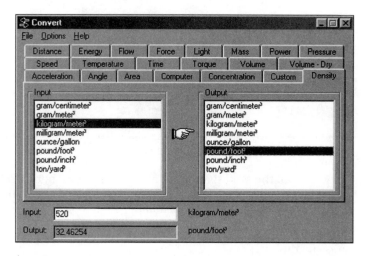

Figure 28-1: Conversion from metric to English units of density using Convert.

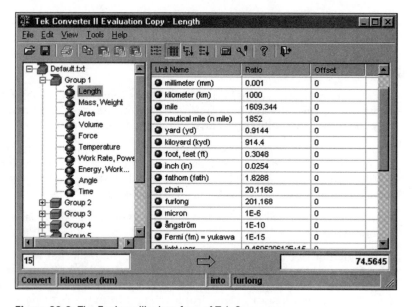

Figure 28-2: The Explorer-like interface of Tek Converter.

While its interface was, well, cute, what we really liked was the fact that you could add any conversion units that you like and group them in any manner that makes sense to you. You could also get rid of conversion units that you would never use.

Tek Converter II is shareware, but there is a freeware version available at the same site. You'll find it at village.infoweb.ne.jp/~tek/index.htm.

Calculator with paper tape and unit conversions

There are plenty of shareware calculators available on the Web. If you are looking for something special, you should conduct a search and check out a number of different ones.

You might take a look at the CDML Advanced Calculator, shown in Figure 28-3. It has three nice features: a paper tape, a financial calculator, and a unit converter. This is not a scientific calculator, but it does calculate net present value, annuity payments, double-declining balance depreciation, and other financial functions.

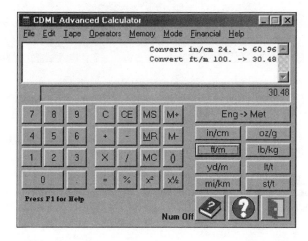

Figure 28-3: The CDML Advanced Calculator offers lots of functions and a "paper tape."

You'll find it at members.aol.com/cdml.

Print graph paper

You can't keep every type of graph paper on hand. Graph Paper Printer prints a sheet (or more) of graph paper for you, based on your settings. How about log paper with sixteen sets, as shown in Figure 28-4? Or just a linear one-millimeter scale on the abscissa and the ordinate? Perhaps a polar graph? You get to choose a scale that is linear, logarithmic, quadratic, or gaussian.

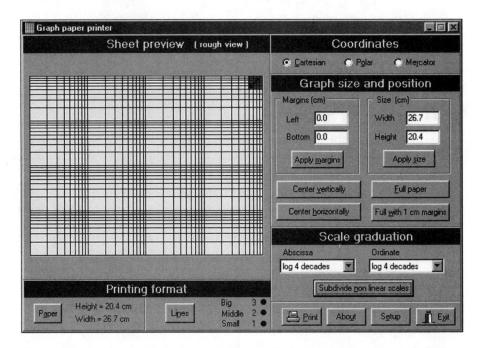

Figure 28-4: Graph Paper Printer lets you print more kinds of graph paper than you might have known existed.

All of these types of graph paper, and many more, are available in this freeware package. You'll find it at perso.easynet.fr/~philimar.

The program consists of one executable file, and its installation doesn't add any DLLs to your System folder. Uninstalling Graph Paper Printer consists of deleting the program, its folder, and any shortcuts to it that you may have created.

Know what's going on outside

While you're pressing your nose to the computer screen, it might be nice to know what is going on outside, and maybe what will be happening over the next few hours or days. While it is not exactly a Windows 98 secret, Cli-Mate is a handy little piece of shareware that sits in your system tray and periodically goes out on the Internet and updates itself with the latest weather.

You can choose which weather server to use. It shows current conditions (see Figure 28-5), and you can click it to display the NOAA forecast and the extended forecast. It can keep track of multiple cities as well as the radar. It doesn't provide everything that some of us weather fanatics want, but for painless weather data gathering (without having to open your browser), it works great.

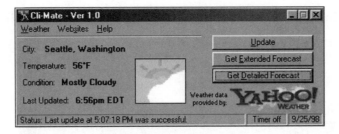

Figure 28-5: Double-click Cli-Mate in your system tray to see an updated overview of the weather. You can choose your preferred weather server.

You'll find it at users.nac.net/splat/climate/index.htm.

You can also get the weather e-mailed to you. You get an HTML-formatted e-mail message every morning (and afternoon, if you like) with a basic three-day forecast. Click one of the links, and get detailed current conditions, a five-day forecast, and radar and satellite images. The server is much quicker than other weather sites. Bob Kaplan told Chris Pirillo about this site: www.weather24.com.

Look back at earth

While there is an endless variety of themes available on the Internet, this one is especially cool, as you can see from Figure 28-6.

Figure 28-6: A Desktop view of the Earth View theme.

You can find the Earth View theme at www.mo-net.com/~recurve.

Download an answering machine greeting

Another of the endless possibilities of the web. You can go to The Answering Machine web site (see Figure 28-7) and download any of their long list of answering machine greetings. Courteous or not, that's up to you.

Figure 28-7: The Answering Machine web site.

The files come in the *wav* format. You can play them into your answering machine or use them on your computer-based voice mail system.

You'll find The Answering Machine at www.answeringmachine.co.uk.

Buy low

How about a little comparison shopping made easy? If you know what you want, you can find it cheap on the web. It's always nice to have a little web page front end to do that dirty work for you, too. One place to check out, and there are many, is Bottom Dollar, shown in Figure 28-8.

Figure 28-8: Bottom Dollar's web site, one of several comparison shopping Meccas.

You'll find it at www.bottomdollar.com.

There are other sites, such as www.pricewatch.com. Because of its wealth of online supporting articles, I like Ziff Davis' Computer Shopper at www.zdnet.com/computershopper/index1.html. You'll want to go there if you need to figure out what you want to buy. One other really inexpensive place to buy computer equipment on the web is www.buycomp.com.

Help crack the code

We like secrets, do you? Would you like to participate in the worldwide effort to read a message that has been encrypted with RSA Labs' 56-bit secret key? If so, find your way to the distributed network shown in Figure 28-9, and add your computer to the effort during its idle moments.

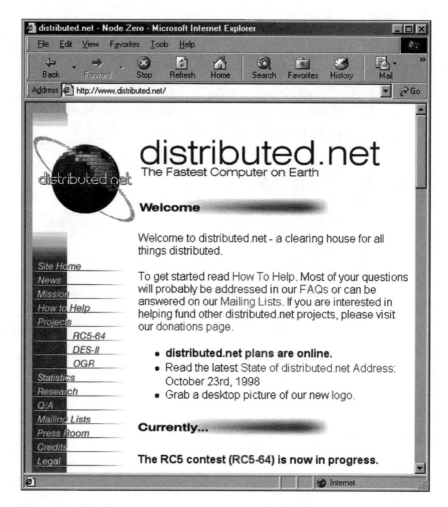

Figure 28-9: The Distributed.net web site, host for the RC5-65 contest.

Here's the story from the distributed network:

> Project Bovine RC5-64
>
> The Bovine RC5 Effort was formed to take the responsibilities of coordinating and maintaining the RC5 servers that are needed to distribute key blocks to work on to all of the participating client programs. We depend heavily — entirely actually — on the participation of people like yourself, as we intend to solve this project via the use of brute force, trying every possible key there is. This is for the most part summarized in our mission statement
>
> We know this method works. On 19 October 1997 at 1325 Greenwich Mean Time, we found the correct solution for the previous project — RSA Labs' 56-bit secret-key challenge (that's RC5-32/12/7 56-bit for you

stats junkies; the key was 0x532B744CC20999, and it took us 250 days to locate.)

RSA Labs is proffering a US$10,000 prize to the group that wins this contest. The distribution of the cash will be as follows:

$1000 to the winner

$1000 to the winner's team — this would go to the winner if she or he wasn't affiliated with a team

You'll find the distributed network at www.distributed.net.

The home of freeware

Programming is fun, or at least it can be. Software authors like to get their programs out there so that others can use them and recognize the authors for their technical brilliance. Let's see, any other good reasons for the availability of freeware?

There is a huge amount of freeware that can be downloaded from the web, and many sites supply it in addition to shareware. While we've covered a number of freeware and shareware products, we could never even come close to covering them all.

You'll find the Freeware Home, obviously a site that specializes in freeware (and makes its income from advertising), at www.freewarehome.com.

Easter Eggs, anyone?

For some reason, Easter Eggs aren't usually available through a choice on the Help menu. You have to seek them out. Here's a method to display the Easter Egg in Windows 98:

STEPS:

Finding the Windows 98 Easter Egg

Step 1. Double-click the clock in the system tray to display the Date/Time Properties dialog box.

Step 2. Click the Time Zone tab.

Step 3. Press and hold your Ctrl key. Place your mouse pointer over Memphis, Egypt (the point numbered 1 in Figure 28-10), and then press and hold your left mouse button.

Continued

STEPS

Finding the Windows 98 Easter Egg *(continued)*

Figure 28-10: The numbers in this figure mark the locations of Memphis, Egypt; Memphis, Tennessee; and Redmond, Washington. (You won't see any numbers on the map in your own dialog box.)

Pretend to drag something to Memphis, Tennessee (the point numbered 2), and then release the left mouse button. (Memphis, of course, was the code name for Windows 98.) Don't let go of your Ctrl key.

Step 4. Still holding down the Ctrl key, point to Memphis, Tennessee, and then pretend to drag something from there to Redmond, Washington (the point numbered 3). Release the left mouse button, and then release the Ctrl key.

Step 5. An animated dialog box should appear listing several Microsoft developers, complete with images of the Microsoft campus and the Seattle, Washington area. If you don't see it, re-try the steps carefully. It takes some people two or three tries.

Our thanks to Frank Condron (worldowindows.com).

No they don't go bad, even though some of them are a bit old. To get the latest in Easter eggs, turn to the Easter Egg Archive at www.eeggs.com/.

Find out stuff on the web

Search tools are good for some things, but not for others. If you want to find out about a historical event, an encyclopedia is probably the place to go. It's nice to have places that bring specific reference tools together. Research-It! provides dictionaries, translations, biographies, quotations, maps, a CIA fact book, package tracking, and a directory of list servers (see Figure 28-11).

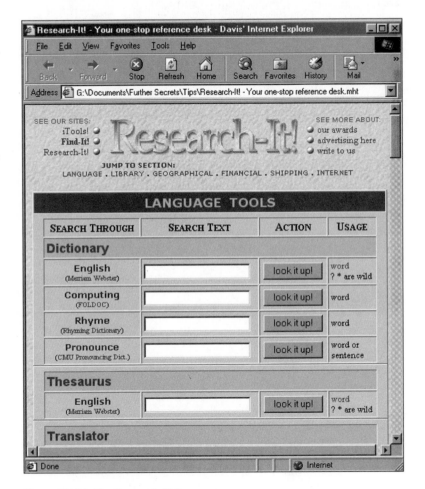

Figure 28-11: The Research-It! home page.

You'll find it at www.itools.com.

If you want to look up words, check out www.dictionary.com, or download Magic Dictionary at www.avalon.net/~rbliss/magicd.zip.

Looking for medical knowledge? Check out www.drkoop.com.

Summary

We show you where to look on the web for fun stuff.

▶ You too can help crack the RSA code.

▶ Freeware in one place.

▶ Easter Eggs, for those who want to know.

▶ The web is a reference source if you can find the right sources.

Appendix

MORE Windows 98 Secrets
CD-ROM Contents

The *MORE Windows 98 Secrets* CD-ROM contains the following items:

▶ The e-version of *MORE Windows 98 Secrets*

▶ A few Registration files that are detailed in the book

▶ A small program for clearing partitions on your hard disk

▶ An HTML index to the Windows 98 Resource Kit

▶ A late-breaking shareware and secrets file

E-version of *MORE Windows 98 Secrets*

You can install the e-version of the book on your hard disk by running the Setup.exe program found in the root directory of the CD-ROM. The e-version of *MORE Windows 98 Secrets* consists of four files that are installed in their own subfolder. The installation doesn't disturb any of your system files.

If you'd rather not install the e-version of *MORE Windows 98 Secrets*, you can access it from the CD-ROM. You'll find it in the \Book folder; just click the Moresecrets.hlp file.

All the files in the root directory of the CD-ROM are used by the Setup.exe file to install the e-version on your hard disk.

Registration files

The Registration files are in the \Reg folder. You can right-click any of them in your Explorer and click Merge to insert their contents into your Registry. To see a *reg* file's contents, right-click its filename and then click Edit. Here is an explanation of what each *reg* file does:

Filename	Function
CMC.reg	All the CMC.reg file does is associate the CMCSend extension with the Sendtox.dll, and thereby associate the Mail Recipient CMC menu item with the functions in this dynamic link library. See "Send To X" in Chapter 25.
Colors.reg	Changes your Desktop colors. See "Your own colors" in Chapter 14
Compressed Folders Zip.reg	No matter what version of WinZip you have, you can re-associate Compressed Folders with zip files. See "WinZip takes over my Compressed Folders" in Chapter 13.
Explorer.reg	Allows you to open My Computer in Explorer view with one click. See "Open My Computer in Explorer view" in Chapter 14.
Logon.reg	Edit this file to insert your own dialog box before users log on to your computer. See "Start up your computer with a dialog box" in Chapter 18.
New.reg	If your context menu doesn't contain the New menu item when you right-click the Desktop or the right pane of your Explorer, it may be because there is a damaged key in your Registry. This file repairs the key and restores the New item. See "Missing New from your context menu?" in Chapter 13.
Notepadhtml.reg	Puts Notepad on the context menu for HTML files, providing quick access to that editor. See "Edit HTML files with Notepad" in Chapter 11.
NT Registry change for NetMeeting.reg	Configures NT to allow Windows 98 clients to receive NetMeeting calls. See "I can't hear anyone through my router" in Chapter 9.
Offline.reg	Works with toolbar button to set Internet Explorer and Outlook Express into offline mode. See "Set Work Offline before you open Internet Explorer" in Chapter 2.
Online.reg	Same as above, but sets online mode.
Owner.reg	Edit this file to change the ownership data on your computer. See "Make sure you're the owner" in Chapter 14.
Regedit.reg	Makes Edit the default action for clicking Registration files instead of Merge. See "Changing the default action for reg files" in Chapter 14.
Sendto Desktop shortcut.reg	Installing Send To X overwrites a Registry entry that associates the Send To Desktop (Create Shortcut) menu item with the DLL containing the function that actually does create a shortcut and place it on the Desktop. This file re-associates the overwritten Registry entry with the correct DLL. See "Send To X" in Chapter 25.

Program for clearing hard disk partitions

The Clear.txt and Clearhd.com files in the \Tools folder are the source code and program file, respectively, for a program that will absolutely clear your hard disk partitions. Check "Completely clear your hard disk" in Chapter 28 for more information.

HTML index for the *Windows 98 Resource Kit*

The Resource Kit Index.htm file, also in the \Tools folder, is an HTML index to the *Windows 98 Resource Kit.* See "Windows 98 Resource Kit Online" in Chapter 16.

Late-breaking shareware and secrets

As the book went to press, we constructed a file of late-breaking shareware and secrets. You'll find it in the \News folder. Click Local Lockergnome.htm.

Index

continued

continued

continued

continued

price lists, distributing, 176
Print button, 214
Print dialog box
printers, 305
    batch files, 334
    different papers, 606-607
    graphics on Hewlett Packard printers, 604-606
    print spooler values, 602-603
    text editor fonts, 603-604
Printers.txt, 415
printing
    directory of files in a folder, 346-347
    graph paper, 733-734
    Internet Explorer preview, 48
    messages, 146
    shortcut, 37, 334
    small networks, 637, 638, 644, 654
    telephone list from Address Book, 214
privacy, 36, 152
private key, 183
processes, killing, 453-454
Prodigy, 5, 35
profiles, 75, 433-437
Programmer's File Editor (PFE), 514
programs
    interfering with Disk Defragmenter, 550
    malicious, stopping, 452-453
    running when Windows shut down, 407-409
    running with Address bar, 318-319
prompt, DOS. See DOS
protocols, 646
    encryption, 201-202, 205
    IPX/SPX, 657
    NetMeeting users, 236-237
public key encryption, 183, 200
punctuation marks, 126
pushpin icon, 86
PWS, 501

Q

qt, 40
QTVR, 723-727
Qualcomm Eudora, 205
Quantum, 520, 572
Quarterdeck QuickBook, 437-438
Quick Launch toolbar
    put Find on, 319
    Recycle Bin, 316
Quick Res utility, 583
Quick View, 683-684

QuickRes, 688
quit
    checking for a CD-ROM, 548-549
    searching for floppy disks at startup, 502-503
quoteCheck
    ending, 520-524
quoting
    enabled, 144
    replies and forwards, 107-109

R

radio toolbar, 718-719
RAM, 417
RAMexam, 386
RC2 encryption, 201
RD, 664
Rea, Steven Charles, 361
Read Only files, 272
reading
    attachments without opening messages, 122-123
    messages, 97-105
    newsgroup messages, 133-134, 136, 137-146
Readme files, 415-416
real-time connections, 228
receipts, 179
receiving
    digitally signed e-mail, 184-186
    encrypted e-mail, 200-206
recording, 221, 223
    AutoMate, 429
Recording Industry Association of America (RIAA), 713
recovery
    corrupted messages, 59-60
    deleted message folders, 62-63
    help from Zip drive, 450-452
    Outlook Express won't open, 62
Recycle Bin, 305
    file storage, 452
    putting on toolbar, 316
    renaming, 298-300
    Thumbnails view folder, 352
red ribbon icon, 184, 191
References line, 144
Refresh button, 621
refresh rate
    display/video adapter, 584-587
reg files, 375-376
    changing default action, 378

S

S/MIME, 201, 205
S10 registry default value, 485
S11 setting, 485
S36 registry default value, 485
Safe mode, 497, 560
SafeInstall, 498, 512, 515-516
Samba, 426
Samsung hubs, 416
Sandeep, Jain, 555
Sandra, 520-521, 554-555, 698-700
Sanford, Shawn, 510-511
Santovec, Mike, 123, 155, 160
saving
    automatic replies, 179
    calling card, 481-483
    choosing file locations, 335
    Dial-Up networking password, 492
    digital e-mail certificates, 190-193, 197
    GIFs, 125
    messages without attachments, 124
    newsgroup threads, 145-146
    Outlook Express documents, 55-59
    uninstall information, 414-415
    user names and passwords, 280
    web pages, 22, 266-267, 269
SCAM (SCSI Configured Auto Magically), 526
ScanDisk, 396, 409, 410, 450, 535, 536, 552, 625, 664
ScanRegistry, 385-387, 387-393
Scanregw.exe, 385, 390
Scheduled Task Wizard, 396
scheduling tasks
    hard disk thrashing, 547-548
    while computer sleeps, 623-626
    web downloads, 17-19
Schneider, Bill, 246, 621
Schnoll, Scott, 615
Schott, Jim, 24
Scoble, Robert, 225
Screeble, 304
Screen Loupe, 581-583
Screen Rip32, 682-683
screen savers, 399
    hard disks, 547
    hot corners, 337-338
    indoor rock climbing, 337
    show your pictures, 336-337
    turning off to defragment hard disks, 552-553
screen shots, capturing, 682-683
scripting, 426-428
    AutoMate, 429
    object models, 265

scrolling
    keyboard shortcuts, 37
    Word 97, 676
Scrows Icons, 300-301
SCSI devices, waking up, 621
SCSI drivers
    Adaptec 29XX and 394X series, 545
    computer won't boot, 544-545
SCSI hard drive, adding, 524-532, 549
    copy files onto, 529-530
    designate active partition, 530-531
    FDISK partitioning, 526-529
    formatting, 529
    Internet Explorer, 531-532
    plug in, 525-526
    swap drive assignments, 530-531
Seagate, 410, 519-520, 524, 535, 561
Search Engine Watch, 31
search engines
    multiple, 29-31
    standardizing, 31-32
Search pane, 28-29
searching, 741-742
    exclusionary e-mail, 172
    jump to site without, 32-33
    multiple search engines, 29-31
    Search pane, 28-29
    for web addresses, 26-28
Second Copy 97, 371-372
secrets, defined, 6-8
sectors, FAT 32 problems, 535-538
security, Registry, 385-393
Security Warning screen, 185
    levels of trust, 186-189
Select Group Members dialog box, 210
self-test, pause during, 498
Send, 95
Send and Receive, 86
    add news account, 134-135
    keyboard shortcut, 95
Send To, 371
    HTML pages, 259
Send To X, 685-687
senders, blocking, 174-175
sending
    encrypted e-mail, 200-206
    messages, 105-112
    messages as web pages, 109-110
SendTo, 316
sent messages, sorting, 179-180
Sequential Folder Creator, 348
Serdy, Steve, 135-136, 144

continued

IDG BOOKS WORLDWIDE, INC.
END-USER LICENSE AGREEMENT

READ THIS. You should carefully read these terms and conditions before opening the software packet(s) included with this book ("Book"). This is a license agreement ("Agreement") between you and IDG Books Worldwide, Inc. ("IDGB"). By opening the accompanying software packet(s), you acknowledge that you have read and accept the following terms and conditions. If you do not agree and do not want to be bound by such terms and conditions, promptly return the Book and the unopened software packet(s) to the place you obtained them for a full refund.

1. **License Grant.** IDGB grants to you (either an individual or entity) a nonexclusive license to use one copy of the enclosed software program(s) (collectively, the "Software") solely for your own personal or business purposes on a single computer (whether a standard computer or a workstation component of a multiuser network). The Software is in use on a computer when it is loaded into temporary memory (RAM) or installed into permanent memory (hard disk, CD-ROM, or other storage device). IDGB reserves all rights not expressly granted herein.

2. **Ownership.** IDGB is the owner of all right, title, and interest, including copyright, in and to the compilation of the Software recorded on the disk(s) or CD-ROM ("Software Media"). Copyright to the individual programs recorded on the Software Media is owned by the author or other authorized copyright owner of each program. Ownership of the Software and all proprietary rights relating thereto remain with IDGB and its licensers.

3. **Restrictions On Use and Transfer.**

   (a) You may only (i) make one copy of the Software for backup or archival purposes, or (ii) transfer the Software to a single hard disk, provided that you keep the original for backup or archival purposes. You may not (i) rent or lease the Software, (ii) copy or reproduce the Software through a LAN or other network system or through any computer subscriber system or bulletin-board system, or (iii) modify, adapt, or create derivative works based on the Software.

   (b) You may not reverse engineer, decompile, or disassemble the Software. You may transfer the Software and user documentation on a permanent basis, provided that the transferee agrees to accept the terms and conditions of this Agreement and you retain no copies. If the Software is an update or has been updated, any transfer must include the most recent update and all prior versions.

4. **Restrictions on Use of Individual Programs.** You must follow the individual requirements and restrictions detailed for each individual program in the appendix of this Book. These limitations are also contained in the individual license agreements recorded on the Software

Media. These limitations may include a requirement that after using the program for a specified period of time, the user must pay a registration fee or discontinue use. By opening the Software packet(s), you will be agreeing to abide by the licenses and restrictions for these individual programs that are detailed in the appendix and on the Software Media. None of the material on this Software Media or listed in this Book may ever be redistributed, in original or modified form, for commercial purposes.

5. **Limited Warranty.**

   (a) IDGB warrants that the Software and Software Media are free from defects in materials and workmanship under normal use for a period of sixty (60) days from the date of purchase of this Book. If IDGB receives notification within the warranty period of defects in materials or workmanship, IDGB will replace the defective Software Media.

   (b) **IDGB AND THE AUTHORS OF THE BOOK DISCLAIM ALL OTHER WARRANTIES, EXPRESS OR IMPLIED, INCLUDING WITHOUT LIMITATION IMPLIED WARRANTIES OF MERCHANTABILITY AND FITNESS FOR A PARTICULAR PURPOSE, WITH RESPECT TO THE SOFTWARE, THE PROGRAMS, THE SOURCE CODE CONTAINED THEREIN, AND/OR THE TECHNIQUES DESCRIBED IN THIS BOOK. IDGB DOES NOT WARRANT THAT THE FUNCTIONS CONTAINED IN THE SOFTWARE WILL MEET YOUR REQUIREMENTS OR THAT THE OPERATION OF THE SOFTWARE WILL BE ERROR FREE.**

   (c) This limited warranty gives you specific legal rights, and you may have other rights that vary from jurisdiction to jurisdiction.

6. **Remedies.**

   (a) IDGB's entire liability and your exclusive remedy for defects in materials and workmanship shall be limited to replacement of the Software Media, which may be returned to IDGB with a copy of your receipt at the following address: Software Media Fulfillment Department, Attn.: *MORE Windows 98 Secrets*, IDG Books Worldwide, Inc., 7260 Shadeland Station, Ste. 100, Indianapolis, IN 46256, or call 1-800-762-2974. Please allow three to four weeks for delivery. This Limited Warranty is void if failure of the Software Media has resulted from accident, abuse, or misapplication. Any replacement Software Media will be warranted for the remainder of the original warranty period or thirty (30) days, whichever is longer.

   (b) In no event shall IDGB or the authors be liable for any damages whatsoever (including without limitation damages for loss of business profits, business interruption, loss of business information, or any other pecuniary loss) arising from the use of or inability to use the Book or the Software, even if IDGB has been advised of the possibility of such damages.

(c) Because some jurisdictions do not allow the exclusion or limitation of liability for consequential or incidental damages, the above limitation or exclusion may not apply to you.

7. **U.S. Government Restricted Rights.** Use, duplication, or disclosure of the Software by the U.S. Government is subject to restrictions stated in paragraph (c)(1)(ii) of the Rights in Technical Data and Computer Software clause of DFARS 252.227-7013, and in subparagraphs (a) through (d) of the Commercial Computer — Restricted Rights clause at FAR 52.227-19, and in similar clauses in the NASA FAR supplement, when applicable.

8. **General.** This Agreement constitutes the entire understanding of the parties and revokes and supersedes all prior agreements, oral or written, between them and may not be modified or amended except in a writing signed by both parties hereto that specifically refers to this Agreement. This Agreement shall take precedence over any other documents that may be in conflict herewith. If any one or more provisions contained in this Agreement are held by any court or tribunal to be invalid, illegal, or otherwise unenforceable, each and every other provision shall remain in full force and effect.

my2cents.idgbooks.com

Register This Book — And Win!

Visit **http://my2cents.idgbooks.com** to register this book and we'll automatically enter you in our fantastic monthly prize giveaway. It's also your opportunity to give us feedback: let us know what you thought of this book and how you would like to see other topics covered.

Discover IDG Books Online!

The IDG Books Online Web site is your online resource for tackling technology — at home and at the office. Frequently updated, the IDG Books Online Web site features exclusive software, insider information, online books, and live events!

10 Productive & Career-Enhancing Things You Can Do at www.idgbooks.com

- Nab source code for your own programming projects.

- Download software.

- Read Web exclusives: special articles and book excerpts by IDG Books Worldwide authors.

- Take advantage of resources to help you advance your career as a Novell or Microsoft professional.

- Buy IDG Books Worldwide titles or find a convenient bookstore that carries them.

- Register your book and win a prize.

- Chat live online with authors.

- Sign up for regular e-mail updates about our latest books.

- Suggest a book you'd like to read or write.

- Give us your 2¢ about our books and about our Web site.

You say you're not on the Web yet? It's easy to get started with IDG Books' *Discover the Internet*, available at local retailers everywhere.

CD-ROM Installation Instructions

1. Insert the *MORE Windows 98 Secrets* CD-ROM into your CD-ROM drive.

2. Use your Explorer to display the contents of the root directory of your CD-ROM.

3. Click (or double-click) Setup.exe to install the e-version of *MORE Windows 98 Secrets* onto your hard disk.

See the Appendix for more details about what is included and how to use the *MORE Windows 98 Secrets* CD-ROM.

Spliffigami

Roll the 35 Greatest Joints of All Time

CHRIS STONE

TEN SPEED PRESS
Berkeley | Toronto

Published by Ten Speed Press, by arrangement with
Elephant Book Company Limited, 14 Dryden Court,
Renfrew Road, London SE11 4NH, United Kingdom

Ten Speed Press
PO Box 7123
Berkeley, California 94707
www.tenspeed.com

Distributed in Australia by Simon and Schuster Australia,
in Canada by Ten Speed Press Canada, in New Zealand by
Southern Publishers Group, in South Africa by Real Books,
and in the United Kingdom and Europe by
Publishers Group UK.

Editorial Director: Will Steeds
Project Editor: Laura Ward
Cover and Interior Design: Lindsey Johns
Illustrator: Adam Walker
Joint-Roller: Paul Malden
Production: Robert Paulley
Color Reproduction:
Modern Age Repro House Ltd., Hong Kong

Ten Speed Press Editor: Lisa Westmoreland

Library of Congress
Cataloging-in-Publication Data

Stone, Chris, 1973–
Spliffigami: roll the 35 greatest joints of all time /
Chris Stone.
p. cm.
Summary: "An illustrated guide to making 35 origami-inspired,
conversation-piece joints"—Provided by publisher.
ISBN 978-1-58008-937-1
1. Marijuana—Humor. 2. Origami—Humor. I. Title.

PN6231.M24S76 2008
818'.607—dc22
2008010426
Printed in China
First printing, 2008
1 2 3 4 5 6 7 8 9 10 — 12 11 10 09 08

Contents

Introduction

In July 2006 in Nancy, France, police thwarted an attempt by a group of potheads to roll the world's longest smokable joint by seizing a work-in-progress measuring 2 feet 8 inches (.81 m). The smokers' aim had been to beat the previous record of 3 feet 8 inches (1.12 m). The giant reefer contained 2½ ounces (71 g) of marijuana resin, but according to one of the heroes (sorry, culprits), they failed to finish it because they ran out of tobacco!

This book is an homage to those French stoners—and to all the people around the world who are similarly dedicated to the art of spliffigami. If you've bought this book, it's safe to assume you enjoy smoking cannabis, and you may even be fairly adept at whipping up a single-skin reefer in the time it takes to recite your favorite line from Cheech & Chong. On the other hand, you might be a novice: well versed in the art of toking but less adept in the craftsmanship of pot origami.

"To be peaceful without being stupid, to be interested without being compulsive, to be happy without being hysterical . . . smoke grass."

Ken Kesey

DISCLAIMER It is a criminal offense in the United States and in many other countries, punishable by imprisonment and/or fines, to cultivate, possess, or supply cannabis. You should therefore understand that this book is intended for private amusement and not intended to encourage you to break the law.

HOW HIGH?: ....The potency of the spliff—the greater the number of leaves shown, the more stoned you will get.

FREAKY FACTOR: ....Indicates the uniqueness of the joint's shape and design.

SMOOTHNESS:..........How the joint feels and tastes when smoked—the more leaves shown, the smoother the smoke.

TOKIN' TIME: ....Approximate duration of the smoke, in minutes.

While the thirty-five joints featured in *Spliffigami* are not all of the lung-busting proportions of the aforementioned French beast, there are spliffs for all abilities here. The joints are neatly arranged into chapters organized by level of rolling complexity, with a great range of easy, medium, and more challenging joints in each. Some require only a couple of papers, others call for dextrous fingers and plenty of practice, but all are kick-ass to make—and, above all, to smoke. A couple even feature a nonsmokable unit that can be reused. And that's not all. The book also includes a guide to assessing bud and hash, and there are full descriptions of the tools of a roller's trade, a list of the dos and don'ts of smoking etiquette, and much more. The spliffigami skills you'll learn in this book might not get you through med school or enable you to fulfill your dream of pitching at Yankee Stadium . . . but they might lead you to succeed where those French stoners failed—and be a world-record holder in your chosen field of expertise. Now wouldn't that be vindication of a misspent youth?

So what are you waiting for?
Get ready to spliffigami!

Chris Stone

chapter 1

GETTING STARTED

"And God said, 'Behold, I have given you every plant-yielding seed which is upon the face of the earth.'"

Genesis 1:29

You're probably eager to get rolling right away, but as with any new hobby, preparation is paramount. So before you start, take some time out to get to know your subject—the nuances of grass and hashish, the role of mixers, the tools of your trade (from papers to pokers), and, finally, some cool "cheats" to set you on the road to rolling greatness.

Before you start . . .

Some of the joints in this book represent the pinnacle of achievement for any cannabis craftsman, but if the smoke is harsh or you just don't get stoned, then you are wasting your time. The purpose of any spliff (however intricate) is to smoke it and get high. And the bottom line is this: your joint is only as good as the ingredients you use.

But how do you tell the good pot from the bad? In days gone by, it was a simple task, since all cannabis was more or less the same. It grew wild and was later planted and harvested for recreational drug use, but it was usually cultivated using organic methods. Nowadays, the grass or hash you buy from your dealer will almost certainly have been grown indoors. Growers use artificial light and heating conditions to speed up growth, and they cross-pollinate strains to increase potency.

Thanks to sophisticated equipment that is now readily available, it is possible, with a little practice, for almost anyone to grow high-quality pot. However, the fact that cannabis is easier to grow isn't necessarily better: because production is illegal (and unregulated), it is also vulnerable to abuse. It is easy to add alien chemicals—particularly to your supply of hashish.

In the early days of your joint-rolling career, your spliffs will not look all that aesthetically pleasing—more knobby turnip than perfect cone. But fear not: if you're using good shit, the appearance doesn't matter and your friends will excuse your clumsy fingers. Still, if you have ambitions to achieve greatness in the art of spliffigami, it is important that you know how to tell the good stuff from the bad.

SPLIFFIGAMI

A NOTE ABOUT TERMINOLOGY

Since this book is written for a worldwide audience, it takes an international approach to pot smoking. There are some key differences between North American and European pot-smoking practices—the gist is that Europeans more commonly roll joints with a mix of weed and tobacco or shredded cannabis leaves, and they insert a piece of rolled card (thin paperboard) into the end to serve as a filter.(*) We'll use these extremely civilized practices in the spliff instructions that follow. Apart from making the instructions user-friendly to international readers, there are two very practical reasons for this: First, many of the joints are amazing constructions and oftentimes need the extra support offered by the filter. Second, you'd have to be either plain nuts or Rockefeller to pack some of these monster doobies full of pure weed. (You see, we have your welfare—and bank balance—at heart.) But if you want to embrace your old-skool side, throw caution to the wind and roll a j with pure chronic and smoke it down to the end with a roach clip. (Just be prepared to blaze past the "How High?" rating provided.) And if you don't want to embrace your inner trendsetter and use the word "skins" for rolling papers (another Euroslang classic) then keep calling them papers—your boyz won't mind.

(*)We know you Euro and Brit stoners out there call this a roach, but for the sake of your cannabis-smoking chums in the U. S. of A, we'll refer to it as a filter in these pages.

Assessing bud

Grass (or "weed") is the natural form of cannabis—essentially the buds of the harvested female marijuana plant. Whether a bag of grass is any good depends on three key elements: First, the strain of the donor plant determines the strength, and type, of the high experienced. Second, the plant needs perfect growing conditions and the hands of an experienced gardener. Third, after being harvested, the buds should be subjected to a drying and curing process lasting at least several weeks. Like fine wine, cannabis improves with age if properly stored.

However, as a purchaser you're not going to know the history of your bag of weed. The following checks will help you to distinguish the best from the rest.

Feel: High-quality weed is soft and light to the touch. It crumbles easily and in doing so releases a strong aroma and sticky resins. Stems should flex but snap when bent; stems that are too bendy indicate a poor or absent drying process.

Smell: For the cannabis connoisseur there is no better fragrance than that of perfectly harvested bud. Great weed can have a wide variety of smells—no two strains are the same—but those with an intense perfumelike aroma are best. If the weed smells very pungent, damp, or like mowed grass, it is best avoided. At best, the bud may have been picked prematurely and will lack the potency of a fully grown plant; at worst, it may not have been cured and may be infested with mold.

Appearance: Good buds are light to the touch and fluffy, and they should retain the natural shape they took while growing on the plant; they are often bright green with orange, red, or purple hairs. They have a crystalline quality that creates a colorful sparkle under direct light. These sparkling dots are resin glands swollen with THC—the active chemical ingredient in cannabis—and the more of these that are visible, the stronger the high. Low-

quality weed usually contains stalks and seeds. If the grass is solid dark green or has a fine powdery consistency, it is most likely made up of shredded fan leaves rather than genuine bud.

Smoke: Top-quality weed smokes well (with a pleasant taste) and burns consistently all the way down to the roach. Low-quality weed often burns inconsistently, produces excessive tar, and fizzles and pops as it burns. This is due to the presence of stalk and seed particles, and also to the existence of toxic chemicals that should have been removed from the plant prior to harvesting.

Quality of high: Finally, you can usually tell a fine weed by the high you achieve after testing a sample. Great weed should inspire you creatively without giving you that heavy, burnt-out feeling sometimes associated with lesser-quality marijuana.

Preparing the bud

Once you have identified the perfect weed, you need to take care of it. Heat, light, and exposure to air degrade the levels of THC in your bud. If you allow your stash to remain unprotected for long, it will become dry and brittle. When dry, your bud will burn too fast and the hits will be harsh. To keep your weed in prime condition, place it in an airtight container or a plastic bag.

GET FRUITY

If you notice your weed is getting too dry, add a sliver of orange or lemon peel to your bag and seal it tightly. After twenty-four hours the weed will absorb the water from the rind and become rehydrated. Be careful not to leave the peel in for too long, as it could turn moldy and ruin your weed. Conversely, if your weed is too wet, add a piece of tissue paper to absorb the excess moisture.

Of course, you don't want to keep your stash in a container forever—you want to smoke it. Before skinning up, the first thing to do is remove any seeds, stalks, and other debris. Then the buds need to be broken down into small pieces. The finer the mix, the better the air will flow through the joint (giving you a good, even smoke). Nail scissors or a bud grinder (see page 27) are perfect for chopping your bud down to size.

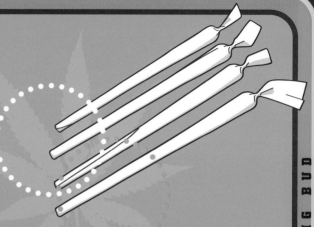

You can either smoke your pot pure (but beware—this will make you very high and your stash won't last long), or you can blend your weed with tobacco or shredded fan leaves from a cannabis plant. Make sure your weed and your mixer are of a similar consistency and fully blended in a bowl, so there is an even balance of weed and mixer throughout the spliff—you don't want to smoke an inch of plain old tobacco!

Assessing hash

Traditional hashish from countries such as Nepal, Afghanistan, India, and Pakistan is produced by rubbing marijuana flowers between the hands or between other implements. This rubbing process causes the plants to excrete a sticky resin. As the resin accumulates, it is hand or machine pressed into a solid piece of hash.

Low-quality hash, which often originates from Morocco or Lebanon, is produced using a four-stage sieving process whereby stalks, seeds, and leaves are filtered out, leaving only premium-grade hashish. Moroccan hash is usually harder and drier than rubbed hashish, and though the top-grade stuff is the real deal, much of the hash on the market has only been subjected to the initial sieving process. It thus contains various pressed debris that should have been discarded.

This low-quality hash is also often adulterated with a variety of substances, such as tarmac and sand, to increase its weight and thereby the profit of the dealer.

Some of the methods used to distinguish the good from the bad are the same as those used with bud.

Smell: Although the smell of hashish is less pronounced than that of good weed, it should still smell like cannabis—rich, sweet, and slightly spicy. If the odor is faint or musty, it is probably because it is either very old or contains little cannabis; either way it is best avoided.

Appearance: Rubbed hash is dark brown to black on the surface. It usually has a lighter brown interior, so it is well worth cutting into it to check this. If you break open a piece of sieved hash, you should see the very small granules of resin. If you cannot see the resin, there is a strong chance it has been cut with other, potentially harmful, products.

Feel: High-quality rubbed hash is firm and sticky, yet quite pliable. After a few minutes of kneading and warming the hash, it should become more pliable—this is the sign of high resin content. However, if the hash is too pliable at the outset, it might mean it has been adulterated with coconut or palm oil, a common imperfection. All sieved hash is dry and hard, regardless of quality.

Burn it: Hash with a high resin content burns slowly and completely, in the way an incense stick burns. Hash that appears too flammable is probably contaminated with oils; if the hash is resistant to the flame, the THC content is low. The smoke it emits when burnt should be milky white or blue-gray in color. Brown or black smoke indicates that contaminants have been added. The color of the ash produced is also indicative of the hash quality—the lighter the color, the greater the resin content.

Eat it!: The best way to eat cannabis is in a brownie or cookie recipe, but you can also assess the quality of hash by taking a small nibble. High-quality hashish tastes peppery and slightly bitter. If the hashish tastes like vegetable matter or contains gritty dirt, it is contaminated.

Preparing your hash

The good news about hash is that you don't need to store it in an airtight container—you can just go right ahead and smoke it. The bad news is that, unlike bud, which is light and fluffy and easy to snip into small pieces, hash comes as a solid lump.

The heating method is the most popular way to prepare hash. Hold a lighter close to the ball of hash. As it gets warm, it becomes powdery and crumbles. However, the trick is to warm the hash just enough to cause it to powder and not actually light it. (Burning or overheating degrades the THC content before you've even rolled the joint.) Joints containing hard chunks of hash instead of powder not only give an inconsistent smoke, but also produce "hot rocks" (lumps of burning hash that fall out of the joint, ruining your best threads or your leather couch).

Alternatively, if you are fortunate enough to have some pliable rubbed hash, you can roll out a narrow sliver, like a strand of raw spaghetti, on a flat surface using the palm of your hand. This is the perfect way to prepare hash for rolling because it results in a guaranteed even smoke.

GLASS LUNG

For a great hashish-only smoke, try this idea on for size. You will need a large glass, a piece of card with a circumference greater than the glass (a bar coaster is ideal), a pin, some adhesive putty, and some willing accomplices. Place the card on the table and fix the putty to its center. Stick a pin in the putty and put a small lump of hashish (to a size of your choosing) on the pin. Then light it and place the glass over this arrangement. When it's full of smoke, tip it up slightly and inhale from under the rim. When you've had your fill, replace the glass and let a friend take a turn.

Rolling with mixers

A mixer is anything that is added to a joint other than cannabis. There are three main arguments for using a mixer. First, it prolongs the actual smoke, making it a more sociable experience. If you want to get really stoned, hit the bong or smoke a j filled with pure weed; if you want a laid-back evening with friends, smoke joints with mixers. Second, like an alcohol mixer, it alters or enhances the flavor. Third, mixers help to regulate the burn of the joint and stop it from going out.

Tobacco is the most common form of mixer. Rolling tobacco is preferable to the chemical-laced tobacco found in cigarettes; it has a superior flavor, and it is easier to roll. However, if you don't normally smoke tobacco—many stoners don't—you might try one of the nicotine-free herbal options available in all good head shops.

gaspers

These Ain't Healthy

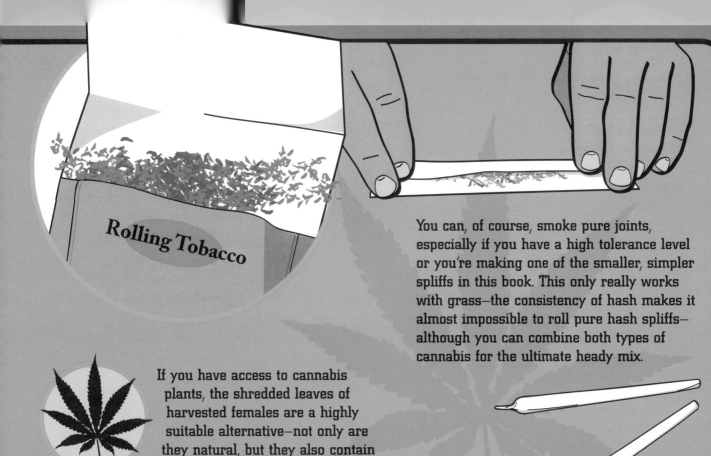

Rolling Tobacco

You can, of course, smoke pure joints, especially if you have a high tolerance level or you're making one of the smaller, simpler spliffs in this book. This only really works with grass—the consistency of hash makes it almost impossible to roll pure hash spliffs—although you can combine both types of cannabis for the ultimate heady mix.

If you have access to cannabis plants, the shredded leaves of harvested females are a highly suitable alternative—not only are they natural, but they also contain minute traces of THC.

Papers

It is impossible to roll a joint without papers. They are the tools of the smoker's trade, and as integral to the joint-rolling process as a sesame seed bun is to a cheeseburger (an analogy that any self-respecting stoner with the munchies will recognize).

GUM STRIPPING

The strip of gum on your paper has additional uses beyond sealing your rolled joint once it's been licked. The bigger your joint, the more you will need to plug leaky holes and bind your creation together. So, in order to create your very own construction tape, rip the gummed part all the way along its length and discard the main paper. Gum stripping is essential for larger joints and can hide a multitude of sins. Get practicing.

The original rolling papers date back to sixteenth-century France, when the Lacroix firm (forerunner to Rizla) was founded. In 1796 Lacroix sealed a deal with Napoleon Bonaparte to supply rolling papers to the French military—the hapless soldiers had previously been tearing pages from books in order to enjoy a good smoke—and the rolling paper business never looked back.

Nowadays, as befits the size of the smoking market (both tobacco and cannabis), you can get papers in continuous rolls (rips), transparent papers, papers printed with an array of shapes and designs, and papers flavored with everything from absinthe to sizzling bacon!

TASTY THC

Little Skins

Big Daddy Skins

Size and weight

The standard rolling paper is small and rectangular, white in color, and has a gummed strip down one edge, but there are variations in size and weight that are relevant, depending on both your rolling ability and the scale of spliff you want to create.

The lightest papers are the favored apparatus of the connoisseur because they are more porous and allow smoke to escape, resulting in a smoother toke. Heavy papers retain more smoke and are potential lung busters. However, this extra weight can be an advantage: because they are sturdier, they are perfect for the first-time roller to practice with and for the more experienced skin-up merchant to create extra-long spliffs.

The size of papers differs both in length and width. For the first-timer who needs practice, long and wide is the way to go, since there is more forgiveness in the roll. Once you're up to speed, the size depends on the scale of the joints you want to roll. If you're rolling small spliffs in a hurry, then small, thin papers are fine; if you are endeavoring to roll a behemoth such as those in chapter 4, then you need to go large.

RIPS

Roaches & filters

The "roach" is drug vernacular for the discarded butt end of a spliff. The name is derived from the Spanish slang term for marijuana, *la cucaracha* (cockroach). Rather like a rolled cigarette, the butt becomes moist, full of tar, and generally unpleasant when smoked to the end. A roach clip (essentially a pair of tweezers or an alligator clip) can be used to pinch the butt and eke out those last couple of puffs.

A superior alternative is to use a small piece of card (thin paperboard ripped from a rolling-paper box, a cigarette pack, or whatever's handy), rolled in a cylindrical shape and inserted into the joint. There are numerous advantages to using such a filter (also known as a roach in Europe): it halts the buildup of tar, stops the end of the paper from becoming soggy, prevents the toker from inhaling bits of the mix, and saves the lips from being burnt.

So, how do you make and use a filter?

I Take a piece of card. Tear off a small piece, approximately 1 inch (2.5 cm) square.

2 Roll it around a cylindrical tool such as a "poker" (see page 27).

3 Or simply roll it quite tightly between your fingers.

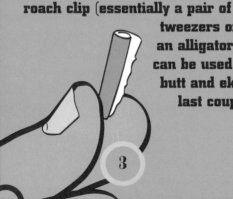

At this stage you have two choices— you can roll the spliff with or without the filter.

Post-roll

This is probably the best method for novice rollers. Lay out your weed or mix in the usual fashion, but be sure to leave some empty paper at the butt end. Roll and seal your joint, then insert your filter into the end. Invariably your filter will be the wrong circumference for the hole, so you may need to do some fiddling around to get it to fit snugly.

Combination roll

Rolling the joint with the filter already inserted with the mix is slightly more difficult, but with practice you will end up with a more satisfactory end product. Try to keep the filter and mix as one unit during the roll. If the two become separated, the result will be a baggy joint.

WARNING

The filter is an integral part of stoner culture in Europe (it's a "roach" to you Euro-savvy folks). But following this trend can have its disadvantages. If any disapproving eyes (such as your parents) see a packet of papers, they may incorrectly assume that you are smoking hand-rolled cigarettes, but if they see a packet of "rollies" with assorted bits of card missing . . . well, it's more of a giveaway! So, hide your packet of papers as thoroughly as you would your bong.

ROACHES & FILTERS

25

Gadgets

Although the purpose of this book is to train dextrous fingers and encourage freestyle rolling, hand rolling isn't the only way to make a joint. So before going any further, we should at least tip our cap to the variety of gadgets on the market that enable those with sausagelike fingers to enjoy a good smoke . . .

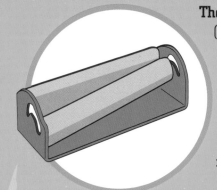

The cone rolling machine (like the one shown here) produces an acceptable, jointlike shape and is infinitely superior, but it's still no substitute for rolling one yourself.

Rolling machine

The basic rolling machine is formed of two plastic-covered steel rods that rotate against one another. The toker opens out the rods, puts the mix in the cavity, and then gives it a few rolls. Then a paper is fed into the contraption and, voilà, you have a prerolled spliff. Sadly, this flat and hard-to-draw-on offering is often no better than your worst attempts at a freestyle roll. Avoid.

Rolling mat

This lightweight flexible mat, purposefully designed to be much larger than the open joint that is laid upon it, molds around both sides of the paper as your fingers roll back and forth. It is quite useful for getting large joints into shape in the early stages of the roll, but when it comes to the "tuck and trap" (see page 36), the spliff needs to be removed and completed freehand.

Prerolled cones

These prerolled empty cones certainly produce joints that look the part, but shame on you for using them. A variation on the pen method described on page 30, these cones can even come with a filter inserted. Simply put the paper in a plastic holder (also supplied) and fill with weed or mix.

page 30

WHAT, NO ROLLIES?

If you're ever stuck in a foreign country with some dope but no papers, fear not. The rice paper that is commonly used for packaging rolls of toilet paper works just as well.

Bud grinder

Not a rolling aid, but nevertheless a useful tool if you're rolling with weed. Consisting of two circular disks, each with protruding spikes on one side, the disks are turned against one another, thus reducing bulging buds down to smaller particles that are better suited to rolling.

Poker

This is a seemingly innocuous but indispensable tool for any wannabe spliffigami master. The poker itself can be almost any narrow implement—a pen, matchstick, toothpick, or sharpened pencil. It's used for those awkward jobs when a plump digit simply won't do, such as packing down the mix or getting the filter to fit snugly. Put one in your stash tin now.

Rudimentary rolling

If you have bought this book, it is likely you have at least a basic talent for spliffigami. But if you don't, you have to start somewhere and this section is for you. Before we progress to your first unaided roll, you'll want to practice two useful techniques that will help you to learn some fundamentals that you simply don't get by cheating and using a rolling machine. These basics will act as a useful stepping-stone to joint-rolling perfection.

Money method

You don't have to be flush with cash to execute this rolling technique, and it produces consistent results time after time.

I Get a regular dollar bill; any denomination will do. Place the bill flat on a table and add your mix across its width, leaving a small gap at either end.

2 Now pick up the dollar bill and secure the mix between the thumb and index fingers of both hands. Roll the mix between your fingers several times, working from the center of the bill outward and using your middle fingers as a support, until it is shaped.

3 Then, with the "joint" lightly secured with one hand, add a small rolling paper between the mix and the bill. Ensure that the bottom of the paper pokes under the weed and emerges on the other side, and that the sticky side is facing up.

4 Now fold the dollar bill in half and roll it firmly upward with your thumbs; the rolling paper needs to move with the motion of the bill and wrap around itself to form a jointlike cylinder.

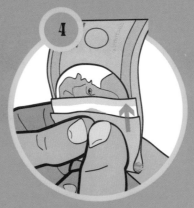

5 When the rolling paper is fully rolled, just short of the gummed strip, remove it from the dollar bill. At this stage be sure to keep a firm pressure on the paper so that the joint does not unravel. Lick the sticky strip of the paper and seal the joint. You're now ready to spark up your smoke!

Pen method

This technique involves rolling and sealing an empty joint, then adding the mix. Sounds easy? It is. Here's how you do it.

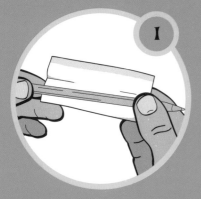

I Take an ordinary pen or pencil and wrap a rolling paper around it until only the gummed strip of the paper is showing. This will provide the basis for your joint.

2 Lick the sticky strip and execute a final roll to seal the joint.

3 Next, pull the paper and pen apart so that only about ¼ inch (6 mm) remains around the pen.

4 Now start loading your mix in small pieces into the exposed end of the spliff.

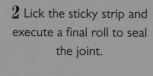

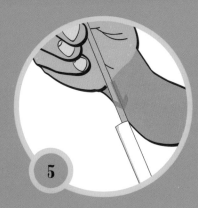

5

5 Use a poker to pack the mix into the joint as you go and continue until the joint is almost full.

6 Next, tear off a piece of card to make a filter, roll it, and insert it.

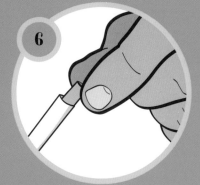

6

7

7 Finally, remove the pen, twist the paper at the end to secure it, light up, and toke away.

ALTERNATIVE METHODS

Of course, the thicker the pen you use, the wider the paper you will require—and, consequently, the fatter the doobie you will produce. There are even specially designed metal cones that can be bought at head shops or on the Internet for this purpose.

chapter 2

SIMPLE SPLIFFS

"Roll, roll, roll a joint, twist it at the end, light it up, take a puff, pass it to your friends."

Tré Cool, Green Day (to the tune of "Row, row, row your boat")

You may be able to fashion a joint using various aids, but now you've got to create one on your own. Starting with a straight joint, this chapter guides you through a series of standard cones. Pay close attention. The skills you learn here are vital for progressing to bigger and better things.

Freestyle

Roll your own

HOW HIGH?:
✻✺✺✺✺

FREAKY FACTOR:
✻✺✺✺✺

SMOOTHNESS:
✻✻✻✺✺

TOKIN' TIME:
3 mins.

Now is the point of no return. All rolling aids should be discarded as you prepare to freestyle your first joint. The finished joint looks terrible, but who cares? You've taken your first steps on a very long journey.

I

I First things first. Take a standard-size paper from the pack and lay it on a flat surface as shown—sticky side up. As a novice, avoid ultrathin papers; a thicker option has a bit more purchase and is easier to roll with.

STICKY SIDE UP

It sounds simple, but it's amazing how many smokers mess it up. The golden rule: Make sure you roll with the gummed side of the paper facing you. The last thing you want is to get your mix in perfect shape, pinch and roll like a pro, go to lick the strip . . . and find it's on the reverse side. Doh! Anyone caught making this faux pas should be made to drink the bong water.

2 Prepare some mix as previously explained and add it to the paper. Place the mix in the bend in the paper, evenly along its length in a cylindrical shape, leaving a small gap at either end. Don't insert a filter; it's not worth it for your first spliff.

GET THE RIGHT BLEND

Pay attention when loading the mix. Too little will lead to a tight roll, air will struggle to get through, and the joint will go out; too much mix will prevent the joint from closing and sealing properly.

3 Gently pick the paper up between your thumbs and forefingers, keeping it level and taking care not to spill any mix.

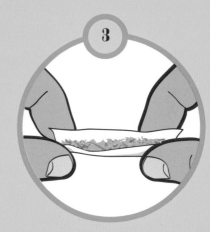

5 . . . then all the way down to the bottom edge, but try to perform this in a continuous motion. Keep your thumbs just above the mix, pushing it into the bottom of the paper.

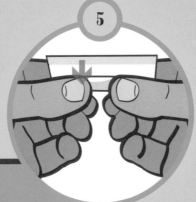

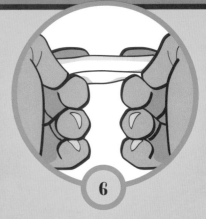

4 Still using your thumbs and forefingers, start to roll the mix into a neat, rounded shape. First up . . .

STICKY FINGERS

Make sure you've got some purchase on your fingers, otherwise they will slide up and down the paper, making it impossible to roll. You don't need to have dirty fingers—just don't wash your hands half an hour before rolling. Licking your fingers in preparation also helps.

6 After four to five rolls, you should be ready for the "tuck and trap"—the key stage of any roll. For this, roll the mix down to the bottom edge of the paper. Then, using the end of your thumbnail, tuck the nonsticky edge over the mix and down the other side, and hold it in place. Start in the middle of the joint and continue outward until the whole joint is tucked and secured.

7 You are almost there now. With the paper tucked over, simply roll the joint up until you reach the narrow gummed strip.

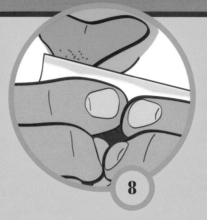

8 Lick the strip, fold it over, and seal it.

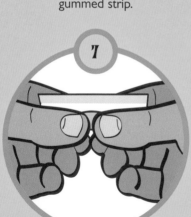

9 To finish off, twist both ends to hold the mix in place. Now admire your handiwork—it may not be the sexiest spliff in the world, but it's functional.

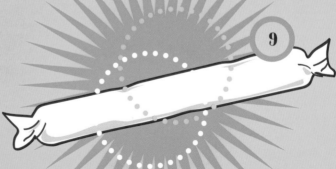

One-Skin Cone

Easy does it

HOW HIGH?:
🍁🍁🍁🍁🍁

FREAKY FACTOR:
🍁🍁🍁🍁🍁

SMOOTHNESS:
🍁🍁🍁🍁🍁

TOKIN' TIME:
5 mins.

I

Now that you've got the basic straight joint mastered, you can progress to rolling with a filter and embark on the path to being a spliffigami master. Don't be alarmed—there isn't a major difference between rolling a straight joint and a high-quality cone. The secret is in the distribution of the mix and the angle of the paper. Watch and learn.

I For starters, use a king-size paper; it's easier to fashion a cone with this. First, add your mix, paying attention to the distribution. Sprinkle the mix from left to right and back again, loading progressively more as you go, to create a triangle shape that is significantly narrower at the filter end.

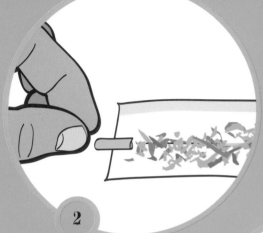

3 Now pick up the paper and cradle it between your fingers. Keeping hold of the filter beneath the paper, tilt the angle of the paper as you start to roll so that it mirrors the shape of the cone—less mix at the filter end equals less paper.

THE TABLE TRICK

Tucking and wrapping is by far the hardest part of joint rolling. Once you've mastered this, the sky's the limit. One way of making this tricky process easier is to place the joint on a flat surface, such as a table. This means you can maximize thumb pressing without having to worry about supporting the joint with your other fingers. A thin object such as a credit card can be used instead of thumbs. When you have tucked the joint along its length, pick it back up and roll normally.

2 Now tear a piece of card from the pack of papers and roll a straight filter. Alternatively, by rolling the filter at a slight angle, you can create a cone shape that makes your mission to create a cone spliff a little easier.

4 Use your left thumb and forefinger as a reasonably steady base on the filter end and, with the right hand, coax the joint into shape along its length. To use a musical analogy, pluck the strings with your left hand, and use your right to move between the chords.

5 Once the mix is cone shaped, pull the front of the paper down to the top of the mix and tuck it over. Work your way from left to right, at first using firm pressure. Then, as you reach halfway, guide the tuck rather than force it—this will help to accentuate the angle of the cone.

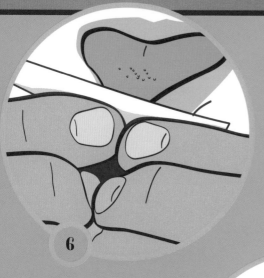

6 Complete the roll, run your tongue along the gummed strip, and seal.

7 Now take your trusty poker and lightly pack down the mix. Twist any spare paper at the end to prevent leakage.

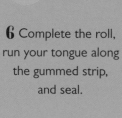

8 Now that's what I call a cone.

Two-Skin

The horizontal high

If you want to cut it as a roller with a rep, you need to think beyond single skin rolls, because there's a whole lot more to the art of spliffigami than that. For instance, what do you do if you want a long smoke but you've only got small papers? You stick 'em together, that's what. This is how.

HOW HIGH?:
🍁🍁🍁🍁

FREAKY FACTOR:
🍁🍁🍁🍁

SMOOTHNESS:
🍁🍁🍁🍁

TOKIN' TIME:
5 mins.

1 Take two small papers and line 'em up end to end.

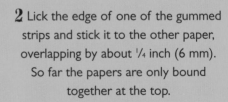

2 Lick the edge of one of the gummed strips and stick it to the other paper, overlapping by about ¼ inch (6 mm). So far the papers are only bound together at the top.

3 Now take a third paper from the pack, fold it in half with the gummed strip on the outside, and lick the glue on both sides.

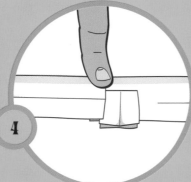

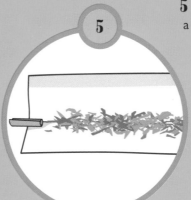

5 Leave this to dry for a few seconds before adding your mix and a filter.

4 Lift up the first paper, place the wet strip underneath, and press down as shown. Leave for a few seconds, but not long enough for the glue to dry. Then whip the third paper out, leaving the residue from the gummed strip to form a perfect bond between the existing two papers.

6 Then roll, tuck, trap, lick, and seal as normal.

Congratulations, you've rolled your first double-skin.

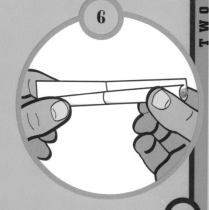

The L-Shape
Angle of attack

HOW HIGH?:
🌿🌿🌿🌿🌿

FREAKY FACTOR:
🌿🌿🌿🌿🌿

SMOOTHNESS:
🌿🌿🌿🌿🌿

TOKIN' TIME:
5 mins.

1 This time line two papers up at right angles. Lick the bottom half of the right-hand paper and join them up.

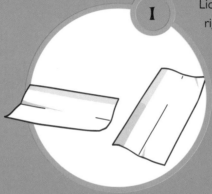

2 Now sprinkle on your blend and add a small filter, if you wish.

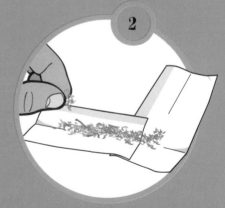

You're probably feeling pretty fly, if not a little high, by now and ready for another challenge. Sticking with the theme of, er, sticking, the L-Shape is a way to play the angles, providing you with plenty of paper at the business end of the joint for a real fat cone. Enjoy.

3 Pick up the joint and practice your rolling technique—let's see those forefingers and thumbs do some work!

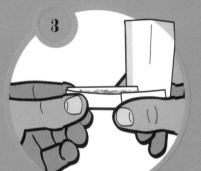

4 Roll the paper to the bottom of the mix, tuck it over, and pinch it.

5 Now you need to treat the joint as two separate halves because of the peculiar shape of the papers. Lick and seal both papers in turn, starting at the filter end. Use a poker to pack down the mix if necessary.

6 You've made it—now smoke it.

OR TRY THIS...

As an alternative to the L-shape, try sticking the second paper at an angle of about 150 degrees. Not only does it produce a slightly different end product, it provides you with much-needed rolling practice, and you get another type of smoke.

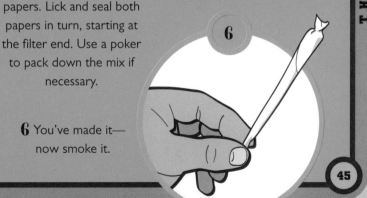

THE L-SHAPE

45

Three-Skin

Sticking practice

The last of the standard cones, the three-skin utilizes three papers to form a square. It's a little more tricky to build than the others, and owing to the square shape, the resulting cone is short and stubby, but it's a popular creation nonetheless. What's more, it's a must for your rolling résumé. Get to work.

HOW HIGH?:
🍁🍁🍁🍁🍁

FREAKY FACTOR:
🍁🍁🍁🍁🍁

SMOOTHNESS:
🍁🍁🍁🍁🍁

TOKIN' TIME:
10 mins.

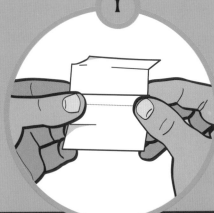

1 First, take two papers and stick the ends together, one on top of the other, ensuring that one of the sticky edges remains at the top.

2 Peel a third paper from the pack, align it so it's perpendicular to the other two, and stick it down the side of the square formed by the other two.

3 Carefully lay out your mix in a cone shape, add a filter, and pick up the joint in readiness for rolling.

3

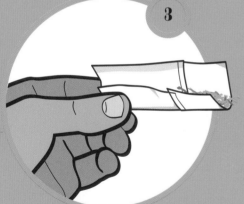

4 Now roll the spliff. Due to the construction of the papers, the top right edge does not have a gummed strip, but lick and seal anyway. With an added twist, it will hold in place long enough for you to smoke past it.

4

5

5 Show off your three-skin wonder joint to anyone who's interested.

chapter **3**

POT PRACTICE

"Roll another one
Just like the other one
That one's burned to the end
Come on and be a real friend."

Fraternity of Man, "Don't Bogart Me"

Now that you are well versed in the art of basic rolling, it's time to try some more ambitious creations. From the Blunt to the Dutch Bud to the awe-inspiring In Reverse, this chapter showcases some doobies to stretch even the nimblest of fingers. You'd better buy some more papers.

Cannabis Cigarette

The real deal

This design is both a covert way to smoke bud without fear of detection and a great rescue smoke if you're clean out of papers. It's quick and easy to make, and hits the spot as either a solo smoke or one to share. To all intents and purposes, it looks like a normal cigarette but, of course, it doesn't smell like one— so make sure you are downwind of any disapproving noses.

HOW HIGH?:
🌿🌿🌿🌿🌿

FREAKY FACTOR:
🌿🌿🌿🌿🌿

SMOOTHNESS:
🌿🌿🌿🌿🌿

TOKIN' TIME:
5 mins.

1 First, take a cigarette from the pack and, rolling it gently between your fingers, empty all the tobacco out of the paper. Discard about one third. Add grass or hash to the remaining tobacco and break it all down into a fine mix.

2 Next, turn the cigarette around and use a pair of tweezers or nail scissors to remove the filter padding from the butt. Work your way around the edges first to make this easier, although it's likely that it won't all come out in one go.

3 Roll a suitably sized filter and place it in the freshly emptied butt. Given that this is a straight joint, it might be a good idea to roll another, smaller filter to fit inside and offer added protection against mix falling into your mouth.

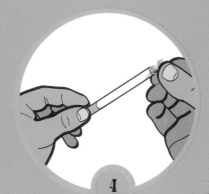

4

4 Now turn the cigarette around and start loading your spiced-up mix. Use a poker to tap down the mix as you load it, to ensure good distribution.

3

5 Voilà. One modified cigarette, ready to savor. Twist the end to distinguish this specimen from the others in your pack. You don't want to spark it up by accident in the wrong company!

5

FOR THE PERFECTIONIST

If you have greater time and patience, and are actually in possession of some papers, you can roll a more professional-looking version. First cut the cigarette with a fine-blade knife and then use the empty butt as a filter to roll an all-new doobie.

Two-Tone

Colorful cannabis

With the staggering array of colored and flavored papers available to buy on the Internet, it seems a shame not to break with convention and combine two in the same joint. The key here is to get the angle of the papers just right before you add the mix. So go on, roll one for a special occasion. It won't get you any more stoned, but it'll look mighty fine.

HOW HIGH?:
❋ ❋ ❋ ❋ ❋

FREAKY FACTOR:
❋ ❋ ❋ ❋ ❋

SMOOTHNESS:
❋ ❋ ❋ ❋ ❋

TOKIN' TIME:
10 mins.

I Take two different papers. Here I've used a plain one and a camouflage design, but you can use any style. Browse your local head shop for ideas. If the chosen papers are different sizes, cut them to match.

2 Take a pair of small scissors and cut the nonsticky edge of both papers along the length at an angle of about 30 degrees diagonally.

FOUR TIMES THE FUN

How about the Four-Tone? Prepare your skins as explained here, but this time affix another two papers (in different colors or designs) to the longer end before adding the mix. Then roll as normal. The result will look so impressive it will almost seem a shame to smoke it.

4 Roll the joint as normal. It's only at this point that you can assess the joint's appearance. You may need a few practice rounds in order to determine the exact angle needed in step 2.

The work of a craftsman is before you.

ART CLASS

Create your own look by drawing a design of your choosing on white papers. It's vital that you use nontoxic ink pens.

3 Stick the papers together, ensuring that one of the sticky edges remains at the top, and add your mix.

CHOOSE YOUR FLAVOR

Whether your preference is cherry, chocolate, or cheese, why not try one of the assortment of flavored papers available? This option is a real treat—not only is the joint aesthetically pleasing, but it tastes good, too. However, this may make your munchies worse.

TWO-TONE

53

In Reverse

The joint for fancy dans

HOW HIGH?:
🌿🌿🌿🌿🌿

FREAKY FACTOR:
🌿🌿🌿🌿🌿

SMOOTHNESS:
🌿🌿🌿🌿🌿

TOKIN' TIME:
10 mins.

Forget everything you've learned, because this reefer turns the accepted practice of joint rolling on its head . . . and upside down. Back-to-front rolling is a great trick to master and, when well executed, is a sure sign of someone at the zenith of the art. Practice it at home by all means, but roll it in public at your peril. No one likes a show-off, so if you mess it up you'll look like a dumbass.

1 Take a fresh paper and, ignoring previous lessons, ensure that the sticky side is at the bottom of the paper and facing down—upside down, in effect.

2 Prepare your mix in the customary fashion, tear off a strip of card for the filter, and add to the upturned paper.

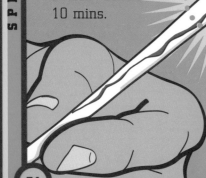

3 Pick up the joint and roll it between your fingers. However, when you reach the point of tucking and wrapping, pull the sticky side of the paper as far down as it will go, then push it over the mix.

4 Twist the joint around in your hands and lick the reverse of the paper. Then twist back and make at least one complete roll. The moisture from your lick is enough to seep through and seal the joint.

5 Now for the final flourish. Owing to the nature of the reverse roll, you will have a spare flap of paper protruding from the side of the spliff. Take a lighter and burn it off.

Spark up your fancy creation and inhale, leaving your friends gaping in admiration.

BOW DOWN TO THE KING

The trick here is to light the paper before the glue is fully dried. If you execute this maneuver properly, the flame will shoot up the length of the spliff, and you'll be feted as a hero. Now, isn't that something to tell the grandkids?

Blunt

Hip-hop high

HOW HIGH?:
✹✹✹

FREAKY FACTOR:
✹✹✹

SMOOTHNESS:
✹✹✹

TOKIN' TIME:
30 mins.

BIG BLUNTS

Smaller than a cigar, but more rewarding than a cigarillo, the blunt is a smoke for the connoisseur. But the blunt is more than just a hearty joint; in the music industry it's a fashion statement. As every self-respecting hip-hop star knows, you need the right look to make it in the rap game. You need bling, you need a crew, you need to wear the best threads, and you need to smoke blunts. Period.

I A fat blunt is deserving of a special occasion, so scour the shelves of your local tobacconist for a top-quality brand. They're not cheap, but they're worth it.

2 Take a blunt from the pack and, using a fine-blade knife, slit it end to end. Take extreme care when doing this—don't do it when you're already spaced!

3 Open out the split blunt, taking care not to crack any other area of the wrap, and gently remove all of the tobacco.

IS THE BLUNT FOR YOU?

If you're the sort of person who genuinely believes wearing sunglasses indoors is cool, then this is the smoke for you. Roll yourself a fat one, lie back, and count your bills. If, however, you're more "rusty nickel" than 50 Cent or think that Dr. Dre could prescribe something for your ear infection, another spliff might be more your style.

4 The wrap will probably be brittle and not very conducive to rerolling, so a little moisture might be required to make it more pliable. Hold the wrap over a steaming kettle for a few seconds.

5 Now it's showtime. Add your mix. Pure weed or a weed and hash combination is the chosen blend of the connoisseur and is encouraged if you can afford it. Don't overfill the wrap, though.

PREMADE BLUNT WRAPS

You can buy prepared blunt wraps off the Internet and in all good head shops, but, frankly, they're not the same as the real deal. Avoid if at all possible.

58

6 Roll it like a pro and lick it. You'll need plenty of spit to seal your doobie, since some of the edges might have flaked away. Don't be afraid to use those saliva glands.

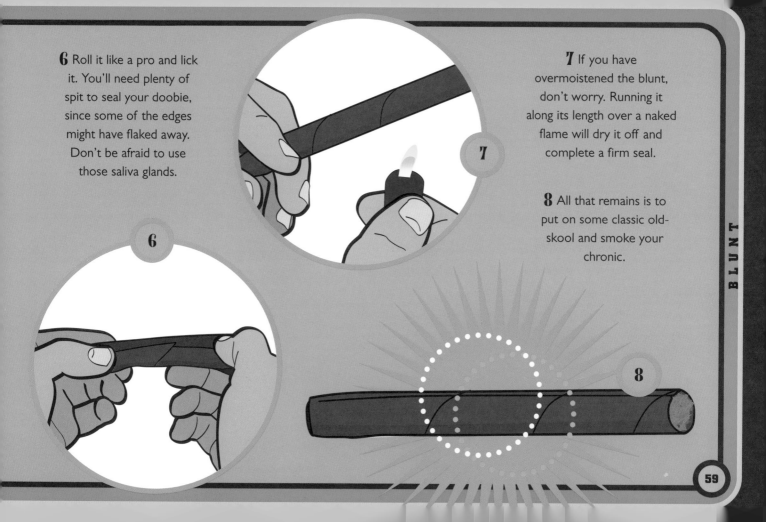

7 If you have overmoistened the blunt, don't worry. Running it along its length over a naked flame will dry it off and complete a firm seal.

8 All that remains is to put on some classic old-skool and smoke your chronic.

Dutch Bud

Let your mind bloom

HOW HIGH?:
✿ ✿ ✿

FREAKY FACTOR:
✿ ✿ ✿

SMOOTHNESS:
✿ ✿ ✿ ✿

TOKIN' TIME:
30 mins.

For parents and courting couples, a weekend in Amsterdam equals canal boat trips, tulips, and diamonds. For everyone else it means forty-eight hours of smoke-filled coffee shops, enjoying endless large skunk reefers. Pot heaven, in other words. The tulip joint (so named for its resemblance to the Dutch flower) is an Amsterdam specialty. It's certainly not for the fainthearted, and it requires practice to roll well, but the high it provides is well worth the effort.

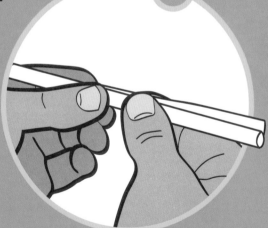

I Make a tube out of card, about 8 to 12 inches (20 to 30 cm) long and with a diameter of ½ inch (1.3 cm). Seal the tube tightly along its length with tape. This is your filter.

3 Fold the bottom left-hand corner over toward the sticky edge but leave the sticky edge exposed.

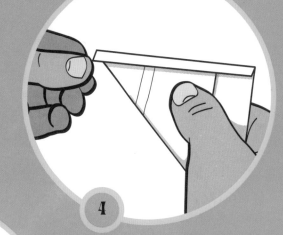

2 Stick together two papers to form a square. You can use more papers to make a bigger bud, but they should always be an even number to form a rectangle.

4 Lick the sticky strip, fold it over, and seal. Leave for a few seconds to dry, and then open out your cone.

5 Prepare some blend and add it to the empty cone, using either your hand or a paper funnel.

6 Next, push your filter into the cone.

7 Wrap the excess paper around the stem of the filter.

8 Seal the top with a number of gum strips or a piece of string.

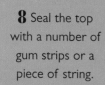

9 Fold the excess paper back over itself to form a petal, and then sit back and admire the product of your green thumbs.

DOUBLE DUTCH

No one of sane mind could possibly argue that one tulip fails to hit the spot. But be warned. One day, while merrily high, you might lose all sense and consider it a good idea to fuse two together. Think long and hard about this—and then don't do it.

Heart-Shaped High

A love bud for sharing

HOW HIGH?:
✹✹✹✹✹

FREAKY FACTOR:
✹✹✹✹✹

SMOOTHNESS:
✹✹✹✹✹

TOKIN' TIME:
20 mins.

The aphrodisiac qualities of cannabis are well-known. A joint between lovers is the perfect end to a romantic evening. What better way to get you in the mood for "lurve" than a heart-shaped joint to share with your significant other? But beware of the tipping point. Puff on it to excess and the only thing you'll be getting intimate with is the couch.

I

I Stick together papers to make a square in a method similar to that used to make the Dutch Bud (see page 60), only this time use four papers.

2 Fold the bottom left-hand corner over toward the sticky edge but leave the sticky edge exposed.

4 Open up the resulting cone and make two holes in opposite sides, about 1½ inches (4 cm) down from the open end.

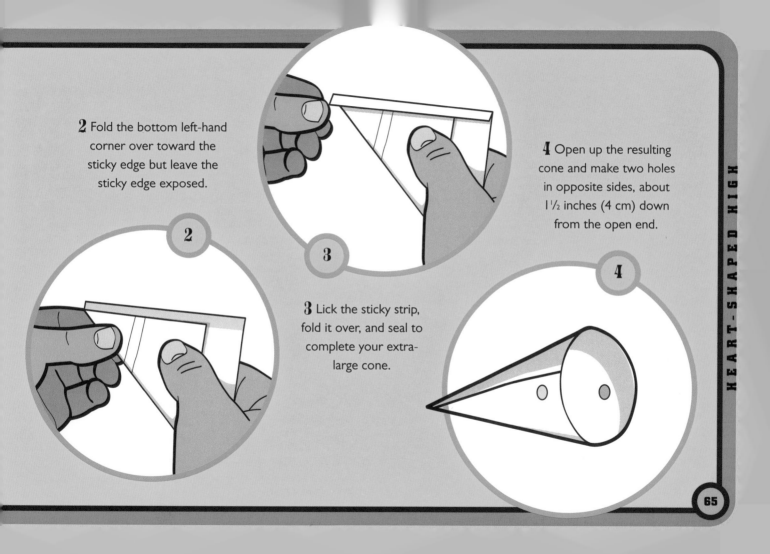

2

3

3 Lick the sticky strip, fold it over, and seal to complete your extra-large cone.

4

5 Now prepare a large amount of grass-tobacco mix. Roll two medium-sized reefers with half of the blend, and leave the other half to one side.

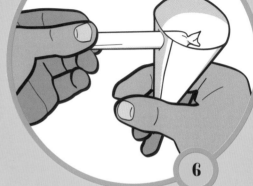

5

MIX IT UP
For a fresh twist, why not vary the mix? Use a hash blend in the tulip and weed in the joints, or vice versa.

6

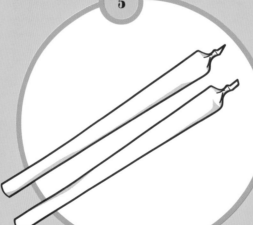

6 Poke your reefers through the holes in the cone so they meet in the middle. Secure the joints in place on the outside with liberal use of gum strips.

7 Add the remaining half of the mix to the cone. Then twist the end and secure with string if necessary.

8 Now turn your lovely creation right side up, light the top, and puff away with your special friend.

KEEP IT BAGGY

Both joints and the tulip bud need to be fairly slack rolls to allow both tokers to draw on this spliff sufficiently. If you pack the mix, or twist the ends of the joints too tightly, you'll be going red in the face before you even get a hit.

Round the Twist

Weave yourself high

This is another killer way to smoke two joints simultaneously, and it's so easy even a pothead can do it! Choose rolling tobacco over cigarette mix for this concoction, since the former tends to be more pliable—perfect for twisting. As you smoke your creation, the joints will gradually unravel, a bit like your mind.

HOW HIGH?:
✷✷✷

FREAKY FACTOR:
✷✷✷

SMOOTHNESS:
✷✷

TOKIN' TIME:
20 mins.

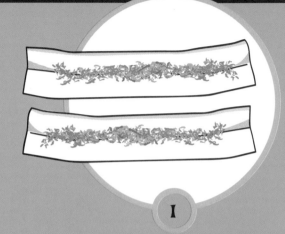

I

I Prepare two joints using king-size rolling papers. Tear off some card and make two filters, slightly longer than normal.

2 Roll the joints, leaving a small gap the width of a thumbnail at the end. Pinch the paper to stop stray mix from falling out, but do not twist the ends.

2

3 Using gum strips, bind the two filters together. You need a firm base, so use more strips than you think are necessary.

3

4 Then take one of the joints and fold it over, and then under, the other one. Continue to weave until you reach the end. Then twist the ends around one another to seal.

Hey, presto! You're ready to twist and shout.

4

BIG BERTHA

Those with more weed than sense should note that Round the Twist has the potential to go large. By using three or even five joints, you can weave the doobies together, as you would when plaiting hair, and in the process fashion a real brute.

Snake Bite

A forked-tongue treat

This one is a bit of a slippery customer, requiring you to bind together three reefers. Your gum-stripping prowess will be severely tested and you'll need a steady hand, so roll it with a clear head. Get a friend to load the mix with plenty of "venom" at random intervals to keep you guessing, then light it up and wait for it to strike.

HOW HIGH?:
❋❋❋

FREAKY FACTOR:
❋❋❋

SMOOTHNESS:
❋❋❋

TOKIN' TIME:
15 mins.

I Prepare and roll three reefers: one a king skin with a filter, and the other two with standard-size papers and no filters. Leave the end of the large joint open and quite baggy.

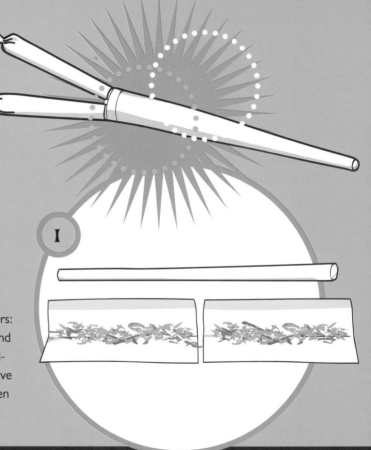

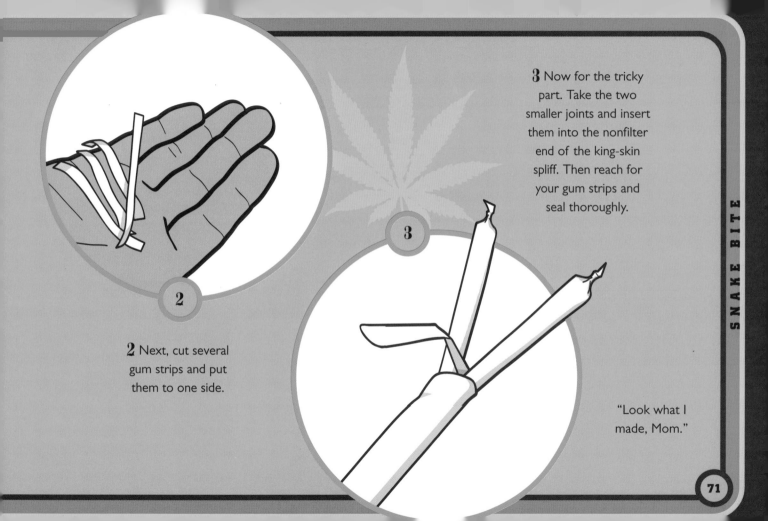

2 Next, cut several gum strips and put them to one side.

3 Now for the tricky part. Take the two smaller joints and insert them into the nonfilter end of the king-skin spliff. Then reach for your gum strips and seal thoroughly.

"Look what I made, Mom."

Pipe of Peace

Far out, man

Peaceful living and smoking have always been inherently linked. Back when the buffalo ruled the Plains, Native Americans, believing tobacco to be a sacred plant, smoked the ceremonial peace pipe (I think they missed a trick with the cannabis plant). Then in the swinging sixties, hippies hijacked the "V for victory" sign as a symbol of peace. Now you can continue this admirable tradition. Make doobies, not war.

HOW HIGH?:
🌿🌿🌿

FREAKY FACTOR:
🌿🌿🌿🌿

SMOOTHNESS:
🌿🌿🌿

TOKIN' TIME:
10 mins.

I Take a long piece of card and roll it into a filter at least 6 inches (15 cm) long. Seal it with tape.

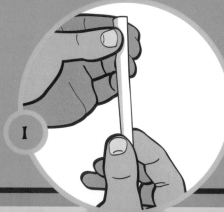

I

2 Carefully using a fine-blade knife, make two holes side by side, about ½ inch (1.3 cm) apart, at one end.

2

3 Next, roll two small cones from card, a bit larger than a standard filter, seal them with tape, and insert them into the holes.

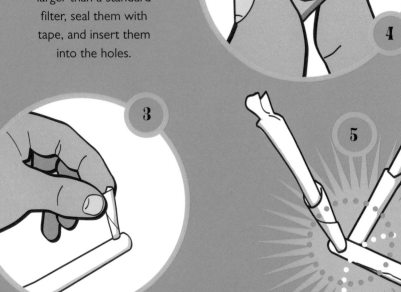

4 Use gum strips to seal the holes around the card, and use an additional piece of card to block the end of the filter stem.

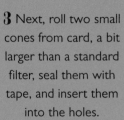

5 Roll two joints, pop them into the receptors—the cones—and then stage a weeklong "bed-in" with Yoko Ono.

T-Bar

Double trouble

What do you do when one joint is simply not enough? You make a T-Bar, of course. The secret of the T-Bar, an old favorite, is in the quality and, above all, sturdiness of the filter. It can be reused until such time as you get bored or lose it down the back of the couch. Once you have smoked this, you'll never look back . . . at least not with anything approaching clear vision.

I Cut two pieces of card about 6 inches (15 cm) long. Roll them into tubes, making one slightly thicker than the other, and seal with tape.

2 Using a fine-blade knife or small pair of scissors, cut a hole at the halfway point of the thicker tube.

HOW HIGH?:
✹ ✹ ✹ ✹ ✹

FREAKY FACTOR:
✹ ✹ ✹ ✹ ✹

SMOOTHNESS:
✹ ✹ ✹ ✹ ✹

TOKIN' TIME:
20 mins.

3 Insert the thinner tube into the hole to form a T shape and seal with tape or gum strips.

4 Place reefers in each end of the thicker tube and light 'em up. Don't set fire to your beard.

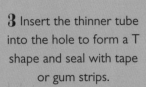

Hammer Blow

It packs a punch

With the big, bad brother of the T-Bar, only those with serious intentions should apply. This design ups the stakes with tulips instead of joints, so you will definitely need two or three stoner friends to lend you a hand. Spark it up, then take the rest of the day off; it's called Hammer Blow for a reason.

I Follow steps I through 3 for the T-Bar, but use thicker card and don't roll the tubes as tightly.

2 Now make two meaty tulips. (See Dutch Bud, page 60, and Heart-Shaped High, page 64, for full instructions on how to make tulips.)

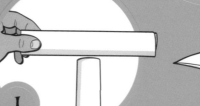

3 Seal the tulips in place with tape, grab a lighter, and make yourself comfortable. This could get messy.

HOW HIGH?:
🍁🍁🍁🍁

FREAKY FACTOR:
🍁🍁🍁🍁

SMOOTHNESS:
🍁🍁🍁🍁

TOKIN' TIME:
30 mins.

chapter **4**

HIGH
ROLLER

"Victor proceeded to roll the biggest bomber anybody ever saw.
He rolled . . . what amounted to a tremendous Corona cigar of
tea. It was huge. Dean stared at it, popeyed. Victor casually
lit it and passed it around. To drag on this thing was like
leaning over a chimney and inhaling."

Jack Kerouac, *On the Road*, 1957

If you've gotten to this stage of the book and you haven't passed out yet, then you're either superhuman, or you're Tommy Chong. Either way, you're now ready for some truly frightening joint-smoking action—from circles and triangles to airplanes, ships, and even a spaced station. Read on at your peril and don't say I didn't warn ya.

The Carrot

The vegetarian's choice

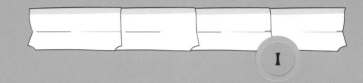

This spliff might look like a bumpy and baggy mess, but that's the idea—after all, few prizewinning vegetables are perfectly straight. Based on the joint made famous in the cult movie *Withnail & I*, this one requires a steady hand and a lot of papers . . . not to mention a whole lotta pot. It might not be orange, and it certainly isn't good for you, but (if you smoke a whole one) it will make you see in the dark. Probably.

I Take four standard-size papers from the pack and stick them together end to end.

2 Now you need to seal them together. Take a fifth paper, fold it in half with the gummed strip on the outside, lick both sides of the gummed strip, and place it underneath the first join. Press down, wait a few seconds, and then peel away the fifth paper before the glue has dried. Stick down the join, then repeat twice more.

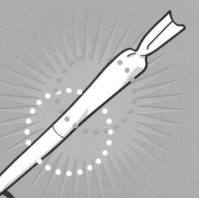

HOW HIGH?:
✳✳✳✳

FREAKY FACTOR:
✳✳✳

SMOOTHNESS:
✳✳✳✳

TOKIN' TIME:
25 mins.

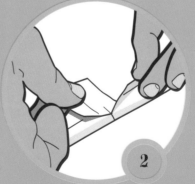

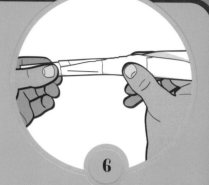

3 Add three more papers (leaving the filter end free) and seal the joins by following the instructions in step 2.

4 Next, remove the excess paper from the bottom end of the joint. Think of a 20-degree angle running from the filter end.

5 Add your mix and tear a strip of card for the filter.

CREASE UP

This trick is handy when removing excess paper from large reefers, as in step 4. First, fold to make a crease along your chosen line, then lick the edge of the crease, and then unfold and tear. The result is a smooth tear from end to end.

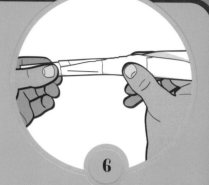

6 Roll the joint between your fingers. Because this is a longer-than-average spliff, keep your left hand fairly steady on the roach end and move your right hand up and down the joint to ease the mix into place before licking and sealing.

Your Carrot is ready: "What's up, Doc?"

Flaming Fork

Straight from hell's kitchen

Are you ready for the devil's own reefer? Of course you are. This contraption, in the shape of Lucifer's trident, utilizes a complex interlocking filter. If you're brave or foolish enough to tackle it on your own, you'll find the hit from all three cylinders to be otherworldly. But hey, you're going to hell anyway, so why not travel first-class? Give my regards to the earth's core.

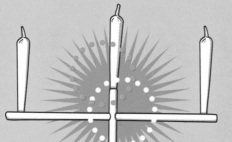

HOW HIGH?:
✿✿✿✿✿

FREAKY FACTOR:
✿✿✿✿✿

SMOOTHNESS:
✿✿✿✿✿

TOKIN' TIME:
20 mins.

I Roll two pieces of card, one (the filter) about 1 foot (30 cm) long and ½ inch (1.3 cm) in diameter, and the other about 8 inches (20 cm) long and ¼ inch (6 mm) in diameter. Use tape to seal. Then roll three medium-sized joints.

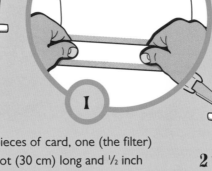

2 Take the shorter tube of card and, using a fine-blade knife, make holes at both ends and in the center. The two holes at either end will take the roach ends of two joints, so should not go all the way through.

3 Now take the long filter stem. Mark a position about 2 inches (5 cm) from the top and make a hole through both sides of the card.

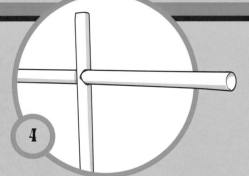

4 Slide the narrower tube through until it's in a central position. You have now assembled your reusable trident.

5 Use gum strips to seal the join, and card to block off the holes at the ends of the narrow tube.

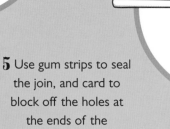

6 Insert all three joints, spark 'em, and prepare to sell your soul.

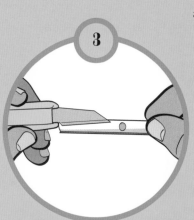

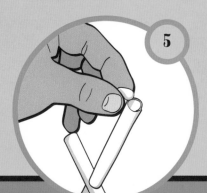

Bemused Triangle

How to disappear completely

Like its Bermudan namesake, this spliff is a black hole. But instead of causing ships and airplanes to disappear without a trace, this joint can be responsible for a vanishing mind. For sure, this is a potent creation that uses a trio of joints (there are three sides to a triangle, right, kids?) so team up with a friend or three to puff on this one.

HOW HIGH?:
✳ ✳ ✳ ✳

FREAKY FACTOR:
✳ ✳ ✳ ✳

SMOOTHNESS:
✳ ✳ ✳ ✳

TOKIN' TIME:
20 mins.

1 Roll three equal-length doobies. Two of the joints should feature long filters and should be rolled so there's no mix in the last ³/₄ inch (2 cm) of paper; the other should not include a filter. Don't tightly seal any of the nonfilter ends.

2 Take the two filtered joints and, using a pair of small scissors, cut away a segment of the paper on each as shown.

4 Next, grab the two filters, pull them together to form the third point of the triangle, and bind together with plenty of gum strips.

3 Take the third joint and push one end into the open segment of paper at a 90-degree angle. Fold the flap of paper over and seal thoroughly with gum strips. Now repeat for the other side of the triangle.

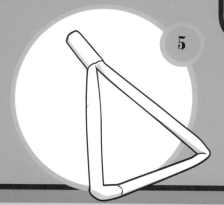

5 Light this sucker halfway along the straight edge directly opposite your mouth.

BEMUSED TRIANGLE

Wheel of Fire

Ever-decreasing circles

HOW HIGH?:
✹✹✹✹

FREAKY FACTOR:
✹✹✹✹✹

SMOOTHNESS:
✹✹

TOKIN' TIME:
15 mins.

The concept of a circular joint might appear to defy the laws of physics, or be merely the product of a permanently stoned mind, but it works. This doobie needs to be a minimum of 1 foot (**30 cm**) long and you might require the assistance of another pair of hands, but if you can pull off this roll, then you shall be feted as a spliffigami master. Take a bow, my child. You've come a long way since the pen method.

2 Now prepare a very long reefer. To make your life easier, use rips (the papers that come on a continuous roll) instead of conventional skins. Also, use rolling tobacco rather than cigarette mix. Don't use a filter, and leave a gap at each end.

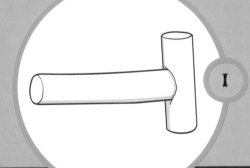

I Build a three-way filter, basically a shortened version of the T-Bar filter (see page 74).

3 Tucking and wrapping this monster is a real challenge, so you might need to enlist the help of a friend to hold the joint at specific intervals.

4 When you're done rolling, start bending the joint around so it forms a neat circle. Be gentle. Then fix the ends of the joint onto the T-Bar filter.

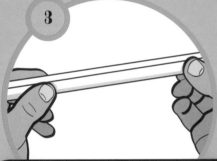

THREE-WHEELER

If you struggle to make the Wheel of Fire as a single joint, don't despair. This design works just as well with three smaller joints (loosely rolled) thoroughly gum stripped together.

You've now completed your wheel. It might almost be mistaken for a miniature halo . . . if you weren't so darn naughty.

Reefer Roulette

Do ya feel lucky, punk?

Far safer than its Russian equivalent, and less expensive than the casino version, this is a great game for up to six potheads to play. The replica gun takes a little time to make, but once done, it can be reused time and again. Roll six joints, then spin the chamber and prepare to take your hit. "Do ya feel lucky, punk? Well, do ya?"

HOW HIGH?:
✳✳✳

FREAKY FACTOR:
✳✳✳

SMOOTHNESS:
✳✳

TOKIN' TIME:
35 mins.

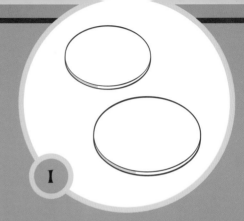

1 Take some thick corrugated card and, using a template, draw two circles about 4 inches (10 cm) in diameter. Cut these out using scissors. Tape these two circles together to increase the thickness.

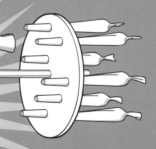

2 Find the center of your circles and make a filter-sized hole in the middle. Then mark and cut another six holes around the outside of your disk—which will form the chamber of your gun.

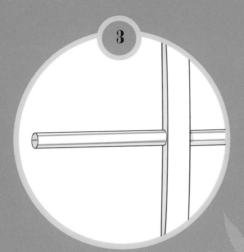

3 Take two drinking straws. One straw needs to have a larger diameter than the other. Using the bigger straw, cut a 4-inch (10 cm) section. Put this through the central hole in the chamber so that about 1 inch (2.5 cm) protrudes through on the other side. Seal this in place using tape or adhesive putty.

HANDY HINT

If you are struggling to find drinking straws with different diameters, note that most bars and clubs use thin straws, while most fast-food outlets favor the thicker variety.

4 Take the thin straw to be the "barrel" and insert it into the straw already in the chamber. Then carefully heat up the end of your barrel with a lighter and press it down with any blunt object. The chamber will be able to slide up and down the barrel but not fall off the end.

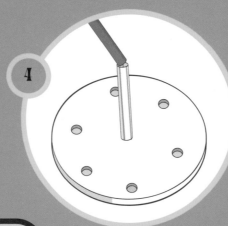

5 Using another thin straw, cut two equal segments that will cover the length of the end of your barrel, approximately 2 inches (5 cm).

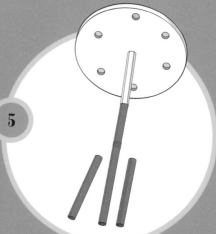

SHOOT 'EM UP

If you don't have the time to make the roulette wheel (or are simply too stoned to care) why not make the Six-Shooter? Roll six ultraskinny joints, neatly bind them together with string, and smoke in one hit. If that's too much for your modest appetite, try two joints (the Double-Barrel) instead.

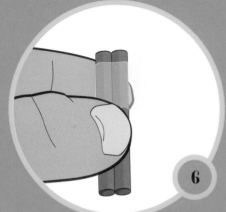

7 Into your barrel straw, you will need to insert a chopstick or something similar. This will stop your barrel from bending.

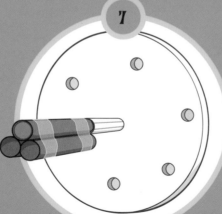

6 Tape these two straw segments together, then tape this section to the bottom of your barrel straw, creating a triangle of straws.

8 Now for the butt of your gun. Measure and cut out a 4 by 4 inch (10 by 10 cm) square of card. Roll this quite tightly and tape it down to form a tube. Then take some scissors and cut one end of this tube at a slight angle. Tape this to the triangle of straws.

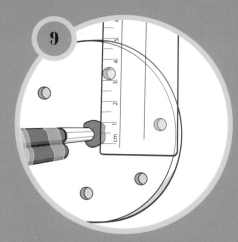

10 Cut a strip of thin card as long as the figure you've just come up with and 1½ inches (4 cm) wide. Fold this strip around the triangle end just past the butt of your gun, so that it fits snugly around the triangle and the two ends meet equally, then tape in place. Fold each of the top ends of the strip at 90 degrees away from each other. Do this so the fold is level with the bottom of a chamber hole.

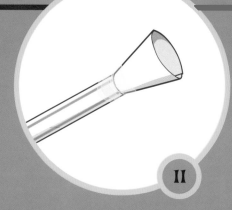

9 Take a ruler and on your chamber measure the distance from just below the bottom of the lowest straws on your barrel, up to the bottom of one of the holes on the outside edge (where your "rounds" will go!). Add a further ½ inch (1.3 cm), and then double that figure.

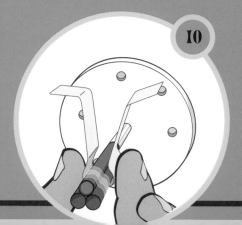

11 Now take another segment of the larger diameter straw, approximately 4 inches (10 cm) long. Cut the corner off a piece of thin card, roll it around to make a cone, and seal it with tape. Cut the point off of your newly made cone and tape this cone to the end of your new straw segment.

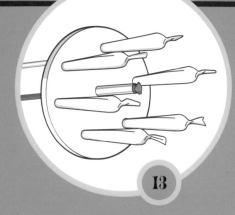

12 Now place this cone segment onto the support and tape it in place securely.

13 Roll five mixed spliffs and one with pure weed. Spark up all six spliffs (or rounds) and then put them into the six holes around your chamber.

14 And you're ready to go! Slide the chamber to the end of the barrel, spin, wait until it stops, and slide the chamber back so the round goes in the cone straw. Then suck on the straw to get blown away.

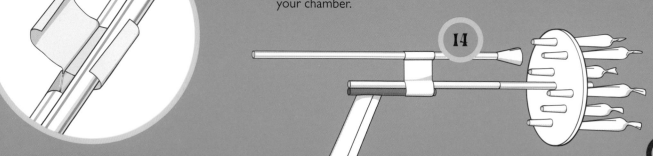

Pot Propeller

Three times the fun

HOW HIGH?:
✸ ✸ ✸ ✸

FREAKY FACTOR:
✸ ✸ ✸ ✸

SMOOTHNESS:
✸ ✸ ✸ ✸

TOKIN' TIME:
30 mins.

Are you still with me? Good. It's time to introduce you to another multiple-joint smoking device. The design of this one centers around a solid cone made from card to which you affix three loaded bombers. It resembles an engine propeller (or maybe a windmill). Call it what you like, it gets you stoned just the same!

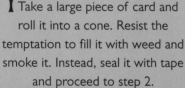

I Take a large piece of card and roll it into a cone. Resist the temptation to fill it with weed and smoke it. Instead, seal it with tape and proceed to step 2.

2 Using a fine-blade knife or small pair of scissors, make three holes (at equal intervals) around the cone about three-quarters of the way up.

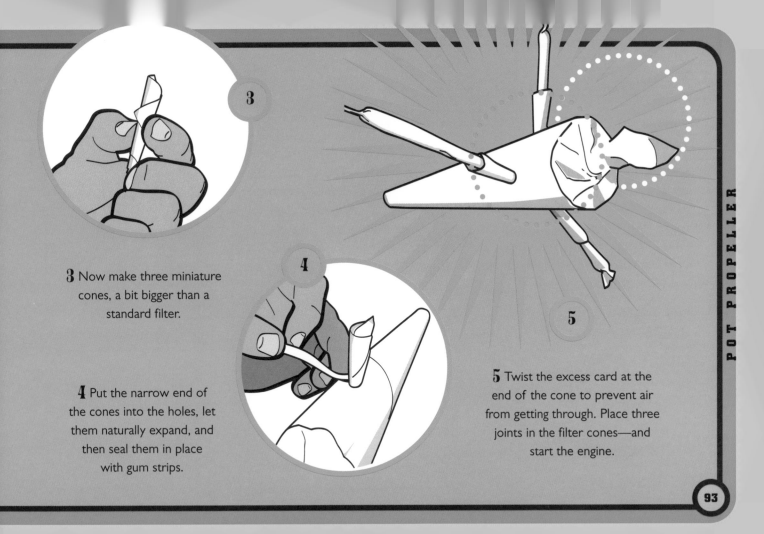

3 Now make three miniature cones, a bit bigger than a standard filter.

4 Put the narrow end of the cones into the holes, let them naturally expand, and then seal them in place with gum strips.

5 Twist the excess card at the end of the cone to prevent air from getting through. Place three joints in the filter cones—and start the engine.

Burning Man

Festival freak-out

You've heard of the festival, now here's the joint. The principal attraction of Burning Man, which takes place every September in Black Rock, Nevada, is the torching of a large wooden effigy—well, that, and sitting around smoking lots of bud. Now you can create your own mini festival every day of the year. Pretend the spliff is your local congressman, who so vociferously supports the War on Drugs.

HOW HIGH?:
🍁🍁🍁

FREAKY FACTOR:
🍁🍁🍁

SMOOTHNESS:
🍁🍁🍁

TOKIN' TIME:
25 mins.

I Make a narrow tube about 8 inches (20 cm) long. Measuring from one end, mark two points with a pencil at approximately 2 inches (5 cm) and 4 inches (10 cm). Then cut two holes all the way through the tube as shown.

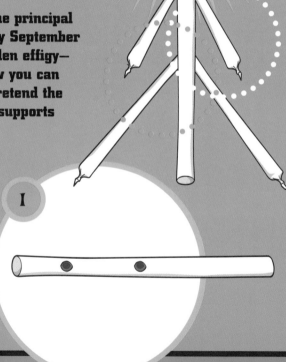

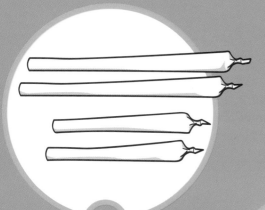

2 Now roll two pairs of joints, all fairly skinny—two with standard-size papers, and two with king skins.

3 Now make a tulip. If your stoned little mind has forgotten how to do this, refer to the instructions for Dutch Bud on page 60.

4 Insert the five smokes (representing the head, arms, and legs) and away you go—burn the man.

Star Shape

Seventh heaven

SPLIFFIGAMI

HOW HIGH?:
✿ ✿ ✿ ✿ ✿

FREAKY FACTOR:
✿ ✿ ✿ ✿ ✿

SMOOTHNESS:
✿ ✿ ✿ ✿ ✿

TOKIN' TIME:
45 mins.

Featuring a long stem of card and seven protruding spliffs, this is a real cannabis challenge—both to make and to smoke. It might look implausible, but the key to this creation is in the design of the improvised clay filter. It does take a while to make, but it is time well spent to fashion an airtight center. If you get bored, you can always roll up a fattie while you wait . . .

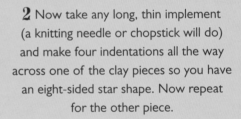

2 Now take any long, thin implement (a knitting needle or chopstick will do) and make four indentations all the way across one of the clay pieces so you have an eight-sided star shape. Now repeat for the other piece.

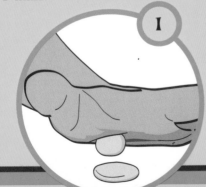

1 First, you need some modeling clay. Take a decent chunk and roll it into two round balls. Then flatten them with the palm of your hand and ensure that both are the same size.

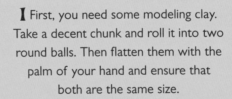

3 Now for some cooking. Put the clay pieces in the oven for about an hour. (Time and temperature will vary depending on the clay used, so check the instructions.) When the clay has hardened, remove it from the oven and let it cool.

3

4

4 Next, roll a narrow tube of card about 8 inches (20 cm) long and place it in the center of the clay as shown. Make sure it's thick, since it needs to support the weight of the clay disks.

5 Roll seven fatties and place the filter ends in the indentations. When everything is satisfactorily aligned, take the second piece of clay, place it over the top, and glue with superglue.

5

Be very afraid.

Jolly Roger

The ship of fools

Hoist the mainsail and man the rigging, we're taking to the high seas. Make your hull, which, like the fuselage in The Jumbo (page 102), can be reused, erect the mast, and gather together a hearty crew. Then it's time to set sail on the pirate ship to pot-puffing paradise (try saying that after you've smoked one).

HOW HIGH?:
✹✹✹✹✹

FREAKY FACTOR:
✹✹✹✹✹

SMOOTHNESS:
✹✹✹

TOKIN' TIME:
45 mins.

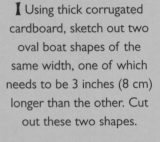

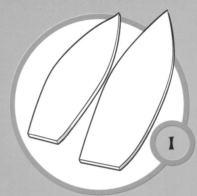

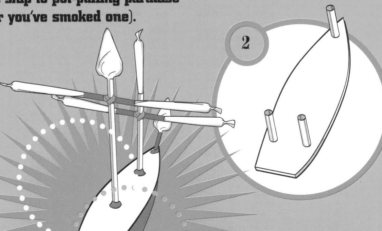

1 Using thick corrugated cardboard, sketch out two oval boat shapes of the same width, one of which needs to be 3 inches (8 cm) longer than the other. Cut out these two shapes.

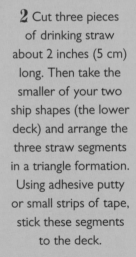

2 Cut three pieces of drinking straw about 2 inches (5 cm) long. Then take the smaller of your two ship shapes (the lower deck) and arrange the three straw segments in a triangle formation. Using adhesive putty or small strips of tape, stick these segments to the deck.

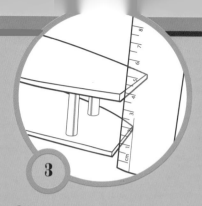

5 Take four drinking straws (two of thick diameter, and two of thinner diameter, as in Reefer Roulette, page 86). Cut one of the thicker straws to approximately 5 inches (13 cm) and the other (the forward mast) to 3 inches (8 cm). Trim the thinner straws to approximately half of these lengths.

3 Place the top deck on the straw supports and, using a ruler, measure the height and length that your sides need to be. Take a piece of thin card and cut out two strips to those specifications.

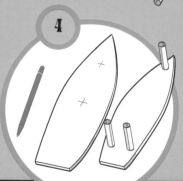

4 Place your top deck next to the lower one. Pick two points for your masts to go. Mark them and cut appropriate holes.

6 Just below one end of the masts (the thicker straws) cut an X with a fine-blade knife. This needs to be done on both sides of the masts—you should be able to see through your X cuts.

7 Find the central point along the length of the two thin straws—the crosspieces for your masts. Cut small holes on both sides of each thin straw. Carefully slide the crosspieces through the mast holes. Twist the crosspieces until you can see all the way down through the masts.

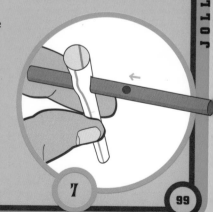

SHOT HOLE

You may experience a buildup of smoke in the hull of the ship because there is no escape hole. If this is the case, remove the tulip from the bow end of the ship and use this tube as a shot hole. Now you can "clear the decks" after every toke.

8 Using gum strips or tape, affix these crosspieces in place, making sure to seal any small holes. Take your masts and place them just through the holes on your top deck, so they poke through. Remember, the smaller mast goes in at the bow end (for you land-lubbers, that's the front).

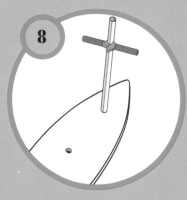

9 Using a small lump of putty, roll several small sausage shapes. Take one and curl it around a mast, molding it in place and firmly sealing the seam without blocking the hole. Seal both seams of each mast—above and below deck. Now make another small hole at the pointy end (bow) of the deck. Insert another small straw segment in this hole and seal it with molded putty.

10 Put small bits of putty on top of the supports and affix the top deck. Now take your two side strips and, using tape, attach them along both upper and lower decks. Snip off any excess card at the bow of your ship. Use lots of tape, and make sure there are no gaps.

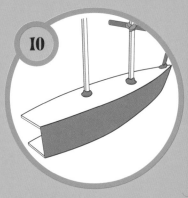

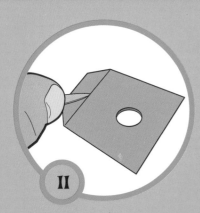

11

11 Place the stern (rear) of the boat on a piece of card, then draw around it to get the exact size and shape. Now cut this shape out, but leave enough card at the lower end to form a securing tab. Cut a round hole in the middle of this piece of card, and use scissors to score the fold along the tab.

12 With another piece of card, make a small tube that will serve as your sucking mechanism. Place this tube in your new hole and seal it in place with more putty.

12

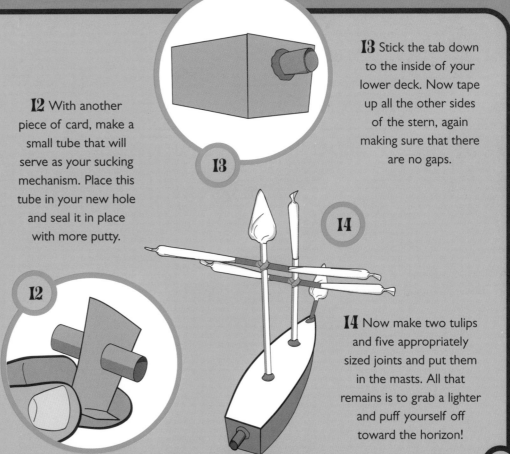

13

13 Stick the tab down to the inside of your lower deck. Now tape up all the other sides of the stern, again making sure that there are no gaps.

14

14 Now make two tulips and five appropriately sized joints and put them in the masts. All that remains is to grab a lighter and puff yourself off toward the horizon!

JOLLY ROGER

SPLIFFIGAMI

The Jumbo

Taking you higher

This is a great joint in more ways than one. Built in the shape of an airplane, the spliffs represent wings, while the main body (fuselage) of the aircraft can be decked out with your chosen logo and reused. Nervous passengers may wish to overlook the fact that the wings are set on fire. Keep your seat belts fastened—there may be turbulence ahead.

HOW HIGH?:
✹ ✹ ✹ ✹

FREAKY FACTOR:
✹ ✹ ✹ ✹

SMOOTHNESS:
✹ ✹ ✹

TOKIN' TIME:
30 mins.

I Using a sheet of card, roll a straight tube at least 12 inches (30 cm) long and with a diameter of approximately 4 inches (10 cm). This is the fuselage.

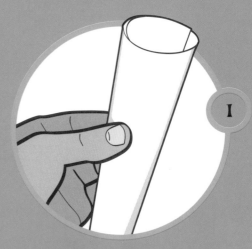

I

102

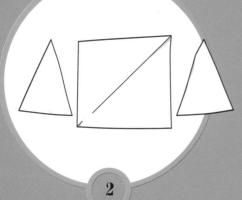

2 Cut out a square piece of card measuring about 5 by 5 inches (13 by 13 cm), and two triangular-shaped pieces about half that size.

3 Cut a V shape in the end of the tube, fold the piece of square card in half diagonally, and affix it in place with tape. This is the plane's tail fin, which also doubles as a cover for your nose during the smoke.

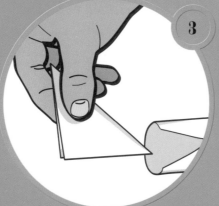

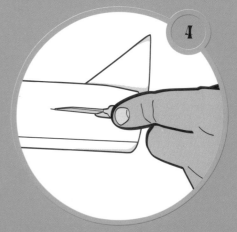

4 Using a fine-blade knife, make a narrow horizontal slit on each side of the tube just below the tail fin.

5 Insert the two card triangles and seal with tape. Your airplane is beginning to take shape . . .

5

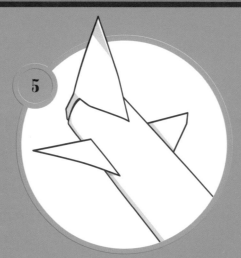

6 Now make a cone from the remaining card, larger than the average tulip.

6

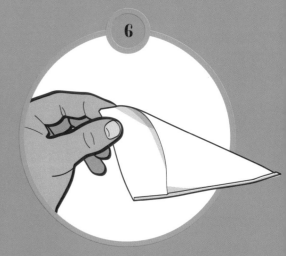

🌿 **THC** Airways...

Tokin' you higher

PIMP THAT PLANE!

Why not customize your plane with a specially designed logo, then invite all your friends over for a maiden flight?

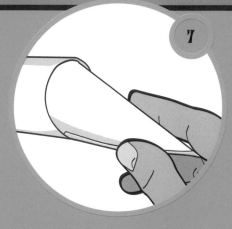

7 Position the cone in the opposite end of the tube, but do not attach it with tape.

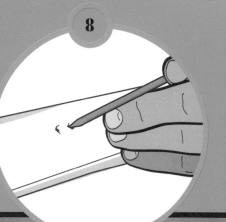

8 Now punch some holes on either side of the fuselage, about halfway up, for the wings. (Start with two wings, especially if this is to be a solo flight.)

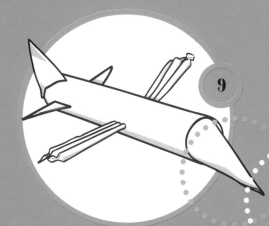

9 Roll some reefers, insert them into the holes, and prepare yourself for takeoff!

NOSE CONE

The removable nose cone serves a purpose. When the cone is in place, the passage of air is restricted, forcing the air to be drawn through the joints. But by removing the nose cone after every toke, you can clear the excess smoke from the fuselage.

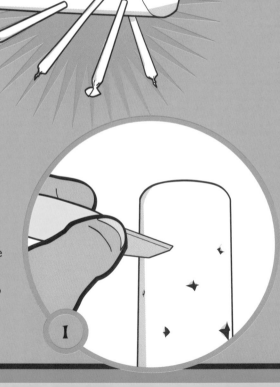

The Mace

Let the battle commence . . .

Like its namesake, a weapon wielded by battle-hardened warriors in medieval Europe, this one is highly destructive. You'll need an army of people to smoke it, too, so save it for a big party. The good news is that it's relatively simple to make and you can tailor the number of joints to suit your needs. Just watch where you put it—you could put someone's eye out with all those spikes.

HOW HIGH?:
Off the scale

FREAKY FACTOR:
❋ ❋ ❋

SMOOTHNESS:
❋ ❋ ❋

TOKIN' TIME:
Hours, probably

I Roll a wide straight tube of card at least 1 foot (30 cm) long. At one end, make a series of holes in the card. The number of holes is up to you, but it should be in proportion to the size of your party.

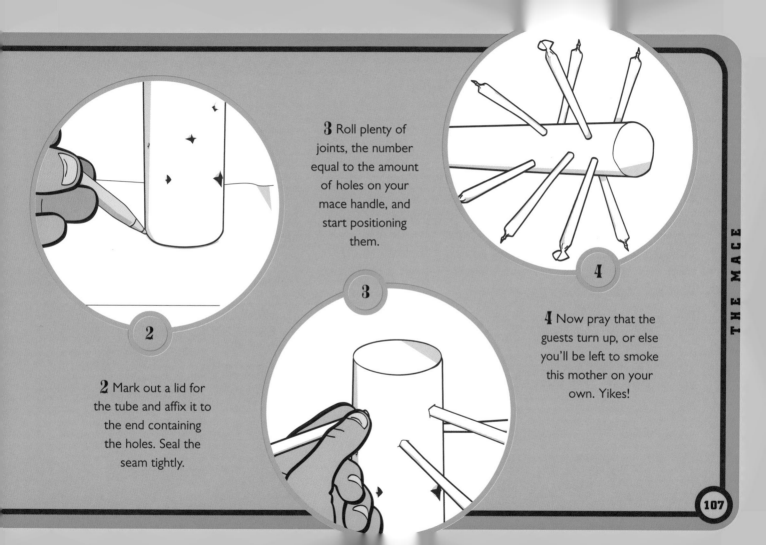

3 Roll plenty of joints, the number equal to the amount of holes on your mace handle, and start positioning them.

4 Now pray that the guests turn up, or else you'll be left to smoke this mother on your own. Yikes!

2 Mark out a lid for the tube and affix it to the end containing the holes. Seal the seam tightly.

Spaced Station

A galaxy of ganja

In 1794, when George Washington proclaimed, "Make the most of hemp seed, sow it everywhere," it's fair to say he didn't envisage this, the magnum opus of joint rolling. Featuring an array of pipe cleaners, drinking straws, and more doobies than you can shake a stick at, this creation will tend to make you very high. Remember: In space, no one can hear you scream . . .

HOW HIGH?:
Off the scale

FREAKY FACTOR:
🍁🍁🍁🍁

SMOOTHNESS:
🍁🍁🍁

TOKIN' TIME:
Don't make any plans

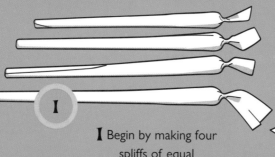

I Begin by making four spliffs of equal proportions.

2 Now begin to make a tulip of gargantuan proportions by using five long rip skins sealed together. (For further instructions on making a tulip cone, refer to Heart-Shaped High on page 64.)

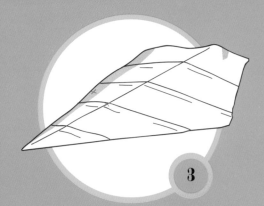

3 Once your tulip cone is sealed, open it up and fold it again so the previous creases are in the middle. You will now have four creases in your paper. Mark a hole at an equal level on each of the four creases for the spliffs. Using a fine-blade knife or scissors, carefully cut a small X on each of these marks (in the illustration the fourth mark is on the underside).

4 Now, taking a potent tobacco and grass mix, fill your tulip up to the level of your holes. Stop every so often and take the time to carefully press down your mix to make a nice firm fill.

5 Now take your first prerolled spliff and carefully push the filter end through the first X from the inside of your tulip. Slide it through until there is only ¼ inch (6 mm) left inside the body of the tulip. Repeat for all four spliffs and thoroughly seal in place using numerous gum strips.

6 Next, put in more grass mix. Then place a good amount of plain tobacco on top of that. There's no need for weed here. Once you get past the spliffs, the tulip is unsmokable, the spliffs will come out, and you'll have one each. Hurray! When you're done filling, twist the surplus paper to seal your tulip up. (When you invert it into its final position, it will look like the illustration.)

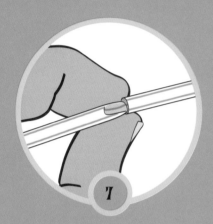

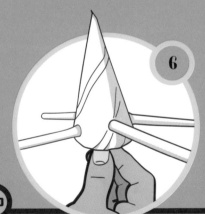

7 Take eight flexible straws and cut them in half, retaining the flexible portion. Using a blunt instrument, crease the longer end of this piece, fold it using your fingers, and insert it into the longer end of another straw segment. Repeat this so that you have four double segments.

8 Take a pipe cleaner and fold it in half. Make a 45-degree fold halfway along the top half of the pipe cleaner; make another 45-degree bend about 1/4 inch (6 mm) along; and then repeat on the other side to make a triangular hole in your pipe cleaner, as shown. Repeat this with three more pipe cleaners.

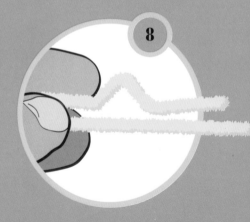

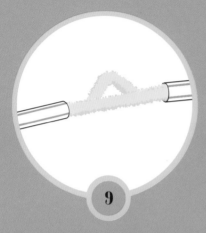

9 Stick each of these into your straws to form an octagonal shape.

10 Finally, carefully fit the octagon around your four-pronged tulip, push the filter ends of the spliffs through the holes in the pipe cleaners, and raise the whole thing up using a toilet paper roll. Voilà, you have a space station set to send you to another dimension!

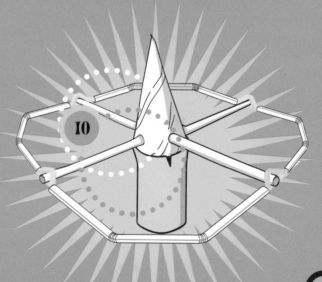

SUPER STATION

If you make an even bigger tulip at the outset, it is possible to have room for an additional ring around the station hub. It'll knock the Galactic Empire's Death Star totally outtasight.

Other ideas to try...

...and get you high

If you believe those medical guys, toking on Mary Jane all day saps your ambition and makes you lethargic. So why not prove them wrong by getting off the couch and exploring some other ways to get high? Here are a few suggested projects to tempt you further from the path of righteousness. I didn't have time to make them, and I can't be certain that they'll work, but you can have some fun finding out.

Crisscross

In fact, this is a simplified version of some of the other joints already outlined. Take two long filter stems, one of a slightly narrower diameter than the other. Make holes all the way through the center of both filters, then insert the narrower filter through the wider one and line up all the holes. Bind them together to form a cross shape. Stick prerolled joints into three of the ends and puff away.

Spliff Shapes

First, using a long piece of card make a mold that is square or triangular in cross section. Stick some papers together and wrap the paper around the mold. Crease it around the edges of the mold so it fits neatly. Next, pull the paper off the mold, place it inside, and fill with prepared mix. Push down hard so the blend is well compacted (try placing the mold in a refrigerator overnight). Then pull the joint out of the mold and smoke your misshapen delight.

The Long Smoke

If you can roll the Wheel of Fire (see page 84) single-handedly, then why stop there? You might benefit from using a rolling mat, and you'll definitely require an extra pair of hands, but the potential exists to roll some super-long spliffs. Remember: Rolling with a pack of rips, which come on a continuous roll, is far easier than licking fifteen papers and sticking them together.

High-Handed

This is a highly intricate design involving a large tulip and five joints. First, make a tulip with at least four large papers (see Heart-Shaped High on page 64). This represents the palm of your hand. Before you twist the spare paper at the end, insert five joints (with the nonfilter ends inside) in a fan shape across the width. These joints represent four fingers and a thumb. Seal thoroughly and get four friends to help you out.

Black Box

Mark out a template for a small box on a piece of card. Cut a small circle in the lid and punch several small holes on all four sides. Now build the box and insert drinking straws through the small holes. Next, get some aluminum foil, make some tiny holes in the center, and place it in the circular hole. Put some grass or hash on the foil, light it, and inhale through the straws. Party fun.

chapter 5

POT-POURRI

"Yes I smoke shit, straight off the roach clip
I roach it, roll the blunt at once to approach it
Forward motion, make you sway like the ocean
The herb is more than just a powerful potion."

Cypress Hill, "I Wanna Get High"

As a new, full-fledged graduate of rolling college, you might think you know all there is to know about cannabis culture. Think again. This chapter sets you on the right road to smoking etiquette, reveals some tricks of the trade, explains a few side effects, and rounds off with a summary of stoner slang.

Joint etiquette

If you want to impress (or at least blend in with) your smoking circle, there are some matters of smoking etiquette you need to abide by. You don't want to roll the greatest reefer your friends have ever seen, only to pass it on the wrong side or, worse, be caught bogarting it. So follow these dos and don'ts of pot smoking practice.

Butt out

What do you do when the joint has burnt down to the end and there's nothing left to toke? Maybe nothing, other than stub it out, but in many smoking groups there are penalties for being caught holding the roach or filter. In some circles, the unfortunate individual is made to swallow it (known as "eating the peanut"); in others the person may be obliged to skin up, or perhaps make drinks for everyone.

Sleeping on the job

2

Similarly, it is a cardinal sin to let a joint go out on your watch, especially one that was roaring along nicely when it was passed to you. If you are guilty of this, it means you're already way too stoned and should never have accepted the doobie in the first place. Expect some swift justice from your so-called friends.

Munchies

3

You might be overcome with hunger, but don't sneak off and eat all of your host's food. Being caught at three in the morning covered in strawberry sauce and clutching an empty tub of Ben & Jerry's isn't a good look and won't lead to repeat invitations.

Passing out

Like drinking alcohol until you vomit, passing out due to excessive toking is not good form; nor is feigning the effects of a session and sloping off to bed early. If you commit either of these faux pas and you wake up in the morning to find some expletives stenciled on your forehead or a missing eyebrow, you've only got yourself to blame.

Sponging

Like that guy in the bar who never quite gets around to buying the drinks, sponging pot is mean and won't endear you to the smoking circle. Make sure you take your rightful turn at scoring the bud. On the other hand, you must not let others sponge off you. When you're having to share your stash around all the time, it becomes a burden to smoke at all.

Dirty hash and seedy weed

Don't try and pass your dirt off as top-dollar draw, even if it smells and looks great. Everyone will soon tell the difference once they've tried it, and they'll be less inclined to let you toke on their top-grade stash.

Don't slobber

One of the side effects of smoking pot is a dry mouth, so chances are you won't have this problem. But if you do happen to generate a lot of saliva, keep it to yourself. No one wants to receive a soggy roach after you've been slobbering all over it.

7

8

Which side?

So, which direction should you pass the reefer around the circle? Musical Youth would have you believe it's the left-hand side, but generally speaking it doesn't really matter which way you pass the doobie. However, once you've started in a particular direction, make sure to keep the hit traveling the same way until everyone has had a turn.

9

If you rolled it, spark it

Many potheads will go by the following law: if you rolled the joint, you get to light it—after all, it's your stash. But this isn't always the case. Getting high is about peace, love, and sharing, man, so don't be scared to offer the "green hit"—the first toke on a new reefer—to your neighbor.

Include everyone

As the doobie goes around the circle, some people may not want to smoke. Nevertheless, you should offer them the chance. It's a mistake to assume that because they didn't want a hit during the last round, they'll pass it up again.

Puff-puff-pass

In most cases it's appropriate to take only one or two tokes on a joint before passing it on: this is known as "puff-puff-pass." By following this rule, you ensure that nobody smokes more than his or her share and that no one waits too long between turns.

Sometimes it's practical to take three or four long drags before passing. This is a great way for small groups to smoke when there are no pressing time limits.

Toking on the joint for longer than this, or simply hanging onto the joint without toking, thereby wasting good weed, is known as "bogarting." It is named for Humphrey, who was never without a cigarette dangling from his lips, yet very rarely took a drag. This is one of the worst smoking violations. Don't do it.

Don't roll for yourself

12

Some unscrupulous potheads pack the front of the joint (the bit they will be smoking) with all the good stuff and leave the rest comparatively empty. Your fellow smokers aren't stupid; if you do this, they'll soon suss you out and you'll be rightly ostracized.

More speed, less haste

There's nothing worse than waiting half an hour for someone to roll up. Don't rush, but don't lose focus, either. If a single-skin joint is taking you longer than two minutes to roll, then you need to go away and practice on your own for a few nights before rejoining the circle.

13

Cutting in

14

Joining a session as a first-timer is a tricky business. If you jump in at the wrong time, you could lose your chance to become a part of the circle. Rather than just butting in, try to be smooth. Try telling a story, supplying some munchies, and skinning up regularly to make yourself part of the crowd.

Tips and tricks

Hole in the roll

Have you ever tried to suck through a straw with a hole in it? This is the same effect you get when your joint has a tear. You can fix a tear by gum stripping or by rerolling the joint completely. To avoid this situation, remove all stems, which have a tendency to poke through the paper, and break or grind the buds into small pieces. It may take an extra minute or two to prepare the weed in this fashion, but it will save you time and frustration down the line.

Blowback

A neat way to turn on a loved one, the blowback requires you to put the lit end of the joint into your mouth, close your lips and blow smoke through the filter end into the mouth of another. The two mouths need to be pretty close together, and by cupping your hands around the joint you'll better direct the smoke. This technique is best avoided with hash joints: if the cherry falls off onto your tongue, you'll sober up pretty quickly.

Sidewinder

Thoroughly preparing an even mix before you roll is important for achieving a consistent burn. However, sometimes even the best-rolled joints will burn more rapidly on one side than the other—this is known as the "sidewinder." It's important to remedy this as soon as possible, otherwise you'll soon lose the cherry. Fortunately, the solution is simple. Using the tip of one finger, apply some saliva to the fast-burning side of the joint; this will allow the slower-burning side to catch up, and your joint will burn evenly again.

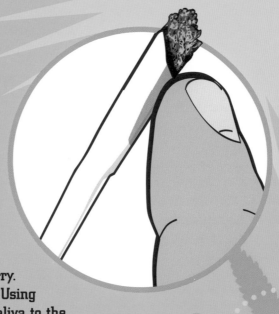

Side effects

Blim burn

One of the telltale signs of cannabis use for suspicious parents the world over, blim burns are the holes caused by falling "hot rocks" (small particles of burning hashish) landing on clothing, seating, carpets, and skin (ouch!). As well as being destructive and painful, they are a waste of hash. Thoroughly heating and rubbing your hash into powder at the mix stage is the way to avoid these troublesome fellows.

Cotton mouth

A dry mouth is one of the common by-products of a good session, particularly when you're smoking weed. And the more stoned you get, the easier it can be to ignore. Banish dehydration and a tickly cough with regular sips of water or fruit juice.

Munchies

It's an unwritten rule of pot smoking that the more stoned you become, the greater your propensity to seek out junk food, irrespective of how full you felt before smoking. The medical explanation is that the cannabinoids activate the hunger receptors in your brain. Whether it's nachos, fries, potato chips, ice cream, chocolate, pizza, or burgers, if it's unhealthy, you'll crave it . . . and it will taste fantastic. In fact, the only thing that will stop your frenzied eating is if you're passed another joint.

It goes without saying, prolonged exposure to pot smoking and binge eating equals health issues. Vary your lifestyle.

You've done it—you've negotiated every joint in the book and you're still standing (sort of). All that remains is for me to welcome you to the brethren: you are a full-fledged spliffigami master. By rights, I should present you with a certificate, but you'll only pack it full of chronic and smoke it. Peace out.

Glossary

Abe–a $5 bag of pot, in reference to Abraham Lincoln's appearance on the $5 bill.

Blim burn–the small burn holes left on clothes and seats caused by burning particles of hashish.

Blowback–a way of smoking whereby one toker puts the lit end of a joint between his or her lips and blows smoke into the mouth of another through the filter end.

Blunt–a big fat joint made by rolling pure weed in a cigar leaf.

Bogart–to hang on to a spliff for longer than one ought to.

Card–thin, bendable paperboard used to make filters.

Cherry–the lump of burning hash at the end of a joint.

Chronic–a generic term for very potent grass.

Cone–the ideal joint shape, narrow at the filter end and progressively wider toward the lit end.

Dime bag–one costing $10; traditionally $1/16$ ounce (1.8 g) of cannabis.

Dirt–low-quality weed, usually containing numerous seeds and stalks.

Doobie–alternate name for a joint.

Dub–a quantity of weed costing $20.

Filter–a cylindrical piece of card, approximately 1 inch (2.5 cm) long, positioned at the narrow end of the joint to stop the smoker from inhaling the mix.

Hand pressing–the traditional way of making hashish by rubbing the glands of marijuana flowers together between the hands.

Hashish (or hash)–term for the pressed form of cannabis, which dates to the assassins (Hashishin) of twelfth-century Persia, who ingested large amounts of cannabis before embarking on raids.

Head rush–a loss of control, dizziness, and/or euphoria caused by an overindulgence in cannabis.

Herb–a common Rastafarian term for cannabis, drawn from the Bible: "He causeth the grass to grow for the cattle, and herb for the service of man."

Hit–a puff of cannabis.

Hot box—to smoke marijuana inside a vehicle with the windows rolled up.

Hot rocks—small lumps of red-hot hashish that drop from the end of poorly made joints.

Grinder—a small circular tub in two halves used for grinding buds into powder for better distribution in a joint.

Kind—a word used to describe high-quality cannabis.

Loading—the practice of concentrating more weed in a certain area of the joint.

Mix—the blend of herbs smoked in a spliff. Grass joints can be smoked pure, but we recommend that cannabis be padded out with a burning agent, commonly tobacco.

Munchies—the overwhelming desire to eat large quantities of snack food, brought on by cannabis use.

Pinner—a very thin joint.

Poker—generalized term for an implement used to pack down the mix in a joint.

Pothead—an aficionado of cannabis and prodigious smoker of the drug.

Roach—the butt end of a joint.

Session—two or more pot smokers gathered for a common purpose: to get high.

Side lick—the application of saliva to the faster-burning side of a joint to regulate the overall burn.

Skin up—a phrase meaning to "roll a joint," from the term "skins" (rolling papers).

Stoned—being intoxicated with cannabis; a person who is often stoned is referred to as a stoner.

THC—tetrahydrocannabinol, the primary psychoactive element found in cannabis.

Toker—one who smokes cannabis.

Tuck and trap—the method, crucial in the joint-rolling process, of tucking the bottom end of the paper over the mix and pressing down.

Weed—variant term for grass; also a reference to the invasive nature of cannabis and its ability to grow almost anywhere.

GLOSSARY

AUTHOR'S ACKNOWLEDGMENTS

To me, there are few greater pleasures in life than rolling a nice fat cone, and settling back in a comfy chair to smoke it. But to get paid to do it as well—as I have with this book—well, what can I say? . . . It's every stoner's dream. Now I know why proper authors often describe their literary works as "a labor of love."

It hasn't always been an easy ride—the publisher droning about something called a "deadline" really freaked me out—but overall I'm happy with how the book shaped up, and I hope you readers enjoy it, too.

This book wouldn't have been possible without the invaluable assistance of many friends and colleagues. You know who you are (which is just as well, because I've smoked so much chronic in the last six months that I've forgotten the names of most of you). Of those who I can recall: thanks to Will Steeds and Laura Ward at Elephant Book Company for the opportunity; to Adam Walker for the illustrations; and especially to Paul Malden for helping me roll and sample an array of spectacular joints.

Finally, to James, Paul, Ben, Andy, Tom, et al—thanks for the hazy memories of youth.

EDITORS' ACKNOWLEDGMENTS

The editors would like to thank all those who have provided help and advice—Lisa Dyer, Mick Farren, Paul Palmer-Edwards. Particular thanks go to Lindsey Johns (not only for her great design, but also for her patience) and, of course, Chris Stone, for his dedication to this subject! Finally, thanks go to Lisa Westmoreland, editor at Ten Speed, for her eagle-eyed input.